Inherent Solutions
to
Spiritual Obscurations

Inherent Solutions
to
Spiritual Obscurations

Richard Chambers Prescott

Originally Published By
Grascott Publishing
Seattle Washington

ISBN 1-58721-867-4

1stBooks - rev. 5/17/00

About the Book

Swami Sarvagatananda, The Vedanta Society of Rhode Island: "I am glad to receive two copies of your wonderful book Inherent Solutions To Spiritual Obscurations. Thank you very much for sending us these valuable books."

Swami Chetanananda, The Vedanta Society of St. Louis, Missouri: "In this materialistic age, it is always good to create a spiritual vibration, either through writing or speech. What one thinks that one becomes. Your thoughts may inspire some sincere seekers in this world. May the Mother bless you."

Swami Gokulananda, Ramakrishna Mission, Ramakrishna Ashrama Marg, New Delhi, India: "This will indeed be a valuable addition to our Library. We deeply appreciate the monumental work that you have done in bringing out this publication. We shall be thankful if you kindly send a copy of "Inherent Solutions to Spiritual Obscurations" with the new addition of a final chapter entitled "The Ancient Method" (Ramakrishna, Janaka and the Upanishads), as and when it is published. With all my best wishes."

Swami Jnanadananda, Sri Ramakrishna Math, Mylapore: "The book would be of great value and interest to our Library members."

Swami Krishnarupananda, Ramakrishna Mission, Vacoas, Mauritius, Africa: "This book will be added to our public Library. This is a good work. I hope our readers will be benefited by this book. Thank you very much for the book which you have so kindly sent to us. May the blessing of Sri Ramakrishna be on you."

Swami Jyotirupananda, Ramakrishna Society - Vedanta Centre, Moscow, Russia: "Ample references of Ramakrishna and Swami Vivekananda there as I found at a casual glance gladdened me. Wish you the best from my heart."

Swami Jagadatmananda, Ramakrishna Mission, Singapore: "We express over appreciation and thankfulness for the same and we are sure the volumes will be very helpful to many readers."

Swami Nirmalatmananda, Ramakrishna Vedanta Ashrama, Sao Paulo, Brasil: "Thank you very much for the kind gift of your new book... They will be kept in our library for the use of devotees here."

Scott Bennett, Yale University Library, New Haven, Connecticut: "I gratefully acknowledge receipt of the gift mentioned below and extend to you our sincere thanks. Faithfully yours."

Dr. Stanley Krippner, Saybrook Institute: "I read your splendid book this week. It is a solid contribution to the literature and I will recommend it to our students."

Swami Nirmalatmananda, Ramakrishna Vedanta Ashrama, Brasil: "I am sure the spiritual seekers will benefit much by the contents of the book."

Swami Murugananda, Satchidananda Ashram, Virginia: "I am sure that those who read them will find them of benefit." (On Inherent Solutions to Spiritual Obscurations and The Ancient Method)

Swami Shivamayananda, Belur Math, West Bengal: "We found the book quite interesting and informative. It will be added to our general library. Thank you very much for sending this book to us. We are sure that the blessings of Sri Ramakrishna and Swamiji are upon you."

This text is Dedicated to the Great Soul,
the Pure Mind within you, the Reader,
hidden and yet Ever Present
in Service, Humble and Surrendered
to the Happiness of Pure Mind.

Other Works

The Sage
Moonstar
Neuf Songes
The Carouse of Soma
Lions and Kings
Allah Wake Up
Night Reaper
Dragon Tales
Dragon Dreams
Dragon Prayers
Dragon Songs
Dragon Maker
Dragon Thoughts
Dragon Sight
Kings and Sages
Three Waves
The Imperishable
The Dark Deitess
Years of Wonder
Dream Appearances
Remembrance Recognition and Return
Spare Advice
Tales of Recognition
Racopa and the Rooms of Light
Hanging Baskets
Writer's Block and Other Gray Matters
The Resurrection of Quantum Joe
The Horse and The Carriage
Disturbing Delights: Waves of The Great Goddess
Kalee Bhava: The Goddess and Her Moods
Because of Atma
The Skills of Kalee
Measuring Sky Without Ground
Kalee: The Allayer of Sorrows
The Goddess and the God Man

Living Sakti
The Mirage and the Mirror

Part One

THE WONDER OF THE DAKINI MIND

Part Two

LETTING GO AND SOARING ON

Part Three

RESOLUTION IN PURE MIND

Part Four

THE ANCIENT METHOD

Introduction

The more you identify with Pure Mind the less you identify with the sleep of deep sleep, dream and waking. Pure Mind is Original Awareness never lost. Discovering the Awareness of this Original Awareness is Rigpa. Letting Go, Cutting Away or the Immediate Complete Decision to be Pure Mind is Trekchod. One may think Trekchod is an act in mind that cuts away or lets go, yet, it is more a sudden total seeing that Pure Mind has no conceptual barrier at all and You are This. Thogal is to Soar On from Here without moving from Here. Pure Mind! Trekchod and Thogal are two very deep and powerful spiritual dynamics. And Tayi (All Light) is a Step Further.

As much as Pure Mind is Ajati (Not Born), that is, the not birth in body/mind, it is also the not death of itself. The appearance of death or birth only come on or over the surface of Pure Mind which always remains in the deepest depth of Original Awareness untouched (Asparsa) by the surface appearance of death or birth. This awareness produces the feeling that the world is dreamlike, yes, but the dream feeling also must be quenched and exhausted away (Alatasanti and the fourth Thogal) and this just naturally, effortlessly happens the more Original Awareness of Pure Mind proceeds dream, dream-like feelings and appearances in general or all together.

It is no less, Pre-Sleep, Pre-Dream, Pre-Waking. Pure Mind remains the Spiritual Constant never having made the leap into the display of sleep, dream and waking. Yet ever Abiding in a somewhat divinely adjacent fashion as the Illuminator of all that goes on in the display. Yet its thought is not dualistic in this adjacent description. Its Sight is Non Dual Sight. A Great Oneness if you would. You may think of this Great Oneness as Immense Mind or Universal I-ness (the Bhavamukha of Sri Ramakrishna) but it is Not a cosmic state of I-ness in conceptuality for you See, it is nothing less than Pure Mind free of all conceptuality which has apparently taken the form of an appearance of an Immense I-ness!

Losing oneself in the Immensity of Great Wondrous I-ness

can and most certainly is a pleasure. Yet this spiritual pleasure may simply be a way of continuing the display mind. Not then exhausting pleasure, though spiritual, into Natural Great Bliss (Dakini's Sahaja Maha Sukha) in Original Pure Mind! If one presumes immensity forgetting Pure Mind that is simply arrogance which is nothing less than presumption itself. The antidote is Humility which in its Genuine Depth is not presumptuous in the least. Then Surrender spontaneously comes in the Soaring On (Thogal). Here, in this context, Trekchod is the Cutting Away of all presumption of ego's conceptuality of its self importance within duality. When this is so, Pure Mind or the Energy (Sakti) of Pure Mind which is as it was said a moment ago, to be the Abiding Spiritual Constant, is Seen and Realized to be the best spiritual friend, guide, teacher and illuminator. If you have become sensitively aware of Pure Mind and then arrogance about it arises, that presuming self feeling will in fact make you feel unwell. When Humility is restored the unwell feeling will disperse.

When it comes to teachers who believe that they have learned every thing there is to learn and have presumed that thought to be their self reality, you will find that teacher is not a very good one. There are severe problems and there are blessings with all teachers in history. It is the hope for the Perfect in the imperfect. And for just that reason it should be clear that Pure Mind is the best teacher and is the teacher no less, of even the very best of the good teachers. Though from Pure Mind viewpoint there is no teaching, teacher or taught. It is only from the imagined dreamlike conceptuality of the taught that the appearance of a teaching and/or teacher appears. A teacher too should see this way in regard to the teacher's teaching itself. Develop this Attitude Now, because once you attain the Dignity of Enlightenment that will be your Attitude then! For the real meaning of the teacher/elder/mentor is that they are Knowledge holders in the Continuance of the Tradition in Human Heritage for the living, so that Wisdom follows on and does not disappear with their death. So this Wisdom is handed down to the next generation. To worship them is Insanity. To have Loving Respect and Honor for them is True Humanity! To Know Pure

Mind is to be a Real Human who has Awakened from the Sleep! And it is Pure Mind alone that should be worshiped, if you must make a dualistic separation where alone any kind of worship is a possibility.

What Ramakrishna said, "Sometimes I say to myself in the Kali temple, 'O Mother, the mind is nothing but Yourself.' Therefore Pure Mind, Pure Buddhi, and Pure Atman are one and the same thing." This is the inspiration for this elaborate explanation of Pure Mind to myself. It was on Friday, December 21, 1883 that Sri Ramakrishna was telling M. "many secrets of spiritual discipline" when he said "that the mind at times becomes one's guru." This great Truth is conveyed to even a further depth when Ramakrishna says, "It is the mind that becomes at last the spiritual teacher and acts as such." Pure Mind is Ubiquitous whether body/mind is in New York, Chimphu or Dakshineswar. Whether you are a great non-dualist like Gaudapada, a great Dzogchenist like Garab Dorje or a great awakened poet like Walt Whitman, this Pure Mind is the Unchanging Reality.

People say, "Let Go and Go On." It is the Trekchod and Thogal dynamic, but mostly directed to the effect or affect, not the Cause (ego based identity) which if not Let Go of will only continue to become effected or affected by something else. That is not Thogal, the Confidence in Soaring On with Identity in Immensity, which, though better, may also be just greater ego in a larger complex. So Humility as the Cutting Away of Trekchod must proceed Surrender within Immensity. We seek to become a Grounded individual within Immensity through the Unity of Trekchod and Thogal.

Let me relate four dreams. I dreamt a dream of Pure Mind as the Vast Expanse of nothing but Pure Light. There was no support in my mind about its Nature, Essence and Energy. I thought within the dream I can do this without a teacher. That was wonderful. Yet this Immense Light within the Pure Mind with no support gave me a jolt of fear and I awoke. You see full Trekchod to the ego based identity which is effected by insult or assault, not only from the outside but even from one's own mind in doubt that it still needs support had not been fully applied. In the next dream I felt a comfortable amazement. I was sitting in a room with other souls who were practicing in the dream mind the Great Gesture (Maha Mudra) on the Dzogchen of Clear Light. This was beautifully perceptible within the dream. This dream was a comfortable amazement because of the support of the mind expressed in this dream, by being with others and by the act of the Great Gesture. The Pure Mind dream had none of this support and so it was a jolt to the fabricated mind support system. I hope you can see the difference. One is a dream of Asparsa (No Contact) and the other is the path of Contact!

In a third dream I was talking to a saint/sage about the second natural Tantric Power, the Voice or Speech. The first is the Body. The third is the Mind. I was saying that this second Tantric power leaves indelible imprints on the mind as to making us what we think we are. I said that removing these indelible imprints is the thing. The saint/sage agreed but when asked how to do this he did not know. But is not the location and the surroundings and the very nature of the dream itself an indication of how this is to be done. Not forgetting the resplendent thoughts of Sambhogakaya overwhelms all imprints and so cures their indelible markings. It is to see that all this conceptuality of identity and such has about only the tenacity of a dream. In the fourth dream I dreamed of Atma (the Real Self). It was an excellent sensation. Nothing in my dream mind could define Atma, yet I was aware within the dream that I am Atma. Nothing could measure out the Atma. Though it was a conceptual feeling, not quite like the Pure Luminous Mind dream. The You Feeling, the Me Sense, this is not an objective thought, thought about by a subjective thinker.

All conceptuality is mis-conceptuality compared to the Unfabricated Pure Mind. Misconception creates fear which becomes anger that then sinks into despair where Peace is lost. Keep thought (conceptuality) tuned to Pure Mind. May we all come to Serve the Purpose of Spiritual Happiness. With this Spiritual Power being so Wonderful and Indescribable, can any claim (a person or religion) to have the direct and only word on Something so Ineffable?

One's Sense of Perception is everything when it comes to

understanding one's own innate and inherent solution in the Pure Mind. A popular story from Tibet illustrates this very well. Six beings, one from each of the six worlds were standing together on a river bank. Though the water in the river was always the same water, each being's perception of the water was different. The benevolent humble gods perceived the water as nectar. The arrogant egotistical gods perceived the water as a weapon, I suppose they could drown an antagonist in the water. Human being's perception of the water is to quench the thirst. The animal being, here a fish, has the perception of water as a home. The ghost being's perception is that the water is lava, I suppose that they might think it would suffocate or consume them. And the hell beings out of their fearful perception see the water either as burning fire or icy pain. The whole point to the story is that the stand from where one perceives creates the nature or quality of the perception itself.

The Katha Upanishad gives its version of this sense of perception as well. Human beings see or perceive as in a mirror through their intellect (buddhi). The perception of the departed ancestors is said to be like seeing in a dream. The gandharvas (celestial nymphs and satyrs) see or perceive as though looking through water. And those who are in the world of the creator God Brahma see quite distinctly through light and shade. It is said that these are various ways that various beings see the Pure Mind (or the Infinite as the Brahman Principle to quote the Upanishad.) Whether it is a mirror, dream, water or light and shade; these are all within conceptuality and so even these fine and interesting metaphors still veil the Pure Mind with their poetic tastes.

One morning I awoke out of dream I was realizing the hollowness and silliness, the transparent and translucent dream-like nature of all experiences and with that the sense of humor or spiritual comedy within this translucent hollowness of experience and it sent me into a Place of Joy. I had another dream, the Aum Dream, I was standing forehead to forehead with the individual who first gave me the Mandukyo Karika of Gaudapada. This person asked if I would write down the Upanishad for myself and I did. I wrote down the two hundred and fifteen verses of Gaudapada's four part Karika. My friend only thought that I would write the twelve Upanishad verses. In the dream we were repeating the sound of Aum as it was reverberating within our entire being I felt like all four of the Karikas were being fully conveyed.

In another good and beautiful dream my friend Swami Bhaskarananda was reading some information about the Pure Mind to me. That sweet feeling came to me as I listened, tears in the dream state, deep tears, as deep and sweet as any tears in the waking state, for there is no barrier in regard to this feeling. I was moved so I saluted Swami with praises of greeting and to my surprise and amazement Swami saluted me with the same praises of greeting. It was Pure Mind in each of us that was greeted and why should it not be so. Ramakrishna would take the dust of others feet in complete Humility and adoration of the Pure Mind within them. Why should not the teacher greet the Pure Mind within the student as much as the student greets the Pure Mind within the teacher?

There is a spiritual state of understanding called Vijnana. Jnana is Knowledge of the Eternal, the Nitya, but Vijnana is Something More. Vi, the prefix, means a vision that has gone past the usual levels of consciousness, it means to go far past the usual realms of thought and to gain a visionary knowledge. You ask of what. Of the Eternal and the Relative, the Nitya and the Lila. Ramakrishna asks and answers, "What is vijnana? It is to know God distinctly by realizing His existence through an intuitive experience and to speak to Him intimately." So this vijnana is an intuitive experience which knows that what was found in the Nitya is also pervasively all present throughout the Lila. The word intuition not only means contemplation but also to gaze at and so this is to gaze upon the relative Lila from the Height of Height in Pure Mind, where the Lila no longer has the obscuration of the maya/mirage upon it and so one may have the feeling of intimate communion (speaking) with the Pure Mind as it is expressed in the relative. Then everything in the Lila that appears is the poetry of Pure Mind since it is the Central Core of all experience.

Let it be demonstrated. "Ramakrishna closed his eyes and

said: "Is it only this? Does God exist only when the eyes are closed and cease to exist when the eyes are opened? The Lila belongs to Him to whom the Nitya belongs, and the Nitya belongs to Him to whom the Lila belongs." So you see this is very wonderful and interesting, for You who are Pure Mind are this One expressed as "whom." We tend to think of the Eternal, the Nitya, with the eyes closed, where there is no dreaming going on, like as if one is in deep sleep, yet, you are Awake to the Infinite as a feeling or an awareness. This could be simple Jnana. But Ramakrishna tells us much more. "Then one throws away both the thorns, knowledge and ignorance, and attains vijnana." You see he is telling how the thorn of ignorance is removed by the thorn of knowledge, but you must throw away both if you want vijnana. How can this be? Vijnana is neither conceptual knowledge nor conceptual ignorance. We all understand what it is not to have ignorance, but who understands what it is not to have knowledge, that is, to throw away the thorn of knowledge. Both ignorance and knowledge are merely conceptuality compared to the Unfabricated Pre-Primordial Pure Mind. Our ignorance about it is certainly understood but even our knowledge of it is a conceptual limited barrier to its Innate Reality!

One who has knowledge of it in this regard also has ignorance of it in the same light as the symbol of paradox in the light/dark duality, does not explain the nature of the non-dual itself. We can only speak (or write) at the level of Conceptual Advaita because in Pure Mind (Absolute Advaita) there is no speaker nor listener! Perhaps the Vijnana of Pure Mind itself is Seeing All Knowledge within All Ignorance, not just the avidya or non knowledge of the spiritual, but even the maya/mirage of vidya, which is knowledge of the spiritual even as teachers, books, practices and deities, is still also, that is both ignorance and knowledge, and as such is still within the occurring of the maya/mirage of conceptuality, which is nothing but the barrier of the mortal mind's horizon.

We are born into this World with all its various Belief Systems and I don't think they tell us all we want to Know of What We Are! Yet, I must confer with Ramakrishna and

Whitman, that we may indeed know but a very little in fact, as What We Are and its Spiritual Wonders before this World and What We Are and its Spiritual Wonders after this World, that while we are in this World perceiving it with our little mind contained inside a skull, we may actually, indeed, comprehend very little of the Wonder!

You may ask why I go to this length to write all this out. Two reasons. One is to put in one place all the best thoughts as ideas and facts, processes and methods, on Advaita and Dzogchen that I could find, which are only found by sifting through numerous texts which are centuries and millenniums old. And the second which is of more importance is to affirm the occasion of the stupidity of this smiling buck toothed fool of an ox grinning with his own feeling in the Clarity and Happiness of the Mother Light, who in fact is too stupid to know that he should breathe, without the Mother Light!

I gave myself November 1997 to March 1999 to recreate the poetic voice with Sakti for this Inherent Solutions... I am serious, but I do not take myself (ego) or even my writing seriously, for how could I keep the Feeling of Humility if I did.

May you be granted Dakini Awareness in Death

I do not seek Refuge with the living or the dead. My Refuge is Dakini, the Pure Mind. I really and truly, completely and absolutely believe (know) there is no death. The Consciousness of Her, Here Now is There Then! That is what I am, it will not change, so why grieve. Grief can create massive illusion about the Continuum as projections to protect you from your fear of your own death.

I am waiting for my feelings and mind to catch up with what my soul and spirit know. Use this mind feeling to gather there. Do I grieve the death of motherhood or the person of the mother? I think of motherhood, as Garab Dorje's Mother and son meeting in the Clear Light. But that is not physical nor bound to death's arena, yet the physical reflects the Spiritual feeling and it is this spiritual feeling of dividedness that one grieves in truth. All these precious dakini women, mothers of world, power and spirit, will die, what madness you must enjoy Mother Kali! The Kali Tantra brilliantly states the highest insight into the Divine Goddess, "At first, one should reflect on the Consciousness alone, then one should think of that as their Real Nature. 'I am alive, I am dead'; such thoughts are evil. The Self has neither birth nor death. The grief of separation from relatives is false; it is only a distortion of Consciousness." Why? Both thoughts deny the Reality of the Mother Light. I am alive, I am dead, I am a guru, I am a disciple, all equally evil. A Truth as True for your own self as for the self of another. And evil is hell for hell is illusion, and illusion is deception, deception of what you are, the Pure Mind. That deception is the "welter of lies" that Padma Leks Krub speaks of and I call the upside down world.

In three watches or periods of observing Sakyamuni got enlightenment in one night. First; observing the wheel of birth and death illusion, with pots/buckets, each a soul turning through many worlds spreading forth as this great wheel.. Second; taking full account of the illusion of his own life and five hundred and fifty other births and deaths in one extraordinary sweeping glance and other being's lives and deaths too. Third; watching and thinking over the twelve causings, forward and backward, backward and forward until "I, who am here, at this moment, I know, What Is," dawned as the Pure Mind Womb of Suchness in this What May Come, and then Compassion for ignorance Arose Fully like a Blossom.

It is just the five super sensible perceptions that keep mind from Pure Mind, even as the belief in their apparent existence, that they make up the pots (jiva/dharmas), yet Pure Mind is never contained by them, in birth or death. I see different souls, yet the same faces coming back again and again, to realize their own Pure Mind, what other reason could there be for this strange and wonderful vision in mind. Do I then mourn the death of motherhood (maya creatrix) which gave birth to the mind in a body which made heavy the feeling of distance from the Mother Light (Real Creatrix) which was the cause of agony, misery, despair and the fast turning dance toward death, in the first place.

Even so, when I depart I will not have parted. I will see and hear you and when you feel that warm feeling of Delight, know then that it is I as Love who embrace you! If you can, as Ramakrishna says, realize God in a dream, then why not the Continuum of me which is such a lesser knowing realization, even as I a spirit am dancing as Dakini! Blessed Be all my precious and dear dakini mothers who have been dancing on the thin precarious crust of Mother Earth in many shapes since the time of Rodinia and then to Pangaea and all to now and tomorrow, many lives. Blessed is the Circle of the Dakini Goddess, birth, life, death and rebirth, human, spiritual or not at all. Dakini! May I now be permitted to charge this spirit of my own in body and mind with Power Pure in Spiritual Assertion! Truthfully, all you must do is allow yourself the Extraordinary Dakini Thought of Your Own Reality.

The dead love music, so sing for them and the living! Do not grieve, for the dead do not like to see the living in grief since they have just now been opened into a Wonder never known before. All sorrow is but hate in the unknowing of death's illusion, which brings you back into the display, the memory of illusion, yet it melts away in Love, the Memory of Love itself which knows nothing of a barrier or a mortal horizon. Amani Bhava is to freeze, paralyze, even kill mind thought (mani) with God thought, Dakini thought, Pure Mind thought, where only that feeling (bhava) is left here. The poet Tennyson sings that death is a "laughable impossibility" from this Point of Seeing in what I am calling Pure Mind.

May you be granted a Bright and Joyful Passage into the Pure Mind free of dream conceptuality. "Who were you before your mother's mother's mother was born?" Neuf Songes. The Garbha of the Awakened Mind is my Real Mother. As much as others have cast off I too have cut my significant connections! Everything has been cremated before my cremation except contact with my beloved. Gaudapada says that one like this does not salute a superior teacher/person, nor praise any deity, nor do they perform funeral rites or ceremonies that propitiate the departed. None are born so none can die. It is a contradiction to believe or honor death. Sugata Garbha (Womb of Suchness) is Life Positive as Spiritual Affirming, not belief in death as real. It is a dream. Never deviate from this Real Sight.

To even acknowledge a mother's birth is to acknowledge her death and one's own birth and death which do not and never have existed in Pure Mind! Your Pure Mind (Sugata Garbha) that is Aware right now of body and mind is the Same that is Aware in the What May Come in death phenomena. It is Great Benefit now to meditate on Trekchod and Thogal styles, methods, sciences and arts of death techniques, for death is a technique as is the illusion of rebirth. Suddenly Aware in the Bardo Mind, my own death as intimate as my mother's, outer, inner and secret. Who lives or dies, when, how or where? She too is Pure Mind! How much can you understand of this Bardo method? Wake up, it happens to us all! Familiarize now so that in the Bardo it will not be unfamiliar to you! May the subtle bodies of all my dakini mothers Rest in Luminosity!

Boundless Joys! How many mothers I have had of past life bodies! How many dakini mothers of future life bodies will I have, human or Thogal like! Indeed, the Truth is that My Mother is the Deathless Divine Mother and no other. And yet She is embodied in all women! So shall I chase out to the ceremonies of all these mothers of mine, past and future, as they depart this world or some other dimension! Blessed be Death, the Form of True Mother Kali, that She may grant to the mother of this body here, a Bright and Joyful Passage!

Have my thoughts found a place in my voice where I may speak? What is this strange and unique question mark of my life? There is no answer, for this life has never been apart nor away from Dakini!, and the question itself imposes the question! May we all remain unguarded, and unprotected by thoughts that keep us from the Divine Mother, our One and True Mother. Who ever reminds us as Death, how Swift She Is, so do not wait. For eventually, She makes us all become just a memory, yet for Pure Mind, indeed, what is your memory!

In Humble Surrender to Whatever May Come, May we all as all my mothers and yours who are There, Now, get real Trekchod and Thogal genuine, doubtless and sure, as each one of us as offspring, Reach the Lap of the True Mother! My heart is heavy and sad in the Waiting Gesture of this Occurring! I see the mirage/maya of death, but I know there is no death. And I see the divine spiritual wonder of the natural world as our Earth turns around a medium star and as I see it I know it is a mirage of extraordinary cosmic vigor and that the true Spiritual Sun is the Divine Mother! Do we, when departed, attend our own funerals? If mind departs or separates from Mother Light, which is really what the laughable illusion of death is! Even with this I feel peaceful sometimes and terrible. It is the Zhi Khro!

It is a strange feeling to know that one of my mothers may indeed meet Chikhai Sakti tomorrow! Or today, or yesterday. May you all be granted more than ten thousand centuries in the Pure Light of the Divine Mother's Mind, with no need for practicing Trekchod and Thogal! Kali Dakini Maha Sukha Trung Pe! Mother Kali, the Divine Dakini, is Great Bliss as She resurrects (Trung) the dead corpse of Shiva by embracing him in conjugal passionate Love union in the cremation ground! This is the Soaring On and Leaping Through death (Pe!). This is the real meaning of Kama-Kala (passion and death) united in the Turiya state! It should not be a shy secret! The Goddess is True Life and there is no death except when mind dwells in conceptuality and it is Kali Dakini that resurrects that mind to True Life in the non-conceptual Pure Mind!

Is it possible to be so tuned in to another person's death that you would know that they are entering the world of human rebirth too soon because they were not comfortable in death? Or is it the conjuring of an illusion to protect from sorrow? Walt Whitman's thought on death was that he does not commiserate with the dying and their grief nor with the sadness of others, but he congratulates them for there are wonders and beautiful Knowing, Feeling and Being just past the mortal horizon that no one has ever even been able to imagine! Whatever it may be, may you be drawn by the pull of the Bright in a yogini's death focused in the high center of consciousness, so that you may wait never to return by the lunar pull toward rebirth. Be a Pratyeka! Solitary! A Yamantaka! Victorious over death!

There are no hard and fast rules for marriage, for birth or for death. Ramakrishna could not perform his own mother's death rites. Latter when he wanted to offer water into the water of the Ganges to honor her memory he could not. His fingers froze open so water could not be held. When one of his mother's sons died he prayed to Kali to give her understanding. Her awareness awakened and she said, "This world is unreal. Everybody must die some day or other. So it is useless to mourn." When Akshay died Ramakrishna saw his consciousness leave the body like a sword being drawn from a sheath. He was ecstatic. Latter he grieved deeply for even though he knew the illusoriness of birth and death his heart was tender. Death rites, funerals are more like weddings than anything else, weddings to the Goddess, so why should one grieve except only when one has forgotten this truth even as we all have tender hearts!

For we all will be Effaced of the dream of death in Mother Light! It is the self effacing Grace of the Goddess. It comes to every body, but not to the Pure Mind within each body. One is forced to see one's face and form in a shape never discovered before! As Swami Aseshananda would often say, "Death tears off the mask!" So, do not put on a new mask of conceptuality. Remain in Pure Mind and practice Humble Surrender to What May Come! Be that Faith, then Experience is yours, Illumination arises without effort, and finally Certainty. Never drop from Certainty. Kuntu Zang Po humbles himself to Her, because from Pure Mind even he is just an appearance. Love is to Know their Non-Dual Perpetually Blissful great Rush of Delight in Equality! It is the True Setting Face to Face in the Mother Light of Pure Mind!

Then the three Precipices in the Bardo will not confuse you. Red, white and black, the three gunas are then like ledges to fall from which are nothing but anger, craving and stupidity. In Death, do not be stupid, nor angry about it, nor craving of the world, the wheel. Rest and Relax in sudden Dzogchen Luminosity, now as much then in the no death realization of the Mother. For death is but great comedy as you live for many years under the delusion of dying yet when you die you realize the joke that What You Are is never subject to death. But if you return without the memory of this then you forget and fall once again into the joker's domain. It is the dance of the fool in April who is reborn in Spring perhaps remembering the Clear Light and perhaps not remembering and thus he is once again a fool!

If Jigme Lingpa had seventeen births/lives, then he had seventeen different mothers and seventeen deaths. Did he remember them all and bury, cremate, put in a river or give to sky burial all of them in death rituals. And Sakyamuni had five hundred and fifty birth lives before Suchness clearly appeared in the What May Come! So many, five hundred and fifty mothers, their deaths and five hundred and fifty deaths himself!

A young woman came to the enlightened Sakyamuni and asked if he would resurrect her dead child back to life. He said, "Yes, I will, but first find me a handful of mustard seed from a house where there has been no death." She looked and looked and no such place could be found. As she rested and thought of this suddenly she too became enlightened. She became a Pratyeka Yamantaka!

From the Dakini Mind anything that Appears in the What May Come, the Pure Mind, the One, or the Many, the Frightful or Beautiful, Recognize Suddenly the Wonder of Pure Mind Ever Accomplished without effort neither with Trekchod or Thogal, Shining Luminous Everywhere in the Eternal Be at Rest in Dzogchen Radiance and the Great Bliss of Love. "Walk with your head erect! Know your Self in the Bardo!"

I can see my dakini mothers in their luminous youthful forms comforting those who are weeping. Have no contradictions of spiritual and emotional parts. Even in my dreams my prayers for Dzogchen continue even as my beloved dakini woman could also see you in her dreams before you left the body. I am not confined to one mother's womb, not physically and not in the Dzogchen Mind! In the mind's eye of the Dakini you can see so many things, exactly what happens at death and even the quality of the death rites. The healing of hearts, the miracle of five rainbow lights, the unfolding of Love! May your mothers and fathers greet you and their mothers and fathers help and guide you through the phenomenal maya of death stages. Yet be blessed by knowing the union of Great Bliss of your true inner parents in the red and white bliss drops of Kuntu Zang Mo and Kuntu Zang Po! Be free of the illusion of flesh parents. Are you egg and sperm or are you Divine Dakini Energy Dancing in the Infinite! May Mother's Mystery in Trekchod and Thogal, please be granted to you! It is all so previously conclusive! Be honest in your awareness and though you now have no bones nor heart, follow the feeling of your bones and heart and not the head, for with the head arises the wrathful Zhi Khro and from the heart (Love) arise the peaceful Zhi Khro. Be not confused by any contraries or gaps for it is mental obligation alone that makes you chase toward the emptiness. Allow the three centers of head, throat and heart, which compose your illusory being, to suddenly melt in the sudden instant of supremely blessed Trekchod and then Soar On in Thogal! Follow your True Voice if you must go somewhere or Rest Now in the Radiant Dzogchen. The Bell's Sound rings, resonates and then is gone! Yet the Bell remains. The Divine Mother is My Only Bell!

I love cemeteries. I am ecstatic at death! Pratyeka Wonder. Inspiration to what is Immortal. But I could not bear to view her dead body and see the box put into the ground. Why this feeling? I am too tender for the Dakini! Indeed it is strange and I agree. My life has been Dragon Sight which is my own Cremation Poem. And all those writings of a thanatological poet, even so, all conjuring aside, I could not bear it. For it is Kali's image submerged into the river which I cannot bear! For once, there was Compassion for my own feeling and being. In the scorch test of death be true to your innermost Reality. Freedom is a great blessing so be honest as it is the greatest honoring of those who were alive and now appear in the mirage to be dead.

I grieve for those who are born! I dance for those who die! In Pure Mind there is always Beauty! Do not tell me you have never felt this way. In the Truth of Pure Mind all this passes, the dream of her death, my death, the dream of her birth and the dream of my birth. We are all in Chikhai, the Mother Light, even as we dream or live. Heal the psychological spiritual duality. No more psychological dream state. Light alone is Real! Tayi! Live in Spiritual awakened Contact, Alive, not falling to the dead in death as they doubt! Did I feel her meet Mother awhile ago or was it Dzogchen? No, it was the Vast Expanse where in so many mother/fathers were dying and being born! Dakini Mind was Dancing in the Clear Blue while cloud lands of birth and death were dancing in Her! To do this alone with Pure Mind where one is never alone, keeping mind in Pure Mind is for me a greater empowerment in Self Testament! And death ceremony. I do not celebrate deaths nor grieve at births, which is the way that it should be! I love the sad joyful tears of death! It has made so Real, the Light with Love!

I heard one of my elder dakini mothers say, "Confidence will take you where you want to go." Who of us is ever motherless, for even the trees are our mothers. Dakini Mothers! May you Dance with the Dakini who has Always Been Dancing. Now in the Bardo, where there is no distance, consciousness being everywhere at once as swift as one's thoughts carry the mind, May you recognize suddenly without obscuration, the Light of the Divine Mother as the Wonder of your Own Dakini Mind! To Let Go and To Soar On, May the Divine Mother Grant you now! Suddenly in the Bardo Know your Self in Divine Dignity! In the Wonder of the Bardo Mind you may now Know the Dakini in the Vast Expanse! Do not create a conceptual barrier. Be barrier free. Trekchod. Do not limit the Vast Expanse of Dakini Experience by saying, "She is There and I am Here." That is mind illusion. Mirage! Soar On in the Light of the Divine Mother. Thogal! Do not be attracted by wonderment nor by fright. Nor nirvana, nor paradise heaven nor return rebirth. Now in the Luminosity of Pure Mind, Direct and True, you can clearly See how wicked is the distraction it is to salute a teacher as a superior, or praise a hero deity, or even be concerned with your own illusory death rituals! Hear my prayers now or if not, may these thoughts remain in the Akasha until they are needed.

Part One
THE WONDER OF THE DAKINI MIND

Self Doubt or Self Trust
Non-Dual Light Phenomena
Nirvikalpa as Personal Death Process
Tantric Levels and Pure Certainty
Dream States and the Bardo Mind
The Enigmatic Dwelling of the Dakini
Sakti, Buddha and Pure Mind
Dzogchen and Pure Advaita
Amanibhava or Pure Mind
Pure Mind as Teacher
Flying like Garuda
Trekchod and Thogal
as the Nitya and the Lila

1

Self Doubt or Self Trust

What it really comes to, finally, after separating superficial surface emotion and as I dive into the deep vortex of personal ego centered doubt, I ask myself the most bewildering question of all. Would I have progressed more in Spiritual Experience if I had stayed with a guru? Something Unknown must be made real (realized) to Know this Answer Truthfully. I believe with all certainty that this question denies the Reality Itself, of What Is Spiritual in the Experience of everyone. It is the dark mind of the guru himself creating bewilderment and doubt. It is the darkness of the guru who makes you feel doubt that without him, Spiritual Reality cannot exist for you. This is an old, invalid and crippling way which brings no Peace, for looking outside of You, you come to expect too much from others, in that they should be symbols or manifestations of your own Pure Mind in the very Self Experience that you always are abiding within.

Really, it is the cause to doubt, to lose Trust in Life Itself, which alone bestows the Depth of Spiritual Experience that cannot be gauged by comparison. A dangerous mind set. And of Greatest importance with Certainty I do not think I would have ever learned to feel the Depth of Humility and Precious Surrender I have come to know. As those genuine examples in the spiritual history of our human heritage, Sakyamuni, who in one night arrived at the Summit of Becoming (Bhavagra) and then at that single sweet moment of pure human love, Knew What Life Is. And as Ramakrishna did, abandoning self to the Goddess, none other than Life Itself, in the fullest comprehension of Life as It is, in the Pure Awareness of the Pure Mind at Peace with Life as much as with Death, (He too experiencing these things in one night), Luminous without light reflected in dual conditioning which has never been lost in the deepest deep of deep sleep where Mother Light is known, experienced, felt, as never has It been in dream or waking.

Suddenly, Life Itself (Herself) reminded me what had happened. Like eyes being distracted by a fancy flash of light or a piece of paper blown by the wind across the pure sight of my

2

clear vision, my attention became obsessed with the enchantment of the phantom wizardry of the guru's darkness-- and like the ear being lost to an echo of what is the Real and Original Sound, I lost Awareness and real contact of the sweetest simplicity with Real Light within, in you, in me, the True Teacher within, without, above, below, in front, behind, the Beauty and Truth that makes all Life what all Life Is. I was paralyzed, stunned by that distraction, so much that I could not until now, this Moment, be Alive to Life.

Simply, it is the problem of Looking for Self in Others. Imagining the dual in the non-dual, we go further into the distraction of imagining and to seeking the other.

Everything in the cycle of day and night stands forth as our personal creation of Samsara, the dark/light paradox, the doubt/certainty dualism. Only Naked Awareness stands forth as the Uncreated, the Unborn Non-Dualism, the Pure Mind, the one to be trusted now and in the end, and from the beginning.

One can learn from Pure Mind when one is open and without expectation. Looking forward, looking backward or looking outside yourself is a break with Pure Mind. Let us say you start looking outside yourself toward a mentor who is going to instruct you somehow, well you are not going to ever learn anything new about Pure Mind for that is your Primordial Intrinsic Awareness, all you will get is perhaps some new ideas. Besides, in the Dzogchen school Samantha Bhadra, the first primordial buddha, and Vajrasattva, the deity reflection of your own Pure Mind are there to remind you that it is all within you from the first point and to now in the reflection of your own enlightenment within you. Moving out of the complete moment of now is losing it. Even if you look forward to seeing a Dzogchen lama or listening to a holy woman saint from India sing her songs of the Divine Mother or just meeting again an old spiritual friend, these encounters will only express in themselves, spiritually or otherwise, what you take with you from your own Pure Mind. Even when looking backward into the past we can only correctly interpret things and encounters that have happened when we look through Pure Mind and the meanings of those events are only correctly seen when seen through Pure Mind.

3

Always it is the Sweet Simple Moment of Peace Right Now that one wants, that one leaves Pure Mind for looking elsewhere, which was ever abiding within you as your own Pure Mind.

In the third vision of Thogal one sees the tiny spheres where in all world systems are contained and within those systems are lamas and gurus and holy beings and deities and all that, but in the third vision stage they all appear as apparitions of non-duality, very tiny and very small compared to the Immensity of your own Pure Mind. Never lose sight of that fact!

Keep your counsel with Ma! (not lama), with Real Light (not guru). Otherwise the Essential is forgotten in the chase for footprints. This is the Whole Thing. Mother is free from the bardo cycle. She is free of the samsara wheel. Human beings are fragile fruit and they circulate in the wheel cycles. Mother is Constant. Yes, Never changing. The Perfect Teacher, Always the Reality.

A strange thought! Sometimes I think everything is produced by mind phenomena and when you are dead you are dead and you don't even know it. So there, Existence, Consciousness and Bliss are aspects applied to a living ego, so much so, to protect this ego and guard this ego from the Great Uncertain. And when ego focuses so much on these three aspects, when the mind-world is wiped out in that focus, what is called samadhi (either savikalpa or nirvikalpa) then comes there to that mind so deeply immersed in that guarded focus into those three aspects of Existence, Consciousness and Bliss. Even within such a deep doubt we are still protected by this focus, for the Universe proves the Invisible Indivisible Power by Its Immense Presence (Behind and Within)! If I did not believe it to be so, I would lose all respect and gratitude for what my life is, all faith and trust in what life is, and all sense of humility and surrender which is all the good I can find. Know those Parts of Consciousness that we have yet to touch and to recognize.

Atma and the conscious/unconscious psychology are just two drawings on the same Water, ever just defining Self (Atma). It is all that is happening there at that level. And with that, those drawings on Water, doubt and trust come and go on the shining and glowing surface of Pure Mind.

Know the real content of what you may envy, as the pride, power, attention and esteem given from one person to another or given by a person to her/or himself. But we all suffer the ego as we are human beings forgetting our own True Being!

Actually, embodiment is a strange comfort, where the Pure Mind Light is so natural! If only everyone of us could say to each other and to ourselves, "Poet, I Empower you to know your True Identity!" What a world it would be. Everyone really knowing what is. The Dzogchen writers that we remember were really high class excellent poets. Through the Vast Expanse of Pure Mind I Empower Myself by Myself to Know Myself in the lineage of poets within the Vast Expanse itself. Whitman the Wonder. Tennyson the Tremendous. Shelly the Superb. Sappho the Supreme. And they are all Dakini! Not many! But One Brilliance! Dakini is Always Present, yet certain mind forms can make mind alert to this Dakini Ever Present!

Enjoy the Light by Love. No pushing, no pulling on the Light. In this state or the next. Delight in the Bardo of the Now and fill its emptiness with Love! Excellent! Now the bardo mind, the birth mind, the child mind, the young mind, the middle mind, the old mind, the dying mind and the death mind are no longer a comfort. I find my ease in Pure Mind, Dakini Mind, Garuda Mind, all in Mother Mind, the Light that causes the Lighting Up!

I have on many occasions impaired my spiritual Peace by hoping, waiting and looking for teaching, initiation and empowerment from another human being. When all along what was hoped for was to be directly taught by Reality and is it not this and this alone that is real to the Reality of Self. And all along what I was waiting for was to be initiated by Peace itself into the peace of my own mind not via some other necessity of human arrangement. And what I was looking for was the power to Give Power to my own self in my inner-most and own-most deepest sense of Being as what I simply am without expectation, hopes, looking, waiting or measuring the power and energy of myself to only give energy and power to myself by something or someone that is not myself. You see, when you are exploring such high systems like Dzogchen thinking or Advaitic thinking,

5

when it all does not yet click into place or you are still confused about some point of it or find yourself in a waiting stance expecting Truth to come from somebody else, you have just set yourself up in one of the most powerful places of potential despair. More than any other cause of despair really because you are standing at the door of the Ultimate Spiritual Region and knocking and nobody is opening that door. You have to do it yourself, don't knock, just go in, it is Your Own House. But usually we just stand on the other side of the door waiting in our worries. And if you wait there too long without doing anything pretty soon your worries have made you to feel you have lost your power. And with that loss of power you know what despair is and then your entire world view exists in the repeating mental cycle of despair (worry) without answers and soon you feel insane or worst yet, empty.

Dzogchen gives the four Confidences which come with singular reliance on Pure Mind. 1: No fear of hell because you know it is an unreal delusion created by a closed cycle of mind generated by hate and resentment. 2: No expectation of results from the Karmic domains (whether they are pertaining to the desire, form or formless realms) because it is all Samsara anyway and you have unlocked the links in the twelve karmic chains. 3: No hope of attaining Nirvana because he/she who attains Nirvana does not exist in any way as a permanent being who attains a Permanent State, and hope is a distraction anyway like looking at an elephant's footprints wondering where he is when the damn thing is standing right behind you. 4: No desire for joy (thinking that it would come from others) so you are equal to all beings in kindness, compassion, love and equanimity (the Four Boundless feeling vectors) because all are as Pure Mind in Reality, friends and enemies alike.

It all boils down to finding that Love that does not fear. I think Love is the only thing that does not fear or doubt or lack that Spiritual Trust that is cut free of all barriers and makes the final leaping and soaring to what Really Is. And it seems that the five traditional poisonous emotions all come out of fear. Fear is the break from Reality, you are caught in its illusion and you think you are no longer Real in the sense of Pure Mind. Out of

6

fear arises anger because you are naturally angry at what causes you this discomfort. Out of fear comes desire for you think by getting momentary pleasures that you may escape from that fear and you do for the moment but when the pleasures are over you go back to fear. And fear is the cause of stupidity because it blunts and paralyses your mind. Jealousy comes out of fear too because you are afraid that you are not like or equal to the thing or person you envy, when in Reality as Pure Mind we are all quite the same, Divine, if I may reluctantly use this word. And so too pride is the exact same mechanism, but here you try to boost yourself above others because you are afraid they are better than you. So fear is the obscuring and Love is the clearing, the Solution.

Materialism doubts materialism because of the presence of the Spiritual. The Spiritual doubts the spiritual because of the presence of the material.

Within one bolt of thought it struck me yesterday that twenty-nine years or more is not a long time to wait for Love. Then I remembered the beautiful thought that there is not only birth and death in the physical world but also in the subtle (astral) world one certainly comes and goes. As well as entrance and exit in the causal world. Death as Trekchod cuts away the bundle of all three layers of ideas about this world or the next. It is beautiful really. One can Trekchod the astral form or take birth in the astral form. One can Trekchod the causal idea forms of self or take birth there. It is really a condition of ideas. Thinking, I wondered, am I a dakini who has wandered back to Earth to translate a few religious cognitions in the light of the advaitic principle. With that thought I became psychologically happy and no longer felt self doubt but became filled with self trust. So it is good, true or not. With this I realized as it became real to me that Trekchod and Thogal are not so difficult to comprehend and experience. Trekchod is essentially Humility that cuts away the hold on all ideas so that one may then Let Go of those ideas. With this comes the Soaring On of Thogal as Surrender, to all that one may vision one then automatically surrenders.

I seek the Spiritual experience without cognitive illusions.

7

That is what I want and nothing less. With thoughts of the rainbow body, the light body and the great transfer of consciousness at death it becomes evident for the thoughtful person that these may somehow be true to experience not only in this physical world, but again in the astral (subtle) and causal (more spiritual) dimensions. One may Trekchod the astral body leaving in the wake the rainbow spectrum of the energetic astral form. One can Soar On in Thogal as well with the newly created or old form astral light body as well. These two, Trekchod and Thogal, again may be applied to the dimension of causal ideas as well. Indeed they may, they must, and should be practiced there at that causing idea, first and foremost, for that is where the rest, astral then physical, takes origin. And one should not think that the great transfer of consciousness at death is just from the physical point of view, for the practice applies equally as well to or out of the astral subtle cognitive forms of self and the more spiritual causing ideas of a self form. These cognitive forms are amazing really and vast. One may generate consciousness or assume massive identities in meditative states as well as after death, even more so, whether it is Ramakrishna style or Yukteswar style or Tibetan style, Buddha style, Jesus style, personal archetypal style or finally and joyfully with the blissful logic of Gaudapada.

Devotees of Ramakrishna speak of the after death condition of Ramakrishna Loka (A Realm of Heaven). Those of Yukteswar have written (see Autobiography of a Yogi, The Resurrection of Sri Yukteswar, even so, here Yogananda's endearing and sweet description of his encounter with Yukteswar may be indeed a little forced to align or fit the Christian context.) of Hiranyaloka, an astral plane where Yukteswar works with those who have got some grip on nirvikalpa samadhi but are still holding to their astral shape and have yet to go to the causal dimension or they have died out of the causal domain of pure thought and are now reborn in the Hiranyaloka. Which is a luminous golden astral plane, a name of a condition which comes from the older name of Hiranya Garbha, the Luminous Golden Womb of all subtle (astral) forms. Well it is certainly interesting. Or you can generate Tibetan style visions filled with peaceful and wrathful shapes and forms. And again there is pure Buddhistic or Christian elaborations. Certainly the Christ/Jesus dual view in the truth of it is similar to Pure Love and Pure Buddha (A State of Mind) before the additions of complex elaborations through the centuries. No doubt these are experienced in the astral and causal worlds if one's mind form is accustomed to that thinking in life. Or one may be bold enough to find one's own Poetic Reality that expresses all this in personal loving simplicity. But at last Gaudapada solves the whole problem II 8. "The objects perceived by the dreamer, not usually seen in the waking state owe there existence to the peculiar conditions under which the cognizer, that is the mind, functions for the time being, as with those residing in heaven. (It is here that I refer to the astral and causal cognitions selected by the dreamer's personal preference) The dreamer associating himself with the dream conditions perceives those objects even as a man, well instructed (or conditioned in this world of the waking state) goes from one place to another and sees peculiar objects belonging to those places." So if one is bedazzled by the complex bewildering cognitions of these fantastical dream worlds, these regions of mind it will create self doubt, eventually, after the exotic effect wears off, because the fantastical descriptions of imagination may only cause the suspension of belief. When in reality it is always more than the experience of any assumed mis-identity through imagination. That is the Trekchod (cutting away every illusion of mind) into the Thogal (to Soar On in the Spiritual beyond and free of every imagination). Spiritual self trust is free of illusions. When reading such accounts of the after life whether it is Yogananda's Resurrection of Sri Yukteswar or some other remember that there is no last word on the truth-nature of this experience. Imagine if you could get outside the Milky Way Galaxy and look back on it what would it look like. Now increase that experience to getting out of the entire universe where you could look down on the spiraling arms of the galactic superclusters turning like petals of a fluid flower around the core without circumference, then what would it look like to you? So where is the "last word?"

9

In a Trekchod death from whatever sphere, one may or may not leave a rainbow body in the wake of death. It depends on the direction of the Trekchod impact on the spiritual, subtle or physical environ (toward Pure Mind or toward energies in the display). The re-manifestation of the Thogal light body is, if it is considered, very well demonstrated as to what that might be in The Resurrection of Sri Yukteswar, even though Yogananda claims that this was an actual remaking of a flesh and blood body by Yukteswar. It may or may not be so, but it is an illustration of the Thogal light body. And Ramakrishna demonstrates very clearly the Thogal Light Body in the case of Vivekananda when he appeared in this apparitional light body to Vivekananda six years after his death in 1892 before going to America, though it was described as a symbolic dream. That too is of clarity and interest about the nature of these things. Elsewhere he says, "Several times in my life I have seen returning spirits; once - in the week after the death of Ramakrishna Paramahamsa - the form was luminous." That is no less the beautiful Thogal Light body. Others too have seen Ramakrishna's light body, even while he was still alive there was one who saw him elsewhere than where his flesh and blood body actually was. But here in these examples, neither Vivekananda nor the others, claim a remaking of atoms and energies into the form of flesh and blood.

Nevertheless the Thogal Light body is described. "God cannot be seen with these physical eyes. In the course of spiritual discipline one gets a 'love body', endowed with 'love eyes', 'love ears', and so on. One sees God with those 'love eyes'. One hears the voice of God with those 'love ears'. One even gets a sexual organ made of love." At these words M. bursts out laughing. The Master continued unannoyed, "With this 'love body' the soul communes with God." M. became serious again." This Love Body may be the Bhagavati Tanu, the Pure Body of the Goddess Sakti. But it certainly is very Thogal-like! As he says at the beginning this type of God experience is not seen with physical eyes. So experiences of this nature are something spiritual. But this Thogal light body can be seen in the waking physical, the dream subtle, or the causal spiritual, one may cut away (Trekchod) or soar on (Thogal) with a light body

10

in any of these dimensions it seems. One cuts away all that is not Love and then soars on, coming back as Love. Love is first found in Humility then comes back as Surrender.

The Tibetans consider resurrection as a dark science. The reanimation of a corpse is no doubt very strange and weird, if not gruesome no less. Trekchod melts or explodes the solidity of the physical with attending rainbows and other signs but is very rare like spontaneous combustion. Thogal emanates the light body composed of the energies of the five pure lights. In Phowa Chenpo, the great transference of consciousness, there is no death, it is not experienced. Consciousness is too high to even notice death. Physical substances melt back into atomic/quantum energy light, which is the case anyway when death occurs though in a more common and naturally recycling way.

I had a Dakini Dream where a Tibetan lama woman told me that the spontaneous births that take place in these emanation worlds (subtle and or purely spiritual) after death, are not flesh experiences. They are bardo subjects and potentials of the bardo, not flesh body experiences.

A Dzogchen thinker loves to practice death and rebirth. They can fearlessly and vigorously as well as enthusiastically Abide in Pure Clear Mother Light, assume a new body and not lose it (not lose awareness of the Mother Light). "In the work of waking up Atman in my fellow men I shall gladly die again and again." And, "It may be that I shall find it good to get outside of my body - to cast it off like a disused garment. But I shall not cease to work! I shall inspire men everywhere, until the world shall know that it is one with God." Vivekananda. We come to an interesting thought on the Thogal light body. On one hand the Buddha (Sakyamuni) was said to have extinguished all karma and that would mean even the karma of remaking a light body. But Swami Vivekananda says, "I saw the extraordinary figure of a monk appear suddenly, from where I did not know, and stand before me at a little distance filling the room with a divine effulgence. I have seen many monks but never have I found such an extraordinary expression in any other face. That face has been indelibly printed in my heart. It may be an hallucination, but very often it comes to my mind that I had the good fortune of seeing Lord Buddha that day." Perhaps he did see the effulgent Thogal body of Sakyamuni and perhaps it was out of the intensity of his own consciousness that this vision occurred. But Swamiji is so clear headed about it and describes it in such an open ended way that it does not engender doubt but only trust and respect. Why all this about the various forms of death and states after death? Because it is here in the most primary sense that self doubt or self trust is made. Of course, self trust is found when the Clear Light is discovered as one's own Self, and doubt is the trouble we feel when that is not known.

So if sweet Jesus really resurrected from death you would think he would have told us more about death, and God life, there in that place where the body is gone. For Tilopa the art of resurrection was considered to be a black art for lifting life back into the flesh that is dead is creepy to say the least. But not rainbow body death, in this body flesh dissolves. It is death like fire going into fire. Compare it to the rare phenomena of yoga style spontaneous combustion. Then a Thogal light body may reappear, but out of spiritual substances, not the dead flesh, that stuff is buried, burned, eaten by vultures, gone. Then there is death which is like space melting into space, the Dakini style death, pure Trekchod, pure mind into Pure Mind, no phenomena projected outward on the environ. Just Pure Letting Go (Trekchod).

The third form of Dzogchen death methods is Phowa Chenpo, that is the Great Transfer, but nothing is really transferred, it is a misleading word cognition. It is a beautifully enlightened condition where Pure Mind has already surpassed or even by passed the three Kaya bodies or dimensions and the three Bardo states. But it becomes confusing after that thought because of the impossible suggestion that the body stuff itself melts back into the Pure Light, but it is magnificent poetry for the soul. In Trekchod death unusual signs appear, the body over days disappears leaving only hair and nails, rainbows are seen in the sky at the time of leaving the body behind, earthquakes happen (as with Sakyamuni), even images of deities are seen on

12

the bones (if in this case the body is not cremated, and does not disappear and some bones are left). But in Thogal death a luminous body composed of the five dakini/buddha light energies is emanated. Did Sakyamuni do this? Did Ramakrishna do this? Or were and, will be these appearances, just in the mind of those who experience such things? Nature speaks, not man!

Be at Peace for all these death methods are nowhere in Pure Mind, in the Mother Light that doesn't even know (cognise) death, bardos, light or rainbow bodies, phenomena, kayas, transfers, cutting away or soaring and surpassing on, even so what could be even called an innermost secret, a base, path, fruit, an essence, nature or energy to the One who is that Secret. No, nothing of it at all! I will not have Trust confused by so much doubt!

But doubt may come from the other direction. Those who may say there is no religious god creator of the universe, the galaxies, planets, bodies, brains, the self or no self idea, no lever puller and nothing after death, but wait before you go off into the deep end of despair, they have the Deist Idea, you see, the Creative Force Idea (divested of all religious myth) as Light and Energy is the Spiritual Stuff we are talking about. No ego and ego. Pure Mind encompasses even this idea of Light Energy Creative Force. It is Evident as Light Energy by the Evidence/Existence of Creative Force by the presence of the World/Universe before us. We speak of our Non-Duality with this Power that has made us, that we have become out of and so are! Duality is the question, not religion. We are Non-dual with this Great Power (Sakti), all the rest (universe, living bodies, brains, brain center identities in the self/no self constantly adjusting neurons and neural calculations, genetic continuance (as human development one half a million years old) and that no inner divine lever puller survives death (which is fine/fantastic, eliminating the ego/soul idea and finishing it off) is all the incredible astounding power of Maya (the Phenomena of Amazement in the Occurring). Besides, what do Near Death Experiences show us when body and brain (ego) are dead, but a Light Energy Force is Experienced? Is it not a contradiction to

13

the strictly empirical view of experience (Life) opposed to the one that mixes a transcendental surviving Principle (here named Light Energy Force). Again, the amazement of Maya, which makes mind thought look through finite duality (a broken apart life death picture) which in Reality is the Infinite and Non-Dual Consciousness/Love/Existence (Vedanta's Satchidananda), the Light Energy Creative Force renamed. It is again the duality of ordinary/divine appearance. Really, is this Universe in anyway ordinary? So, What Is the Experience we are having Here? I Answer with a Question so you will think for or of your Self (even in the context of thinking as a temporary no self idea which is the Buddhist concept of the no self idea of the five conjunctive aggregates of mis-identity so similar to the genetic/neural/socio/bio/ evolutionary idea of no self and as to what may happen from one moment to the next, we are brought to Wonderment at all that is in front of our minds and that mind melts into the Void which is Dzogchen's Mother Light in Perfect corresponding analogy to Light Energy Creative Force ("His own body, mind, and I-consciousness, not to speak of those of others, seemed to be but a component wave in that immense mind. In that state the Master had the direct experience and vision of the real nature of universal consciousness and power as the "One without a second" - as the one living and wide-awake Being, as the source of all will and action, the Mother of infinite grace. It is the same Being who the self-styled materialistic scholars of the West, looking through their clouded intellects and scientific instruments, view as inert and insentient, though admitting its unity." Swami Saradananda on Ramakrishna). What is more Creative than Her? She who is Light, Energy and Power. Here, one is no longer dreaming, as dreaming is the mere conscious vibration of dualism. The Non-Dual Light Energy Creative Force was Here, what you have been all along, before (that is pre-primordial in reference to the space/time creation and pre-subjective in reference to mind as conscious living activity occurring) the finite appearance of a merely 18 billion (a finite number concept) year old universe. Again, Hindu/Buddhist cosmologies take account for these vast though finite expanses. And though modern astrophysics and

14

cosmologies have given us a much farther reaching range of ideas about the universe out there as galaxies, etc, and in here as quantums and so forth, we are still confronted with a finite system/cycle potential. And much of the Deist/Science ideas are addressed to the Judeo Christian beliefs about Life and the Universe. However you see it the Universe is not ordinary, for everything in it or on this planet is the condensation or expansion of Pure Light Energy and so we achieve the perception of Divine Appearance in all approaches.

There is a place in the human mind that psychological science cannot describe for it is Pure Consciousness this very same Creative Light. They have given it the name of Zone of Convergence for this is where the describable mind converges with the indescribability of Consciousness. Somewhere along the event horizon here in this Zone of Converging the materialism of mind, memory, ego, intellect, neurons, nerves and energy all collect and give rise to the idea of an "I" which arises in this event horizon. Within this event horizon there is buddhi (intellect), when bodha (Consciousness) is known that becomes buddha (Awakening).

Generally, it is said that to humanize the lama/guru is the wrong direction, but if we are to take the spiritualized direction, then it is best indeed to move beyond the mere lama/guru, forward into the entire universe and every being that appears in the six rotating worlds. Then, where not does She Shine! The Entire Field of Experience more than Mirrors Her Pure Mind!, for it may indeed all be Her.

Experience is the Content of experience. It is just remembering your own Self is the Experience. What it All is, just layers in the circle of Dakini Knowingness, the Rigpa of Yeshes (Kuntuzangmo) Ma! The Unfabricated Primordial!

Is Love perhaps the intense awareness of time's passage causing this feeling to rise and expand, in that we are all going to Death, so that Death teaches Love if anything at all. Or is Love that longing, that missing of what has gone or will be gone. Or is this definition simply sentimentalism. As mental (mind) sentiment is not Pure Mind (Love).

When I look and listen, I can clearly see and hear the "child

15

within" looking outward to find the mother/father in every being I encounter.

King Arthur did not worship Merlin. They did not worship Socrates, Keats, Shelly, Wordsworth, Whitman or Tennyson. And all are considered to be Enlightened Beings. But those now ask you to worship gurus and lamas. If you want a little time with Whitman or Merlin, fine, but do not worship anyone! Be pure and true in what is Human Heritage. "The one hopes to show what all may strive for, the other, what none may hope for or attain. The one inspires. The other degrades." S.G. One causes self doubt. The other causes self trust. This is the true Karana or Cause of Spirituality. Even Shankara ended with poems to the Goddess. She appeared to Shankara removing his stupid Brahminical arrogance which is hypocrisy, not seeing Reality everywhere, but holding powerful prejudiced distinguishment (that is the case with most gurus too). So should have all of Shankara's guruism also have fallen away at Her feet, the Goddess, no longer holding to the attitude of arrogant opinionated brahmin gurus, who cause self doubt by their preposterous proclamations! Love is what gives Self Trust and the Power to go on.

In many cases, gurus as with all and any of us have tremendous Super Egos in regard to their Atma (Self) being Brahma (God) or Brahman (the Infinite). In such cases of event it is very important to remember Sakyamuni's definitions of Atma as a misconception of True Reality. Atma dristi (self belief). Atma moha (self delusion). Atma mana (self conceit). Atma sneha (self love). It is the delusion of loving one's own narcissistic self belief.

Non-Dual Light Phenomena

I have no doubt burdened myself with too many thoughts as even two thoughts are a burden. It is a phenomena, that is an unreality, a delusion of imagination that the offspring mind thinks and believes that it looks back and inward to the Mother Light. This is the start and the end of all phenomena. For She is the Non-Dual Light!

16

Ultimately, you empower yourself to permit these experiences to happen. The beauty of Dzogchen and Bardo instructions is that Kuntuzangmo (Mother Light) in instant Dzogchen can happen at any stage along the way. It is a limiting illusion to say that one only experiences Her Light in the death moment, for how do you define death. Is it not but the release of one's hold on life, on the here and the hereafter and all ideas pertaining therein? Who can own this Mother Light and who can define Her? Does She not wait for one and all and is She not within one and all. There is no higher or lower awareness of Her!

For Kuntuzangmo, the Mother Light can be experienced in any of the Three States of waking, dream or deep sleep, in any of the Kaya dimensions, any of the Bardos, or between any two thoughts, two feelings, two actions or movements. These teachings raise you to look at your self beyond death, birth, becoming and so forth. Wonderful!

The Chikhai (The Clear Light at Death) Mother Light is Purely Subjective. The secondary Offspring Light is Mother Light becoming Objectified and then Dream Dualism stirs up. But is it ever so, in Pure Mind Non-Dual where Subject/Object are One and not two, never two as Mother Light and Offspring Light. So does this Mother Light only become named "Mother" in regard to the presence of "Offspring"? Yes and No. She cannot be described by any thought, nor contained thereby with any idea, so we call Her Mother. The Tender One taking hold of us at the death moment. We are filled with emotion for this One and that helps remove the fright of death's transport from one place to another, from the comfortable to the unknown. But in those who stay with Pure Mind none of this happens. The Offspring Light does not come forth or if it does it is immediately recognized as the Mother Light. These go no further into the Bardo.

The Mother Concept? The Offspring Idea? Do either comprehend this clear Reality that has no mind thought that can describe its Nature, its Essence, its Energy? Does Mother Light only have the true capacity and skill to comprehend the Mother Light? Can the Offspring Light ever contain within its mind

17

creation the full content of the Mother Light? Must this offspring idea die completely in order to stay aware in the Mother Light? If it exists at all then it is a secondary observer of the Mother Light as one looking into the Mother Light, not as Mother Light alone and pure as Pure Mind itself. As long as you create the offspring idea within the Pure Mind the possibility of roaming about through states, conditions, dimensions and bardos still exists within the potential of the offspring consciousness. The Pure Consciousness of Pure Mind in Pure Mother Light is never caught in the amazing maze of the roaming and the wandering! When one awakes from a dream the roaming and wandering there stops and at that sacred moment Mother Light in Pure Mind as Pure Mind shines as awareness in the conception-less. Offspring is conception. Mother Light cannot be contained by the offspring's conceptions. The personal melts into the Principle but the Principle can never be contained by the personal's conceptions.

In the Chikhai Bardo one experiences Full Mother Light without any subjective or objective reference point whatsoever. In this regard, the Chikhai may not even really be a bardo strictly speaking since here we embrace Complete Perfect Mother Light, at least for the snap of the fingers, or the time it takes to eat a meal, or three or four days as the Bardo Thodol says. In the Chonyid Bardo, when the subjective and objective reference points begin to stir up I believe we experience what is a very clear, vivid and lively vision of those pictures and projections that come up out of the karmic mind one is carrying somewhere within the illusive mind stuff that makes up identity. I was thinking this is not like the dream state ordinarily speaking because consciousness is now without the limiting body reference point to constrict its so called dream activity. I think that consciousness out of the body is going to have a much wider view. Think of it, when you dream it is really confined within the small arena of your head, but when that arena is expanded through death of the confining space of the mind then you are going to experience a wide screen panorama. This is why I thought that the dream state is perhaps more like a television screen and the Chonyid dream condition is much more like a

18

wide movie screen. Silly as it might sound but I think the point is carried through. Now in the Sidpa Bardo we are no longer in the experience of personal dream emanations of any kind, well perhaps some traces surely in visions or flashes of various worlds one might be incarnating into, but you see the Sidpa has a relation to the fixed realness of the waking state, at any rate, for now consciousness is considering to reestablish itself back into a living body through the vehicle of conjugal making. Here now our consciousness is not just in the personal dream experience but is actually coming back into relationship to the physical world. But of course it only seems natural that these bardos would at times intersect, these ideas only being maps of the world of the death mind experience.

When one has actually come back you go through the whole rebirth experience to find yourself helpless as an infant now remade into the waking state and this waking state has the very clear and wide visual reality division of extreme subjective and objective dividing lines. Duality. Where has the Mother Light gone, forgotten through all this passage? So within this waking living bardo we again experience the dream bardo or the smaller free flowing dream content within the confined and consciousness attached waking condition. Thinking on the Mother Light, the child/son/daughter-mind, that is the offspring subjective/objective thinking visionary dream mind so busy conjuring up duality, has at times moments of peace and serenity and clarity or energy which connects it in various stages to the Mother Light and that is samadhi bardo. Once again in the cycle death approaches and when the severing comes the consciousness so attached to the confinement of the waking birth living bardo, the dream mind projection bardo and the small Mother Light experiences of the samadhi bardo is destroyed and so there offspring consciousness returns to the Mother Light of the Chikhai Bardo, which is the exit from the cycle and not really a bardo (a between two conditions state) at all, since here is where Complete Perfection in Mother Light Consciousness or Clarity of Pure Mind is originally and best experienced.

By uniting Concept with person and experience one comes to know. Is it really only in death that the son mind completely

19

knows Mother? Because it is the complete letting go (or Cutting Away: Trekchod) of waking and dreaming states. So no hold is there in the son mind as to make it or still be the son mind. But Mother Light is in deep sleep. So then even in the encounter there, there is still some holding of the son mind as the son mind. Can it only be in Chikhai Bardo then that full Mother Light is known as they say. I think not. After that, then the Chonyid Dream stirs from there. The Zhi Khro. When one actually begins looking for a waking state birth that is then the Sidpa Bardo and the son mind has separated further from Mother. When birth in a new waking condition begins that is the Bardo of Jati (Birth). Consider, imagine what are waking, dreaming and deep sleep for the Humble Gods, the Egotistical Gods, for ghosts and hell beings. We only know the waking, dreaming and deep sleep states for human beings and animal beings. But where is the son mind in complete Nirvikalpa? (Non-Conceptuality) The hold is busted even if karmic remains continue until death's dissolution. There is no end to the depth one may go! Mother Sakti!

In Chikhai, like Nirvikalpa, real death has not yet occurred, for death comes when consciousness steps down from the Mother Light and begins movement in the Chonyid dream mind. So death, technically speaking, is movement out of the Primary Clear Light of the Mother as it enters a new journey, hmm, not until then. So death is no death, only new movements. Where should there be fear? One wanders in the Sidpa state looking around for new life, when one leaves the Sidpa condition, Birth in a new bardo now begins, then the Dream state arises and the Samadhi Potential is again reached in the human plane of Mother and offspring alliance.

A Non-Dual Light Phenomena. Mother gives to father (intellect) son which becomes father. An absurd formula for how can One (Mother) produce two, so in Reality there is no duality. I am my own Mother, or I am just Mother, making my own dual problem play or Being my Own Non-Dual Peace, when the "own" concept slips off, then Naked Self, Aware of (its own language description problem) Non-Duality! Awareness Stands Alone, Here, none are aware as with duality.

20

It is the extraordinary miracle of psychological harmonizing with Experienced Spiritual Content for as you give in and give over to Trekchod, Thogal continues to arise as Self Arising Appearances, because the three Kaya dimensions are ever within the Wonder of Inseparability. The Mother of Mother Energy is experienced in the Son Energy which is the Energy of Advaita Sakti, the "Primordial Power" as She was called by Ramakrishna!

Nirvikalpa as Personal Death Process

Ramakrishna spent six months in nirvikalpa samadhi, only barely coming out of that state to be force fed a little nourishment. At all other times he appeared outwardly as if dead. His consciousness going so deep past the mortal horizon's border of life and death. I have heard the spiritually illumined say that they believe that Jesus went into nirvikalpa samadhi when he was on the cross. Later when his friends took him down, after a few days he returned to normal consciousness. This has been interpreted as the phenomena of resurrection. The art of resurrection is practiced by a few Tibetan lamas (Shankara too, raising the dead king Amaru), but generally it is felt that this is a black art and should not be engaged. And to them the entire thing may indeed be myth. As something to stimulate curiosity about spiritual powers.

As the story goes, Sakyamuni right before enlightenment went through the observation of the three watches. In the first watch he saw the great wheel of the worlds turning and souls on it like buckets. In the second watch with lightning-like sweeping thought he remembered his five hundred and fifty past births, identities and deaths and that of others too. In the third watch he contemplated the twelve links of causation in the forward and backward sequence, then at that time it came to him, "I, who am here, at this moment, I know what is." The mystery of enlightenment is made so simple! Now as it says in the Tibetan Book of the Dead that the soul wanders for 49 days before rebirth. You see, Sakyamuni after his realization of knowing "what is," paced (walked) back and forth around the seat of his enlightenment for 49 days thinking about what he had realized. That is the metaphor of the 49 bardo days. After one realizes Clear Light at the moment of death, one spends a symbolic forty nine days in the Chonyid bardo pacing as it were and thinking about what was experienced at the moment of the Clear Light of Death. It is poetically beautiful.

Many have known the moment of their death, when it would be. Jigme Lingpa would contemplate and calculate the wonder of how much time he had left. Vivekananda knew he would not live to celebrate his 40th birthday and he left his body a few months before that date. Ramakrishna knew his life extension would be coming to its fulfillment when he could only eat porridge and he told people of this long before it came to be. Shankara knew his life span would be 16 years, but the Goddess doubled that time to 32 years so he could finish his writings and teachings. All these and many others have been aware when they would awaken from the dream of this life.

In the Death process, the dark stage before the Clear Mother Light comes up just like the Prajna state of Deep Sleep. So everyday you apply yourself to one of the ultimate spiritual questions and the answer is right there in your experience. The actual states of waking, dream, deep sleep and Clear Consciousness where no subject perceives no object in Radiant Emptiness. Pure Mind comes forth!

Should I not be so humble as to think that I am so unique that Death would pass me by? Every moment is precious, so fill the here and here forth and here after with Spiritual Thought. Know my mind, my Atma (Self) quenched of Vaitathya (Illusion).

Can I like a lama choose my next birth? And what would that be? If I were dead what would I miss the most from this life? Would I die with insecurity? Or will the Great Mother of Transcendent Wisdom fill me so that this "I" of "no I" would know not fear? The Quest of Earth has been walking Sacred Ground with my loving Goddess friend!

Would Ramakrishna greet me? Aseshananda and Bhashyananda guide and comfort me? Would my consciousness then in the sushumna tunnel be cognizing all the dreams of

22

recent? Or would Mother in Her Great Wisdom Love Compassionately Embrace Me? As I venerate Sakti, Sakti generates me into the divine pride of Her Consciousness.

Would I be able to still Love and Watch my Goddess friend? Do I Love her that much? Yes! A gross body is found easily enough! The subtle body continues, Mother keep there my memory of Your Tantra, Advaita and Dzogchen. Forget not me in what I have found here in this life. The causal body has not the effect of death within, being Pure Cause, a cause within, which has the Inherent Right to Mother's Turiya! OM Sakti OM!

But would there be poverty, loneliness and despair as I've known in this life? Or will there again be Poetic and Sakti Sentiment and enough Provision to freely create with words something that might help others? As a Bodhisattva would do!

Would I become a man or a woman or remain for a time Joyfully Disembodied as Joy itself would close the womb doors to dualistic bodies!

The four ego fixations cause all problems with death worry. Let me cut (Chod-pa) these away. The ego's fixation to the pleasure of the physical body. The ego's fear of the death of the physical body. The ego's emotional possessiveness of the physical body. And the ego's holding to an idea of identity in the form of the physical body, with its perception, feeling, volition and consciousness. Come drink the Immortal nectar of my inevitable corpse sacrificed to you all!

Enough of this fussing and figuring. Kali come quickly, quickly now and devour the "me concept" with Your Death! Drain every drip of Nectar from Life. Death then Come and Love Yoke Me! It is just the accustomed feeling of the body which causes the distraction and dread of death! Graduate from Her School!

Am I really so pleasure bound (attached) to all these previous things? So easily my mood changes! Happy with my Goddess, I want to live forever and that want makes me afraid of death. Unhappy with my Goddess, then I am more than prepared to die. How easily I am influenced, based upon the happy and the unhappy of my life! So many people spend their whole life

23

lamenting, brooding and mourning their death, pretending it does not exist or hiding from it and so never come to really ever be fully alive! So why should not I write of what Heightens our Awareness to the Extreme?

I weep, Tears of Love, for all that is Precious to be preserved. This Quickened Emotion of Love is all the Truth and Meaning I know. The rest of what is here left of Earth is an empty cup, void by its own pain. So move along quickly, quickly as you arrived now depart into Love Quickened by the Pleasure of Its Own Knowledge! The One Object without form that can forever and eternally be held in Consciousness as Real Being Embraced!

Mother, if I must return let me be of Loving Help! Oh how we die for, go to war over, disregard some, defend others, all for our idea of Love! But what is Love, the Mystic Secret Core of Human Spiritual Nature and Essence, the Energy of Life intensely known as much felt. We suffer, bear, change ourselves, compromise, embarrass, humble and surrender ourselves until we Know Love freed of the body idea bound to limited pleasure (feeling)! The orgasm of death could be our greatest spiritual pleasure! Shankara yogically raised the dead king Amaru to experiment with sex pleasures through his body in the king's harem. Janaka, the father of Sita who was the divine Wife of Rama the Avatara, was said to converse on spiritual subjects with dead/disembodied siddhas and sages while in sexual orgasmic embrace with his wife. Janaka was a highest Realizer of Advaita as shown in the Ashtavakra Samhita. (See also Tripura Rahasya.) A moment free of body feeling (proven by the great pleasure of mystic states). The paradox of Joy and Pure Mind's spiritual powers we forgot when we returned to this heavy flesh and bone feeling!

In one's own personal death process each step is a buddha, an enlightenment, or if you wish, a dakini, a powerful Tantric Goddess. It is a way of giving self light and divine dignity to the process of dying, or even of just simply passing from the waking state, into the dream condition and to the black non-dual state of deep sleep. And so also to the process of return, either from deep sleep or death as both are equated as similar in nature and essence. Either process is no longer ordinary but is filled with the clear appearance of divine meditation or better yet, immediate contemplation (the natural condition of Dzogchen awareness).

As consciousness leaves the earth buddha/dakini, the awareness of the physical body and senses diminishes. Again as consciousness passes through the water buddha/dakini that awareness leaves the emotional stages of contact. Then consciousness goes through the fire buddha/dakini and the ordinary mind is left behind. When consciousness passes through the level of the air buddha/dakini, then one is leaving behind the intellectual interpretation of their condition. The bardo of the waking state is now gone.

One now enters the space of the bardo of the dream state where the white creative thought wave of male energy is said to descend from the top of the head down to the heart. And the red creative thought wave of female energy ascends from the root of the central canal of the spinal tree trunk to arrive at the heart. These two energies of the white buddha/dakini and the red buddha/dakini are forces of consciousness moving up and down in the dream mind or as the case may be in the bardo of the intermediate mind that is aware, after death and before rebirth. These two energies of consciousness separated in the head and heart are the cause of the peaceful and wrathful dream appearances that occur when one is no longer in the consciousness of the waking state or when that consciousness in the dying process is in the free floating state of being between worlds (bardo). When these two energies are brought together non-dualistically one has unified the two forces of dualism and there by no longer experiences the confusion that comes with two thoughts in one's conscious thought process.

Now, as consciousness leaves all this behind one's self awareness enters the beautiful and extraordinary depth of the black light of deep sleep or profound death. This is the black buddha/dakini light. It is black because it is the wondrous absence of any cognitive state of dual thinking either of body and mind or waking and dream. At this stage one is technically in deep sleep, but one is not thought to have died in the personal death process until the Ground Luminosity has shown itself in the Pure Mind and then whatever is left there in consciousness by the shaping of thoughts moves onward into the next world or state of consciousness.

This is the death process described in Tantra, in the yoga chakras and in Tibetan yoga. If one has been drawn deeply into the Ground Luminosity it is the same as nirvikalpa samadhi, the final absorption into the Pure Consciousness of Pure Mind where not the slightest trace of thought is left in that Pure Mind. It is called Turiya in the Advaita, the Fourth Pure State in relation to the three conditions of waking, dreaming and deep sleep. The Tibetans think that this process not only occurs by arriving into deep sleep, or the process of death, but also when one thought passes away and consciousness is clear and pure, before another thought arrives. Or when a feeling fades and the Pure Mind (Love) appears before the waves of another emotion arises. Also it is thought that this beautiful process occurs in the loving embrace of sexual orgasm to those who have trained their minds to recognize this Pure Mind during the state of union with the loving consort.

You see, the Pure Luminous Mind is your own Pure Mind. You must be your own Buddha. Nothing less will do! Have no fear. In this way where Pure Mind appears in death, or out of the black oneness of deep sleep where then is the Teacher Now, none other than You, Pure Mind, True Buddha! Now when one comes out of death or back from deep sleep with this awareness of Pure Mind in regard to the now non-conditional state of that deep sleep, dreaming and waking, or in the beautiful and fearless loving awakened death bardo state, the intermediate bardo mind state and the process of rebirth, one no longer perceives these as described just now. They become the enlightened dimensions (kayas) of the Pure Mind. Waking state or rebirth is now the full awareness of Nirmanakaya, the emanation of the Pure Mind. The Dream state as well as the intermediate Bardo mind is now known clearly to be the Sambhogakaya, the dimension of pure enjoyment or resplendent thought in the Pure Mind. And so likewise are deep sleep and the clear light of death nothing but the innate and ever true self experience of the dimension of

26

Truth known as the Dharmakaya. This is the real meaning of Divine Dignity in Pure Mind!

At the death moment, in phowa (consciousness transference), in the sudden samadhi of Pure Mind, as in the Dzogchen style suddenness, the power of the conscious you that makes up your human identity slams up the central canal (it can be gentle, gradual as well) and experiences the Clear Light of the Pure Mind. This explains the High Conscious Feeling. The return is by the backward throw down, back into the dual paradox, when energy comes out of the central canal (sushumna) and starts circulating in the right and left nerve canals. Figuring shuts off Maha Mudra (The Great Gesture of Pure Mind). And Maha Mudra shuts off figuring. Figuring is the thinking currents moving in the dual nerve canals. This brings mind back to the world. Or if you are dead it starts up the return process of traveling back into rebirth somewhere. If phowa is performed successfully one's mind stuff drops and the primal particle of "I" within the border of death's event horizon, crosses the mortal horizon and then enters the Mother Light. Then all mind wandering and traveling in the bardo is finished. There is nothing to go anywhere. You are in the Everywhere of the Great Gesture. When Ramakrishna was passing out of the body he called out, "Kali, Kali, Kali." His hair stood on end. His eyes looked upward. The sushumna shook and he entered the Pure Mother Light. That is what is meant.

Nirvikalpa Samadhi is nothing but Pure Mind as the Ground Luminosity. Ramakrishna actually saw within himself the Divine Power of the Mother, She who is Life Itself, go up the Sushumna (Central Canal) and reach the Seventh Plane producing Nirvikalpa. "He felt that the parts of his body left behind by that Power, at once became still and insensitive and dead to all appearance." (The Great Master. By Swami Saradananda). As the Sweet Life Energy of the Divine Mother moves up and out, the earth chakra sinks into the water chakra which sinks into the fire chakra, in turn which sinks into the air chakra, then the mind space chakra of the red and white spiritual energies, sinking upward as it would be into the depth of the black luminosity of deep sleep death in the ajna or Prajna

27

Chakra. This again is the process of death. When Her Sweet Power comes down, those sinking processes unfold as the chakra flowers now full of Mother's Life Energy. This again is Her True Empowerment. Or becoming Vajrayogini Dakini Sakti in terms of Tibetan practice.

In the Instant of Death, mind energy slams up into the Nirvikalpa Mother Light. The Offspring Light (relative mind light) as daughter/son energy stirs the emanation series which starts when mind energy moves down the central canal and into the solar/lunar channels. This is also described in the Bhagavad Gita, the Brahma Sutras, and the Upanishads.

Intense awareness of the ever possible presence of Death Experience always reminds at every moment of the uncertainty of the impermanent transitory human forgetful world, the very up and down sinking and revitalizing process just described. It Keeps You Humble. So Surrender to this Beautiful Awareness. For Death is a very good Spiritual Teacher viewed from Pure Mind where deep sleep is death, dream is after death-like and grasping for waking state characteristics and conditions is seen to be the one ego centered obscuration, to the View in Pure Mind or the High Vantage Point of Pure Mind. Have faith in Death, the Chikhai Light, everything is Impermanent! You can Trust that! Peace!

At death point, first, the bright pictures or samskaras (latent tendencies)) arise, latter the darker ones surface, even so all with the Dzogchen of death (mind death). It was the same with Ramakrishna's sadhana and your own. There were times when he too saw quite frightening things in the mind surface.

All these things are just a compensation to the living mind which holds so hard and tight to life in the grasp of fear. Who knows, who really knows what lies there beyond. Maybe we all just wake up in some Beautiful Way! But a human being is an amazing thing created in that knowing in consciousness or in the denial of the fact, that this human being is spiraling through time, through birth, age, fragility and then to death, that still and yet still this human being will do good things, self sacrificing things, compassionate things and loving things giving up all into death in some unknowing certainty and out of Love for Others!

28

This is the true Wonder of being human and this makes nothing of human life ordinary as it appears and as we think it to be, since we have ground below us and we can explain birth and survival and daily functions of life and that we argue and fuss with each other and so we think this world is ordinary when it is not. It is a plane of divine dimension in itself. A precious living dimension but not the only dimension.

You see, the fear of death arises from this awful limitation of identification with the body and the mind's clinging to hold on to this phenomenal compounded transient thing. If I worry about my teeth or eyes, my feet or legs, my stomach or sex organs, then fear arises in correspondence to those organs to which the mind has become attached. In death as in spiritual understanding that hold on the body is naturally just given over to the Divine Something which is greater than the little thing of the body that the mind is holding on to. Let everything at once die and then you are truly Alive in the Consciousness which is Formless or Void of holding and clinging, Luminous in itself.

The ever present Presence of Death causes (karana) us to Wonder about the Spiritual. The inevitable direct approach of Death upon us effects (karya) us to find the Immediate Solution to the Spiritual. The first may make us feel we have some time to find the Answer, the second makes us drop everything within the mind and go right for the solution to the Karmic "I." This karmic "I" is the sense of self within the flood of time and the ocean of space that sleeps the sleep in the deep of unknowingness, and dreams the dreams of life and death, and then eventually awakens to the state of the waking state either by simply waking up or by becoming reborn somehow. This is all the entangled fascination of cause and effect with the identity of the karmic "I". Pure Mind is ever free from these conditions! The karmic "I" is the obscuration and Pure Mind is the Immediate Solution.

Blessed is Mother Death who pushes me to work the work of the Spiritual, otherwise I would just sleep and dream my life away. Her Nirvikalpa seeks me, as I know nothing but the Simple Life.

What can we really know of Death. Those who tell us what

29

they know have only reported the beginnings of Death. And the meditation itself effects and affects the meditation on Death. Know matter what you Know you must be free to Know there is always more to Know. And that doubt blinds us and Trust opens our eyes. Only the One who has made Death knows what Death Is and what waits there. And Only That One Knows how much Love that One holds for us now and in Death. It may be like a perfect dream imperfectly translated back into the waking mind. Where parts are remembered and not the whole.

"Chikhai is not of this world," I was told by Lama Geshela and then another Lama friend said, "Phowa is not a shadow going or moving up the sushumna." This is because the body and mind just drop away. Nothing rises, moves or goes in real phowa (consciousness transference). Pure Mind or Consciousness stays just as it is! These two lamas expressed these truths in the not so, negative description, it is not this and not that, perhaps because no words describe. I want Chikhai Phowa now and when I die. This is the High Spiritual Desire, but failure brings inferior feeling even here. Should I not reenter Chonyid and Sidpa (even as this bardo of the living, is the between state of a death behind us and a death in front of us)? This is not the Vow of Love. This is not the Patience of Lifetimes. This is not the Real Embrace of All Kayas. Nor is the simple desire to just get myself out of the cycle the true meaning of the High and the Low OM of Gaudapada!

That self idea complex of inferior failure reflects in dream maya as the Chonyid itself of wrathful self ego directed intellect and the same as loving heart response, the Spiritual Voice Lotus (Sambhogakaya Speech) manifest in dream state self talk. Chikhai is not attained in this dimension of ego self effort. It is Reality without question or striving. Simple Familiarity does it, by grace, faith and ego-surrender Chikhai (Turiya) appears here and then!

If one frees the mind of envy in regard to the four desires (pleasure, position, power and paradise) and the four stages (early life, marriage, retreat and death preparations), then those unreal Chonyid dream emanations and those insignificant unreal Sidpa waking birth state feeling-thoughts will not obscure the immediate constant recognition of Chikhai (Turiya), within the mediatory non-cognition of Chikhai, as the Chonyid and Sidpa (Dream/Waking) states of the self/soul who as a self contained embodied being is the neurotic self illusion, due to the confining feeling in the idea and experience of self!

Love those Things, People, and Feelings that bind you and you are Released. I Take Leave in Chikhai of this World and my complex self idea multidimensional problem mind. Gaudapada IV 10. "All the Jivas are, by their very nature, free from senility and death. But they think they are subject to senility and death, and by the very power of thought they appear to deviate from their true nature."

Death is naturally occurring Trekchod, but unless you have learnt some Thogal what arises now and in death after may be those moments of dropping down from Mother and may assume the distracting quality of appearing to be a dream state or the bardo mind, which are something other than what they (those moments) Really Are as What You Have Been all along. But American Near Death Experiences report their recall of a Spontaneous Guiding Principle through the fifteen or so stages of after death experience so even Trekchod and Thogal do not define everything. A Trust higher than mind work brings Peace with all this.

Ignorance (maya) has no beginning therefore it does not exist, so why use mind to search it out, when Mind is Rigpa Clarity. The twelve causal links in the chain of productions stop when Mind remembers this, "I, who am here, at this moment, I know what is." I am now Silent within. No poetry to here extend. In Pleasure's Peace my hunting thoughts have Ceased!

31

Tantric Levels and Pure Certainty

Set Om, the Mystic Mantra and the Venerable Friend in the One. Then Full Sudden Complete Sakti. Sakti is the Real Content of the Three in the One! Mahavayu prana (the great wind of vital energy) makes the sudden leap up the sushumna (central nerve canal), the prana enters quickly into prajna (deep sleep) with unmani samadhi (sudden awareness). It is like quick death where one remains alive in the body. Could this be Dzogchen Suddenness!

You can ascend in the Holy Ghost through the seven layers of the angel mind into the Heaven of Christ Consciousness or dive deep into the blissful serene equanimity of High Nirvana but when you come back, even if it is in the Pure Reason of the Great Reality, if you do not hold Love in your heart for others regardless of the belief system in their head, then your so called experience is just imaginary.

Mother, I know none of Your Mantras or Tantras, none of Your illumined sages incarnate, only You in Pure Mind do I know and You are named Mother as Death Light because of the Sweet Comfort and Ease lifting away all fears and loneliness. If sages and poets write of Truth, whether they try to or know You or not, You, Your Name as Wonder always Comes through their words. Yours is grace made so by diligence!

In the Pure Mind appears the bija, then from bija (seed of concept) the visual experience of the Goddess arises. That appearance goes back into the bija and that bija returns to Pure Mind. She is Pure Mind in both Voidness and Manifestation!

My consciousness increases to know the Creator is Voidness, so nothing is created and when anything appears it is the Goddess and no longer illusion.

Seeing Void (Dharmakaya) in Manifest (Sambhogakaya, Chonyid Bardo and the Dream Mind, even More as the Waking State of Sidpa Bardo and Nirmanakaya) brings Sudden Dzogchen. This is Svabhavakaya. This is Amanibhava. Also Mahasukhakaya or Sahajakaya. All in Pure Mind. All in this Abhisambodhikaya. Abhisambodha, the special, unique, super,

32

rare Bodha (Consciousness of the Tathagata, one who has understood the Tathagata Garbha, the Womb of Suchness, the Womb of Reality) The Buddha State. It started with Voidness in Pure Mind and ended there.

If the love of Tantric Practice (except for Dzogchen Tantra) causes one to return, then who is there to remember who has returned? Again if one applies pure Dzogchen Advaita and does not return, then who is there to know it is true? We are left in unknowing either way with no recourse but to surrender to the True Self in Pure Mind at this very right Right Now, not the ever returning self which is a cloud in the cloud world of the six chronic and inveterate spheres of reincarnation.

Pure Certainty is the Increase of Sakti, the Ability, the Skill, or the Power of Pure Mind. This is the Inherent Solution to every obscuration. This is what brings real answers into one's life when one opens up to the evidence of Pure Mind and the Certainty of its Profound Ever Present Existence. "All truths wait in all things... Only what proves itself to every man and woman is so, Only what nobody denies is so." Walt Whitman Song of Myself 30.

Through and out of the nine levels, and passing the Buddha fields of incredible dream activity, it is within the individual alone that the experienced content of Pure Wonderment is known.

At the Spiritual Level of Pure Certainty, pure orgasm, pure death and Pure Mind are brought together into the Pure Mind which knows not the border of dualism between the relative and absolute Experience. That border of dualism is a mere shadow within the mind content and has no real existence. Even the act of bringing together is a shadow illusion as well.

As long as the sexual twinning of woman and man remains a somewhat pleasant feeling the production of human bodies will be guaranteed and insured more or less. It is a very beautiful and clever design by the Great Power of Life and will continue until every being has realized the ever undivided union of the inner God and the internal Goddess whose Bliss State is further on than some moment's pleasure but is the reach and range of Pure Openness in Pure Mind.

33

Complete Decision that you are Rigpa Enlightened (Pure Mind) is Pure Certainty above the eight Tantric Levels. It is the ninth level, Ati Yoga Advaita Tantra.

Mother is the Light that is Sakti. The son mind is really the consciousness embodied in OM, the three states of waking, dreaming and deep sleep, sleeping there in those states like a five year old child. Energy is the power movement of OM. This is Mantra Tantra. Real Compassion. Primordial Power. And this Primordial Power of Compassion, this Pure Energy expresses itself in the three: Base, Path and Fruit. The three Series: Mind, Mind Space and Reality as it Is. In the three: View, Behavior and Attitude. The three (Tri) Kayas: Dharmakaya, Sambhogakaya and Nirmanakaya. Also in the three: Trekchod, Thogal and the Rainbow Essence of all energies. Mother is more than the Kayas. The Son Mind is the Comprehensive Background Witness Experiencer of the Three Kayas. And Energy is the Primordial Oneness of the Whole Thing. The Dzogchen Moment that is Rigpa Clarity as Non-Dual Energy.

Tantra is there to open you up so that you can Dance with the Dakini, then as the Dakini, the Sakti Goddess, even so, as Mother Kali Herself. There are those who have heard of the Dakini. There are the Heroic Solitary Practitioners who alone attempt to embrace the Dakini within! There are those who are so Kind in the Kindness of their heart that they refuse the appearance of perfect liberation until everyone is free to dance with the Dakini. That is the three stages of embodied soul minds. Then six levels of Tantra, making nine vehicles to Enlightenment. First Tantra is to debase oneself to the Dakini, giving rise to the tremendous spiritual powers of gratitude and respect of and for life, trust and faith, and profound humility and surrender, the true keys to Liberation and freedom from confining attitudes. Second is Friendship with the Dakini or any Deity one might desire. The need to debase oneself is gone and one begins to gain the dignity and esteem of friendship with the Dakini. Third is that one still continues to have a sense of the Dakini as entering and exiting one's spiritual condition. One greets Her then one leaves Her in one's mind. Fourth is the beginning of the inner Tantric levels as opposed to the former

34

three which are practiced in an outside state of mind. At this fourth stage of Tantra one no longer feels an entrance nor a departure of the Dakini. One sees Her always as She is and has been, that is Ever Present in the Dance of Pure Mind. The fifth stage of Tantric leveling is that one now sees clearly that one has always been in the embrace of and embraced by the sweetest conjugal mystery of the Dakini Goddess. The ideas of there ever having been any kind of duality between you and Her are going. At the sixth level which is Dzogchen itself you see with Absolute Decision and Confidence leaving no doubt whatsoever that the Dakini is in Herself Ever Perfect and Complete as one's own Pure Mind. To make it even more simple. The six Tantric levels round up as Debasement to rid ego, Friendship to feel near, Entering and Exiting with the Dakini. Then the Always Existent Awareness of Dakini, The Consort Awareness of Her Ever Present Love Embrace and then Primordial Mother (Dakini) Awareness. Pure Certainty begins when you start thinking and being Your True Self! You have to become Pure Certainty about this, everything that you need is already here, only this attitude is what is our Re-Enlightenment! It was never lost and now you are Dancing with the Dakini!

The six stages of Tibetan Tantra correspond deeply to the six stages of Indian Tantra, with open outlook you can see the direct relation of both systems saying the same thing. Untrammeled Loving Liberation and Freedom whether in this world or the after-death plane may be said to be of five kinds. First: Salokaya. Here the Soul Shares the Same Plane, Realm, Region, Dimension, Field or Place of Spiritual Habitation with the Goddess Herself. Second: Saristya. Here the Soul Shares in blessed similarity, the Same Powers and Divine Magnificence as the Goddess. Third: Sarupaya. Here the Soul Shares the Same Form as the Goddess, in the Spiritual Sense. Fourth: Samipya. This is the attainment of Nearness, Closeness, Proximity or Parallax with the Great Goddess Herself. Fifth: Sayujya. Here, the Soul has Contact or Union with the Self of the Divine Goddess. The differentiation of I and Thou melts into the Eternal Thou. Her Supreme Self Shines. All sense of otherness melts into Unique Universal Identity. This is the Freedom of

Kali, the Clear Self, the Clear Love, the Clear Consciousness. Yet, one may even go a step further (corresponding to the Sixth stage of Dzogchen) into the Pure Absolute Kaivalya or Ultimate Singular Unity and Aloneness with the Goddess where even the idea of the Goddess Herself melts into the Wavelessness of Nirvritti (free from mind waves). This is Standing in the Self Without Support, a Stateless State that many souls might fear because It is Absolute Unconditional Love Itself! This is a Love that consumes the Relative Circle, the Eternal Circle and the Threshold Borderline of the Crescent Moon Facing the Two Which Have Always Been The One. Vijnana and Bhavamukha! From Disturbing Delights Volume V.

Not just physical and psychic but the Spiritual Embrace as Samantha Bhadri! Sambhavi Mudra! Look In, Eyes Outside, even thoughts, no matter their quality are outside. Ah, the spinning mandala of life! Behold Mother Kali's child, servant, Her slave! With this in the mind the simple most gentle kiss can become the dynamic spiritual embrace and non-dual encounter of Samantha Bhadri and Bhadra, of Kuntuzangmo and Kuntuzangpo.

Dream States and the Bardo Mind

The first dream that came across the stuff of my mind that started the ideas for this text was one of Aseshananda who was observing the twenty-one issues of Disturbing Delights: Waves of the Great Goddess. The second dream state that started all this was one where the same Aseshananda said, "Yes, Richard. You Read. I shall very quickly interpret."

I think that perhaps spiritual dreams occur in the Sambhoga Kaya, the illuminated radiant dimension (Kaya) of pure enlightened enjoyment (sambhoga), not in the ordinary dream mind. So here we are in contact with enlightenment perceived through the dimension of beauty and its enjoyment ever within me and you.

This world realm of ordinary appearances drops in the Chikhai, Chonyid and Sidpa Bardos, but we do not see this now due to the habit of embodiment. In spite of this blindness to

36

what is, the Bardo Mind is here now. The Bardo Mind is the Pure Mind in the clear condition of the death state, it is the after death mind full of clarity to what is.

It is from nowhere else than your own Pure Mind that the Bright Lights that guide you to enlightenment or the Dim Lights that pull you into the comfort of rebirth, come from. From your own Pure Mind in the Bardo, there then, as even now, when you look! It is choosing your Reality! The true spiritual freedom that everything is within you now and in death!

Those Unborn Buddhas (Samantha Bhadra, Samantha Bhadri, Vajrasattva, and so forth) that come, that appear to help you in the Chonyid dream mind, once Consciousness has left the physical body when you really need them, are coming forth from your own Pure Mind. It is like Longchenpa's fantastic field of Awareness pictured in Pure Mind that expands as your awareness of Rigpa expands in the potency of Rigpa itself, You are Helping your own Self. Rigpa in Rigpa! If you can contact your Bardo Mind now then instant Dzogchen comes to you! In the last ditch effort to realize Rigpa before taking rebirth in human form, the Bardo Thodol (Evans-Wentz) states, "Walk with thy head erect. Know thyself in the Bardo." I weep with Blessed Joy when it suddenly comes to me now that I must walk erect and know My Self in this Bardo of living before death arrives or rebirth comes.

Clinging to and craving the future corpse to be now in the form of the fetus, becoming animated and resurrected by body form, feeling, perception, impulse and consciousness, to the madness of names and forms, to mind now standing erect, awake and yet dreaming, diffused into five sensory experiences rainbow broken out of mind not knowing the origins of these psychic impressions named ignorance in contact with world and time, tasting it, wanting it, only to die and begin the madness again. As such does my Goddess dance without taking a step out of Herself!

Ego wants others to submit to it. When they don't ego works itself into anger, pride, envy, stupidity and greed, these dull emotions then lead consciousness out from the Loving Chikhai (Rigpa) to enter the dull lights of the six symbolic

37

dimensions psychologically speaking as our now time bound Bardo Mind slips into the psychological dream states of those dull light states even without dying, once this Bardo Mind is loosened from the waking flesh it is said to be nine times more lucid and nine times more capable in comprehension, more than it is in the dream state, but we must know that Bardo Mind is here now, working through the heavy waking body and the psychological junk world interplay of the dream mind. Entangling relationship with others can cause loss of alertness in Rigpa, unless the bright lights of self radiant Rigpa are applied assertively to them in daytime practice where other people's sense of reality is experienced.

A dream Empowerment? In every room, whether embodied or disembodied, the secret mantra was practiced filling all space and produced the same Fifth Level Tantric Bliss on the face, just as Ramakrishna's Fifth Plane where one can no longer speak in words or if one speaks one can only speak of God. So what is then left but for Pure Transmission (Pure Empowerment) in Pure Mind from Pure Mind.

Songs from the Bardo, Poems from the Bardo, Dreams from the Bardo. Pure Contact! Yea, don't let any one tell you no! Is Pure Mind limited for anyone?

I had a dream of someone I knew. I said, "You need a psychiatrist." He said, "Don't be the guru around me." Be the guru, can anyone just be the guru? Is giving advice like that, guruism or is there something more to this dream? Is it a principle that appears? And what does it mean as 'around me' as such when opposed to elsewhere?

Again I had another dream. More interesting. I arrived in India and took a bath. A Dakini came up to me and spoke in a language I could not understand. I followed her to a temple of enormous size where monks in brown robes were prostrating in front of a chair. Some were joyfully wrestling with each other. Latter I found myself observing a procession of beings which I thought were the disembodied dead. I thought to myself, "Did I die in my sleep and now am meeting others in the death plane?" One of those beings in the procession said, "No, you did not die. You are dreaming." Another said while passing me by in this way, "You do not have enough experience to die just yet." I questioned this asking, "What is experience?" This person threw back their head and said' "Who knows?"

Latter I saw the procession moving down a hill and through a very large gate. Above the gate was a star field I had never seen and many meteors shooting through the sky. Then a large square cube made of light and energy was floating above the gate in the star field. I thought I am now dreaming so let me control the movement of the light cube. I did so with some success. Then for a moment I was aware of the room I was sleeping in and the cube of light I was dreaming about. One eye was on the waking state and one eye was on the dream state. That was curious. Then I entered the huge temple again. Many being were there. The walls were covered with old paintings of enlightened beings. In the chair was a teacher. An old woman was sitting next to the teacher. The teacher person also threw their head back but this time I thought, "So he is in Samadhi."

Any person familiar with the most basic dream language could clearly interpret the Mind Sakti expressed in this dream content. But the most interesting element of the dream is that it hit me with the understanding that the difference between the dream state and the bardo mind is that the bardo mind cannot and does not return to connect with the former physical body consciousness. It just goes on, moves onward you see, as what is called the Chonyid of experiencing Reality, but the question of what is Reality is still left there really speaking. For is the Chonyid dream movement a Reality in the purest and highest sense of the Pure Mind? The answer has to be No.

You see, it is within Vajrasattva that much can be realized. Vajrasattva is the mirror-like or reflective energy of Pure Mind itself. Remember it was from Vajrasattva that Garab Dorje realized Dzogchen and this Vajrasattva is the subtle mind itself as it mirrors Pure Mind but is also aware of dream states and the bardo mind as well. Vajrasattva is the way out of the bardo and the dream state, as it is the non-dual thunderbolt (Vajra) of one's own pure mind (sattva) as the pure dream mind or subtle mind now mirroring the actual Pure Mind which is never caught in the fascination of dream states or bardo conditions.

Do you ever have thoughts to which no word forms describe? That is where my job is, to translate those thoughts into concrete words which may be utilized. You see Vajrasattva is the reflection of Pure Mind which teaches the human mind (the metaphor of Garab Dorje) the Truth of the Pure Mind (Samantha Bhadri/Bhadra). Of course this is in the context of the Dzogchen tradition. Remember, though tradition speaks of Pure Mind, this Pure Mind is not defined nor contained by any tradition and is accessible to all. Garab Dorje means the Blissful Dorje or Vajra which is the thunderbolt of your own mind and intelligence ever capable of grasping in a single second the Truth of the non-dual Pure mind. Vajrasattva has just been explained. Samantha means, like the stone certain Ground, yes, and Bha is to shine, beam, to be resplendent, luminous, and to Show Oneself! Yes, so this is most often translated as the Ground Luminosity which should and will show you Yourself in Pure Mind which is what it is. Dra and Dri are God/father and Goddess/mother designations respectively. With Dri or Dhri having the special meanings of to hold, to bear, carry, convey, cling to, keep, observe, support, design for and allot to, so, these are what the Mother Luminosity in Her Changeless and Unchanging Ground is ever doing for one and all.

Even as the Bardo Thodol states that Pure Mind is accessible to all. And out of its great Compassion brings this forth to anyone, in the after death conditions and in the now experience of waking, dreaming and deep sleep. Yes, so let us take a gradual surveillance of the relationships of these spiritual principles. One could say that the sidpa bardo is indeed the return to the plane of the human mind. So the Chonyid bardo is the subtle mind. And the Chikhai is the Clear Light of the Pure Mind or the first encounter with the Mother Light. So the Vajrasattva method deals with understanding the Pure Mind from the level of the subtle mind's condition here and in the after death state. And it is most fascinating because it brings sudden immediate recognition of the Mother Luminosity now or in the after death bardo mind. Vajrasattva is the ultimate spiritual form of the Vajrayana vehicle of spiritual stages, but I think that absolute pure immediate Dzogchen is in fact one quick step

40

above this vehicle as it is called the adamantine spiritual vehicle and Dzogchen goes a quick step to Pure Mind which is not categorized in any definition, adamantine nor impermanent.

One is dealing with two principles here, the Pure Clear Mother Light and the subtle dream or after death conditions (the secondary offspring light). In its deep Wisdom, the Bardo Thodol brings in this most powerful Dzogchen teaching at various stages, but especially during the darkest of the buddha and dakini reflexes on the Chonyid dream mind which is the Zhi Khro (Primordial dreamland of the peaceful and wrathful deities) or Clear Light of the Mother Luminosity during the Chonyid bardo which is the dual combination of Light and dream as a non-dual inseparate Reality different but not opposed to the Pure Rigpa Light as Clear Pure Mind, the Zhi Od-gsal (Primordial Clear Light). The Zhi or Primordial is the element of Sameness. Or it is the mind state of reconciling the Pure Mind with the spectacle or marvel of mind in dream or subtle motion. A "primordial" side is given to both to try and convey non-dualism (advaita). But I do not think it means that the Chonyid dreamland (Khro) is an eternal state but only that the stuff out of which it is projected, the Pure Mind or Clear Light (Od-gsal) is, yes, Primordial (Zhi). This Zhi is the Dzogchen Base or Foundational Reality, which is different from the Kung Zhi (Alaya-vijnana) where in the Zhi Khro is stored. So there.

Well, to me it is a subject, yes, a spiritual subject of great importance, that is the method of Union in the Four Wisdoms within the Inner Translucent and Lucent, Hollow Passageway of Vajrasattva. It is a powerful teaching. This hollow void passage way of Vajrasattva in the Bardo Thodol, that is Garab Dorje's Illumination itself in Dzogchen. I do not think it is only related to the deities and dakinis appearing in the bardo with Vajrasattva uniting these into the experience of sudden oneness. Nor just to the first four of the meditational practices. Nor to just the second four samadhi practices of Sakyamuni (please see the Totapuri and Rudraka chapter), but if you would remember that Sakyamuni did die at the fourth meditation practice in consciousness mentioned earlier, well that does not mean that his consciousness did not continue through the other levels after leaving his body. So he did most likely, I am sure go through or went through the Space samadhi, the Consciousness samadhi, the Void samadhi, into the fourth samadhi which is Bhavagra (the Height of Bhava Feeling), the Summit of Becoming. And from here what can we say.

Well you see the fourth innermost of the Wisdom dimensions here in this Vajrasattva practice is that of the Svabhava Kaya, which is again Bhavagra, so Svabhava is the spontaneous spiritual mood (bhava) of Self (Sva). This is the point or summit of becoming. Yes indeed. All these mediations and samadhi conditions are thought to be transient states. But this Vajrasattva realization comes as the union of the Four Wisdoms. The realization of the Pure Light of Mother Wisdom in the Four Kayas. The Mother Void which is the beautiful translucent and lucent luminosity of the void expressed in phenomenal appearance as Nirmanakaya which does indeed relate to the samadhi of infinite Space, the perfect expression of all extensive Nirmanakaya. So the second wisdom comes as the Mother Void expressed in the pure radiance of the Sambhogakaya, which is the radiant consciousness of the samadhi in infinite Consciousness. And then the third stage of union in this wisdom comes forth as the actual realization of the Mother Void expressed as Pure Bliss in the Dharmakaya or Bliss of Self Uncovering as it is when the Void of Bliss expresses itself in the Pure Mind itself and so we come up to the fourth union of the four wisdoms which is again the Svabhavakaya or Bhavagra samadhi which is beyond, beyond, beyond awareness or no awareness, void or no void, consciousness or no consciousness and space or no space! All four of these are instantly realized in the Maha Sukha Kaya, which is also Sahaja Kaya, and the same as Abhisambodha (Final Highest Awakening) Kaya, as One in the Great Perfection which is ever perfected (Dzogchen) mentioned there in the text. Further symbolized at a little lower level is the Maha Mudra (Great Symbol), for it is a symbolic gesture in the mind of what Pure Mind is and perhaps not the instant of the Pure Dzogchen Mind as it ultimately is. But we must decide for ourselves before death arrives, if the Union of the Four Wisdom Empowerments within the Four Psychic Centers (chakras) in the Four Kayas are what is intended. Anyway, the Great Symbol gesture (mudra) blocks the womb door into the dream state of the continuous stirring of psychic forces in the intermediate condition.

But it is all so sweet and simple when you realize that it is the Light of the Mother Void that is indicated by what is meant in the expression of the "inner, hollow or clearly lucent passageway." Which is where we bring it all together. I did not know that it was so but now I know. The Divine Mother Light is also called Kuntu Zang Mo and the Father Light is Kuntu Zang Po. She is the Watcher, the Observer of what happens and he is the what that is happening as the watched or observed. He is the consciousness of the phenomena of space or what is spacious and She is who perceives it. He is the consciousness of the radiance of consciousness or radiance of intellect, even as supreme intellect, which is simply radiant intellect which has nothing before it to obstruct or obscure and She is who perceives it from the higher inner point. He is the consciousness of the bliss of the void and She is the who and the what that comprehends it and perceives it. He is the consciousness of the Self Mind (Svabhava) and She stands above or beyond and so perceives it. Everything goes into Her. As She is the Great Pleasure of Maha Sukha Kaya, the Spontaneous Liberation of Sahaja Kaya and the Final Wisdom of Abhisambodha Kaya. Absolutely! She is the Tatha Gata Garbha (Womb of Suchness), the True Awakened Being! At any and every moment we are in a bardo of some kind and so we can suddenly come to this Pure Mind in the Mother Light at any of those moments.

What is true here is also true in the context of the Dual Light Phenomena. It is phenomena because it is never dual. The offspring consciousness or all that is expressed in the Kaya dimensions is never separate or dual from the Great Mother Light of the Pure Mind. That is the implication and the reality of it.

Within Vajrasattva is the entire field of the Zhi Khro, the peaceful and wrathful deities and deitesses as well as all the wisdom holding deities and deitesses. The Mother Light is never distracted by this, perhaps the consciousness of the father light

43

will engage this as phenomena, radiance, the awareness of void and even the self-mind, but the Mother Light is never lost to this current of appearance. She never needs instruction, nor direction as to what is here engaged as She (Pure Dakini) is ever Helping, Teaching, Instructing without ever needing any Help, Teaching or Instructing! She is that Chikhai experienced at the first moment of actual death, or in nirvikalpa and in the purest moment of Dzogchen. The thought is almost inexpressible in that She is what you are in the Reality of Pure Mind and so all that goes on in the levels of the father light (Samantha Bhadra), the reflection of the Zhi Khro (Vajrasattva) or the human mind (as Garab Dorje) is as such a non-engaging nothing, yes, really. Since there is only the One Mother Light ever in Clarity to Light. So, no Bardo mind nor dream state arises to the one who knows Her, even the appearance of anything like this is seen in the purity of sight seeing only what She is, Pure Mind. Nothing but Pure Mind is seen. Even that fails to describe Pure Mind.

The Secret Meaning of Vajrasattva's Four Wisdoms in Oneness is the Void of Mother. She is the Secret that brings the Four Kayas into the Great Pleasure Kaya. But know that these Kayas are not like steps in a ladder or planes of existence but are more like circles within circles, the greatest circle being Mother encompassing all the others, with the Pure Pleasure of Pure Mind as the Maha Sukha Kaya, which is not really even a Kaya or Dimension since none of this can really be defined by the limited mind. In Mother (Void) there is no death. She is the Uncreated, the Unmade, the Unformed, the Unshaped (Primordial Unfabricated) (see Bardo Thodol) and not even the circle concept can contain this that is Her. Vajrasattva is the Void Mirror like Reflection wherein these Four Truths (Kayas) are seen in Pure Mind (Mother)!

As to the Four Empowerments within themselves or within the four psychic centers in this thought of these centers which brings the empowerments home so to speak. You see, they are the head, the throat, the heart and the base of the central canal. That base is the idea of the foundational reality within that does not change, but the real beauty of these four empowerments is that the three Tantric forces of body, speech and mind are

44

brought all together as One, the three primary kayas are brought together psychically or within realization as the fourth. Body, Voice and Mind are the three Tantric Powers. Are we all not empowered this way, by the gifts that are natural to us all. But how can we put it in words one can easily understand? What is Dharmakaya? It is Truth as related to the Mind which in its real nature is the Void, Luminous and Loving. What is Sambhogakaya? It is Beauty as related to the Voice. And Voice is what is filling the Mind Voice with concepts, as these should be filled with Beauty And Nirmanakaya, what is this? It is Life itself as the Body. These are all brought together in the One Great Awareness. As simply as it can be asked, do you ever really need anyone to give you Empowerment to Truth, Beauty and Life! No! These are for everyone at all times.

When you let Dzogpa Chenpo, the Great Perfection perfect from the beginning of forever, just happen here in the Chonyid bardo mind dream state, and then instantly it is no longer dream but is what it always is, the Dimension of Beauty. When Mind is filled with its naturally imbibing Voidness it is the Dimension of Truth. And when Body as all bodies extending through the vastness are accepted finally as one's own Body, it is the Dimension of Life.

The Four Visions of Thogal are the mystic secret of the Four Unions in the Mother Void as Vajrasattva's sudden salvation in the Light while in the Bardo. Dzogchen is simply the Decision. Trekchod is cutting the bundle of involvement in any kind of Trikaya action, the three Tantric forces of body, speech and mind. The Four Wisdom Unions in the Pure Void of the Mother Light are again confirmed even while one may be in the Chonyid Bardo but is this not but the dream mind.

I had an interesting dream where a psychiatrist was examining my poetry and said, "It shows that he does not want to be reborn." This meant something to me. In another dream three lamas were offering me to sit in a chair, I thought, "The chair is Reality and the three lamas are the illusion that the three Kayas are three separate realms, when it is non-dual." Like suddenly remembering a dream, The Depth of Self! But it is not a dream. You create your own atmosphere when conditions in

45

your mind are right, that is, conjunctive with and for Pure Presence, Non-Dual Peace.

The psycho-sexual death-horror-fear symbolism in the dream stuff of the Chonyid Bardo, love-making like the gods and goddesses, the angry Heruka (a compassionate yet violent and sudden surfacing of psychic conjunctions permeated by the interplay of fear and anger, of what? at what? Illusion!) forms of the same peaceful Dakinis and Buddhas (a god and goddess love-making on a mountain peak... is it an idealism, a memory, a psychedelic conjuring, a powerful recall of Tushita-like memory? Or some other Desire or Form region in the after death state? Who Knows?) In Dzogchen there is the confession or the admitting of all of one's faults to Vajrasattva (one's own Pure Mind reflection)! Vajrasattva, I confess only one fault which is responsible for all of the million others and that was Self doubt of my own Reality which was ever Real in and as Dharmakaya!

I wonder if the dreams I had while I was starting this book were a push from Somewhere deep within causing me to write of these subjects or if it is just the work of my mind thrusting some meaning or cause upon the dreams themselves. But there is a harmony between the writing and the dreams.

"Yes Richard. You Read. I shall interpret quickly," Swami Aseshananda in a dream. Ricky Remember what you are doing here! In this dream I saw Swami also examining Disturbing Delights: Waves of the Great Goddess and I have wondered what that means if anything. I had another dream where I visited a Tibetan monastery and on a wall in a hidden garden I found the Mystic Name of Ramakrishna. This dream surely shows some of the comparison of content between Vedantic thinking and Dzogchen thinking. Was it there before the work or does the work project it there? Again I saw a Goddess beautifully adorned and there finding serenity "like never before." I also dreamt of a Vedantic teacher and said, "But since I question everything, when realization comes to me it will be great." And he shook my hand, laughing in agreement. I dreamt of a gentle Judo man who lived without fighting and of Jesus who was lying on a stairway telling me, "how he did it." But the best dream I had was of Swami Aseshananda which was so vivid I thought I

46

was awake. People were visiting Swami and as they would say hello their bodies would rise in the state of levitation. Was this a Sambhogakaya Dream? The best part was not magical but the sweetest and most empathic face I have ever seen was there as Swami smiled at those people even so my own rising self! It was after the series of these dreams that the contents of my present writing came to me. So I wonder.

Sometimes, no dream memory is better, only vague or free recall of Prajna! She said, it is a "thin word" for Becoming One with the Ideal! Kalee! The Tibetan Vajrayogini and the Indian Maha Kali are most Similar, yet one tradition will set a head higher. If it is true that the Bardo mind is nine times more lucid than the dream mind or ordinary waking consciousness, well what then do these ordinary dreams mean at all. I dreamt that I was one of three friends (waking, dreaming and deep sleep), symbols of three spiritual selves, and then this Spiritual Column or Pillar. It was invisible but its powerful presence was felt. Was it the Sushumna? As we pushed on it, it pushed back, stronger, more powerful and irresistible than either three of us. We could not see it but we could feel its shape. It was taller than any three of us and about two and half feet round. Out of fear there was aggression and lack of Surrender so the idea of fear was projected by the three ego levels, the fourth being projected in the Column. It was a dream of Vajrasattva's Hollow Passage and since this is a spiritual method in the Bardo state, fear arose out of fear of death. The three friends and the invisible column of power are the four wisdom unions in Vajrasattva's passage. I think these no less relate to the Four Thogal Visions. This is it, this is what is meant in the Bardo, finally. Phenomena is the Waking Friend symbol. Radiance is the Dream Friend symbol. Bliss is the Deep Sleep Friend. Consciousness is the more Powerful Invisible Passage to Non-Duality free of after death phenomena. That fourth Thogal or fourth wisdom union is Gaudapada's Alatasanti, the quenching or exhausting of all dualism as then one is Free. Yet from the point of Ajati Advaita (the Non-Dual can never be born as the dual) this is all imagination, this quenching or exhausting, even so there can be no talk of duality, nor soliloquy with duality in the fourth

47

Thogal.

The content of another dream, "Superstition begins with the sense of separation and ends up on the 13th." The mantra from the Avadhuta Gita continued over and over in the dream state, "Jagrat Svapna Sushupta Abheda Turiya Bhoga Sambhava." Waking Dreaming Deep Sleep Non Different as Turiya Enjoyment the Self Mood." I feel asleep sitting in a chair and from the dream mind I could see my waking mind observing surrounding conditions. It felt like death, there was no fear. I thought from the dream peak of sight that both Arada and Rudraka (Sakyamuni's two teachers) were time and space, cause and effect bound. Coming out of the dream state to the waking state in the space Bardo between I thought this is the Nirmanakaya, so generate Joy! In a dream I visited a Ramakrishna Ashrama and there I saw an amazing dancing Dakini girl. It is your own Joy that teaches You Yourself (Discovery). Quickening all emotion to Love as Amanibhava (Pure Mind). This comprehends Gaudapada! The teacher is Emptiness, and Emptiness is the teacher. As it is with the teacher so is it with the teaching and the taught (your own self conjured idea/conception). There is no transference and there is no transmission from any of those three, teaching, taught or teacher. Everything is always within You. Find this larger form of Experience!

In the dream state I saw and heard the words, "Amani Bhava. Amani Bhava. Amani Bhava." But my attention was weak, I became fascinated by a strange terror so I did not Recognize Pure Mind here where the dream mind is more lucid and fluid to recall itself into that finer and more refined state as the dream mind or the subtle mind in waking state may more easily shift there. Gaudapada writes of those who have fear of the fearless Pure Mind for they seek to strangely grasp at an illusory support for the Experience. If dream is practice for Bardo then what shall I do. Relax my fool, relax and be Here without grasping at supports for conceptions for the passage is Hollow without conceptuality.

Again, there were three sweeping dreams in one stroke. I dreamt that I was envying the Dead that they might know what I

48

seek to Know. I dreamt of meeting the Makers of thunder, lightning and tornadoes. Were they Human? Gods? Or even Greater Forces! The third dream was an answer to Eastern spiritual questions in America. Those guru/lamas, they are like tribal leaders. Sakti, keep my sakti in Sakti. Keep my practice simple. Mind my own world! You are even more than Dzogchen's Vajrasattva and the four unions. Here or there, in life and in death, Trekchod is to Let Go, to Cut Through to the Infinite, Thogal is to Soar On and Back, lightning the lamps of mind and consciousness, of dreams and perception with this Infinite itself.

Lighted dream stuff. The luminous mind everywhere in this dream, the whole of the Zhi Khro, the Sidpa bardo, etc., all have no form. This Mara-Kama (death and sex) complex is but the peaceful and wrathful Zhi Khro. Then I dreamt of the Three Watches same as Sakyamuni. The buckets of life and death as souls turning on the Wheel. My own bucket of identities. The twelve Causes of the Maya Dream. Then Peace. "I know what is." Love extends self in suffering to all other buckets. Four meditations. Four depth experiences. It is just the memory remembering "What Is." Pure Buddha Mind before any fabrications.

A Way of getting there to Emptiness is not the final solution. That is Trekchod with no Thogal. You must Soar Back with Compassion. So mind complex appears as kama and mara saying you are defected, but this is mind illusion. Mother comes up and says, "I witness your Truth." Sakyamuni was a person, the Buddha is not. This is a mind state, the Tatha Gata Garbha. Mind Gone to the Womb of Suchness where all compassion arises. Compared to this the six teachers of the six Indian doctrines and their gods appear to have demon egos. Now the Buddhist Tantric observations on Hindu teachers and limitations, the deceptions, the dark side of gurus. The lord of limitations (mara) the architect of ego view point is not the Pure Direct Manjushri (The Gentle Lord). Isvara is thought to be the demon of controlling other's emanations. And the Vajrayogini Goddess destroys the egotism of worldly gods like Brahma (a Creator who appears to have created the maya of the ego you) and Indra (ego's intellectual power). These ideas satisfy me for they are honest in their insight that there is both truth and deception, control, limitations and pride (ego) in the Hindu powers, gods, gurus and the six teachings, Vedanta being one of those teachings. Sakyamuni rejected all that to get to a Truth free of ego and so did Ramakrishna by holding to More than mere traditions.

Even the Trikaya or the Dakini Country in the spiritual or material dimensions have no form. From the kama (six desire worlds), rupa (form planes) and arupa (formless spiritual dimensions) levels, Move On! To Prajna Paramita Mother Wisdom. Venerate your own higher perceptions, holistic (non-dual) experiences, and deep calm of non-dual peace, venerate everyone, disparage none. Walk, move with your head held high while in the Bardo or in the dream. May all beings find ease and comfort. The trainer (your own mind) disappears into the inherent heritage of naturally existing Rigpa (Clarity Light Intensity) after all have been trained. "I, who am here at this moment, I know what Is." Sakyamuni's experience is your experience. Void is Luminous not emptiness and Wisdom Consciousness Knows It. But Love even as Dakini Prajna as to Thogal Back On is the Final Solution as Ramakrishna said "charged with the Love of God." His highest opinion and final solution! This Luminous Dakini Rigpa Mind is in everyone, no less in me. And the inherent Sakti Dakini Rigpa Knows "what is."

Sakyamuni's last words, "Atma Deepo Bhava," but if Atma is a compound of the five skandhas (form, feeling, perception, impulse and consciousness) then Where is this Lamp in Reality? So how is this type perception of Atma negated from spiritual sight? Waking, Dream, Sleep, Samadhi! If I can die from this ego now as I here dream, then I won't die later in the Bardo as my awareness can stay at this Pure Level, where ego does not grasp at sleep and the rest, waking, dreaming, returning or even the bindings of heaven! But the four ego fixations on Atma must be gone over! Atma dristi (self belief). Atma moha (self delusion). Atma mana (self conceit). Atma sneha (self love). These are Buddhist complaints on the Vedantic Atma. And

50

again Sakyamuni Buddha said at the end, "Atma (Self) Deepo (Light) Bhava (Mood)." His final opinion. But with Deepo, some translate as Light, others as Lamp, others as Island. As Light it would be Trekchod. As Lamp it would be Thogal. As Island it would be Pure Absolute Self Reliance, the way of the Pratyeka Buddha who practices the best path of Yamantaka, the Solitary Hero Path, or the Path of Inner Light, Lamp, Island Self! Yama is Death and so this path takes one's own death as the teacher enlightener where one must say that whatever happens is just fine and whatever comes to arise is the Supreme Teacher! "Be Light to Self," there are versions to the meaning, the truly human crisis and enlightenment, the purely historic, the glorified myth. Some say worship, rely, and depend Not on outside assistance, yet Self manifests everywhere as Assistance! No transmission, no transference comes from the outside. It is You.

Dream teaching. "Those who are progressing forward (spiritually) are only Remembering. They are not Reflective." What does it mean. There is no progress we only Remember what we are, "what is." As the Real Teacher, the Real Itself, Mind as the Womb of Suchness, it does not even reflect into the mind content as it is in an Ever Free Pure State. True Joyous Luminosity! In Itself, ever Itself, never in mind imagination!

A Chod thought on the limits of Atma, self belief, delusion, love, conceit. Trekchod is a step further than just Chod. In Chod (Cutting) one sacrifices all one's fixations to these architects of the ego who made these fixations as if these fixed things were a feast. One dies away from the psychic fixing on the four gripping problems of human existence. The fixation on pleasure (sexual and sensual), the loss of which we fear. The fixation on death in that we fear the loss of the compounded idea of the body, emotions and mind. The fixation on the five toxic emotions that cause our dream delusion; desire (craving), anger (hatred), stupidity (as ignorance is an emotional attitude of grasping at the unreal temporary), jealousy (envy) and pride (ego). Then the fixation on the love or affection for the compound of form, feeling, perceptions, impulse and consciousness as our idea of self being. These are given up and cut away. Machig Lapdron is the Dakini who made the Chod

51

practice. To rid out ego, for ego's hold (fixation) makes for madness which is the fear. But if as Gaudapada says that all these kinds of things as being needed to be "rendered ineffective" or "rejected" are indeed just imagination that we have covered Reality with, then why sacrifice something that is merely Vaitathya (imagined illusion)?

Buddhism can seem dry. Christism overbearing and depressing. Atma assumes by appearance what is projected on it! Religions are motherless children compared to that Pure Perception. Death studies cognize fear. Life affirming studies cognize peace. Mind (Atma) assumes what is put before it. People gage spiritual truth by the historical acts of great world teachers.

I dreamt of "particles of qualified ego consciousness" that were coming back from the Depth into the waking and dreaming states. There were two views about their nature. One, they were truly ego particles. Two, they were now something not egoic but conscious. The last two verses of Gaudapada, the final Quenching, say that there is nothing but Tayi (All Light), everything else is imagination and that within our human nature we salute this Light as best that we can. But saluting is dualism for how can All Light salute itself. So in our imagination we drag the All Light into some form, shape, person or ideal in order to salute this Light. This is a fascinating question, perhaps the need to worship (the inner need to honor or respect something as being worthy) itself drags us from the Height of All Light beyond all conceptuality, down back into dualism. This pulls us back to the level of ideas in Consciousness, instead of remaining in just Consciousness. It is said that Sakyamuni's experience was beyond asti (that everything exists) or nasti (that nothing exists), indeed it must be so for these two extremes are still ideas in Consciousness.

Why do I seem to dream mostly of people I feel inferior to, or have longed for at one time, do I not value my own self? I do not tend to dream of people I feel superior to, it seems honestly, or those who have not devalued me in some way. Is it the wound of the impermanent gift of precious life bound to the suffering of all this karma? But then within the extremes of the

52

dream mind I can dream within the dark black deep vast expanse of space filled with distant orange galaxies! Or of silly theatrics with human egos. Or contemplate Sahaja Kaya which encompasses as it is itself the Dakini Kaya (Maha Sukha) the other four Kayas while dreaming of nirvikalpa samadhi, knowing that it is not the final solution, but that compassion is the answer really, for us all. So what then is this Power of bright dreams, an inner guide itself, but a guide is a guide and not the Goal. While awakened beings, other Sakyamunis, innumerable, may become the Maha Kali Protector or one of the twenty one Tara Goddesses. What does it mean that in non-duality all identities are yet indescribable to the logic of the conscious waking mind? Where for example, in the dream stuff of my own bright mind, one stated to me, "only a narrow person would ask that question." And then that "one" becomes me in the dream asking myself if I, "am being too mechanical?"

And I would diagram a dream (as a clarity practice) for sixteen years of personal history and see within this diagram my own fear of being thrown away, the fear of the unpredictable, the hurt and the Love, the insecurity of organic life and material fears, seeing how the subconscious insecurity of how life is like a dream distortion, self valued as an impermanent and transient reflection of Something Greater and more real than this dream of life that fills us with hurt as we fold blindly into the accepting of this hurt, unpredictable and never the same. One level of this I have called Sidpa Mind Wrath having to do with our returning to this world. Some get to God with passion, maybe we all must. Ignore that passion and its denial becomes frustration and then anger. Accept that passion and its desire becomes pleasure and then radiant satisfaction. Give in to guilt and then you get regret. There is no shame in being a passionate human being. Krishna, Tilopa, Nagarjuna, the Sixth Dalai Lama, even Shankara was said to practice the black art of resurrection in the dead body of king Amaru so he could experience all these sexual joys. Then there is the level of Chonyid Mind Wrath, where envy and worry distort consciousness with inner conflict that may drive you unnecessarily to its strangest fate. But it is all your own emotional imagination and exists only with the tenacity of a

53

dream, a dream which can hold you in the thought shape of its grip where you cannot stop thinking of what your mind is captured by. It is the wrath of family and the injury of childhood coming up and the way to release it back to its own illusion is to show compassion to oneself. Why compare yourself with anyone which will only make your ego feel high or low in reference when in the end we all experience the Bardo of Clear Light where none of this nagging karma has any strength to its existence.

After death, when the forty nine metaphorical days of the Bardo are done, you view your new parents in sexual copulation. Now. Stay in the Sushumna. Stay in Sakti. Stay in Shunyata. Stay in Maha Shunyata! What a Thought! Ended are the dualities of the Six Bardos. Birth and Death. Dream and Waking. Sleep and Dream. Death and Rebirth. Samadhi and Stupidity. One Thought and Another Thought. So the pull to enter the Six Worlds, is now Gone. Even the ideas that there are the Chikhai, Chonyid and Sidpa Bardos are Now, dispersed. It is nothing but the Kayas of the awakened mind and not even that. Gaudapada said it a moment ago, Tayi is Real, all else imagination. In this Tayi imagination comes to rest.

For there in Tayi, the Unfabricated All Mother Light, one sees "what is." The Clear Bardo Mother Light is seen at that utter perfect moment of True Death when all mind contact with the former old life is released and it is there in the bardo between space before any contact with the new and future life begins that this Mother Tayi is seen. No waking, nor dreaming mind comprehends it nor deep sleep. She is Turiya. Yet in deep sleep we know Her as Being and Bliss, but as the Light, She is yet to be known, to Come up to Consciousness. In Turiya She comes to be known in Consciousness, yet all the while Her Reality is ever present abiding even so during the dream and waking conditions, the deep sleep state and then even in death. For some this Bardo Light lasts the length of a finger snap, others the length of a meal, others for three and a half to four days, but there are no hard rules and who can say what occurs during death when the red and white thigles meet in the immortal thigle as conceptual currents moving in the left and right nerves come together in the quiet of the non-dual and conceptuality stops. There prana flows up the central nerve and stops when this mind energy meets Samantha Bhadri, the Mother Light centered high above the central canal (Sushumna).

That is the method of not returning to the Chonyid or the Sidpa worlds, the easy way of closing dream mind wombs and physical mind wombs. But also not being contained in the phallic or vaginal mind conjunction. Even if you are having visions of the parents in sex embrace at the gate door of the Birth Bardo, it is not too late, if you are not wanting to return to the waking state in any of the six world dimensions, excepting for the occasion of a Nirmanakaya which are already there as the Nirmanakaya guiding images in the six worlds themselves. But whether consciousness is born through moisture, eggs, or wombs or even finer yet, spontaneously born by mind birth in higher heavens, it is as Gaudapada says all dream/waking imagination.

In a Poet's Dream, the elements, stars, atomics, and quantum powers, from there, the Poet goes on and on to more and More! In a dream of "Amazing Continuity," the five Pranas (energies) the five elements, the nerve/nadi circuitry, the organs that relate to feelings and the five toxic emotions, (as anger to the heart and bones, as pride to the breath and lungs, as craving to the life heat and liver, as jealously to the blood and kidneys, as stupidity to the flesh and spleen), the five pure emotions: love, humility, serenity, happiness for others and wisdom, the Five Kayas, the demons of negative feeling and the deities of pure feeling all rose and sank as the five Pure Lights. The rainbow body might just be these five Pure Lights as one, as the pure light body in one's own seeing and being! This rainbow and pure light body might just be a metaphor of Enlightened Perception. Just like seeing Tara or Vajrayogini. Did Sakyamuni show a rainbow body? Signs! No dissolving! No lights. Best of karma blasted! And why should it not all be "amazing continuity" when the center source of all this is Prana as Pure Mind Energy which Gaudapada says is the Prajna (Deep Sleep) itself, and furthermore that all such things like "Prana and the rest" are imagined in the Atma (non-duality).

I dreamt of thunder, tree, mountain, lake, earth, water, fire, and wind. The sixty four combinations born of the eight coming out of the two which are One (Tao). "I do consult and practice this all the time," saying to the dream inquirer. Who? It means that all this as World in whatever arises to presence is the Self State of Guiding Images as Spontaneous Nirmanakaya, always present as dream state Wonderment Called Sambhogakaya. The Non-Dual Energy is the Real Karunam (Pure Compassion) or Mother who is the Svabhava Essence while the offspring Son mind is nothing but Prakriti (Natural Prana, the Supremely Creative, the Mother's Energy) innately and inherently ever existing as Inseparability! Essence (Sva Bhava)! Nature (Prakriti)! Energy (Karunam)! One! Is this the Dharmakaya ever present? Yes.

In a Goddess Dream I saw lights coming from my hand. A good sign. And heard different names of the Goddess such as Kali-rulini and Kali-lana. My body like a corpse lies down, letting go comes easily. There is no figuring mind here. The flood gate of Humility, Surrender and Faith rushes sudden. Knowledge. Wisdom. Love. This is all that matters. All surroundings and all signs teach me if my ego is interfering! Dreaming and dying are not so different. Nor is awaking in the morning and entering a new life. In Dzogchen when one is about to dream one thinks of the letter "Ah" (or "A") with the five Pure Lights surrounding and dissolving into this "Ah" and so one dreams good dreams filled with Power and Import. When one awakes immediately one thinks of Kuntuzangpo (Samantha Bhadra) the primordial Buddha who is the one true and highest teacher and the Reality Essence of True Self. Such is the way to dream or to die and the way to awaken back into this waking life, or be reborn in another life, or here in the awareness of this waking life, as Vigorous Dakini Light, Vajrayogini!

A Thigle is a drop or nucleus essence of dream material and may hold a dream within it. These points or bindus of information appear at the conjunction of emptiness and awareness, of openness and nothingness, where clarity and the operation of the dream mind conform with one another. In a thigle dream I saw the White Flowing Current in the Central Canal of Tara the Goddess. Above it was Her bija (a mantric

56

seed nucleus) Dom and below, Pom. On each side of the central canal were numerous thigles flowing up and down on both sides. These thigles did not enter the central canal but flowed efferent and afferent on either side.

Now a dream of Honor and Respect. It was very clear to me as I saw a Mystic Awakened Being sitting crossed legged. It felt sweet to give honor and respect, not worship, to this being. Before any offensive blows were thrown I said, "I cannot throw any blows." The reason being that here finally was the clarity of just honor and respect in human heritage without the taint of worship. Yet, it is not just this, for one must Venerate your own Dream State as the Imaging Power of Pure Mind itself.

In a Lama Dream, one of the Dzogchen lamas I met was waving to me to come over to where he was. I awoke and thought about it, then drifted back to dream. I showed the lama a gesture of respect and he touched my chest. It felt spiritualiy reassuring. He asked if I remembered the mantra of Garuda Trung Pe from the Yidam Cycle of the Longchen Nyingthig Treasures. The other two Cycles are the Lama and the Dakini empowerments. I recited with clear sharpness the Garuda mantra that is filled with the Trekchod and Thogal secrets of Cutting Through and Leaping Onward! I asked the lama if he would make a phonetic chart of all the other mantras in the Three Cycles. He turned his head with the gesture of no. Why? Perhaps the Power of my own Dream mind did not want to do all that thinking work.

Reflecting on one's own Dream States gives you a tremendous and immediate power/awareness because these come from you and from nowhere else. Even if you dream of other humans or of gods and goddesses or of spiritual heritages it is you who are the Assimilator! This is the meaning of Dzogchen Vajrasattva as a subtle reflection of the Vast Expanse. One more step higher is Samantha Bhadra, leaving all dream content behind. The shape of the Most Direct Dzogchen Rest in the Primordial. Rest? Because the shape of all conceptuality is Now left behind by even leaving away the image shape of Samantha Bhadra (Kuntu Zang Po). Your Own Energy in your own Dream no one can touch. Taijasa is the Dream State as the Inner

Luminous Fire of Consciousness in the Mirror of Consciousness, which is ever Non-Dual, where yet all ideas of all dual relations vibrate upon the surface of the mirror of mind fire (taijasa) and here, though it is imagination, one may find the relationships with gods, goddesses, humans, etc. For you see as Gaudapada has written, the Truth, the Reality is like the Vast Expanse of Pure Space (Maha Akasa) and it is in everyone, but more refined than the finest idea of Consciousness. And again, from my point of view there are two methods. That of Opening Gently and that of Entering with Force. Of course these two seem masculine or feminine. From the waking state the harder solidity is Exploded (Trekchod). From within the dream state the thoughts are more subtle and easy to disperse, change, transform and enlighten. But the dream mind exists in the waking state, the same imaginative power, yet with the addition of the solid material of waking experiences, and indeed so strange it is how the belief that we are flesh and bone, alone makes us doubt some much of the Spiritual Power we are so truly capable of! One must also Trekchod through the subtle reflections of imagination for to think one has done Trekchod is but imagination since its purity in direct spiritual feeling really cannot be put to words. Then one may Leap Onward (Thogal) knowing the sweet Womb of the Suchness of Pure Mind.

If you receive empowerment/initiation (understanding) in a dream is it not coming from Pure Mind reflected within the subjective source of Self within the dream content of your Real Identity! Then why not Give Your Self the same empowerment reflected from Pure Mind into the objective source of content in identity in the waking state! One is as the other, as real and important or as unreal and unimportant. The Ramakrishna initiation/empowerment is so simple and sweet to the Point! Sometimes Tibetans get so complicated. Is that really necessary?

Yet, the Goddess Tara empowerment is so sweet and simple too. I like that. All the Principles are there. Surrender! The Bodhichitta Heart! The Four Immeasurable Feelings! The Luminous Void! The Image of the Salvation Goddess within the Luminous Void! The Sudden Reappearance of the Goddess

Always Smiling! The Goddess in our own heart and body continually making Her Mantra circle in our heart! Drawing Her Back into Luminous Voidness! Inseparable Awareness of Her Manifestation and Luminous Voidness! The Victorious Significant Prayer that all beings may become the Goddess and so be separated from their suffering! And is it not She Who is the Primordial Power of all Empowerments in any of the conditions (waking, dreaming, deep sleep, death, the after life mind, or rebirthing oneself), the One and only One who gives the Real em-Power-ment. Vajra Yogini and Kali, and Tripura Bhairavi, their sister in such similarity or Tara, the True Power of the Avatara, the Mother Compassion that Descends to Saves us all from Stupidity. She is the second of the ten Maha Vidya Goddesses in the oldest of Tantric Tradition. They are all the Same as Pure Mother, as Pure Goddess, Pure Dakini in Pure Mind! The Pure Mind is untouched (Asparsa!), the dream designations are our own mind dance.

It does seem true that all empowerments, visualizations, (Bija Bindu Thigle; Pom, Ah!, OM, Hri, Hum, Etc.) stages, practices, etc. are to bring you to a place where you can move through the Six Bardos easily and without fear. This is the True Kindness of the Mother's Teachings in Pure Mind or Primary Clear Light! Even more, that you can get out of the Six Bardos, Six Worlds, and the Desire, Form and Formless Regions of what boils down to be just stupidity or spiritual obscuration! Yoga Advaita is Ati Yoga for Non-Duality is the Primordial State. The Mandukyo Upanishad and the Tantra of Sri Vidya (Mother's Shakti Knowledge) are used to bring about the same Easiness and Liberation.

Dream state initiations are not person to person transmissions. They come forth from the unexplainable Pure Mind. If you dream of a boatman, a goddess or a mantra, these all arise from your Pure Mind making its efforts to make itself clear and real to your sorry soul!

Explain it to yourself clearly. There is a causal consciousness that is Pure even before Samantha Bhadri appears and that is Pure Mind before any cause whatsoever! A subtle being like Vajrasattva is a dream state cognition in

59

consciousness. And here is the waking being in this state.

The journey of a child to get here is amazing. They have gone through death and the three bardos of the other side. Is it not truly a peak experience when the conscious mind meets womb consciousness within the birth/death bardo mystery? Deal with your own karma, the body/mind contact with space/time in Pure Mind. How else with skillful means (in the now and then too) could you be a Dzogchen Awake lama-mind returning (in the now and the then) to help others, not yourself, who are ever being harmed by the three state illusion and amazement, the wonderment of forgetting, the divine Occurring!

On the Bright and Dark Light Paths in your own Pure Mind, remember these five are the Unborn Buddhas. So one may know in waking or dreaming that Vajrasattva is the single one image including all five Unborn Wisdoms; the Clear Sky of Pure Mind, the Many, the One, the Mirror that glows with the Reflection of Truth Everywhere and the Ever Accomplished nature of Pure Mind as Reality! Find your own Chonyid dream meanings to the Bardo Mind in the Thogal of your life practice before the sweet moment of death! The five senses and the five Wisdom concepts gather together and withdraw from the waking state. The Udana prana, the rising energy, moves fast or slow yet swiftly upwards. The dream state ensues. Then the death moment. Ah Now the Mother Light! No more wandering!

The Dream State is a wondrous example of the creative intelligence/imagination within us. Imagine that if this is an example, then what Inner Potential is within the Bardo Mind as an example and even Further Onward in the Inseparable Awareness of Pure Mind in Trekchod and Thogal. Here the Dream State and the Bardo Mind have become Trekchod, Cut Away or Let Go of and so what Soars On is Pure Mind Itself.

The Enigmatic Dwelling of the Dakini

Pure Sakti is the Same in the Bardo Conditions or in Avasthatraya (The Three States), or the Three Kayas as the Dimensions of Her Expression. Pure Mind is the Enigmatic Dwelling of Sakti Dakini! That is what Tilopa did say! She is Pure Mind encompassing the Turiya, Prajna, Taijasa, and Visva. That is the Goddess.

Sakti is the One encompassing Pure Consciousness, the Depth of Prajna Wisdom yet to know what is here at this Moment, the glowing luminous reflection of consciousness in the dream state and the outward turned world mind of the waking state. The Goddess contains these within Her, not the other way around. As Pure Mind She is like Pure Space that appears to be enclosed within the position of a cup. The cup would then be the three states of consciousness and Pure Space is the metaphor of the Pure Consciousness of Turiya. · Yet Sakti is in a dimension of Her Own. Would you think it is the fifth, sixth or seventh dimension? How dare you blessed fool! She cannot be contained as it was said before, again and again.

I have no need of pilgrimage or retreat, searching for something or of changing something, teachings or teachers. Adorned as I am with the Energy of the Goddess all places and ways of Power (Sakti and Dakini) are within me. My own Pure Mind is the Enigmatic Dwelling of the Goddess whether I embrace Her as Dakini or Sakti.

In this flesh bardo the mind is thick with disbelief, but in the free mind death state I will become again, that is regain myself as Dzogchen Dakini Advaita. I feel drawn to my Dakini Self even now as to what I am. If this view is not the master liberator then how indeed was the first primordial wisdom being enlightened in the first place? It was my Dakini then and now! Yours too.

Once in a while I wake in the morning and think to myself what a precious gift this life is, it is all God. But when I die I shall think the same thing. It is all God. When I wake up in death I will realize it is all God. There has never been anything but God. How amazing is my mind when it dances with God. All the galaxies, all life, all appearances, all death are but the demonstration of this. The Wonderment of God. Blessed be the Dakini who dances through the Sky of Pure Mind.

Embodiment! What stupidity. Sometimes I perceive all human beings, men and women both as the embodiments of the beastlike stupidity. How ignorant to wander into this dimension and become caught up here. But I too am embodied and stupid. And taking this knowledge with me compassion for myself and others arises. And the strangest most comical sense of our condition I ever experienced. Now I am dancing in the Dakini Mind. Oh what sweet arrogance is this beautiful pride.

It is the Stupidity of Mind-Sleep that runs so much of this human world! When you Know the Answer Within, but never bring it Up, by Self Energy, Sakti Dakini, for you feel you need "someone" to come along and kick it out of you! And that feeling of need is a wasting of your Dakini Energy!

I think that waking and dreaming cover us with doubt and stupidity, shadow us and frazzle us and yet we go on with the misplaced Supreme Teacher Within, call that One Truth, Manjushri, Dakini, Sakti or whatever you like, for it is nothing but Pure Mind! We leave the Elephant at Home and go out looking for the footprints. What madness and stupidity like an insane person looking for their own face in a crowd of people! What is this tendency? Strange! Hilarious as well! Death is just the disintegration of waking and dreaming conditions and contacts! Realization is understanding what waking and dreaming are in their natural fact! In both we return to Pure Mind, Manjushri, Mother Light, Dakini! Whatever you name it!

Trekchod is cutting to the Pure Spiritual. Thogal is Living Spirituality. In terms of Dakini Power only, Trekchod is cutting away the bundle of everything that is not Dakini. And Thogal is Living (even as) Dakini. Dakini is Kha Dro Ma. Mother (Ma) who goes (dro) in the Sky or Space (Kha) of Pure Mind. That is where Dakini Dances the Dance of Illumination!

The problem with Emptiness and Void is just that. You eliminate and annihilate everything into Nothingness and you feel a deep desperation. When you start to realize the unbelievable power of Maya (the Occurring) and how truly Impermanent Impermanence is you can become wrapped into a state of great spiritual fear. You start to realize the illusion body gained at birth, that just because the body and mind aggregates have arisen into waking and dreaming conditions resting on the ocean of deep sleep, they are still not lasting, they are an occurring impermanence. Is it real evidence of our true existence? You see that all human beings around you at some time must die and leave this impermanence behind. What is Real? You wake and dream with your beloved friends and family in this in-between impermanence and wonder what is the purpose. The world is upside down, we who are Reality Unborn and Un-contained are apparently (that is temporally) born and contained and destined once again to death. And the idea that it is all just an illusion is a haunting despairing illusion in itself. That is where Dakini comes in to save your mind from this despair. For when that Void is filled with Her Energy (Love) then the Magic happens and the World is filled with Great Bliss (Maha Sukha). That is why She is the Sky Dancer. The Sky is the Pure Sky of Emptiness and She is the Love Energy that is Dancing in that Emptiness and thus it is no longer empty. Now there is purpose to all that was annihilated. It all happened only in your mind and there is where the Dwelling of the Dakini exists! All that elimination and annihilation is simply the custom of death, this universal custom which happens all the time. But there in the Clear Emptiness the Dakini is Dancing, so Embrace Her as you would the Most Beloved and then the fear, despair and emptiness vanish!

This Uncreated Nirvanic Part of My Self never needs nor is deluded by the Six Yoga Doctrines: Heat, Illusion, Dream, Light, Bardo and Pho Wa. This Uncreated as Me has always been so, "I" consciousness appeared for a moment (as many lives) and got in the way!

Tilopa gave us the Interval Between Two Thoughts, When and Where Mother Light is the Experience, even as She is there in the Clear Light of Deep Sleep, clear as to the loss of all deep dark dualism. Now Sakti Rigpa. Vijnana is when there is no breach in the Unitive Experience of Samsara and Nirvana as both

63

Samsara and Nirvana are Mind (Consciousness).

More than a Soul in a mortal body; to View this World itself, between Birth and Death, as the Pure Realm of Gods and Goddesses with no break in this view, Living, Alive, yet as an apparition of Truth. Illusory body transformed! This Higher View. Immediate Heaven Consciousness. No waiting. You see Everything without exception as Opportunity for Self Arising.

Live Now in my Big Self larger than the movement of my bones, my flesh, my skin. Touching all, Being All, Feeling All. I Know Their Minds as My Own.

Denial is not admitting one's pain and holding to the need of the object of one's pain. It is the cause of breaking the View of Non-Dual Gods and Goddesses. The Sweet Bhava comforts me and lessens my fear. Passion too, is a Path to Truth.

On a planet, in a body we are unconscious, in Samadhi or at Death for a Sacred Moment we Awake and Become Conscious. If your Bhava Wish is to Feel and Know What the Immense "I" Is, it will Be So! I don't have to figure everything out right now. Deep within, it is already known. Besides, peculiarities and uniqueness in the waking/dream self complex are nothing (void) in Turiya. The Mother Light Void perceives intellect (mind) unfabricated, unshaped, unmade, unbecome! (see Bardo Thodol) Here, nothing is lost and we speak like madmen compared with logic. This is the Reference, it is the rest of the world that is imbalanced.

True Communion (Communication) or Eternal Delight (Nitya Sukha) is when female comes out of femaleness and male comes out of maleness and the true essence meets in union in the Loving Center (Pure Mind) for that blessed moment. Is this a metaphor of Kundalini?

With the Dakini comes the most beautiful of all spiritual ideas and there are many. One is the terma (a hidden text). The Dakini can hold a terma for centuries or more, until you are reborn. Then She can give this terma to you, recite it to you from within. It is a complete circular cycle of Pure Mind as Dakini. Garab Dorje was helped in his writing by three Dakinis. And there is the interesting idea that Her poetry or Dakini script is not limited to the human idea of cognate language but that Her language can be seen in the air, sky, clouds, fire, water, earth, leaves, trees and rocks appearing first in the Pure Mind Space and then reflected into those appearances. This kind of inspiration is a Moment of Precious Epiphany Sakti. As Sakti Dakini is the Highest Epiphany teaching in this kind of learning or more accurately, remembering.

There are many ideas about the Dakini, the Sakti, the Goddess. First, one must have the proper concept of what Dakini is and not harbor false ones. M., in his translation of The Condensed Gospel of Sri Ramakrishna gives us the best ever meaning of Dakini. Ramakrishna describes what She is, "Those Sacred Books, the Tantras, speak of the Goddess Unconditioned, the Absolute. When nothing was - no sun, no moon, no planets - nothing but darkness deep, there was my Divine Mother alone, Formless!" And here it is given in the footnote that this is "Dakini." This is the best description of Who She is.

An Exquisitely Important Dream came into my mind. Sitting in Dzogchen Ecstasy! There was the remembering of all the Dakinis, even Bamkini and Ramkini. Then Ultimate Dakini! Pure Ecstasy in the Dream Mind. Pure Mind there! Aware this was happening in the dream state. Who supported my back with their arm while I was in Ecstasy? Was it Dakini Herself? Impersonal and Formless, yet most Personal. Faceless (Trekchod) and yet Comforting (Thogal). Now have it in the Waking State.

The Bija-Bindu-Thigles (Word Seed/Point/Concepts) of the Dakini are these. Hakini is the All Good Consciousness (Sive or Samantha Bhadri). Sakini is the Goddess of Great Abundance who delivers us from difficulty. Kakini is the Goddess of Desire who expresses herself through Kamadeva, Krishna and Kali. Lakini is Indra manifest as the thunder lightning of pure buddhi (intellect) which is what pervades the conceptional expanse of all that can be known. Rakini is spiritual wealth, the power of the natural world, the creative force and energy that makes everything as well as that same creative power that provides the internal and external circumstances for salvation and liberation. Dakini is the Pure Goddess and the One who destroys all obstruction and obscuration as well as clinging to any kind of

65

body, gross, subtle or causal. These are shapes of the Dakini descending from the sixth chakra to the first chakra at the base bone of the spinal column. This is how She is already within you as this unfolding spiritual system.

Of course the Pure Sakti, the Pure Dakini is the Formless Free Dzogchen Consciousness of the highest seventh Chakra expressed as the thousand petaled center-less center. Descending down to the sixth comes Hakini who is Siddha Kalini who is elated from drinking draughts of Ambrosia. This ambrosia is Amrita Thigles, or Immortal Drops. Then at the Sleep Gate designated by "M" is Sakini the white Sakti Sakini whose form is Pure Light (Jyoti Svarupa), the Light as Background to Everything. She is the Gateway to Liberation. Then at the Dream Gate designated by "U" is Kakini garlanded with human bones whose heart is softened by the drinking of Immortal Nectar Drops. And these Drops move as Energy Currents through all Her nerve channels thus softening the chronic hard conceptual world to the fluid dream state. Then at the Waking Gate designated by "A" is Lakini who is fond of animal food, (a symbol that the physical flesh is not permanent) her breasts are covered with blood and fat which drop from Her mouth (a symbol of the physical body's eventual destruction). Sir John Woodroffe writes (The Serpent Power) that all these Dakinis are actually the Saktis of the Yogi himself or herself which is the Great Secret to be touched, known and digested. That is that all this power is within you as the Dakini already present. Then comes Rakini who in furious aspect is showing Her teeth fiercely and this is a symbol of the emotional sexual energy of the second chakra center. Then at the ground floor of the central nerve channel is the Dakini again as She is here the Keeper of the Door, of either the beginning of liberation or of the return descent from the liberated pure feeling that you touched at the highest position of Dakini Consciousness.

We go again at it, within a slight variation. Dakini at the highest is She who grants the Bright Pure Mind (Nitya). Lakini is the Beautiful Play or Display (Lila). Hakini is the Energy within you of the Divine and Spiritual A-ham which is the Divine "I" knowing itself as the Divine Self or Pure Mind.

Sakini is the inherent or innate Sakti Ability of your own power or skill in this power of Sahaja, which is the Sa-ham or Spiritual Sakti (Sa) Self (Ha) which is born as You (Ja). Then there is Rakini who protects, guides, guards, keeps and watches the ordinary mind center as She is the natural teacher of the ordinary mind. Ramkini is next and She is the Fire (Ram) as cremation of Body/Mind mis-identities at all levels gross, subtle and causal. She is Ram too as the Beauty of this liberation. At last is Bamkini, She who is the pure Energy that Brings about (Kini) a Vajrayogini Rebirth either in a human or divine realm. So really this Bamkini is the Goddess who guides and empowers the birth process in any form, spiritual or materially manifest.

In regard to the Four Dakini Thogals. She is the One who flies in Turiya gone of all Samsara. Who moves (M) where not even the Trikaya can touch Her. Who dances (U) and so cuts away all mis-identities. Who walks (A) and with Her step kills away all useless verbiage.

Dakini is Khadroma and here She is Pure Space (Kha) that Walks, Flies, Moves (Dro) as Mother (Ma). This Naked Awareness of the Goddess Dakini is the Self Liberating Principle within you. The precious Padmasambhava was taught by Dakinis, as the precious Ramakrishna was taught by Mother Kali, by Sakti!

The Dakini Sakti is called Bhadra Kali, make note of how much the same is Samantha Bhadri as this Bhadra/Bhadri is the All Good, the Universal Goodness and the Auspicious Power of the Jiva (the Atma bound in Dharma conceptuality and so She is that Good Power that frees us of that limited conceptuality).

There is more. So beautiful! The Secret Innermost Meaning of the Dakini is not found in common language for it goes back to forgotten dialects of the Sindhu valley region where sprang forth Tantra, Dzogchen and other amazing spiritual systems almost now lost to the world. I do not want these to be lost. So I write. Bear with my patience and learn who She is! It is said that the Dakini is A-Yoni-Ja, that is that She is not (a) born (ja) of a womb (yoni) of any kind, whether physical, subtle nor in the spiritual causality. That is that She is before any of those. And She is also the Atma Yoni, that is the Birthplace

67

(womb) of Atma (the Spiritual Self in all its true Dignity). It seems a contradiction but it is not when one once begins to think without the dual mind conceptuality. So that is why She is Kali Dakini, the Formless which has no birth place and is the only place of Self Birth! So She is the One who resides in Shunyata and there the dual problem paradox is solved. Then solution is now evident. For Dakini is She who is Eternal (Nitya) and She who displays the play (Lila). What is higher than This Dakini!

But then came the Aryan denigrations with their invasion of the Valley region of the Goddess. Now these Hindus find ways to denigrate the Buddhists and the Buddhists find ways to denigrate the Hindus. It started a long time ago. The word Daityas refers to a yaksha or mythological genii/daiman who can fly (dai). Even fly to Tushita, the highest Buddhist heaven of spiritual satisfaction. But latter developments arose and dakini became a mermaid, an ogress, flesh eaters, attendants of Kali who poisoned baby Krishna (he survived), but all this is such a mess to get through. More is added as sakini (or saktis who are able ones) became reduced to vegetation spirits by the Aryans, and were called demon witches attending to Durga, a Destructress Goddess. It is all made to sound awful when it is no such thing. Then rakini: a guardian, protector, keeper and watcher was associated with the fierce bhairavi yoginis of the region and their reputation was darkened by being named of the rakshasa class. These rakshasa demons were said to be of three classes with their overall identification with the people of India who were there before the Aryans. Ravana was said to be one of these demons. And they were given to three classes. First, the harmless yakshas. Second, the jealous gods (asuras). Third, demons who were the people of the Valley and Mountains and Rivers and Forest of the land before Aryan/Kurgan arrival. Kashyapa who was one of the six or seven Buddhas before Sakyamuni was held by these invaders to be one such demon. So, much was lost and outright intentionally corrupted to destroy a previously existing spiritual system in order to replace it with another.

Yet, in Reality, Dakini like Garuda can go in the Sky (Pure Mind). Both are of such conceptual capacity, skill and power.

The very idea of Dzogchen in the Sanskrit language is Maha Sandhi, Maha meaning Great and Sandhi meaning Fulfillment, Gain, Acquire, Possess, Bestow, Wish, Enjoying, the All Great Experience of the Already Present Dakini.

Hindu, Tantric and Tibetan definitions of Dakini can vary deeply and widely. The Bardo Thodol speaks of the Dakini as the Divine Mother who appears as the Clear Light of Death and with potent meaning on the seventh day (a symbol) after death. Ati Chitti Dakini is the Highest Sudden Pure Consciousness! Pure Thought is Dakini! The Pure Blue Tibetan Sky Dakini! Dzogchen! The Longchen Nyingthig is nothing but Dakini given. M.'s Dakini is my favorite, what a thought is in that entire sentence. Before even ideation conceiving Samantha Bhadri and Samantha Bhadra, before Kuntu Zang Mo or Kuntu Zang Po, before, before!

Dakini, the most singularly perfect ever expanding word/meaning (Tantra) truly. Ever Comprehensive and Incomprehensible! Dzogchen is not grasped without becoming yourself, the Dakini! Goes in Pure Mind Sky! Heroine (Bhairavi) Vira Yogini! Pure Bhaga (Pleasure and Joy). Thought is Pure Thought Dakini! Pure Womb Mind Sakti! Stable Orgasmic Flow! Never losing Joy! Secret Knowledge! (Guha Jnana) Compassion to Great Bliss again and again sealed into and made Real in the Knowledge of Sahaja Pleasure! Again and Again!

Mistress of the Red and White Thigles, closing the return in wombs moist or mind generated! Clear Light above the eight deaths of five sense contacts and three mind layers. Gives Pure Certainty. She Who (Dai -To Fly) is Sky Dancer, Walking, Goes, and Does Fly in Pure Power Space of Pure Mind. None But Kali Dakini. Single Self Liberating Principle, Pure Power, Epiphanic Thought or Feeling of Sudden Self Recognizing! Kali Dakini is Formless Mother Essence, Nature and Energy without single, dual or triadic break! She Bestows Suddenly, by eating up resolute flesh formed concepts, chronic ideas, habitual non-exalted emotions, fears, desires. She who cannot be brought down by any denigration, modern or of old Aryan impositions on Kali and Chandi by their renaming Her, dagini, as the old retinue of the Goddess Kali. She is the Tantric Dzogchen Goddess. Non-Dual Awareness Herself! Moving through Khechari (the Sky Space) and thus as Khadroma is momentarily touched in Khechari Mudra (Sky Space Gesture)! But Her Space (Vast Expanse) of Reality cannot be touched by any in free surrender as She is all that touches anywhere and the only One who is capable of Trekchod and Thogal! Find Her within. The entire Trikaya takes its Final Refuge in this Dakini for She is the Epiphany Teacher, who is at the Epiphany of all Spiritual Occurrence, the best and highest Teacher as that Epiphany Itself! She destroys all resolute flesh concepts (Trekchod) and then Soars On (Thogal).

The Vajrayogini Dakini must be there for success in Pho Wa, in Chodpa, in Naropa's Six Yogas (tummo and illusory body dissolution), in Dzogchen Suddenness, in Her Empowerment which remakes or re-enlightens the Three Kayas and the Three Bardos. She is Trekchod itself which destroyed the ego at the deep sleep level of ignorance and darkness. She is Thogal as this very intense remade Dakini you have now become by remembering. All thoughts in the ordinary mind are but illustrations drawn in water having no staying power of their own. Dakini stays, She never left. "Why reason about the path?" Ramakrishna asks for ordinary mind will not hold water! They say Jigme Lingpa had a disturbing and unsettling relationship with the Dakini. Blessed be that or things would be stagnant. The thoughts written in Disturbing Delights were also driven forth by Dakini. I have always been a Dakini man. She is the enigmatic dwelling of what is Your Mind Essence. Da is the Bright Light of the Chikhai Awareness. Ki is Trekchod. Ni is Thogal. Dakini is the Search Through, To Perceive, To Observe, To Decide, To Be Certain or Become Certain as All that can become or be Certain at all. Da is the Giver, the Bright, the Pure, the Able as She who Grants anything! Ki is Resolution. Ni is the Eternal which is what is Innate and what is your Own. Kini is She Who manifests, brings forth, brings out, who emanates the mind energy that comprehends Shunyata (Ma Herself). She is the Self Bestowing Power in the Space of Pure Mind (Prajna/Wisdom Para/Supreme Emptiness, empty of all

70

resolute concepts). Dakini is Pure Mind. Dakini is the Space of the Pure Mind. Dakini is what Manifests as Pure Mind in that Wondrous Free Feeling That never ceases Spacing Out of, or Away from, all ordinary conceptual states. No doubt, the Dakini is the Epiphany of Spiritual Joy! If I may borrow an expression from a dear friend, Mr. Curt M. Pavia, I will say the Dakini is the highest and ultimate "Altruistic Affirmation" of our Spiritual well being, ecstasy and joy! Dakini is the most Altruistic Affirmation of Maha Sukha which is Herself! Dakini, as the single most Pure Direct Empowerment can never be repressed!

Sakti, Buddha and Pure Mind

The secret is in the power of veneration. It is this power of veneration that brings out the Self to be realized. It happened to Ramakrishna in his astounding veneration of the statue of the Goddess Kali. It happened to Vilwamangal in his veneration of a prostitute. It happened to Dattatreya in his veneration of twenty four principles in the natural world, two of which were human, one being a maiden, the other a prostitute. Your level of veneration creates your level of contact with the ever-present awareness within you that is constantly teaching you at every level.

Not too long after Sakyamuni's Moment of Enlightenment he met Upaka, the ascetic, on the road to Benares and the ascetic asked him, "Who is your guru/master/teacher?" Sakyamuni then made this remarkable reply to the ascetic, "For me, there is no guru/master/teacher, for I have reached Enlightenment on my own by instructing myself, so whom should I call guru or master or teacher. Who is like me, who is my equal, for by teaching myself I have attained Enlightenment. I am the Tathagata (Gone to That, the Pure Mind) which is the teacher of all beings, gods or men. Other conquerors (Jinas and Pratyekas) like me have done the same!" Here Sakyamuni speaks as and from Pure Mind itself, that is as a representative of Pure Mind itself. He expresses the full potential of Pure Mind. This is your Pure Mind. This sacred statement should come from the voice of your own Pure Mind as well. Otherwise you have not yet lived as the

Tathagata that you are. This Tathagata is the Pure Mind thus Gone to the Pure Mind. Go there now, today! Why would you settle for less than your fullest potential? The Tathagata of your own Pure Mind even goes back further and deeper than the historical Original Experiencer! Whether it be Samantha Bhadra, Vajrasattva, the Bon Tonpa Shenrab, Sakyamuni, Kashyapa, Garab Dorje and so forth.

You may call this Sakti, Pure Mind, Rigpa, Dakini, Prajna, Turiya, the Wisdom of Self or the Original Self Sense. But once you have given away this subjective Sense of Self as we may call it now though it is not even subjective, well then, that sense of self becomes lost in the external, in the outside and that weakens you and so you go out of your Self seeking assistance, tradition, psychology, whatever. You lose that contact with the Innate and Inherent Spiritual Solution of your own reality as it becomes spiritually obscured. It is always with you, even as you go into deep sleep you feel and are this but you do not know it. Once you know it you have arrived at the introduction to Turiya. Then you continue until you cut away all the psychology and memory of the inveterate mind, that is the old chronic habit of the mind. The Reposed One Sakyamuni said, "Be a Lamp unto Your Self." And Issas said, "The kingdom of Heaven is within You." But it does not have to be a kingdom for one can just say Heaven is You, more than a subjective condition of being within. Even from the position of the Non-Dual Oneness of deep sleep one gives away this Lamp of Heaven when one gives consciousness to the cloud land of the dream state or the sensory experiences of the waking condition, unless one is full of Pure Mind upon the return to objective consciousness. Then it is the same whether one thing comes up or another. Don't throw away the Power of Pure Mind. Keep your own counsel. Keep your own Power. In other words do not reverse or turn upside down the subjective content of your own self sense for that is where the confusion of delusion first begins to stir, then it expands, then it repeats itself and you have lost contact with your Original Sense of Self. But this never happens to Pure Mind. Yet, spiritual mind, subtle, or human mind can call you out, as an imagined spiritual or subtle being or your human mind, yes, even as you have found a state

72

of Peace in Pure Mind, yes, or in the Bardo mind as well. Let us say you have died and are at one in Pure Mind, everything cut away, or some excellent state of spiritual Peace in the Absolute with Pure Reality (Is this Trekchod?) and so from There you start to think or feel that a spiritual or subtle being says to you that you must now return to the Dimension of Human Birth. Well, in Truth, those spiritual or subtle being's commands are nothing but projections of your own mind. And as such, Pure Mind, even then, in the event of your following an arising of those projections will remain as Pure Mind. (Is this Thogal?)

As I Empower Myself in Pure Mind as Pure Mind as Dzogchen Vajrasattva, as Samantha Bhadri and Bhadra, as the Sweet Protector Tantric Dzogchen Vajrayogini, then where is the need or want to run there or there or there anymore!

"It was an Infinite Stillness in which Self communed with Self. Sri Ramakrishna had reached the highest pinnacle of spiritual realization, and all this without the least effort, for his pure mind was now habituated to dissociating itself from all finite things, which throw a veil, as it were, over the absolute majesty of Brahman -- the One without a second." (Life of Sri Ramakrishna) This is what the Pure Mind is, as Pure Mind communed with Pure Mind, the highest pinnacle. Ramakrishna always knew his own Pure Mind. "He knew that he had always been a free soul; that the various spiritual practices through which he had passed were not really necessary for him..." A free soul is always in the Pure Mind, this is the highest potential itself expressing itself at the highest pinnacle. Ramakrishna's existence and purpose in this world was to show this clearly to those who are yet to believe this.

I will have no dialogue with any but Sakti even if I appear to be speaking to others in the waking and dreaming states. It is She who is the One Significant Point in the entire field reaching and ranging through all events and meanings. This is now done even if it takes vigorous psychically violent, aggressive repetitive prayer. Her Voice is Pure Mind.

I do not practice, She practices in me, with no imagination, rumination, nor calculation! It is just a natural state of spontaneous attraction to fifth stage Tantra, where Atma is

73

drawn by the Pull of Sakti.

She is the Doer of every waking and dreaming instrument
even as our psycho-sexual-somatic ego mind imagines this to be
our own, as these aspects or characteristics so compose the
conditions of limited waking/dreaming identities. It is Mother's
Maya Form appearing as the twelve links in the chain of cause
and effect, efforts and results. This attitude, view, behavior is
much easier than trying to control the cycle of day and night, that
is of waking and dreaming.

You see, perhaps we have not stretched the imagination
enough in the spiritual sense, to allow ourselves to be in the Pure
Sakti Mind. In this sense imagination has become limitation
instead of reaching into the range of Wonder and Wisdom
inherent within the Pure Sakti Mind.

In the Pure Mind which is Mother's Divine Suchness, not
objectified, nor even subjectified, Just as She Is, then Her
Teaching comes from surprising places and this illuminates
ordinary mind, but without Love it is but a beggar's
bewilderment.

Put Truth where there was delusion. Put Pure Mind where
there was bewilderment. Why substitute human contact for
Divine Contact? It is like trading a beautiful woman bride for a
monkey and then marrying the monkey. Get beyond the
atma/guru dual complex, the atma/god ratio complex and even
the dual imagination of an atma/goddess separation and so then
go direct into the Pure State of Pure Mind in Pure Sakti. It is
insanity to substitute the worship of a human being for Pure
Worship in Pure Mind. What are you doing? Do you think a
human being can give you grace (Kripa)? Do you believe the
human form is the divine form (Murti)? Do you believe words
spoken in the human voice are the divine voice (Vakyam)? Do
you worship the feet of a human or the divine lotus feet (Padam)
of the Goddess which are the nectar fountain of Pure Mind
Energy! Even a reincarnated high lama (a tulku), or a special
yogi/sage on a spiritual mission in this world is still just a human
being!

Ramakrishna sings out and proclaims this Reality in
Excellent Truth! "Sometimes I say to myself in the Kali Temple,

74

'O Mother, the mind is nothing but Yourself.' Therefore Pure Mind, Pure Buddhi, and Pure Atman are one and the same thing." (The Gospel of Sri Ramakrishna) Indeed, the thing, it is to get to this thing, Pure Mind which is not a thing. For it is nothing but Yourself, Herself, the Sakti, the Kali, the Divine Mother. Here too you may clearly see that Pure Buddhi (that is the Supreme Luminous Intellect) which is the Ever Awake Buddhi, is the True Buddha Mind so often taught. From here, it is nothing other than the Goddess, the Mother Herself that ever is and also becomes the Pure Mind as the True Tatha Gata Garbha, the Real Buddha? Yes! Sakti, Buddha and Pure Mind all the Same.

I have examined and reexamined birth, life, death, rebirth, the body/mind complex, memory, subconscious impulses, emotions, that the six senses are the waking state and the sixth (mind only) is the dream state, always turning in impermanence, heaven mind, hell mind, ghost mind, animal mind, human Earth mind, by the twelve conjunctions of causing body/mind ego connection and that deep sleep equates with the acceptance of ignorance without beginning. And I have found that this simple Awareness of "I, who am here, at this moment, I know what is," is good, is best. It is the pure psychological crisis and its Solution, when consciousness faces its own captivation with the twelve nidanas (the links in the chain of causes and effects) and their self explanation through the Three States (Avasthatraya) with their resolved decision into Pure Mind (Amani Bhava) which is Turiya, the Shunyata. The twelve arising links in the chain of causings come out of the doubt/stupidity complex (ajnana, the deep sleep of not knowing) which is nothing but forgetting your own awareness of Pure Mind. 1. Avidya (ignorance or stupidity about your own Pure Mind), 2. samskara (past and present impressions of things and experiences other than Pure Mind), 3. vijnana (here meaning a consciousness other than Pure Mind), 4. namarupa (the cognition of names and forms other than Pure Mind), 5. shadayatana (the six sense projections away from Pure Mind), 6. sparsha (touch, contact with phenomena other than Pure Mind), 7. vedana (a sensation of something other than Pure Mind as being real), 8. trishna (the thirst, the craving for phenomena other than Pure Mind), 9. upadana (the clinging to, the grasping for and the taking hold of a womb birth other than the Womb of Pure Mind or Tatha Gata Garbha), 10. bhava (the becoming or feeling that you are other than Pure Mind), 11. jati (actual birth somewhere other than the Womb of Pure Mind), and 12. jara maranamh (the old age and death of that phenomenal creation which has distracted you from Pure Mind, yes, Sakyamuni wrestled with mara, the psychological crisis of death prior to illumination for it was embracing this death reality that brought about his Illumination, for a Pratyeka he was!) are the links in the chain of captivation. The inherent solution to the spiritual obscuration is Compassion, which is nothing less than Pure Love, not just clear emptiness.

Dzogchen and Pure Advaita

In Advaita Vedanta the three principles come up as the Teacher, the Teaching, and the Taught.   In Dzogchen and simpler levels of Buddhism these three components of the Pure Mind manifest as the Buddha (the Awakened One), the Dharma, (the Teachings, the Way), and the Sangha (the Community of seekers and practitioners). From either point of view these exist only in the appearance of non-awareness of Sakti (Pure Power) Rigpa (Pure Primordial Awareness), or the unenlightened mind.

The Question of Consciousness in Dzogchen Buddhism as an illusion of self reality? Well, it is Wisdom Energy that comprehends the Luminosity of Void, Shunyata, the Prajna Paramita (Supreme Mother's Wisdom), yes, so this is Consciousness and there can be no disagreement in the conclusion.   Is not what Dzogchen calls the Void but the Formless of Advaita? Is not Void directly Formless in its Nature and is not the Formless also Void in regard to having no forms (sound, touch, shapes, etc.).

Dzogchen appears vacant, a trance, but is not so, for Pure Mind holds no world object in particular, but recognizes and knows all of them (world objects). The Buddha's criticism of grasping at the Atma as self-belief, self-delusion, self-conceit and self love is solved by destroying the grasping at these four in the Luminous Love Void. Love is the Compassion that freely and spontaneously comes forth from the Luminous Void.

Emptiness in the Void is not enough. One must be identified with the Happy Dakini. Otherwise it is only emptiness. Mother Joyful Dakini, give this functional corpse of mind just enough vital longevity energy to finish this text on the nature of Pure Mind as I dedicate the work to You!

Trekchod and Thogal in the Three Bardos is Facing and Going through Death Now, Before you die. This may be True Thogal Dzogchen, the Stage that is Final, accomplished in the fearlessness of Pure Mind. Trekchod is Cutting the Bundle or Cutting to the Essence, which is the bundle of lesser identity. Thogal is the Instantaneous Arrival or Surpassing of the Utmost.

Before you die, in this now, explain to the Self in Pure Mind what the Four Visions of Thogal are in this bardo of life and in the bardo of death and there after. First is to hold your head high and know your Self in Pure Mind. The second is to Increase the Sensation of this Awareness of Pure Mind where one becomes Sensitive to what Pure Mind is and so there is no returning to inveterate thought patterns. Third is the clarity in Pure Mind that no thought can describe the experience of Pure Mind, not even the farthest reach and range of the imagination can contain this Pure Mind. Four is Pure Mind aware that every appearance in Pure Mind is nothing but the Non-Dual Pure Mind.

Everything I have ever thought about for forty-six years and perhaps more is and always has been the Self Radiance of Rigpa. Thogal. Dharmata, the Mother Light. To see nothing but Dharmata is the Fourth Vision of Thogal. Or is it to see nothing but Dharma Dhatu, the Never Dying Indestructible Truth. "I dote on myself, there is that lot of me and all so luscious, Each moment and whatever happens thrills me with joy..." Whitman Song of Myself 24.

I have been through the Three Bardos before, how many times, as also the Three States that now bring both of these Three Conditions into the Awareness that they have never been distinguished by discursive dualistic figuring from the Three Awakened Dimensions, from the Dzogchen Outlook it was never not so! "And as to you Life I reckon you are the leavings of many deaths, No doubt I have died myself ten thousand times before." Whitman Song of Myself 49.

Third Stage Thogal is that no thought in the whole universe can contain Dharmata (Your Pure Mind's Luminosity), not your waking meditations, not your dream states, nor any non-dual recognitions in the intermediate state of the Chonyid Bardo. Dharma Dhatu is Pure Mind before it goes into the Cause State of becoming a Seed of Everything Manifest. Dharmata is the Light of Pure Mind manifesting in the Manifest! This is a very important point! Because Fourth Stage Thogal is nothing but the Non-Dual Dharmata and Dharma Dhatu. In Pure Dzogchen there is no duality between the Pure Clear Light and the Moving Light manifesting the Manifest!

No stirring, repeating or expanding of thoughts or memories for these are not in reality the Reality of Pure Mind, but they should serve Pure Mind, let these become radiant spiritual thoughts, the good servant disciples of your Pure Mind. Ego and all attending thought forms and memories will become the servants of Pure Mind. Ego is a power that brought about rebirth! These thought powers are potent disciples of Pure Mind and yet Pure Mind is never lacking in Compassion for these. With so much Love, will you bring this down to dualistic devotion, or show True Compassion Keeping Love in Pure Mind!

The True Master of the Art of Thogal is Dharma Dhatu, the Clear Light Itself, yet as Pure Mind before the event of Consciousness manifesting as a seed-cause or even the limiting idea of an Eternal Principle in dual relation to a relative one. Your Best and Greatest Spiritual Friend is your own Pure Mind.

Trekchod-pa cuts the bundle of memory obscuration, memory of ego being the strongest part of that obscuring bundle of causes to be cut. This is similar to Chod-pa practice.

Thogal consumes the Three Bardos in Itself. One arrives at the Six Instantaneous Accomplishments. Body. Speech. Mind. The Rising of Ground Luminosity. The Rising Door of the Eyes. Spontaneous Breathing. This Breathing is that the In and Out Breath are Filled with Clear Light. The Eyes Perceive Everything in Rigpa, they are Open to all sight as nothing but the

Dharmata. Rising Ground Luminosity consumes Everything in that Light. Mind is nothing but Light once it is Known and this is Dharmakaya.. Speech is the Sacred Vehicle of Sambhogakaya in that speech produces the cognates of words and these produce waves in consciousness producing enjoyable images in the mind. The body is also consumed in the third Tantric power or force, as body is realized suddenly to be the Body of Light or the Divine Rainbow Body of Nirmanakaya. Body, Speech and Mind are the Three Tantric Powers of the Awakened Dimensions. These Six Arrivals give the Four Confidences to the Dzogchen practitioner. The Confidence not to fear any hell or suffering and so be Compassionate as Loving to all. The Confidence to not expect any result in this here or hereafter other than the Pure Experience of Pure Mind. The Confidence of having no expectation of other attainments outside of Pure Mind or of anything better than Pure Mind. The Confidence of Pure Happiness and Pure Enjoyment in the Essential Sameness or Non-duality of the Pure Mind.

Of course these Four Confidences of Thogal come by the practice of the Four Visions. First Rigpa. Second, More Sensation of Rigpa. Third, No thought can contain what you Feel/Experience in Rigpa. Fourth, Dharma Dhatu, nothing but Dharma Dhatu, all cause (that is any reason or force within oneself for creation/phenomena) now brought into the awareness of Rigpa, nothing but Rigpa, which is Clear Mind as Pure Mind. One has no Offspring Mind, there is now only Pure Mind in Mother Light before any creation stirs or expands.

It is the most Beautiful Practice Imaginable, the Dzogchen Method of Instantaneous Arrival! You View Your Self as the Awakened One, You Behave, Act and Be in the Attitude of the Awakened One. In the Pure Sky of Pure Mind in Pure Heart you start and finish in That which has no start or finish. It is Incomprehensible and that is why the Pure Heart is the seat of the Pure Mind. Only the Heart comprehends. It is the place of Love and it is the center of consciousness where Sakyamuni left his physical emanation behind. He rose through the four conditions of meditation then up through the four states of awareness and back to the fourth condition of meditation which is in the heart then the body ceased. You see, you must now in

79

the Pure Heart know the Pure Mind of the Awakened One as your True Self. Why put it off? The eyes, luminosity, the heart and wisdom are all Open as the Open Pure Sky without a trace of cloud land within it. The eyes are Open to all awareness not closed in the contained circuitry of inner locked up energy, emotion and thought. You must experience Pure Mind with the eyes open as even then nothing can distract that Pure Mind. With Eyes Open you are aware of the three major nerve channels in the body, speech, mind and breath. With Open Eyes the mind knows only the word/sound of Pure Aaahh, the Pure Sky. Here then even phowa is unnecessary, as it is redundant, a back step, superfluous, for there is nowhere to go, nowhere for consciousness to be transferred to, no other world, no new body, no bardo experiences and no more any sting to what was Death. This Thogal is the Dzogchen Art of Surpassing All Immediately, Now in an Instant! And then you get the Four Confidences.

Vajrayogini is a Dzogchen Goddess empowering Divine Pride in Dzogchen Empowerments! I worship the Goddess as Dzogchen Wonderment, as Pure Amani Bhava, even within my own body and mind (reflection) as waking and dreaming yet even the finest region of consciousness in deep sleep is still materialistic. As causal material, as subtle material, as body flesh material, all this is materialism. So it is also true with the guru or ishta or God, at these levels, until the sweet moment, Pure Mind, Pure Buddhi, Pure Atman are perceived, worshiped and realized. This was the Refuge that was for Always sought and once there everything below appears as delusion or reality or nothing, whatever the eyes hold at that moment.

At times it seems to me that the idea of the Void is there so that you will never limit what is Experience by any conceptual judgment. If you keep making your mind void and at the same time you keep experiencing this living reality of life which is not void but living flesh and bone and earth and rock and so forth, well what happens, you never conceptualize the experience you are having and that is good because all that can happen in the void is an increasing and ever expanding awareness of what is. And "what is," hardly seems void or empty at all. In fact, really speaking what more often seems void is our so called living experience in many ways, how often do we think it is hollow, empty or at the very least all too short in its impermanent time span. So, this Void as it is said is called the Luminous Void and the Mother Light and the Clear Light and is often times distinguished as being quite different from what is indicated by Sat Chid Ananda. But you see, the Chid is also translated as being an indication as well for the Light also, or the Light of Consciousness which gives light to all ideas and concepts but is itself ever beyond any idea of concept. So Sat Chid Ananda is this indication of Existence Light and Love. Three words that can only at best give us a peek at the Pure Clear Light of the Luminous Mother Herself being the True Existence. Also Dzogchen Buddhism teaches that both Samsara and Nirvana are seen or come out of, or exist as ideas or concepts of cognition within this Clear Light of the Mother Principle. So even the reality (nirvana) illusion (samsara) complex of duality still exists only as a cognition within the high and final Mother Light of the Pure Mind. Something Primordial and Perfectly and Completely Original backs both ideas being foreground concepts in the mind content. Pure Mind backs all mind content, where in Samsara and Nirvana rest or exist, but Pure Mind stands for itself.

Longchenpa gives us the wondrous thought that at the Climax/Fruit/Result of all spiritual searching and practice, you your very Self become the Supreme Refuge for all beings in all the six worlds. (See Kindly Bent To Ease Us) That is you as Pure Mind, not as a person. Yet, this includes you as you are never excluded from this. From the beginning, not the end. No becoming. You are this. Pure Dzogchen. You are an embodied being if you need Refuge. Maybe Compassion comes First to you from You. So it can be given (shown) to others (without doing so as ego). Be Complete and Greatly so, as Great as it can be for it is so (As You), from now, the beginning. Study in anything generates various mind states all of which have some dual doubt. Non (Nir) Conceptuality (Vikalpa) of ordinary Pristine Awareness (Pure Mind) is everything. Now, back then and tomorrow! In Pure Mind arises the appearance of nirvana, and as much as, the arising of samsara. They are both projections on Pure Mind. Do you get it yet?

Trekchod is going into the Nitya, the Innate Eternal Being, the Mother who is Pure Light, Pure Mind. It is cutting away into the Chikhai Bardo but not as a bardo of intermediate and changing conditions. It is the cutting or sweeping away of everything that is not that Light. Thogal is working with the Lila, the Spontaneous Arising Play of whatever happens and being comfortable with that and seeing the Pure Mind Light in that Play that arises from the moment of its appearance, to the increasing of its sensation, to the knowledge of its full scope and to the fourth Thogal stage where one has exhausted every possibility of expression in Pure Mind. Pure Mind being all that is left. So even when or if one experiences the Chonyid dream mind or returns to the Sidpa bardo there is only the Full Light of Thogal. Even in its four stages. This is an aspect of these two practices. Trekchod sweeps away the "I" consciousness. Thogal brings back, sweeps back with the True Spiritual "I" Consciousness. Deathless and Beautiful! One cuts away into the Pure Mind of the no ego. The other comes back as a new being.

Trekchod is Chikhai practice. Thogal is Chonyid practice. Now with this the five pure wisdom lights appear as one's own self. The Pure Mind, the One, the Many, the Mirror of Pure Mind which Glows everywhere and fifth, the Ever Accomplished Feeling that Reality is always Reality. Sometimes this is called the Five Buddhas, Awakened Ones. I prefer the Five Dakinis, the Goddesses of the same Five Wisdom Lights. All these, even with the five elements, the five emotions, the five pranic energies, all these flow out of, that is come out of forgetting Pure Mind. That is the reason for this demonstration.

The Three Kayas are more the Spiritual Dimensions within and behind the Three States of Consciousness, Waking, Dreaming and Deep Sleep. Trikaya can be personal, universal and even something more! These are three ways to See you were always Pure Mind.

Trekchod is Neti Neti (Not this, Not this) until one has completely made the decision to burn down the house of the "I" into the Ground Luminosity of Mother Light (Chikhai). Thogal is Iti Iti (This This) rebuilding the new House out of Mother

Light in the Chonyid and even the Sidpa Bardo. The Real Three Kayas are now Awake. Non-Dual Kayas as One Self Kaya Dimension. Trekchod is cutting into the Absolute. Thogal is back again in the Relative. Yet more dynamic than just thinking about it.

Dzogchen is a Circular (Path) in the End (Fruit/Result) you reach the Start (Base). I never stepped out of or down from (Myself) but Now everything is Brighter in the Lamps of Visions, by the Lighting of these... Finally, the amazing spiritual Dzogchen layout is becoming clear. You get it in one beautiful sweeping stroke of comprehension and then the suddenness of self arisen recognition comes out of the Pure Mind when your Dakini Dances for you!

Poetry is Fine! Dzogchen poetry is better as Dzogchen is mostly taught through poetry and verse. Yet, Illumination is best and from there comes the best poetry! If you cannot contemplate Pure Mind (Turiya) then contemplate the three states, eventually the Constant will Show Self to You, the Self. When all forms and names fall into the wayside and are no longer pregnant with significance, then every experience, is the experience of Self (Turiya).

As Trikaya, the Book is the Nirmanakaya emanation or surrounding manifestations. The Wisdom within it the Sambhogakaya of luminous energy or thought energy in enjoyable movement. The Truth within this is the Dharmakaya which Shows Clearly at that Moment, the Place where there is no self apprehension, where thought is cleared out, emptied of content. Maha Mudra (the Great Gesture of Truth) is a gesture. Dzogchen (Pure Mind) is not a gesture in the thought dimension.

Pure Mind is Ever Complete, so there is no need to lose it in seeking perfection. Listen here, "The Perfect never becomes imperfect." Swami Vivekananda. From such a Height, to even think of seeking Truth and finding it as a birthright is losing it. "There is no "birthright", we were never born." Swami sees clearly from that Height. The Unbelievable Power of Maya, the Occurring, makes you believe in containment, embodiment, ego, dream, the Measure of what measures Infinite into finite, even to believe in a reality of planets, stars, galaxies, universe, livings beings, deities, deitesses, to that extent, the measure of Rigpa, which is Inseparability itself in Dharmakaya cannot be contained by any thought. This is the 3rd Thogal Vision (the 1st and 2nd are obvious). The 4th Thogal is the exhaustion of every imaginable possibility in the same inseparable Dharmakaya. Rigpa no longer functions adjacent to imagination. It has extended past all possible things and now rests in Itself Complete (Dzog, as it always has been, that is why it is Great, Chen). Have you ever thought about how much hurricanes look like galaxies. It is that we are living within one and are so small to its motions that we don't feel it. There is no place to go, everything is right here in front of you. Even death, rebirth, other worlds, are imagined in relation to what Pure Rigpa is! Even if land extended to every direction and it was never dark for any reason to explain the fact that light was constantly present, that creation would still be as unbelievable as this one is. Nothing real is perceived in the finite contained perspective. Everything has burst forth before you in its own Rigpa.

Advaitic Theory is the three states and Turiya, an idea, a theory until I become Conscious of the "I" within the theory. The theory becomes practice and practice becomes Experience! Yet, what is "I" as Experience never has gone away. So, even just theory is good as the "I" is also there! Besides, AUM becomes (is) the Trikaya of Wondrous Field Experience! Ordinary waking, dream and sleep becomes (or just is) naturally divine and spiritualized as Blessed AUM, no longer ordinary, but Pure Mind Wonderment. I am not of mind, even as a subjective source of guidance, as in what one might say or think next or do and so forth. I am saying Pure Absolute Mind as the Intensely Direct Revelation of Revealing Itself as to What Reveals Itself to Itself Alone! This is Satchidananda, the Purest Refuge of and in Sakti.

Dzogchen is to jump out of the known universe to a View of the universe surging with Wonderment. A friend of mine spent time too in the third ring of hell, then Joy and Love came to her in Mother's manifest vision filling her. A beautiful friend. The Mother is this Wonderment.

Amanibhava or Pure Mind

Amanibhava is this Pure Mind, the Real Refuge/Teacher, Ever and Ever Within! Bhava is Pure Feeling here, Pure Love. Mani is mind, the jewel of the little mind engaged in the dream and waking states and the dark light of deep sleep. The letter "a" here means without. So Pure Mind is without or not this little mind as such, not really. This Feeling or Mood of the Pure Mind is the Great Primordial Mind that encompasses the little mind. But then you are not worshiping a guru or a god or even a principle. You are worshiping Pure Reality with Pure Feeling which is your Pure Mind to begin with. Every single thought and every single feeling has this Pure State at its very beginning, but in the quick rapid firing of thoughts and feelings the later analysis and reasoning about thought and feeling kicks in, and you apparently lose contact at that moment with what is Pure Mind. It is an extremely subtle process going on all the time.

What is it that happens to my mind in Pure Mind? Sometimes Great Expanses! Sometimes narrow corners. In the Mood of Free Mind, Pure Mind, O Mother Ultimate as Pure Goddess Mind, what is it that You wish to constantly teach by the lesson of dualism at one moment expansive and the next so narrow? Is it that no mind is best for that opens the way for Pure Mind to come forth? In Your Pure Mind I can see everything at once, from Whitman to Dzogchen, to the mountains of the Himalayas where accomplished children of Your Doctrine have walked and died and will be born again, to the Temple in Dakshineswar to the Region of Ramakrishna's Deathless Wonder! To those inner death movements, to the indestructibly residing Mind that is the Buddha Tathagata Garbha, Your Own Self, oh Blissful Mother First and Singular Power Light seen at death! What is it that You are doing to my mind. Her Pure Mind is always here, the narrow corners make the impermanent moment of doubt.

You see, arrogance attracts arrogance, if only I may let myself surrender to Life as Teacher, Vivekananda's ever present reality of what is inside OM and what Joe Campbell describes as that awareness when one need not go anywhere for within OM is

85

everything. With that deep freedom in real Humility, then learning is everywhere. If I raise my head of ego, in superiorism, guruism, knowing-ism, ageism, well then Life teaches me through those things the nature of my arrogance. I humbly surrender to the lesson that one should seek Humility First! If it is fear, fear of disease, fear of death, fear of impermanence, then by that ego fear I am taught. It is a real spiritual gift to be able (Sakti) to look within and see the subtle workings of the ego's tricks. It is even a greater gift of and in the Pure Mind to stay alert, attentive and astonished in Rigpa, and not engage the complex of ego tricks, but what of emotions (betrayal, insult, etc.), they must come to rest in the surrendered self-radiance of all feeling arising in Love Itself. Love is the Rigpa of emotions. Stay astonished in Love, then one does not descend to engage pride, fear, craving, anger, jealousy, stupidity.

Mani is mind even as in the great mantra OM Mani Padme Hum. "A" means no, not and non. So you see Amani is no mind, not the mind, even non-mind, as in the sense that the active figuring of the mind is indeed the loss of Pure Mind which knows What Is automatically and arrives to this Wisdom Energy (Sakti) instantaneously and spontaneously. Bhava is the Mood or Feeling of this. So it is simply the Spontaneous or Instantaneous Mood of Pure Mind that comes up within us all the time but we have not conditioned ourselves, generally speaking, to recognize this immediate gift of Presence in Pure Mind.

So Enlightenment or Centered-ness in Pure Mind, if it may be called such, or Suchness itself as the Mood of Suchness in Pure Mind may simply be our own most ordinary awareness conscious of the three states of everyone's ever present experience in Prajna, Taijasa and Visva (the Avasthatraya states) as they are now aware to be the Suchness Itself of the Dharmakaya, Sambhogakaya and Nirmanakaya, as the barrier of the "I" complex is no longer dimmed as to what it is, Luminous Simple Awareness - Aware of the Aware - and the three states and dimensions. Loving every minute of it. Treating everything as Suchness, no flash of light, no message from the sky, no miracle, no amazing encounter with a deity or teacher, just

Peace, the simple Peace of your own mind knowing the Three States as they are in the most unexalted way!

Immense Mind (Bhava: Mood Feeling, Mukha: As the True Face of Reality) is there after coming out of the Dzogchen Pleasure, Radiance, and Non-Dividedness or the Advaitic Sat Chit Ananda, it is the return to the entire field in the reach and range of relative awareness.

Pure Mind may not even have an Awareness of Immensity for what could be immense to Pure Mind: the world, the galaxy, the universe, God, deities, living beings, the twenty-four cosmic principles are indeed only a point drop (thigle) within the Vast Incomprehensible Expanse of what is the Reality of Pure Mind!

Dharma Mind is what is happening to the jiva self concept at this moment in time. The concept of what you believe you are at any given moment, not just your purpose in the world, but all dharmas (jivas) whose purpose or reason is to realize the Self Awakened. Once done you are no longer a dharma as the Dharma has been fulfilled.

Isvara (God) Koti and Jiva (Soul) Koti (Class). Can the jiva class become a God Aware class? Yes, it can be so. It must be so otherwise what is the Universe doing? Then to return! God Class is born Aware, no loss of the Amani State, by being blurred with the mani state.

Mani Bhava, mood of mind (or manas bhava) is as what is cognitively wrapped up with the twelve causing links, even the illusion of self, as Amani Bhava is not even an idea of a self concept, perhaps not even the Atma, but it is an Aware Mood of the Something More than mind may conceive. That is why Void is given in Dzogchen and Annihilation in Advaita.

Amani (not mind) Advaita (Not Two) Bhava... Mood of Not Mind, so where does one mood end and the other begin since This is the Already What You Are State from the very moment the first thought in the universe came into being!

Pure Mind encompasses, expands and extends throughout mani bhava, surpassing its influence as an imaginative obscuration over inherent innate spiritual awareness. The obscuring factor is only an imagined one.

Amanibhava is simply this Mind now, that is aware of

waking, dreaming and deep sleep. It is the same Mind, Pure Mind, as Ordinary Awareness, but as Amanibhava it is Felt without the limited consciousness grasping to identify with the three states.

The Innermost Secret Essence is Pure Mind in Divine Wonderment (no apprehender/apprehended) living non-dual radiant pleasure. Pure Mind is not a subject which views the Three Kayas like an object, thus perhaps better than the Vedantic Witness, as the Three States are a living sahaja advaita. It is as Longchenpa says that the Lama is inside as One's own Self, not external. Then the entire Three Kayas appear everywhere and as always the one Absolute Teacher.

So someone said that God is beyond all thoughts and words, then Ramakrishna replied, "No, that is not true. He can be known by the pure buddhi, which is the same as the Pure Self. The seers of old directly perceived the Pure Self through their pure buddhi." But Girish protests that God must take human incarnation to teach us spiritual mysteries. And Vivekananda restates that God is in the heart and, "He will certainly teach us from within the heart." Ramakrishna confirms, "Yes, yes. He will teach us as our Inner Guide." Some amazing things are here. In the living presence of one who is considered an incarnation he affirms the Inner Guide and not himself. Also we wonder about these seers of old. Perhaps, Sakyamuni, as one of the original and earlier of the three types of spiritual beings, gives us another clue. The simple buddha, the solitary buddha and the supreme buddha. As the awakened buddhi is the Buddha. The simple buddha follows the doctrine of an Already Awakened Buddha. Latter they were called Hearers. Now the Pratyeka Buddha, like the "seers of old," by themselves alone and alone following no other Buddha they became enlightened. These are those seers of old. But the latter description of them became those who merely practice by themselves, when the more of it is that they found Reality all by themselves. Beautiful. Then were the supreme Buddhas once bodhisattvas who promised to help others learn to help themselves. So it goes back all to Pure Mind. You find it by your self alone, even if at one time you followed another or even if you have promised to help the world know that it must be found on its own.

So in the whirlpool of contradictions on the subject Swami Vivekananda lifts us out of the water in which we are drowning. "Christs and Buddhas are but waves on the boundless ocean which I am. Bow down to nothing but your own higher Self." There, he said it and that is it. And, "Nonetheless, we must not pin our faith to any man , however great; we too must become Buddhas and Christs." To this it seems Walt Whitman speaks in echoes, "And nothing, not God, is greater to one than one's self is." He adds, "Nor do I understand who there can be more wonderful than myself." (see again, Sakyamuni's remark to Upaka)

To this we add, "Buddha never bowed down to anything - neither Vedas, nor caste, nor priest, nor custom. He fearlessly reasoned so far as reason could take him. Such a fearless search for truth and such love for every living thing the world has never seen." Vivekananda applauds the path of the Pure Mind which is no less what this is. Swami says, "You are God, and whatever else you may think is wrong." And Whitman returns with, "None has begun to think how divine he himself is..." Wonderful, wonderful am I! "You must worship the Self in Krishna, not Krishna as Krishna." Vivekananda makes clear that it is the Pure Mind example in someone like Krishna, not the person Krishna. Whitman also makes the point, "I see the place of the idea of the Deity incarnated by avatars in human forms." and "The saints and sages in history -- but you yourself?" It is you your Self, that is the place... Swami adds, "Never fear what will become of you, depend on no one. Only the moment you reject all help are you free." Walt Whitman echoes again, "He that by me spreads a wider breast than my own proves the width of my own, He most honors my style who learns under it to destroy the teacher." That is depend on no one, that is the spiritual style that takes you to Self proving even a width greater than what was thought possible within this place! So we hear Swami now echo this spiritual style, "No books or teachers can do more than help us to find it, and even without them we can get all truth within." Excellent! "Until the inner teacher opens, all outside teaching is in vain." Swami again speaks from the

89

height of Pure Mind and would you want anything less than that, "As men, we must have a God; as God, we need none." Said from the highest Amanibhava advaita, "So long as you hold yourself separated by a hair's breadth from this Eternal One, fear cannot go." And who is this Eternal One, "Until Mother releases us, we cannot get free." There is no other than that, so, "The greatest sin is to think yourself weak. No one is greater: realize you are Brahman. Nothing has power except what you give it. We are beyond the sun, the stars, the universe. Stand up and say, I am the master, the master of all. We forge the chain, and we alone can break it." These are all spoken from Pure Mind by Vivekananda.

In praise of Humility I shall repeat again and again that one who thinks they know everything never learns anything. The Secret is held and kept subliminal until it becomes liminal, that is reaches the threshold so the solution is no longer obscured and so it is then no longer a secret. This all happens within Amanibhava, the feeling state of the Pure Mind and it happens no where else than here!

This Pure Buddhi, this Pure Mind is your own Buddha Mind. That is it. And Swami Yatiswarananda's insight is perfect in saying that guru worship is a form of spiritual materialism. So, all drops off, sleep and mind, dream and space, waking and the words of the waking world, and you are left with Swami Vivekananda's Principle which was forgotten in the person, that is the condition of the three states of consciousness (waking, dream and sleep) your own or another's. If you compare Amanibhava to Shunyata, then "Who" is the Experiencer of Shunyata? A "someone" speaks of this Experience. After the experience of Pure Mind a "someone" comes down to speak, that is not the ego, that is Primordial Energy and that Energy now plays as your own mind and body! Here, in spiritual materialism with whoever, cultural practices and emotional responses, Western or Eastern, give me a break. For a moment I felt the guru attitude in my response to A., "The Great Reality over the idea of God." Even ideas are material. I praised. Immediately there, Mother showed me the limits and faults of the human mind forgetting the Principle in a person. Divinize none! Or

90

All! Indeed, how true. Actually, Aseshananda healed the wound of the guru crisis, the wound of looking elsewhere other than where Reality Is! I thank him for that. In his last days and months on Earth, so indeed it must be an important cure, perhaps needed by others as well as me, who have forgotten Pure Mind at one time while dwelling on a person.

Pure Mind as Teacher

I give homage to Compassion, to True Humanity, to Love! Love is the Ground, the Path, the Fruit! I will always show the gesture of my respect to those who demonstrate True Humanity. But never to those who want to be worshiped as gods!

Pure Mind is with You as You, for generations so hold no fear of many deaths or many lives regenerated through Sidpa Mantric Rebirth (when you consciously choose your next existence through the force of mantric focus). You are the Deitess through Divine Pride generated out of Mother Light (Sakti Chikhai) in death's deep sleep, into the dream mind, into waking mind. Ever Pure Mind it was!

The very act of looking (outside of Self) for something or someone (external to Self as an assistance) distracts from the Pure Art of True Seeing (Spontaneous Rigpa Astonishment). It is like leaving your Elephant at home while going into the forest to look for his footprints. Or more so it is like a madman looking for his face on other people's heads in a crowd. Just let mind wander in the self radiance of Rigpa. It is most relaxing.

It is in Heroic Solitary Practice that the Truth of Pure Mind is discovered and continued. Heroic Solitude is for those who are no longer dependent on traditional teachings and whose spiritual passion has brought them to the desire to experience the final solution that is inherent within the Self, the Pure Mind in reality. Ramakrishna demonstrated this Heroic Solitary Practice alone in the Kali Temple as he was resolved to use Her sword on himself if She did not reveal the Truth to him. She did. Sakyamuni also made the highest spiritual example by going to sit under the Tree resolved to starve and die until Truth was revealed to him. And it was through his own diligence as it was

91

for Ramakrishna by the same power of his own diligence.

Have the Darshan (Sight, Insight, Instruction, Teaching, and Revealing) of your own Pure Mind. No Janaka! No Ashtavakra!

Scientists study things. Psychologists study people. Lovers study feeling. Philosophers study thought. Seekers study God. Poets study things, people, feeling, thought and God. As a poet living in Pure Mind, I study Life right in front of the awareness of my eyes that taste Life like tongues searching for color and the Goddess of Life teaches me what I must know at this precious moment.

Can we say that Pure Mind is nothing less than Supreme Intellect, but not the intellect of the intelligent only, but the Intellect which is Supreme in Knowing the Heart. The Heart which knows and is Love. This is the superior Power within us all that guides, reflects, becomes and Is just "What Is." Is it not the Tathagata, the Pure Mind as Such, in Suchness just as it is? Is this not the Chikhai, the Pure Light at death, death of the body, death of the mind and mostly the death of the ego when its grasping dies and Real Life comes up to embrace you. It is the Pure Nature of your own Pure Mind and not just the mind that goes here and there as it does in a mere dream.

So what is the Pure Mind and what is the pure mind versing the impure mind. Pure Mind is not a pure mind verses impure mind dualism. Whether or not you feel your mind is pure or impure the Pure Mind is there present in either identity or practice. I say practice because if you are a disciple of your ego space then you are in the discipline of the impure mind, you are listening to the voice of selfishness. This restriction upon your consciousness goes away with the practice of genuine Humility and Surrender to Pure Mind. Yet, in the dualistic sense of it to think you are working with the pure mind as opposed to an impure one is also no less being a devotee of the ego space with just a different face to it. Pure Mind must be something more and it is. It is even Something More than a God idea reflected in the buddhi (intellect) or of a Supreme Self (Atma) reflected into Bodha (Consciousness). It is not a duality as these two examples which contain more than one principle. When Bodha (Consciousness) becomes Buddha (Awakened) who can say

92

what that Is? It certainly cannot be expressed in the dualism of word, gesture or mind. Yet we all feel it as a bhava (an energy of emotion or of loving presence). At any rate, though Pure Mind is the non-expression of any ego space, it is nevertheless still present even when the ego is present for where else would Pure Mind seek to give its compassion but to the sad and pathetically confined ego space.

The True, the Real, the Divine Teacher is Compassion Itself. The Pure Mind Ground Stratum of the Universe Appearing everywhere, Arising everywhere. Even as Longchenpa has said, this is in books, food, clothes, warmth, comfort, rest, beds, blankets, actually anything that protects you, everything that protects you, the entire Buddha Fields which are nevertheless but a dream to Pure Mind. The six teachers (symbols of the Self Arisen) of the six worlds all are but the Response of Pure Compassion that appears in correspondence to the need of the trainees. It is not applied compassion as a human person might apply or do compassion. It is the very Founding Stratum of the universe when the universe appears and is as a causal or acting agent or energy disappears into itself as Pure Love, when the trainees have understood. Then, no conceptualized duality exists. It is the ever present, always perfect Primordial Awareness that has never left you, there, there ever and even in deep sleep, dream and waking. Ever "Inscendent" (as my Blessed Companion in this Life has described this Reality in her own words and spiritual discovery). It does not transcend, descend or ascend, the, into, or above the waking, dream or deep sleep state. But is the ever dynamic Primordial Energy which is dynamic only when the duality of the trainee's need for "It" appears. Always present as Pure Mind, the very profound and true nature of the Tatha Gata Garbha. Even the Buddha himself, the Dharmic teachings, the Sangha of seekers, Hearers, Solitary Practitioners, Kind Ones, the path itself and all that, is negated (or better yet Inscended) in the Primordial Pure Mind described in the full Prajna Paramita. Tatha Gata Garbha is the sweet precious jewel in the history of human heritage stripped of all myth about it. Be the true, genuine, real and authentic human being in the Pure Mind that you are, in nature, essence and energy in the Primordial Awareness that you are (Tatha Gata Garbha)! So what Sakyamuni said about having no masters is true for you in the Real State which is never not so!

"You are your own Guru," Dadaji of Calcutta. (See Mystics and Men of Miracles in India by Mayah Balse) Consider this at the finest level which is nothing short of Pure Mind. Even if you have many lives and deaths, or just one, there is never not a time when the Real You (Pure Mind, Turiya) is not there. Turiya is always reflected down into the waking and dreaming states, its essence is what makes them alive with conscious energy. And in the finest level and deepest depth of conscious experience the Existence, Consciousness and Love (Turiya, your True Self) is experienced there in the prajna or dreamless sleep state. So, never are not You there with You. You are your own Teacher, and it is a matter of you diligently working out your own energy to the awareness of this. It is the essence and energy, as the extreme nature of Primordial Energy (Sakti) in Turiya itself that has become you, the pure nature of deep sleep and the very essence and energy of your own mind and body now here as your dream and waking state. So, from both points of view, that of Pure Reality or that of the ever present awareness of Pure Experience in the dreamless, dreaming and waking experiences, you are your own Guiding Light. Brahmajna Ma a self-enlightened woman also says that one does not need a guru's help who asks such questions of their own Self, like who am I, where was I before the world, what is the world, where shall I be after the world and what is Peace, Truth and Life! (Daughters of the Goddess by Linda Johnsen) This is exactly the same thing Ramana Maharshi practiced and advised others to do!

Only You (Pure Mind) are with You all the Time. If you want permanent union with a Light that takes away all darkness and doubt it must and can only be this You, as Pure Mind (Tatha Gata Garbha). The Buddha is Shunyata (Void). Void is the Buddha. The Dharma is Void, Void is the Dharma. The Sangha is Void and Void is the Sangha. The Three Tantric Forces; Body, Speech and Mind are Void. Void are Body, Speech and Mind. Waking, Dreaming and Deep Sleep are Void, Void are Waking, Dreaming and Deep Sleep. The Rope is Void, Void is the Rope. The Serpent is Void, Void is the Serpent. At the end, or where Spirituality begins, what we have is Pure Mind.

You see there are three rivers of Consciousness from which my mind no longer wanders. Pure Sakti, Ramakrishna and Dzogchen. In this Flow of Power my Spiritual Friend is Suddenly with me in Pure Mind. No limitation! The ordinary waking, dream and deep sleep states are now manifesting as Nirmanakaya, Sambhogakaya, and Dharmakaya. It was always so I just could not see this Reality until Pure Mind became evident. Pure Cultivation of Pure Mind shows the natural ever present reality of these dimensions (Kayas) that were not even ever obscured by the waking, dreaming and deep sleep states of consciousness that had temporarily forgotten reality for thousands of centuries back into the delusion of past time.

You have to realize that your life is your own Life. It is your Life. It sounds so simple and obvious but there is no final depth to the knowing and feeling of your own Life and of course this is discovered in Pure Mind. Your Life as You is Your Own and not another's domain.

We are wrongly told that we are not free (as it is our own very Pure Mind in its natural state of Primordial Awareness simple and true) from the moment of birth, from within the claws of impermanence, from the grip of stupidity, etc. and that causes fear and that fear makes you run to a teacher, a church, etc., but the whole time you were in the True Refuge of the Primordial Awareness of Pure Mind. Now you remember this Rigpa in Pure Mind. Yet, you might need to cut away the bundle of former ideas pertaining to experience (Trek Chod Pa) and to go deeper and deeper into It's Immeasurable Wonderment (Thogal)!

Is it in fascination then imagination, these dream like conditions where mind wanders outward? Perhaps at moments when the thunder of Pure Mind exposes itself within those processes. But you see, I myself make my own limitations on Pure Mind by the act of mental preconception about what Pure Mind is in fact and the potential I feel it has. That is self created limitation and there is no limitation to the experience in Pure Mind and the Power of Pure Mind as Teacher but we often do limit this Power by distinguishing discursively where, when and in whom Pure Mind may make itself known. We say it exists in this particular person and it does not manifest in that person and we never realize Pure Mind in itself for it is never a particular nor a manifest objective thing, being ever existent in its own right. Nothing can touch it! Asparsa!

This is my constant and perpetual continuing wish for you! May your own Pure Mind never be clouded by stupidity. May you never have fear of fear, nor ever be angry at anger nor ever desire to desire. May the external dimension of your waking state always be filled with the word power of Pure Mind. May the internal dimension of the space of your dream state always reflect the power of Pure Mind. May your mind itself within the dimension of deep sleep always be luminous with the luminosity of Pure Mind Wisdom. May you spontaneously know Pure Mind as a Self Arisen being never in need of receiving teachings nor of being taught. May you know Your Self as Ever Spontaneously Arisen never needing any arising!

We think that Pure Mind becomes the Teacher, no not really, for Pure Mind always was the Teacher and no one else even if your own Pure Mind was engaged with some other method at one time. In the Immediate Perspective of Dzogchen, the Pure Mind is Here and Now and there is no becoming, you see, Pure Mind, the Core of Reality is the Excellent Leader, the True Helper (even of the Three Jewels) it is the True Jewel Teacher, the Real and Highest Potency of Greatest Import, what Longchenpa refers to as the Unsurpassable Level. For Garab Dorje, Pure Mind came up and showed itself to him as the subtle mind being, Vajrasattva. For Ramakrishna Pure Mind came up as the Shiva Sadhu, as an image of his own self who taught him everything, Tantra, Advaita, Nirvikalpa, even before his redundant encounters with those traditional teachers. (See Ramakrishna's Solution to the Obscuration of the Guru) Vajrasattva is the adamantine thunder bolt reflex of Pure Mind itself charging mind itself with the power of Pure Clarity free of the images that appear in the consciousness of the bardo like dream state to which Vajrasattva is a part. Yet this principle of Vajrasattva is the introducing, discovering and continuing in what is called or appears in the three states, as the being named

Garab Dorje or You! This Ordinary Simple Awareness, even so, even here in the three states, appears to what appears to be Garab Dorje, Gaudapada, Ramakrishna or You! Why waste your swift precious life span on fundamentals? To do so is the most strange exchange of what is Real for what is dream.

Pure Mind as the Potency of Highest Significance is your own Ordinary Awareness, clear of subjective ownership. This is very important not to have even the feeling of subjective ownership in regard to the feeling of being in Pure Mind. This feeling is the Amanibhava, known at the Simple Moment, your Ever Awake Nature, which then first Appears Awakened, yet has always been so, the Most Precious Jewel, most valued, far more than the "three jewels" (Buddha, Dharma, Sangha) which are there out of Compassion, so people may have something to relate with! So why not take Refuge Here in your Pure Mind Jewel, before all that other. Bend to this and this will bend to you, teach you how to live well, to die well, take you out of your ego, and show you the Secrets of Non-Duality. What more is there but that you will Love well!

Sweeping across the layers and fields of thought I clearly realized for one moment that whatever appears in mind is at that moment Pure Teacher as Compassion at the stage of the moment itself! And this Pure Compassion (Love) at that Moment in Pure Mind is always and permanently has been Dharmakaya, Sambhogakaya and Nirmanakaya, which never needs to transform or replace Chikhai, Chonyid or Sidpa Bardos, for those Three (even as AUM) are nothing but and never have been anything else other than or different from the Inseparable and Non-Dual Kayas, Dharma, Sambhoga and Nirmana, even as the Immediate Self Arisen appearance of these Three have never been anything but the Energy of Compassion as Rigpa in the Son Mind and as Mother Essence (Yeshe: Primordial Wisdom) of the Whole Thing. And this is how Base, Path and Fruit are brought together as One Experience in View, Mediation and Result which are Mother, Son and Compassion in all three fields and stages.

Regard Your Self even Now, wherever you are, with the Dignity, Esteem and Humility of an Enlightened Being! By so

97

Surrendering to This You Become This in the Becoming (less) Reality of What You Are. There is nothing that is not there in your own Pure Mind!

I am Aware in Dzogchen (Pure Sakti), but still I can speak and write, think, walk, sleep and eat. I am not yet dead, Beyond, or am I? Amazing! The Wonder! The Dakini Mind!

I am tired of living and I am tired of dying. What shall I do but be in Pure Mind! A most astounding thought is Jigme Lingpa saying that the Buddha, Padmasambhava, Longchenpa, his Dakini, himself and all his experiences in his life as Jigme Lingpa and his previous lives as well, are one and all nothing but projections having no substance. Everything is the display of exasperation! Pure Mind is the only refuge but even refuge is an exasperation.

The thought about the state of Amanibhava is still a thought dimension though a very refined one at that. With this thought you are still in the student/teacher duality as a student of this thought. Though in Reality you are nothing but a student of your Own Self, for that is what is Final in the Soaring On. But you see, the thought alone of Amanibhava which is the Mood of Turiya without the mind obstruction of the Avasthatraya (no-mind of the three states, no more little mind thought of a cognitive ideal of what Aum embodies, you Feel its Power you don't think about or over it) is not the Experience. Are you yet Experienced? When can you say that it is So? Long before it was misplaced! Knowing it then, Joy! In the moment Undefined and Unfabricated. You Let Go into Mother and then Soar On as Mother! Where was duality? Where ever was it not Reality? Amanibhava is the Immense Mind of Mother who has never lost Her Self in the delusion of waking (A), dream (U) or deep sleep (M)!

Don't think, don't imagine, don't calculate, don't dream, don't figure, don't worry, don't wonder, don't identify with the mind that is misapprehension in waking and dream, don't identify with the mind that is non-apprehension in deep sleep. Be awake as you are. Don't be distracted by the tossing about of the mind attracted to waking phenomena, don't be grasping to the deep desires that rise in the reflections of the dream phenomena, don't sink away into the dissolution of deep sleep and don't be satisfied with the joys of lower realizations. That is the message then Pure Mind is there. Don't compare your journey with the journey of others. Unique, yet in common examples shared show the way. Mind the spiritual dimensions of your own body, mind and soul or body, speech and mind as you prefer. I have found that this brings Happiness.

I am Crushed by the Immensity. I see everyone already dead, gone, in their future lives, Now! The six worlds turn, the three realms hang loosely in Pure Mind! Yet all Apparition! I too see what you see Jigme! No Buddha, no Ramakrishna, no Gaudapada nor Garab Dorje, no Longchenpa, no Totapuri nor Rudraka nor Arada, no Ashtavakra, no Janaka, no Me, no Jigme Lingpa! Wonderful, this Liberating Sight!

Flying like Garuda

Resistance to Pure Mind is useless Every effort is useless Empty. It is the cause of thousands of lives wandering in the Samsara. It is in Pure Mind that everything happens, the cycle of birth and death, and the feeling of enlightenment that comes serene when the waves of mind calm and move out of the wonderment with the cycle.

My body happens within Pure Mind, its coming and going, as if it were indeed all bodies. Yet I am not a body, nor a Kaya of dimension. I am Pure Mind, arisen from the beginning, born fully grown like the mythical bird, the divine chariot of Vishnu, Garuda.

Pure Mind as the Seat of Pure Sakti is where and how the Ava (Descended) Tara (Mother) moves. Mother becomes Vishnu, the Preserver who Incarnates as Working the Savior Consciousness. Yet it is She, the Divine Mother, who is the Real Protector. The Tara (Ava Tara) meditation, empowerment, cognition or visualization is the power of preparing one's mind for Pure Mind. She is the Savior Goddess. The True Energy of Compassion as Compassion itself and as the Consort of Compassion. Your own Pure Mind is Her Mind sublimated now into this mind you are experiencing. Clear the way. The

Goddess is the Teacher incarnate into the stuff of the mind. All other teachers, doctrines or families of enlightened beings are but ornaments upon Her headdress. Surrender here first and last, generate the Compassionate Promise and Boundless Joys. This clears the way for Pure Mind to enter and stand forth. Out of Pure Mind the cause-thought of the Goddess springs forth, then Her Beautiful form, then the circle of Her sacred teachings. Her Victorious Knowledge and Love. This is drawn back into Pure Mind which is Her Ultimate Nature. But it is not finished yet. One must see Her simultaneously in Pure Mind and in manifestation, from the view of the Non-Dual. Then one is empowered with Her Helping Power. The only phenomenal difference between you and the Goddess as True Essence is that you as ego retain either or both human and spiritual selfishness and She does not! Do you live within or respond to mind or Pure Mind?

It is said that Tara always has a smile on Her Face. Why? Because She knows the True Nature of you, of me and of Herself. From time without beginning to time without end. And She is filled with this Wisdom Knowledge and the Love and Compassion to make it known to you, what She knows. The Truth of the Pure Mind! I too would always be smiling if I could always see Pure Mind within every living soul, and have the Love for each soul to know that real reality of Pure Mind for them.

Like in Vajrayogini practice empowers your mind as the Pure Mind of Garuda when consciousness moves out of Prajna, into Taijasa, into Visva, and back again. With this, the free flying divine bird of Pure Mind sees and even changes death, the after death dream mind and rebirth into the waking state, as the consciousness of Pure Mind. What else is there!

The Garuda Mind, is it not the same as the Parama Hamsa, that is the Supreme Swam, also a bird. Yet Hamsa is Mother's Mantra, as a-Ham is "I am" and Sa is She. Hamsa is Pure Mind. The Garuda Mind is the metaphor of your Fullest, most Expansive Purest Potential!

Garuda's (Pure Mind) Body contains all the Vedas and Vedanta as nothing but the teachings of the Atma. So, Garuda's

100

Body is nothing but the Atma. That is Pure Mind in Full Self Potential.

There are the six Beautiful-s of the Garuda Mind, the products or offsprings of Pure Mind in conjunction with Pure Sakti. The Sakti who contains the Garuda Mind is Anita, She who is Progress, the Queen of Knowledge named Vinayika. She is the Voice of your own Pure Mind that is always speaking to you to manifest Beautiful Face, Beautiful Name, Beautiful Eyes, Beautiful Vigor, Beautiful Brightness and Beautiful Strength. You may find Pure Mind in the beauty of your own face, the covering of Self. It is in your name, that identity of you, that Pure Mind is known. In your own eyes and from nowhere else does Pure Mind perceive what is before you. In Pure Mind alone does any find the beauty of spiritual vigor! And Brightness comes from your own Pure Mind and from nowhere else. And of course, from Pure Mind we all find our only source of beautiful spiritual strength!

Garuda is said to be Courage incarnate, which indeed is the Pure Mind alone that is capable of courageously carrying Divine Principle incarnate into the heavy load of flesh.

Garuda is born forth fully grown, such is your Pure Mind, as Such, needing no teaching nor training! Ever Being (Moving) as Help, Teaching and Instructing, Never Needing Help, Teaching or Instructing!

Garuda moves anywhere in the Universe (the Six Worlds, Form and Formless Realms) in the twinkle of a thought, quick and not bound by time or space, just the same as the Bardo Mind is said to be, which is here even now with the flesh.

What in Truth this mythology tries to remind us of and speak to us, is the spiritual capacities of your own Pure Mind expressed in the myth or maybe even the celestial heaven dream reality of Garuda.

The youngest part of the mind is submissive to established tradition. The middle aged part of mind feels connection with universal family. Yet the oldest primordial mind shows itself in the Garuda man or Garuda woman! Its all only mind, and it is a blessing to see that, by high Garuda Mind perception. Who does not love the high flight of clear thinking in Independent and Free

101

Pure Mind!

Blessed Goddess in and as Pure Mind, Elevate my Practice for I so much indeed do most certainly Love the Sweet Emotions You Give. Place Their Power in this Body and Mind so I can see and feel pure body and pure mind as Vajrayogini!

The metaphor (Garuda Mind) of Pure Mind is not Pure Mind in Itself. It is metaphor, myth, symbol, and so forth.

In the body-seat of Garuda the Bardo Mind is hidden. This Pure Mind stripped of even a trace of bardo ideas instantly accomplishes the comprehension of all, all teachings, even those never heard. Garuda is the body/seat/vehicle of the enlightened power of Buddha Amoga Siddhi (The All and Ever Accomplished Power).

The Garuda Mind in its all encompassing power encompasses pure mind, pure space and pure word. The essential threefold methods of Dzogchen contact. The Garuda Mind encompasses the prajna mind, the dream mind and the waking mind. Garuda Mind encompasses and circles the three Kaya dimensions as the Full Bliss Pleasuring of the Self Awake Pure Mind! If one has any movement, feeling or thought from Here, the waking state body becomes the pure illusory body of Nirmanakaya. The dream mind becomes the radiant subtle mind of pure enjoyment as Sambhogakaya. Even deep/sleep/death is recreated as Dharmakaya, in the firebrand of the new Garuda Mind! These are the Three Worlds and it is said that Garuda can stop the rotation of the Three Worlds with the wind of his wings! That is the Pure Voice of Pure Mind! For Garuda moves like quicksilver, goes where he wills, lives as long as he pleases and vanquishes the thunderbolt movement of intellectual cogitations.

A Tibetan lama once told me a story which I consider a powerful Dzogchen teaching if not the very Nature (Mother), Essence (Son) and Energy (Non-Dualism) of Dzogchen itself. Garuda came to a village of young children and taught these children to fly in the air. They could fly just fine when Garuda was there flying with them. But when he left and was gone from their sight they could no longer fly. Until one by one they discovered within themselves, Independent Confidence (Yes,

Garab Dorje's Continuing in Confidence in Pure Mind or Gaudapada's unwavering non-hesitation in Pure Mind). The lama went on to say that the True Teacher is the True Mind, that is the Pure Mind no doubt and that this True Mind is the Open, Primordial Space of Luminosity where everything else is but an ornament: teachers, doctrines, ideas, practices. And this Primordial Space of Pure Mind is the Advaita Vajra, the Divine Non-Dual Thunder Bolt which protects us us all! This is the Vajra Kaya of the Pure Mind of the Buddha Mind before it seems to break up, emanate and expand into Samsara, which it never does in Reality and that again is Pure Mind. So be Free and Fly like Garuda.

Trekchod and Thogal as the Nitya and the Lila

So you see, getting to Amanibhava is Trekchod, anything that appears There is Thogal. Even as the Firebrand is Quenched (Exhausted) in the Advaita. Now you are Soaring On like Garuda! When anything Appears (Thogal) you Let Go (Trekchod). Whatever comes you Soar On, you Let Go. For why in the world would you hold to any apparition of the Firebrand? Therefore, Trekchod and Thogal are Inseparable (Non-Divided Advaita). Even as two practices of essential Advaita, they arise together as one (Non-Dual), but as Pure Mind Alone you Soar Past even both ideas of practice. And for this reason they should be engaged (taught and studied) together. Not kept in esoteric hidden divided rooms. That is a contradiction in Advaita (Non-Duality)!

The Four Thogals (the Four Soarings) are only four points of distinguishing or measuring how much of Mother you have comprehended! Trekchod gets to Mother Alone, Thogal brings, soars back as Mother, but these two views, methods or ways do not contain Mother in either approach. Can you cut away anywhere where Mother is not, can you soar on anywhere where Mother is not! In a way, these are two of the most absurd ideas, from Mother's View, but to you who are stricken by dualism these two efforts may provide some unique help. Mother (Reality) does not need this help, unique or not!

Letting Go in Mother. Soaring On with Mother. Are not the two ideas intrinsically dualistic as efforts made within what is the Unsurpassable Unspeakable Non-Dual Mother!

In a Dakini Dream, She was teaching me about Trekchod (Chikhai) and Thogal (Chonyid). Nitya and Lila cannot be practiced as Cutting Through and Surpassing All. Gaudapada says we cover Reality with imagination as our ideas, even Trekchod and Thogal are ideas that cover. Those who relish practice more than Reality will reject this. "In truth, all such ideas are always imagined in Atman." Gaudapada II v.28. Mother (Kali) is Inseparable as Pure Mind and Pure Energy (Pure Love is Her). The idea is the cause of the problem. You imagine you can Trekchod to Pure Mind and that Pure Energy is the Thogals of That. Longchenpa says that you are a stupid fool of a donkey if you separate Trekchod and Thogal. Does he mean what I mean? To separate the two as practices? Or that it is the height of stupidity to dualize the Non-Dual! Emptiness is in Appearance. Appearance is in Emptiness. The Prajnaparamita Goddess says the Same, Form is Shunyata and Shunyata is Form.

Empower your Self! This is what I again have learned over and over and over, to Which must be Surrendered! Humility is the Finest Treasure! To think (cover or imagine) that you can Trekchod into Pure Mind (Nitya) and Surpass (Thogal) as Lila (Pure Energy) may be a great illusion! Totapuri could not do it. Go beyond Mother's Evidence. Nitya and Lila are Her. An ego thinks it can Cut Through, Explode Solidity or Let Go to Pure Mind. An ego is one that in thinking generates visions, optical phenomena and dream like conditions, but ego can never exhaust Lila. So both thoughts of practice bind and cover Pure Mind. Love has never known those bindings or coverings.

Can you Trekchod into or away with Pure Space? In explaining the Nature of Advaita, Gaudapada says that the jiva/egos are imagined like vessels in Pure Space (Akasha). Same with Pure Mind. So also Thogal may all be "imagined in Atman." Meditating on illusion makes me feel unreal! Mediating on Emptiness makes me feel empty! Both are imagination! So, the Positive Sat Chid Ananda is of Great Value! Supreme Affirmation! Not negation! And Love, most

Supremely So! "The way of the Sunyavadins (believers in the Void) and other Buddhists of making the mind absolutely vacant is not so healthy. It is dangerous, for it allows old impressions to arise." Aseshananda.

Even the concept that there is something to Cut Away (Trekchod) is Dual, as is, that there is something to Vision as Appearance! (Thogal). Trekchod is getting to Advaita by Letting Go, Exploding or Cutting Through the Barrier to Free the ego jiva-hood as a dharmic/karmic confluence. Thogal is Alatasanti, the Quenching or Exhausting of the visions or illusions of the firebrand circle.. Though they are useful, holding to the Four Visions, the Six Accomplishments or Four Confidences are grasping at what should be Exhausted! Even the channels (nadi nerves), winds (pranic energies) and drops (the thigles) are still firebrand distractions. Reality is the Fire. On the end of a torch, at night you whirl it about in a circle and so on and it produces appearances, but all the while what is There is just Fire! Alata is literally firebrand. Santi is Peace. It is the title of the fourth and final part of Gaudapada's Advaitic Brilliance!

In the three statements of Garab Dorje the entire process of Dzogchen is shown in the simplest way. If you would call Dzogchen a process! First is the Encounter or Discovery of the Mother Light by the offspring mind. Second is the Total Decision to Let go in the Mother Light. This is Trekchod. Third is the Confidence to Continue in the Mother Light in whatever arises. This is Thogal. All this happens in Mother Herself. It is as simple as that! In the Kali Temple the Goddess, Mother Kali showed Ramakrishna this Pure Mind or Pure Consciousness. The Encounter, the Discovery. He Let Go into Her as Pure Mind. And then She revealed that Consciousness (Herself, this very Being) within everything that was there, the image, door, ceiling, floor and so on. Is this not Soaring On in whatever arises? All three stages are there. The Discovery of Pure Mind beyond all materiality. The Total Decision to Explode to Freedom the barrier of all solidity and one must realize at this moment that the physical is not the only solidity, but the subtle and the causal or spiritual levels of existence also have a materiality or solidity to them, though more refined. These three levels are the waking, dreaming and deep sleep state. Whenever they arise in whatever way they arise when Pure Mind watches these states, that is Soaring On in Thogal. Then, Whatever happens is Fine! Now, Whatever comes to Presence is the Supreme Teacher's Display! This is the exhaustion of all visions in Mother. It is bringing the Alata to Santi! When nothing is left but Her then your task is finished! It is knowing Reality (Jnana). Cutting to Reality (Nirvikalpa). Soaring On as Reality (Sahaja or Vijnana). Again, in Absolute Reality, the three presentations all happen in Mother!

Trekchod is the Ultimate Act of Rejection (Negation), Cutting Away. Thogal is the Ultimate Act of Acceptance (Affirmation) as Surpassing All as Arisen Appearance. Dzogchen is neither rejection nor acceptance, nor any of the spiritual tactics of arrival. That idea is anti-Dzogchen, really. The Whole Thing! Remembering Gaudapada I v 18, "If anyone imagines illusory ideas such as the teacher, the taught and the scriptures, then they will disappear. These ideas are for the purpose of instruction. Duality ceases to exist when Reality is known." The teacher, the teaching and the taught are the same ideas as the buddha, the dharma and the sangha. Looking outward to the teacher for satisfaction there, is not Dzogchen, not Pure Advaita! Is Trekchod, Letting Go or is it Total Decisiveness? Both? Really the two acts are different. An impossible contradiction? But most Beautiful during the Bardo! And useful maybe. Thogal, Surpassing All, Soaring On, Supreme Vision, Spontaneous Experience or Instantaneous Arrival. You are All This in Dzogchen, but these two ideas can limit you, for where does Pure Mind arrive, surpass, soar, decide, let go or cut to? Even the idea of spontaneous or instantaneous is a limitation by grasping at a notion that something is going to happen! And are they not yet to be exhausted visions, yet to be quenched by Peace, anyway? Looking anywhere or to anyone outside of Pure Mind is the Cause of Despair!

Trekchod is cutting to the Infinite, the Nitya, letting go of the Finite, the Lila, to get the Infinite. Thogal is Lighting Up the Finite in the Infinite. It is simple as that. Thogal is exhausting the Lila in the Nitya, exhausting the Finite in the Infinite and really is it not always so, the Infinite being the nature of what It Is has already exhausted the Finite. Further speaking, Thogal is to Light Up the Finite in the Infinite, to Light Up the various lamps of consciousness, the eyes, the nerves, the breathing energies, the drops, or seed points of various manifest awareness/appearance points in the mind, the six attitudes of accomplishment, the four certainties of confidence, the four expansively surpassing visions soaring on to see the world in greater and greater and vaster and vaster expanses, all this, and the Kayas and Everything that arises in waking or dreaming or the clear light arena of deep sleep, even death and every quality of dream, the immovable stances, the waiting gestures, the three types of death, all as Lila, all Lighted Up by the Light of the Infinite. But as the Infinite is the Nature of What It Is then all this is already so. That is why Thogal and Trekchod are a paradox if thought of dualistically. They only make sense in the Comprehension, even suddenly so, of the Non-Dual. Remember, here the Infinite is meant in the most Absolute Sense, not infinite space, infinite consciousness, infinite void, or infinite becoming.

The third Thogal is to be so satisfied with Pure Mind that any other ideation in conceptual cognition is of no interest. This is what is meant by the Full Measure of Rigpa, So the fourth Thogal is the Exhaustion of Visions, but it simply means you have yourself explored all potentials in the spiritual dimension and have reached a state where you no longer build conceptual models or psychic structures of what you think your life or life as a whole should be. You simply have no more expectations of events in samsara or accomplishments of nirvana. For one, nirvana cannot be accomplished for it is Pure Mind the innately perfect and complete in itself (Dzogchen, its very import) and two, what strives for nirvana never reaches nirvana. You see it comes this way, let go of your body, let it fall to the ground if necessary, let it die to its mis-identity. Let your mind do the same, no more words to yourself in comparisons over the self, that is dichotomic disaster and the form of despair. You are as you are and have been so all along. That is good. Let your mind become lost in the Immensity of Pure Mind that you discovered

107

for yourself in the first Thogal (or the original Trekchod when you first cut through and let go). The sensation of this discovery overwhelms the sensation of all you have sensed before (the second Thogal) until nothing is satisfying to you but Pure Mind (third Thogal) and now you are so aware of What has been all along that you give up and surrender every effort to build any psychic construction or vision about your True Being (the fourth Thogal). These are the four Thogals and the four Confidences (the promises of Dzogchen) mixed together in explanation here. 1: You no longer fear despair (life, death, hell, heaven, anything that you could despair over). 2: You have no false hopes in reference to samsara (for there is nothing here that is going to last anyway). 3: You don't even expect nirvana (the expectation itself of nirvana being a strong obstacle to the peace of nirvana). 4: And everything is simply reduced to its focus in Pure Mind. It is all the Same and so you have no despair, no fear, no hope, no expectation. Why? Because you have re-enlightened or rediscovered your True Self.

That side of Thogal which deals with optical phenomena or dream mind visions is simple delusion to me. I suppose to some those visions may restore once lost confidence in the Reality, but really seeing things like vajra chains, radiant lights like a peacock's tail, bindus, thigles, points or drops of creative light energy or psychic breath energies moving along the nerve paths, well are they not merely the vibrations of the dualistic psyche in the dream mind or visionary hallucinations in the eye nerves, cortex or fissure of sylvius in the waking state. They are the increase of delusion, not the quenching or exhausting of it. The natural presence of the Lila here is enough to deal with in our waking, dreaming and deep sleep states. Why would one need more vision, dream and phenomena except to generate the reason for ego.

The here, and the hereafter, come to the Thogal beyond the concerns of these two thoughts. Then you are Now, in Pure Mind, not somewhere else! Even in the Trekchod of these two concerns.

The Nirvikalpa Samadhi is a small state compared to Bhavamukha. One mind melts like that, but in Bhavamukha all beings are seen in their True Immediate State, in the Awareness, here and now, of Mother, ever liberated, dancing and not dancing, so it appears to be more than the Thogal visions of thigles, vajra chains, lights and faces. But the Fourth Stage Thogal may be the same where all visions are exhausted and only Reality is seen. "Atman is realized through Atman alone. Pure Mind, Pure Buddhi, Pure Atman -- all these are one and the same." Ramakrishna. Such is not the state of expansive visionary imagery. Or what is the image if not Pure Mind itself.

In this shadow land of stupidity, this world called human, beings know that death comes closer with each moment, still they do not contemplate the Great Perfection methods of Trekchod and Thogal. None dies. We all Spread Forth! We all Let Go! We all Soar On! Sakti (Turiya) is Always Powerful, Brilliant, Alert. The activity of waking and dreaming and the non-activity of deep sleep have given the sense of duality and thus the illusive thought of separation from the Rigpa of Turiya (Sakti). Nothing in the current of waking and dreaming or the still water of deep sleep ever effects That (Turiya) Mother. One thinks there is the Mother Light and here is the Light of the son-mind, and between the Dakini Light dances. Over the surface of Light these ideas are imposed. There is only Her Light in Pure Dzogchen Advaita solution. Trekchod has been translated as the Barrier Free Approach. The barrier of all problem obscurations are let go of, left just where they are like a river or a mountain, an ocean or your body and all bodies and your mind and all minds. Then just the Light of Mother. Thogal has been called the Final Leap. Is it so, a final leap to where, when all is Mother! You are, she is, he is, everywhere, the entire field of events is Mother from the Pure Mind View She empowers you!

What comes back as Thogal? It is not ego, that was just cut away with Trekchod: all ego content, all ego identity, ego emotion, ego fear, ego thought, all let go, free of the barrier of ego. One has clarity in Nitya. So what comes back is not ego, it is Atma, but not as ego self sense. Here one finds only Mother (ma) Moving (at), thus the atma as Mother Moving. She is the Direct Experience, the Pure Sensation, the Full Measure, the Final Exhaustion. Thogal is nothing but Mother in the clarity of

Lila! Only a foolish buck tooth stupid smiling ox like myself would ever separate the Nitya and the Lila into Trekchod and Thogal.

It is only Pure Mind (or if you break it into lesser degrees, the true Lama Mind, the real Dakini Mind, and the genuine Garuda Mind) that is capable of Trekchod and Thogal, not ordinary mind. Only the Amanibhava Mind feeling can make Trekchod and Thogal a Reality. It just happens once the ordinary mind is Surrendered to Pure Mind which is the Spontaneous Feeling of that One Reality that is imagined to appear as the Nitya and the Lila. And what is Pure Mind but Love. And what is Love but Pure Feeling Empathic into every living being, even those who are not living in terms of what we define life to be as death and other worlds. Love feels no difference for there is none!

When I see a person sleeping in deep sleep I think to myself, how Near they are to nirvikalpa enlightenment, without conceptuality, to nir thigle (without appearance). When I see a person dreaming I think to myself that in a Moment their dreaming may turn into savikalpa awakening (with conceptuality) or sa thigle, with appearance. When I see a person waking, if it is a woman, I remember what Ramakrishna would say, that all women are embodiments of the Sakti, Divine Mother and if I see a man I think the same, then there is no more dualism between goddesses and noblemen. In Pure Mind appears both the Nitya Mind and the Lila Mind. It is only Pure Mind. In the Immense Mind which Faces outward the Pure Mind is still there in the Non-Dual, without conceptuality in Awareness, even though there is that outward Facing, in seeing the Sight, it is Non-Dual. Trekchod Cuts Away or Explodes Away all materiality or solidity from the finest thought form to the grossest thought, then remains as Pure Mind. Thogal reaches the same Pure Mind but through the course of Exhausting all visions or Quenching all dualities into the Dharmata which is the Mother Truth!

Part Two
LETTING GO AND SOARING ON
(Trekchod and Thogal)

Gaudapada's Advaita
and Garab Dorje's Dzogchen

Garab Dorje
Three Conveyances
Three Series
Chikhai
Atma
Heritage
The Occurring, The Mistake
Effortless Amanibhava
Nirodha
Dakini Mystery
Audulomi Or The Rainbow Body
Heart Essence
Three Methods
The Most Secret
Three Statements
Re-Enlightened
Mother Light and Offspring
Suddenness
Kung Zhi
Barrier Emotions
Pre-Primordial
Maya
Conceptuality and Infusion
Prajna
Nerves, Energies, Thigles as Five Wisdoms
Abhi Sambodhi
The Summit
Four Visions
Dakini Eyes, Thigle, Awareness, Self
Thigle

The Cosmological Extent to Thigle
Ask Dakini

Letting Go and Soaring On
With Gaudapada and Garab Dorje

Dakini Lamps
Eyes, White Silk Nerve, Heart
Illuminating The Lamps
Dakini Lights
Spontaneous Arrivals
Sixteen Illuminations
That Mind Pure Mind
Bindu Thigle
The Spiritual Friend
The Garuda Mind As Trung Pe
The Height of Height
Dakini Given
In You Yourself
Gaudapada
Advaitic Light
The Extreme View
Misery
Handling Objects
Thoughts
The Magic Elephant
Best First
Best of Bipeds
Firebrand Visions
Tayi

Gaudapada's Advaita and Garab Dorje's Dzogchen

I salute and praise only the Divine Formula OM within every living being that wakes, dreams and sleeps, so that out of this Great Love may be born in them the wisdom in deep sleep, the body of divine pride in the new dream state and the full recognition of reborn new flesh living the wisdom and love in the OM Formula! (Only a habit of forty-six years has made me feel limited to this power!)

"Beginningless Maya'" means it never had a beginning, not that it is very old. The Rope was never a serpent. Turiya, the One, is thought of in three ways. Yet, no thought has ever made it the "serpent," as it is just the very nature of the "Effulgent Being." So even the level of Qualified Non-Dualism is extinguished now. Who feels the One, but the One who was never the other experiencer. The "serpent" (the three states) was never the Rope (Turiya)!

Religion is still materialism, the material stuff being ideas (ideals). Spirituality does not drag Truth (Pure Mind) down to be a Person (oneself) or a Teacher (another self). It is still materialism. In considering Trikaya, the Three Vehicles or Dimensions. "The Tathagata Garbha is not a person. Worship no one!" Paraphrasing Vivekananda and Aseshananda. Nor the Three States, still materialism in non-apprehension or misapprehension. Gaudapada says, "This one does not praise any deity, nor salute any person." Longchenpa calls them stupid people. Gaudapada says these are to be pitied for they are of "narrow mind" and "afraid of the fearless." I call them idiots. Perhaps it is this "materialism" that "pricked" Ramakrishna's flesh, that this is "mean intelligence" for it denies Pure Reality and that this heaviness weighs the "balance" down, people who attend to this material idea, even if you think guru is Pure Atma, the human image is materialistic, even if everything, through the cognitive force of Sakti, vanishes in Pure Light, like a fool you come back to worship the material image. This drags you (the person) and the other (teacher, ishta, yidam, god or goddess) also down, back to materialism.

113

Garab Dorje

It is said that Garab Dorje was the first human teacher of Dzogchen, yet it is also said that Sakyamuni was the twelfth of twelve teachers of Dzogchen. It is also said that Dzogchen is practiced on thirteen planetary worlds, but one must remember that the definition of these worlds in Tibetan cosmology may be spheres of consciousness and perhaps not other planets like the Earth. It is fantastic. But who can measure the level of this Great Teaching? Again in the descent of this instruction, Garab the human received it from the subtle deity being, Vajrasattva, who received it from the pure heaven being, Samantha Bhadra, but he receives it from his Pure Sakti ultimately, the Mother Samantha Bhadri, who in Her, there is no teaching, that is no need for teaching as She is the Ultimate Perfect! This final ultimate is most important to keep in mind as we go further and further into the subjects we engaged, especially that of the inner passage of Vajrasattva and the union of the four Wisdoms in regard to the immediate recognition of liberation in the time of the bardo of dying and becoming. (Refer back to Dream States and the Bardo Mind)

Three Conveyances

So here Dzogchen gives Three Forms of introduction, transmission or conveyance (these conveyances are not the Three Series which will be encountered a little later) which relate to and are the three Kayas at their Core. In conveying Pure Mind, even so, the the first actually has very little, if no form at all. It is Pure Mind in direct contact with Pure Mind. It is You the Real Thing directly speaking, though sometimes it has the context of one who is already in Pure Mind then transmitting messages on Pure Mind to another, but this is scattered thinking because there is but One Pure Mind for it is Non-Duality itself. So it does not go from one person to another, one subtle mind being to another or even from one purely spiritual being to another in its Purest Context. It goes from Itself to Itself in Pure

Reality and not even the expression "itself to itself" is accurate as that conjures up a duality of transmission from one point to another. There is no point or place from which Pure Mind makes contact with another mind as it is, for this is Primordial Awareness (Rigpa) as the Real Thing, You who are never lost, out of contact or separated from Pure Mind. This is one of the purest most direct spiritual teachings around.

So the second introduction takes place in Space, a Space within Pure Mind or the space of existence in front of or before, as in standing before Pure Mind where spiritual beings like Samantha Bhadra may be seen or subtle mind beings like Vajrasattva are seen, also the yidams and ishtas or the five dakini or buddha powers. Yidam is like one's Ishta or Spiritual Ideal but the yidam also has the added quality of being a direct psychological counter reflection of what is within you as your spiritual make up and the Ishta Ideal is maybe a little more like a spiritual principle that you might wish or try to become like or be guided and taught by in your spiritual pursuits.

Then the third form of introduction is quite naturally the spoken or the speaking of words that indicate and express the potential existence of Pure Mind within oneself. Even to the awakening of those who have never alertly considered the existence of Pure Mind in the first place at all. This is the mental dual speaking and thinking relations between one person and another within the level of teachers, teaching and the taught within that state of human heritage and its ongoing process. So Dzogchen has given a very comprehensive explanation of how anyone may be introduced to Spiritual Awareness, through the mind transmission, the space conveyance, or the word introduction.

Three Series

After much mind effort to grasp the Three Series, in a flash, I realized that before all figuring ever began or I ever realized grasping, I realized the Primordial Perfect, the Spontaneously Ever Has Been Accomplished. Figuring to grasp got in the way. Dzogchen is the Great or Complete (Chen) Perfection or

Accomplishment (Dzog), an amazing way of thinking that thinking does not grasp or does it really, for eventually it becomes your own. And so three series are given to exercise your mind towards Dzogchen thinking. Semde, the mind series, which is mind analysis, how will you understand Pure Mind without studying your own mind. Londe, the space series, which is the effortless symbolic encounter with Pure Mind through the mirror of the mind space vortex. And then Mangagde, which is surveying Reality in Reality or just letting be in Reality as Reality (Pure Mind). These are not Kaya, or Essene, Nature and Energy related as I had thought. A common blunder and confusion in Dzogchen. These three series as well as First Encounter, Trekchod and Thogal are thought to be based on the three essential statements of Garab Dorje which I simplify here as Get It, Keep It, Stay It! But these are so choice and non-elaborate that it is hard to make everything in a triad arrangement correspond to these early statements presented with such simplicity. But you could say that the Semde is mind analysis through first direct word introduction. Then Londe is the vast expanse of discovery in how to keep it. And Mangagde is the secret essence of continuing or staying in it. But these three system series are more elaborate than that. I really give my own thoughts here just as the historic formations of these belief systems give different lineages. There are different opinions over the spiritual effects of the three series, basically, which are disagreements with whether are not they are of equal value. Like the highest is the third, and the first and second are not of that much value. But the mind/oral Semde is essentially the self study/observation of thought projections within the mind itself. The mind space or vast expanse Londe is the practice of keeping the mind in the Ultimate. And the secret esoteric innermost Mangagde is staying in the Ultimate Sphere as the Ultimate itself. But I suppose that if you are unfortunate enough to divide the Undivided dimension into the three dimensions (kayas) then it would seem that you have the outer mind method as the Nirmana Emanation. The inner mind method as the Resplendent Conceptual Horizon. And the essence of the Essence method as the Incomprehensible (from the first and second dimensions) of

116

Truth, Reality, Pure Mind. In truth these three methods ring of such similarity to the three Advaitic methods of conveyance to Experience. That of hearing about it. That of reflecting over it. That of meditating on it as an authentic actualized experience. My regard should be equal to Advaitic and Dzogchen methods, because for years it was not so and how can we have such divisions over the expression of Non-Dual Reality. Arguing over the methodology of philosophical contents is boring. It is like arguing over the symbols of Trekchod, the Pure Crystal, and Thogal, a Peacock Feather representing the Full Spectrum of Arising Light and which of these may have more meaning to you as a person.

Is there really a presentation in Dzogchen that is so utterly unique that it goes beyond all other teachings? Is it so different from Pure Advaita? Is the utterly infinite Sat Chid Ananda so different from the Luminous Void (Shunyata)? Is not this Shunyata simply the final existent (Ta) which is blissfulness itself as a Consciousness which is void of any idea, concept or object? Maybe it is simply definitions and designations. Arguments are there to no end, over these subtle definitions. Even hair splitting. Even that Satchidananda (Existence Consciousness Bliss) is admittedly only an indication of what is a Reality beyond those designations, just like the void or emptiness idea of Shunyata, something beyond any conception so we call it void, that is, of any thing or idea we can place there. Are Garab Dorje and Gaudapada so different in their conclusion. They both are direct, they both get rid of all superfluous content, they both say to continue without doubt in the Reality which they have presented to you. In Dzogchen ignorance is call ma-rigpa and its unique Advaitic equivalent is Avidya Sakti. Again Rigpa, the knowledge of the Mother Reality is Vidya Sakti. Both schools are speaking of Sakti the Mother. She is the Inner Guide.

If you follow the exhausting process of emptying thoughts from the ocean of the mind drop by drop with a blade of kusa grass as Gaudapada says, well then, I become tired just thinking about it and Gaudapada does not recommend it for it is the path of fear. If you really tune into the secret method of just watching

117

thoughts as they arise and disappear even so self liberate themselves in the instant of their disappearance, hmm, in this you must not fixate on any thought, grab any thought as final, but especially one must be careful not to fixate on the thought that one is not fixating for that is a fixated thought. Neither in the waking state nor the dream state, for fixing on a dream as of spiritual importance can often times be just fixing on egotistical self importance. Garab Dorje speaks of being introduced into and continuing in Primordial Awareness. Advaita speaks of the Witness. Yet, is not that which is first (primordial) and which is an Awareness of something, as it were, a thought, the Witness? Being the Witness is what you are as Primordial Awareness but both systems speak of something higher than the Witness or Awareness and that is a state where everything that comes is seen in its non-dual nature. This is where the flow, the arising, the coming and dispersing of thoughts is really free! Dzogchen says thoughts are like drawings on water, they disappear as soon as they are created into the water which they are made. This is the Non-Dual impact of the teaching, the sudden blow that awakens you. Advaita says Jivas, that is conceptualized conditions of souls as separate beings, or the Dharmas, that is the momentary conjunction of various conditional factors which give rise to the concept of an identity in space/time with a purpose that this identity is seeking, are but waves in the water. It is the same non-dual expression.

The flowing mind is not Dzogchen it is just poetry. But the Advaita Flow that is it. Where in the Relative (Lila) the Absolute (Nitya) is seen, felt, experienced. Yes. It is the same when Trekchod is practiced and experienced in Thogal. The cutting away (Trekchod) into the Absolute Mother Light is experienced in the manifest wonderment of relative emanating powers, energies and presence. This is the direct approach into surpassing all (Thogal) that is living the Advaita. As Gaudapada conveys in the sacred transmission of words, that everything is imagined in Advaita (II 33). Even Garab Dorje makes it clear eventually as you absorb his transmission, that even the introduction to Pure Mind, the Decision upon this singular unique state and Continuing in Pure Confidence in this State of

118

Rigpa in the Mother Light as the son mind especially are ultimately also imagined conditions or stages imagined in the Pure Mind which is Non-Dual Advaita itself. It is only the non-existent imaginings within the state of the son-mind that dreams up ideas about a cause (karana) or an effect (karya) that is going to bring about the mind state of the Primordial Pure Mind. It is Dzogchen, the Great Perfection and needs nothing to make it perfect by way of a cause or effect. It is the Great Completeness (Dzogchen) and needs nothing added to it to make it complete. Nothing you do will do it. Like Garab Dorje, Gaudapada gives three imagined stages of bringing about Pure Mind, that of being identified with Pure Mind, delighting in Pure Mind and being unwavering in one's state of Pure Mind (II 38). Is not identity real introduction? Is not delight to be in such depth of decision about this discovery that there is no more doubt about it. And is not to be unwavering from Pure Mind the real continuing in Pure Certainty and Pure Confidence in Pure Mind. As to be unwavering is to no longer flicker or flutter or hesitate! But all these stages are only imaginings in the son-mind for the Mother Light is Herself the Great Perfect!

Chikhai

Indeed, sacred transmissions are there. Two of the most powerful and direct transmissions that have come to me were both received in a matter of two and one half seconds. "Chikhai is not this human world." Lama Geshela spoke and conveyed the whole thing at that moment. Chikhai is the Primordial Mother Light. The son-mind is this human world. She is not in the duality of relation in the son-mind. No concept there can comprehend Her. She is met with and only in non-duality with complete death or cutting away of all waking, dreaming or the sleep of deep blissful non-duality. Chikhai is not this sleeping death. Everything was cut away (Trekchod) then at that moment. The Mother Light, is not this human world nor any world, the world of the humble gods, the world of the jealous egotistical gods, the human world, the world of animals, of ghosts, of hell. She is not any of the Realms of Desire, or the

119

higher Paradise worlds with form nor the even higher Paradise worlds that are formless. She is not the four stages of concentration. Not the four stages of meditation. Not even the Summit of Becoming. Become what when all is Ma, the Mother Light? And this Summit of Becoming is neither the perception or non-perception of either Samsara or Nirvana, which both arise from the Primordial Pure Mind which is none but Chikhai, the Mother! This was all empowerment, all initiation, all view and all meditation given in two and a half seconds. There. Another time the Dalai Lama, Kundun, the Presence of the Ocean of Wisdom not the human person, Tenzin Gyatso, generated Extreme non-duality at the peak of Dzogchen, the Pure Blue Dzogchen Sky where in both Samsara and Nirvana are seen as what they are. Neither being nor non-being. Again another lama performed the Tibetan finger snap where there is total sudden recognition of the Dzogchen Awareness given in one second. But the perfect Chikhai was pointed out by the words, "Chikhai is not this human world." And that was the Trekchod of everything, everything ever arisen, everything self-arisen and everything ever to arise again. It was pure perfect introduction to Rigpa. The son-mind's awareness of the Pure Awareness of Pure Mind as the Mind of the Mother Light. It was the Decision to discover this unique and singular state. And the continuing without doubt in Pure Confidence, Pure Certainty of this unique state.

Atma

Yet it was Swami Aseshananda who said, "Your own Atma is the Divine Mother." And that conveyed to me exactly what is the Thogal of Dzogchen even though he was speaking of Advaita. You see, "At" means to go, wander, roam and "Ma" is nothing but the Pure Mother Light. So the idea of any arising thing or thought is automatically self liberated in that very instant of spontaneous surpassing in the direct approach of Thogal by realizing that all ideas, manifestations, or visions as an Atma (self) are nothing but Mother Herself. Even Phowa is unnecessary for Mother is Mother in Mother and there is no son-

120

mind consciousness to be transferred here or there! It is nothing but Mother and so you have the Living Non-Duality of all Thogal experience. You see, the Rainbow Body of Light is realizing and putting to practice this realization that it is Mother Light manifesting here and there as everything. The world is a Rainbow of Her Non-Dual Joy. The bardos of birth (waking), of dream or of enlightenment no longer exist for they are the ever present Rainbow which always has been so. There is no transformation here at all. How can you transform something that already Is. And indeed when all waking/dreaming attachments are in the cutting away (Trekchod) of death at that moment where the son is Gone and all is the Mother Light, yes and even as the son-mind may regenerate and start to form projections of the Chonyid Zhi-khro dream state it is again but Her Rainbow of Thogal where every arising is nothing but Her. A living non-dual Mother experience. Even the idea of Mother is gone. No Void. No Manifestation. And so what then is the re-arising of self birth in the sidpa bardo of the waking state but this Sameness of Mother going, wandering and roaming as the apparent self in Samsara. No Samsara. No Nirvana. Dzogchen is not a state of analysis. Advaita is not a state of analysis. This is the Innermost Secret Essence as it is the instant and simultaneous practice of Trekchod and Thogal non separate at Once (Nyingthig). One cannot underestimate the generosity and beauty of these instantaneous or gradual transmissions that have a life long effect through even the apparent Maya/Samsara of lifetimes. I am not bound by any tradition, Advaita or that of Dzogchen. Longchenpa says that those who separate, Trekchod and Thogal, dividing the practices, are just the friends of donkeys. So, is it not so even if one separates traditions, transmissions or reception of Pure Mind Truth from whatever source it may arise. That is the point.

Longchenpa has conveyed that it is the kindness of the lama that helps bring about this state. But is it not really an inner Kindness to oneself as the son-mind which comes from the real Lama, who is Ma Herself, the Mother. She is Kind and one can only be kind, experience kindness and feel kindness when one is in the Pure Ma (Mother) Mind. It comes from nowhere else to know it.

For Garab Dorje this is called Ati Yoga. For Gaudapada this is called Asparsa Yoga (IV 2). Ati Yoga is highest Primordial Yoga. Asparsa Yoga means that it has no contact, no touch, nor relationship with anything at anytime but for the Primordial Reality. How similar! In both systems there is no imagination with duality. Neither system touches or has contact or any kind of relationship with duality. There is only the Primordial Non-Dual Pure Mind.

Heritage

It is hard to say really where exactly Dzogchen came from historically. I am not bound to rigid speculation. As the Bonpas, who say they have a seventeen thousand year tradition of Dzogchen with their twelve remembered Tonpas (teachers) and the Tibetans, like the Japanese and the Siberians are originally Mongolian people. Well perhaps the Siberian reindeer people are actually older than the Mongolians. Well, also in the Himalayan region you have a most fascinating collection of spiritual teachings. There was of course the very old Tantra and Goddess worshiping society of Mohenjo Daro (which goes back thirty to forty thousand years) and the other cities there that were all connected. There was pre-Buddhist Buddhism as there were six or seven famous Buddhas prior to the advent of Sakyamuni. There was Vipashyin, Shikin, Vishvabhu, Krakuchchanda, Konagamana, Kashyapa and the fire meditating Buddha, Dipankara. Sakyamuni even met one of these in a former life and was told by that one that he would attain Enlightenment. There was of course Jainism, Samkhya and Yoga. And there was the arrival of the Vedic tribesmen that later evolved the mysteries of the Vedanta. So where Pure Pristine Awareness begins historically speaking may be a redundant speculation. But, somehow somewhere there has been a tradition of it always in our human heritage.

The Ashtavakra Samhita and the Avadhuta Gita are very good texts on the Pure Advaita State, but they are more exclamations of that State, where Gaudapada's Karika to the

Mandukyo Upanishad is a perfect description of the Arrival of Awareness in Pure Mind, that is, Pure Advaita, and how one gets there. It is pure and direct and it is simple. One cannot get out of the obscurations by meditating or thinking on the obscurations. One gets out by Pure Mind. The problem/obscuration only cycles in the problem/obscuration. This is a good thing to know. One's entire perception can change in an instant by the influence of Pure Mind. Then the sense of Self is retrieved as a phenomenal event in the mind, phenomenal because it was never lost. The thinker of the thoughts contemplating all this is Pure Mind. Yet, Who takes this moment, this precious gift of this instantaneous moment, to Notice?

The Occurring, The Mistake

"...All of the living
Make the mistake of drawing too sharp distinctions.
Angels (it is said) would be often unable to tell
Whether they moved among living or dead."

Rainer Maria Rilke (1875-1926) First Elegy

If I separate myself from death it is the worst dualism as I have then separated from life in which death is contained, nor do I break apart Love, joy, sorrow or pain as these too are total to the togetherness, the Immense Oneness of Life. Really, we all become terrified in the Mistake. From here, the mistake, comes fear. One has taken the unreal to be what is Real, one has mistaken regular mind for Pure Mind. It is like hearing a cat call out in the night and thinking it is a baby that is crying. It makes one afraid, but that fear goes when one realizes that it is only a cat. It is the same when one mistakes the Rope (Pure Mind) to be the serpent (the three states), a serpent kills and so you are afraid. But a rope does not harm you as it lies thére on the ground. Deeper is the horror that the Self ever even makes this mistake. It is the Game of Mother. This side of Her you should know well. It seems to be everywhere.

Pure Mind is the most excellent human potential fulfilled. If

123

you think that you are something else even in the smallest most infinitesimal subtlest quantum way that will start the whole mess of mistaken identity. If you recall yourself to be something someone called you in your childhood, or latter in life, or if you think you are the disciple of someone or the student of something, or if you believe in one religious thought construct or another of some kind all that mistakes you out of your own Pure Mind which is the high result of all Spirituality! At once with the arrival of the awareness of Pure Mind there is no attention to all the thought waves, flashes, currents, as they come and go. Pure Mind is the most excellent potential of what should otherwise be called the Happy Mind without thought. Thoughts and their attendant emotional currents rise and set but you do not attach these to a mistaken identity with the Loving Center of Pure Mind.

The world is a dream before and a dream after, that which Vedanta calls Maya (Illusion), may leave a confusing and uncertain taste, where Dzogchen calls the same, the Occurring, without particular things in focus and attention. It is just the Great Occurring.

For Gaudapada, the jiva state is dharmahood, jivas are dharmas and so your purpose and path whatever and wherever you are, like me, where I am at and what I am going through. Yet your Jiva-hood leads to your Dharma state of Atma or Dzogchen. Dharmas are that which hold, as holding together the jiva (the individual soul). All dharmas are free as the one Tathagata Garbha which is the Dharmakaya, the real Dharma of all beings. These dharmas hold together as the atma ideas of many individual beings, they are attributes of mis-identity really until they know their true Dharma. Reality!

The atma/dharma complex is done with when one no longer believes in the five skandha identity. Take alert note of your own Shunyata Prajna (Luminous Wisdom) with no ego, there, even numerous Buddha forms are empty. Don't even try to figure it (or anything) out with your mind (a mind). It is just what Happens in the pure Precious moment that Shocks time out of its mind.

I come back to Gaudapada who is even less complex than

Padmasambhava. I seek the simple. What is called the Bardo in Tibetan thought is called Antara Bhava in Tantra. It is the mood of the bardo or the Inner Mood after death. This bardo mood carries you through the inner death light (Chikhai) the dream journey (Chonyid) and rebirth (Sidpa). Yet the Great Delight of Amanibhava is the non-dual Mood beyond all mind Samsara.

Effortless Amanibhava

So Amanibhava is the mood free of mind dualism, where Mahamudra is a great gesture of the mind in At Oneness with Reality. Amanibhava is free of any mental gesture. Even as Amanibhava is experienced within Antara Bhava (Bardo Mood) it is free of any dual experiencing of birth, dream or samadhi experiences, or on the other side, of light, consciousness or return experiences. It is even more than the Summit of Becoming (Bhavagra) because there is no mind dualism there to become anything as a becoming of something. So Amanibhava, which is no less than pure direct Dzogchen, is the best way to transfer without transferring anything at death and there after. What happens? When you are in the feeling mood without mind structure what can happen!

Amanibhava is compared to Nirodha, the arresting of duality, where all thought process has sank into a dream free like condition and there and then before any thought or mood or dualism re-arises one is experiencing the Nirodha of Amanibhava. Now all these Bhavas are in Bhavamukha, Mother's Immense "I". Kali (Goddess) Bhava, Sakhi (Friend), Vijnana (Special Sahaja Wisdom), Sakti (Primordial Power), Advaita (Non-Duality) Bhava, all of them. So too are Avasthatraya (The Three States: Waking, Dreaming, Sleeping) Bhava, Antara Bhava, Amanibhava, Madhura (Sweet) or Bhakti (Resplendent Love) Bhava. These are all consumed again in Gaudapada's four Prakarana (Supreme Causes) Bhavas, that of OM, that of Illusion, that of Advaita, and that mood of Quenching the Firebrand which is all the motion of dual mental illusion.

This text I am writing is an exercise in Mother Kali's unique and novel doctrine. So, at death one experiences the Chikhai Bardo and gets a glimpse of the Primordial Clear Light of the Mother. If this Energy of the Universality of Mother that was you, in Primordial Death, floods back down the right or left nerves or the central nerve canal you may experience the great gesture (Maha Mudra) of your mind trying to attempt an understanding of the Mother Light that you became for that moment of death. It is a throw back down of the death energy, that is the death of duality, and if mind is thrown back that energy will be trying to understand what had happened in the non-dual death experience. An Ishta or Chosen Ideal of a God form or a Yidam (inner true psycho/spiritual reflection) may appear during this process. These are losing It and are unsuccessful Phowa or transference of the mind death energy into the Non-Dual Mother State.

A further deeper problem then arises which is the cultural context of the bardo experience. There are peaceful and wrathful Tibetan deities as psychological reflections in the context of the Tibetan experience, but then there is also superstition which can influence the bardo experience. The personality contents in the mind complex come up in the bardo of the after death mind cognition. It raises the question what is mind. Of course, it is more than brain. Yet, in the near death experience, the brain and body are dead, but there is cognitive experience. If that experience of the bardo mind is influenced by the Apocalypse of St. John then the experience will be colored to the extent of what is presented as a reality in that book. Gaudapada is clearest, leaving nothing to color one's experience with but the Non-Dual Consciousness, so death and after death are bypassed or seen through or lived through as an awareness of Pure Mind. But if your mind follows such Vedantic descriptions of cosmological deities and elaborations of sense fields and mind principles then the after death light of consciousness may be influenced by those thoughts. Pure Mind is the best influence not all these cognitive elaborations.

Gaudapada states that all objects are imagined in Non-Duality and that all objects are imagined in Atma, this would include the imagined ideas of Samsara and Nirvana too. Even so

126

the Offspring Light (objective) and the Mother Light (subjective) are also imagined in Non-Duality. They are dualities trying to grasp the grasp-less Reality, that is what Gaudapada calls his method, Asparsa (no contact, grasping no duality). It is Tilopa's paradoxical example with Naropa when he keeps asking him what is wrong with you and why aren't you happy? There is only one thing wrong. The dual identity. The "I" bound to body/mind deserves to be killed, ground up, beat up, etc. (which is what Tilopa does to Naropa) Tilopa is then the constant work of death on the body/mind "I" from the birth bardo onward through the other five bardos and back again until we are done with that false idea of it all.

When someone dies, people here and there might squeeze out a tear or two, but the new dawn comes and they will go on. Universal recognition of the great fright of death (Sakyamuni's motivation and purpose of the search he underwent) comes to one and all, therefore at every Precious Moment practice Precious Love and Compassion, for without This Loving Compassion, emptiness, death and cruelty would rule this world dwelling. "All the jivas are, by their very nature, free from senility and death. But they think they are subject to senility and death, and by the very power of thought they appear to deviate from their true nature." Gaudapada. IV 10.

Stress background tension release! Dzogchen style. Eyes Open because the Chikhai Light is Bright, more than the eyes and the Chonyid or sidpa bardos are nothing from There, so far below! Not to mention (to your mind) waking, dreaming, and deep sleep as the AUM silent in Chikhai for then there is no subjective or objective sound clash duality, nor light dualism nor emanation at all! The channels, nerves (nadis) are all on front line alert yet Relaxed in the Dzog Chen orgasm/death let go. Conceptionless Ecstasy!

People and religion are not the problem. Dualism is the problem and yet not a problem since being in dualism is void, nothing, only a moment occurring in Dzogchen, then it never was. Eyes Open and Alert to all foreground experience in Dzogchen's Primordial Background, the six accomplishments, the four confidences and four visions arise automatically.

127

Behavior is a result of Attitude and Attitude of View, for Bringing All Points Together and Nailing it Down. Dzogchen Style Surrender is Open Heart/Mind Sky! The Vast Expanse. Can I Relax myself (the "I" in duality)? No! The opposite is always there as tension. That is why Surrender to Pure Mind Open Sky makes it (Relaxation in Spiritual Power) most important. But even an idea/effort of importance can stress you out. Bringing together in One Moment all the primary principles. This is Dzogchen! Causing the son mind to Real Make and see the Mother Mind! Kali! Sages and Buddhas, as one sees them all in the son mind, may be sitting still in Nirvana but Mother never stops working on you as long as the son mind is your conceptual basis. May not even once, will you let it go (Trekchod)! The dual anxiety tensions Relax completely in Mother Mind. Even in death when the tension of waking/dreaming connection Goes! Naked Awareness (Mother), no clothes, (mind naked in Her Nakedness) the son/mind/ego/concept/judgment/tension clothing all gone! That is surrender which brings Sweet Humility!

Is the sweet relaxation and pleasure bliss known at orgasm but a prelude to the Bliss Light (Maha Sukha Dakini) in death when one is released from the heavy mortal flesh. Ah! Pure Moment when Pure Mind stands clear, on its own, and non-dependent! Now I can do whatever without dualistic anxiety/tension. Are not all those spiritual friends and the rest, everyone, is it not transmission, in sweet spiritual and human heritage. Same ideas, different words. "What you call Brahman I call Kali," Ramakrishna. Besides, who is our "Inner Guide," if not Pure Mind. So why should you or I chase for footprints anymore? Everyone's life is a wisdom story of their own pilgrimage to the Divine Mother. You make it within your Own mind to Mind Pure journey.

In Pure Mind, concepts of Samsara and Nirvana or Maya and Advaita Nirvikalpa are imagined. Gaudapada even says that non-duality is imagined in Non-Duality, as perhaps our ideas of the non-dual are but imaginations compared to the Reality Non-Dual. "Atman is imagined as the unreal objects that are perceived to exist and as Non-Duality as well. The objects too, are imagined in the non-dual; Atman. Therefore Non-Duality is Bliss." II 33 Garab Dorje's concept of the Void is not void. It is the not Self as no ego. Gaudapada says in Self they cover Reality with the idea that they imagine a void. Both bring us deeper and deeper Experience, both in Pure Mind, because Pure Buddhi is Pure Atma.

Trekchod is relaxing all dual tension which is the "I" of the son-mind. Gone! But with an "I" feeling of doing it, it cannot happen (holding to that feeling of "I") for it is really Chikhai Death Practice. Thogal is Seeing and Being this result at the Innermost that is surpassing even a process of this result, by this in waking/dream/sleep, in Chonyid and sidpa, or birth, dream and samadhi of course. Because Chikhai is that Light and Relaxation. The four Thogal visions are Seeing as Self Born (Sahaja) the Self Arisen. The Peak Through! The Cloud Away! Everything Burnt up! Delusion Never Was!

Nirodha

It is said that Tilopa was not enlightened by any human teacher, but by becoming into oneness with the Vajra Goddess, who could this be but Pure Dakini. Some have said he had telepathic communication with the Dakini Goddess but this is misleading because such a direct enlightenment is not a communion between two parties like speaking on a telephone. It is the highest Spiritual Conveyance and wherever you are She is Present. You are fine just where you are! Gaudapada also appears to not have had human teachers. He salutes one called the "best among men" in the fourth chapter of his text, which some believe to be Sakyamuni to whom he gives his respect. In sacred writing it is common to salute the teacher at the beginning of a work, but here it is not the case. Again it is claimed that Gaudapada was taught by Suka, but Suka is the narrator of the Bhagavata, the son of Vyasa who lived when Krishna lived. So it is an almost mythical relation because Gaudapada lived around the seventh or eighth century C.E. and Krishna lived anywhere from fifteen hundred to three thousand B.C.E. So you see, it seems that Gaudapada was posthumously awarded a mythical teacher later in order to maintain the traditional dependency on the human teacher. I think the examples of Gaudapada and Tilopa are so important to us in finding pure spirituality for oneself. We make the great gesture of Pure Mind on our own. The Dakini, the Advaita is ever present here in the true power of thought. Whether thought is luminously void as in deep sleep (prajna). Or bright with energy as in dream (taijasa). Or moving as the usual current in waking (visva).

Tilopa is one of the first to give us the ideas of where to find Dakini in Non-Duality. He speaks of the Clear Light of Mother being found in the deep sleep state where all thought as the usual current or as bright energy has come to rest in its Luminous Splendor. And that between two thoughts or two feelings, as one sets and before another rises again, in that Pure Space between, the Dakini Mind is resplendent! There is the Place you find Her. This is the Great Bliss (Maha Sukha) of Self Feeling (Sva Bhava) beyond any yidam or ishta. This is Her Sakti Rigpa, the Mother Clear Light where no offspring duality remains. If one is blessed with Pho Wa from this position, then there is no Bardo experience and no dream experience. The Tibetan practice of staying in this Clear Light for six months straight reminds me of Ramakrishna's six months in nirvikalpa samadhi. What Tilopa describes is none other than what Gaudapada describes as Amanibhava, the mood where mind duality is gone. He calls that Nirodha which just naturally happens between two thoughts or two feeling currents and in deep sleep. Yet there is a conscious knowing of what is happening as Nirodha is to imprison, suppress, or to restrain the mind from seeing (or getting lost) the serpent (the three states) in the Rope (the Self metaphor). Sakyamuni's Nirodha is the Cessation of samsara, which is the third of the four noble truths as the way out of suffering. This Nirodha or Nirodhika is just naturally the Unmanifest State (Avyakta Avastha). This not manifest state is naturally occurring without effort and that it occurs without effort is a very important point to remember. This occurs individually in deep sleep and universally as cosmic sleep, the wholesale withdraw of all universal phenomena back into its seed or potential and original condition before manifestation.

This Amanibhava is also called Unmani (beyond mind) Bhava (feeling) and there are degrees of its consideration through the four states of consciousness. Regarding the waking state it is Manomani (supreme mind) Bhava. Regarding the dream state it is Ananta (infinite) Bhava. Regarding deep sleep it is Sakti (Primordial Power/Goddess) Bhava. Regarding turiya it is Pracaya (Universal) Bhava. And regarding turiyatita (beyond Turiya) it is Maha (Great) Pracaya (so even more expanded). Many other ideas can be layered into these by different systems but the supreme point is that Pure Mind (Amanibhava) is what is of foremost importance!

Saraha drives this golden nail Home for us so we may be secure in this Truth. "Since all things are born of the mind, Therefore is the Mind itself the guru." This aligns perfectly with what Ramakrishna says throughout this book. (Pure) Mind is with us always, always present with us in the waking, dreaming and deep sleep states. We must simply come to know the nature of these three conditions and thereby know Pure Mind as it is. Even in the manifestation of some dream image Milarepa confirms that it is still just Mind. "The dream dreamt last night, Wherein phenomena and mind were seen as one, Was a teacher, didst thou not so understand it?" Pure Mind is always speaking to us as the oneness of our own Pure Mind within us. This is none but Mother (Dakini) Kuntuzangmo who in this reflection is the Subjective Seer (Pure Mind), but not caught up in the dualism of the subjective mind. And so Kuntuzangpo is the intellect as the object or objective seen. But we shall not descend so deep into dualism at this time.

Again, with all this dualism whether dream or waking, the Atma itself covers itself with all this bewilderment. "First of all is imagined the jiva, the embodied individual, and then are imagined the various entities, both external such as sounds, forms, etc, and internal such as pranas, sense-organs, etc., that are perceived to exist. As is one's knowledge so is one's memory." Gaudapada II 16. Pure Mind at first appears to be lost (though it is not) when we begin to imagine something other (a duality) than Pure Mind. Tilopa augments Gaudapada with his thought. "Do not think, imagine, analyze, dream. reflect, calculate, let your innate Natural (Pure) Mind (or Sahaja as he names it) come forth." My own paraphrasing. Just be in your own Pure Mind is his highest opinion.

Dakini Mystery

Actually Tilopa attributes the whole thing to the Enigmatic Dwelling of the Dakini which is the Goddess of your own Pure Mind, and that was Sakti or Kali for Ramakrishna so each verifies the other. Your own Mind is the Secret Home of the Dakini. And in the Dzogchen empowerment that is what you are taught. Your own storehouse mind of Alaya-vijnana (memory) is burnt up and what is left goes into the mouth of a symbolic deity and then that deity ejects that essence as an energy which is reborn with the divine pride of a goddess within whom is another Goddess, the great Tara (Savioress, for Ramakrishna She was Kali Bhavatarani) and then, even deeper into the mystic circle of the Goddess, one becomes the Dakini Vajrayogini. This is your own Mind.

You see many are familiar with Naropa's six yogas: psychic heat, illusory body, dream body, clear light, pho wa (consciousness transference) and mastery of the bardo experience, but Tilopa taught him twelve methods all together and that each of these techniques came from the Goddess Dakini. The additional ones are: the wish fulfilling power of one's own mind, the mind value of oneness, the mind commitment, the art of resurrection (a dark and not recommended method), karma mudra (the inner spiritual profound sexual union of the goddess and god within one's own mind) and maha mudra, the great gesture of the Dakini Mind that holds Reality while on the border of the Infinite Pure Mind. So now that you know this, where can all your ego's subconscious spiritual bewilderment still be imagined to exist? Your dilemma is answered! Actually, if you focus only on a single human teacher alone, it can dim your Perception of the Goddess Dakini whose teaching is everywhere as the Universe itself. I do not limit myself, for my teachers are everywhere. I humble myself to everyone of you, as I am the dust of your feet, even here now as you, the reader!

132

Again, the beloved spiritual friend Gaudapada projects further and deeper into the reality of Pure Mind. He tells us that all efforts but the Pure Mind itself are but the fancies of ignorance (imagination), all our ideas of what is to be rejected or accepted, or to be rendered ineffective or even the object of realization are only products of imagination for here our object of realization can only be imagined and not Pure Mind itself. Gaudapada IV 90. Again this blessed friend tells us that the waking state and the dream state are wrong apprehension and that deep sleep in non-apprehension. If you see this and adhere to this, you yourself cannot but be Pure Mind. Even if you dream of a Great Swam as a symbol of the Primeval Atma embedded within the OM symbol that dream or any like it "exist only as products of imagination."

In Gaudapada's Asparsa Advaita there is no contact with the support system of any possible imagination whatsoever. You are Reality. Garab Dorje is just the same. Gaudapada gives four obstacles to this Pure Mind experience/awareness. Laya or Deep Sleep when the mind is not alert. Viksepa or when the mind is tossed about or distracted in the dualism of the waking and dreaming subjective/objective dualisms. Kasaya which is the affect of the cause and effect potentials that still lay within the deep subconscious mind, call it your dream mind if you like but it is what pulls you to continue to experiment with possibilities that you think might bring Truth into your experience when in reality it is only Truth that brings Truth into your experience and that is always present within your experience. Then Rasasvada is the memory of savikalpa or saguna like states of realization where you mix Pure Mind with other phenomena and because it is enjoyable you hold on to those experiences as something that you want to return to and repeat which is a delusion because Pure Mind is always here and now and not in the repetition of some past pleasurable spiritual state. Immediate Clear Now is the Thing!

Audulomi Or The Rainbow Body

So if we have come to This what happens when we die?

133

Thinkers in the Advaita say different things. "Audulomi says that the liberated soul becomes established in Consciousness as Consciousness itself, that being its True Nature." This is like the Trekchod Death. Jaimini tells us that the subtle body attains the attributes or characteristics of the Infinite, like omniscience and omnipresence. "Jaimini asserts the existence of body (subtle) and sense organs..." This is like Thogal Death. "Badari asserts the absence of body (subtle) and sense organs for one who reaches the Brahma Loka, the world of Brahman, for the Upanishad says so." But in the same text, the Brahma Sutras, the Advaitic thinker Badarayana considers both possibilities for released souls. So that seems reasonable. Total Gone-ness into Absolute Here-ness (Trekchod) or Subtle/Causal Light Body Continuing (Thogal)! Trekchod as the Great Transfer works through Preexisting Pure Buddha Mind. Thogal as the Light Body can only be seen by those who possess "pure eyes" as the Bardo Thodol states, or those who are dead and so are not limited by the fleshy eyes alone. But the Rainbow or Light Body is more Reasonable as just the Sambhogakaya (or Chonyid bardo itself filled with resplendence) which works as a Conscious Helper naturally as its own Spiritual Dimension. The dissolving of the physical body as fantastical as it is claimed (the rainbow body), leaving rainbow signs, hair, nails, little sacred stones, images on the bones, may be similar to the equally fantastical spontaneous combustion. The thing is that Light Bodies, Rainbow Bodies or Pure Great Transfer (Transformation) all happen only in Highest Mother Light. And so you can make your own Great Transfer either to Pure Mind itself, or to continuing phenomena as rainbow subtle light bodies and all that! (See Chapter: Self Doubt Or Self Trust)

Heart Essence

I feel that Gaudapada like Dattatreya and Garab Dorje, had no human teacher but learned by looking at what is around. "Na guru, na sishya, na tvam, na me, sahaja paramartha tattvam." Avadhuta Gita. No guru, no pupil, no you, no me, the Spontaneous Inherent Self is the Supreme Principle. If someone

134

before has done This then you can do it.

The Dzogchen Heart Essence (Nyingthig) of the Vast Expanse (Longchen) empowers you in three sacred treasure cycles. (The fourth Cycle is the Foundational Text itself, Longchen Nyingthig Ngondro.) It is somewhat secret but may be spoken of. It seemed to me that the first cycle, the Lama empowerment actually empowers you to become your own Lama, since, for one, in the end of the ritual there is Inseparability here with the Supreme Lama. Second is the Dakini empowerment which takes you a step further where you not only have inner contact with the Dakini but ultimately become the Dakini Herself. This leads to the third empowerment which is the Yidam cycle where here you become one and inseparable with the Garuda Trung Pe who is nothing but Pure Mind in my interpretation of this. To become a spiritual master of others? No! Never! To master oneself Spiritually? Yes! Ever On!

Three Methods

This poet, this writing, is but a fool's knowing in Dzogchen and Advaita, a spiritual greeting from a buck tooth grinning ox in the state of his own brightness. There are three Dzogchen presentations based on the Three statements of Garab Dorje. Semde, Londe and Mangagde are the methods through Mind, Vast Expanse and Essence of Essence. Again these follow the line of Yogas, Symbolic(s) and As It Is. As these are stages in the Vast Expanse, even so such unions are but symbols. The four stages within the Mind method are; step one, Calmness, two More Calm Insight, three the Watcher (the Witness) of thoughts without the maintenance of thoughts, four is Self Perfect Arising. In the Vast Expanse method the four symbols are; one, the Eyes are caught, two, the Eyes that see the Eyes (the Void) are caught: three, is the Bliss Sensation churning in the Base of the central canal, four, is actual Union of mind in the Vast Expanse or Great Void. In the As It Is method or the Just Letting It Be method the first step is Becoming like the Mountain, second is Becoming like the Ocean, third is just letting be Whatever Arises

135

without being caught by it, and fourth is that all thoughts, experiences, events and feelings are but Ornaments of Dzogchen.

In these Three Series thoughts are viewed or approached in various ways. Like water in Water (which is most Vedantic in its thinking) or like fish jumping out of and returning to Water, or like Ornaments hanging in Space, or like Meeting Old Friends (when they come as enlightenment) or like the snake that uncoils (metaphorically that your own thoughts naturally uncoil and so reveal Reality to you as Enlightenment) and again, thoughts are like Drawings or Illustrations made in the Water, disappearing as soon as they appear. These views of thought essence are there so that thought does not get caught or becomes lassoed into negative emotions like fear, anger, hatred, resentment, jealousy, craving and pride, or distraction, worry, fixation or obsession on what is unreal (samsara). Perceiving thought essence in such ways help bring about the three series. Semde as the Calm of Pure Mind (nirvana like in nature). Londe as the Active Thought of the Pure Mind (samsara like in its nature) and Mangagde which is Neither (of the first two) just Being As It Is Pure Mind in itself.

So these are also called the Outer Secret, the Inner Secret and the Secret Essence, to which is added a fourth, the Most Secret Essence which deals with the Nying Thigle or the Mind/Heart Essence. Mind logic, the Vast Vortex, the Secret Essence and the Most Secret Essence are again these method/series.

Again, Semde is Analysis with mind, the mentality series with its four engulfing sensations of separating what is mind from what is Pure Mind. It comes first as Calm Insight that penetrates, then as more of this Penetrating Calm Insight, third as the recognition of the Pure Mind as the Witness of thoughts and fourth as the Self Perfect Pure Mind. This method appears to be Waking Mind State related.

The next series is Londe which is As Effortless no mind contact within the Vortex, Pure Space or Vast Expanse. It is to become one with activated thought movements in four attuning within phases where one sees thought essence but just lets it hang there in the Vortex of Pure Space. The first is the

136

recognition of what the Eyes see. The second is the recognition of the Great Void, or the Eyes of Eyeness itself which is to perceive that which is doing all perceiving on a deeper level. Then comes the Blissful Sensation of this recognition which also along this line develops a kind of symbolical embrace or conjugal union of bliss with the Great Void. Finally that becomes complete Union as Pure Mind is One with the thought screen. It is within the vast Pure Space that these four symbols are contained with the practice. In seems that this series/level is Dream State related to the Dream Mind in the Dream Vortex of the Vast Pure Space.

The third stage method is Mangagde which is the secret information about stabilizing the Non-Dual, As Reality In Reality. It is Just Letting Be and as such is crucial to understanding both Trekchod and Thogal. First is to Be as a Mountain as the mountain body of the waking state is left wherever as is. Second is to let mind become like the Ocean where the dreaming mind is vast like the sea and just left wherever as is. Third is the non-dual thought feeling without the sensation of even attuning to a harmony within such as the prior example of the sensation of being in union, for you have always been in union and to think you have just become in union is really a fantasy as such. This step is also compared to peeling the bark off a tree to get to the pure wood itself. The bark is all our chronic habitual tendencies to view Reality in a conceptual way and not As It Is. This is truly a Trekchod method. The mind just arises like Prajna (Deep Sleep) as a void or emptiness or mass of one pure light without conceptual context. The fourth method/step is really the secret of Dzogchen Non-Dual Pre-Primordial perfect identity/knowing of Pure Mind itself where all thought essences arising are but friendly non-dual ornaments. This surely is the beginning of Thogal practice in this stage/series. Relating it to Vedanta, it is just as it is, the seeing of Pure Consciousness (Turiya) in all consciousness.

The Most Secret

The Most Secret Stages also called the Unsurpassed and

Unsurpassable stages are the four Trekchod style visions which cut into Turiya. The Four Thogal style visions are those which bring back Turiya without ego/dream conception. And the Four Nying Thigle style Lighting Ups are Illuminatings of Mind in Non-Dualism. This is Non-Dual Light Infusion Empowerment. The four Trekchod visions are first to get a Perception of what we are talking about. Second to increase this Perception, till third, everything that is not this Perception is Cut Through, until the fourth Trekchod vision where all that is not this Perception is absolutely exhausted. The four Thogal visions are the same in reverse. One first takes the Pure Trekchod Perception into a direct and immediate context of a living and living right on through experience. Second, this increases to a point of diminishing all else to the third stage/vision where nothing can contain or measure the vast greatness of this Perception, to the fourth where all the world before us is exhausted or quenched in Turiya (The Pure Perception). The spiritual layout of this is brilliant. If you consider the Waking State as the Woven. The Dream State as the Interwoven. The Deep Sleep State as the Unwoven and Turiya as the Supremely Unwoven and then multiply each state by the same four states (four stages within each state) where one condition has the characteristics of all four penetrating within it, then you get sixteen stages of Turiya Perception. This will become clearer as we go along.

Three Statements

Of course, it is thought that the three series are inspired by Garab Dorje's three profound statements. The first is the Introduction (Directly) into the ma-rigpa/Rigpa dualism so as to know what is not Pure Mind. This is to recognize Just the Witness with Bare Attention where there is no thought and just the Calm of the Mind. Second is the Discovery or Decision which is to decide with total decisiveness to exercise the Cutting Away (Trekchod) of all that is not Pure Mind. This is the watching of the Witness of all arising thought as thought excitement exciting in its decision to no longer be obscuring to what is your Pure Mind. Third is Continuing with complete absolute undaunted Confidence as so to be Coming Back or Returning as Pure Mind in Thogal, the Soaring Onward. The four confidences, the four visions, the three gazes and the six accomplishments pertain to this and will be explained further on. This is just the letting be so of the Non-Dual Appearances of all thoughts. Pure Mind in the concept of its being a Witness is gone here as that concept no longer holds or catches or lassos the mind. The fourth Most Secret Stage (Nying thigle) is Living Non-Dual Awareness! Not just Cutting To It by Total Decisiveness (Trekchod) but this is Living It (Thogal). It is no less what Ramakrishna describes his "most mature spiritual opinion" which is to be charged with Love and see that in all the cosmic principles and by so seeing in this way there is no longer any duality to obscure.

The Whole Point is to get into the Mother Light of the Turiya. Cutting Through (Trekchod) the Waking Semde mind analysis, the Dream symbols in the Londe Vortex, and the Mangagde as it is of Deep Sleep. We arrive at Turiya, Pure Mind. Again one cuts to it with the four stage visions of Trekchod and then brings back into one's living-ness, this Turiya, by the four Thogal visions. The four Nyingthig Lights come last as final Empowerment Infusion. This excellent spiritual maturity is when one lights one's own Lamps of Self, Great Expanse, Thigle (Mind Essences) and Eyes. We shall go further into it.

It is all Pure Mind. It always has been Pure Mind. It never was not so. Three statements, but even here there is still conceptuality attending the ideas of all, always and never not so. The effort of Dzogchen is to take one beyond all conceptuality and experience the Dzogchen Mind! I feel a saving connection with Something I cannot describe as so many insight/feelings that connect to Pure Mind. But the idea of connection is itself still conceptuality! We are dealing with Rigpa which in Sanskrit is Vidya (Knowledge) and its opposite powerful obscuration, Ma-rigpa or Avidya (not-Knowledge). This again is a potent conceptual duality, potent in its distraction. The vidya/avidya thought comes from Advaita, so are Dzogchen and Advaita so different. With more exact parallels than divergences,

139

Gaudapada and Garab Dorje come at last to the same Place it appears to me. Is it so different? Of what? Of Mother? Of Sakti? Of Dakini?

Re-Enlightened

We get Re-Enlightened, not enlightened. The six distracting thoughts cease (The thought that one is unenlightened, that one is mind/consciousness alone, that one is seeking enlightenment, for it is already in the palm of your hand, always, the thought that one must detect, determine, encounter or discover, the thought that becomes emotions like stupidity, pride, jealousy, yes stupidity is an emotion since it is an attitude, and lastly the thought that one needs to meditate or contemplate, for what indeed does the thought/need to mediate have to do with Pure Mind?). The eight ever inherent and accomplished truths of Pure Mind arise! The essence of Pure Mind as Ceaseless Compassion! The Ceaseless Light of Pure Mind comes forth and may diverge into the five rainbow primordial wisdom lights! The Ceaseless Primordial Wisdom arises without thoughts! The Ceaseless Dharmakaya arises and may at times become the peaceful and wrathful Sambhogakaya! As the Ceaseless Non-Dual arises there is no place for the analysis of a dual and not dual thought! As Ceaseless Liberation arises it is clear as Self Essence (Sva Bhava)! As the Ceaseless Primordial Pure Mind (Nirvana) arises it appears above like a Clear Cloudless Sky! As the Ceaseless Samsara arises the six worlds turn below! (And it is in these that Nirmanakaya manifests non-dual with those worlds.) The Kung Zhi (Alaya-vijnana) where all conceptuality has been for long stored up is realized as different from Pure Mind in its Wisdom Pre-Primordial which has always been So with us, Originally So!

Mother Light And Offspring

You see, Rigpa as just Pure Mind is Mother. Rigpa as the Awareness of Pure Mind (Mother) is the Son-mind or the Daughter-mind (the Offspring). This is still dual in its conceptualizing, yet, ever so, the Non-Dual Energy Background (The Ground, Foundation/Base) is Always Present. And because this is So, Non-Duality, it is only a buck tooth laughing fool who separates Trekchod and Thogal. They are one and together in living spirituality ever cutting through and soaring on. Trekchod is really just like Neti Neti in Advaita, the Not This Not This process of exhausting all dualities and cutting them away. One, reaching the awareness that there is really nothing to accept and nothing to reject, goes into nirvikalpa, the peaceful state of mind without conceptuality. So then Thogal is like the savikalpa where one has living peace even though conceptuality arises. But then the Nyingthig or Secret Mind Essence is more like Vijnana (unique comprehensive experience which is basically just like bhavamukha but not as vast in its expanse) or sahaja-like (or our natural, innate and inherently born spiritual condition) or in the greatest capacity even so, Bhava Mukha which is the Supreme Pure Mind that faces (mukha) the Eternal and the Relative (the Non-Conceptual and the Conceptual) with one sweeping breath of Mood Feeling (bhava) that is knowing both as inseparable and as coming both from the Same Pure Mind!

So the Nyingthig is the Innermost Secret Spiritual Practice which brings together both Trekchod and Thogal as One. Trekchod is the Cutting Through or Cutting Away of all Samsara into Pure Mind (Nirvana), it is complete total decision to Let Go and Leave all Samsara, even the four vision stages of Direct Experience, Fuller/Further Increase, No Measure and Final Quenching. While Thogal comes as a Direct Surpassing with Nirvana into Samsara where Pure Mind expresses itself with Samsara as Four Confidences, Six Crucial Accomplishments, Five Radiant Wisdoms, Five Enlightened Dimensions (Kayas), the Thigles of Bindus which are spiritual points of

141

perception/knowledge like Tara's "Pom" bija which manifests Her entire being out of the Great Luminous Void. In fact the Tara practice really has both Trekchod and Thogal and even Nyingthig in its beautiful simplicity. Trekchod is there by dissolving the Goddess into the Great Void. Thogal is there by manifesting/emanating the Goddess out of the Great Void. And Nyingthig is there in the heightened Awareness of the Goddess as both the Great Void and the Manifest being simultaneously Inseparable and Non-Dual.

Again, Mother, the Light, the Pure Mind, Unconditioned and Unfabricated is Love! Thogal brings the Mother (This Love Itself) back but now the son-mind as an offspring in duality has been cut away (Trekchod). This Thogal is the Pure Arising of Love. Trekchod has cut away the bundle of the offspring ego mind where now only Pure Mother (Love) is, and so Trekchod is what gets to the Ever Pure and Thogal Soars On or Back as the Ever Pure. These two conceptions of Trekchod and Thogal are still dual until Nyingthig is Realized or Re-Known!

Suddenness

Sri Ramakrishna spoke of Unmani Samadhi or Sudden Samadhi which is exactly Dzogchen, for it seems that Dzogchen practice is the progressive exercise of this Sudden Awakened Awareness. More and more. Un-mani is no different than A-mani, both are where the mind disperses to God knows where and what is left is just the Wonderment. Ramakrishna again spoke of Shiva Yoga and Vishnu Yoga and it appears that these two methods are exactly like Trekchod and Thogal. In Shiva yoga "you must wipe out all that you see and hear" contemplating only the "Inner Self," "one directs one's look to the forehead." Trekchod is really Death itself in the Purest Finest Sense of Pure Death where everything is wiped off and Let Go! This is no less a Shiva movement. Thogal is so much then like Vishnu Yoga where the eyes look partially outward while one is still highly aware of what was discovered in Trekchod. Here, Thogal or Vishnu Yoga is very much like the Return to Life. So it is Death and then back to Life to share or

142

express what was rediscovered! In Vishnu yoga it is the dance of Pure Mind coming forth as the Pure Mind uncovered in Trekchod. But Trekchod is a Living Experience and not a death-like one. And Thogal is a Living Right On Through or Direct Surpassing Experience, for when it relates to the vishnu yoga concept it is the returning or descending of what has ascended to Pure Mind with Pure Mind coming back to protect, guide, sustain and maintain all that was past, is present, and now to be future, with its Wonder and Luminosity. This is the true meaning of Tara and of Ava (Tara), the Descending Saving Goddess.

So we equate Trekchod with Pure Death of all chronic dual conceptuality, all of it, gross, subtle and causal! Then Thogal is the Continuing Natural Principles! But are these "principles" not involved with visions and miraculous death phenomena so warned about by Advaita? Yes, there is that aspect of it where what Gaudapada warns us about which is lingering too long on the rasa vada pleasure of lesser wonders in the samadhi states. You see we are looking for Pure Mind not miracles and phenomena. The idea of a border between the Nitya and the Lila is an illusion in conceptuality. Between Trekchod and Thogal there should be no border idea, only Ultimate Continuing. Yet, Thogal must also be practiced before death otherwise consciousness will be carried along on its own projections, even as currents of rasa vada. The pleasurable wonder states.

Every illusion must be cut away in the death-like Trekchod! True Trekchod gives no room to any duality! Real Trekchod, what a wonderful thought, is Exploding Solidity and this is to Cut Away even Subtle Solidity as that of even the Bardo Bodies! As it is explained, in the after death state, the past bardo body form is based upon memories of the previous body and the future body form in whatever bardo may arise is a projection from that point in the Bardo to the future becoming of that Bardo mind. Real Trekchod Lets Go of even this! So then what indeed manifests as Real in the Thogal recreation of a Light Body or Rainbow Body? Is it the Five Pure Primordial Lights? The Trikaya without ego self? But then most of the time when people claim to see a Thogal Light Body of someone who has passed on, they see a former past body. So here that is surely a confusing aspect.

So you see, Trekchod is to get to Mother Light in all Her Nakedness, naked of all conceptuality! Trekchod is like cutting into and through the Lila Cloud as the four far ranging visions that dive deeper and deeper through even death itself to find the discovery of what can only be the ever present, that never has left you, Mother Light. Thogal is the four far ranging visions bringing back Mother's Naked Light through the Original Direct Point (Bindu or Thigle), to the Increasing Sensation, to the stage where nothing can measure Her, to the Full Rise of the Dharmata Joy, which is the Great Bliss of True Self! This Thogal is Mother Adorned with Lila! These bindu/thigle lamps may be as The Point, Filling All Sensation, No Measures, and Full Blown. These thigles are information drops of Advaita Knowledge (but still dream conception), Pure Sakti Information in these four thigle Clear Light nuclei which are ever expanding as Self Kindled Advaita Information packets, drops, points, circles, and great all-spheres encompassing. But do not be daunted in your experience by the influence of Tibetan imagery such as the vajra chains and links or Tibetan faces and and architecture or ornaments that are said to be seen in the process of these expanding visions (but still dream conception). One's own imagery is naturally applied from the well/pool of symbols therein. Again, the thigle may appear as chains of drops or points linked together in Non-Dual Information that comes to you. It means that this information is running through your very own nerves and through the five pranic energies circulating with this nerve system which is elaborate and beautiful! But still dream conception.

Kung Zhi

Again, Trekchod is Pure Process to Pure Mind and the Death of all belief systems which chronically inhibit the Expanse of Our Freedom. It is strange how people so fiercely adhere to their inveterate beliefs when in the end those beliefs only restrict them. It is voluntary slavery to one's unfree ideas! Pure Mind in

Trekchod is above all the Bardo processes. All the eight dissolving consciousnesses. The universal ground as the eighth stage of death is called near attainment for the blackness or darkness of deep sleep in the Kung Zhi (the universal unconscious or Alaya-vijnana, an interesting word which can mean that special knowledge or consciousness of things which has not yet been dissolved or even just the deep sleeping consciousness within us all universally speaking). That is the last to Let Go! It is called "near or full attainment" because one step more out of this deep sleep like stage is the Clear Luminosity of Mother Light and here is the source point of the most refined subjective level which continues until Mother Light is clearly known. Before that is the radiant red increase of the consciousness of the mind looking back on the Kung Zhi (and it is this looking back at Kung Zhi that is the birth point of our inner subjectivity) and it is this mind that becomes the Zhi Khro manifestation of thought essences in the forms of peaceful and wrathful deity forms. It is called "increase" from either direction, that of progressively dying closer to Mother Light or in the return path of coming back to another life it is the increasing of cognitive awareness outwardly and this is the birth point of objectivity. Before that is the white mind of appearance which only is seeing itself in context of the mind alone (objectively isolated) as it is unaware of the above two stages, that of consciousness looking increasingly deeper and that of consciousness being near to attainment. But here it is called "appearance" as the coming from the direction of dying, what appears now is the white mind consciousness separate from the five senses and so forth down below. Consciousness has raised up from there. The red thigle and the white thigle of those two stages (referenced to the waking and dreaming states) become One Thigle and that thigle becomes stabilized in the sushumna which is the Great Void. From here there is no dropping down from or going out or sallying forth from Pure Mind. Now if there is a sallying forth from Here, the other five consciousnesses break out into the Occurring of mind, as the Primary Prana diverges into the five senses, the five Wisdoms, the five guiding images, the five pranas and other wondrously

145

amazing continuities of spiritual dimensional expressions. Trekchod actually cuts away and lets go of all this getting to the heart of Pure Experience as Pure Mind and stays there, stabilized as that Pure Mind which actually needs no stabilizing in its inherently pre-primordial Nature, Essence and Energy which are ever Non-Dual!

So to clarify. The mind consciousness of white appearance is no less connected to the Waking State of consciousness and this comes up either coming back into or leaving that state. In this Tibetan system it is related to the thigle of male energy. The mind consciousness of radiant red increase is related to the coming back into or the leaving of the Dream State, and it is this Dream State where things like the Zhi Khro are seen. In this system this red radiance is related to the thigle of female energy. The darkness of near attainment is no less the Deep Sleep state itself and here what is called the Immortal thigle may indeed only exist on the conceptual side of Deep Sleep for in deep sleep no image of waking or dreaming is seen or experienced. It is parallel and equated to the Great Void and Void is void, there are no thigle there, for these thigle are conceptual points and concepts exist only in waking or dreaming. So really speaking, the Primary Clear Mother Light or the Ground of Infinite Luminosity could be considered a ninth stage from the view of the analytical mind.

When we die (or practice Trekchod or Pho Wa for that matter) and rise up from the first five stages there is a natural cutting away or letting go of the eighty misconceptions. They are severed away through this Trekchod death. If they come back while alive they distract the mind. If they re-arise in after death they cause new birth. From the rising up or going toward the death direction these eighty emotional misconceptions begin to be cut away in the naturalness of the Trekchod of death at the stage of the fifth element, Space or Akasha, but their full letting go of is considered to happen in the progressive stages of appearance, increase and attainment and are only fully left behind when Primary Clear Light is Realized or Stabilized and no dualistic conceptuality is left to be thought about by the thinker in either of these three final stages: appearance, increase

146

and attainment. It is a thought to consider that this break up or cutting through (Trekchod) occurs here when mind consciousness in the dying process of consciousness projection reaches the region of just pure space. So it is obvious that the physical human body goes in the letting go of death. But it may be so that also the subtle body goes with its innermost composing principles of the nadis, the pranas and the thigles. Certainly the red/white thigles that have held together the human physical body start to move up and down the central nerve canal before they unite and move forth to another life or stabilize in the Great Void of the Sushumna Canal. What moves from here soaring onward is what Tibetans call the very subtle body and mind as opposed to just the subtle body and mind. And this "very subtle" is what the Advaita refers to as the causal. It is this causal consciousness that moves through appearance, increase and attainment. But it is universally agreed that what is there in our re-enlightenment is just the Primary Clear Mother Light alone! In another life we get a new body, with new nerve/nadis, new prana/wind energies and new thigles perhaps, well of course, from the new parents, but it is also believed that the thigles, you carry from one life to another, contain (especially when the red and white become one and move onward) the conscious and spiritual impressions of what the new life will be as the soul (or causal mind consciousness) goes to one of the six worlds, or a form region or a formless region. Or even to uttermost Freedom. Ah, so many opinions and thoughts on it all. So Trekchod even this!

Barrier Emotions

So anger, desire and ignorance are the three primary emotional obscuring forces as told by Sakyamuni. These are the three precipices in the Bardo and in the Now. (Refer to the Introduction) In Krishna's system in the Bhagavad Gita, the three emotions given are fear, anger and desire, so it varies from system to system. This Tibetan system considers fear an offshoot of anger (but it may be that anger is an offshoot of fear, noraphinephrine - anger is a biochemical subgroup of adrenaline

147

- fear and we tend to have anger at what we first fear), which makes much sense and they deal face to face with this wrathful quality within us. Nevertheless when Trekchod reaches the white appearance the thirty three emotions of anger are cut through. Certainly who could categorize all the emotional side shapes of anger, but of great interest is that even thinking the conception that you are a knower or that you are knowing or that there is an object to be known is under this heading. Indeed, the ego, thinking it knows, is the essential source of anger. So is the fear that perhaps one does not know. The other thirty three misconceptions are mild, medium or intense, and they are as you might surmise, such things as jealously, hatred, pride, resentment and so forth. But even compassion, mercy and the wish to meet the beautiful springs from this arena and it is not so strange when one realizes that it is because one has anger at what prevents compassion, mercy or beauty. With the Trekchod of the red increase goes the forty emotions that are desire or lust based. And they are as you would assume such things as blood lust, sex lust, fame lust, power lust, all these that Sri Ramakrishna tells us are strong obscuring emotions to spiritual life. But all are not negative, there are those which are the natural desire to enjoy what is pleasant, virtuous and attractive. At the stage of the near attainment is the Trekchod of the seven offshoots of stupidity (ignorance). Yes, stupidity can be an emotion in that it is the highest ignorance when one thinks that one has known or learned everything there is to know or learn when in fact how can you ever feel that in regard to Infinite Knowledge or Unfabricated Consciousness in the Pre-Dualistic or Pre-Primordial State of Itself. That emotional attitude can only make you depressed, doubtful, lazy, mistaken and forgetful. Yet the Wonder of Trekchod cuts all this away into Immediate Clear Light.

Pre-Primordial

Really, the most important principles here in realizing the Pure Dakini Mother Light are appearance, increase and attainment. Mother Light is Pure Jnana (Knowledge) and is much more than the Rigpa of the Jnana of the Mother Light for the Mother Light is Pure Pre-Primordial Wisdom, before any duality appeared. Where this duality first appears is the point of entrance/contact between Eternity and Time, for it is in time space that the offspring comes to be and to look back at the Mother Light feeling that this offspring is now the apprehender doing the apprehending of the apprehended which is the Light and all this process takes place in time and this is where the duality begins in the illusory dreamtime of separation. Does this triad of apprehender, apprehending and apprehended exist in the deep sleep of near attainment. No, not in its true form because there is no dual dream/waking energy going on there to start up apprehension or separation. But this deep sleep near attainment is where the apprehender first appears and so drops down to begin all the rest. This of course is the red increase of dream and the white appearance of waking. Now when this red increase and white appearance take the shapes of thigle, these create the hard to get over duality of a created physical and subtle body which is just further identity, deeper and grosser, of the apprehender who feels duality and separate self sense (offspring) from the Mother Light. So if in Trekchod or death these two dual red and white thigles come together and form that Amrita Bindu or Immortal Thigle it is still an idea of conceptual identity within the Great Luminous Void of Pure Dakini Bliss and since it is a concept it does not comprehend the Nature of the Void (which is clear or empty of all concept/ideas) that supports the concept or the thigle itself!

Some thinkers have thought that these thigle (red/white) are the bringing together in One Thigle the non-dual quantum genetic nuclei which returns to the depth of near attainment and so hushes or ceases the rebirth process or if rebirth takes place from there due to impressions or influences within the storehouse of Alaya-vijnana, then one comes back as an already enlightened being. Extraordinary thoughts like these can make you somewhat inebriated, so one must take care not to follow the lasso of that inebriation and keep the Eyes on Dzogchen.

It is said that true death actually takes place the moment one's consciousness returns down from the Mother Light and reenters the flow of thought to start up the next existence. You would think that death was in the Mother Light but if one is in the Mother Light one is not dead, but in the Highest condition of what may be called true Life. So, That is Chikhai, Primordial Clear Mother Light. If one moves out from there, the Chonyid Dharmata is now no longer like a dream but arises like an old friend within whom one only sees that True or Actual Reality (Dharmata). Now if one has come to this then one has really changed the ordinary Bardo experiences into what is called Antara Bhava (Inner Mood), in the Pure Awareness or the Feeling of this Inner Experience is now nothing ordinary at all for one is in the Inner Feeling/Mood of the Mother Light (yet even this still has a tinge of offspring duality). If one brings back this Antara Bhava from the after death condition or from a high Trekchod, into life again one is now reborn with Bahir Bhava or Outer Mood/Feeling which exhausts everything in the field of experience called Life and this is a great insight/clue to what Thogal can be in some of its very high profoundest possibilities. But this is not all that Thogal is, for it is Soaring On in the most excellent Non-Duality where no dual word forms of conveyance can really describe it completely. You are flying like the Solitary Garuda bird who is discovering spiritual secrets that have never been written or spoken by anyone. You are a true Pratyeka (Solitary or Inner) Yamantaka (one who has Death as their teacher and who conquers or rises above Death)!

And it would seem that part of this Pratyeka Yamantaka is to understand your own death even as Trekchod and this will involve the sweet Letting Go or cutting through to the Barrier Free Approach (Trekchod). This is to know what the Lights of White Appearance, Red Increase, Near Attainment, the Offspring Light of itself, which gets its own Luminosity from nowhere but the Pure Mind of the Pre-Dual Mother Light. So it seems that is five lights if you are counting. These are all the Antara bhavas of your own death experience and they come up all within you when you die or at least as this Tibetan metaphor expresses and as explained before in the above paragraphs as Trekchod.

Since for most of us, death is a terrifying and all finality delusion causing no end to anxiety, let me go once again at this

Trekchod of the death fear. It seems that Laya Yoga is very similar to Pho Wa if not exactly the same. One drives Consciousness upward through the seven chakras in the idea of this Consciousness as the Kundalini (Even as the Coiled Up Pure Mind Energy as a conceptual identity (thigle) now uncoiling.) Goddess Dakini rising upward to the highest State just like the Consciousness Transference of Pho Wa. Pho Wa does this in twenty one vigorous breath expulsions. For those of you not familiar with the seven chakras they are in simple form; earth, water, fire, air, space (Akasha, for without space/time they would not exist having no ground to stand on), then mind and finally Pure Consciousness. This kundalini consciousness rises reaching at each stage a no contact state with each element and then finally having no contact (Asparsa) even with mind conception it just naturally reaches the advaita of Pure Consciousness. This is when the offspring of Rigpa Awareness reaches the Pure Rigpa in Mother Awareness which is none but the Primordial Wisdom (Yeshes) of the Mother Light. Even in Trekchod or death one dissolves (Laya) contact with each progressive element that forms the waking condition (earth, water, fire, air) then reaches the border of the dream condition as an experience of pure inner space of the mind also, yet when this contact is dissolved (with space) then mind is now in the deep sleep condition. One more step, or rather dropping away of contact, or letting go (Trekchod) of contact with the just mind state of deep sleep and the Light of Pure Mind sets in without exertion or effort, Her Primordial Presence (as Eternity without time and Infinity without space) is uncovered as Pure Rigpa (yet was always already here even as the most ordinary awareness). Getting Through to this as Trekchod and then Going On with this, is really the "Pe" of Garuda Trung Pe, the "Leaping and Soaring" Out of the Death Maya, the Illusion of Death.

Maya

Maya is an Inscrutable Power which covers everything and experience (cognitive or otherwise) with the idea or conception of duality, separateness and division, really Maya is the Goddess

151

who creates the World in Total as we generally see it. What we generally do not see is that the entire total idea of a World complex, from atomic to cosmic, is ever always inseparable and non-dual with the Power (Mother) who apparently created or made it. I once had a dream of Her Great Mystery. Swamis, Aseshananda, Bhaskarananda, Dayatmananda and someone else who was with me were discussing "Maya as Primordial Energy which is as the Manifestation of Glory (Luminosity) in all you see, think, hear and feel." At that point Swami Aseshananda said, "This conversation itself is Maya too!" All of us present in this dream were in open eyed agreement. I said then, "Whatever you see, think or hear is maya," quoting Ramakrishna directly, "The Chitsakti, Mahamaya, has become the twenty-four cosmic principles.   Take refuge in Chitsakti, the Mahamaya."   I continued within the dream state, "The idea of Maya was yet to be developed in Rig Vedic times. Though Maya as Vac (Speech or Voice) would be all that is between the Create and the Uncreate, and the sense of between-ness itself, here as Vac is thought of as this Primordial Energy." Aseshananda listened, open eyed, agreeing. So you see simply, all conceptuality comes into the form of Voice or Speech and that creates the ideas of separateness.

So the Rigpa of Mother is not in the three states, Waking, Dream or Deep Sleep. It is there but one does not find it there (of course, as the Ever Present). Rigpa is a step above alertness! One is thinking of all that goes on in the waking, dreaming and deep sleep states. You see, but when you are really in the contemplation of Higher Reality, you are not in any of those three states. This state of consciousness has even been clearly measured by instruments that show it is not like simply being awake, or dreaming or being in deep sleep. It is a clarity more than alertness and different from those three conditions of consciousness. So again it is nothing less than Turiya and to make more comparisons, there is the Tantra saying of "Kama-Kala in the Turiya State" as the state of enlightenment. Here, in this study, I would compare this Kama-Kala to the union of uniting the masculine and feminine thigle energies, as well as, the passion (kama) kala (death as time) dual complex.   This

152

duality as Kama-Kala becomes stable in Turiya which is Pure Consciousness or even as it is also described in the Shiva Samhita, as being Maha Shunyata, the Great Void. That means there is no more going out from There, from Turiya or the Great Luminous Void. The idea is that the Immortal Drop is stabilized thigle which no more will break apart and divide into the red and white thigles or bindu points as the solar and lunar, red and white, feminine and masculine (yes, the red thigle is feminine and the white is masculine, but the moon/lunar is white and the sun/solar is red, so the usual solar/lunar ideas are reversed here which is good because our projections of gender identities on Nature are self limiting thoughts, so the sun can be feminine as creative source and the moon masculine as receptive vessel) forces of the Maya of coming and going, of waking and dreaming or ever even falling into the state of deep sleep again! That the efferent and afferent currents of thought energy becoming stabilized within the sushumna is another actual as well metaphorical illustration to demonstrate the return to Non-Dual Luminosity.

Conceptuality And Infusion

So Trekchod is the cutting away to get to Turiya. It is cutting through the entire Trikaya misconception which we understand as the ordinary (A) Waking, (U) Dreaming and (M) Deep Sleep States. Aum being the designation of these three states and their Unity in Turiya. But the entire misconception of Aum as separative states must be Cut Away. As well as the Trikaya misconception that Emanation, Resplendence, and Truth are divided from one another as dualities or different levels when they are all Non-Dual in Reality. Then Thogal is the Soaring On or Back as Turiya (not as the divided offspring ego, but as the Pure Light of Dakini Mother) to Infuse AUM as Trikaya in its Real and True Understanding or Innerstanding! This is the real meaning of the Longchen (Vast Expanse of Innumerable Non-Dual Rays of Light) Nying (Mind/Heart) Thigle (Essence or Point of Extreme Spiritual Knowledge). This is what becomes the Brasbu Lamp or the Climax/Result/Fruit of all Dzogchen. It

153

cannot be described.   Yet it is to bring the Lamp of Zhi (Primordial Luminous Ground) through Lam (The Path or Transition through the Lamps of Bardo or In-between Lamps and this includes the various Bardo Transitions) to the Lamp of Brasbu (End Result) and yet these three appearances are a mirage in the thought of their being separate/dual.   The awareness of this may indeed be the Mind/Heart Thigle of the Vast Expanse itself. The Immortal (and ever present) Bindu.

So really Trekchod cuts through all the six bardos (as path or paths) and even the thigle of mind essence that comprehends the total understanding or grasping in knowledge of the six bardos. That is, Trekchod cuts away the idea/illusion of coming and going through the six bardos. You must cut through it or it just happens over and over again as the same dragging or pulling current, just like our experience of redundancy in ordinary waking, dreaming and deep sleeping. Trekchod cuts away the redundancy or ordinary view and then Thogal is the Surpassing Onward of all this as the exquisitely Luminous, Beautiful and Loving. The six bardos are nothing but waking, dreaming and deep sleep (or the Luminosity within this Deep Sleep) in forward and reverse.   Birth bardo is Waking, the Dream Bardo is the Dream State, and the Samadhi Bardo (Enlightenment which is still in transition) is when deep sleep reveals her innate and inherent Light/Luminosity. So then the Death Bardo (Chikhai) is this same Light in continuance but now on the side of death. And the after death dream state is the Chonyid Bardo. And then the point of coming back into contact with a new waking state is then the Sidpa bardo. So you are back again at the birth Bardo. So many transitions, (bardos) and yet the final climax is the Lamp of your own Self Generating Acumen and Appreciation of Illumination. From either side, life or death, the near attainment of deep sleep is seen to be in its Real Light (the Primary Brightness of Chikhai). The conceptual ideas of a red and a white thigle moving into the one Immortal Essence thigle are consumed from the dream bardo of the Chonyid as the True Tummo or Luminous Heat Fire of the Mother Light consumes the duality idea of a red and white duality. The psychic heat through the nerve/nadis is not true and final tummo but only a starting! All the five moving Primordial Prana energies are bought into One in this Luminosity! That is the Real Tummo (inner fire/heat/luminosity)! When these five Primordial energies now One, then break up, this reappears as the Five Wisdoms in the formless sense and as the five buddhas or dakinis in a form sense and this again is an aspect of Thogal when one knows that this is what is reappearing! But even all that, nerves, energies, thigles, tummo, five energies and five Wisdoms as amazingly congruous as it all is, is still within dream mind conceptuality and so the idea of duality may still come back. So one must still practice Trekchod even though the Thogal vision is attained in order to keep that vision in the Never Dual Light of Pure Mind.

Prajna

May the Dakini Free Us of all conceptual blocks to the Pure Mind! Let me dive deep in search of Spiritual Treasure. So, Gaudapada equates prajna with pure Prana. It is called prajna (deep sleep) and it becomes Prajna (Wisdom). Now, in Sudden Dzogchen, see that this is so! As prajna this condition is the unified state of individual energy (prana) where and when this energy does not become the stuff of dreaming nor of waking cognitive varieties. In the universal cosmic sense this energy state is the unified field of pure Prana before creation. This Deep Sleep is "Ekibhuta" where all experiences are Unified. It is "Cetomukha" as it is the Doorway or the Face of Consciousness that can turn, enter or face toward Turiya or in the direction of dreaming and waking consciousness. It is called "Prajnanaghana" as a mass of unified consciousness. It is "Anandabhuk" the experiencer of Bliss, but not the Maker of Bliss, that is Turiya Atman or the Maha Dakini Sukha. Again we see that it is "Pralaya" or all dissolving of contact with the outside dreaming and waking in both the personal and universal experience. As this Pure Prana is deep sleep, for one it shows that deep sleep is not entirely passive as such but is the concentrate of Pure Energy, when this energy (which is an innermost core) realizes or Faces or looks at itself it becomes

155

the Self Generated Bliss or Pure Dakini Consciousness. Again, Prana in this state of complete unified Energy is the Unmanifest (Avyakta or Avyakrta), from this springs all that is seen, heard, or thought about. Referred to elsewhere in this text Avyakta is Nirodha (when waking/dreaming imagination are held from sallying forth) and this Nirodha is where and when mind makes real to itself, the Pure Mind (Amanibhava). Again this prajna is avidya (ma-rigpa or not Awareness) yet when turned to Face its Pure Energy it becomes the intensity of the ecstatic Rigpa (Pure Vidya). This prajna is the womb of the sleep of not knowing and the Womb of Self Knowing. It is "Bijanidrayuta" as the seed or cause of the sleep which gives rise to varieties (duality or waking and dreaming stuff). In Turiya or Rigpa this sleep (nidra) does not exist so Turiya Rigpa is not sleep and so does not dream or become befuddled by the waking mind either. It is Pure Awareness (Dakini) and so there is no bija, thigle or bindu, no cause, no drop essence, no point for cognition to arise, so there is no sallying out nor giving rise to anything objective nor subjective in the thinking of thought which just naturally stays as Pure Thought Epiphany which is another name of the Dakini! This is "Anidram" which is without sleep or thought, does not go out to the seed cause of sleep and so does not drop down into the imaginative display of diversity or the many. Deep Sleep is "Apitih" or Becoming One. And it is "Miti" the Measure and "Prastha" a kind of measure from where the coming and going of waking and dreaming can be measured.

The importance of this Prana and the prajna to Prajna leap or adjustment will be shown. You see the Pure Energy of Dakini Sakti is what you are. She is the Arrival-less Arrival to Where You Always Have Been, even as before the becoming of any display or occurring. Now once that Pure Awareness which we here call Dakini moves out forth from Pure Mind or Turiya Space this One Energy (Sakti) appears as the Five Prime and Primordial Wisdoms (often called the five dakinis or the five dhyani buddhas). Never the less, the Energy goes out from the Pre-Primordial to the primordial and then manifests as these five Wisdom Powers which are in my own words: The Pure Mind, the One, the Many, the Ever Successful Accomplished Truth and the Mirror Shining Everywhere. (To students of the five meditation buddhas these associations should be obvious and yet more simple). The first, Pure Mind display is naturally always Pre-Primordial (Amanibhava) yet here Pure Mind makes its Face known even within the cognitive display or the break up of Pure Energy into the rainbow spectrum of radiant consciousness. These are the five First Best Wisdoms and they are what we return to at the time of death (Tibetan Book of the Dead). I believe this is what becomes or more so, what Actually Is the Thogal Light Body which is always here and ever present if you can see with Pure Wisdom Eyes (which the Tibetan Book of the Dead says comes to you when consciousness is released from the cognitive view of the material world of the first four of the five elements). We naturally possess wisdom eyes though the welter of distractions usually keeps us from using them. This Thogal Wisdom Light Body is not the ego you, it is the Pure You! Or the display of what is Pure Dakini Awareness.

Nerves, Energies, Thigles As Five Wisdoms

Now I want to relate these five Wisdom Powers as they manifest as the five Prana energies, their function currents as the wind energies through the nadis (nerves) which are not just organic but subtle current channels and canals (something like String Theory is to the Actual existence of the Universe in all its material/physical form). And of course how the five Wisdoms are five thigles that make their appearance in the developing spiritual mind.

These five essential thigles spread forth in display from the One essential thigle rising out of that unified mass of consciousness which is a drop down from Pure Mind. This is the Immortal (Amrita) Thigle Bindu (Essence/Drop or Point/Seed/Cause) which is a shape of consciousness in feeling/understanding that comes out of the Formless Dakini. Thigle is a form and so it is still conceptuality and thus is not the Formless Dakini, yet it is She who gives birth to the thigle of Self Generated Wisdom, that comprehends and feels the Formless Dakini (Pure Mind) within you. And then this One

157

Point of Comprehension spreads out and becomes the point/drop or circle/essences in the manifest thigles of Pure Mind, the One, the Many, the Ever Successful Accomplished Reality, and the Mirror Shining/Reflecting Truth Everywhere. I will call these the dakini thigles.

Now as to whether the dakini thigles appear in creation before the dakini pranas is a question and answer of favoritism for they most likely appear spontaneously together in simultaneous manifestation. But if we go to the Upanishads we find that before Hiranya Garbha, the Pure Prana was first present. That Hiranya Garbha is an excellent example of what the universal thigle is on the cosmic scale of a single universe for it is the Golden/Luminous Womb/Egg/Seed of the first Dream State of an Energy Force (Prana) out of which comes everything we see from the atomic to the cosmic. An excellent example of a supreme thigle. But returning to our original thought it seems that with the thigle of Pure Mind comes forth the simultaneous Prana which is the Life Energy of everything atomic to cosmic, it is what makes us breath and gives us living energy and luminosity to our thoughts; heat, fire and power to stars and galaxies. There you have it and this Pure Prana is the Energy that gathers all diversity together into the Unified Point which is the prana of prajna where no dual conceptuality as dreaming or waking is there to sally forth the mind into the display of occurring. This in relation is the energy that moves up the center canal/channel of the sushumna that gathers everything into the One (Pure Mind). Next is the downward moving prana called Udana which spreads the One out into the Many (the diversity of display occurring). This is the carrying away or efferent prana current that spreads out to the waking state and is associated to the right dakini nerve which is called the pingala (in Sanskrit the hot solar nerve that leads to the diversity of the waking mind). Next is the dakini thigle of the One that is expressed in the energy prana of the Samana currents that is the assimilating power or digestive power that brings things (diversity) back toward Unified oneness but is itself not that unified oneness. This is the afferent current which is carrying toward the unification and expresses itself as the dream state

158

which between the diversity of waking conditions and the unified deep sleep is a carrying toward indeed, as thoughts are within their own current, turned toward the within state which is dream. This is associated with the ida nadi or the dakini nerve that is carrying toward the dream and the assimilation of the Many toward the One. It is called the cool lunar nerve and indeed this is the current that cools down for us the heat of diversity observed in the waking state. So we go on now to the Ever Accomplished dakini thigle which is simultaneous with the Udana display of the Original Prana. Udana is fascinating for it is the Energy that without effort on our part carries consciousness from the waking state into the dream state and even further into the restful state of deep sleep where no dual dream mind is stepping down or sallying forth. The Udana is what carries consciousness out of the body at the moment of death and so its importance should not be underestimated and in spiritual life it brings about that Sudden Dakini Awareness either in some Dzogchen mind states or in that Unmani samadhi and even perhaps Amanibhava which have been mentioned before. So Udana dissolves the duality we experience in our dreaming and our waking mind. It brings consciousness right up to the Clear Mother (Dakini) Light at death and is thus important in the practice of Trekchod when rising up and letting go is taking place. (I would say that Thogal pertains to other currents like the next one I will deal with). This pure and sudden arising energy of Udana no less must be associated with the White Silk Dakini Nerve of Dzogchen practice that goes directly from the center of consciousness as the Heart itself upward spreading forth to the two eyes in Open Awareness of Pure Dakini (A perfect Clear Light Death) or where and when dream states as duality disperse into the Non-dual essence light of the Pure Mind. To realize this Ever Present and Accomplished dakini energy and thigle in the white silk nerve of direct and sudden Dakini Awareness is a blessing of Great Awareness. The dakini thigle of the Mirror that is Shining and Reflecting Reality/Truth Everywhere is no less associated directly with the dakini prana named Vyana which is the energy that spreads around everywhere through the body (whether the living human organism or in the subtle

159

spiritual context as all these nadis and pranas do) and as such is relating to the remaining dakini nerve network in their ordinary and spiritual function and these will be mentioned later on. This spreading around everywhere is truly a Thogal like dakini energy, dakini nerves and dakini thigle. But you must remember that though these three, dakini nerves, energies and thigles, are fascinating, they are still at the level of conceptuality! When contact is dissolved with these Five Dakini Thigles, these Five Dakini Energies and these Five Spiritual Dakini Nerve networks then death occurs or Dzogchen Trekchod. Coming back to these Three principles of Five Energies, Five Dakini Wisdom/Powers and Five Dakini Channels with Heightened Awareness is Thogal!

Abhi Sambodhi

In Dzogchen one finds a general, an essential and an esoteric meaning to the Three Refuge Jewels. In general they are the Buddha (the enlightened one), the Dharma (the teachings) and the Sangha (the fellowship). In the essential these are the Dharmakaya (Truth dimension), the Sambhogakaya (Bright luminous dimension) and Nirmanakaya (Emanation dimension) corresponding to the general refuges. Now the Dzogchen esoteric meanings are best. The sangha and Nirmanakaya are really the Five Dakini Nadis (your own spiritual nerve system). The dharma (path) and Sambhogakaya are really the Five Dakini Energies. And the buddha (enlightenment) and the Dharmakaya (Reality) are really the Five Dakini Thigles. This is not given out ordinarily for it encourages pure independence in one's own spiritual system. All the refuge Jewels of the Dakini are within You already and have ever been so. Interesting and upside down from what is in the Vedanta Upanishads is Aum in the three jewels. A is Buddha and the rest. U is Dharma and the rest. M is the Sangha and the rest. So M is the Emanation and the nadis. U is the Luminous and the pranas. And A is the Truth Realm and the thigles. It is just the opposite of the direction which AUM leads one in the Upanishad Advaita in the sequence of going from waking, to dream, to deep sleep and to Turiya.

160

Nevertheless Turiya equates with the Kaya of Sva Bhava (Self Awareness/Feeling), the Youthful Manjushri Vase (youthful as a Pre-Primordial before the break up into duality), Vajra (as Absolutely Permanent and Indestructible) Kaya and Sahaja (as Inherent and Innately Natural to you) Kaya. Just different names for the same level. And these are represented by the sudden expression "Ah." Then is the Maha (Great) Sukha (Bliss) Kaya which in Dzogchen Empowerment is taught as being nothing but the Pure Dakini Bliss which surpasses all previous conceptual states. The word empowerment is "Hum." And this finalizes into the Abhisambodhi Kaya or Abhisambodhana as the Last! This is also called Samyaksambodhi or just Sambodhi. It is a name given to Sakyamuni's Final Realization. Sambodhi is two words, Sam and Bodhi. Now bodhi (enlightened mind) comes when buddhi (intellect) is lighted up or infused with Bodha (Awakened Consciousness) and that is the true Buddha (the Awakened). The word Sam means calm, peace, tranquil, quiet, satisfied, cease, allay, still, gentle, died out, extinguished. Now if we take any of these ideas and place them in front of Bodhi we come to that insight on what this high enlightenment may be. But as in regard to the fourth Thogal it may even be the allaying or satisfying or the extinguishing of the mind that is enlightened itself, which is an extraordinary thought. And it certainly means something similar but less in regard to bodhi-ta as admonishment, communication, rendering, intelligence and instruction, so with this it would be to cease or satisfy all communication, intelligence or rendering. Beautiful. Both buddha and bodha mean to awaken or arouse, revive or restore to life, cause to open or expand, attract to one's attention, bring to one's senses or to make known. When this happens it is bodhi, the buddhi (intellect) is lighted up. So bodhana is skill in the awakened or aroused mind and "abhi" is fearless" so one gets the Fearless Awakened Knowledge or fearless extinguishment of mind. (Which is so much exact to Gaudapada's Amanibhava, A Mood not of the mind.) And with the word Samyak one gets Continuous or Uninterrupted Awakened Mind (or extinguishment of lesser mind or what is not Pure Mind in the first account or primary sense of it). And this is exactly to

Gaudapada's Alatasanti as santi is again that peaceful ceasing or the quenching/extinguishment of the fire brand or burning coal of the mind (alata). Take note of the similarity of sambodhi and samadhi, sama (peace) in dhi, the one point of concentrated or meditative focus, the buddhi (intellect) itself being the arousing or focusing of that one point in the very nature of mind as it is really just one point or thought at a time which is the essence of the experience of buddhi, bodhi, bodha and buddha. Yet with the full Thogal of Alatasanti all thought of the mind/intellect ceases in the Amanibhava. So this is truly the Fearless and Uninterrupted Dimension (Kaya) of Pure Mind. Also take note that when one makes Bodhi Chitta vows it is a promise in one's consciousness (chitta) to get to Bodhi (for the sake of others even more than self) and Bodhisattva is a degree of peaceful harmony (sattva) within the mind on that state. So go from dhi to Dha making it Bodha-na! Go from dhi which is the splendor of one thought or one conception, insight or intention to Dha which is to convey, grant, bestow, cause, produce, hold, grasp or carry, to take to oneself, receive, obtain, conceive and resolve in mind or thought the Vast Expanse of Bodha, then by making it Na, that becomes strongly empowered or strengthened by Strong Affirmation (Na).

And is not this Abhisambodhana the very admonishment, the strongest affirmation of Sakyamuni at the last, to take to Self Skill and Self Diligence in "Atma (Self) Deepo (Lamp/Light) Bhava (Be, Become, this Mood)!" Is it not the way of the Pratyeka Buddha, the solitary inner arousing of the Bodha Mind, who are those capable of Direct Perception (Pratyak), so again this Samyak Sambodhi is the Uninterrupted Perception of the Bodha Mind! These solitary heroes retreat into their own Self Initiation, into the Fire of their own Knowledge. To them that is the Light and the Lamp. They are of the Primordial Experience reflected in the Gentle Wisdom of Manjushri! They are Yamantaka, Destroyer of Death (who is actually the ferocious or wrathful emanation of Manjushri, which only further affirms non-duality in the reflex of dualism), their teacher is death and it is death they conquer. This is also known as the Vajra Bhairava Tantra of the Diamond Terrifier. Like Whitman, "He most

162

honors my style who learns under it to destroy the teacher." Who as it is said was first self assertive but learned humility, then humanity and immense and vast spirituality by seeing and observing death. These heroes embrace the three deaths which are the outer death of the waking state body, the inner death of dream state delusion and the inner secret (guha) of the deep sleep death of the dualistic mind itself! Then there is no death! No more can death teach us. That is the secret (guha)! "Who dares misery love, And hug the form of Death, Dance in Destruction's dance, To him the Mother Comes." From Swami Vivekananda's Kali The Mother.

When we come to this the ordinary mind (waking, dreaming and deep sleep) is shown in Pure Mind and that there was never any separation in what this Is. Ramakrishna makes it perfectly clear, "... at that time this ordinary mind does not function. When all impurities of the mind are removed, you may call that mind Pure Mind or Atman." The "impurities" are just obscurations. Yet, as "that mind Pure Mind," it was never separate and though appearing ordinary, it never was! So ordinary mind slows down from its captivation when all obscurations are quenched or extinguished (santi) then the burning coal of the mind (alata) is shown to be Pure Mind, Pure Atman, Pure Buddhi, "all the Same," as Ramakrishna says. The Rope (Pure Mind) is no longer taken to be a serpent (ordinary mind) to apply Gaudapada's illustration.

But remember the utterly direct Dzogchen reminder in regard to the three refuge jewels being (A) the lama, (U) the yidam and (M) the Dakini, that their Empty Nature is Realized. That this Is Inseparable with one's Empty Awareness in Trekchod and Thogal! Our Own Awareness is the Foundation (Zhi) and the Result (Brasbu)! That all phenomenal stages and practices are Absolutely Empty! And that Buddha, Dharma and Sangha. Body, Speech and Mind! Nirmana, Sambhoga and Dharma Kayas! And Lama, Yidam or Dakini are in Essence but Emptiness. That is everything drops away from contact when the Pure Pre-Primordial View is Re-Found!

163

The Summit

To continue on the same ground I will look at some of the Sakyamuni's spiritual practices, his method or art of death and these also pertain somewhat to his enlightenment process. Proceeding through the eight consciousness states in the death process or the enlightenment process he came to experience the four mind/insight states and the four almost mind free (A-mani) states. These are explained in greater detail in the chapter Totapuri and Rudraka. Finally consciousness rose to the Ninth State, the Cessation of Mind which is Bhavagra meaning the Summit of Becoming, but more accurately meaning Mood or Feeling's Summit. The five senses, etc. and the five elements, pranas, wisdom deities have all been dissolved of their contact. Also of importance is that contact with the five aggregates of form, feeling, perception, will, and consciousness itself has now dissolved. At this level it is a dissolving of contact with the particle field of each element (earth, water, fire, air, space), their innate cosmic/quantum, atomic energy systems and so at this occurring there appears eight signs. Yet even through this, whatever comes to Presence is just fine as Dzogchen will be the same. In the process of the death ascent from consciousness contact with earth then proceeding upward the first sign is as a mirage. Then smoke as the next, fireflies or the like (particles), then the flame of a butter lamp with the air element (as the flame goes out, air contact is extinguished with the simultaneous entering into pure space (Akasha), then comes the white appearance or the white moonlight mind which is the isolated objective view. After this the red increase arises as the white appearance slides away. This red/orange sunlight is the increase of the awareness of subjective mind, but now mind is not looking outward or back at what it has already passed through, but its direction is turned and focused inward and subjectively at the Kung Zhi (Alaya-vijnana). Note, Zhi is different than Kung Zhi. When this subjective viewing drops away mind enters that Kung Zhi (universal ground) without any subjective feeling or apprehension and this is the stage of near attainment. It is so

164

near because here the Mother Light Pure Mind actually dawns now but even the concept of this dawning still retains a subjective feeling to it because we think this Pure Light is coming from above or outside or from somewhere else when all the while it is the True Self of our most intense Being and so it seems to be revealed by the death process or dropping away, sliding away or the very Trekchod of all that has obscured this non-objective and non-subjective experience.   When one becomes familiar with this the eight wonderments arise spontaneously in the sense of what the World either in the life view or the death view appears to be in context of the illustrations that all is like phantoms, a cloud land, an echo, the Moon's reflection in water, a mirage, illusion (the occurring or maya), bewitching enchantment or wizardry (and wonderment) and dreaming.   These were Sakyamuni's own eight poetic illustrations of this experience. With these eight Wonderments within this Pure Clear Awareness, the Four Thogal Confidences or Reassurances are produced naturally in consciousness. One: No fear of hell because you know it is a delusion or No fear of suffering because you Know You are What Pure Mind Is! Two: No expectation of results in karma because you know its all Samsara (and the twelve causes are busted). Three: No hope of attaining Nirvana because he who attains does not exist (as you can see from the dissolving of contact in that death process or Trekchod) and hope/expectation is a distraction as a sliding out of Dzogchen immediate awareness anyway. Four: No desire for joy, as one is equal to all, as all are Pure Mind. This means one finds one's Joy in spiritual desire fulfilled which is the Joy of Heightened Awareness. So, from this heightened awareness and filled with the Confidences if one were to go back into the birth descent as one was approaching the Sidpa Bardo descending through the Chonyid dropping down from Chikhai, the eight signs would appear in reverse order. Attainment, increase, appearance, flame, fire particles, smoke, mirage and then one is back in the dream state within a mother. The important thing is to keep in mind the Clear Light of the Real Mother so that when passing through the Chonyid the five primordial wisdom powers spring up around the "Ah" symbol just like in the Dzogchen

Dream Practice. This is said to direct consciousness either to a Spiritual or favorable Human dimension with the application of certain mantra bijas like Bam, Om, Ah, Hum and others. I recall a dream, "Bamkini or Ramkini, Which way to Go? My choice? Oh this upside down sex world! Why reenter the sex dimension of waking and dreaming duality?" Bamkini is a bija of favorable Vajrayogini rebirth in a spiritual world or a human land. Ramkini burns up like a cremation fire the entire storehouse of Alaya-vijnana (Kung Zhi) and so there is no reason or cause for rebirth. In truth both are the extremes of dualism and not flying free in the Garuda like Pure Mind. In the Dzogchen Dakini empowerment there is a stage between the Ramkini and Bamkini which is Tam (Kini) and this Ta is representative of Pure Being (Tat=That Reality or True Self). This is what remains when everything is burnt in the Alaya-vijnana. It is taken into the mouth and then ejected forth from the mouth (of the lama/deity image/visualization, but you must implicitly remember that you are empowered to be your own lama/deity and you are, by accepting the real meaning of Om in your own head, Ah in your own throat and Hum in your own heart, again and again, not just with Lama, but with Garuda and Dakini) to become the new being of the goddess, of Tara and of the Dakini. Here one realizes for their own Self the Sva Bhava of Maha Sukha!

In Pure Mind arise Samantha Bhadri and Bhadra, Vajrasattva and the Hollow Passageway of the Four Thogal Wisdom Unions. (See chapter: Dream States and the Bardo Mind). There is here no evaluation (conceptuality) in Pure Mind. Mirror-like is Pure Mind reflecting in the evaluating mind. From Pure Mind, equality (non-duality), the One comes forth. Pure Mind alone discerns the Real from the Unreal (the Many). Pure Mind alone is the Ever Accomplished. Pure Mind is Dharma Dhatu (The Eternal Stuff of jivas (dharmas). The symbol "Ah" is all this in One Sweep, getting to the bottom of it or even just catching it by the nose!

Divine Mother, You have Given the Tantra of Pure Mind. Assimilated Here and then the Exertion of Pure Mind Practice, designated in the higher traditions but transiting (crossing over) even these! You as One have become the Five Dakinis moving

166

as energies and thigles through the nerves. But even this will be gone when the Real Om is known, not the Agama description which is Vaitathya (imagination/covering), Advaita is the Meaning, when you have come to Alatasanti then Mother is Immediate!

Ah, now heaps and heaps and heaps of the Dharmakaya (Mother Utterly Simple), the Sambhogakaya (the five pure energies as the five rainbows around "Ah") and the Nirmanakaya (all and every surrounding which includes the five elements all within the Great Expanse) are offered up and sacrificed again and again and again. Until Gone (Gata)! The six bardos have dissolved contact in "Ah" as Chikhai is true mind, as Chonyid is true speech, as Sidpa is true body. As samadhi (realization) is real mind. As dream is real speech. As the birth bardo is a real body again. Ah, it is body, speech and mind, hit by the Dzogchen bolt of Om Ah Hum and Hum again! The passion of embracing rebirth is no longer a fear!

In Dzogchen what you get are the Three Kayas in One Experience, the Immediate Impact comes directly but it does seem to take time to develop. The six bardos are but the three states (waking, dreaming, deep sleep) forward and reverse, coming and going. Even in the Six Worlds there are the three states, so there is waking, dreaming and deep sleep even in heaven or hell, and any where else. These are all entered or left behind in my awakened Vajra Kaya on full alert to Trikaya!

Four Visions

Oh Mother, this worthless fool of Your's puts off the task of translating spiritual feelings into written thoughts! Must I continue? "Yes." So I shall just Soar Right On with it. The four Thogal stage/visions may be thought of in various ways. First Thogal: Direct Experience in the Unfabricated Primordial. Second Thogal: Increase of Sensation in the Unfabricated Primordial until this Feeling Sensation is more than the fabricated world. Third Thogal: Full Measure of Rigpa even as the Three Kaya expanse is Gone (Gata) in Rigpa. Fourth Thogal: All (Samsara) idea Exhausted (Alatasanti, the burning

167

firebrand of dualistic display thought is Quenched). Turiya is known as the only Experience, the three states exhausted!

One may compare these stages to first seeing the Moon, then watching its increase, then it is Full to its Measure but there is no analogy in this picture of the Fourth Stage unless you realize the Moon as completely disappearing. But with music one may find a better illustration. A Single Note of Dakini Self Awareness. Some Chords of Dakini Self Awareness. A Full Song of Dakini Self Awareness. And then Silence in the Self Awareness of Dakini.

Of course, these four Thogals are in the Four Kayas. First Point seen in Nirmanakaya. Second, the Sensations of Sambhogakaya. Third, Rigpa in the Dharmakaya to Full Measure. Fourth, Svabhavakaya is All and here all of the phenomena before is Exhausted in Sva Bhava (as Self Feeling). But Dakini (Maha Sukha Kaya) is further on and deeper on Within You!.

Dakini Eyes, Thigle, Awareness, Self

Now in terms of the Lamps (Dakini Lamps as I name them) where each Thogal is the infusion of Dakini Awareness within each Lamp. Briefly, for I shall give more detail latter, these Lamps are first, from the outside and moving then further and deeper within, comes Dakini Eyes, then Dakini Thigle, then Pure Dakini and then Dakini Self. So first comes the Dakini Thogal being Shown What Reality Is (To Discover) in the Eyes, Thigles, Pure Awareness and then Self Awareness. Second Dakini Thogal is Illusion Diminished and Sensations Increased through one's Dakini Eyes, within the Dakini Thigles, to Pure Awareness of Dakini, to Self Dakini. Third Dakini Thogal is Advaita Dakini to the Full Measure within Dakini Eyes, within Dakini Thigles, to Pure Dakini Awareness, and deep into the core of Dakini Self. Now the fourth Dakini Thogal is Exhausting all conceptual Momentum in Ultimate Luminous Dakini through the Dakini Eyes, the Dakini Thigle, the Pure Dakini Awareness, to final Dakini Self! In simple terms these are the sixteen Thogal combinations. Four Visions through Four Lamps.

To me the four Prakaranas (supreme causes) of Gaudapada's Karika (treatise) are actually the Four Thogals. Agama (scripture) Prakarana explains the Direct Experience of understanding the Meaning of AUM. Vaitathya Prakarana increases the Feeling/Sensation of this understanding by diminishing imaginative illusion (Vaitathya). Advaita Prakarana brings the Non-Dual meaning to Full Measure where nothing within the imagination can compare to the Advaita Experience. And then as the Fourth Thogal (Exhausting all conceptual visions), one has Alatasanti (Quenching the Firebrand) Prakarana. These four treatises make great sense with this. One cannot but see clearly that the Four States of Consciousness relate to the Lamps and the Thogals. Direct Experience in the Waking State. Increased Sensation in the Dream State. Coming to Full Measure in the Deep Sleep State where nothing in waking/dreaming can contain it, measure it or describe it. Gaudapada even describes this State as the place where everything is measured (refer back to Ceto Mukha under subtitle Prajna) And then the Fourth State is when all consciousness is quenched in the Pure Self Consciousness of Turiya. Again, with the Lamps one realizes the Waking State Eyes. The Thigles as Appearances like the Dream State. The Pure (emptiness luminosity) Awareness of Deep Sleep where there is no duality. To the Self Generated Lamp of Turiya.

You see this is the same old story as with the Seer and the Seen in Advaita Vedanta. The Lamp of the Eyes perceive or catch the world. The Lamp of the mind/dream catches or perceives the lamp of the eyes. The Lamp of Awareness catches or perceives the lamp of the mind/dream. And the Lamp of Pure Light (Consciousness or the Real Seer) catches and perceives the lamps of awareness, as well as the lamp of mind/dream, and the lamp of the eyes. A Lamp illuminates something still dual. Even the Witness (Sakshi or Kutastha) still acts as a Lamp illuminating something before it. This would correlate to the third lamp of Pure Awareness. In my essay The Lamp of the Turiya written a few years back, I wrote that this Turiya Lamp is the Light of Self Evident Consciousness and that is very true. But you see, even Turiya is Lamp-like only until the Exhausting

169

(Fourth Thogal or Alatasanti) of even the concept of a fourth conceptual stage. For we speak of What You Have Always Been and not what you become! You are not a stage. You are the State, you/one has been all along.

So in the same manner that the Lamps themselves are actually Extinguished/Exhausted/Quenched, so are the thigles. And it might be wise to say a few more things now about the nature of the thigle. As the Nitya and the Lila are only two aspects of the Same Reality as Ramakrishna says time and time again, so Trekchod and Thogal are a practiced Unity. It is this Unity that is the target we seek. So do not lose Self in the stirring of the thigle. It is a Thogal caution trap for that can lead to only more and more phenomenal rebirth experience in the drama of the relative Lila, Lila is but a dream without the Awareness of the Nitya and this is to say that Thogal is but a dream without the Awareness of Reality in Trekchod. For these Thigle are the same as Bindu and bindu is the same as Prajnata or seeds of what comes out of deep sleep, at this stage, or seeds of consciousness in terms of relative cognitive awareness of phenomena. And so you get those two states of Samadhi in regard to this idea. That is sam-prajnata samadhi or Pure Awareness combined and with those conceptual seeds of consciousness. And a-samprajnata samadhi or Pure Awareness only of Pure Awareness which is not with or is without these bindus, thigles or prajnatas of consciousness.

Perhaps I should mention the samadhi states of Patanjali at this point. Vitarka is samadhi on physical objects, persons, deities. Vichara is samadhi on subtle pre-atomic or quantum states of the five energy fields. These two samadhi states can be either "sa" or "nir," with or without contact. Sananda is samadhi on the super sensible state of the five senses where no physical vitarka or subtle vichara samadhi is applied. It is a free condition of the five pure senses merging into one consciousness. When this happens one gets asmita samadhi which is samadhi on the pure ego "I" without any contact to the phenomenal sensory world. It is very interesting, as ego, isolated from everything else, with the meditation (samadhi) that God or Pure Mind is there within this ego (asmita)! When this expands out of the individual into the Universal it is called Mahat (Cosmic/Universal Mind). Realizing this one has approached what Patanjali in his Yoga Sutras calls the Dharma Megha, the Truth Cloud, where the real nature of the jiva is known as Dharma, here meaning its Reality. (See subtitle Spontaneous Arrival, the tenth stage)

Thigle

These Thigles are Points of Appearance in changing mind, where you comprehend/feel the Un-Changing (Pure Mind). The Thigle is a Measure of Spiritual Knowledge. And as a Measure they only appear on this side of What Cannot be contained or measured (Pure Mind). One can have thigles of Bhakti (Love), Jnana (Knowledge), Karma (What To Do), Vijnana (Sahaja Pleasure), Immensity, Rainbow Thogal Light and who knows without knowing what limit there can be!

So the Amrita (Immortal Nectar) Thigle/Bindu (Drops/Points) are conceptual shapes of feeling/understanding that come out of the Formless Unfabricated Primordial Dakini. The Appearance in Awareness of these Amrita (Immortal Non-Dual Nectar) Drops seem to come forth or be born forth from the Eternal/Infinite Dakini, but this is only in the face of relative time/space for the Eternity as Infinite has no concept about itself, so the thigle appearance is only from this side. A thigle/idea of the Eternity of Unfabricated Dakini can only be a limited concept from this side of the mind. But when this idea/concept, from the most inwardly directed subjective sight, then turns around on itself it becomes the first primary most creative Prajnata/thigle out of which comes the Universe, a Big Bang Thigle if you like. From this original bindu/thigle comes Siva and Sakti or Kuntu Zang Po and Kuntu Zang Mo, and from these two original parents of all other thigles come the Kama-Kala Vilasa, the occurring display of the two efferent and afferent currents of birth and death, kama and kala, passion and time/death. This is the beginning of the cosmic Yantra that comes out of that original thigle/bindu as a one inch (or smaller) cosmic quantum drop to create and engulf the entire universe,

171

the three Kayas, the Five Wisdom Lights and all the rest. It is this original drop/point that becomes the red feminine and the white masculine energy quantums that split into making the human body (or any other). When they reunite that Non-Dual thigle is gained.

So we have the concept of an Immortal Drop, the Prajnata as original and then comes all the rest. We cannot limit the Immortal by concept/thigle or any idea. It is the Vast Expanse (Pure Mind or Dakini) and cannot be caught by conceptuality. A dakini thigle is just a small point of understanding the Formless Goddess. These thigle/bindu and even bijas (seed sounds) are but Particle Drops or Point Spots of Understanding/Feeling in Relative Context, since no one Knows Ma (Mother) all together! Yet the thigle idea is an expression of the Unmanifest and Unknowable! It is much the same as when Tibetans say that during life only the Offspring Light (Bu) may be experienced and not the Primary Clear Light (Ma). But this is a barrier of conceptuality and it is misleading for is not nirvikalpa samadhi indeed real death where not only all conceptuality is wiped out, but also all Sakti is pulled out of the body/mind connection. One is not fully dead, as to know Ma then, in that way, but there is the full experience of the Primary Clear Light without inner subjectivity, the seed/womb or Prajnata idea or any duality of red/white thigle and all the rest that follows. That conceptuality is wiped out! The offspring mind/light (Bu) is the most subtle ego idea projection in dual subjectivity encounter. This is wiped out in nirvikalpa which means, without conceptuality, and when there is no conceptuality, there is Ma, the Primary Mother Clear Light!

As mentioned a moment ago, the bijas, are seed forms of mantric power and they are to sound, in its four levels, what the bindu/thigle are to the drops/points of Comprehension in Knowledge (a knowable nucleus of Knowledge). These bijas are the Tantric sounds of the Dakini and they are your essence as: pre-atomic, pre-quantum, pre-samskaras (mind characteristics), pre-vasanas (unconscious desires/wishes/potentials), pre-white father drop/thigle, pre-red mother thigle/drop and before everything in your spiritual journey ever began and certainly all

172

that you have made of it now in your own force and way, before any of those stairway listings were mentioned (pre-this, pre-that). So we are always connected to the Dakini even as you lose oneness in the subjectifying of the Silence of Turiya, as it becomes lost in pre-ideation and that ideation becomes the thought to speak and then one speaks and makes sounds with the mouth and usually identifies with what is being said or with the saying of it by oneself or others and mis-identities are then set up in that moment and one slips off into the display of occurring before the mind! These are the four bhavas (mood affects) of sound. Dakini is still there but you are wrapped up with the something elsewhere in sound going toward the display or following the trail back to Silence.

Again in the Hindu yoga systems you find the Bindus which are the Thigles to Tibetans. So that Highest all encompassing originally first and primary appearance Thigle is Maha Bindu and that is Maha Karana the Supreme Cause of all the display. This Karana Bindu splits into the Karya Bindus (effect points) of the Sita (White) Bindu and the Sona (Red) Bindu. Interestingly the male/female energy display is the opposite to Tibetan imagery and visualization and that only shows that no system is absolute at all. Sita, the white drop is feminine and Sona the red drop is the masculine. And when the two are mixed together it called Misra bindu and this is where you get the human body. Going back to Maha Bindu you are again at Para the Supreme or very near to it. And this Maha (Para) Bindu is the source/seed of the sukshma and the sthula which are the subtle and the gross and related to the mixing of the Sita and Sona bindus.

So, where does it take us with what the thigle is? Traditional Tibetan ideas of the four increasing waves or stages of Thogal and the expanding thigle concepts are described with such classic descriptions as first appearance being a thigle one square inch, second about the size of a warrior's shield, third a size engulfing the village to the country, fourth the country to the world. These are filled with vast sky and mountain ranges characteristic of Tibet (with architecture, banners, designs, faces and deities that are Tibetan). But this high level of awareness in the appearances (thigles) is poetically described even as thigle within the pores of the skin where in immense buddha fields are seen, that is, as in tiny places as much as in large places. Infinite Vastness is only limited to one's sight/perception by a personal reference point which should go or be gone in Dzogchen Sight. Even to the point where one clearly sees there is no death and that death as we generally think about it never happens, only appearances (or thigles of awareness) change.

The Cosmological Extent To Thigle

We can expand into the Expansive this conceptual thigle. What the Universe really is like, is more than any creation story has ever given us! Cosmology and such, gives us physical evidence for and of Wonderment itself! If you think of the Vast Expanse as the ever expanding balloon or bubble of space/time then you have tied up and restricted your reference point to less than going into the Vast Expanse of Pure Mind. Even so the multitude of galaxies, each one themselves, are but single thigle in Mother's Immense Pure Mind. These galaxies are but point/drops (thigles) within another thigle, as our scientific concept of the big bang point and the bubble of space/time that comes out of that thigle. You see, that is just another and yet just one thigle in Mother's Pure Vast Expanse.

So it is such an immense thought. The Dakini's Blessing. To think of the known cosmos, or the known universe as being all there is, is a closed cycle of perception or a closed cyclic perspective. In the Vast Expanse of Pure Mind one may get out of the closed cyclic perspective and see with the imagination all that is within the big bang thigle concept of universe as just being one point drop in Mother's Pure Mind. Then one sees other point/drops of other big bangs in different stages of progress from the original point of bright luminous power to a stage like the thigle that we exist in, with beautiful innumerable galaxies spreading out in every direction weaving webs like fine white powder filled with red and blue around the inner rim of a Huge bowl, but you are looking at this from outside it now. Not with the old view of being within this concept of universe. You are making leaps and soaring past barriers of conceptual thigles.

174

Out in the Vast Expanse you see all that we think of as universe in space/time as really just a small thigle. There are other big bang thigle/bindus spreading out through the Vast Expanse and they are as innumerable as the galaxies within our own thigle concept of universe. But the Vast Expanse cannot be measured! Nothing can contain it for all concept is but thigle within it!

Every star is like a single thigle of energy, light and power! As hurricanes on the Earth viewed from space look so much like spiral galaxies, those cosmos' (as multiple big bangs) look similar in the patterns within the Vast Expanse. Yet all those cosmos' (or full universes in themselves) as many thigles, are still nothing to the size of Pure Mind Vast Expanse! Thinking in a confined singularity spiral within the big bang time/space is a trap catching the mind by the architect of the ego! Limitation is not elevation! A Single Drop of thought (thigle) from the Pure Dakini Mind becomes the Primary Prana Life/Light or the Dakini's first tummo heat/fire! This is before the cool places and the heat signatures on the original form of the tiny big bang point ever appear. Time nor space even do not exist yet. Latter the cool places on this primary thigle become the vast spaces between galaxies and between galactic superclusters while the heat signatures of this thigle latter becomes those same galaxies and intricate weavings of the webs of galactic super clusters. It is all within the original thigle point! Dakini is before all that! Dakini is Pre-Free particles. Pre-quantum energies. Pre-atomic formations before electrons, neutrons, or protons bind. Dakini is Pre-Proto galaxies in super cluster families or individual. She is Pre-Quasar. Pre-Galactic. Pre-Supercluster Webs. Pre-Star. Pre-Planet. Pre-Dna which now makes up your ego's body and brain! And that was there among the first heat signatures of Her tummo! Dakini, is Pre- the Moment Now! Dakini is Pre-Primordial! But all this is just one thigle of concept and is not the Vast Dakini Expanse!

The quasars viewed through the vast distance of space are also viewed through time and over the curve of space. We see them as the early swirling light/energy pools that latter became the centers of galaxies that we see now but when we look at galaxies or even just stars in our own Milky Way galaxy, what

175

we see through the distance of space is really what was in the past of time, for in the actual present we are only catching the light from years of traveling images that left long ago and the place from where it was sent is no longer the same as when it was sent. All we see are conceptual ghosts of light images of the past. Even the red and blue shift of stars and galaxies approaching our place in the galaxy or the universe (as blue) or moving away from us as red light (as most everything appears to be moving further away from our perceptual reference point) are but phantoms, mirages, cloud lands. All but conceptual thigles of appearance.

The theory of the big bang and bubble balloon universe ever expanding is obviously a thigle concept. The steady state theory of the universe is one of continuous prana flow, where matter and energy are constantly being made a new. The pulsating universe theory of a cosmos which comes out of the creation point (bindu/thigle) of the big bang and expands until it reaches its limit until gravity pulls it back to it original shape is very much a concept influenced by the outflow (bahir vaha) and inflow (antar vaha) of prana or breath energy. You see there are comprehending relations between the cosmological reality and the spiritual reality. The energy of knowledge has certain directional flows, conveyances, bearings and drawings through, into or towards. This is the meaning of vaha. So we see that the big bang concept is really inspired by the conveyance of a thigle singularity. The string theory where energy moves in string like patterns below the quantum levels is really a directional knowledge flow through the nadis or nerve webs. The quantum theory which is as coherent as the fine grain rivers of polished wood is a bearing through of energy knowledge from pure prana. The theory of the relativity spiral which is smooth as glass comes out of the knowledge conveyance flow which is drawing forth from pure Akasha (space/time). You see, Knowledge is Awakened spontaneously and then comes back through systems of drawing, flowing and conveyance (vaha) in such ways as the nadis, the pranas, the thigles and that is how it happens. The restriction of a referential point of perception between a macrocosmic wonder and a microcosmic astonishment is all that

176

holds mind from Vast Expansiveness. Let Go and Soar On!

A closed cycle of perception is the one limitation. I suppose that one can see not only what has been described but also thigle wherein past lives may be contained. And future lives also. Or what one was dreaming while within a mother's womb. Or the moment of one's death, the quality and time of Clear Light (Chikhai) experience/perception and what one will experience in the Chonyid and the next Sidpa all by the help of thigle. Modern psychiatric science believes that we learn the extent of emotional possibilities (what we are capable of feeling) or pattern potentials within the flow of the nervous system all by the age of two years. If that is so then Dzogchen seeks to extend the potential and possibilities not only of emotions, but of nerves, pranas and thigles. When I was contemplating the Wonder of the Dakini Mind in Vast Expansiveness as a seeing within my mind's eye this Great Space outside the big bang, and then other thigles of big bangs in the Vastness of the Dakini, I felt fear for a few moments. But it only reminded me of the Fearless Yoga, Ati or Asparsa which has no contact with any support thought of conceptuality (vikalpana). You are the Vast Expanse which is so Immense in the Great Infinite, you may be afraid for want of conceptual support, but there is no need for fear as you work this Non-Contact Yoga. Touching concepts causes fear when you look back to hold or grasp something for support. The upside down welter of lies (mis-conceptualities) is the anxiety, not our Unfabricated Pure Mind.

I am going into these thoughts about the cosmos for the sake of greater expansion of awareness in Thogal and Alatasanti. I think that the study of the speed and the distance (time and space) of light is not quite accurate about the age of creation (the universe), for then this big bang seems so limited. Astronomers/cosmologists even admit to the existence of objects so far back in time and distant in space that they cannot be seen. We have not seen the actual big bang itself, but only the evidence of its Presence in a ubiquitous background. If there was indeed an original big bang it could be further back and more ubiquitously distant than presumed. The general speculation is that the universe is 15 to 18 billion years old but now there are theories that double this age to 30 or 35 billion years. Will it double or triple again as observers see more and more. Still it does not approach Eternity. It is relative measurement not Eternity! The new look is still conceptuality though very wonderful. The factors of measuring keep changing or expanding as various constants of light moving through space/time. And no one agrees completely on one answer.

The quasars as the most distant objects visible and as the core of galaxies, are called the firstborn or the earliest lights of the big bang (thigle). I think they are dead galaxies, now ghosts, from the beginning, but they might not be from the beginning but simply the ends of something long before. So what is the theory of age with that thought? Looking back in time and through the distance of space at these aging or even dying galaxies or that these quasars are indeed infant galaxies from the beginning of time one must wonder. A quasar may be the entire mass of light in a galaxy being pulled into its core in a blackbody of gravitation (black hole) and that is an acceptable idea. Is that what we see through the distance and through time into the past? I do not see Space/Time as Vast Expanse as having an edge to it or as being contained within a big bang bubble (thigle)! I think there are innumerable big bang bubbles throughout the Vast Expanse and they are many in variety as much as no two stars are exactly alike and no two galaxies are exactly alike (similar but not exactly, even though the harmony of things as being similar in creation spreads through the display of the immensity).

You see, galaxies have halos fifteen times the size they are now which shows how large they were in their proto-galactic stage. Elliptical galaxies are filled with old red stars. Spiral and Barred Spiral galaxies are filled with young blue stars. What was believed by Hubble that ellipticals become spirals now seems quite the reverse. Spiral like galaxies with young stars seem to tighten up as they become ellipticals with old stars. (So, Irregular galaxies have yet to reach the Spiral Condition and are more the shapes of protogalaxies). As ellipticals become tighter and tighter around their central core, all the mass, energy and light becomes pulled in to create a brighter and brighter core. If we are looking at quasars at the edge of the Event Horizon of the

178

big bang it is likely that we are seeing galaxies that have lived their births, lives and deaths from long before. The Event Horizon is what we can see up to and then the border of the Event Horizon is what we cannot see. Most likely there is so much in the time and age of this big bang that is imperceptible to us now. Just as it is believed that only one percent of the mass, energy and light is visible to us in the form of quasars, what is falling into black hole event horizons and what is in them as amazingly dense material, as well as stars, planets, galaxies. There is so much Unknown! The postulate is that the rest of mass or matter is in the form of dark matter which is a misleading term because it is not out there hiding between galaxies in the great spaces betwixt them but is below the visible surface in the form of pre-quantum particles, an energy field below the surface of the seen, one percent, which is ninety-nine percent larger, greater and of potential power to do whatever it wishes in the universe or somewhere else. It is the same principle with visible light. What is seen is one percent. The full electromagnetic spectrum above and below that referential point is the ninety-nine percent which is unseen. Infrared, microwave, radio waves below the reference point. Ultraviolet, X rays, gamma, and cosmic rays above the reference point of optical perception. So much is Unknown, unseen and yet to be and yet ever here as the Pre-Primordial Pure Mind. Even as the idea of origin from a Singularity (big bang) is the same as Non-Duality, the Where and How of Our Beingness. We don't really need to travel to others places (and can't, in the sense of the inter-galactic) since the light from "other places" has traveled to us as images of the tremendous universe and many life forms are here on Earth already that express the diversity that so many crave to meet. It is astonishing to think where we are. "The same Perfect knowledge, again, makes him realize that the one Consciousness has become the universe." Ramakrishna.

With this Consciousness having become the universe in mind it is interesting when one considers that quasars may be the burning cores of dying and dead galaxies visible at the farthest edge of the universe (with some quasars spaced in places not quite that far away, maybe half that distance) and that dark matter is a yet to be manifest inexhaustible source of energy and matter, we come to reexamine the steady state theory of creation of the universe. Or to conjunctively reexamine it along side the big bang. Generally only half of the steady state theory is given as that the universe expands infinitely into infinity until all galaxies are so far apart from one another that they cannot see each other and eventually they all fall out of existence as dying embers. This is massively a long time from now, but if quasars are dying lights of galaxies, more like crones than like maidens, then we may be seeing this very thing at the farthest edge of the visible universe. Now the other half of the steady state theory is that the universe is itself an inexhaustible source of energy and matter and so new galaxies and all that is within them, though imperceptible to us now, may be in the making, as a universe that is constantly expanding toward amazingly infinite dimensions but is simultaneously and continuously creating new galaxies in a never ending eternal process! Even big bang cycles or pulsating universes which burst forth from a singularity, reach their peak and then collapse back into the singularity, would fall within this conceptual view. It is like a Fountain of Continuous Prana which makes more life than there is death. In some ways this is much less fearful than an eventually collapsing universe in a big crunch as they call it where time/space actually moves backward into the singularity. I see it like an immense Fountain, a huge column of water coming up from a well pool of inexhaustible energy and at the top is this flower like pouring out of galaxies, universes and big bangs that fall back into the inexhaustible dark matter only to continue once again in this extraordinary, breath taking and inebriating creation. The water of the fountain, like Prana, is inexhaustible life energy! Even space/time is created in a big bang which is unique to that big bang. All this is within the Vast Expanse which is more ample, spacious and extensive than energy which created space/time and its creation flow.

There is no center point of where the big bang happened for it happened everywhere and everywhere is the center point and this must be understood as that all space/time were within the condensed thigle or primordial fireball. There are about 33 stars

180

within a distance in every of direction of 13 light years from our perceptual center point of view. There are 170 stars within 30 light years of the same upon our far edge of the third spiral of the Milky Way. It takes 200 millions years for our Milky Way to turn or rotate once. Human like and human beings appeared in the last 2 to 1 million up 10,00 years ago up to now during the Pleistocene to the Recent Quaternary. That is only 1 to 2 percent of one galactic rotation. The creation of us is certainly a peak experience for us but in comparison to the immensity we are humble. In Dragon Sight I wrote, "To this Milky Way galaxy, this immense chakra wheel, existing within Mother's Mind, suspended in the Great Space, the Maha Akasha knowing no limits, dwelling upon the outskirts of this wondrous flower, we are but a moment in eternity, more than two hundred million years for her four arms to turn upon herself merely one single time while we humans appear in but a fraction of one turning on yourself. On the edge of the third arm, Mother, we are little toys in a moment of your pastimes, one rotation, one single day, in less than an hour of that day, in one sweeping movement, the grand fun of your amusement, Ramapithecus, Rama's ape, Neanderthals, the first humans, Cro-Magnons, our ancestors, but merely your next new toys, Homo Sapiens, the wise humans, and now, your newest toy, an Omega Prototype, a new emergence, a little fresh entertainment."

But what is strange to me and what seems like not enough is this. One rotation of the Milky Way is 200 million years. Five rotations is 1000 million or 1 Billion, If the known Universe is only 15 Billion years old that means the Milky Way has only rotated 75 times since the beginning of creation. (The stars and planets within the galaxy of course turn much faster and many more times in their past to present formations.) If you multiply that number of rotations for even an older universe of 30 billion years then you have 150 rotations of the Milky Way. Still it seems like not enough for a galaxy to form! Something so Huge and Wonderful forming by gravity's pull on cosmic dust clouds, light and energy to shape a galaxy in only 75 to 150 rotations?! Like a finger in Water making Illustrations!? This seems anomalistic!

Our conception of time and space is relative to the pull of gravity upon our stellar and planetary position. That is the idea of position in space is relative to conceptional focus when in reality everywhere is present everywhere or every place on the bubble is the same. Space is infinite and ubiquitous. Time is broken into past and future only by reference to planetary/stellar location in a galaxy and in reference to, or of one galaxy to another, or to many innumerable galaxies! We bring Eternity down to our little gravitational conceptions of Eternity. I know the Buddhists will now accuse me of being an eternalist, or one who believes everything is forever (or its opposite, a nihilist who believes nothing exists at all, two extremes), but I like the idea of eternity! And I know it is conceptual as an idea that exists within the Unfabricated Pre-Primordial, as is the idea of space as infinite. A cluster is a bunch, or a gathering of things of the same kind being held together. With this we are thinking of galaxies. These are galactic clusters. Like a bunch of grapes. There was at one time thought to be about 2,750 of these clusters. Now super clusters are gatherings together of a bunch of clusters. One cosmic map maker thought there were at one time about 50 superclusters with 11 or so clusters in each. This only accounts for 550 clusters. The figure should read that the entire universe as what is now visible to come to more like 247 to 250 superclusters! Each are thought to be about 250 million light years across (superclusters). But even this is elliptical, though round calculation, even in every direction. Still conceptuality, though beautiful. Except for those who love beauty and immensity innately, most people would not pay much attention to this kind of thinking if it could not lead to exploding an atom.

Ask Dakini

At the Dzogchen empowerment I asked Lama Sonam four questions. He answered every one of them in a sincere, humble and honest way and I appreciated that. He sat low on the floor and was not pretentious (putting to practice, Sakyamuni's 8th moral code, which is that a teacher monk should use no high seat/mat nor a throne), yet he was of an affirming nature and genuine to the core. "Will you tell us of Dakini and Thigle?" I asked and he said, "Why don't you explain." "Me? Why me?" "Dakini has to do with Emptiness. Thigle has to do with Appearance," his answer was simple and to the point. Latter he told me I asked questions he could not answer and said, "You ask the Dakini. You ask Her." This reminded me of when I asked Swami Aseshananda about becoming the Sugar (Infinite) or tasting the Sugar, and he answered, "Pray to the Divine Mother. She will Guide you." So, whether thigle appear or not, Mother is the Unchanging Present. Trekchod is cutting to this Dakini Emptiness and Thogal is coming back to the appearance with the Luminosity of the Dakini Emptiness (through the four thigle visions infusing the four lamps). It is seeing Emptiness/Luminosity (Mother) in all Appearance! The psychic essences (thigles) are nuclei/nucleus of Appearance(s) of the Reality (Mother Emptiness/Luminosity) in one's Rigpa. The 1st Point Drop of Appearance could be Trekchod itself. The 2nd is the Sensation of the Body (The Three Kayas of Body, Speech and Mind) becoming filled with that Appearance. The 3rd is the Full Measure of this Appearance which engulfs the entire Trikaya (the entire universe of Emanation, Splendor and Clear Actuality) in Total Rigpa. Rigpa as Vast Expanse is more than all the Trikaya universe. The 4th is even the idea/conception of Trikaya stuff (the measure of it as an other or dual or relation in size) is Exhausted! These four Thogal phases happen in the four lamps as four cognitive expansions happening in each lamp. The 1st lamp here I will call the Eyes of Garuda (same as Dakini Eyes). The 2nd lamp is Rigpa And Thigle where you have an inner conjunctive feeling/awareness of Clarity/Luminosity with Luminous Appearance. The 3rd lamp is Pure Shunyata as Emptiness Luminosity without any appearance or thigle arising. The 4th lamp here I will call Atma (Real Self) Sakti (Dakini Goddess Power) Jnana (Knowledge).

That you can sit here in the Milky Way and Get It, Feel It and Never Lose It is an amazing thought that makes life like a dream, like a wonder, like an experience of which you are free to return to or not, even as in the Face of Immensity, one life seems

183

so humble and small.   Remember, the Power that made this world/cosmos which you dwell within and are passing through and of which you are yourself made is ubiquitously everywhere! So nothing is insignificant!

If I must return from Mother Light, now or in the next life, Dakini give me the Spiritual Vigor of a Bear or a Dinosaur, so that I may find You again and do Your work!

Letting Go and Soaring On
With Gaudapada and Garab Dorje

Must I tell you that when I speak of the fourth Thogal of Dzogchen or the Alatasanti of Advaita I mean full coverage to the furthest stretch of the Universe (our Known Cosmos). To this extent I seek the Letting Go and the Soaring On.

A human body has a life and a death. A human's Being is Something Else! This all pervasive duality is the perplexing bewilderment from a body to a galaxy, from a galaxy to a cluster of galaxies and to a supercluster of galaxies, endless as they are while being pulled around the bowl of the cosmos by the unseen Great Attractor. So too our little humble lives. As it is still within phenomenal visions a disembodied consciousness may perhaps look down on the the thousand petaled lotus of consciousness, as it would be the same if you could project consciousness out of the known dimension of the cosmos looking down on the clusters of superclusters from above and it might look like a lotus blossom filled with the string filaments of galactic superclusters spreading forth in the indestructible light of Pure Mind! Now we should bring our Alatasanti awareness to that level at least.

Dakini Lamps

The First Lamp is called the water distancing capturing lamp of the eyes that lassos all. To the full extent of the cosmos in my view. Simply this is the Lamp of the Eyes or the Luminosity of the Eyes, or the Wisdom of the Eyes. Do not be confused when it is said that this Lamp has three phase/levels. The eyes which do the seeing itself. The cognition of the mind which catches what is seen. And the Rigpa awareness (or Openness/Emptiness) which catches from even deeper within what is seen by cognition and what is seen by the eyes. Those three, eyes, cognition and Rigpa function as the first lamp.

The Second Lamp is the Lamp of Thigle/Appearance. Or the Wisdom Lamp of Appearance or the Lamp of Luminous

185

Thigle. This is when conceptual points of understanding appear within Openness/Emptiness itself. The third lamp gives a better understanding of the second.

The Third Lamp is Pure Openness/Emptiness as it is Open and empty of any thigle or conceptual states. Or the Luminosity of Openness or the Wisdom of Pure Openness.

The Fourth Lamp is Self Generated Self Wisdom Luminosity which is neither emptiness (openness) nor appearance. I hope these simple explanations will clarify what is often presented as quite difficult to grasp.

Let me attempt simplicity again. 1st Lamp is Perception (seeing, hearing, etc. and if eyes are handicapped then why not catch or lasso by the ear?). 2nd Lamp is mind with or in Appearance. 3rd Lamp is pure buddhi (intellect) absolutely empty/open/void of conceptual obstructions which catch the mind into looking at what is not Pure or Immediate Awareness. The just Awareness state. The 4th Lamp is then Pure Consciousness. These Lamps do not go through the conveyance paths of memory or ego! The Lamps themselves are the four Thogal stages or if you prefer, the Lamps are how Thogal is carried through. Very simple. They are what is infused with the Awareness of Thogal.

I make it simple for myself by naming the Lamps to my own taste. Dakini Eyes. Dakini Thigle. Dakini Rigpa or Pure Dakini. And Dakini Self. The first relates to the Waking State (A). The second relates to the Dream State (U), of which even the Sambhoga and Nirmanakaya are but a thigle (bindu) compared to the third which is Pure Dakini (or Rigpa/Dharmakaya) beyond any measuring or containment and signified by (M). The fourth is that you begin and end as Self and all other Lamps are but within Self. Where you begin as Base/Foundation is where you end as Result/Fruit and the apparent path between are the Lamps. Each step as it appears is but the Dakini. Dakini Base. Dakini Path. Dakini Fruit. AUM (OM) is the symbol.

The water distance capturing Eyes of the Dakini that lasso or catch everything is like being or seeing while submerged in an ocean. All surroundings are Dakini. Dakini Thigle is a condition of mind/dream stirring. Pure Dakini is a non-stirring of mind/dream. Dakini Self is where all seeking, searching or practice has ended.

The Dakini Lamps and the Dakini Thogals or Light Infusions of the Lamps are not understood by diagrammatic thinking, but it may help. These lamps are your very stuff. It is what makes up your finer being. The First Thogal is Direct Dakini Experience and this relates to the Agama understanding or introduction to the meaning of Aum. The embodiment of Reality. The Second Thogal is is the Increased Sensation of the Dakini by diminishing the weight of Vaitathya (Illusion consisting of all that is in sleep, dream or waking). The Third Thogal is that there is no containing measurement of Pure Dakini, nothing phenomenal can describe Her in this state. This is Advaita. The Fourth Thogal is Everything Exhausted, all dual illusion, that is ending where you began which is with the Dakini Self. This is Alatasanti or Quenching the Firebrand of the dual dream/mind which make things appear other than or outside the Self.

Eyes, White Silk Nerve, Heart

Before we continue let us clarify the meanings of the Eyes, the White Silk Nerve and the Heart. For if we do not then some bit of confusion may arise when they are spoken about in regard to latter Thogal thoughts. The Upanishads speak of the one hundred nerve spokes around the Heart wheel (chakra) with the one sushumna coming up out of the heart center and rising all the way up and out of the head center (thousand petaled lotus or sahasrara) to Liberation. This is not the White Silk Nerve. Ramana Maharshi spoke of a nerve of awareness that went from the heart to the thousand petaled head center, but this is not the White Silk Nerve as it is internally focused within. Ramakrishna spoke of the "nerve of memory" which is most likely the sushumna (central nerve) as we now know that the cerebral spinal fluid (CSF) that holds our memories and the dreams we turn over during sleep, that are not up in the brain neurons themselves, are stored in the CSF. This is not the White

187

Silk Dzogchen Nerve which runs directly from the Heart then up to the Eyes, as it separates going to each eye. You see this is Open and outward focused not inwardly turned and that is important to remember about Dzogchen.

Now, in the Tantra they speak of the Jnana Vaha Nadis. Jnana is Pure Knowledge. Vaha is conveyance either moving inward or moving outward as in drawing toward or pulling out. These nadis or subtle spiritual nerves, come forth from the Ajna chakra in the midpoint of the forehead. Ajna (which is deeply related to prajna/deep sleep) is the Wisdom Command or What Directs (as True Prajna). The three main nadi/nerves that rise out from the Ajna are the Mano vaha nadi, the Svapna vaha nadi and the Prana vaha nadi. Mano pertains to the waking mind. Svapna is the dream mind. And Prana vaha is the wisdom that directs or commands the flow of vital life essence/energy. These are not the White Silk Nerve, but they are especially interesting, as in the ordinary sense, they do what has been described, but after the increase of spiritual awareness they begin to convey (vaha) a new sense to life, well being and so forth, how the mind works, the quality of dreams and the flow of spiritual energy. In a dream I was given a thought, this White Silk Nerve is Saham Kini Nadi, that is the Direct Dakini Nerve to the Pure Awareness of the Dakini as Saham (I Am She), Sa is She and aham is the sense or feeling of "I". As this feeling of Saham rises forth first from the Heart, indeed, all our feelings of who we are starts here and is given birth first here from the place of the Heart and this is what Bhava (Mood/Feeling) is. It is where illusions are born and reality apparently dies and in the favor of the turnaround, it is where illusions die and reality is born (as an apparent phenomena)!

Understanding can be gained looking at Gaudapada I.2. "Visva (Waking State) is the cognizer through the right eye; Taijasa (Dream State) is the cognizer through the mind within; Prajna (Deep Sleep) is the Akasa in the Heart. Therefore the one Atman is perceived threefold in the same body." The idea is the same as in the Dzogchen: Eyes, White Silk Nerve and Heart, except the dream mind within is substituted for the white silk nerve. But great light will be shed when we look into the

188

meaning of the Dzogchen Dream types which are also indications of Death types or the quality of Dying. For as we dream so do we die or it is that our awareness of what dream states are in fact gives us the awareness of what is death.

Eyes, White Nerve and Heart are the practical and usable methods of Open and Immediate Dzogchen Awareness and it is this Open Awareness which is both the Base (zhi) and the Result (brasbu). It is also the path. It is a conveyance from both directions; from the eyes to the heart and from the heart, to and then out the eyes. The Heart Lamp in Tibetan is tsitta which is a variation of chitta which is Sanskrit for Consciousness and it is in the Heart that Consciousness really identifies. So you see, what comes in from the eyes, becomes sense to the heart and what goes out from the heart spreads forth from the eyes. The Heart is Pure Love, it is Pure Mind in this immediate Dzogchen state. What travels or draws as conveyance through the white silk nerve? If we follow Gaudapada the answer is dream. And if we look at Dzogchen there are three kinds of dreams (and deaths). What one sees through the eyes is taken in as information in the dream and that produces an emotion. Second, what is seen with the eyes is taken in as cognition in dream but there is an instant let go of that dream material. And third, there is no seeing or what is seen is all light and so no information cognition comes in except for it being preemptively recognized in Pure Awareness. Whether the light is objective as in the first dream stage or whether the light is subjective as in the second dream stage it is all just accepted as Energy/Light in the third stage and so has no other hidden meaning to self but for That! From the Eyes, through the White Nerve and then in the Heart you discover what it is that you are seeing.

Dzogchen is the Wonder Study of Your Own Completeness, once you begin to comprehend. To those of sharp acumen they may here relate the three Conveyances (which are different from the three Series: Semde, Londe, Mangagde; the Conveyances are more related to the Spiritual reflex in the three Kaya dimensions) to the three Dream types. Consciousness in sound, words, music, wherein one finds or looks to find meaning. Then the subtle dream reflex of one's own Vast Expanse. And then Non-

Dual Pure Mind. It seems there is a relation to these and particular dream types in that in the first stage, one feels they should find meaning in dreams. Then one realizes that Light (Self) is the only meaning in dream. And finally whatever comes to presence in dream is seen and known only as this Light. We shall speak more on this as we go deeper into the Thogal.

Illuminating The Lamps

Now in regard to the Lamps there are different systems which give different numbers and sequence layouts. In regard to these lamps, as a place to begin, there is the sushumna and the two nerves around it that are described. Really the sushumna is two layered. On the outside is Vajrini with some Goddess form and inside is Chitrini which is Pure Goddess Consciousness. This is called the sushumna and she runs from the the spinal base up out the top of the head. (So necessary to Pho Wa.) Intertwining around her in a dual dance going upward are the efferent and afferent nerves which when gathered together as energy currents in immediate awareness then produce a very pleasant feeling. These are actually preliminary yoga and may possibly not be strictly Dzogchen, but they are part of the layout. Again we come to the three: Eyes, White Silk Nerve and Heart. After that as part of the Eyes, there is the distance capturing water lamp of the eyes which catch and lasso all. Again this lamp has the three layers to it. Eyes, Cognition and Rigpa. Its feature characteristic is Luminosity. Now in regard to a varying system layout one comes to the Ecstatic Pure Rigpa Lamp as the second whose feature characteristic is the spontaneous awareness of the non-duality of the three Kayas: Dharma, Sambhoga and Nirmanakaya. Then there is the Singular Thigle/Pure Openness Lamp as the third whose feature characteristic is Primordial Wisdom. Fourth is the Self Generated and Self Kindled Lamp of Original Highest Acumen/Insight and Appreciation/Gratitude for this, whose feature characteristic is Never Lost Clarity of Pure Mind (meaning it has always been with you). Added to these is the

190

Bardo Lamp and the Brasbu Lamp. The Bardo Lamp is the Transitional Between Lamp, what lights the way there, not only between the six common bardos but also between the sixteen spreading out stages of Thogal, as the lamps and the visions in leveled out combinations, all of which are Illuminated by the Mother towards the son/offspring mind which is the first and final bardo, that sense of duality between the Mother Light and the offspring mind. The final leap back into this Non-Duality or the exhaustion of the offspring mind as the fourth Thogal, is the ever present never lost Brasbu Lamp itself which is the Lamp of Climax, Result or Fruit. Varying on how you count all these lamps (including the three yoga nerves) you may come up with four, six, nine, twelve or more lamps.

In Bonpo Dzogchen the Lamp sequence is Eyes, Thigle, Awareness and Self Wisdom. The Tibetan Buddhist Dzogchen gives Eyes, Awareness, Thigle and Self Wisdom. It seems the inner two are reversible in cognition or are so closely related they cannot be clearly distinguished. But in an entirely different system, that of Garab Dorje's the order of the Lamps is first Pure Awareness, then Heart, the White Silk Nerve, the Eyes that Catch or Lasso, the Thigle Lamp, and last, Self Wisdom. A total of six lamps in sequence. At any rate, however you look at it the Self Kindled Wisdom Lamp of Pure Mind is getting it All in One Sweep from the Peak Towering Over and Independent of Anything and Everything, as Irrepressible Light.

These Lamps, it seems, are not the usual Tantric chakras but appear to be deeper systems of Self. Though they may relate exactly to the Ajna Chakra, Manas Chakra, Soma Chakra and Nirvana Sakti in the Tantric system. Anyway it seems that the Eyes, the White Silk Nerve and the Heart are in a sense the three outer lamps (three inner lamps: Thigle, Awareness, Self Wisdom) which are essentially connected within the First Lamp of the Eyes. The Eyes catch the Distant Luminosity. The Luminous White Silk Nerve I feel is Vajrasattva's Secret Hollow Passageway through the Bardo. And the Heart is the Consciousness that comprehends. This is discussed further in Dream States and the Bardo Mind.

The Base or Foundation (Zhi) Lamp is added in some

systems. And the Path (Lam or Bardo) Lamp is also added which results in the Brasbu (Climax/Result) Lamp which is the same as the Self Wisdom Lamp, both being when the bardo of separation is crossed and the offspring mind meets Mother in the Fullness of the four Thogal stage/visions and to this, the fourth Thogal really has no end to it. Whereas, the Bardo Lamp, through the four increasing Thogals (even as four deaths, one dying away as another is brought forth with more and greater awareness) through the Four Lamps is a Transitional Between Lamp up to this Fullness without end! And that is Self Kindled Self Wisdom which is appropriating an Innerstanding in Pre-Subjective and Pre-Primordial Pure Mind.

Dakini Lights

Again, as the Dakini Lights each of the four Lamps through the four Thogals (Immediacy. Sensation. Full Scope. End Result.) it constitutes four lamps with four visions running through each and so making sixteen stages of illumination from the Pure Mind View. These are themselves sixteen bardos which could be said to constitute one bardo of before realization or the bardo of non-realization, as until the sixteenth phases, one has yet to reach the stage of no more bardos or transitions between. Again these sixteen inner spiritual bardos differ from the common six bardos of the ordinary life/death cycle.

Simply, the Four Lamps are nothing but Receptors of Vijnana which is that special Knowledge (jnana) that sees or brings back the awareness/knowledge of the Eternal (Nitya) to the Lila (the Relative) and so it is bringing back Sakti through these Thogals into the Relative as the four receptor/lamps hold with or light up with this Pure Awareness. The Advaitic text, the Pancadasi gives its clue to the Lamps in even far different terms while speaking of Five Lamps: Lamp of the Picture. Lamp of Unending Satisfaction. Lamp of the Witness Consciousness. Lamp of Mediation. Lamp of the Theater.

Pure Mind is Turiya Amanibhava (the Nitya) and it is only from here that the Thogals may be achieved without effort as Trekchod has been asserted. Really, in accordance to Garab

192

Dorje, Trekchod is Total Assertion and Thogal is Flying On in Total Confidence. It is the Dzogchen wish that you may acquire or get Trekchod and Thogal as a Unity as easily as a child gets up in its Mother's Lap. This was Ramakrishna's attitude of being a child in the Mother's Lap and everything was acquired by him in this attitude. This Unity is symbolized when the crystal (Trekchod) and the peacock's plume (Thogal) are brought together. It is the same Unity as Tara in the Void and Tara in Appearance. And the symbol tool of the Vajra which brings the infinite void and the infinite manifest into the Unity at the center of the Vajra. Dzogchen happens here!

So, Trekchod is Total Decision (with Garab Dorje), the Barrier Free, Exploding Solidity, Letting Go, Cutting Through, No Contact (or Dissolving Contact) with the madness of endless thought processes leading out to the display of phenomena. Trekchod Cuts Away Instantly or Immediately Lets Go of thought itself into Pure Awareness, Self Kindled and Self Generated, to return to thought configurations (or emotional configurations) is to come back and try to empty the ocean drop by drop with a blade of grass or even with a bucket, it will take you so long you might give up or go mad. Thogal is Continuing On in Total Confidence (with Garab Dorje) and this means Spontaneous Arrival, Spontaneous Perfection (Great Completeness which equals Dzogchen), the Final Leap according to Guenther, Soaring On according to Lama Sonam. And the Crucial Charges or Crucial Infusions (of Light into the system) as it is. Total Thogal is equal to Gaudapada's Tayi which means All-Light. And of course, we will approach this latter.

Spontaneous Arrivals

Now we will enter the Thogal of the Six Points of Spontaneous Accomplishment or as they are also called the Six Crucial Charges in the sense of command directives but also as in being infused, fired up or charged up. Briefly, they are the arrival of: Body, Speech, Mind, the Eyes, the Breath and the Ground/Sky to this Dzogchen Trekchod/Thogal Unity. The title to my book Measuring Sky Without Ground was conceived while contemplating these.

I will give two descriptions of the Spontaneous Charges. The first one will be more simple than the second. To me these are really Vijnana Methods or Vijnana Practices. In regard to Body there are three gestures relating to actualizing by imitation, the three Kayas. The highest Dharmakaya body posture is that of a sitting loin. The intermediate Sambhogakaya body gesture is that of an elephant lying down (no effort). The last is the gesture or posture of Nirmanakaya, which is that of the seer/sage or the awakened being (perhaps sitting like Garab Dorje with the right leg tucked up and the left leg down, right hand in front of the heart and left hand open palmed on the left knee, the head tilted slightly to the left with an expression of astonishment on the face). Now in regard to Speech, all speech becomes silent even as the speech of innermost thoughts. Mind becomes Pure Mind as if the entire deep field cosmological map of the universe were but mind itself which is nothing in comparison to any possible imagination of what Pure Vast Space is. Then there are the three gazes of the Eyes (sometimes called the rising door of the Eyes) which again like the body gestures, relate as a spontaneous awareness of the three Kayas. Looking upward are the eyes in Dharmakaya. Looking straight forward are the eyes in Sambhogakaya. Looking downward are the eyes in Nirmanakaya. Next comes the arrival of Breath. The body is just dust without breath. Breathing is Open. The inner, and outer, and the inner space of breathing or holding the breath, arrives at the Dzogchen of Infinite Breathing where in there is no longer finite in or out! All conveyance is hushed in the Unceasing Energy of one's own breath. Last is the Rising Door of the Sky/Ground which is just what it sounds like. The sky/ground duality is devoured up in the Pure Non-Dual Sky which is actually the great natural and living symbol of Pure Mind!

Now we should approach the more extensive imparting of Thogal's beautiful Arrivals at Total Confidence (Soaring On without ending)! Pure Mind is again nothing but that Amanibhava gotten in Trekchod. When it rushes back as Thogal

194

there are the Arrivals of Vijnana into the system expressed as the following: Three Waiting Gestures. Three Immobilities or Stabilities (which I would call the Three Groundings or the Eyes, the Breath and the Sky/Ground). Three Death Obtainments. Three Dream Types (which are signs of what Death obtainments have arrived). Then Body arrives, Speech arrives, and Mind arrives, each through the four Thogal phases (again, in truth, Body is Nirmanakaya, Speech is Sambhogakaya, and Mind is Dharmakaya). With all this comes the Four Confidences. In Thogal all this arrives without effort in a spontaneous fashion to appear in the display of appearing as one's New Field Experience. Furthermore comes the ten awakened levels and the eleventh, twelfth and thirteenth, which are Dakini Given! With this the four Thogals through the four Lamps arrive fully accomplished as the Sixteen Phases all at Once in the Pure Suddenness of Dzogchen! The seven behaviors happen without effort as Signs of Thogal. Then one can truly say that whatever happens is just fine and that whatever comes up to arise or comes to presence is the Resultant Supreme Teacher (of one's Self as one's Self in Immediate Dzogchen Self Presence or What Has Always Been So). Here the Trikaya Absolute arises in Sva Bhava Kaya and this is Where Maha Sukha comes to us as Great Dakini Bliss, while everything else is left by the wayside. All Thogal is Lila!

Now to explain each of these signs of Thogal in detail, for the sake of immediate comprehension.

The Three Waiting Gestures: Waiting for the illusory waking state body and dream state body to dissipate into Pure Mind. Waiting for the welter of misconceptions in regard to everything in the upside down world to dry up and return to Rigpa (Pure Mind) or waiting for Samsara, Maya or Lila, which appears ordinary but is actually super extraordinary, to return to Pure Mind. Waiting for Pure Mind to engulf all that does not see Pure Mind.

The Three Immobilities, Stabilities or Groundings: The Eyes perceive only Luminous Luminosity, seeing everything within this. The Breath is no longer in finite entrapment but flows Infinite. The Sky/Ground duality ceases in the Non-Dual.

The Three Death Obtainments (Types) or Three Styles of Liberation or Three Death Awareness States. Pure Mind Directly. Pure Mind during the intermediate bardo. Pure Mind later accomplished after spontaneous parentless birth in a pure emanation realm (a heaven).

These of course are intimately related to the Three Dream Types or Three Dreamers. Remember dreaming is a dream and death is a dream and the one who dies is a dream or a dreamer of dreams, so death only appears to occur as a dream. 1st and highest; Liberated from dream states or after death states as they are Known to be nothing but Pure Mind. 2nd or intermediate; Recognizes or Liberates (self in Letting Go) immediately during dream (or in the after death state) into Pure Mind. 3rd or last; Once dreaming (or in after death), eventually recognizes dreams (or that one is dreaming) by Pure Mind. Or putting it in other words: 3rd; By Self Light you see, you recognize you are either waking or dreaming (or both). 2nd; You see Self Light is all that is being said, conveyed or experienced in waking or dreaming. 1st; So waking/dreaming have no more interest/learning or meaning to you since it is All Self Light. In Death Awareness: 3rd; You see death around you or happening to you and look for its meaning. 2nd; You see that Self Light is all that is said or conveyed or experienced in death. 1st; You realize there is actually no death ever happening as it is all Self Light (Pure Mind) and only the dreamer is appearing to go somewhere (phenomenally, remember the Waiting Gestures). See last subtitle Tayi, (All Light) to understand the depth of this.

Furthermore, Body goes through the four Thogals. One, the Body does not engage in extra activities being at peace and not craving just to do something else. A turtle in a metal bowl. Two, Body is like one stricken by illness not giving off pride nor being ashamed. Three, Body is like an elephant that can pull itself out of the mud of internally imagined materiality or external concrete materiality. Four, Body is like a bird that has flown free from the cage of material feeling altogether.

The four Thogals through Speech are: One, like a mute's talk is silent, one no longer is just pouring forth verbiage. Two, all one's talk is like that of a madman for you are no longer

196

speaking in context of the world's mis-identity. Three, one's speech becomes like the music of a goddess filled with countless messages. Four, speech is like an echo, others may gain some meaning from it, while from your standpoint there is nothing to talk about or explain and no one is even talking or explaining or listening. All is an echo in the Luminous Void!

The four Thogals through Mind are: One, mind is like a bird in a cage, it is caught and cannot go off into thinking in terms of dualistic spinnings. Two, like the mind of one who is drugged, thought does not pass away or out from radiant non-dual pleasure/light into the display of mistaken dualistic identity. Three, the mind is like one cured of the plague, it no longer has anxiety or worry and never falls prey to false identity in conceptualizations. All that comes to presence in mind is pre-subjectively known as Radiance/Light. Four, mind is like one struck in the heart by an arrow. It suddenly dies and never comes back again with any dualistic notion within the Vast Expanse of Pure Mind. All is quenched. All is exhausted.

These four Thogals through Body, Speech and Mind are methods as well as signs of Actualizing the Dharmakaya, Sambhogakaya and Nirmanakaya as Soaring On with Confidence in the Radiant Pleasure Light of Pure Mind.

As one embraces the Encounter in the Unity of Trekchod and Thogal the ten spiritual levels arise spontaneously with the eleventh, twelfth and thirteenth coming up, as one at last encounters and embraces the Dakini. These are all the stabilizing of Pure Awareness in degrees. First is the Joyful One. Second is the Flawless One. Third is Unlocking Light. Fourth is Emitting Light. Fifth is Difficult to Practice. Sixth is Coming into the Open. Seventh is Going Far. Eight is No More Shaking. Ninth is Clear Thinking. Tenth is the Cloud of Real Meaning (Dharma Megha). These poetic descriptions of states should speak for themselves as to the increasing depth they indicate. But after Dakini Awareness arises forth one comes to Radiance All Over (11th), the Never Touched Lotus (12th) and the Pure Mind Holder (13th). One sees nothing but the Light of Dakini all over, which has never been touched by duality and that She is the Holder of Pure Mind.

These progressive depth states are also summarized as the Ways of Preparation, Linking, Seeing, Creative Imagination and the Full Scope or Getting to the Bottom of all Learning (if one can so say that one has learned all that can be learned, for what it means is more to the point of being completely familiar with Pure Mind).

Sixteen Illuminations

Now let me proceed gently with the description of the Sixteen Phases all At Once. A High Awareness of the Totality of Experience. The four Thogals through the four Lamps are here the four Stages of Consciousness: Waking, Dreaming, Deep Sleep and Turiya. It is to be considered as four Leaping Through(s), each of the four stages of Consciousness, but we will also consider the four Leaping Through(s) in regard to each single stage of Consciousness. So we will get sixteen inter-spiritual levels or bardo transitional states.

In regard to the Waking State, the four Thogals proceed as 1: Waking Thought Thick with Woven Waking State Thought. 2: Waking Thought Inter-Woven with more Refined Dream State Thought. 3: Waking Thought with Unwoven Deep Sleep Thought. 4: Waking State Thought has become Supremely Unwoven. So here you have four Thogals of Immediacy, Sensation, Scope and End in regard to Soaring Through the Thick Cloud of the Waking Core Experience and this could be also thought of as just the first Thogal. Immediate Direct Experience Encountered in the Waking State.

In regard to the Dream State, the four Soaring On states proceed as 1: Dream Thought interwoven with the Thick weave of the Waking State Thought. 2: Dream Thought interwoven with Refined Dream Thought. 3: Dream Thought becoming Unwoven Deep Sleep Thought. 4: Dream Thought gone, in Supremely Unwoven. Again this is the four Thogals through the Dream State. Or Soaring On Through the Thin Cloud of the Dream State in the second stage of Thogal, or Increasing Sensation, as there is then a Diminishing of the Dream Cloud, the Sensation of Pure Mind Increases.

In regard to the Deep Sleep State, the four Thogals run like this, 1: Deep Sleep Thought becoming Thick with Woven Waking State Thought. 2: Deep Sleep Thought becoming Interwoven with Dream State Thought. 3: Deep Sleep Thought Unwoven in its own Unwoven Thought. 4: Deep Sleep Thought gone, passed over to or soaring through to Supremely Unwoven. These four Thogals are Soaring Through the Thinnest Cloud of the Deep Sleep State Thought. Or simply the third Thogal of Going past anything that can be measured or contain. It is interesting too, that Gaudapada gives the Deep Sleep State as that of What Measures (See subtitle: Prajna) for here everything goes into the Non-Dual and so cannot be measured for it is then a Singularity which has no comparison. But even saying it cannot be measured infers what could be measured and so there is still dualistic conceptuality. One has reached the Full Scope but has yet to get to the bottom of Reality. Yet looking back from Deep Sleep one can see that nothing in the Waking or Dream States can contain the Immensity of this Singularity. So the third Thogal does apply to this stage of Awareness, that is, nothing can contain or measure what you have just experienced in the Non-Dual!

Finally one comes the the Fourth (Turiya) which is the Atma or Genuine Truth in Self. The four Thogals are easily seen as being just what they truly are in regard to this Fourth State Consciousness or Reality in Pure Mind. 1: Atma has exhausted/quenched all Waking State Thought (Immediacy). 2: Atma has Exhausted/Quenched all Dream State Thought (Increased Sensation). 3: Atma has Exhausted/Quenched all Deep Sleep Thought (No Measurement to its Scope) And finally at last 4: Atma has Exhausted/Quenched Atma, which is Alatasanti or Quenching the Firebrand which is no less the fourth Thogal of Exhausting all dualistic imagination in regard to an Atma or the Atma, the sense of it being outside oneself is exhausted. This is Soaring On Through the Cloudless (the Atma) as Self is all that has no cloud of conceptuality about it in its Just As It Is phase.

That Mind Pure Mind

What appeared as mind in regard to the bardo transitions of all the proceeding stages are no longer regarded as between or separation states. The mind never was not and has really become what Ramakrishna says, "that mind Pure Mind." Now all Bardo (between or separation states) has been crossed. The Climax or Result Lamp/Light of Mother Light shines. The offspring is gone, no more, no more going out into the display of bardo transitions occurring. The signs of this Awareness has seven, or more behaviors, of those who have broken through social and spiritual concepts. One: Like a bee who goes only for the honey of Dzogchen. Two: Like a bird settled in the nest who has done away with flying out to the display of conceptuality. Three: Like a wounded deer who goes for a place beyond (either within or a location) the upside down world. Four: Like a mute who does not talk with wasting words. Five: Like a madman who sees all as the same: friends, enemies, blessings, obstacles. Six: Like a dog befriending any person who comes along without distinction. Seven: Like a lion afraid of none, this one Lets Go and Soars On past all hope or fear, which are indications that the Four Confidences have set in. These are no fear, no hope, no expectation and equal heart to one and all as the One and The All! The person who has these behaviors and confidences can die without fear not hoping for heaven, nor fearing hell, having no expectation, resting in Pure Mind, their heart at One in the Heart of All. Like a dog or a wounded deer they may die in their own dignity wandering off to be alone for that event-less never really occurring event. Or like a lion through the gate of death, Fearless, Letting Go of the upside down world and Soaring On as the Infinite!

Now one can say that Whatever Happens is Just Fine and that Whatever Comes in the Arising, the Occurring, whether display or Pure Mind, is nothing but Pure Dakini. The threefold separation of the three Kayas is busted and Self Mood Arises Alone as the Great Bliss of the Dakini! This is when all the Thogal stages themselves have been fully Quenched! You have now Exhausted all Bardo imagination and Rest in Pure Mind!

This is the Unity of Trekchod and Thogal! Dakini Given!

So if we are at the Height of Height we find Pure Mind free of all conceptuality. This appears to be the Mother Light from the first start of conceptuality, and yet then dropping further and farther into conceptuality as this becomes the Offspring mind/consciousness. We are flying and spreading out now. But remember no matter what the Pre-Primordial Pure Mind is ever present, and here, as mind thought, the Awareness of this (Rigpa) appears to come or to go. This is all a Singularity of Unity as the Base, the Path, the Result, for where you start, or go upon or end up is Here in the Mother Light. Its Essence is Sva Bhava. Its Nature is Prakriti. It Non-Dual Energy is Karunam. There is no Bardo of separation or between-ness at any time, nor to this Pure Mind any Climax or Result in Awareness as it is always Aware. The Four Lamps to This Mother Light (or Pure Mind) are ever shining and illuminating the way. As Self Kindled Pre-Primordial Wisdom Awareness. As the Openness of the Vast Expanse. As the Intensity of Ecstatic Awareness in Appearances. And as What the Eyes Catch as a Distance Outshining (toward the inside or the outside). Trekchod and Thogal Come at the Same Time. This is the Total Meaning of the Nying Thigle as the offspring consciousness, which is the original thigle, is engulfed in the great Openness of the Vast Expanse of the Self Kindled Mother Light. Here duality has Gone.

Bindu Thigle

The bindu/thigle package essence is a disclosing or uncovering of what is Invariable and Never Changing even though these thigle/appearances appear to come and to go. When the offspring mind/consciousness which is Aware of itself as being Pure Mind Light, Pure Energy and the Dynamic of Indescribability, loses primordial contact with this Blessed Awareness, this Awareness itself spreads forth as the Five Wisdoms Lights/Powers/Energies. The Awareness is Never Lost and Yet Ever Found in the Intense Ecstatic Evident Awareness of Itself. When it spreads out even further it becomes the action

201

or work as an act of the Three Kayas and these spread further out as they work, act and play in the three Regions of consciousness which are the Desire Fulfillment Regions, the Form Regions, and the Formless Regions. These conditions are brought about by contact with the five conditional identity aggregates of form, feeling, perception, will/impulse and consciousness which cause one to lose their True Identity in the circle/cycle of the twelve chain links of causation. This produces entrance into and the coming or going through the common Six Worlds by coming and going through the Six Common Bardos. Each of the Six Worlds in fact have a Waking State, a Dream State, a Deep Sleep State and a True Self (Turiya) Awareness, though similar to ours in the Human condition, may vary a little bit in context to the World that is there in the display of consciousness that has spread forth. To wit, a Heaven World of the Generous and Humble Gods with its own waking, dreaming, deep sleep and Turiya States, or the Animal World with the same states present in some way we may not perceive, or other World/States (Angry and Unhappy Souls, Nomadic Wayfaring Ghosts and the Arrogant or Angry Gods, yes, it is interesting that one can attain this god-like status but still have anger or jealousy). These six worlds are the Tibetan view. So indeed we all share a common delusionary state of spreading out into the display of four seemingly separated conditions of the One Singularity. As we have become so lost in the Six Bardos (Birth, Dream, Enlightenment, Death, After Death and Rebirth/Return, which is to turn back to the display, cognitively, and as actual body birth) of the Six Worlds (Generous Gods, Humans, Arrogant Gods, Animals, Ghosts, and Angry Sorts), the Six Yogas arose as an attempt to End the Cycle of moving forth into the Display. The Yoga of Psychic Heat, Tummo, Vital Life which includes nadi, prana and thigle. The Yoga of Purifying the Impure Illusory Waking State Body (Tantra seeks to change or purify, but Dzogchen sees What Always Has Been Real). The Yoga of the Illusory Dream State Body. The Yoga of the Primary Clear Light in the practice of day and night (or waking and dreaming). The Yoga of the Bardo (Primary Clear Light at Death, Intermediate Bardo methods, Rebirth techniques). And the Yoga of Pho Wa (Consciousness

Transference) which proceeds or comes before the act of death even prior to any physical, subtle form or causal level of death and thus in such a way bypasses death itself as consciousness is so high it does not come down to a level of one who experiences waking or dream body death (or causal death as in some sort of dying away in deep sleep). Yet this Pho Wa is not the Beautiful Clarity of Dzogchen or Pure Advaita, for in these two there is no identity left with the die-er, the one who identifies with the display of death. This is the Pure Awareness in Pure Mind where we started at the Height of Height!

All this is the creative imagination of Pure Mind Itself which never loses Itself in this creative imagination. It is the Height of Height. And all this creative imagination (the Maya or the Occurring) is just like cosmic dust clouds within the Vast Expanse spinning or stirring into the shapes of galaxies within which are more stirrings of stellar and planetary bodies in smaller and yet faster turnings. Or, as the same process reflected in even greater dimensions as Big Bang Bursts within the Vast Expanse, all of which are in the shapes of conceptual appearances (thigles). As the Vast Expanse in which all this is happening as occurrence never loses itself in those individual and universal thigle shape appearances, so too, Pure Mind never loses Itself in the conceptual appearances of the thigle. That is the twelfth Dakini stage as mentioned a while back. Never Lost to Appearances. The thirteenth stage being Never Losing Hold in Pure Mind, but there is no effort there to hold. The more you Cut Away to this Pure Awareness (Trekchod), the more you Soar On (Thogal) and it is all Dakini Given.

The mind that displays itself in fabricated creative imagination is the same mind that becomes, is and always has been the Unfabricated Pure Mind. Otherwise Non-Duality is contradicted. It must be the same, even from the perspective of viewing as to different things, like "I" and "Thou" which are only ideas in the realm of creative conceptuality. Even from the lowest physical standpoint we are all made of the same cosmic star dust evolved to have the sense of "I" and "You". But in the Moment beyond conceptuality where indeed does it all go! Even if we maintain a conceptual Non-Duality that is aware of

Oneness but sees things as having distinct conceptual identities within that Oneness, those conceptual states of self must go in the end of Awareness, but we do come back to that awareness of concept identity or do we. I had a dream where I saw words of poetry written on paper which said, "If the Self is What I am..." then where is the end to potential once this Reality is kept in mind!

In another dream state it also came to me, "The tedium of the Waking and Dreaming cycle. That We all Share Equally in God as Parts of God like the Cosmic Form of Krishna or the Bhavamukha of Ramakrishna, as Lovers all Equally Sharing. Even as we are now holding to conceptuality and so feeling unenlightened, who have given up the Unfabricated Enlightened state, even so it is the same Sharing." The Generosity of True Reality holds back nothing from this Equal Sharing, but this dream with its concept of God and of sharing is still at the level of conceptual Non-Duality and so there is a religious or spiritual ego there that is still again holding to a conceptual support system and has not yet Thus Gone!

The Spiritual Friend

So I asked Swami Bhaskarananda about these concerns when I visited this True Spiritual Friend which is a wonder relation to have. He spoke about the Absolute which is nothing but the same Pure Mind. I was concerned about complete realization in one life but he explained that even from Ramakrishna Loka or Brahma (God as supreme Creator power) Loka (a heavenly dimension) one may get to Pure Mind from there. Is it a law of nature that one must come into the human state to complete this Brahma (God) Jnana (Knowledge)? It seems apparently not. No samadhi is needed and there is no rebirth with this though it still sounds like conceptual samadhi. He even stated with conviction that not even coma, or stroke or loss of organic memories could subtract from the inner gain of experience in regard to this Spiritual Wisdom. Swami told me what I hoped to hear, "With this there is no return to an embryo." It gives Peace to know this and it is similar to the Power of

Belief it seems. He explained the four Brahma Vidya (Knowledge) states. First the Knowledge of Brahman (this Brahman is the Infinite Unfabricated, but sometimes Brahma as Creator God is exchanged with this higher term) causes the world to be like a dream. Second, others might or may come along and without trying may distract one from this State. Third, others must have an intention to bring one down from the Consciousness of this State. Fourth, no one even with intention can bring one down from the Consciousness of Brahman. This is the state of jada (as if outwardly dead) samadhi or nirvikalpa (without conceptuality) samadhi, Swami stated, "There is a little warmth here at the top of the head." This is to say in my understanding that in this fourth stage of Brahma Vidya the body itself appears cold and dead except for the "little warmth" because all the pranas moving through all the nadis and all conceptuality (bindu/thigle) have gone to the Unfabricated Pre-Primordial, Alive and Non-Dual Living Luminous Loving Pure Mind. All energy is focused there and no where else and the meeting junction is there at the top of the head where all the tummo has gathered in that point. I said, "So many states of Consciousness." And my beloved friend said, "But it is One Consciousness that appears like the Sky through the clouds." Swami's words were a comfort and ease to my mind. But as we all speak, is it not within conceptuality, even as we may creatively imagine attaining Pure Mind somewhere else, like another life, or in a heaven or a plane of consciousness somewhere other than here in Pure Mind. With this Awareness there are Isvara Koti (God Class) and Jiva Koti (Soul Class) as to types of persons who are aware, but Pure Mind is More than a "class" of beings. Of course, Swami is completely aware of these stages in all this.

I asked Lama Sonam about Trekchod and Thogal and it is from him that I learned the meanings of "Letting Go" for Trekchod and of "Soaring On" as Thogal, which I refer to over and over again. The night before I was blessed with the most wonderful and excellent Dakini Dream where I saw written down in Dakini script, a large amount of information about Trekchod first and then Thogal second. I felt very good from this dream, for the truth is that all this information in the form of Dakini writing (which looked like writing on paper yet in etheric space, sort of like shorthand, like animal markings and maybe Arabic) came up out of my own radiant dream mind. Lama Sonam was very humble and sincere and I thought he was genuine in the same way that Swami Bhaskarananda is, in fact, soon before this meeting I dreamed of Swami with long silver hair and he was saying that Spiritual Power is within everyone but expresses itself through a kind or type of social shape which came to me latter as meta-social in its meaning. Nevertheless Lama Sonam was humble to say that he did not know much about Trekchod and Thogal (but it was not so). "There are different opinions about Trekchod and Thogal. Some say that if you get Trekchod then you don't really need Thogal." I thought on this latter and it came to me that this thought is because Thogal just naturally rushes back in as Life Infinite on any level, without ego effort, like air into a vacuum or water in a crevice. Lama Sonam, just being open about these two practices, was a tremendous empowerment in itself. I asked him about the further practices of the rainbow body, the light body and Pho Wa Chenpo. He explained them all in detail, the dissolution of the dying body into the rainbow body, the recreation of the light body after death, the merging of the physical elements of the body and consciousness in the Great Death or Pho Wa (Consciousness Transference) Chenpo (Very Great). But he went on to explain the body we have as a meditational body, the body one has in the bardo and the Vajra body which is indestructible. All this was helpful and I am grateful, but now I see that each concept of various bodies and so forth is still within the realm of conceptuality itself and none to be the Pure Mind itself! My own dreams included.

Perhaps it is a dream like Thogal vision to see that all these bodies, human, bardo, vajra, light bodies, all of them are just hanging out there in the Vast Expanse as concepts and yet all the while Pure Mind is ubiquitously Here! So it seems in sudden splendid Moments! I asked Lama Sonam another question about Rigpa and Dharmakaya and he went into a beautifully detailed exposition of Rigpa (Clarity) and Dharmakaya

(Actuality or Reality). Then he surprised me, "I want to ask you a question. What do you think?" I described what I felt that Dharmakaya was as the Mother Light, Ma, always and ever present and that this Rigpa was as the Bu or offspring mind that goes through most of life or through lifetimes with the Mother Light simply unnoticed, but that even as Padmasambhava speaks that this Light is constantly there even as Ordinary Awareness and so we are never without It." "I feel you still separate Rigpa and Dharmakaya. In Reality it is imaginative separation only that gives us an idea of Rigpa and Dharmakaya as different," Lama Sonam suggested, and perhaps it is so being that I am too much a thinker and so seldom at rest in just Dzogchen! Again it is only our conceptual imagination that gives power to the idea of "separate" from Pure Mind.

One other question I asked this very good unpretentious and sincerely genuine lama was about Goddess Vajrayogini and the Awareness of Her as changing or replacing the ordinary three bodies of body, speech and mind and the ordinary three bardos of death, intermediate state and return or turning again to birth, so being changed in this Awareness of Vajrayogini to Dharmakaya, Sambhogakaya and Nirmanakaya? It was a lengthy question but he answered it skillfully, "Yes Vajrayogini is a Buddha of the Dharmakaya, like Samantha Bhadri. Leaving the three Bodies and the three Bardos aside," he continued in detail describing the retinues of the Sambhogakaya and the five ever present certainties or conditions within the Sambhogakaya (Supernal Place, Time, Teacher, Audience and Doctrine) and then went on to speak of the occasion of manifest Nirmanakaya happening now and then, while the Sambhogakaya is always present as the Resplendent Realm. He showed expertise here, at shifting my thoughts from an idea of changing something to an idea of what is Ever Present!

207

The Garuda Mind As Trung Pe

But is it not still the conceptual mind that speaks and thinks of all these yet only as on the surface and not down to the depth of the Unfabricated Primordial! But how do we get there? We Let Go and Soar On as the Garuda Mind, which is a metaphor for the Pure Mind. It is in Pure Mind alone these things are already done. Oh Mother Kali Sakti Dakini please help me to write for this feeble buck toothed fool even though he is happy cannot explain everything to himself and so much less to others! The Heruka Yidam of Garuda Trung Pe is extraordinarily powerful! The Tibetans are masters of psychological symbols. A Heruka is a violent or fierce symbolic composition of the mind content arriving at the conjunction where Compassion Arises. Garuda Trung Pe really Gets You There! Shakes you out (Trung and Pe) of dependency on others. And actually resurrects the dead mind, which is dead by the boundaries of conceptuality! This Heruka Yidam image is different from a God/Goddess Ideal (Ishta deva) for in truth it seems to be the very bottom of your own dark mind, in Oneness not only with your own deepest darkness but also with the dark teacher principle, the shadow of the mind, by which when Non-Duality is here so experienced frees you absolutely in Garuda Trung Pe's dance itself, making duality obsolete. What can I say? Until you see it and live through it you will still be in duality.

Pe is Cutting or Leaping and Leaping or Soaring, yes, exactly Trekchod and Thogal. Trung is a fascinating word from Trung Jug, the dark art of resurrection. But it not only means raising, resuscitating or resurrecting, but also and more appropriately, Translation, Transference and Inspiration. How shall you apply the idea to yourself? It is the translated, inspired, transferred experience of the mind which is dead within the limitations of conceptuality to the Living Luminosity of the Unfabricated Primordial Pure Mind!

This beautiful conceptual figure reflecting back at you your deepest sense of duality also brings back to you the Non-Dual! Here one gains what is embodied in the sacred mystic teaching

208

that one may now be Wandering, Going and Roaming as Help, Teaching or Instruction, yet Without Help, Teaching or Instruction! It is the Beautiful Free State! It is like mouth to mouth resuscitation from your own Luminous Free Self! Indeed! This is alone praiseworthy! You get the Deity Mind as your own Pure Mind. You have dissolved duality here by becoming one with what has obstructed and obscured you! To negate darkness as the other will always be perplexing. This itself is the Secret (Guha) of the divine horse (Hayagriva) neighing with Great Bliss as each neighing sound breaks up the construct of conceptuality! One's own Pure Mind is Vajra, that is Indestructible, and so this Vajrapani takes the form of the Garuda to subdue or even trick the rain garudas from showering their wet distraction on the Buddha's enlightenment. Pure Mind becomes Garuda to conquer the rain garudas. It is Non-Duality again which answers the question of dualistic distraction! The Many rain garudas are as the many thoughts we have that are purified from distraction by non-duality becoming now the Unfabricated Pure Mind, now your own Deity Mind which is itself the Unbearable Wisdom Fire! The Unfabricated State of Pure Compassion Arises. Heruka Garuda Trung Pe is dancing within the inner consciousness over the twelve causal links, grinning and smiling, the Wise Garuda your own Inner Wisdom! Blue, Red, and Orange! The three disks of heart, throat and head, blue, red and white, with all syllables of all language (conceptuality) dissolve into the Self, your own, as Garuda like a hail storm into the divine lake of one's own mind. The three Tantric forces: body, speech and mind in the three disk centers: heart, throat and head, become Light Rays (Longchen)! Dissolving into the Unfabricated! Trekchod! The four visions arise without effort! (Trekchod and Thogal a Unity in Nyingthig.) Thogal! This one is the Great Teacher and this one is within you! Inseparable! Has dissolved into your Heart! A red fire has burned away all conceptual speech/thought. And here a prayer is said that you may be granted and have the blessing of realizing the View of Primordial Pure Mind in Trekchod and the Four Visions of Thogal as Spontaneous Vision Arising At Once.

There are Two Tastes yet they are One in the Final Tasting! The Lama is Outer. The Yidam is Inner. And the Dakini is the Secret, Kuntu Zang Mo, the Highest Dakini as Samantha Bhadri. It is Pure Dakini for Me! Or there is Lama the outer, Yidam the inner and Daka the Secret. He is Samantha Bhadra the Primordial Awakened Buddha who has never lost touch with the Enlightened Pure Mind! The four empowerments make You your own Lama really. What else could it mean, but only the fierce conjunction in Non-Duality as Trung Pe will make it real to you, for as long as you separate, so long you are dead in conceptuality. So come to your own Life itself here and now forever more Soaring Through With It! Om. Ah. Hum. Hum! The vase empowerment puts you into your Vajra Body with the awareness of the destruction of the skull of impermanent being. The secret/mystic empowerment gives you the Nectar of Pure Mind. The wisdom empowerment is the ringing of the Bell of Inner Self seeing that Self in the Mirror of Pure Mind. And the word empowerment is the sound of your own True Voice now reclaimed in the power of Pure Mind. It is the the Crystal of Clarity (Trekchod) and the Peacock Feather of Colored Lights (Thogal) United as One. For me it is Pure Mind. Pure Garuda Trung Pe. Pure Dakini! But you only come to the Fullness of Vast Expanse, when the three Kayas, the three Forces, the three centers and nadi, thigle and prana come to the Emptiness of Luminosity or Pure Oneness.

One, Sakti is the Formless Dakini, the Wisdom Woman of Pure Clarity! Two, Your Own Buddha Self is the Real Supreme Teacher! Three, Pure Mind is the True Garuda Yidam! These are Three Cycles, yet the Fourth Cycle is itself the Inseparable Awareness in these three and the Unfabricated Primordial. The bindu/thigle are the true Buddha teacher. The five pranas and the luminous heat of tummo are the true Dharma teachings. The nerves/nadis themselves are the mystic Sangha company. Your own nerves are the Lama! Your own prana energy is the Yidam! Your own thigle/concept is the Dakini! The field of Refuge is in front of you but it is Emptiness Luminosity. The Sangha/Body, the Dharma/Speech, the Buddha/Mind all Emptiness, and yet Luminous. The Nirmanakaya, Sambhogakaya and Dharmakaya

210

are at Root the Emptiness of the Primordial View in Trekchod. Soar On with It if you can Stay with it. It is your own Confidence and Total Decision. Dissolved into the Unfabricated!

Think of it! You Become Vajrayogini in Her Empowering, so why should it amaze you to become your own True Lama as the Root of Self Teaching! This Lama Deity Mind, now You, helps you to go further as Dakini and Garuda! So you achieve Awareness of Inseparability in the Four Kayas: they are One, Emanation, Resplendence, Actuality and Self. You in your waking state are Nirmanakaya. Be awake to this. You in your dream state are Sambhogakaya. Be alert to this. You in your deep sleep state are Dharmakaya. Be aware of this. You in your Turiya Self are Svabhavakaya. Be this, relaxed, without effort!

Do not be surprised as you are now more than one with, more than ever before, the Supreme Precious Lama. The Four Rainbow Lights from the midpoint of the forehead, from the throat, from the heart and again from the heart of the precious lama have entered and become the Lights within you in those same four wheel centers. In the Dzogchen Consciousness of the Rainbow Body of the Precious Lama you are Conscious of the Real Rainbow Light Body of the Four Kayas Inseparable. Nirmanakaya in the midpoint of the forehead. Sambhogakaya in the throat. Dharmakaya in the heart. And Svabhavakaya there in the heart again. Aum. Ah. Hum. Hum. Do not be astonished that you are your lama, the root of yourself, for it is the same in the Vajrasattva Empowering, you Become Vajrasattva (who is even higher than the lama). From the sacred union point of embrace with his Vajra Goddess, bliss nectar flows and floods your head crown center spreading out through the thirty two nerves. The same bliss floods the sixteen nerves in the throat center. Then the eight nerves of the heart wheel are filled with their nectar bliss. To the floodgates of the sixty four nerves of the navel plexus center. All your regrets are feasted upon by the vengeance of regret itself and you are Pure as the Pure Mind of Vajrasattva, who is the symbol of the Full Teaching Power of the Sambhogakaya. You as your own Lama are that in the Nirmanakaya. As Dharmakaya, Samantha Bhadri and Samantha Bhadra, embracing together the Great Bliss of Maha Sukha, represent the Truth that Actual Truth is never a forgotten state, always present as the Self Essence of that Feeling. May it be Blissful with the Dakini!

The Height of Height

This is Ati Yoga, the Highest Primordial! This is Asparsa (No Contact) Yoga (Union, but here without the act of union as that is only emptiness like the vapor of a dream yet even less)! This is Chitti (Pure Consciousness) Dakini Yoga! To Come Back with This is Yang Thig in Dzogchen, which is like Thogal, but it is Forcing the Entrance of the Clear Light of the Primordial back into the Seen World of states, bardos, kayas and the rest! It is more than just Non-Dual Light visualizing. It is the pure tummo of Clear Light pushed back down! The fourth practice melting all this into One Inseparability is the Nying Thig. The Mind/Heart Essence (Nying) and the Mind Packet/Bundle Complete with Advaita Pure Mind in the excelling Emptiness within Appearance (Thigle). Trekchod and Thogal through all four of these, Ati/Asparsa, Chitti Dakini, Yang Thig and Nying Thig in Pure Unity as the Ever Has Been So!

It is the Secret Knowledge of the Dakini's Great Bliss, which is none but Compassion/Love that would return ten billion times to help others while knowing return itself to be Emptiness in the Luminous. It is the Height of Height in Wisdom/Knowledge of the Dakini Vajra Varahi. She who embodies the Bliss of Sahaja Pleasure as She is the Essence of Great Bliss (the Ananda Bindu/Thigle) who enjoys Herself in the Sahaja Pleasure while resting on Her bed, of which the four legs are Brahma (Creator), Vishnu (Sustainer), Shiva (Destroyer) and Isvara (Godhead) and the bedding of which is Sada Shiva (Ubiquitous God Essence). These are the five Wisdoms of Her Sahaja Pleasure as She is the Essence which is Ever Knowing their Emptiness in Luminosity! Thinking of Her, the Dakini, a dream came to me and I don't mind telling you that I saw a secret mantra written there in my dream mind which gave me ease, rest and comfort, "Maha Kali

212

Yana" which means Great Kali Vehicle!

It is the Indestructible (Vajra) Power (Siddhi) of Your own Lama Self that makes you your own Lama empowered to See your Self Inseparable and in Luminous Emptiness with yidam, lama and Dakini! Get Real Clear, Absolutely So, about the Depth Meaning of it! It is not just visual imagery! As much as you empower the Image of Dakini, Garuda or Lama you Empower Your Self in return! The cognizance is Inside You, Not Outside in the Dakini, Garuda or Lama. It is Your Consciousness which is the Unfabricated Primordial! It is Dakini for me! She is the Encounter in Unfabricated Mind and She is the One who says that you are now so permitted to practice Trekchod and Thogal! It is this Inseparability with Dakini that is Inseparable with one's Empty Awareness in Trekchod and Thogal! One's own Pure Mind, the Ultimate! Trekchod and Thogal come in with the Dakini and Trung Pe Garuda Deity Mind, not with the Lama stage.

It is more than visual seeing of images outside the Self of Pure Mind! One experiences true Oneness Inseparable with Dakini, Garuda and Lama, bold and fierce to go on to more than trust or faith! The thinker of the thoughts contemplating all this is Pure Mind! But Who takes this Moment to Notice! Pure Mind, Happy, without thoughts, no attention in thoughts as they come and go! The Delight of Light in Enlightenment follows you and so too me, around. There is no seeking for it. Who is it that is emptying the deep of hell, a metaphor of this world, if it is not the Dakini who is One. It is Ecstasy Now, there is no long way to go. You are floating, flying and Soaring On in the Infinite Right Now!

Ramakrishna describes Dzogchen without ever saying so. "The mind of the yogi is always fixed on God (but in Dzogchen it is the Luminous Void), absorbed in the Self. You can recognize such a man (or woman of course) by merely looking at him. His eyes are wide open, with an aimless look," and he says it is like the vacant eyes of a mother bird thinking of her little ones. In Dzogchen the eyes are wide open completely aware but the look has no aim due to not holding to the conceptuality of thoughts. The look in the eyes is such, for it is not vacant emptiness, but Luminous in itself! Ramakrishna's thought that he will be reborn one more time is a relaxing thought. Nirvana? Heaven? Return? What does it matter for what you Know Now is What Is So. The rest Mother Knows and Does, so why get stressed for stressing out is not Surrender Nor Humility! Mother Trust is like the wide open eyes of the kitten. Doubting the Mother is the little grasping monkey of concept shivering with eyes shut.

I had a thought one time that made me relax. It came to me that I might have been responsible for the death of a number of people in a previous life and that this may be why I write so feverishly about what is Death and what is Spiritual. The creative imagination is astounding. I bind myself to the twelve links of causation by this, do I not? Is it the logic of the psyche, analysis, or mysticism? What does it really mean? What is beyond this point? You see, the mind weaves its justifiable loop with causation, while Pure Mind has none! Trekchod, that is the thing! It gets you out! Gaudapada describes Trekchod! "All the multiple objects, comprising the movable and the immovable, are perceived by mind alone. For duality is never perceived when the mind ceases to act. When the mind, after realizing the knowledge of that Atman alone is real, becomes free from imaginations and therefore does not cognize anything, for want of objects to be cognised, it ceases to be the mind." III 31-32. What is the mind then? Pure Mind and this is not only Trekchod but it is Amanibhava! The same, and it is Nirodha, the Cessation!

Another day my beloved asked me with a kind and tender inquiry, "What is your Experience?" And I described to her this Loving Trust that I feel in the Deepest Darkest Depth of Mother (Kali the Goddess), Where a Moment Is that I know waking and dreaming are not What I Am and there at that beautiful Loving Moment the sense of separation is gone. This too is a conceptual pegging or nailing of an identity with Pure Mind and so it not the moment "it ceases to be mind" for it is mind describing what cannot be described (it seems). I listened to my beloved friend/wife speaking and it came to me when she said the one word "Self" that this Vajra Sva Bhava Self is always Here, but

214

how we define it by how we define the idea itself of the Self is how we experience the ever present Vajra, Bhava, Sahaja Pleasure for our own! Sakti! Dakini! Om!

Dakini Given

It is the Garuda Mind, not the regular mind that Soars On Through the Four Thogal Visions and this Garuda Mind, this Pure Mind, is the First Vision. The Second Vision is More Field Like Intensity of the First Encounter as Pure Mind. The Third Vision swallows the entire Measure of the Zhi Khro. The Fourth Vision Extinguishes all Vision of Dual Phenomena like Alatasanti, exactly so. And though Gaudapada uses this expression as the description of his fourth and final thought on Advaita, it is well known to be a high Buddhist expression or term for the Spiritual State completed. Trekchod is Getting into Advaita Light, the Pure Mind in the First Vision. Thogal is Light Alone Everywhere and this is an exact tally with Gaudapada's thought of Tayi, the Extreme Answer which we are coming to! These matters as the 11th, 12th and 13th stages, Light Alone Everywhere, being the 11th are Purely Dakini Given! Not to be found externally in an outside teacher or teaching! The 12th is knowing the Never Defiled, or rather never contacted by duality, Pure Mind. The 13th is Pure Mind without holding on to a conceptually knowing knowledge of Pure Mind!

So here is a good place to remind you of the Nine Tantra Yanas (Vehicles). The first three are those types of spiritual people, being those who need to hear or listen to teachings, those who are solitary in spiritual pursuit depending on no external someone, and the great generous souls who care more for the enlightenment of others than for their own. These are three significant stages in the spiritual personality. Now the other six Yanas. Three outer ones, the lesser ones as they represent stages of dependent need until the Soaring Through with the three inner vehicles. Of the first three, the first represents a relationship with Deity where in the first stage one debases oneself (all too common). The second is establishing the intimacy of friendship with Deity (some religions never even get here). Third is the feeling that Deity comes into Presence and goes out of Presence. These are Kriya, Carya and Yoga Tantra vehicles. The inner three are free of dependent contact expressions. Independence in the Sugata (the Suchness of Pure Mind) is where they are at, for you have "cut" or dropped the outer need for dependent contact! In the first of these three (Maha Yoga, the Great Path) what was seen as a coming into and going out of Presence is now realized to be an Ever Presence of Moving Forces in what I call a Non-Dual Circle, but what is said in the Tantra is that one realizes the Deity and Deitess are ever present in the Mandala. Then the next stage (Anu Yoga, the Path of the Awakened Inner Grace) is a somewhat secret/mystical knowledge of the awareness that you yourself are both the Deity and Deitess engaged together in the Radiant Pleasure Embrace of Spiritual Union (or in a lesser degree that you are the offspring of their Bliss). It is a Deep Wisdom of the Non-Dual which then verges up to and then merges into the highest vehicle of Dzogchen! That natural great innate and complete perfection (Ati Yoga, the Highest Path or Maha Sampatra in the Indian tradition, Sam meaning entireness, totality, completeness and Patra meaning vessel, receptacle, recipient, as a person abounding in this) which has always been right here in you, no, as You! Of course all this is the key to the dual problem in relationships of any kind, human or spiritual. And this duality is first gotten over when the offspring mind (Bu) Encounters the Mother Light (Ma) in the Pure Clarity (Rigpa) of Pure Mind. All that is in the way to That Non-Dual Oneness is gotten rid of by Cutting to the Essence (the Mother Light) in Trekchod. Then comes the Spontaneous Arrival of all parts of our being if I may be permitted to say so, in that complete arrival as spontaneous accomplishment of the Six Crucial Charges, the Four Thogal Visions and the Four Confidences again come to the Fore of Experience as one's Own Self Arrival and the Joy of Living in that Arrival! All this has been explained in detail previously. The important point is that with this Arrival you have moved through the three levels of conveyance and are now quite naturally able and without effort to express them. Gone, through

216

the Word/Gesture level (lama). Gone through the Vortex of Mind Space (yidam). Gone through the Mind itself as highest conveyance to itself through Pure Mind by the Dakini. And it all takes place in Her Womb of Suchness as it is your spiritual birth or rebirth or re-enlightenment of what you just forgot for a few hundred lifetimes or a few seconds.

Again, signs that this is now so are the Three Dream types which forecast the Three Death types in the Great Imagination! First: Recognizing Dream/Death in Ordinary Appearance. Two: Liberating Dream/Death into Divine Appearance. Three: At the Loft, Remaining in the Seeing of Divine Appearance. But I ask you to ask yourself; Does Pure Mind need any "dreaming" to be where it is without the conceptuality of Great Imagination?

In You Yourself

It is so important to note that Tibetan cultural influence on the nature of Thogal Visions is a limitation to their expression in personal and wider universal context and use. One must use one's own Matrix of Visions, Dreams, Ideas and Ideals, not another's.! Shall you try to be Tibetan with that imagery or be Yourself? It is like Music or Poetry made in one's Own Light. One Cuts Through (Trekchod) To the Meaning and then Soars On (Thogal) with this Meaning in Expression. It is the Very Same Trekchod/Thogal Dynamic! No Doubt. In Walt Whitman's Song of Myself the Trekchod and Thogal are there as; The Cutting Away of small identities and Expanding Self, Out to Exhaustion, and in the exhaustion he reached Love, Empathic Compassion. It went through his own four stages: ego Assertion, Humility by recognizing death like a Pratyeka Buddha, his own Humanity by Love/Empathy for humanity and then that Immense Identity exhausting out past the Edge! Take time and make your own deep and indelibly imprinted truth in understanding, on thought's meditation natural to you inspired! Trekchod and Thogal were there in Whitman though he never heard the particular Tibetan words as they have just recently become published openly. But in my taste I am filled joyfully with the thought of the Inner of the Innermost, being Ma!, the

Mother, the Light! Vajrayogini!, as the Active Sakti, the Dakini Energy. And Garuda as the thought sign of Pure Mind! Find and make you own from what is within you already. Chase out for nothing!

As it seems that spiritual dynamics are often very similar in their deepest context wherever they are discovered one may see with Open Eyes, the beautiful principle practices of Letting Go of the bundle of conceptual complex dualities and then Soaring On with that delightful Freedom in many systems. For example, the ideas of salvation in Spirit may parallel Trekchod and then surrender to Spirit and living in Spirit to Thogal. But the difference is that these are still conceptual experiences. True Trekchod has cut the bundle of all conceptuality away! And Thogal has exhausted all conceptuality! But here are partial parallels, the Tao and the Te, letting go into the Oneness of the Way (Tao) and then moving on and through as its Power (Te). Actually a beautiful example especially because most people want power in their spirituality and are so seldom happy and joyful with Love alone. Again, one may surrender to Allah, and then live on for Allah. The deep mystics of this religious persuasion have done this. Even though politics are stressful nowadays, the idea of One God here is something that Ramakrishna appreciated in his spiritual experiments. The idea of Letting Go into the Holy Ghost is another example. Then Soaring On with the Holy Ghost. Sometimes the ideas that are within one's spiritual (or religious, psychological, etc.) conditioning may touch the heart of these two dynamics. It is a curious thing that the Western oriented mind responds to the spiritual feeling of the ideas of Spirit or Ghost more than to the ideas of Void or Consciousness in the East. Could we cut away everything into Letting Go in the Ghost and then Soar Onward spiritually in this Ghost that is Holy (Hagia), Wisdom Sacred (Sophia), the Breath (Pneumato/Greek Ruah/Hebrew) of Life itself. The conditioning of one's spiritual equipment is interesting and though ideas do respond to the inner content of the mind complex as the ghost thought satiates the need for the sense of spiritual continuance (even with ancestral energy or the company of the beloved departed/disembodied), also that a super

218

Presence might engulf us like a spiritual vapor, giving us courage or vigor which is again to have spirit. Trekchod and Thogal are not the mind complex that feels a dual conceptuality with a Ghost/Spirit that is Holy. It is a start but there is More! Even as the Oneness of the three sacred forces (a trinity) Unite in the Extreme Height of Height.

One could also move outward back into the display consciousness in the consideration that this Holy Energy is the Unified Field Heat of the Big Bang Burst that is Ubiquitously Everywhere the Same. It is interesting but one has here dropped down into cosmic thought (the Display of Samsara) which is not the Unfabricated Pre-Primordial Mind! A ubiquitous energy is grand in concept but is still material and so, is it then Ultimately Sacred! Here you are still thinking in dualism nevertheless. And there is the East Indian idea which believes this Holy Energy is the Consciousness/Power that Unites the trinity of waking, dreaming and deep sleep into the Abstract Unfabricated Turiya, as a Sound force that ultimately exhausts itself in Superior Silence. But here again one is sallying back into conceptuality in the form of sound concepts and their captivating charms. And the Great Spirit in Original American's Spirituality is the super Presence that unites all humans, the Earth, the Wind, the Sky and Stars and other beings all together, yet it is possible that with this thought one is still moving within cosmic thought which is like the unified field heat, a remnant of creation and what is Pre-Primordial proceeds before creation either cosmic or ordinary, if one can say that anything is ordinary! Or say that anything even proceeds Something that has never not been present!

Gaudapada

So Gaudapada says that "Atman is imagined as Prana and other numberless ideas." I 19. This includes not just prana, but nadi and thigle, even the acts and arts of Trekchod as well as the six accomplishments, four confidences and even the four visions of Thogal! Where does it leave you? In Pure Mind! You are not anything that your imagination presumes or assumes. Again,

"Things to be rejected, realized, accepted and tendencies to be rendered ineffective, of these four, all except the goal to be realized, (the Pure Mind), exist only as products of imagination." IV 90 Trekchod is the "rejection" of what is not Pure Mind and "rendering ineffective" the bundle of dual complexes. Thogal in the sense of accomplishments, visions, or confidences may be those things to be "accepted" in a spiritual state. But what is this? All imagination! Only Pure Mind is Real! Even more directly, "When Consciousness is in vibration, the appearances do not come to It from anywhere else. Neither do they go anywhere else from Consciousness when It is at rest, nor do they then enter into It." IV 51. How can that be? The Great Imagination makes it seem that those things appear as appearances, even as the acts and arts of Trekchod and Thogal, for Gaudapada gives his insight into what we are in Truth/Reality as Pure Mind and here "There is not the slightest imagination of conceptuality among them anywhere, even by a jot or tittle." IV 91 What is meant by them, is all the jiva/dharmas in their innate Reality! And who is that but you! So where is the need for Trekchod or Thogal?

So it is that all doing, going, work, effort or accomplishment, is all the great imagination from the perspective of the Already Enlightened Pure Mind! "Nitya! Suddha! Buddha! Mukta!" (Ever Eternal, Ever Pure, Ever Awakened, Ever Free!) as Swami Aseshananda would often say, quoting Ramakrishna. With this we may also reach Sakyamuni's conclusion in a Pure Psychological Awakening Experience that took place in the Third Watch of his Enlightenment. Gaudapada expresses this State! "As long as a person clings to the belief (the mental preoccupation) in causality, samsara will continue to expand for him. But when this attachment to causality wears away (is exhausted), samsara becomes non-existent." IV 56 And "Realizing the absence of causality as Ultimate Truth, and not finding any other reason for birth, one attains that state which is free from grief (sorrow), desire and fear." IV 78. This brings us not only to understand the "Suddha Buddha," but to see that "All Atmans (Dharmas as the apparent confluence of identities in jiva-hood) are to be known, by their very nature, to be beginningless and like the Already Pre-Primordial Vast Expanse (Maha Akasa)." IV 91 "All jivas are by their very nature, illumined from the very beginning. There can never be any doubt about their nature. The person who, having known this (Pure Mind) rests without seeking any further knowledge (or to whom ensues in this way the freedom from the need of any further acquisition, seeking, searching for knowledge) is alone capable of attaining Immortality (as Pure Mind)." IV 92. And it is from this State that such a person "has no appreciation or greetings for others (that is teachers or deities), and who is free of rituals" II 37. Independent in Pure Mind in the life of Whatever Arises! As the same verse elsewhere translated says that the "illumined does not praise any deity nor salute any superior." II 37. Are you not illumined as Pure Mind, as this can never be in doubt, then what or who shall you praise or salute! As the act itself takes you outward into the display of dual conceptuality!

Advaitic Light

You see the Advaitic Light (Pure Mind) is not an idea, not a theoretical realization, nor an intellectual concept. You Are the Suchness of This! You are Moving in Advaitic Light, as this Advaitic Light, and yet that thought is a Thogal concept. It is the most extraordinary amazing feeling to feel that you are moving, feeling, being, waking, eating, walking, talking, thinking, dreaming and even in the depth of deep sleep, you are this Advaitic Light. Oh, the more it is made known in your clarity the more is the joy of living or dying or just ever being this Advaitic Light! The most extraordinary simple act of waving one's hand in Advaitic Light is Amazing! It is Gaudapada's "firebrand" moving in Consciousness for what appears as our body of waking conditions, or our dream minds, or deep sleep, is but the firebrand which is in Actuality the Fire Itself (Advaitic Light). One has Cut the Bundle (Trekchod) of dual concepts that keep one from this Sensation. To the Full Measure it goes Soaring On to its Exhaustion! It is not intellect, we are Real, Moving in Advaitic Light! What Garab Dorje says in the three

221

precious statements: Direct Encounter. Trekchod of Total Decision in this Delight. Continuing in Confidence (Thogal) with This Decision, Gaudapada also clearly states in parallel. ""One should become identified (Encounter) with Reality, should have his Delight (Trekchod) in Reality and should not deviate from Reality (Thogal)." II 38. Is it not the same to your now Open eyes!

The Extreme View

If we move onward we will discover exactly where Gaudapada Is! It is the remarkable and extraordinary spiritual view. Just like Dzogchen, Rigpa is always ever present in the Encounter with Clarity even in the most Ordinary Awareness as Pure Mind, Original and Pre-Primordial! "The Birthlessness that Consciousness/Mind attains when freed from causes is constant and absolute; for all this duality and birth was perceptible to Consciousness/Mind that had been birthless and non-dual even before." My rendering. IV 77 Excellent.

Nor do the four extreme notions have any effect (or causality) on Pure Mind! Hiding it from Real View as either Existence or non-Existence, or the conjunction of Existence or non-Existence, or Total Non-Existence. Which are Change, Changelessness (immovability), a combining of these two, or absolute negation (Void), anything you put on it misses it for if you say it is one thing and not the other it will show you it can be both and then more. "These are the four theories regarding Atman (Pure Mind), through attachment (contact or holding on to) to which It always remains hidden from one's View. He who knows the Pure Mind to be ever untouched by them indeed knows all." My rendering. "Hidden" does not mean gone for it is always here as Rigpa, even as such, in the most Ordinary Awareness of Consciousness/Mind. These four extreme notions in conceptuality also apply to other arenas of the display dimension: good, evil, both good and evil, or neither; also female, male, both female and male, or neither. You see, once display thinking begins it flows downward, and one begins to question outward; is it dual, or non-dual, both or something else.

222

The limit of one's imagination is the limit of how many places these four extremes arise.

Is it born, unborn, both born/unborn or neither? "since in accordance with the conclusion arrived at in the scriptures of the other schools, the soul undergoes birth from the empirical point of view, therefore in pursuance of that fancied empirical view it is said by the non-dualists (advaita) that the soul is birthless (ajata), but from the standpoint of absolute Reality (Pure Mind), it is not even birthless." IV 74. You see, the fancied view that Pure Mind is born or unborn is still conceptuality in the meshes of dual thought. Does it not recall within you the formless Dakini who is as She Is, A-Yoni-Ja, not ever born within any womb dualism. Pure Mind! What can be said! After the four notions are gone! Then where are you left? "The humility of the awakened is natural (sahaja). Their peace is also natural (sahaja). Further , the control of the senses (that is mind and all the rest that has the tendency to move out toward conceptuality) is natural (sahaja) to them. The one who has realized Pure Mind Is peaceful." IV 86

So, Humility and Peace are just Natural (sahaja) to the already awakened Pure Mind which is oneself in Reality. Sahaja is Always Just As It Is and this is the very true nature of Amanibhava or Pure Mind. But what is the cause of all the misery people feel? "On account of the mind apprehending single objects, the Bliss which is the Real Essence of the Self always remains concealed and Misery Comes To the Surface. Therefore the effulgent Pure Mind is not Realized (Remembered, Felt (Bhava), the Notion of which is ever within You)" IV 82 It is not that the single objects in themselves are the cause of misery, it is the apprehending, as Dzogchen has said, when Pure Mind breaks forth into beginning conceptuality and the offspring mind arises separately from the Pure Bhava (Amanibhava) of the Mother! It is simply the moving out into the display (samsara) that causes misery by bhava focus on single objects.

223

Misery

Further clarity is demonstrated in regard to these moods (bhavas) of apprehending conceptuality. It is a great secret here how the mind goes toward imagined misery. One must keep in mind that it is Amanibhava originally speaking and that this Pure Mind Mood never goes out toward the misery of single objects as identity but remains Blissful. "This Pure Mind (Atman Self) is imagined to be the unreal things and also to be non-dual, and these perceived things (Bhavas = Objects) are also imagined on the non-dual Pure Mind. Therefore non-duality alone is the highest auspicious Bliss." II 33 Most interesting because in the first part of the statement you find "unreal things" which are the single objects in the mood (bhava) of contact with them, combined with an image or imagining of the Non-Dual, as a dual perception of two things, the Non-Dual and the object/bhavas. This will not do, for Pure Mind as your mind will make contact in the mood bhava with objects, then go outward, or downward into that imagination of duality/conceptuality. As this Amanibhava is the Mood/Feeling of Pure Mind, so the other bhava moods, feelings, bring one back to duality where the conceptual misery is once again felt (as a bhava) but not as Reality. It is all the bhava of imagination in Pure Mind. But it does not really exist in the Reality of Pure Mind. It is, no doubt, an extreme testament to a powerful spiritual state which is your own potential.

Handling Objects

Even as we imagine that we are handling objects, "As a person (someone) in the waking state, through false knowledge (or the lack of knowledge of Pure Mind) appears to handle objects (or who appears to be in contact with the bhava of actually fancying objects) whose nature is inscrutable (as if they were real), so also, one sees the object/bhavas in the dream state alone." As in the dream state we handle or have contact with dream objects, in Reality, it is all Consciousness and nothing but, in the waking state too we handle or have contact with objects that are nothing but Consciousness. It is the mood alone in waking or dreaming that makes this Ubiquitous Consciousness appear to be this and that object. If you keep this in mind while "handling contact" it produces an interesting feeling (Bhava). You see yourself and everyone moving in the Advaitic Light! Even science says we are all beings who have come from star dust and star light, take that thought another step further into the Consciousness Light and where are You but in the Joyful Light! Even as the firebrand whirls around, what that firebrand is, is Consciousness! One does not destroy the world in their mind, one sees with feeling/bhava what the world Is! You are Spirit with no duality about it, "not a jot or tittle," not even as a conceptual apprehending of an offspring from its Source (the Great Light of Creation), for there is no duality in this experience. Amazing! You see waking and dreaming only appear to exist apart from Consciousness or at all!, by the mind contact (bhava) that you have with them. Otherwise, just as in deep sleep (or Nirodha or Amanibhava) where no mind contact is in outside Bhava, there is just Consciousness! Again I am amazed! The beauty of religion is the sweet peaceful feeling of simply coming home or returning and re-linking/rejoining with your Source. Yet this view is a little bit more extraordinary than that! But that conceptual sense of reuniting is a matter of personal taste, preference, and even a bit of the prejudiced imprint of one's cultural upbringing. But let us get back to the Pure Subject at hand.

Thoughts

Dzogchen teaches to not accept thoughts and to not reject thoughts. Where does that leave you? In You, the Pure Mind. Any movement either way, saying yes to this, and no to that, pulls mind into duality. Instead of coming at it from the practice of not accepting or rejecting any thought, Gaudapada explains Pure Mind from its own point (in reference to thought). "There can be no acceptance or rejection where all mentation stops (Amanibhava). Then knowledge becomes established in Pure

Mind and is unborn and poised in the sameness of equality." I am using "Pure Mind" where Gaudapada uses "Amanibhava." So you come to see that Pure Mind where all accepting/rejecting duality/conceptuality has no thought grip, rather than saying to the mind, "I accept this and I don't accept that," within an endless loop like circuit of insanity, trying to empty the ocean with a blade of grass. That method will make you go crazy, still strangely enough, it is the one that most people are so fond of, the comfort zone of religious process (yoga) not Reality. The paradox of yoga (the effort act to reunite) is that one seeks to reunite with That which has never been parted or separate from you! As I am now comfortably familiar with Pure Mind that too amazes me!

The Magic Elephant

If we use Gaudapada's illustration of a magician creating a magic elephant, the actual "evil" (deception) of the magically produced elephant is really rather "insignificant" for it has never and never will harm Pure Mind (who in the great imagination is the producer of the elephant of creation itself). "As the elephant conjured up by a magician is taken to be real because it is perceived to exist and also because it answers to the behavior of a real elephant, so also objects (bhavas) are taken to be real because they are perceived to exist and because one can deal with them." IV 44 "Those, who, because of their fear of the truth of absolute non-creation (Ajati) and also because of their perception of objects (bhavas) deny Ajati (non-creation of duality; that it has never been real and that you in reality have never parted into a dual sense of separation from This) are not affected by the evil consequent on the belief in creation (the feeling/bhava of separation). This evil, if there is any, is insignificant." IV 43. Beautiful, so now who of us is not Free in Pure Mind. The deceptive appearance of the elephant of duality is superfluous, immaterial, meaningless, irrelevant to Pure Mind. Insignificant! (to your real and true spiritual State).

Gaudapada's elephant also reminds one of Padmasambhava's elephant where he says that going out of your

226

Dzogchen Awareness, out of you your Self to search and seek for the teacher to explain the Self to you is just exactly like leaving your elephant at Home and going to the forest to look for his footprints. Lunacy, madness, foolishness, the fugue of separation, a spiritual aberration from your Reality, but this evil is insignificant. Looking for those footprints is going or sallying out into the display to seek the doctor of samsara that can only also be samsara (a magic elephant). This high spiritual view in its immediate power and presence is not for the ordinary seeker who thinks of following as a follower. The ordinary don't Get It! "They alone are said to be of the highest wisdom who are firm in their conviction of the Pure Mind, unborn (to duality) and ever the same. This, ordinary persons cannot understand." Blessed is the truth of that firmest conviction in Pure Mind which is not deceived by the magic elephant!

Best First

As Ramakrishna has said it is the Pure Mind that is the teacher at last, so that must be the Best and so why not go to the Best right at the first. Forget process, get the Result and if the process comes latter or not, what does it matter in its total insignificance. Amanibhava is this Pure Mind! And Gaudapada is the good poet of it. "The mind (Pure Mind) does not enter into the causal relation (that is with causality as duality) in any of the three periods of time. How can it ever be subject to delusion, when there is no cause for such delusion?" IV 27 No cause being never entering, so that, your Pure Mind may guide you in its natural freedom and end you in itself! That is, take you to the End! When shall you be free, when the "I" shall cease to be. Ramakrishna. (And that is the karmic "I", the jiva/dharmahood confluence.) "Therefore neither the mind nor the objects (as bhavas) perceived by the mind are ever born. To see their birth is like seeing the footprints of birds in the sky." IV 28 What you think and feel, is not Amanibhava, it never was! Do you believe/see footprints of birds in the sky!

These footprints (object/bhavas) are amazing and extraordinary to Pure Mind. "The mind (Pure Mind) is not related to objects or to the ideas that appear as such objects. This is so because objects are non-existent and the ideas that appear as objects external to Pure Mind are not distinct from mind (Pure Mind)." IV 26 Remember what it means to "handle" objects as bhavas. The leap back from object to an idea (bhava) of an object to mind as really Pure Mind is sweet to the Heart as the Eyes Open to the Wonder of True Seeing! In these verses is not this wonderful advaitic poet describing the Pure Feeling of Amanibhava which is no less, Trekchod! "The mind (Pure Mind) is never subject to birth. All beings, too, are free from birth. Those who know this do not fall into false knowledge." Here he Cuts Through and Lets Go of that conceptual fall or subjection, (which never happens to Pure Mind) as the idea of being bound into a birth or body/mind dimension. You are not contained! Trekchod Cuts Away the contained, the container and the ridiculous idea of containment!

"No jiva (that is dharma conjunct, or dual mind identity, or offspring mind separate from the Mother Light) ever comes into existence. There exists no cause that can produce it. The supreme truth is that nothing is ever born." IV 71 There is no cause to produce it because the dualism is not real and even if one feels the separative conceptuality one is still, in Reality, moving in Advaitic Light. What produces the offspring idea has been Trekchod (Cut Away)! Real Trekchod is the wonderful state of mind which sees in the great moment that, that offspring, in fact, never was! It was only imagination if that. But Trekchod is applied in case of this imagination. "That which exists on the strength of false knowledge (avidya/ma-rigpa) based upon imagination does not really exist. Again, that which is said to exist on the strength of the views advanced by other schools of thought does not really exist." IV 73. But he goes more into the Trekchod of duality! "The world of duality, which is perceived to exist and is characterized as subject/object relationship, is verily a movement of mind (imagination). The mind again, from the standpoint of Reality has no contact (Asparsa) with any object (bhava or idea). Hence it is declared to be eternal (not time related) and unattached (Free from conceptual contact)." IV 72 And that is pure Amanibhava

228

Trekchod.

There is further testament to the ideas that are exquisitely similar to Trekchod. Profoundly, the poet in Advaitic Light does write. "On account of attachment (bhava contact) to unreal (imagined) objects, the mind pursues such objects. But it comes back to its Pure State when it attains non-attachment (non-contact to the bhava), realizing their unreality (imagination))" IV 79. It is to realize unreality which is in itself a recognition of Pure Mind, amazing. But it must not be an empty realization, Humility and Peace must be there when the unreality of imagination is Trekchod. "The mind free from attachment/contact to all object bhavas and undistracted by fresh object bhavas attains the State of Immutability (meaning it does not mutate back to conceptual feeling). The wise realize such a mind to be Pure Mind. It is undifferentiated (Unfabricated), birthless and non-dual." IV 80. "Knowledge (Pure Mind), the essence of the Jivas (the dharma confluences as offspring mind) who are unborn, is admitted to be unborn and unrelated to any object/bhava. This Knowledge (Pure Mind) is proclaimed to be unconditioned (Unfabricated) as it is not related to any other object/bhava which, really speaking, does not exist." IV 96.

Gaudapada's Advaita is what Swami Aseshananda has pointed out as, "It is a timeless realization where the sparkling radiance of eternity floods the whole being of man." And as swami says, "Gaudapada speaks of it in his Karika as Amanibhava." This too is pointed out as Asparsa yoga and this is free from contradictions (abadhitatva). It does not contradict itself and so it turns our heads around from its height because we are so used to a contradictory world (dualism). Or because it does not contact (Asparsa) those contradictions which intoxicate us with delusion. When that intoxication wears off we see What We Are. This is pointed out, "I bow to the yoga known as Asparsa, taught in the scriptures, which promotes the happiness and well being of all creatures and is free from strife and contradiction." IV 2. It is a profound thing, this Asparsa is just like Dzogchen. There is no surprise to that for neither school has any relation (contact) with duality!

229

It is said that Gaudapada was at the Badarikashrama when this purest revelation of Advaita (Pure Mind) Knowledge, the four chapters of the Karika as it is called, came to be written. Other texts are good certainly but they so often leave one in the feeling that the dharma jiva is still a vessel-hood of embodied containment for the State! With Gaudapada it is not so. Again it is common practice in every text to salute or bow to the guru/teacher at the beginning. With Gaudapada it is not so, he simply breaks forth into the Three States of Consciousness (Avasthatraya) and proceeds with incredible power to explain them directly without hesitation. His love for humanity wants that you will not be deluded. But we come across something very interesting in the first verse of the fourth Prakarana (Great Cause) for the Alatasanti which means to bring Peace (Santi) to the notion of the Firebrand (Alata) or the notion of its movement. This Alatasanti is a Buddhist expression alone and that is important especially in that it is also the final Thogal. "I bow to the dvipadam varam, who, by means of Knowledge (Pure Mind) which is like Akasa (Vast Expanse) and which is non-different from the Goal of Pure Mind (Knowledge), realized the nature of the jivas (dharmas), which, too, are like Akasa." IV 1. To me this is fascinating. Who is dvipadam varam, "varam" means the best and dvipadam literally means "biped." Who is this Best of Bipeds? A realized being, but not the teacher of Gaudapada, for no teacher is mentioned at the start. There are quite a few divergent thoughts on who this is. Everyone insisting on their own convergent idea. I suppose I will join the ranks of limited convergent thinkers. Shankara felt that this is Nara Narayana, the Man God, as Narayana (which in itself is also purely just the Great Spirit) here in human form. This may be a contradiction as we will see later in that it was thought that Gaudapada worshiped a human form! Does it mean Krishna? Does it mean Rama, both of whom were thought of as nara-Narayana, the Great One in human shape! Perhaps, perhaps not so. Again the person of Suka has been assigned by Shankara as Gaudapada's guru/teacher, but if you look you will ask how can this be so.

230

Gaudapada lived at the end of the 7th to the beginning of the 8th century C.E. Suka (and this is the Suka he means) was the narrator of the Bhagavata and the son of Vyasa which puts his life time/span contemporary with Krishna. Estimating Krishna's life existence we see him living anywhere from 3,000 years to 1,500 years B.C.E. So there is a mythological fabrication here at work trying to contain Gaudapada by the hierarchy of tradition when he obviously stood on his own outside the containment of the religious system itself. If you are thinking that he was communing with the subtle soul of Suka that too may be a fabrication. He was not into delusory mystical experiences they too being but imagination. He gives a warning to us about those delusory conditions in his cautionary advice on Rasasvada (the pleasant attraction for lower mystic/vision/samadhi states). Ramakrishna told Vivekananda that the same soul who was Rama and then Krishna is now Ramakrishna but not in you "Vedantic sense." This brings in a whole other way of looking at this comment. If it is not Vedantic as the Great Oneness as that which incarnates as divine/great helper, then what can it be? Ramakrishna says it is not that. So if he is the nara Narayana (as Rama and then Krishna) then in Reality was he the One that taught Gaudapada? How can one know such things without mental preoccupation with fantastic fabrication and so remain honest with oneself? I do not doubt Ramakrishna's genuineness! But like Swami Vivekananda himself felt, that Sakyamuni Buddha was the most "sane man to ever live", this too I believe is what Gaudapada is saying in his salute to the Best Biped and that is Sakyamuni whose Love and Compassionate Wisdom shown forth without the tremendous fabrications that go with most religions. It is simply be Kind to others for you are One with them even as your True Self. All right.

Even so, any of these beings are just jivas/dharmas in the strictest sense and so Gaudapada sums up all of us as jiva/dharma imaginations, "As the dream jiva comes into existence and disappears, so also these jivas perceived in the waking state appear and disappear." He says this three ways substituting "dream jiva" for "jivas conjured up by the magician" and once more with "artificial jivas" so as to make the point

Clear! IV 68-70. For indeed this Dream, this Magic, this Artificiality is "footprints in the sky," and just a huge "magic elephant." In all its waking and dreaming variety we so easily believe the fabrication to be real! As Gaudapada states, "The jiva, betaking himself to devotional worship, abides in the manifest (conceptual) Brahman (Infinite). He thinks that before the creation all was of the same nature as the birthless Reality. Therefore he is said to possess a narrow intellect." III 1. A different translation says that such a person "is considered pitiable or narrow in his outlook." Wonderful as those who betake themselves to worship of deities in devotion or bowing and groveling before teachers, are indeed most pitiable in their narrowness of outlook. Also why would you worship devotionally such beings when, "No jiva ever comes into existence. There exists no cause that can produce it. The Supreme Truth is that nothing is ever born." III 48. So if you worship something (a deity) or someone (a person, prophet, sage, messenger, guru, lama, teacher or subtle being) then you are worshiping the dark shadow (conceptuality). The Imagination! Also Gaudapada clears it up with, "There is neither dissolution nor creation, none in bondage and none practicing disciple. There is none seeking Liberation and none liberated. This is Absolute Truth." Who is bound as they are Pure Mind and how can you, a Pure Mind practice or have need for discipline! It is just as it is natural to you. There are no seekers they are imagined, as are devotees and their devotions and those who worship teachers, deities and so forth. Even more profoundly there are no jivas who are liberated (and are now teachers or even gods, etc, as some schools believe) for what appears to become liberated is but dream! Why would you worship that dream shadow? But here, "If, as the dualists contend, the world is beginningless, then it cannot be non-eternal. Moksha (Liberation) cannot have a beginning and be eternal." IV 30. Amazing, Liberation ever has been and so it has no beginning and is endless to you now and always so. So, how do you... go there?

232

Firebrand Visions

We Soar On without soaring Anywhere! Experience! Pure Mind has always been all that is the Experience! We Soar On in the Final Quenching Exhaustion into Peace of the Firebrand Visions. Thogal! In the Karika Gaudapada repeats these verses twice to make the Emphasis. " The disputants assert that the unborn entity (Atman/Pure Mind) becomes born. How can one expect that an entity that is birthless and Immortal should become mortal? The Immortal cannot become mortal, nor can the mortal become Immortal. For it is never possible for a thing to change its nature. How can one who believes that an entity by nature Immortal becomes mortal, maintain that the Immortal, after passing through change, retains it changeless nature?" IV 6, 7 & 8. III 20, 21 & 22. Everything and everyone are as the offspring of "a barren woman" not born "either really or through maya" the Great Imagination, for, "As in dreams the mind acts through maya, presenting the appearance of duality, so also in the waking state the mind acts through maya, presenting the appearance of duality. There is no doubt that the mind, which is in Reality Non-Dual, appears to be dual in dreams; likewise, there is no doubt that what is Non-Dual (Atman/Pure Mind) appears to be dual in the waking state." III 29 & 30. IV 61 & 62. The Immortal (Pure Mind) even through the dual imagination within appearance has never actually become mortal. Lost in the Display! We Soar On Free of the mortal conceptuality consisting simply of waking and dreaming appearances.

Tayi

And so we come to the last step in the Quenching. And this is Gaudapada's Tayi, the All Light View which sees that, "All Dharmas (Jivas) are ever free from bondage (conceptuality) and pure by nature (Pure Mind). They are ever Illumined and Liberated from the very beginning." IV 98. "The Knowledge of the wise one, who is All Light, is never related (never in contact) to any object. All the jivas, as well as Knowledge, (which are

233

non-different) are ever unrelated (that is untouched, no contact, Asparsa) to objects. This is not the view of the Buddha." IV 99. So you see, he has saluted Sakyamuni as the best biped at the beginning of this chapter but now he says his All Light (Tayi) is not the Sakyamuni's view! Even if the best biped be Sakyamuni, Gaudapada has a different view. There is of course, humility and respect there toward the "Best Biped" but no, never ever any worship of mortals or bipeds! Not even in the slightest idea or principle. "To those ignorant people who believe that Atman (Pure Mind) can deviate from Its true nature even in the slightest measure, Its eternally unrelated (no contact) character is lost. In that case the destruction of the veil (of conceptuality) is out of the question." IV 97. "The ordinary person cannot grasp that (Reality)" or "does not understand their way." IV 95.

The All Light (Tayi) as last Thogal in Alatasanti is exquisitely beautiful! The last conclusion to be quenched or exhausted into Peace is that there has never been anything but All Light! Soar On! I have thought about what this means "not the view of the Buddha" and perhaps it is that Pure Mind as Witness of the three states never makes an extension from there in its Pure Light. Or again, as Pure Mind is Amanibhava it never extends itself into a deluded conceptuality. The soul is unborn so it is always Enlightened and that is what is Real, where this may not have been Buddha's view in a belief that the jivas actually become entangled and not merely imaginatively so. That Pure Mind is always this and that the jivas too are always this may not be what he saw at first. That Pure Mind may not even become a Witness for a Witness gives rise to a conceptuality which is then Witnessed! Much less any extension of the All Light into three conceptual Kayas, as it may be, the Dharma, Sambhoga and Nirmanakaya. Would that not be extension into the imagination of contact causality with the twelve causing links, which is the very cause source of being pulled into the question itself of conceptual dualism that then blindly becomes itself the Path! Perhaps ideas (concepts) were thought by the Buddha to be there at least at some point. But even these jivas or self-ideas ultimately have no existence. There is no extension of Consciousness (Pure Mind/Tayi/All

234

Light) given whatsoever to the jiva! The idea! It is Void, nothing, Never Existed! Really speaking, a non-no-not self imagined yet not really ever being. So what you thought/imagined you were was never separate from the All Light. Tayi is What Is, not the imagination, not the dharma/jiva ideas as their own ideals of self are all nothing but conceptual constructs. Maybe one says "yes" and the other says "no" to Samsara as ever having a "birth" in Nirvana, if that is the view then where has non-duality gone? How will you Soar Through? Tayi, it seems, is more than Trekchod or Thogal! Arrival-less Arrival at Where You Always Have Been! Tayi! All Light!

As this is All Light and nothing else, there is no multiplicity, duality or conceptuality in it. How can you salute what is your Self! If you subjectify the non-dual then objectify this as the dual, a salutation is possible. Gaudapada speaks out of respect for Reality! Recall verse 37 II, he salutes no one, not as deity or teacher. The last and ending verse of the 215 verses of Gaudapada closes with, "Having realized that condition, that is the knowledge of Pure Mind, the Supreme Reality, which is extremely difficult to be grasped, profound, birthless, always the same, All Light (Tayi) and free from multiplicity, we salute it the best we can." IV 100. This phrase, "the best we can" leaves one with the hidden feeling that in his voice he is saying, with almost a bittersweet sense of sadness for dualists, that only in duality is this salute possible even at one's best.

Part Three
RESOLUTION IN PURE MIND

America
Tibet
India
Ramakrishna and Sakyamuni
Totapuri and Rudraka
The Obscuration of the Teacher
The Dark Teacher or
Worship of the Shadow
Ramakrishna's Solution
to the Obscuration of the Guru

America

"A worship new I sing."
Walt Whitman

There is the spirit of song in America that rises to touch and become the Atma, the Luminous Shunyata, the Self without ego, Whitman called it the "Song of Myself." If I have the thought, "I am here and these are my surroundings," in a country or in a heaven, in America, Tibet or India, it is all what Gaudapada calls dream and imagination. I travel in the Currents of Dakini Country! No matter where one is (in Heaven or on Earth) nine characteristics occur in the Region of Pure Mind known as Dakini Country. We move out of our psychotic delusion, (as a break from True Spiritual Reality), through the psychodynamic awareness, to cognitive actuality, and then to the acumen of aesthetic peak consciousness and when this comes into us or out forth from us, the nine arise: Unity, the sense of Non-Duality. Transcendence of time and space. The feeling of the Sacred is all things. The intuitive High Insight. The amazement of the Paradox of dualism. Alleged Ineffability (for if you can say anything about the experience it is no longer ineffable). The Transient nature of life which creates Humility. And Continuous changes in behavior and attitude, which become Surrender. (See Clinical Psychiatry And Religion)

It has been said that the poet Walt Whitman (1819 - 1892) had no fear of death. Can it be true? When death approached someone his thought was congratulations. "I am more than nurse, more than parent or neighbor, I absolve you from all except yourself spiritual bodily, that is eternal, you yourself will surely escape, the corpse you will leave will be but excrementitious. The sun bursts through in unlooked - for directions (Is Walt speaking here of the Chikhai Bardo? It seems so.) Strong thoughts fill you and confidence, you smile,... I exclude others from you, there is nothing to be commiserated, I do not commiserate, I congratulate you." They say Socrates fearlessly drank the hemlock. But they do not say that hemlock was well known for its numbing effect on the emotion of fear of death and its quality of bestowing a fearless death. Issas (Jesus) is well known for begging God to take away this "cup" of death. If it were to be so willed. But he had to fullfill some great expectation. Yet it is history true and sure that the Buddha Sakyamuni did knowingly thank the man that caused his death addressing him as "brother" in gratitude for his release. It does not matter where you live or dwell, what matters is your spiritual comprehension of death.

Geographical associations should not condition one's conception of Truth in Experience for the Experiencer is Here wherever you Are! It is a great limitation in experience if one thinks that one can only be spiritual or have spiritual experience, if one goes to some, or such and such a Place. "Passage to more than India! O secret of the earth and sky!... passage to you! O daring joy, but safe! are they not all the seas of God? O farther, farther, farther sail!" Whitman. Indeed it is a passage to more than India.

I have heard Yogis say yes to Walt Whitman's Knowledge of Reality, but then disparage his realization by saying he was a sensual man. If you don't love woman (or man, as the case my be) enough to see her flourish, then your love is but a form of hate (dominance). They forget that their Krishna was perhaps the most erotic and sensuous man that history has ever known. Yet those deceptive gurus and lamas who tend toward that direction of sex abuse, whether female or male, may delude you to think you are having an amorous encounter with the Goddess or God by embracing with them. Amazing really, to think someone could be that audacious and egocentric, but these things happen and astoundingly some people believe it. Nevertheless, Swami Vivekananda called Whitman "the sannyasin of America" feeling that he had reached identity with all forms of life and had felt the same feelings that were nearest to his heart. "I am larger, better than I thought; I did not know I held so much goodness."

I was talking with two Native American shaman dancers and asked them what they thought of the Trickster Wateo, they said, "Wateo changes forms, he is a shape shifter and changes into an eagle, a wolf, a coyote." I asked, "Is not Wateo the Creator?"

And they said, "Yes," so then I continued by saying that Wateo the Trickster Creator's greatest trick was changing Spirit into World, that is people and all, the stars and all. My two Native American friends were then quite deeply surprised by what appeared to them to be the first time this notion came into their minds. People anywhere are just people, wicked and wonderful. Just let go of them. Forget about it, Trickster takes care of these things.

Whitman writes, "What is known I strip away, I launch all men and women forward with me into the Unknown." This is the essence of Trekchod, that cutting away or letting go, here a stripping away. Whitman is practicing Trekchod without ever knowing the Tibetan practice. He goes on, "You must habit yourself to the dazzle of the light and of every moment of your life." Song of Myself 46 And it does seem that here he is practicing Thogal, that soaring on, that final leap surpassing mere awareness of the Eternal (Nitya). He is seeing the dazzling play of the Eternal within the Relative (the Lila). And more of Thogal is expressed, "Wandering amazed at my own lightness and glee." But it is not just romanticism, it is an awareness of the Pure Mind giving deathless courage, "All goes onward and onward, nothing collapses, And to die is different from what any one supposed, and luckier." And as to his experience of uniting Trekchod and Thogal in the Nitya and the Lila, "That mystic baffling wonder alone completes all." And more so, "This the far-off depth and height reflecting my own face, This the thoughtful merge of myself, and the outlet again." This "thoughtful merge" is Trekchod into Nitya. And through the "outlet again" is nothing less than Thogal into the Lila. But it does not stop with just his own state, it moves into the Immense Pure Mind, the Mood of not just his "own face" but of all living beings and more, "I am the mate and companion of all people, all just as immortal and fathomless as myself, They do not know how immortal but I know."

Americans who become exhausted with materialism turn to the Spiritual (or religious, there is a difference). Tibetans and Indians sometimes have the opposite problem. Are humans in India and Tibet so different than in America in regard to miracles, prakaya pravesh/ trung jug (raising the dead), pho wa (consciousness transference) and in Spiritual Insight without the mess of miracles? Swami Aseshananda (1899 - 1996), a spiritual friend in the truest sense, was asked if he would return to India, he said, "No, I am here to serve (help) the Americans." And he did just that for one half of a century. Quietly, absolutely without pretense! Walt Whitman was no doubt a Vijnani, (one who is in the Unique State, when one has thrown away both knowledge and ignorance to Experience the Being of God) one who had realized the Great Truth but also brought it back down into the Immense Field of Universal Identity. Dynamically, it is just like Bhavamukha, the Great Facing in God as God acting One with God, but a step down for bhavamukha is considered the exclusive Highest God or Real Self Identity State of the pure God man or Goddess woman as the case may be. Swami Vivekananda felt deeply identified with his Poetic revelations of Self Reality. As I mentioned before, he called him "the Sannyasin of America" which is to say Illumined American Sage! This American Sage reached the state of Love which is Empathic Compassion! Convergent thinking is to have only one conceptual answer. Divergent thinking is a thousand possibilities with any one thought, like the crown of Sakyamuni! Was Whitman a Pratyeka Buddha? It does appear to be so, for all alone with Self as the only Guide he went through the stage of ego Assertion, into the Beautiful Depth of Humility by observing the teachings of death around him, on to that Empathic Loving Compassion for Humanity, and then into Awareness, Vast, Immense, Expansive! (See The Cycle Of American Literature) For humiliation can be Sweet as it pushes away ego assertion. Then there is Humility! Then Surrender and Sweeter to Sweetest Emotion! Pure Spiritual Feeling, a Oneness without words.

Did Jesus die in the Essene mountain cave as it is written in a quiet letter which speaks loudly a lost truth? Or is his and his mother's body actually buried in Kashmir as I have heard a Swami swear that this is true? (Both alternatives are given in Christ the Saviour And Christ Myth) What is the truth and what is a weave of fantastic fabric? A prophet opened a sea so the

241

people could walk through, another prophet supposedly stopped the Earth from orbiting around the Sun for a day, we believe another raised himself and one or two more from the dead (if they were actually dead and not just in deep states of consciousness) and that one said, that latter those who believe in him would do "greater things" but no one has done so. When was the last time someone raised the dead? Many near death returns have been recorded, but that is not the same! Walking on the Moon, is this greater? Hubble has looked at the Edge of the Visible Creation expanse. Robots have flown to and have rolled around on the surface of Mars! But these are not "greater things" and they are explainable, unlike waving one's hand in prayer to stop the orbit of Earth! It is anomalistic!

Interesting. In the Jesus/Yahweh formula the human is worshiped. In the Allah/Mohammed formula God is worshiped. Where God is worshiped may be healthier. Remove the rust from the mirror of the soul so the Light of Allah may be seen. It is a good spiritual thought. But I am not a religious man, I am an Advaitic/Dzogchen thinker! But there is sound spiritual advice in the Koran, 3rd chapter v 79-80 which says that a real messenger of Allah would never instruct others to take prophets or angels as God! They have messengers, not gurus. No worship of human beings or subtle/causal spiritual beings! Excellent. Perhaps I am a Moslem, as well, at least in this regard. Ramakrishna practiced Islam (Surrender) to Allah and found the same Reality as Vedanta, though outwardly it is different in culture, tradition and so on. It is the same as what Swamiji Vivekananda says, "The Buddha is a State (A Realization) not a person!" Very Good! The president Thomas Jefferson was very sane about biblical writings. "In the New Testament there is internal evidence that parts of it have proceeded from an extraordinary man; and that other parts are of the fabric of very inferior minds. It is as easy to separate those parts, as to pick out diamonds from dunghills." This is true of every religion, of lamas, of gurus, of saints, of followers and leaders, of followings and leadings. (See Letter to John Adams, January 24, 1814)

And so often, the followers in their devotions may actually

242

ruin for others the Spontaneous Natural Spirituality of those Self Arisen beings in humanity regardless of their cultural surroundings! "The truth is that the greatest enemies to the doctrines of Jesus are those calling themselves the expositors of them, who have perverted them for the structure of a system of fantasy absolutely incomprehensible, and without any foundation in his genuine words. And the day will come when the mystical generation of Jesus, by the supreme being as his father in the womb of a virgin, will be classed with the fable of the generation of Minerva in the brain of Jupiter. But we may hope that the dawn of reason and freedom of thought in these United States will do away with all this artificial scaffolding, and restore to us the primitive and genuine doctrines of this most venerated reformer of human errors." Thomas Jefferson. (See Letter to John Adams April 11, 1823) An amazing statement from a Spiritual American mind!

Again he clears the religious air filled with myths and artificial elaborations that intoxicate us in their wish to see what is Spiritual in human nature! "Among the sayings and discourses imputed to him by his biographers, I find many passages of fine imagination, correct morality, and of the most lovely benevolence; and others again of so much ignorance, so much absurdity, so much untruth, charlatanism, and imposture, as to pronounce it impossible that such contradictions should have preceded from the same being. I separate therefore the gold from the dross; restore to him the former, and leave the latter to the stupidity of some, and the roguery of others of his disciples. Of this band of dupes and impostors, Paul was the great coryphaeus and the first corrupter of the doctrines of Jesus." (Letter to William Short April 13, 1820) If you release from your imagination an apocalypse that is forced to fit the older concept of a Messianic kingdom that has conquered and destroyed all the unbelievers of their doctrines, if you realize that maybe the resurrection is a metaphor of life cycles, and that miracles can be explained by medicine and healing arts and that Mary was a woman of the Temple of Isis and so, her conception was sacred, but not what Jefferson just described so well. If all this is free in you you might see that young man who was the son

243

of a Goddess woman in a different light. And that it was perhaps unfortunate that the prophecy of death was thrust upon him, for perhaps his life might have gone on like that of the Sakyamuni for another one half of a century.

I think Jefferson would have liked The Gospel of Thomas which was discovered in a cave and has been determined to be authentic. It has now been translated for many years, discovered back in the 1940's. It describes a man of Love and Wisdom, not of miracles, nor of resurrecting dead bodies, nor magical births nor a messianic destroyers of others. Some thinkers believe that the entire "doubting Thomas" records, with him touching the wound of the dead and arisen man, was in fact, entirely a fabrication of others who were angry with him because he wanted to write of a human being and not a God in the context of a messianic deity incarnate who in his loving grace has come and will return to destroy all the unbelievers of Earth! There are people who have also thought that he purposely got himself crucified to fullfill prophecies. I do not know nor do I accept the thought of an intentional death for some glorious religious purpose, but people have certainly sacrificed their lives for much lesser causes, in wars, in saving people's lives, in many cases. The point is as an American I want to know the Truth without all the fabrication no matter what religion or science, or philosophy or psychological system I look at or explore, embrace or practice and believe! Don't You?

To Go where Love Is, is alone the great journey! Whether your soul/spirit/self/individuality returns completely as in melting itself back into the High Ruah, or Nirvana or the Great and Infinite Satchidananda where heaven and hell do not exist, or whether that same soul of the same stuff returns to the rotating of the Six Worlds described in Tibetan Buddhist Tantra, or becomes a powerful Ancestral spirit like in Taoism, Confucianism or Native American tradition, or melts returning into the Great Spirit or the Tao, or whether that spirit thought of identity goes to drink of the four rivers from the Throne of Allah in paradise, or your belief carries you to a heaven with angels and cherubs and sons of God or you dance joyfully in Sacred Circles with the Goddess!, or if you seek to wait in some shadow world of promised expectation until the Cosmic Arrival of Love which has mystically and even naturally within the Universe, Already Arrived. No matter where, the one journey is the Journey to Love, which as Infinite has never been dual with us even as our minds float in and out of finite conception. We discover that we are Unstifled by conceptuality! That Here, We are Love!

"Love is never redundant. To try to define Love is as attempting to define the ocean, water, but water moving in more ways than one can think, and every emotion is but a shape in this water. Water being its substance, its cause, its very existence.

Goddess, if I learn the skill of Love, then whenever shadows surface from me, as they will always do, until sometime unknown to me, then I shall be capable in embracing those shadow helpers and they shall become one with Love. Love loves truth telling, the sharing of the real story within each of us which is never so different one to the other. Love is not god-like, Love is not justice from on high, Love does not measure nor punish. Love is ever Self defined, yet humble as the excreta that has become humus. Love never resends nor replays resentment, for Love ever lets go of the old to embrace the new. Love is more than ever grateful. Love, having no measurement, accepts and takes in everyone. Love is not exclusive. Love releases pain and brings one home. Love is ever discovered anew. Love always gives back what is needed in others, gives for and forgives. Love is selfless yet the most powerful assertion of self. Love is responsible for everything and Love has never betrayed anyone. Love is the one and only independent emotion in the world that can and may successfully confront every other miscellaneous feeling. Love is the most powerful of all, yet Love has no resistance. Love does not compete, Love does not manipulate, Love alone is not superficial. Love is the pure power of Now, Love thinks not of what has gone down nor what shall go down. In Love there is no escape, nor any holding on. Love is the only true knowledge out of which everything is written. Love is real wisdom. Love is the only ever changing inner freedom. Love is sometimes ecstatic, sometimes sorrowful. Love denies nothing. Love is relaxed and never

245

wastes. Love is felt in the gut and the bone, in the spirit and the soul and yet no one has defined what is Love.... Love does not generate misery nor regenerate old misery. Love is one step in front of every function of the psyche. Love is not logical, rational nor reasonable. Love does not procrastinate for Love is always now. Love is the cure for dualism and the source of all seeing, feeling, being, knowing and healing. Love is the source of all courage and truth! Love is the most serious feeling in the world but Love does not take itself seriously in the face of the world. Love is what is left here in you after consciousness is cleared. Love is the identity of the true 'I'.

The boldest move you can make is to walk out of the front door of yourself and become what You Are. Love is Reality. Love is the Direct Power of Reality. The whole world circulates and surrenders to Love. All thoughts dream of Love and all voice tries desperately to speak of Love. All efforts in consciousness and all desires for ecstasy and bliss are the wish for Love.

Love makes no sacrifice and Love accepts no sacrifice. Why should Love be so involved, being the One all embracing sagacious emotion. Love has already made everything sacred and Love has already taken in everything as sacred. Love does not preach and Love does not teach, for Love is the quiet power ever knowing itself as real, needing no instruction as to what it is.

If one goes through the path of consciousness or the examination of being and existence, it is much more difficult to arrive at reality because the stress of mental dualism is there in this course. But take a person in Love. They wish for, think of and feel nothing but Love for the beloved. This lifts them off the ground. They do not desire to quarrel over what is the right or the wrong, they do not wish to celebrate the joys of life with a friend, they show no egotistical pride being humbled by the great force of the most potent feeling, and they do not even enjoy the pleasures of the senses. Love has pulled them directly and immediately into truth, into Love. All else is discarded as having no importance in the face of the Direct Power of Love. Love is the Immediate Recognition of Pure Mind!

When one somehow begins to realize how deeply and solely important Love is, either through or for someone, a person or an ideal, or in the pure sense of Love as Absolute Reality beyond every dualistic concept, then, the first step has been taken to feel and then see your way clear in Real Trekchod! The grand sensation of Love spreads and stands forth inside and out, going beyond even the comfortable familiarity with one's own mind. It goes beyond even that idea or experience of the All One or the Great Universal, Love comes back from there, so to speak, and becomes in the living sense, a living reality of functional spirituality in Real Thogal!

Love sees no dualism. Even in the experience of the lover and the beloved, the entire wish, want or desire is to be One and this Oneness is Love. Love is the non dual reality of the lover and the beloved, the sole fulfillment of Love. This is expressed most commonly as the conjugal physical achievement of lovers as an eternal symbol of oneness. Yet there is the attainment psychic emotional non dualism as in the peak emotions of creative and poetic consciousness. And in the high course, there is pure unfettered spiritual non dualism as the all embracing, the great perspective of endless feeling, Love.

The Primordial Power of Love is so great that some realized beings, souls through history, have given up or let go of their waking state bodies and have melted into death, due merely to the Primal Power of Love. Out of the intensity of serenity in Love their bodies have just dropped away. The poet Ramprasad is one such example. Out of his intense love for the Goddess Kali, knowing his life here was done, he entered a river, left his body there and was never seen again. But if one were to discard the physical body out of the tragedies of Love, the result is not serenity. This is because to forcibly shut down a body's functions is the denial of the learning of Love, but when a physical body's functions just naturally shut down, that is the harmonious accordance of Love pulling you onward.

The need for self affirmation is the denial of Love. Love needs no self affirmation being the most comforting and assertive feeling. The need for self esteem is also somehow quite funny, for what makes us feel good about ourselves is when we feel Love within ourselves. Esteem may also be a circle of the ego continually needing to estimate itself and assert itself to the ego. But the ego's need for recognition must be there in the first step in order for the ego to be and become healthy enough for the ego to let go of itself. It is strange and beautiful, when at the end of the course, what the waking body becomes is just three pounds of ash, dirt, what and where is esteem then, for every single self as consciousness has the same value. What matters here, is character, and what is character alone is what is guileless, which is to be without deceit to others or self trickery, and the one guileless characteristic in the entire world is Love. Love is the source and being of all true and real character, so what is this thing called self esteem. To come, to do, to be done, to let go, to move through the surface of things and release them. This is the skill of Love. Can you live this? From the deepest depth of Love, to let go of any person, principle, idea, concept, feeling or experience, where only Love alone is held. Love is what we wish to hold and be held by, anyway you look at it, and so to hold or be held by, or to try and control or roll against or be attached as staked out by any other thing in this world besides Love is the one cause of what is commonly called suffering.

The poet Keats wrote from his spiritual experience, "Beauty is truth, truth beauty,- that is all ye know on earth, and all ye need to know." Love is truth and Love is beauty, that is all you need know and all you can know. That is the one transcendent movement in consciousness. The typical and atypical profound idea forms that come from the collective pool of divine intelligence are but drops of water from the ocean of consciousness. But this is Consciousness itself, which is Love, the Power of that Consciousness, not just awareness, it is living feeling, an awareness which is perpetually alive. This is the gift of the Divine to the human mind and this is what is in the human mind that comprehends the Divine. Love.

The deepest fear a human being may entertain is that we might somehow be abandoned by Love. This can never be so. It is mental illusion in the conscious and subconscious dualism. For example, in one's waking mind one might be very clear about one's feelings for another, but then in the dream state the subconscious speaks as one may dream up some terror of being pulled away and abandoned by Love. This is dualistic fear, at one level you are fine, at another you are not. That is why all traces of dualism must be cleared out at the subconscious level. And here, deeper meanings come up to the observer of the dream surface. The fear might be that inwardly one doubts one's own capacity to Love or feels in some place inside an inability to let go and Love for real. Or such things could also be subconscious doubts over another person. Love assures. Love heals. The fear complex of this anxiety exists even in the herculean intellect, for even though one may deeply comprehend great things, that tremendous intellect may deep down feel alone and abandoned. But Love is there, the mind is just ignoring the wonder.

In one life, a former enemy may be one's best friend and in the next life, a best friend may be an enemy. Love keys up to see no dualism. It is the great empathic perspective of Love that does not take definitions nor experiences as personal. Love knows we are all continually changing. Yet, Love sees even beyond this, beyond all those forms of dualism.

Love is the true anchor in the calm sea of serenity, but on the surface of that sea the waves of the relativity paradox continue in motion. People make judgments, people have opinions, seek affirmation, want esteem, desire to have recognition and so forth. Personally, I prefer to be a simple guileless fool, putting all that silliness behind me. What worth has that for me. I live in my own power, Love. I keep sorrow in the front of my skull and ecstasy in the back of my skull and by this I know the reason for and within every human reaction. I never forget, that, if you go looking for your own light in the light of another, that just might be a fool's darkness." (From The Skills of Kalee)

Tibet

"We have thus far exhausted trillions of winters and summers, There are trillions ahead, and trillions ahead of them. Births have brought us richness and variety, And other births will bring us richness and variety. I do not call one greater and

249

one smaller, That which fills its period and place is equal to any." Very few holy men, fewer saints and even fewer sages have this level of pure insight that Whitman expresses here. Regardless of where you are or on what ground you may stand, "All truths wait in all things.... Only what proves itself to every man and woman is so, Only what nobody denies is so." Again Whitman leaves the ground with his words. From the height of Pure Mind he expresses Reality, "Divine am I inside and out..." And from that sane pure perspective, "Copulation is no more rank to me than death is." And to it most directly he states, "And as to you Life I reckon you are the leavings of many deaths, No doubt I have died myself ten thousand times before." In Tibet, dying and the directive to a new birth is nothing less than an art form really. The Dalai Lama is said now to be fourteen times reborn. He himself says he may or may not be the same soul. When one begins to see the imprints (samskaras) and latent desires (vasanas) that might lead one to a rebirth, it is good, for one will be getting ready for Trekchod!

The first and second Dalai Lamas were named so retrospectively after the title was given to the third by the Mongolian king Altan Khan, a descendent of Genghis Khan. His name was Sonam. The fourth Dalai Lama was born a Mongolian as he had promised Altan Khan. The first, the second, the third, the fifth, the seventh, the thirteenth and now the fourteenth Dalai Lama were and are considered to be very good and great spiritual people. It is sad, but the ninth, tenth, eleventh, and twelfth Dalai Lamas all died around their early twenties. Some believe they were murdered (poisoned) because of political intrigue. The sixth Dalai Lama was a romantic poet, a sensual man and I think he was fond of wine. He wrote Tantric love poems that are still famous today. Some say too that he may have been done away with when he was still a relatively young man. They built him a separate house off the side of the Potala palace. The eighth Dalai Lama was thought to be not a strong link in the chain because he did not like politics. He was a good person as all the Lamas are and have been and established a health system for the people of Tibet. I do not know if it still exists. Once a Dalai Lama dies it takes three or four years to find the next one.

Jigme Lingpa (1729 - 1798), the composer of the three cycles (and yet a fourth is there too) of the Dzogchen empowerment had memories of seventeen former lives. (See Apparitions of the Self) One being that of Garab Dorje (born sometime between 184 B.C.E. and 55 C.E.) himself who was one of the original Dzogchen thinkers. He also thought he was the eminent great Longchenpa (Longchen Rabjampa 1308 - 1363). Now the three cycles were received in three visions Jigme had of Longchenpa. Can one have visions of one's former self in another lifetime as in Jigme's case, where that previous self, Longchenpa, was his greatest teacher? Amazing, it stretches the nerves of the mind to think in these terms. Just like thinking of the common Tibetan mantra, Om Ma Ni Pad Me Hum, as it corresponds to the six worlds on the wheel of life and death, their entering, exiting, and sealing off from reentering, all at once thinking of this, stretches the nerves of the mind!

Again there are those who believe they are the reincarnation of Jigme Lingpa now and in the recent years past. I shall not say their names out of respect, but their life spans often cross one another and I wonder how can someone who is still living be reincarnated into a new life of another while they are still living. If you live from 1820-1892 how can you reincarnate as someone living from 1800-1859 (or visa versa) or someone living from 1808 to 1887? It seems one would have to first die to be reincarnated as what the word means. It goes on with the believers who think they are Jigme Lingpa living from 1896 to 1959 and yet another lives from 1910 to 1991 and now there is another young lama who is thought to be Jigme Lingpa who is only around thirty years old at present which puts his birth in the late 1960's while the other Jigme was still alive. Will the real Jigme Lingpa please stand up? Some try to explain this question by saying these are separate incarnations of the body, speech and mind of Jigme Lingpa but that takes quite a stretch of imagination it seems, but who knows?

A lot of what is in The Mirage and The Mirror just came right out from...!, where?, memory?, which tallies so well with discoveries and verifications in Tibetan Tantra, before seriously studying those special features. Did I live in Tibet before or is it subconscious self empowerment memories, or mental fabrication, or the Harmony of dynamics within Spiritual Truths?

Dzogchen and Love? Love must be there or it is vacant! Excuse me, I was just Spacing Away and Letting It Out into the Vast Expanse with Jigme Lingpa! Please pardon me, I did not hear what you said. I was singing the Song of Self with Walt Whitman! Forgive me for not paying attention to you for I was off in the Wonder, Quenching the Firebrand with Gaudapada!

I wonder, how many Tibetans died around 1949 to 1959 or so to become Americans? The same question with those who might have been with Ramakrishna (1836 - 1886), even though my beloved Spirit Friend said those who reached him have reached their last life! He himself said he would come back around one more time two hundred years after his death (Great Samadhi) in 1886! So the Wonder transports me!

I very much like the story of a previous life of Longchenpa. He is a reincarnation of Princess Pemasal! You see she lived at the same time as the Dakini Woman Yeshe Tsogyel and Pemasal was a Dakini Woman too. They got some Dzogchen teachings from Padmasambhava. When Princess Pemasal died the teachings on Dzogchen were hidden. Latter, the Princess Pemasal reincarnated as a man named Pema Latrotsal who rediscovered or uncovered them. When this man died he was reincarnated as Longchenpa who wrote some of the best and most profound Dzogchen Thoughts that have every been written. The beautiful idea of transcending the identity of the two gender minds is there in the story. Ramakrishna also expressed the transcendent soul (Atman/Self) as being without gender duality in his madhura bhava practice. Convergent thinking confines one to this or that identity. Divergent thinking raises us out of that locked in conceptuality to show that we could be a man in one life, a woman in another, a man again. Why not? It goes further into the level of Letting Go of an "I" and "Thou" concept duality where mind becomes Immense in the Vast Expanse. For in this Vast Reality, "the non-dual state of consciousness is something non-relational." This becomes the Advaita. Then the Vijnana or the Bhavamukha. The Sva Gata Bhedha, the Self

Gone past all conceptual differentiation. The Achintya Bhedha Abheda, the Inconceivable Unfabricated Absolute in the Fabricated or Differentiated Immensity! Swami Saradananda again writes, "Some of the anceint seers described the Indivisible Non-Dual Reality in Samadhi as the 'Void' (Sunya, the Great Emptiness of Being) and others as the 'Full' (Purna, the Plenitude of Being)" Within the Inner Essence of this Sweet Mood one feels and knows something more than being a Princess Pemasal or a Longchenpa. Swami Saradananda writes. "continually diving deeper and deeper into one's own personality... Mining, as it were, into the deeper and deeper strata of the inner world, the Sadhaka experiences subtler and subtler realms of ideas until at last he strikes the Ground of his existence and remains one with it -- the Immutable Reality Without a Second, which is devoid of sound, touch and form, and from which all ideas including his I-sense spring and have their being. This is the experience of Samadhi. If the subtle impressions of the mind have not been completely eradicated, a trace of ignorance is still left, and consequently the Sadhaka comes down from Samadhi, to experience the external world again by reversing the process through which it attained the Immediate Knowledge of the Non-Dual Reality. Thus does the mind of the aspirant continue to descend from the superconscious to the normal consciousness and again ascend from it to the superconscious, over and over again." Amazing! All within the Wonderment of Immensity Itself!

The sweetest secret wisdom of the Tibetans is Bodhi Chitta which goes to and becomes Maha Sukha and Maha Sukha is in the Bodhi Chitta. Maha Sukha is Great Bliss and Bodhi Chitta is the promise one makes in one's consciousness to reach the enlightened state of mind not just for oneself but for every living being. In that joy of self for others and for self in others is where the Great Bliss exists! And maintaining awareness while moving through the phase transition of the interval between waking and dreaming or living and dying is another sweet wisdom. To know that loving compassionate promise even during the "interval" is the real journey to Tibet. It is the Certainty of Nirvana when one can hardly tell if waking has ended and dream has begun, or life has flowed away and death has started to arise.

India

So sail on further and farther than India. As the saying goes that all tamarind trees are the same everywhere, this is true with evergreens too. A dear friend of mine, Alan Berger, said that, "India is an anti-universe. There you will find a group of cows standing around watching a human being, barbecued (cremated) while here in America you find a group of human beings standing around watching a cow being barbecued." Well said, well said. And does it really matter how one disposes of the dead body. It should not and death should be an awakening to us all anywhere we are. I love the saying that if one has no longing for God and you go to Benares then it is just an ordinary city. But if you long for God then wherever you go is Benares. Ramakrishna tells that story. To me thats the thing. One swami told me that going to India is not much different than going to Mexico, except there are temples. And I remember an Indian friend of mine saying that he thought that Krishna was the smartest man ever to live because he convinced everybody that he was God and had all the women he wanted. Whitman says it so well, "Old Brahm I, and I Saturnius am; Not Time affects me - I am Time, old, modern as any." And to it, "And if the corpse of any one I love, or if my own corpse, be duly render'd to powder and pour'd in the sea, I shall be satisfied, Or if it be distributed to the winds I shall be satisfied." The new worship he sings, "Yourself! yourself! yourself, for ever and ever!" Shall we be bound by any place in this spiritual quest when, "The whole universe indicates that it is good, The past and the present indicate that it is good... and I say there is in fact no evil... And I will show that there is no imperfection in the present, and can be none in the future, And I will show that whatever happens to anybody it may be turn'd to beautiful results, And I will show that nothing can happen more beautiful than death, And I will thread a thread through my poems that time and events are compact, And that all the things of the universe are perfect miracles, each as profound as any." Most wonderful! So then where shall you go to find the song of your own Self.

There is only one true Pilgrimage, when Prana and Manas rise into the Shunyata, that is the real pilgrimage when Energy and Mind go up to the Ajna Chakra (sixth center) and from there the Vast Expanse of Turiya is seen clearly. One more step and there is no more pilgrim. So whether I am sitting here or there, I am not impressed.

So often, but not always, there is a powerful ego fix in going to Sacred Places like India or Tibet. Watch it if you want Humility. Like a dear Moslem friend was saying that those who go to Mecca have big religious egos from their journey thinking they are now better than others. Even racing to see who has gone there how many more times. Just like with India. The obscuration to real spiritual feeling has been increased not decreased. Ego has become heavier, not lighter. What we also call, "Holier than thou." Be aware of psychological issues and how they influence behavior and mind attitude in self consciousness from the subconsciousness. Know your stuff. If I may forgive the twice or thrice wicked then also I may forgive the dark teacher and so set my Soul to Peace and to Rest! If anyone addressed Ramakrishna as God or Teacher, he would say, "Never say that!"

As I would replicate myself in the smallest unworthy resemblance of the Epitome Wonderful Example, Ramakrishna, in my unique way, in meaning to me personally I assimilate Buddha, Issas and everything else! If asked, a good lama would say, "Buddha is your best guru!" "Beyond him?" "Your Own Pure Mind!" The sacred sound of Aum pervades mystic India (and the entire universe), so, to travel the trail that moves from sound to silence within the center point of meaning (Atma) within the Aum is the true journey. Other movement is just walk about, wandering.

255

Ramakrishna and Sakyamuni

Ramakrishna and Sakyamuni both went further into Truth than their teachers. Ramakrishna went much further than the nirvikalpa samadhi he engaged in with Totapuri. Ramakrishna went for and was more. Further on he went into Universal Love, the Divine Mother's unique and novel doctrine. Sakyamuni too went on past the nirvikalpa samadhi he engaged in with Rudraka Ramaputra. He went deeper to embrace the Truth of suffering and its end, with Universal Compassion.

The idea of the incarnation or the descended being who comes out of Pure Mind to deliver, save or enlighten, or help the world of human beings is there. But look at this idea. Is it that the incarnate one is within Pure Mind, that is standing forth from within Pure Mind, yet not claiming an absurd exclusive right to Pure Mind as raising human self importance to that state. We are all standing in Pure Mind and Pure Mind is all there is whether we know it or not. If anyone is an Avatara or a Nirmanakaya of this Pure Mind they do not say they are. When Ramakrishna was declared an incarnation by a counsel of scholars what he said was that he was happy to find out that it was not a disease. And so deflecting all self importance! What humility! And Sakyamuni said time and time again that the enlightened one, the Reposed One, is a spiritual state, not a human person. Both examples stood within Pure Mind but did not assume an ego about being Pure Mind. How remarkable.

Ramakrishna could shift from one guru practice to another, one religion to another with such ease. Goddess give me this Ease. It was all within him (See the Sadhu Story in Ramakrishna's Solution to the Obscuration of the Guru) anyway. What More was in him that could do this? Ramakrishna and Buddha, both are Examples of "what Is" within Us. What that "What is", is Love!

Vedanta often states that Buddha could not find the words to express his Experience. Hmmm. I think he did quite well. "I, who am here, at this moment, I know what Is." And this is a Positive inference of Reality, not necessarily like the Void, but

256

we can go on and on in the debate. But why waste energy?

Dzogchen is complex, complicated even though it says it is not. You need the intellect to comprehend all its designations. Even all the Tantra levels prior to it. So much figuring. You don't have to figure it out, even right now. How can you, when it is past and before all figuring was ever there as the immediate experience experienced immediately and figuring would only get in the way of this immediate experience. As Ramakrishna says that it is "beyond reason." And, "Come down a note or two."

Dzogchen is to know that you are the indestructible youthful vase body of the gentle and tranquil Manjushri, before diffusion into the five prana energies, Wisdoms, emotions and so forth.

With Ramakrishna Trekchod may be compared to when the sharp glass was applied to his forehead to Cut Through the apparent saguna level. Then Thogal was just as Bhavamukha and for the ordinary person it would be vijnana, which is to see what was found in Trekchod throughout the entire field of the Vast Expanse. So the secret heart essence (thigle) of the Vast Expanse is just this. Then the entire field of the Lila is one beautiful thigle drop on the forehead of the Goddess.

Sakyamuni gave only Five Worlds when he drew them on the ground (for the Sangha). The Tibetans give six. They added to Sakyamuni's Heaven, Human, Animal, Ghost and Hell realms of soul rotation by putting in the realm of the jealous gods. I would call the Goods Gods the Humble Gods and the Jealous ones are the egotistical Gods. Perhaps the Tibetans did this to account for such gods as Yahweh who is admittedly a jealous God over his kingdom. Or perhaps as an interpretation of Brahma the Creator, who is a controller lost in his ego's reflection and consequential idea of control over the fate of other beings, etc. and so forth.

Trekchod is like Death. Thogal is the Continuing Natural Principles. But are these not involved with visions and miraculous death phenomena so often warned about by Advaita as psychic delusion. Dzogchen speaks of the Mother, the Offspring (Son/Daughter) and Energy. Ramakrishna always spoke of Mother, and of himself he felt he was a five year old child in Her Lap and that the Primordial Power itself is Her

257

Sakti. Not so different, all paths. Mother's unique and novel doctrine. Same ideas, different systems. Mother is Base, Path and Fruit. She is Dark, Non-Dual, Without Form. She is Childless, Without Offspring, Without Duality.

Non-Dual Mother Energy is Always Here. It is an illusion that the son/daughter energy is born separate as an experiencer which gives birth to the phenomenal magic of wonderment wherein the six bardo worlds appear to turn around the Center Always Here. What a game! From Birth then to Dream then to real nirvikalpa Samadhi where the body appears dead outwardly, then real death in the Chikhai (the Mother Light at Death) then to the Chonyid bardo and back through the Sidpa on the bordering or touching of consciousness in the Point between, before the conceptional embryonic birth again. What magic Mother weaves. Respect for what it all stands for inwardly is the Whole Thing!

I seek to empty the depths of hell, my own and yours. That is the Dzogchen way. The Kayas are Vehicles that don't go anywhere, but are everywhere just as they Are, even in Pure Non-Dual Mind. The Natural State of Mind is Pure Mind, Mother, sahaja too! For everyone, so hell is now empty, we must just see it and be free of our own hell. The four Dzogchen Thogal confidences are no fear of hell because you know it is delusion but even more so you do not fear suffering because you know You are What Pure Mind is. The next is no expectation from Samsara. Then no hope for Nirvana because you are never separate from Mother. The fourth is equal joy everywhere because what is not Pure Mind! Enemies? Friends? Now you Soar On.

The Look, the Expression, of Garab Dorje, of Ramakrishna, of Sakyamuni, of Padmasambhava, practice this Look and produce in oneself what it is that they are Seeing! Sakyamuni died in the moment of the fourth meditation (not in the four higher samadhi states). Why? Energy entered the Four Boundless Feelings which bestow the Four Confidences!

Both Ramakrishna and Sakyamuni sought a Power Focus not deluded by the Atma idea. Ramakrishna would say it is not me, it is not me, it is all Kali, all Kali. And Sakyamuni spoke of the delusion of self belief and self conceit, self love and self delusion in regard to the Atma which is a real problem with those who use Advaita with no Humility!

As Ramakrishna says, "You will go beyond all this and will be able to understand everything yourself," for where it all leads is here, "It is the mind that becomes at last the spiritual teacher and acts as such." And only from here is it known to be Sakti/Dakini/Kali in Which one can say like Ramakrishna, "O Mother, the mind is nothing but Yourself. Therefore Pure Mind, Pure Buddhi, and Pure Atman are one and the same thing." He relied only on this! "His Pure and Holy Mind Became his Guru." That is how it should be! "Without any external aid, he was, by the sheer intensity of his yearning, able to attain the perfect vision of the Divine Mother and thus have the only ambition of his life fulfilled." And is it not just like Sakyamuni whose Enlightenment in Pure Mind came without any external aid. "Atma Deepo Bhava!" As it is said too of Ramakrishna, "Without a teacher, guide, or helper, with no great knowledge of the scriptures, and even without passing through the prescribed forms of asceticism, Sri Ramakrishna carried everything before him by this adamantine faith and sincere yearning to realize God." And it was this alone that led him to the full realization of the Mother, the Goddess in both form and formlessness which is no less than the Unfabricated Primordial! If it was so for Ramakrishna could it be so for me or you, if we regard him as the other wonderful example of highest human potential to realize that which never dies and is ever living as the Pure Mind! For Sakyamuni it was the same Experience even though he went through prescribed forms of asceticism. In his own energetic diligence and self reliance he came to the Tatha Gata Garbha, the Sugata, the Womb of Suchness and is that not the same Mother in the Unfabricated Primordial!

Totapuri and Rudraka

A lineage, a tradition, a spiritual connection that connects you to your belief in the power of your own power, the Mother Light, in Energy, Radiance and Non-Duality! For this, one would naturally have respect, gratitude and deepest spiritual admiration. For these feelings enlighten you yourself. Enhance you, bring about You Yourself, the state of your mind in the connection, the depth of regard you hold for Yourself, but it is fatal if it becomes egotistical. Yet the long strength of traditions can make you forget the Spiritual Power of your own Pure Mind, as mind becomes what mind here and as the Bardo Mind, dwells upon.

It does appear to be so, that the Experience of Oneness (Advaita) does occur within progressive stages of the Void or being aware of the Void (Dharmakaya). For as long as there is physical contact or subtle visual awareness that secondary awareness obscures the Non-Duality of the Void. Pure Mind stands forth always above all this. The weight of memory, the shadow of the dream mind and the inability to enter the Openness of Pure Mind becomes less and less by far.

It is so interesting to know that when Rudraka showed Sakyamuni the four samadhi states, that when he had experienced the fourth and final one his comment was, "Is this all you have to show me?" One cannot underestimate this. The four progressive samadhi experiences are all conditions of consciousness and so they may come and go, being experiences within the realm of time as the experiencer does contemplate these states of consciousness. First is the consciousness of Infinite Limitless Space. Second is the consciousness of Infinite Limitless Consciousness. Third is the consciousness of the Void itself where nothing is within that consciousness but consciousness itself and so there is not even the feeling of something being infinite nor limitless. So the fourth samadhi state is said to be consciousness which is neither that of perception or non-perception. It is called the Summit of Becoming (Bhavagra) and it is called Nirvikalpa Samadhi also. Here, the Consciousness is in a State which does not perceive the former conditions of space, consciousness or void. Nor is there non-perception of these. It is complete Non-Duality. So there is neither a presence nor an absence of what Is, in the way that it cannot be described. Sometimes the metaphor of an abyss is given, but even that is an opposite in comparison to the fullness of life in the consciousness of something else, infinite, limitless, void, spacious, or something conscious of something other than the Experience of Oneness! Which may be thought of as a Ninth Stage when all eight are described. It is the Cessation (Nirodha) of all perception, sensation or imagination!

You see this is so interesting. That Nirvikalpa is indeed Nirvana in its purest sense. But if you enter Nirvana as that great immense stillness, as long as consciousness is still confined or attached to the body, that Stillness will not stay, for you will be pulled back by cause and effect to the body mind in time space. So this was not a satisfactory final Truth for Sakyamuni nor Ramakrishna either as it is so commonly thought and even misunderstood that Nirvikalpa/Nirvana are final. They both went deeper for Something More. Love and Compassion!

Also you see the first state of Space (Akasha) is different from the third state of Void (Shunyata), for Space is really an objectification of a condition within the Void that engulfs space. And the second state of Infinite Consciousness (Vijnana) is different from the fourth state which is neither a perception nor a non-perception, an awareness or a non-awareness, as infinite consciousness is more like cosmic consciousness and in the Bhavagra, nothing of a cosmic nature is objectified as it is Non-Duality. That is Nirvikalpa and that is Nirvana's Liberation, but to liberate oneself is not enough in the ultimate Spiritual Sense!

Rudraka Ramaputra was an actual descendent of Lord Rama and as already stated he was Sakyamuni's nirvikalpa teacher, but before he encountered Rudraka he studied with Arada Kamala who was his savikalpa samadhi teacher. This is so much a parallel you see, with Ramakrishna as Totapuri was the nirvikalpa instructor and Bhairavi Brahmani the savikalpa mentor. Nevertheless you see, both Ramakrishna and Sakyamuni went further than either set of teachers. Sakyamuni, leaving those teachers as they were to be limitations to his most mature and final spiritual experience. And Ramakrishna with the help of Mother's mysterious ways sent his mentors away as they were originally only there as a way of standing tradition. This is also true with Sakyamuni, we must conclude in both cases.

So you see the Brahmani was sent away because she became

arrogant as to her self importance in Ramakrishna's life. So he released her because she had become possessive of the disciple. Whereas after Totapuri the guru, was taught by Ramakrishna the disciple about the Mystery, Wonder and Beauty of the Divine Mother, he, Totapuri was sent away for reasons that may indeed only be known by the Divine Mother. But it can only be that he would now experience and share the Spirituality of the Goddess Kali as the 'Something More' than nirvikalpa. Two immense and vastly important spiritual truths are present here. One is that gurus should never ever try to possess disciples. The other is that they should never think that they cannot be taught by the disciple. All so true!

But here it is important to give the information that Sakyamuni picked up on savikalpa samadhi meditations from Arada Kamala because you see when that one named Sakyamuni died, that is dropped the body or left behind the composite of what was called the Karmic "I" or self of Sakyamuni, he did so at the fourth level of these meditations. This was to emphasize the great importance of the Four Boundless Joys which are perfectly generated at the fourth level of the savikalpa meditations.

These meditations are really and simply a process of things, feelings, ideas and concepts that drop away. The last stage is when the former concepts and feelings drop away to reach what is equalness of mind, balance, or equanimity itself. There Sakyamuni dropped the body/mind named Sakyamuni, to enter, as it would merely appear on the outside experience of death, to be, the Tatha Gata Garbha. That is the Pure Mind. So his karmic experiences attached to the identity of the Karmic "I" just finished and he became as it were just the Pure Mind.

The Four Boundless Joys will be described but first let us tackle the mediations themselves. In the first stage meditation is contained all five affects of that mediation. Vitarka and Vichara, two words Patanjali categorized in Yoga. Vitarka is to be with question in the mind content. Vichara is conceptualized thinking in regard to the discursive and discriminating mind content that says this and that to itself in process. Here also are present Priti (Fond Pleasure, Joyful Interest, Rapture), Sukha (Pleasure

Ecstasy, Well Being, Deeper Rapture) and this Upeksha (Equanimity). So when question and discursive thinking drops off one is left with fond pleasure of emotion, pleasure ecstasy and the equal feeling (And how often is it so true that questioning and too much discursive thinking subtracts from our inner pleasure experience in the forms of Joy?). That is the second stage. When there is just Sukha and Upeksha that is the third stage. When there is just Upeksha one has reached the fourth stage of this meditation. And it is here that the Four Boundless Joys are experienced.

When Sakyamuni dissolved contact with the body/mind he did so at this level to emphasize these four joys. Of course at the final moment he went through these four stages of savikalpa meditation, then, through the four higher samadhis to the Summit, but it is said his consciousness then returned down through these four higher samadhis to rest at the fourth stage of meditation, Upeksha. Here are the Four Joys. Boundless Kindness toward all beings because at one time or another all beings will be or have been our mothers (parents) so we return kindness to them. To experience joy at seeing all beings released from any form of suffering is Boundless Love. Boundless Compassion is to take more joy at the good fortune and spiritual accomplishments of other beings than one's own, but really it is to lovingly care for other being's enlightenment more than one's own. Then Boundless Equanimity is knowing that in the great karmic cycle at one time or another all friends will become enemies and enemies will become friends who in turn may become enemies who may in turn become friends so eventually you realize that you should feel equal to All. Indeed, but what Joy, once done! This is really the mature spiritual solution that Sakyamuni discovered and practiced as a solution to the end of suffering, indeed, and part of the "Something More" than nirvikalpa/nirvana.

You see again, it was called simply the Summit of Becoming because there is More To Become. That is not to just Realize Reality (Pure Mind) but to become a Compassionate Being filled with Love for others in every way imaginable, describable and indescribable. It was the same with Ramakrishna when he expressed his final and most mature spiritual opinion, that is not simply to melt away into the Nirvana/Nirvikalpa, the Eternal, as he called it, but to return from there back to the Relative, the Maya/Samsara filled with Love or rather "charged with the Love of God," the Reality, the Goddess, even so the Pure Mind, as feeling Love for this in others, all beings, everyone. That is Spiritual Maturity!

So if we now come back to these concepts we are thinking in terms of Pure Mind as covered by space, or by consciousness, or nothingness, or even the beyond. All these clues are learned ideas that do not really convey the nature of Pure Mind. Even Gaudapada's Pure Space (Akasha) can mislead the thought in its search to Reality. That is beyond the idea of being conscious or not conscious, that it is beyond Luminous Shunyata and yet it is conscious as Consciousness. Consult the Prajna Paramita, "Consciousness is Void, Void is Consciousness." Very good. All your reasoning is paralyzed and you are forced to commit to Pure Mind as resolution and solution.

If Sakyamuni practiced guru yoga, the yoga of the lama, as it is now called (or mentor yoga) at one time, he gave it up to find Pure Mind own his own with no one's help. Here Sakyamuni is truly a Pratyeka Buddha, a Solitary Awakened One who by himself alone gets there to the Pure Mind, and not through the teaching of any other being. If one is advised to practice lama yoga on the Buddha as one with the human teacher, remember that Sakyamuni did not do that. He left Arada and Rudraka. So, should I have mentor yoga on Whitman, Swami Aseshananda, Lama Geshela as well as Ramakrishna, Garab Dorje, Gaudapada and Sakyamuni? Now I know Swami Vivekananda as a manifestation of Pure Integrity. Even so in the end I would have to cut through and soar on past these spiritual friends, to find my own, like Ramakrishna in the Kali temple or Sakyamuni under the tree. It is no doubt true. Ramakrishna "could not at all put up with being addressed as a spiritual teacher" and would say that God, Sakti, the Great Reality were alone the Teacher and then take the dust of your feet. "Has anyone witnessed a more humble attitude? And it is this very person whom they are making into a spiritual Teacher and God -- which he was not!"

Swami Saradananda. I feel Ramakrishna and Sakyamuni are the same in this regard. They both Cut Through (Trekchod) and Soared On (Thogal) past the barrier of having or of being bound to the teacher complex.

Sakyamuni left Rudraka. Ramakrishna, by Kali's decree had Totapuri go. Actually Totapuri had quite a tremendous ego which shows the specific problem that ego can still exist even in those who have Advaitic Realization (Nirvikalpa or Sahaja style). The arrogance of Totapuri's ego was revealed in front of Ramakrishna when Tota became so intolerantly angry at the outcast lighting his smoke from Tota's fire. (Shankara had the same problem of anger at an outcast man until he was shown the outcast's True Nature.) Ramakrishna laughed hard. Tota did not believe in the Mother's Power, but when he tried to commit suicide because of physical pain he learned that he could not even do that without Mother's consent. You see, would you want to practice guru yoga on such a soul? Would you want this ego as a connection to your spiritual existence whether here or after death. People do not think about such things and often blindly accept teachers just because they are there.

A teacher can corrupt your sense of the Spiritual Self either by the overestimation or the underestimation of your relation to Pure Mind. So often this happens. We become bound by ideas. In Truth, Pure Mind is larger and vaster than any space of thought imaginable. Larger than any concept of universal space wherein all the galaxies are floating and spreading out. Pure Mind is larger than any dream space imagined and for a moment when we first wake from dream we know that Pure Mind, but then a recall of a dream image comes up or a thought of the waking world arises and the conceptuality of these limited thoughts cover the vastness and largeness of the incomprehensible space of Pure Mind. Even the idea that you are now within an incarnation of life or that you have had previous lives and memories and dreams of this life or another is but a limited covering on the infinite immeasurable Pure Mind. One of the most extraordinary thought sights that poured into my mind one time is this, within and in the immense galactic universe while asleep on this planet (or awake), this tiny

265

subjective dreamer conjures the dreaming mind of dualism and that thought itself within the skull of the dream mind is indeed all that holds us back from the wonderful feeling (Bhava) of Immensity Itself. Here I beg you (and myself) to Cut Through (Trekchod) the barrier, that is our ego based dream thought, and Soar On (Thogal)!

The Dzogchen saying is that looking for the teacher is like leaving your Elephant at home and going out into the forest to search for his footprints. Chasing footprints is nothing but anxiety. You think until you find a footprint you cannot have the Elephant, the Buddha Mind, which is all along what you Are! Pure Mind encompasses all the footprints (lamas, gurus, mentors), any of your Totapuris or Rudrakas.

How beautifully Aurobindo put it when he wrote about how much better is intimacy with the Divine (Pure Mind, Sakti) than with a relation between disciple and guru, "This is a greater and more intimate relation than that of the human guru and disciple, which is more of a limited mental ideal. Nevertheless, if the mind still needs the more familiar mental conception, it can be kept so long as it is needed; only do not let the soul be bound by it and do not let it limit the inflow of other relations with the Divine and larger forms of experience." What do you want? A limited mental ideal/conception or larger and larger forms of experience in Pure Mind. It was also that with Aurobindo that Sakti was his Supreme Guide. None other! And Walt Whitman validates and confirms this whole view, "I am larger, better than I thought, I did not know I held so much goodness." And, "One world is aware and by far the largest to me, and that is myself, And whether I come to my own to-day or in ten thousand or ten million years, I can cheerfully take it now, or with equal cheerfulness I can wait."

Those silly souls who say that within the spiritual chemistry of the student and teacher that all disruptions in that relation are solely the student's neurosis is ludicrous, absurd, for it makes out the teacher, a human being, to be in-fall-able (infallible). Even the present Dalai Lama has said that it is silly and wrong when people worship him as a living Buddha, but respect for a Buddhist monk is quite different.

266

Lord Buddha said there would be no return for him. Karma exhausted. Mind thus gone (Gata) to Nirvana (the Other Shore). But some believe Padmasambhava is none other than that same Sakyamuni. It is a contradiction. Still, the Bardo Thodol (Tibetan Book of the Dead) and Naked Awareness are worthy to be devoured. The three alternatives of Aseshananda are the same as the three in the Bardo Book. Nirvana. Heaven. Or Return.

Padmasambhava says that to know the sugar's taste you need no explainer (guru). If you do need the guru/lama you are like a madman in a crowd searching for his own face on the heads of other people. Yes indeed. You can come into life fully aware, needing no other explainer (some say this Full Awareness is destroyed by the culture and education of upbringing) Again, Garab Dorje did not, nor did Ramakrishna need an explainer. Yet mind and body need the comfort and ease of Sakti but this is not a need for an explainer in that regard. It is Spiritual Feeling. Gaudapada says that Atma covers (hides) and then reveals itself on its own, "The birthless, dreamless, and sleepless Reality reveals Itself by Itself; for this Dharma (Atman) by Its very nature is Self-Luminous." IV 81. "It is the Self Luminous Atman who, through the power of Its own maya, imagines in Itself by Itself all the objects that the subject experiences within and without." II 12. This is so important to understand especially to the imagination of one's bondage and the liberation "by Itself" which means none other than You. You are "Itself." So Know What You Are and do not pretend the act of the madman asking for an explainer to point out the taste of sugar.

Why worry about people's former and previous little worlds, even if they are still entertaining those memories, dreams, illusions. I have reached the Higher Perspective and blessed is the fact that without influence or exertion from others externally, it was all Mother's Work on me. So, I need not nor shall even attempt to exert or influence others by efforts upon them externally. Everyone comes to what they Come To, by Mother Alone, filled in Her Pleasure, it is easy to let this comfort just Be So.

It is Matangi (the Goddess of Intelligence) that should be

respected in the heritage lineage. Jigme Lingpa is said to be the author of the Longchen Nyingthig (Innermost Dzogchen Essence Practice of the Great Expanse) even though it is written by Jigme Trinla, still as it is, if he is the author, Jigme has put his own name with Padmasambhava, Garab Dorje, Longchenpa, etc. in the prayer to the lama lineage, which is strange because the Sakyamuni said to not look to any external for assistance or rely on another for help and here is the reverse of this advice from an Awakened One, Jigme himself. Is it lama lineage ego asserting itself? Or a poetic clue where Jigme is praying to himself for help? That guru/lama/mentor yoga may indeed really be contradictory to what the Awakened Sakyamuni actually taught. Even depending on a Sambhogakaya aspect of Padmasambhava or Garab Dorje is not becoming what Dzogchen says you should Become! Independently Awake!

There is the saying that the most excellent spiritual guide/guru/teacher is one's enemy, from Eight Verses for Training the Mind. Only by Pure Mind encompassing your response can it be made so. Only can it be from the Sight of Pure Mind in Humility, where learning comes in the worst assault to the ego, making you Trekchod the ego base! Should we then seek enemies as the best gurus? No. But some Buddhist psychology says that only by fear of the guru's annoyance will wrong behavior stop. Is this not the stance of an enemy creating fear when you fear this teacher! This is a terrible manipulation, for if we do not seek goodness out of a love for goodness is it then good to seek it out of fear? Should you fear Pure Mind? No, never. Also, the only wrong behavior is non or misapprehension as Gaudapada has explained, that deep sleep is not apprehending and waking/dreaming is misapprehending Pure Mind itself. Besides, the one wrong is to hurt another. What fool would do this and those inclined to hurt others do it anyway, regardless of gurus, lamas, etc. until Karma, Life, teaches them differently and they will not respect or fear the lama/guru anyway. The Power of Life, greater than human teachers will teach them as Ramakrishna has put it, "If they need teaching, then He will be the Teacher. He is our Inner Guide." So even one who has no fearful respect of lama/guru, even as an enemy to spiritual life, is most excellent as guru/lama, if we are to believe that an enemy is indeed the best spiritual teacher. It is Life (Us) that we should respect. That whole idea that we should fear is ridiculous! An enemy, a guru, only fear! As long as an enemy is perceived there is duality. What we perceive as opposition to Pure Mind may be what needs to be assimilated by Pure Mind, it is a source of real power when one "becomes one with the enemy" whatever that may be, once done, then where is the guru or shadow teacher as an enemy! Here is where true fearlessness Begins! Before now, courage was just pretended.

What does it matter if I am a solitary rhinoceros whose death arises as Primordial Wisdom Light and anything thereafter as the Resplendent itself as a rainbow light body of pure bliss. That is just my selfish pleasure and so it is not Compassion. Wherever you are your consciousness levels out there. Don't fight it. Learn from your own strategy that you have conjured with honesty and that will become Grace. The amazing field of embodied being will then reveal itself as the wonderment of Maya. When you think of the three states, the six worlds, the three regions, you begin to see (imagine) everyone around you coming and going through these, where they were, where they are going, the strangeness of their place right now, within death, within dream, within life in the balance. Is it imagination in its strangeness? Death and the three states are real, are evident. It is a strange wonder and I feel no Peace with it until I retreat into my Refuge, Pure Mind. For every religion has their description of different cosmological field experience. But Pure Mind, no one has pegged down (limited) by description, imagined or real. Seeing Pure Mind as Everyone's Reality Essence, then things start to be viewed from the inside out, and no one remains to be seen as ordinary. All are the Retinue of the Kayas, yet More, is that they are all Pure Mind. Within a mind, in a body on a planet, around a star in a galaxy among galaxies that cannot be counted, innumerable as they are! Immensity in reverence. So why should I reason or figure, and where would all that calculation show me where or that I am?

In non-dualism do we become God, the Potter? And if we remain in the dual state are we then just the clay pots? In full

Dzogchen all the Kayas are realized but still you (ego) don't create galaxies. Be Humble. I am just a buck toothed grinning ox of a fool what do I know! We may have a consciousness of participation in the Immense Mind (Bhavamukha) but still there is One making galaxies, life, physical, subtle and causal material of which a human being and body are made with nerves, pranas and thigles, so Humility must be there. Dakini bestows Maha Sukha (Great Bliss). So, no matter how much Non-Duality you feel as Awareness with the Mother Creatrix there still must be Humility before the Principle Reality, for the Immensity of creation is not a human power doing! Even Trekchod's rainbow body and Thogal's light body or the Great Transference are small things, mere manipulations, compared to the One who has made creation. We are left in the State of Wonder, Awe Struck in Non-Dual Pure Mind. When I am not that grinning ox, then it is more than conscious participation, no more the buck toothed fool. Pure Mind is God! Then Who is Doing Everything in Surrendered Pleasure!

In the Pure Mind Perspective all appearance is apparition. The Buddha, Longchenpa, Jigme Lingpa. Who else? Even Richard Chambers Prescott! Wonderful, all mis-identity released, gone, gone, Gone! So now anything that happens is just fine. In a dream I saw the words, "View becomes conduct and behavior," then I awoke with the automatic thought of Kuntu Zang Po, so when I kissed my companion I felt she was Kuntu Zang Mo. Bliss. Jigme was his own Mentor. Longchenpa speaks of the Lama in one's own head. And Khenpo Padma Leks Grub says the Supreme Teacher is Whatever Comes to Presence or Whatever Arises! All Nirmana and Sambhoga Kayas as Compassionate Guiding Images are but Apparitions! What is your View? The Vast Expanse and yourself the Dharma (Truth Wisdom) and Sva Bhava (Self Feeling) Kayas, Spontaneous and Real, your Behavior itself, or some petty smaller something?

The Zhi Khro (the cognition of peaceful and wrathful deities or mind concepts at death or in life) is the entire psychological event field horizon! Take the Mother (Ma) and the Light (Ru) not the la (soul) or the gu (darkness) for that is the shadow

270

worship, the cause of all so called evil which is just the original dropping away from Mother Light. There is the idea that there can be no Thogal without Trekchod of course, do not be intimidated by this system's speaking method! Without Nitya (the Eternal Base) how can you truly understand the experience of Lila (the Relative Play as Path/Fruit/Result)? For the Lila is the Kayas in regard to the Sambhoga and Nirmanakaya, and the Nitya is Dharmakaya. The Dharmakaya is cleared out of all relative (Lila) context to Sambhoga and Nirmanakaya, so it is nothing but Nitya. And that is Vajra (permanent, indestructible) Kaya and Maha Sukha Kaya (Great Bliss). So you can relax now.

The three Kayas are One not three. The Dharmakaya is the Non-Dual and so is the Resplendent Subtle Enjoyment of the Non-Dual in the Sambhogakaya and that everything around us is the Emanation of this is nothing else but the Nirmanakaya and so we come to see it all as the Svabhava Kaya or the Vajrakaya, the Non-Dual Dimension is all inclusive and absolutely One. This Vajra is Vajra Yogini Dakini no less. She is the Prajnaparamita Dakini, the Goddess, empty or free of all concepts (Dharmakaya), Reflected Resplendent in the guiding images and thought forms of all concepts (Sambhogakaya) and inseparable and ever present awake and innate in the guiding images and shapes of all emanated manifest form (Nirmanakaya)!

A simple exchange demonstrates the genuine nature of pure spiritual friendship. I asked Swami Bhaskarananda if he ever needed reassurance that he was loved and he replied, "No. I have always only sought how I can love others better." To me this is an astounding response indicating real spirituality. And with this he told me a story of someone who was asked if a Swami could read his mind with psychic powers and this person said, "If he could read my mind then how could a fool like me be around him." It makes sense.

The lack of Power in the Empowerment has made me turn even More to my own Dakini Power and that is a true blessing of the ritual. But an empowerment impresses you with ideas that stay with you because you! participated by being present! I wanted Dzogchen ritual empowerment because Dzogchen says to get it. I got that. I am grateful.

Deep Gratitude to Longchenpa!, where all credit goes and Jigme Lingpa, but Really those teachings were Dakini Given originally! And realistically speaking most of those in the lama/guru role like to keep the final or last secrets to themselves. How else would they maintain power or authority? But I am concerned with my own sense of respect and gratitude, to honor the Real, but also the teaching. Yet to be honest about human relations, reactions, limits and so forth is the greatest honoring of them! Honesty is Real Honor! Ego cannot measure the Gratitude of the Heart in itself. Since Mother is the Origin of all the World, World is Her! World is Teacher, the Light of the dark soul and that is What is descending, incarnating into us! And so Gratitude cannot be Measured and its Emotional Benefits are endlessly blessing the World as Mother who has Blessed Us! Harm not oneself by lacking the Gratitude! That is what is vajra hell! Nothing else!

By the Blessing of the Goddess may Mind today right now find Ease and Comfort for this smiling fool as it is for Longchenpa, a spiritual friend in the Bardo Sakti of my Pure Mind. Through the cycle of day and night that Pure Contact in the Pure Mind of Samantha Bhadra and/or Samantha Bhadri, that the Clarity of Pure Mind is One's True Teacher even as Samantha Bhadra and Vajrasattva come forth from Pure Mind, is a healthy picture. Advaita insists on one teacher. Dzogchen emphasizes the Unity of all the teachers in the Vast Expanse. This is like Bhava Mukha (the Immense "I")! In the other (the Advaita method) you are missing out! There are systems that insist on one master, but don't forget that they walk with feet of stone (so many are weighted with their ego of being best) and you will become just like that, your feet so heavy you cannot fly free if you follow such ones as these! (see Feet of Clay) Teachers are boats, they are not the Other Shore that you seek!

Vivekananda criticized Ramakrishna's worship of Kali at first and he grumbled about his Madhura Bhava. Is it a healthy thing to do? There should be no delusions about the teacher. The words: master, guru and father pricked the flesh of Ramakrishna, yet still he is called the Great Master. What shall we do to see clearly his True Nature? In the power of imitation I become like what I think is a thoughtful person: a saint, a poet, or a writer or a fool that I see, and so I am not being True as Myself. If just the word "guru" pricks the flesh of Ramakrishna shall I still worship him in the yoga of the guru! Or practice Vajra (Permanent) Siddhi (Power) not only on Ramakrishna, or Garab Dorje or Pure Sakti. Yes, that is right, it must be union with Pure Sakti as the Teacher. No other! For what is it that is said in the story of Ramakrishna, "Even the vision of a Personal God is, ultimately speaking, as illusory as the experience of any other object." (See The Gospel of Sri Ramakrishna) Which tallies with Gaudapada perfectly!

That is why it is so refreshing to hear Swami Bhaskarananda speak of Senior Monks and his teacher Swamis as "Elder Brothers" and what we call the Direct Disciples of Ramakrishna as the Great Disciples of Ramakrishna for in the oneness of Ramakrishna Advaita the idea of those who are direct and those who are not is a thought of separation for what has no separation! Swami had three teachers or elders who taught him: one for Mantra Diksha, one for Brahmacharya, one who gave him Viraja Homa the supreme sacrifice or cremation of all worldly attachment where you are dead to the world but alive to Consciousness! But as Ramakrishna says there is avidya maya (maya of ignorance) and vidya maya (maya of knowledge wherein teachers, books, spiritual practices, devotion and such are contained, even the goodness of spiritual friendship) but do we not seek to be mayatita, free of maya all together! Even the five blessed moods of relationship encompassing all human communion: inner peace with the Ideal, master and servant, friend to friend, parent to child or child to parent, and finally, (Madhura Bhava) sweethearts, as toward the Beloved, (sometimes a sixth mood is given, which is to see spiritual reality even in an enemy) all these as human connections or connection to the Spiritual Ideal are but the maya of vidya when good and the maya of avidya when they drag on you. Get to It. Trekchod! Like a Lion! Nothing gets in the Way. In a dream which to me was sweet wonder, my beloved sweetheart asked, "How do you love me?" "Like a crazy man Loves God!" Even here, my last

273

most loving connection, I know, but cannot say or admit, that inwardly I must have Trekchod even here and perhaps when this is so my Love will be all the Better! The weave of the occurring is amazing, moving everywhere throughout and within, for what is not conceptual binding caught deeper in the triggers of emotion, endearment, fear, any feeling even to the most subtle vanity of religious or spiritual ego which whips back hard with its obscuring and subtle delusion of importance that negates the beauty of Humility and Surrender! So Gaudapada clears the cloud of mind in all this, "The illumined sannyasin does not praise any deity, does not salute any superior, and does not perform rites to propitiate departed ancestors. Regarding both body and Atma as his abode, he remains satisfied with what comes by chance." II 37. No Deity! No superior teacher or person! No worship of ghost spirits! And my friend Gaudapada though you say it here in this context shall I regard the body as my abode, for body too is the maya of imagination compared to Pure Mind!

Even as a time might appear in the illusion of time that I should move through the Bardo, that Bardo body is not my abode! It is Pure Mind for me in Ati Yoga Dzogchen and Asparsa Yoga Advaita. In that Bardo then I shall not practice the Great Gesture of Maha Mudra then which is grabbing, gripping or holding not only to Dharmakaya and Sambhogakaya bodies but the body of Nirmanakaya as these are called the Bodies of a Buddha. Dzogchen and Pure Advaita are not a gesture of gripping or reaching for bodies!

Not to see Buddha in one's teacher! See Buddha is One's Teacher. Tatha Gata Garbha (the Womb Suchness of Pure Mind)! The Real Awakened Oneness, Womb of Dakini Suchness, where all the Zhi Khro yidams are Exhausted! Gone! It is your own Confidence that empowers You, not ritual, not teachings, not prayer. The Encounter is Always Within, so is the Decision to Let Go as Trekchod and the Confidence in Soaring On is Thogal! According to this poet's foolish knowing of the Happy Vajra's (Garab Dorje) Three Precious Statements.

I could have empowered myself if I had believed in myself enough to believe in myself and my own power to know! In

274

regard to those three phrases of the Dzogchen ritual (a ritual is a spi-ritual, something done to inspirit oneself); quoted from the Empowerment, "You are now permitted to practice Trekchod and Thogal" which curiously is literally saying that you may now Let Go and Soar On. "May you be granted the blessing of realizing the Unfabricated Primordial View (which is Trekchod) and the Four Spontaneous Visions of Thogal." "May you have Inseparable Awareness in Trekchod and Thogal." Empowerment is Everywhere in every year and day of my life everything I have ever heard empowers, one way or another. Was it not always a Dakini Dream Exercise in the Great Imagination? Long long before, all this was originally given by the Dakini!

Dzogchen is not a stage! In a Dream, once all dreaming ruminations about Sutra, Tantra and Visualizations stopped, that is ran out, there rose up "Dzogchen" as a dream thought in the dream itself but without the concept of thought. Sudden and Pure!

The second lama's statement, "no use at this stage" can mean his own obsessing with the sutric, tantric and Longchen Nyingthig visualizations, all but obsession with dream which Dzogchen is not. Dzogchen is not a dream, like my dream showed me. Looking at Gaudapada's I 18, you would see that this obsession with imagination/dream continued in this lama. "If anyone imagines illusory ideas such as the teacher, the taught and the scriptures, then they will disappear. These ideas are for the purpose of instruction. Duality ceases to exist when Reality is known." Reality Flashes! Gaudapada's Remedy! Advaitic Medicine! "All these ideas are for ever imagined on the Self." II 28 "Anyone to whom a teacher may show a particular object as the reality sees that alone. And that thing, too, protects him by becoming identified with him. That absorption leads to his self-identity with the object of attention." II 29 "First Atma imagines the individual soul, and then Atma imagines the different objects, external (waking) and personal (dream). The individual gets his memory in accordance with the kind of thought impressions he has." II 16 "Even in the dream state itself, anything imagined by the inner consciousness is unreal."

II 9 "Even in the waking state, whatever is imagined by the inner consciousness is false." II 10 And this includes the experiencer itself in any particular state like "the case of dwellers in heaven." II 8 So when he would imagine he was driving away dark forces the opposites of "dwellers in heaven" it seemed an obsession. Besides does not Dzogchen seek to Empty the depths of hell, even if such things were not just imagination. And where is that true Compassion for all, light or dark? Thinking thus, it was that his ritual obsession became something of a teaching itself, as much as his unexplainable hypocrisy in giving a Dzogchen ritual that teaches Trekchod and Thogal and then not wanting to explain it, but remain at this own sense of stages, visualizations and so forth. Imagination! Dzogchen is not a stage, a dream, nor an obsession, nor imagination!

What karma does one in the teacher role incur by damaging another person's spiritual enthusiasm through mockery? My worst fear about Portland was Disappointment. Yet when Lama Sonam, the other lama, said, "You Ask the Dakini!" That was good yet I have been doing just that long, long before going to Portland. Mocking someone for their desire to know is horrible and not Compassionate at all! You see I asked the second lama about the four visions of Thogal, "Direct Experience, Increasing the Sensation of the Experience, Reaching the Full Measure and the Exhaustion of Visions in Dharmata?" He simply parroted back what was in my question and then said, "I could explain something about the visions, but I won't, for it is no use at this stage." When he heard me ask, saying "Thogal," he deflected the beautiful word back at me with haughty mockery and a twist of his head. I asked again, about the Four Confidences, "No fear, no hope, no expectation and sameness in equality?" Again he just parroted what I said back at me and said once more that "it was of no use at this stage." Such a contradiction since Permission and Blessing to Grant Trekchod and Thogal was given in the ritual, but to not explain any of it. Strange, it didn't feel right. There was rumor there would be no talk about Trekchod and Thogal but I had the nerve to ask of these and when I did I heard fearful nervous chuckles and sighs of awe among those who were there. But there was no answer, it was the keeping of so called esoteric secrets when as we are honest it was so obvious to all that he betrayed himself to reveal his own limitations, hardness and rigidity in the guru/lama role binding himself to his own sense of abusive power, diminishing others in the sense of self righteousness.

What do we know of others and where they are in any space of life? I have seen a couple walking in the town I live. It appeared to me that the man was dominating and controlling of the woman. I thought negative thoughts of him. And then one day my darkness was revealed to me when I saw her walking with a Blind person's long thin feeler cane. I call that lesson Blind Woman Prejudice. Are there others like lamas and gurus who might also have this problem but in their haughtiness will not admit to it. What do we really know of another person's Spirituality or of any other reality in them? Asking such questions that I asked binds and defines you by negative answer. How could the Confidences and Thogal be of no use when they are part of the Innermost Essence of the Longchen teachings? Others who say now, "Yes, teach and talk of Trekchod and Thogal, the Confidences and the Accomplishments, to give that spiritual knowledge before death arrives (and with it perhaps rebirth in this world or another so that we may practice Trekchod and Thogal even there and then) and so that these teachings will not be lost in modern times," these speak as a curing medicine!

To teach all the formulas, rice throwing, mantras and mandala offerings and visualizations without giving Result! Pay for the meal without knowing what the waiter will bring which is to say just believe in Religion with no Answer to be given! I found this second lama insensitive and rigid to genuine spiritual questions (sincere investigations), who preferred sutric and tantric stages, elaborations, sevens, threes, or one rice heap and numbers of this and that, a great waste of energy, denying the Reality of Spontaneous Innately Real Dzogchen (except for what was written in the ritual itself). Are not questions and their answers of "use" if a person has the need, the nerve, and the desire to ask? Yes! And the Compassionate Refuge Response of one in the teacher role Should Be There! Nothing is not in the Past that is not Here Now and will not be Here in the Future.

Mother is the Dancer (Nitya) and the Dance (Lila). We, in mind, do the dividing! So why not speak beautifully, openly, Lovingly, Compassionately and Empathically of Her?

What was learned from this second lama even in the absence of instruction? That my own Confidence and Decision with Inner Encounter is Enough to Empower me to Let Go and Soar On in Dzogchen! There was nothing new with this lama, for really it was the same old story one finds over and over with many spiritual teachers. Poet!, follow your own Feeling and Knowledge! But I do joyfully admit that I feel so connected to everyone that was there, all the people, the lamas too, Anne, all of them. There was a nine or ten year old girl who sat right in front of the lama who diligently took notes on everything that was said in the Longchen Nyingthig cycle/treasures. I thought to myself, what wonderful and remarkable spiritual karma she must have! A yogini lady was there who asked a question and was given an answer and she replied, "That is too general of an answer." A quick response! But I could almost see that even the next answer may have put her into an inner spin of self doubt! Why could I not be so quick to respond with, "Why not explain?" It was because I was depending on an outside answer, so my mind was not relaxed, but this is itself an empowerment in not only knowing what is innately bright, but in knowing what obscures this brightness. Sometimes it is better not to ask questions to spiritual persons for their personality intentions may blind you, like the Dzogchen advice which says don't ask anybody about anything! Should it be so that we should blindly follow and believe in someone or something as if we were in a state of spiritual drunkenness where we have forgotten sober spiritual clarity? Remember what was said about the "Best of Bipeds" (see same subtitle) even Gaudapada felt his conclusion was not that of the Buddha! Yet if Truth be told and if Reality is Reality, then is it not Reality! As human nature or spiritual reality is defined by stage awareness, that definition itself (as an idea only) restricts the True Power of One's Potential Empowerment!

When I met Swami Atmasthananda, one of the three vice presidents of the Ramakrishna Mission out of Belur Math, my thought of him was that he is a Swami's Swami! He had such stories of those two great swamis Vijnanananda and Abhedananda. He told one story of a swami who passed away but even in death was so spiritually brilliant and present that someone said, "Oh No, we have thrown a living swami into the Ganges!" But it was not so. As he was dying, on his lips the words, "Ma, Ma." Another swami who roamed the river at night was asked if he ever felt alone and he said, "No, Rama is Always with me!" But I very much remember the story of the swami who said again and again, "Brahman alone is Real and the world is illusory." He was teaching Swami Atmasthananda this and during one time while emphasizing this to the swami his heart failed and he passed away with these words on his lips and these thoughts in his mind. Swami also spoke of the depth of Eternal Joy that a monk feels. I naturally wondered on this because I am not a monk, but wanting too, that "Eternal Joy" of which he spoke. As I thought on Pure Mind as this Love and Eternal Joy the answer came to me, the very answer itself which made the question arise. Eternal Joy! Pure Mind! Pure Mind! Pure Mind! Even as our only True Mediation constantly without break! Eternal Joy is here as much there even amidst the fully released unconscious contents at death point, where even one's name is gone!

And with that thought, I recall that the swami asked me, "What is your name?" "Ricky." "Ricky? Rishi, you are Rishi! Do you know what it means?" "Yes, Seer or Sage," but I said, "No, No, I am not that." And the swami said back, "No, no, you are Rishi." Now it reminds me of what Swami Ranganathananda said to me when I met him over three decades ago, "Ricky, that is a sharp name." I know it was a play on words, but still it was a wonderful gift for the swami to say. Though when he said it my ego became fearful of its own potential to become lost to arrogance however slight or subtle it might be and so I lowered my head saying, "No, no," as that would bring back to me the memory of Humility. And yet, are we not all this Pure Atma, this Pure Mind, this Pure Buddhi that is the One Seer, and is the Nature of what is within us all as that which alone is Sagely and capable of Seeing with Truth as Truth in Truth! Underneath the

279

taint of obscuration we are all the Pure Mind who is the Seer!

One day it rang like the blessed bell of bliss, in most grateful recall, a memory of Swami Bhashyananda's blessings from over a decade ago. He was teaching me and my beloved what it is to Let Go. He opened his closed hand, fingers out, palm up, saying, "Let Go so you can Surrender." With his huge smiling face and eyes behind thick glasses I felt the Truth in what he was saying but not until now has that Truth become known to be the very teachings of Trekchod and Thogal, though these words were not used by swami.

When I write, sometimes I become so gone in what I am writing. My beloved came up on me once during such a moment. I said, "You scared me right into the Light!" So it seems that even fright, the fear complex of life and death can bring one suddenly into the State. It is no less true for at that moment of intensity we Let Go and wonder how and where we will Soar On.

The poem, Dragon Sight, is certainly that Yoga on the guru/lama/teacher, many of them as it is meant in the fine perception of respect, even when those teachers were not so respectable. It goes through many expanding stages until it reaches Mother Kali dancing in the Dream Mind of the Vast Liberating Expanse! In that practice the keys are Vajra (Indestructible Truth as Original Self) and Siddhi (Power Contact). My dear spiritual friend Swami Bhaskarananda said, "Do we know what Sri Ramakrishna saw as the Divine Mother?" I am at Peace, my friend's words opened Her Divergent Wonder in Oneness once again. Is Pure Mind here just Sattva (the Harmonious Peaceful Gathering Quality of Mind) saying, "Behold!", or the Absolute Itself? I feel right in my heart knowing the teacher is not a physical body, not a human being, but the Power of Powers, Sakti ever Awake in the Stream of Consciousness! With the Self Face of Self Awareness see Kuntu Zang Mo (Pure Mind Mother Light) is the guru/lama/guide, as Buddha (Awakened Pure Mind). Vivekananda saw this very Sight in Ramakrishna and Ramakrishna as this Reality. But Remember, in the Truth of everything that happened, this Sakyamuni Buddha left Arada and Rudraka, as it was with

Ramakrishna also, the Brahmani and Totapuri did not remain.

The Obscuration of the Teacher

That I can have Joy and Realization without the guru shows what damage the guru did! Living under the guru's authority I lost my own authorship. Living in the guru's private world I lost openness to what is the everywhere Self Arisen. Living in the guru's ego I never faced my own ego. Living in the guru's personality I never knew the feeling of my own personality.

Seeking the guru in the other was the cause of my drunkenness with duality! Now I am sober in my True Self. To deny this is still the guru's drunkenness, the lie of intoxication with the poison of toxic doubt. The poet is no longer deluded by the guru's game.

It is true, the guru has tears like any human being, but it is also true the abusive father who is a mono-narcissist can also have tears. Seeking to be part of his journey I shook with fear that I was not walking my own journey. Seeking friendship there I lost what is True Friendship in my self and what that can be to others.

Seeking the death of the ego, I found only the walking corpse of ego returned as arrogance, abuse and the cause of fear in loving parents and friends. Seeking comfort, ease and sanctuary, I found distress, indifference and exile due to self loss. Seeking tenderness I found exclusivity. Seeking openness I found secretiveness.

Listening to the guru I could not hear My Self, contrary to his false promise. Looking for Spiritual Joy I found spiritual jealously. Looking for freedom I found containment. Seeking Spiritual Power in a human being I found the limits of being human. As a child seeking the spiritual mother/father I found only the parents of ego and arrogance.

Seeking to be a loving servant I turned into a slave caught in the clutches of the guru's dominance. Seeking a beloved I lost sight of what is truly to Be Loved. Seeking a master I discovered a tyrant, falling down and further down to worship the guru's feet I could not walk with my own feet on the path of

281

Love.

Thinking Reality was distant and possessed by the guru, I could not touch and hold the immediate Reality that is never far or parted. Thinking that my guru was someone other than my awareness of Pure Mind, I become lost in the intricacies of death and birth, perpetuating the cycle of Samsara, the wheel of buckets turning with life and death.

Seeking truth in a guru became lies and betrayal. Seeking Humility (the true divine teacher within) before a guru I became arrogant in his arrogance, and, then spiritually injured others as he injured me.

Looking for lion-like courage in a guru I lost courage in myself and was thereby paralyzed for a time. I lost Love seeking his love, and searching for his interpretation, I could no longer interpret the pure contact of my own mind in Truth.

Seeking to respect a guru I could not respect my Self and seeking to rely on a guru, that very act of relying prevented me from relying on the Spirituality and Humanity of what is Reliable. Seeking the human guru I lost my humanity and everything else, as I sought to find someone who could remove fear I found someone who created fear and no one who could take it away.

As I sought not to be abandoned I was abandoned, for a guru's love is his own and not yours, and as I looked for someone to surrender my ego to, I found only another ego, back and back into time, until I discovered Surrender true and sweet to the sweet simplicity of Life! I made the mistake of surrendering to the glory of Atma in the glorification of the "Me" of the guru's delusion, so seeking a freedom which was bound by a surrender to a false image, and the damage done was fearful respect for a lie mixed with the formula of Truth!

Seeking the Real "I" beyond the face of the ego, I found an ego so potent with the power of certainty that it blotted out all Certainty of Self. As I sought to destroy the root of ignorance, the stem of ignoring my Self grew into a huge tree in the prison garden of the guru's enormity.

As I would have given this precious life of mine away to find what is Measureless, I found only that I was measured by the guru's measurements. And as I searched out what is beyond Definition I was trapped in the guru's defining. Seeking the Blessed State of never being separate from Sakti by imagined concept, I was deceived in separation from Sakti by the guru's imagination.

Searching to be free of misery and frustration I became perplexed by the heat of the guru's misery and frustration and the uniquely deceptive claim of his, that he was always the same when he was not. Seeking to be free of hell I found the living hell of being constantly disparaged, so much so, that I could not even ask, "What is this hell?"

Seeking for the guru's results and his attainments, I could not see the precious jewel of my own results and I was lost in the lie of being compared as to never having attainment by the standard of the guru and so I experienced the loss of equality wherein it is known that Truth is Equally Present in one and all.

For as I sought the guru's existence I lost my own Existence, as I sought to know what might be there in his consciousness I could not see that Consciousness right in me! And wondering what his bliss might consist of I lost contact with my own Bliss which I had known in myself before the dark day of meeting the guru who dimmed the Light and put out the Lamp of Reality for me.

As I searched for the guru's realization I became unreal, searching for his enlightenment I became darkened, looking for his memories my memory of Reality vanished away. In superstitions perpetuated by the guru, that a river's height, that his health, that these depend upon the disciples' intentions, like the weather, or that one cloth holds less bad vibration than another cloth and that things from the West are so impure they must be picked up with metal prongs or that the deceptions of astrology control us, are all the guru's lies.

Seeking the guru's mind I could not see what was my own mind, looking for what is reflected in his intellect I could not recognize my own reflection reflected in the Ever Awake! And wanting to know the guru's thoughts and the guru's feelings, I could no longer feel a feeling or think a thought for myself! It was tragic indeed, but now, but now finally I Listened to my true spiritual friend in Kali, Ramakrishna, not a guru, who told everyone that "a man cannot be a guru," the very thought of it pricks his flesh, that a guru is a person of mean intelligence and that finally... God (Sakti) alone is the Teacher!

And I listened to the good hearted, wise and awake human being born long ago in the Sakya clan, who told everyone to be a Light unto Your Self, depend not upon external assistance! Work out Yourself from your own darkness.

What these two good human beings expressed for the honor of us in heartfelt human heritage is for me the real union of yoking the Light within one's Self and so there diligently removing darkness, that once and former obscuration gone by bringing up the inherent solution. The rest is illusion. Impermanent. As the wrong thought given to you by a guru is also impermanent, that you have been taught to believe you cannot realize on your own What You Are, to know What It Is that Garab Dorje Knows, to feel What It Is that Gaudapada Feels...

The Dark Teacher or Worship of the Shadow

"Once I fell into the clutches of a jnani who made me listen to Vedanta for eleven months." Ramakrishna

Why do you even want to be a part of guruism? Why not just drop it? Can you not do it because of the hurt, the wound, or do you envy the power? Looking deep into what might feel like spiritual dissatisfaction find You as Satisfaction. To look outward for the teacher is to leave the True Teacher and to look for a lesser instructor. It is to drag down Love into the shape of a friend or something. When Love in Reality, feels Love for all beings (in all the Six Worlds, Everywhere!) in an Incomprehensible Unlimited Way no single relationship can define. So it is until clear in mind, anywhere below, doubt may appear to rise, but Trust, Love is Here. Be warned about the serious and complicated. Here behind is the Beauty of Simple Love. I reject everything but Love which rejects nothing. There is no need to reject when Love accepts everything for what it is. Life as life and Death as death and when you Wake Up in either world you find there is nothing that is not Spiritual! Love is the only Peace and when body dies, Love will be in my Heart (Mind).

Ultimately, everything is the Helper, the Teacher, for everywhere you will find the Dark/Light Paradox screaming at you to Cut Through the Bundle of Dualism with all its impressions. Until you yourself experience the Supreme Moment and then further on you will continue to Cultivate the Divine Sensation of this Moment until you come to a Point where no thought in the entire Universe can describe your Experience to You. But You know the You. Until finally nothing is left but You. You have made the Great Surpassing and in the end as was in the beginning, you as a person become Compassionate, and Loving. You see then that everything in the Great Field of Unity has brought you to this Place of the Compassionate You. The Pure Wisdom Energy of Luminous Love! This is my conclusion and this brings me Peace.

As much as one person may feel good, right and at peace in a monastery, a temple or retreat, I feel good, in the right and at peace when I write. Shall you judge me? How shall that be for we all are aware to some degree of what the human ego is, but how far do you see what the spiritual ego is? There is human pride, but there is also divine pride.

Surrender to God or better yet, the Divine Indescribable is very Natural and Feels Right! Surrender to a human being always has the attendant feeling that something is wrong in this. Follow your Feeling. This is enough to know the way one should go.

A guru who causes fear in a disciple is not a compassionate teacher, since compassion is higher than enlightenment, and Kindness is the Greatest Teacher. A guru who blocks or stifles you is not guiding you. The journey should not be painful if you are on the Course to Love. So a guru who accuses you of having a stout ego is not guiding you to be free from the emotions bound to ego which should melt with Love, but is simply reacting with his own ego blocking your development and speaking from an emotion bound ego of resentment and hard feeling which could be years old. I have seen this.

285

The problem in following a guru is that due to the powerful tendency of human nature toward imitation, you want to become like the guru, but never can this be since this is forbidden, so in hundreds of ways you imitate the guru, never fully becoming yourself and being stuck in an eternal hell of being a servant and inwardly you are given the right to Atma but outwardly you are forever the submissive so there is a duality between your inner and outer nature. You are blocked in both directions. You cannot become a guru which is just the continuation of the tragedy or you must remain sublimated or stifled in the endless discipline of being a disciple which is equally tragic.

You see, again, gurus express themselves in their own terms which may or may not be your terms which is how the Divine speaks to you. They may talk in the frame of celibacy, or of Tantra, of Vedanta or Yoga, or pure Advaita or various levels of Buddhism, dual or non-dual stages and as such their explanations may become your explanations and as such you become colored by the worship of the shadow. We are all shadows compared to the Truth of the Pure Mind. Everything is the dark teacher compared to the Pure Teacher that is Pure Mind.

The worship of anything other than the Pure Mind is the worship of the shadow and everything is the shadow compared to the Pure Mind. Every level. The physical presence of the waking state. The dream reflections of the subtle mind. The spontaneous causes of the causal consciousness. It is all the dark teacher from the point of the Pure Mind. What does Ramakrishna say, "It is all a question of mind. Bondage and liberation are of the mind alone. Bondage is of the mind, and freedom is also of the mind." And to worship the other in someone or something is the greatest bondage of the mind. Whereas Pure Mind is freedom and liberation itself.

All teachers are just human beings like you and me. What is the expectation and the hope of what it is that one should get from a human being? What is the fear that one wishes to get away from or the joy one wants to attain. Indeed, all those are a sign of the lacking of the four Dzogchen confidences. But tradition tells me if I do not venerate the teacher then I will get nothing from the teacher. But this is true of all Life itself, if I do

286

not venerate and have respect for Life I will get nothing from Life. And should I not first venerate the Lama in my own head. Ma (Mother) Herself in my own soul (la). The anxiety of the search exists because one has separated first from Ma and then has formed a separate soul that is caught in the net of the mind.

I am thinking Jesus was born just a human being, but in guru yoga (and in religious myth, etc.) one might project more than is there. In the four empowerments of guru yoga, are not those spiritual energies really coming from one's own open creative imagination? They are just a psychological stairway to your own spiritual energy. I don't worship Jesus. I don't worship Buddha. No human being. But I love the Spiritual Wisdom (East and West) in Sacred Human Heritage. I do Surrender to the Power of Pure Mind, Love and Life and Truth, And that is it!

I think Herman Hesse killed himself not because of sexual propensities but because of spiritual failure or rather spiritual emptiness after looking so deep, then becoming trapped in the idea that there is nothing more. We are blessed by tragic reminder in such an example to stay alert to Wonder and not follow the shadow of those footsteps. But Christopher Isherwood is so humorous, human and sincere, showing the true humanity of his spiritual teacher/friend, the Ramakrishna swami, Prabhavananda in his book My Guru and His Disciple. Again, in mind, bondage... in mind, liberation.

It is the favoring of a thing that creates narrowness and clinging to a guru system and the thing in favor may be purely psychological having little or nothing to do with the belief system itself and that itself can kill out all Wonderment.

The ego is so complex it cannot be overthrown in a one to one fight. It must be just fully held and overthrown with Humility and Surrender (Or Asserted new as Divine Pride.) Even as a sweet arrogance of God himself trapped as a man experiencing divine anger at the illusion of this condition. The Blessed Truth is I (as much as You) can and do have those Blessed Depth Experiences even in my own spiritual experiments, exercises, experiences, the Sun's Light, the depth of thought, nothingness, fullness and More! When I Trust, Treasure and Cherish my own Experience I am Happy and

Joyful. When I imagine my Experience depends on another, particularly a guru, I am depressed. What does it mean? Knowledge of Self is the Way the Universe means it to Be! Knowledge dependent on another is a vacuum of expectation, anxiety, waiting and fear.

I have to speak from my experience. Thank Goddess I got over the one guru control complex. It was never me nor my experience of inner and intuitive rightness. Most people will not admit there can be a problem with their guru. In Humility and Surrender I must simply and honestly admit to myself and to the Truth not divided, that that relation with that guru was just not for me. One benefit of this reflection on my life in relationship to a guru's superego is that it makes all other ego relation problems very trivial.

Summing it up, one guru I knew said, "Compassion is at a lower level." At that moment I felt the difference between his spiritual chemistry and mine. This perhaps accounts for much of his coldness, hardness, strictness, indifference, unkindness and even what felt to be cruelty to those who hurt the most. Advaita says Love is higher than compassion and this is a real problem with Advaita where you have this incredible all encompassing Love of the One Self Reality filled into Love as Love but it just sits there becoming a kind of non-functioning Love State, perhaps so wrapped up in the ego-self (or guru-self) that it seems to care very little at all for the Self Truth in others as they are a Living Reality too. You see in Non-Duality, to love another or show and express Compassion to another is a dualism and that is a contradiction to Non-Dualism. One is Compassionate towards two, the other, the second, the dual. This thinking does not comprehend Advaita Karunam (Non-Dual Compassion) which is perfectly expressed in Ramakrishna's Bhavamukha and Sakyamuni's Void and Compassion together as One! Luminous Karunam is Nirvana Karunam. Without this where is Spirituality? Sympathy, Empathy or Pure Compassion in the Enlightenment of the other, gone to Non-Dualism is rarely discovered there! An example being the Totapuri type who was so wrapped up in his own state Ramakrishna would laugh at him as I now laugh and weep at that guru's concept of non-

288

compassionate Love, which seems now to be quite a hypocrisy. For in Dzogchen it is this Bodhi (Enlightened) Chitta (Mind) that is, that becomes and that ever is so, without never not being so, the Advaita Bodhi Chitta or Advaita Karunam which is Pure Mind itself, is itself Love itself! Maha Sukha! So how could I abide with such an absurd remark in those ideas of Advaitic teachings! Compassion is lower. No! Never! The statement is an excuse to be unkind and say that it is some sort of spiritual thing. Compassion itself may be the Very Energy of Love Itself, never separate from Love, being Love itself in this Reality of this Pure Mind. I think that what was generated was a spiritual practice that did not find it necessary to practice Kindness to others, not even between his disciples. It was hardcore and sometimes actually cruel. Not all of us are like Naropa or Milarepa who need the ever loving living shit kicked out of us to Become Spiritual. To think so is crazy and hardly is it Wisdom.

Even the idea of taking refuge is left behind in Dzogchen! For is it not an effort, a seeking, a thought! Padmasambhava went to empty the depths of hell after his death if one insists on saying there is death. It is so truly wonderful and lovingly compassionate that he did not wish to laze out in heaven. It is emptying the depths of hell which Dzogchen secretly teaches so all suffering might end. For hell is a mental state of seeing things not as they are.

A teacher in the Desire, Form or Formless Regions is still a dark teacher worshiped as shadow compared to the Light of Ma! Formless thought leads to spontaneous birth in formless realms. Form thought leads to form worlds. Desire leads to the six desire worlds of the common cycle of rebirth. You see, the Real Kindness of the True Lama is Ma in One's Self, as this Kindness to Oneself. Yes, True Compassion. Ma shining on la (sometimes meaning the soul), the daughter/son/offspring-mind. From the first moment of the offspring mind's apprehension of the apprehender thought/emotion of Her as apprehended, duality begins. When the duality melts or pops like a bubble then All is Ma. No offspring, no apprehender and no apprehension. She is the One Teacher, the One Reality and the One Truth of the Realizers in all Three Realms or Regions. So why would you attach yourself to something of a lesser degree! Even the Formless Realms have a tinge of thought one must admit, for even the idea of such a level is a form of thought, indeed, though most refined. Any identity as a deity/deitess is thought even as one (who) has gone there to become such a being has to eventually leave that dimension, which is the suffering of the gods and goddesses. So there you see the proof of it being within thought and so that is not Pure Mind. So this Region is attained by leaving the body in one of the four infinite(s); space, consciousness, void or summit. (See Totapuri and Rudraka) Even so the highest "summit" whether Vajra summit, summit of samsara, or Bhavagra, as a summit is a place and so therefore indicates a thought. Also, there is ninth stage of the eight consciousnesses, a summit which is the cessation (Nirodha) of all sensation and perception. Dharmakaya is not a thought, formless or otherwise. The Form Worlds are reached through death in the state of ecstatic rapturous equanimity, spiritual pleasure, or intense mystical fondness where vichara (analytical discernment) and vitarka (the mind's inquiring and questioning) have dropped off. The six worlds of the Desire Realm take no effort at all! As our desires seem so naturally built into our systems. We are here in one right now as we wake, dream and sleep throughout its experience. Until Recognition of the Kaya Dimensions is Recalled in Our Re-Enlightenment in Mother Light (Ma)!

Obscuration! Why? Because if you are looking toward a guru, Your Seeing in Pure Mind is obscured! Pure Mind is Right Here in the three states, but because of fascination with the illustration (the object lesson or person-hood) of the three states, Pure Mind, though ever present, goes unnoticed. So take Notice in a Noticing which is more than elementary noetic insight for this is where that kind of insight springs forth. Know this Place/Point/Dwelling securely!

I know nothing! No! I stand corrected. My (Self) ego (as guru/dark teacher-shadow) is constantly teaching me Humility and Surrender. If I am open to the ego/guru. Is it not true in any case, that teaching, or rather, learning is only there when ego/guru is present! Otherwise, no learner is there to learn, nor

290

ego/teacher to teach!

Be selective who you choose to study with, you will become infected by their personality. Who to consult, guru? Who usually says you are wrong. A psychiatrist, what do they know about God? Two schools with no friend. There is nothing like a true intimate spiritual friend! The Self! Know this in the Heart of one's Truth!

Be complete as You Are, from now, the beginning. Study in anything generates various mind states all of which have some dual doubt . Non (Nir) Conceptuality (Vikalpa) of Ordinary Awareness is Everything! Now, Back Then, Tomorrow!

My mind scatters with the most absurd question when I study Dzogchen. I wonder if a guru could have taught me this when at that "Moment" I am in the Experience of the Content of Dzogchen. This is the crippling effect of materialistic dependence (subtle psychic dependence) on a guru that a guru created, for what should be a pure spiritual dependence in the heart of one's own self. This teacher would say that you can hide nothing from him. I found this very threatening, implying the use of psychic powers, which are the scum in the spiritual quest.

It just goes back to the original cause for my leaving. Why would You want to be with a guru who bites your head off when you ask a question? So you can't even ask any question. You are afraid. And a guru should remove fear (the worst darkness) not make more of it. No matter how stupid a question may be, a guru should answer with light and love! Isn't that the work of the guru as the word's actual meaning, the Light (ru) that removes Darkness (gu). Not to force you into a circumstance where you just sit there abusing yourself, letting others abuse you and feeling humiliated.

This guru that I once knew was never a Kalyana (Beautiful/Spiritual) Mitram (Friend). Never a friend to my Soul, to What I am. Bamboozled, yes I was bamboozled, by hurt, abuse and humiliation. Ramakrishna says if you serve anyone for twelve years you become their slave and have their characteristics. This I did not want. Callous indifference, not Compassion was his. But he was human and with all humans there are moments of recognition. So must I forgive what is human? This is not a question. The Buddhist rule says never criticize the noble ones, the awakened ones, the Buddhas. But the Buddhists say that the six Hindu teachers are demons and their six doctrines are false. These are the famous six schools, Vedanta, Vedic Ritual, Yoga, Samkhya, Logic, and Atomics. So keep your wits about you, nothing is black and white.

This guru referred to my friends as my gang. These were my friends, they did not follow me like hoodlums. There was nothing awakening, insightful, opening or elevating spiritually about that statement toward my friends and me, who sought, discussed and searched for Truth together. It was not coming from Love, the Truth which is just as simple as that. It was a cruel mean-minded insulting strike at friendship, at something he felt he could not control, so he had to attack it and his attack was a success, for none of these friends are friends now. There was no spiritual benefit in that comment and it contradicts the Principle of Love as Truth. This horrible cutting away of friends almost happened in me, but it did not. I kept dear, my friends. I think the guru's truth in what Love is, is just to love the guru and not others or not as much. It is like the repugnant story of the disciple who spent a fortune building a temple for his guru. At the dedication the disciple placed a large stone in the foundation vault. What was the guru's arrogant reply, but to say that he was making too much for himself there, even after he built the temple for the guru! (See The Guru Papers) And the generous devoted disciple was humiliated, successfully. Suffering itself teaches us Humility. Does one really need a guru to add to our suffering?

Sakyamuni spoke of the elders, brothers, sisters, friends in the Dharma (the Path and the Truth), this is good, a good attitude, very human. But when I asked someone I knew how his visit went in India with the guru, what he was most impressed with was the simplicity of washing the guru's shirt, shorts and dhoti. Yet, this guru would put down other gurus, even Ramakrishna, saying they were not fully enlightened. They were karya gurus (path teachers) and that he himself was a karana guru (cause to the end of knowledge). The highest kind. Swami Vivekananda warns that so often the Principle is forgotten in the person. The person he means is the teacher. But that person can also be You. Don't forget it. You can forget the Principle in your own person. Astounding when you think about it. Most wise people should know this is true but rare it is to find one. I realized that in no way did I ever want to become like X, X, X, X, X or any others that were there with this guru. But like a fool I wasted precious time imitating their imitation of the guru. The Principle was forgotten.

The closer they (his disciples) got to him the more arrogant they became toward others and they were even nicknamed the Gestapo. That was a sign of the ego's need to reassert after its sublimation, except for a handful of persons who were just naturally humble, stable, I suppose. It was my signal when I saw how X. had become so arrogant and such a mimic, to get out, no more of this if this is the result. I do not want to become like this, an insane superior minded mimic fanatic, that does not define my Truth experience, but the worst effect that has taken me years to get rid of is that because of all that superior mindedness, I thought I was special, different, above my own humanity. That I once gave my trust to that guru makes me wonder if I can trust myself? The inventory of your own personal karmic history will release you once you have been truthful enough with it. Worst than rape is spiritual betrayal. Worst than murder. Yet, as in all I am writing here, it is just my opinion. If a guru/teacher says you have a stout ego, it is a spiritually vicious act, reinforcing the wrong belief in the existence of an ego. The Spiritual Friend who will shake your hand and perhaps suggest to you that you may be a little too much in the ego when your Humility and Surrender is waning, is far better than a teacher who sits there waiting for you to bow your head or touch and kiss his feet. Is it not a reversing and a blocking of whose ego is really stout?

A guru might express care for you if you show him unconditional love. But you may express what is unconditional love only if you are enlightened. Then you do not need a guru. "It pricks my flesh," said Ramakrishna about just the word, guru. Even an enlightened person who might see Light everywhere surrounding everyone can become motivated by jealousy, anger, defensiveness, possessiveness and so forth. Don't worship such souls, even so, enlightened!

Certainly, from a pure Buddhist perspective this guru and his teachings are a mental stain. God! Why did he have to be so mean minded? And we worshiped him on special lunar days! What a fool I was. Yet, as a stain is only mental, I can see as in a waking dream my own inner Lama (the True Potency of Highest Significance) removing those mental stains. What an interesting journey, the value of which may be more for others as a caution in your course than for myself.

Is it all just ego, and affirmation, validation, evidence of the ego? My ego, guru's ego, even God's ego? If so, then Mother give me Your Ego, a Compassionate Loving Universal Ego! I said to Her, "This guru has damaged my spiritual heart." I felt Mother was near, She spoke in a whisper, "That is just in your mind." How happy I swiftly became again remembering enlightenment (Just Joy) in the Sacred Feminine Power Path. She has said in Truth that you need no guru to Know the Wisdom of Mother. Asking questions to Her within will bring the Reality into the dawn of mind ceasing! What is the World? Where did the "I" come from? What will the "I" Become? What is Peace for the "I"? Indeed, this asking (question) is the guru process itself, not dependent on a false personality, going right into the Principle not forgetting Principle (Self) in person (guru). This guru was not my refuge/ideal, the Totapuri type, enlightened but still angry. Keats, the Poet, had no guru, yet the guru said he was enlightened ("Truth and Beauty") but when I could not deny the feeling and existence of Truth and Beauty within me, his rage was to deny me this.

My record of what I experienced there shows this guru's dangerous contradictions. That is always there with human teachers even as he would dare to state that his enlightenment was on a higher level than Ramakrishna's by saying that Ramakrishna was not fully enlightened. I felt there was something deeply wrong in his comments about Ramakrishna. But I suppose his teachings were rational though rigid, yet what was surrounding him, the people, the worship, the superstitions, I could not be a part of it, at all. We are all just human beings in spite of any prejudice and challenges we face, nevertheless, he was considered to be the highest kind of guru. But it was not so. His disciples by his encouragement became completely obsessed by purity/impurity ritual, a mental asylum, puritanism you would not believe, running around imitating the guru's personality. What else could happen under and overcome by such a powerful personality?

As I keep looking for Peace elsewhere, I find there is no Peace in the elsewhere.

Even the best spiritual teacher has made mistakes. Only a fanatic disciple would think the abuses of a spiritual teacher are a divine inspiration of guidance. But a guru will never admit it, if they did, how could they be a divine mouthpiece? The mistake Jesus made was not openly accepting Mary Magdalene as an apostle even though she had more faith than any male apostle. Magdalene's writings are suppressed to this day because she experienced personal expansive spiritual experiences and guidance from Jesus in the dream state and describes this in her gospel testament. We cannot allow any individual, male or female, to have that much independent power now can we! Buddha's mistake was that he did not make it clear enough, empathically enough, not to worship him or to allow myth to conceal him, the guru is not necessary, you are you own guru and you work out your own deliverance with your own diligence (decision) out of the Natural Wonderment of Awareness present in the Three States of Consciousness. So too, Swami Vivekananda said that Buddha and Jesus were not completely perfect. No one is!

Blessed Goddess (Kali) Please Help Me! My memory is haunted (obsessed) with the image of a guru. Please show me the cause of this haunt and free me of it! Not forgetting, Goddess give me resolution and utter complete Release! What did I want from him that he failed to give, as truth, kindness, anything, and me, did I fail? I apologize, but must God apologize to us for our misery? Save me Savioress!

No more Dzogchen or these years of bewilderment! No thought accepted or rejected. Even with this deeply buried pain (obsession). Be gentle with self obsession. I am too serious. Is

295

it not the Play of Mother (Pure Rigpa) and all mind appearance is but ornament and not Actuality! I am One in Wonderment! "Your own Atma is the Divine Mother." Sri Swami Aseshananda Puri Paramahansa. "Sakti, Sakti! Everything Will Be All Right." His last words to me. "Ask the Divine Mother. She will Guide you," his comfort and ease, his kindness and compassion, in a word, Love.

Swami Aseshananda gave me true Comfort and Ease. What I always wanted but never found in those years. To be Kindly Bent To Ease Us is Longchenpa's Dzogchen. So there, Mother has answered. That is how Spirituality should be. She also says, "The spiritual chemistry was not right for me, with that connection. Be a Mother (Light) to Your Self. Work it out Here, in your own Rigpa. Completion unfolds. Happiness is what you wanted and what you want. You were not happy there and you know well the human faults, funny as they are, and that they are there." Ramakrishna knew the same with Tota! It is all just clouded psychological figuring. Truth is mine as much yours. For I am not-separate from any Advaitic guru or any Dzogchen lama, not in physical history nor even in Subtle Sambhoga Kaya. I enjoy them all in my body, as Suka, as Manjushri. Yes. My mystic nerves are the dwelling of the Sangha, the Nirmanakaya. My psychic prana is the Dharma, the Sacred Celestial Tree of Sambhogakaya. My own Thigle Kundalini (as Pure Mind Energy coiled up into a conceptual scope) is the Buddha in Dharmakaya. It was dualistic obsession in psychological delusion to ever think it was not so.

I give myself to this Sweet Refuge. The teacher is no exchange, alternate or equivalent for Truth or Reality is what Swami Rudrananda would say. Also Rudi would say that the greatest thing beyond finding a teacher is leaving and abandoning the teacher. (See Spiritual Cannibalism) In other words, Satisfy Visva, Taijasa and Prajna with Happy Sakti Bliss (Turiya).

Again, it is not unlike the doubt one might feel in leaving their first or childhood religion. Or the emptiness of divorce where devotion was once given. Yet as True Spiritual Awakening is to simply Become Conscious of One's Ever

Existing Undivided Nature, my excessive and too serious obsessive dwelling on it is echoes of personal delusion.

At best, a person is like a myth or a dream, and is but a symbol of what Great Perfection is. So I am humbled. Dzogchen, the Result (Advaita) is the Practice (Path) as absolute relaxed thought. Ati Yoga (Dzogchen) is the Refined Practice of Prajnaparamita. Rigpa can be exhilarated, excited, creative or at Peace.

Not timid now. My own illusory body is the same throughout, Nirmanakaya. My bright mind throughout, Sambhogakaya. My essence and truth stable throughout, Dharmakaya. What more? The Great Pleasure in Self Bliss. The Bundle Cut! Instant Arrival! Body, Speech, Mind, the Rising Door of the Eyes, Rising Ground Base, Aware Breath is Breathing. Original Ground Perception. Sensation and Experience Developed. What measure is there to Rigpa! Everything is Mother Reality. Now Exhausted in the Vast Expanse. And endless orange galaxies are delightful throughout immeasurable space as thigle specks in Trung Pe's hair, my hair, as I leap into the Unfabricated where there is no "I". No fear of hell. No expecting results. No expectation of attainment. Happiness and Enjoyment are Pure in the Spontaneous Unfabricated Primordial Awareness, The Sameness.

All that makes my ego is Nothing! The Deep Blue Dark with Baba Muktananda. The blue lightning phenomena around the guru during a thunder storm. The blue lightning light (a natural phenomena) around S. The adornments and lights surrounding Swami Rudrananda. The lights and phenomena that appeared when the red blindfolds were lifted with the Dalai Lama. All that makes my ego is nothing, all these physiological/psychological illusions, all the same. What is the difference when they came out of my own mind as cognitive or optical illusions by powerful focusing.

"Nothing whatsoever is Born!" Gaudapada. So do not compare persons one to another, but then the problem, living in emptiness, and my inner Guru answers, "Live Non-Dualistically." In a Dakini Dream, "She was reading the Prajnaparamita. She stopped and said, "I don't believe in seeing

Red Lights and all that." Fear is No Self Trust. A very important fear discovery. In a dream a psychiatrist was analyzing my poetry and said, "It shows that he does not want to be reborn." Amazingly true.

The Reposed One, as Most Excelling World Example, left Arada and Rudraka to Sit Under the Tree of Self, to deal with his own peaceful and wrathful cognitions until the Radiance of Prajnaparamita dawned permanently in that Repose itself! Person is Emptiness. Emptiness is Radiance void of thought, mind (consciousness) released of identity with form, feeling, perception, impulse and body/mind consciousness. Rigpa Primordial. The Bundle Cut Away, Barrier Free. "Oh Mother when shall my bundle be cut?" "When you do it Yourself." "Mother Sakti Prajna, You Are My Tree of Self." "Direct Perception, the Ground of Me. The Growing Sensation Experiences Me. The Entire field of Thought or Event Called Universe, Three States, Six Worlds, Anything cannot contain Me. I Alone Exist, There Everything, Everyone You See is My Womb of Suchness (Consciousness)!" "Sakti, Your Gentle Breasts have comforted my agony, when will this mind be at ease in Your Womb of Suchness?" "When you forget "when" and the cognition of thought in the dual ego mind. Thought is Suchness. Suchness is Thought. The memory forgets what memory wants. Solve the incredible puzzle of spiritual searching." "Sakti, my memory is full of Your Ease and Comfort, the Radiant Prajnaparamita." "Memory is Emptiness. Emptiness is Memory. Repose Now, Here (The magic word!). Never again there!" Sambhavi Mudra is the Gesture of Looking into Shunyata (Emptiness) while seeing other things, people, thoughts, moods... with opens eyes.

Walk through your house (or mind) in the complete dark. Can you see with feeling? Passion gives Emptiness purpose. Compassion gives Emptiness the Profound Reason. Yet Love is More than all of it. The greatest darkness (gu) is within your own deep sleep, which is also the womb of all waking and dreaming life. Do not worship the dark. Do not worship the shadow. Worship only Light (ru). Mother (ru). Self as ru (Light), but not the body/mind shadow, the darkness which

298

appears and disappears over and over as life and death, coming and leaving! Know the Self Meaning of AUM. Know the Illusion. Know your Advaita. Exhaust and Quench all Vision.

I have seen True from the murderer to the depth of spiritual blue. Tibetans regard many lama teachers as benefit, this is very natural. Indians generally believe in only one guru, more than that is heresy. This is very unnatural. Gaudapada's Ist and 2nd verses of the IVth Chapter. Is it the Buddha he calls the Best of Bipeds or is it the Great Non-Dual Spirit that Pervades all beings and is their Sole Teacher, Path and Final Reality? Whichever it may be in the final stage the memory of the firebrand (all Phenomena, People, Everything) must be Quenched Away. Ramakrishna is True, in him, Dzogchen, Ati Yoga, Asparsa Yoga, Advaita, Tantra, Buddha, Krishna, Allah, Rama, the Goddess! and All. Peace Be Me!

Buddha's headache! Study until the head explodes or until the head turns around and it will turn your head (view) completely around. Alaya Vijnana is the universal storehouse of all thought within all minds. There is a turning about here in this deep dark state where everything has dissolved into a sleep that awakens in the deepest seat of consciousness. Even so it is a burning out of all impressions that have been left there. Do not worship the shadow. Come out of the mist into the warmth of Morning Fire! Your Own Self!

Is the horror that I feel, that paralyzes me, that prevents me from moving, that freezes me in my tracks and stops me from being alive, that I feel that if Truth was failed there that it is failed everywhere? Succinctly, this is the core of the darkest legacy of the guru. I cannot believe that such a thought is true or real for if I do believe such a thing then I am dead to the Light. Nor can I believe that India or Tibet are more sacred than America. That the ground there is more vibrant with Truth than here for is not the whole Earth Sacred as it is or not sacred at all. None or All. Where is the Beauty that I seek that I feel sometimes so failed to know at every moment? The rays of the Sun touch the tops of the trees and there, there is my Transcendent Beauty, my Truth, as it shines from pure blue sky around the whole Earth the same. There is only one ocean given

different names. There is only one land given different names.
And sacredness is carried in the heart alone and that is what
gives sacredness to wherever we stand.

When I think upon Pure Spiritual Principle in the experience
of my life I am joyful in this Freedom. When I start to think of
the guru that joy goes away with the thought of the guru. Some
would say this is my dark karma or astrology or some such thing.
This is their denial of the fact that one person (a guru) can injure
another (the seeker) spiritually. People who think it is all their
problem and not the guru's are hiding from reality. It takes more
courage to admit fear, doubt, ego, than to hide it and it is a better,
purer, truer human teaching, by just being human and not
thinking the guru is a god. Love and approval takes you farther
along the way than a guru's abuse. This guru generated in me
such a negative opinion of myself how could I have the vital
energy to engage in vigorous spiritual life. To reach the Love (in
True Self) you must feel good in self. Was this a good method
to rid ego? No! What good can come from damaged feeling?
All this was Samsara (the Dream State) not Nirvana (as the Real
Waking State). I will not entertain (thought forms) in the house
of the mind.

I am no channel, no conduit, no psychic, poet or teacher. I
am transparent. Only Mother is here. If it is true that Mother is
working through me no doubt as one kind and loving Swami did
say, then She is working through everyone. Did She put me
through the agony of guru darkness that I would and could
illuminate Her Reality? If it is so then let me write. I write my
own Tantra to remind this lazy fool not to be forgetful. Do we
make our self what we want? The deep non-dual experience, no
name, no advaita, no dzogchen, no incessant inner soliloquy!
Sakti, my memory goes (dies) in the Moment! Until it stirs out
of the Death Light of Spontaneous Perfection to be reborn (come
back). The very act of meditation deceives! In the Expanse of
Wisdom there is no one who as an ego (thinker) is meditating.
There is no practice. To practice Dzogchen is not real
Dzogchen. Though practice of a participating meditator is
explained in Dzogchen tradition. Imagination is Bright Taijasa,
dream, even with luminosity mixed in mind. This is the silk net

of ego created illusion.

Am I not also in the Presence of the Great Teacher (as you are) even at this Precious Alert Moment. Alert to Sakti, to Tatha Gata Garbha, to Ramakrishna, to all I have known in the Journey? Have I been fighting this True Presence by false memory soliloquy? If I must name this Presence, Nirmanakaya is physical presence, Sambhogakaya is subtle presence, Dharmakaya is spiritual presence, but Tatha Gata Garbha is the Womb of Indestructible Self. Never destroyed by a guru's negativity. Is it not like it was, as I would write and translate what those teacher experiences meant to me.

At the core this guru's teaching was a non-compassionate advaita, no compassion for those who really needed it, steeped in fears and also superstition, exclusive self divining and evil defilements in others. It is sad and it was a sad experience for me. Tibetans say Jesus was only a Bodhisattva, so why can't I make my observations based on my experiences. There is the saying that from Buddha there is no transmission. Transmission comes from you. But so much lama/guru stuff is contradictory to this. Aseshananda never made me feel that way.

Every imaginable thing or person is Mara (illusion) Maya (cosmic dream), even a guru, as the Dharmakaya Reality is expressed in Dzogchen (and you are That) never needs a guru's teaching. Rudraka and Arada are also Mara Maya. Sakyamuni rejected them and nirvikalpa. His first disciples were five reincarnated yakshas (brahmin demons). Amazing. I saw a lama bow to the Dalai Lama, he bows back deeper and the lama goes deeper. The Dalai Lama then goes deeper until both are on the floor head to head. Beautiful. The guru I knew would never do that because of the guru narcissism induced by his form of advaita.

Love flows through and over all these puzzles (mind exercises). In Humility I Surrender to Pure Mind Love for how easily does ego identify with lesser conditions from mind levels inside you, you make up your existence in Pure Existence. In humility I must admit to ignorance. In surrender I give over only to Pure Sakti. May Mind never come down from Pure Love. Even if body or mind may occasionally make traditional

301

salutation to Elder Friends. May I never again inferiorly regard myself, hold to book ego, or an "I" complex. May the gesture of my life be only for adoring Love!

Dzogchen study reminds me of the little Advaita books. This stirs memories of this guru. I must admit my debt of gratitude and not have rejection thoughts. I honestly was never liked by nor comfortable with this guru's community. He was just a man, pure to the core with his form of Advaita, but just a man. Release me now Mother, from regret into spontaneous perfection of Love. All my teachers are only little forms of Her. Even my addictions and obsessions which gradually drove me away, so that many more flowers could be enjoyed by this Bee, who turned into a Lion and then became an Elephant, were but small forms of Her pushing me closer to Her.

It would be easier if X. were not in the mix. But are not all I've known family, in their Essential Self (Being, Bliss, Emanation). Still, this strange undefinable agony is a small form of Her guru-ing me. What does it really mean at the bottom matter of fact? What? A call to Truth? A call to India? No! It is dualistic agony, the non-seeing of Reality Here and Now. Remember the whole story. Transmute the three dualistic poisons. That is the agony left undone. Lust. Hate. Stupidity. Are in Essence. Bliss. Clarity. Awareness. Naropa are you Happy? Ricky are you jealous? Ricky why do you regret the journey put before you now behind you? Can you not with humility and surrender accept what is put here for you by Her!

So why be in agony, my redundant memory of what has been done? I sat in that guru's court. Then left for certain reasons. Now from Dzogchen I get even more Non-Dual Freedom in Felt Awareness than ever from the little books of the guru. That is the past. That was preliminary! Now go farther into the Lion's Mouth! Develop Dzogchen. Joy and Serenity in the Supreme Moment is the same no matter where you are! For Spiritually, I now have what I have always wanted! But his person and words burn my soul. Did he betray the guru's promise to me? Did I betray the disciple's promise to him? Either way is grief! A hell! It is what Ramakrishna describes as the frog (disciple) stuck in the snake's mouth (guru) who is unable to swallow the frog and so they both suffer.

Thirteen years a follower. Thirteen years now in Freedom from following. Ricky it is Time to wake yourself Up in this Supreme Moment of Pure Total Presence. This guru conflict drives me to create my own Free Spirituality. Why? Mother is pushing me, the conflict is Inseparable from Her! Advaita! Excitement! Creativity! When I realize that my own Spirituality is Free for thirteen years now from the clutches of that guru, I am exhilarated in Pure Excitement and Self Joy. Blessed Be! "Once I fell into the clutches of a jnani (Totapuri), who made me listen to Vedanta for eleven months." Ramakrishna. Me too, I know those "clutches" as well my Beloved Friend!

Is writing but weaving webs? Doubting my own power of commitment has been the cause of envy and agony. Is it not sacred to rejoice in other's spiritual accomplishments? That jealousy is a dream image. It does not exist in Love. And what is commitment but to send and give over oneself to someone, some idea, or to pure profound Awareness (Rigpa) itself. Choice or destiny are unenlightened commitment, it is true commitment only in surrender as to render up and give over to Sakti which is All Life.

So there is where my fear has lived, my self doubt in dualistic agony. One feels their spiritual potential before going to a guru, it is the reason that calls you in the stupidity of it. After you have arrived gradually you are made inferior and even that original potential may be destroyed. When S.'s mother was dying I discovered my full commitment to her, to my Love for her, few could understand. Is it to be afraid of death, no, spiritual confidence moves through that, no fear of hell, delusion, others! Is it a fear of separation from, a death of contact (primordial) with the Mentor/Archetype, Lama/Yidam or Guru/Ishta? Is it not the fear of death (and of many memories of death before) more than the fear to live in the Great Completion of Loving Compassion? Rigpa. Trekchod. Thogal. Only when mind generates separative thought illusion. In Reality it is never so, Mind is always Suchness. Is Always Buddha. Manjushri. The three Kayas in Dzogchen Refuge at their Highest. Why settle for less? In a dream three friends (Kayas) asked me

303

"Who?" "Oh Yes, my Dakini (Sakti)!" Is this Mentor/Ishta/Yidam mind related dual level of contact, old and gone, new and better, or Something known of, but yet to be More Powerfully Felt, deeper than either old or new context buried in Sambhoga Dream Mind yet ever Present and Clear in this Dharmakaya!

S. got me stirred into Dzogchen memories. S. functions like Vilwa's Lady guru! Even recollection is benefit as cleansing. Ah, Dr. X. was kind and most spiritual over all of the others it seemed to me. At his house, my first year. I wonder if he left this guru for the same reasons I did. He said he learned about quasars in a dream about this guru. But now we know that the cognitive capacity of the dream mind to find its own answers can be brought up by many kinds of spiritual focus methods before sleeping like meditating on the Dzogchen "A" symbol. It is You, not guru. I liked Dr. X. for he was kind. Right to the bottom of it I didn't ever like this guru's spiritual state, his personality, his abuse. The spiritual union was never there. I tried to force it by my belief in its necessity. But I could never see this guru practice the four Boundless Joys. I left Rudraka like the Prince Siddhartha Sakyamuni.

It was already there. I always felt X. was more advanced (an inferior distortion). X. was said to have... I didn't believe it, latter I heard the same story from a direct family member (a niece) of his, then I had subconscious belief acceptance, but I still could not believe that X. had... Still, did Dr. X. leave for my same reasons? Even my Sakti Life was pre-known to me during all those years of bewilderment. I still want to doubt that X. had actually..., but there was a dark cloud around him. Those spiritual fruits I do not seek from that tree!

Do I still distrust and dread that guru, his picture, his anger, his curses, his assaults, his displeasure, his unhappiness? Is this just basic fear projection into an obsessional form? Am I weak? Why should I fear anything but the absence, the non-presence of Love, which is a fear existing only in mental illusion. So maybe I fear only my own illusion which is not a my-ness of mine in Love, anymore.

I know for sure that I don't want to be an actor in the theater of a guru, being forced by a scolding and even scalding personality into assuming those role playing slave games. What is the difference, William James or Nisargadatta, a conscious level, What? Both are licked out body and mind, everything into Kali Shunyata!

In Dzogchen there are no individuals (ornaments). Thirteen days moaning and groaning about thirteen years of life that ended thirteen years ago. Still justifying my leaving. What I put in mind becomes mind spinning, but Pure Mind is Free in Essence no matter what karma/samsara spins in the ornament. It is the ultimate pleaser ritual! The guru's game over you. Accept/reject in Humility and Surrender what this lifetime is. Always More. Sakti reclaim my mind with Your Joy where I no longer divide You from me and "me" is Gone, Gone, Gata, Gata! Mother remove spiritual competitiveness and jealousy, hierarchal arrogance, the evil faults burned into me by company with the evil guru system, evil even in the best because of its nature of one superior over the other and only good when this disparagement of soul, this murder of the soul does not exist.

I become so insanely focused into my insignificant problems I do not see how Fortunate I am. I Can Love the Goddess and in this Love there is the Non-Dual Peace, no matter if there is Samsara or not, or Nirvana or not! What I have experienced may in some way be applied to anyone's experience with any guru, religion, abuse or delusion. That is why I am writing with painful honesty. No matter what bundle you carry you must Cut Through it to the Reality of Love.

It was truly wicked how the narrowness of this guru could make a person feel. A man was sent away for the clothes he wore. What is more important, Truth or clothes. Clothes apparently. To cause such awful feeling in others out of fear created by such narrowness is wickedly evil when one has set up the promise of Truth to another. No compassion there. Everyone, that is so many of them thought I was defiled, evil and because of fear of this guru's anger no one would carry my letter and story to him for fear of being associated with me. I am happy I am not there. But the wounds, the sick emotions, paralyzing. The superstitions extraordinary. Mother Goddess restore me.

It is what it is, inclusive itself in my own sight, I have always been what I am, suppressed, forced, resisted or manifest. To free my mind habit now of justification and superstition in ego centric mental reverie. If someone turns from the guru to study Buddhism it is superstition to believe that it is karmic fate nor does their death have to do with or because of their study. Haridhosgiri and others never made me feel bad about the quality, nature or essence of my Spirituality, but this guru always did, even in positive moments there was his displeasure. In how, who, when and why I am now free, as S. pointed out, it is a blessing of Kali and Ramakrishna. Kalee Bhava: The Goddess and Her Moods was the pull to Her Saving Feeling of Felt Awareness. Because of Atma became the Real Cause to Peace. The Skills of Kalee and Measuring Sky Without Ground are my Tantra and Dzogchen equivalents. Kalee; The Allayer of Sorrows was a further Confirming of Reality. The Goddess and The God Man was the Epitome Peak of Wonder in Truth. Living Sakti, a Blessing of Clarity and The Mirage and The Mirror the Bringing Together of it all. All this was my sadhana, the writing, my practice. Be at Peace. Open as the Sky, Mighty Garuda, not an entropic bird, but flying non-entropic mind flight in the Open, holding to no thought!

Can one change the flow pattern of mind memory content as the emotional affect experience, the very clarity of causal views? Impulse, energy, etc, is needed. Tantra is transformation. Dzogchen says transformation is not needed. But giving in to something (an ideal or teacher) other than Real Self Being, thats the thing. Ramakrishna did not maintain his four or five primary guru relations (nor I), this is the natural example, only Kali, (me too), child of Her. Advaita jnana is the flavor of my Tantric Dzogchen, not the object, person, prop, external, picture or memory. It is the excitement of one's own advaitic pleasure, radiance and undivided connection. With the Kalyana Mitram, the Kind Spiritual friend, there is no glorification of, nor worship of a person. Absolute Dharmakaya is the shared reflex response and the True Spiritual Guide. Very Good.

I ran to Ramakrishna for Protection from my self imagined

306

superstition of the guru's curse for leaving him and to fill the vacuum within me. With great energy I should think of Ramakrishna for three thousand years. So much of life is sadhana (spiritual practice), it is done with, only in those Moments where one is enlightened, indeed, made light by the True Light of Love. No personality influence memories, it is Immediate Awareness simply as it is the waking, as it is the dream, as it is deep sleep, nor is it vastly unique. When you find yourself in the waking state and then recall the quality of dream consciousness that recall produces subtle spiritual experiences. There is nothing amazing about this. It comes from within you alone, the recollection of the subtle land and its nature, as it is in dream. When again you are in waking (or dream) and you recall the quality of deep sleep, in your mind you experience the non-duality and undivided of that condition and the bliss, joy, happiness and being/existence of that state of deep sleep. No one has given you anything, you have only remembered what is inside you already as the Goddess has made it so. Do not be deceived by external agents, they are not divine doers, it is Mother who has made them and the immense vast waking state. In the same way, yet with greater Awareness when you recall your True Nature that is just you bringing forth You (Turiya).

The guru dilemma may teach better than the dependent relation for you must get Truth on your own. Am I spiritually alert enough to respond to any question mind play any guru could assault me with? The guru of my own mind? Dzogchen! Mother, I know nothing, so just give me the Love to Love Well! Gaudapada states the Truth (III 36) "Brahman is birthless, sleepless, dreamless, nameless, formless, ever effulgent, everything, and a knower. With regard to It there is not the least possibility of ceremony." That is worship. The knower is You as Brahman, how can you worship you? If you go outside or down from this level you worship the dark teacher as that ego or your own ego and that is worship of the shadow.

What a guru claims to be as a human power is the same mistake Jesus and Buddha allowed to happen, or perhaps they did not know it would happen. Swami Vivekananda says that they are both but bubbles in the Ocean of Mother Sakti. So what

307

is a simple guru compared then to Pure Mind (Chitta = Mind Consciousness, Varga = Free From) which is the Truth.

If he was such a high level guru then why did being with him and the memory of him hurt and wound me so much, even as the buried feeling comes up, it can not be that it is all my fault as he would say. This strangeness happens everywhere. A superior denying the reality of their flaws.

Everything (experiences) in Waking and Dream content is nothing, not even my full life to be known. Sakyamuni is but skandhas (compositions). Illumination is never lost. So this is the Truth. But is fear only negative Love, what is called Ravana Bhakti, the demon who loved Rama, the god/guru? They speak of the path of the asuras and the devas. The asuras are the jealous gods and the devas the good gods. They represent two paths. Devotion to the god/guru is the way of the devas. Turning to independence is the way of the jealous gods, but it may be more genuine to human reality. Besides the Real god/guru is the Ultimate Principle, Being Knowledge Bliss, it does not mean an imagined fabricated deity and certainly not a human being. So if you misinterpret this as the deva path where are you? In deep illusion no doubt. So the asura path may help you break free to the one way to see it is illusion, then you give up the asura path and abide in Reality. I do not follow devas nor asuras, I follow Love and this Love is free of both those applied limited courses. If I may be permitted to quote my friend Dr. Alfred Collins from his From Brahma To A Blade Of Grass, which is one of the best depth explanations of all that I am writing about. "As "Sunahsepa" shows, however, it is often appropriate to become somewhat asuric, to decline the role of being a god's (Brahman's, guru's, husband's, father's, etc.) selfobject for the sake of being one's own self." Dr. Collins also makes the extraordinary and astounding insight that the rage of a guru amounts no less to soul killing or the spiritual murder of a disciple, as that one is destroyed by the guru's anger. (See Fatherson)

So if you doubt yourself feeling that you should not break free of that selfobject-hood, then let me remind you what any thoughtful person would remember. The Buddha himself did

308

take that asuric step leaving Arada and Rudraka, he had to, to become the Enlightenment he sought, they obscured it for him. And according to Buddhist viewpoint, Arada and Rudraka were asuric teachers of the six asuric doctrines of Hindu teachings such as Yoga, Samkhya and Vedanta. Ramakrishna too, took this same asuric step, not leaving his teachers but sending them away! It was his choice and it also happened by the guiding power of the Divine Mother's command. Any guru who believes they cannot learn from the disciple is a fool in their arrogant Atmic narcissism.

Am I even the Self of Tantra, or Advaita Vedanta or Dzogchen? These are traditions and my Self is not a tradition. I am my Self, Once Again Self Arisen. Yet Dzogchen thinking frees me, No X., Nor X., not sitting with them and none of their products (disciples). Ramakrishna, my spiritual friend healed me, he says, "A man cannot be a guru." Its amazing how many memories are triggered and almost every one of them is negative. It darkens my spirituality to think too much of the man. It obscures my capacity to see Sakti's Instructions everywhere and in everyone. I did not like his personality. I did not like worshiping a human being. And I believe he could have taught Advaita without crushing the life out of people. Ramakrishna certainly did so. Hierarchal advaitic guru arrogance causes dualistic lesser feeling to anyone else. It does not show the Law of Equality of Kali in Everyone. I no longer live in suppressed denial of those realities, damaging, uplifting or mixed. A great world collective, the dark and light side of guruism slowly turning on a wheel called life in the dimension of Pure Self (Pure Mind). Don't deceive yourself that it will go away on its own.

I remember there was a poet who published his book dedicating it to this guru and his wife. This guru was furious I heard, very displeased that his name would be there with the poet's beloved wife. An excellent illustration of what I am talking about. Maybe you have gone to a guru or two. You can get it without a guru, on your own if you apply yourself to the Self. The joy and knowledge will come as it is what you have wanted in the first place. You must drink yourself, not remain in secondary dualistic practice. Take to, take up the Primary Course. Only fear, mental tremblings, keep you from the Pleasure Radiance of your Innate Undivided Experience. The Great and Sweetest Gesture of Love producing Pure Mind (Amanibhava). Even though I feel deep love and gratitude to Swami Aseshananda, I give him over to Ramakrishna and Ramakrishna goes then to Sakti, my Atma Bliss State. There are hundreds of stories of sages, saints, gurus, and incarnations. You too are in the Spiritual Field of Energy, Nature and Essence as they. Those who think of Atma may think of it as ego until nirvikalpa shut down of thought where no ego exists. Even when you come out of that state as you do out of deep sleep where Mother Light dwells, the ego experience idea returns, comes back. This is the problem with sahaja as divine assertion perhaps, but ego is there as body/mind skandha identity. Sakyamuni saw this problem and so he looked into Shunyata, where no Atma as ego self is as for those who grasp at Atma in ego or relative guru relations, religions, ceremonies, etc. So you have jesus here and guru there and all the universe surrounding, that is why the Goddess answers my need in Loving Satisfaction. Ramakrishna opened the door by my own Love, gave me Love to Love. Love is the one word I have Kept!

It is something about the quality of teachers and the types of disciples. What they want from each other. Yes. Looking back at all that happened in those years is not that profound in truth now, honestly. Love knows no fear. Love is the Truth. It is as simple as that. These last notes were what I heard as the song faded. Yet what is so strange to me now is that these were not his words but the words of Swami Vivekananda and that he did not say who really said them for Swamiji says, "Love knows no fear, knows no rival, knows no bargaining. Love, lover and beloved become one." But what I learned there was so different. Love of who and not who and fear of self, a contradiction. What impressed me most was the fear and submission experienced. S. really hit it when she said that what was paralyzing me, was the learned fear of other's displeasure. And I know that my own Self Trust in Truth that is as much mine as the next was somehow put away (abused) from me

310

instead of a bringing together in the heart experience. But Ramakrishna and the Swamis never did this to me and if I cannot say and speak of me then who shall know even as I am Truth in my Real Self void of all obstructions. To see Tatha Gata Garbha, the Rigpa Essence even in the most ordinary spiritual person or teacher is to receive gifts. But this is really Pure Mind as Suchness perceiving Essence in Everyone. And it is not glorification nor devotional blindness.

The difference in Divine Pride as the Spiritual Everywhere in Everyone as all Gods and Goddesses is not the Ego of Atma, which Totapuri was such a prime example as Advaitic problematic personality demonstrated for us in the Compassion of Ramakrishna's life example who is one of the only ones who speak of the true honest state of guru difficulties. Either ignorance or arrogance it seems. Everyone says their gods and ways are the best. It is astounding in the deception even as a fraudulence through ignorance or just plain arrogance. All that was Buddhist even Shankara aggressively attacked, while his teacher's teacher, Gaudapada, had great respect for the "Best of Bipeds" Sakyamuni.

Still, it was a renunciation of "you", so how can Real You come forth as Self, with the hierarchy of guruism installed no Equality in the Compassion Experience emerges. One can say Everything is Spiritual (Absolute) or one can categorically judge conditions in people and things (Relative). Neither view is Dzogchen. Neither view gets It! A guru who destroys "you" as I heard it said, is not Spiritual. Who will be there to hold Reality as you have been crushed out from being a person. I know, yes, the salt doll (ego) goes, but even a guru has an ego personality and a tremendously stout one at that. That is why Ramakrishna speaks of the ego of knowledge as something that sages have. Shankara had it.

Someone I introduced to this guru could never accept the humanity of the guru as a being who is human, that this person could be unhappy, angry or on a hiss. I also glorified X. and X. and did not question and this went over to the guru to my detriment. Now I see more honestly not brainwashed with glorification, was all the guru's devaluing necessary. Does that

311

treatment bring the destruction of the obscuration of the ego or just produce a hurt and wounded ego where ego is so damaged and paralyzed and so cannot flower into Something greater and more wonderful than ego. But even negative relations can bring joyful whole insight if honest self examination is sincerely applied, if one does not become negative oneself neglecting human fragility, the dream, mind, essence, reality and true ego well being. And truthfully, one does become mean by the meanness of others, like X. who was so mean minded by the meanness of this guru. God, what a mess! You got to let it go, cut through all of it to an environ inside and out, like sitting in a swing on a cool night drinking in the wind, ocean, stars, and the dark. Knowing yourself without parents or gurus, then like never before, memories of the true Self are there, mine and yours I would think. A guru's opinion of you or of anything could be wrong even as they might claim infallibility. What does it matter and in comparison what can bother you after that?

Is the human heart too easily betrayed or is it that because Love is the Truth that the sense of wrong in degrees of Love is our gauge to measure Reality itself. I will peel off every layer in myself to get to Pure Advaita. She, Sakti infuses me with the Energy of this Reality and that is Love. Though everything is contained There, there is no room Here for anything but Pure Mind.

In dealing with this obscuration I must be aware of what is a spiritual problem and what is a problem related to just being alive, age, emotion survival, etc. A mirrored (camaraderie) self reflecting judgment that his (or my own, in reflection) decision to a life of servant/slave devotion to a guru is felt to be wrong. Life is complex, nothing is simple. Idealizing the idea of what a sibling or a mother, child, father, sister, god or guru, any of it, should be, is a problem. Cut loose. Be Now Soaring. Mere depression is nothing, dive into the depth of utter despair and then Cut Loose and Soar On.

Is my resentment that my spiritual karma was that I was deceived to worship what I idealized and what now is to me a dark teacher and that one of my connections I led to him is still in his clutches? As an elder, I trained the younger, in life, which

312

just naturally happens in a family. My younger relation always wanted to be St. Francis, he even created his own religious language of a forest yogi when he was a kid. I am ashamed I feel like I raised a fanatic, but I have pride also over one who could live and give away their life for at least some sort of spiritual reason even if it is hiding from the world under the wing of a guru.

But it finally came to me with ringing clarity that some one who has given their devotion to a secretive cult will not want to hear anything from anybody or any other view, for that would simply deflate the balloon of fantasy that they have built in their mind's conception about the cult. I also at this same time came to the peace of knowing how wrong the method practiced there really is. If every insight feeling one has about their own spirituality is hammered to death, then how will you arrive at the Atma if you have been destroyed on the road to Atma. Or what condition will you be in when you arrive at the Atma. I know, I know what you will be thinking at this point, that you think the ego and all conceptuality must be beaten the hell out of you before you can get There to Atma. But that is not my way. I surely know you can get There through the Joy of our Gentle Insights. Being humble without holding on to ego. And knowing that all conceptions are just conceptions!

I pray I myself am not hammering around too much, I know it sounds that it is so but this problem needs to be thoroughly addressed as it exists in many forms everywhere and is a great obscuration to liberating spiritual development. Is it normal psychology to snap and float even after all these years. Yes, it is said to be natural. One snaps to the clarity of reality about these matters and one also floats back into those memories and superstitions. Is it a psychic calling? I think that is superstition. Or just obsessive? If one must obsess on removing illusions then let it be so. It is not just fault finding for I am trying to get to the bottom of reality without superstition and fear. Am I wallowing in delusion? Did a guru put that delusion in me? Is this all just reverting to earlier training (beliefs and superstitions) as spiritual trauma in the course of self realization? Am I a monkey who is afraid and so therefore is grasping or Am I Mother's cat? Or is writing this a mind terma from Mother and Her cat? I serve only Her. It is for Kali! So Mother if I must be marked with or mirrored within a teacher, let it be You! Let me be mixed with and matched with You!

I have to write with honesty because these kind of things are what we must Cut Through to be able to Soar On. I even Cut Through (Trekchod) the idea that I am writer at all. Then I can Soar Onward without that fetter. Letting Go of idealizing and idolizing is the thing, like a Christian questioning if Jesus did actually resurrect. There are two beliefs. After he came down from nirvikalpa samadhi he revived his body and lived six months in an Essene cave where he finally died a natural death. There is a letter about this secret called The Letter from an Essene in Jerusalem to his brethren in Alexandria. The other idea is that he and his mother went to Kashmir and lived out their lives there and were buried side by side. People can see their graves there and there are those who claim to be their descendants. Also there are seventeen years of his life missing from the story. Some believed he traveled the silk route to Tibet, and India and studied Buddhism and the Vedas and was considered a wise and yet rebellious man. Others believe he spent all that time hammering nails and sawing wood, making chairs, crucifixes and tables. (See Christ the Saviour And Christ Myth)

In my floating I do not deny envy, but I also know we all hate (dislike) in others what we hate in ourselves (mine and his spiritual obsession). Also isn't it ridiculous to be competitive over who may have the longest stable samadhi (Peace) with a person who is not even here except in mind imagining. I am not envious of instruction and daily company. I don't care for that type and I get it in myself, but of extended spiritual states, I care. This is the nature of competitiveness generated around a guru which is also for his attention and approval. I laugh at and even pity others who are there, but with a relation into the mix there is envy, the associative mirror of comparison. Should not my feeling be common and the same in regard to one as to the other regardless of relation types, friends, relatives, bloodlines, whatever? I must completely admit that I think my fantasies (imagined intensity) about India (or a guru) are much better than the reality of it most certainly as every experience in such encounters proves this to be so.

When I am floating into reminiscence I recall the absurdity of psychic screening. A new comer would have to be approved by an older disciple. A friend of mine was thought to be too psychic and was almost not allowed to come and see the teacher. Really how can one tell that about another person? It seems strange doesn't it, like just a control trip over others. My relation never told anyone of his friends or family the reason he went to India. He hid under the pretense of a job and that was nothing but living a lie. This untruthfulness comes up around those who must hide their intentions of being with a guru. But what really kills me is that the hardness of people's belief systems, personal or religious, makes them dread ever having to speak to one another. I know that dreadful hardness is something Ramakrishna wanted to soften by his showing that all paths lead to the Truth. In the end it must come from both sides so neither party would feel the dread.

Once a disciple I knew expressed concern that this guru and his family would go to Florida before a hurricane passed. He snapped back at the man with the usual method of negative self reflecting, not at the concern of the man but that the disciple would even think for a moment that the he (guru) was a fool. This is the classic response of rage that gurus demonstrate when anything about them is questioned and consequently this reaction tends to kill the soul life of the questioner. The disciple's concern was turned to making him feel stupid for even showing care. It is the same with many behaviors which a disciple is not to question, or that person is thought to be spiritually defiled. But it is a game of turn around if you do not eat the guru's trash, his behavioral leavings. An example is that once the guru's airplane had to land in a Mideastern country where he and his family had to go through customs. But what!, the disciples were blamed that their spiritual state was not high enough to prevent this from happening. Things happen, why blame disciples. It is really strange when recently some friends of mine were tying to get a Tibetan lama out of Chinese occupied territory. They

315

couldn't get it to happen, but the lama did not blame them for it in anyway whatsoever. Instead, he wrote that he felt a loving connection with them. In contrast, one person there, given the only position to enter and tend the guru's guru's worship altar was a man whose name means "a little ball of dung," is it not poetic irony as to the treatment of disciples! The high esteemed position is given to one who is thought of as a dung. I suppose it is one way to teach a tragic form of humility. So you see how bizarre some of these things are.

It was the same even if the guru got a cold, the disciple's lack of a spiritual state was the cause to blame. Or in India, if the river near the guru's house is too low, the disciple's spiritual condition has been blamed for this natural phenomena. As I must mention, the very strange practice of making any Western person feel out of it, is that anything brought from the West that is not purified must be picked up with metal prongs so as not to pollute the toucher. This is why Swami Vivekananda has referred to this part of India as an insane asylum of obsessions, that one cannot pick up food with their left hand, that one must count so many times before doing this or that. Very strange. And even these disciples and their guru think that polyester is better to wear rather than cotton because it holds less bad vibrations than cotton cloth. Is this not just superstition and fear.

I remember this guru telling me I had a stout ego, but I also remember that one person once remarked that it is as if the Gods were looking down on a celebration the guru was having and he remarked that it cannot be so (meaning that he is higher than even the gods). I think many gurus must have very stout egos. When I was younger I had a class at a University where we studied and discussed the Upanishads. I asked the guru about it, he hesitatingly said okay, but thirteen years later he bashed me for it, accusing me, that I wanted to be the guru. I never wanted to be a guru, a writer, yes, never a guru. I only want to separate Truth from fantasy and obsession. Yet I did for a time imitate X. who got it all started here in America, because I liked his style. I would were my jacket like him and walk like him, even talk like him. He was more natural to me and it seemed less unpleasant than those who were either neurotic about or at the psychotic

316

level of imitating the guru's personality. My sibling became a raging madman in this direction, spouting out commandments and things like that, purifying everything by sprinkling water in places I had walked or doorways I might have stood in. Ramakrishna has an excellent remark to this psychotic imitation process surrounding those in the role of guru, "Again, if I piss standing, you rascals will do it turning round and round."

X. was as narrow minded as a Baptist who despises a Methodist when they both believe in the same God. I find it is a demented distracting rage. Can one honor a teacher who has such repellent thoughts of you? It took me all these years to salvage my soul, but I was a fool and gave it away. That is the real problem. For one to need such an arrogant figure in one's life is a dysfunction. How important is it for you to hear these things for it is painful for me to speak of them. Did this guru damage my spiritual capacity to Soar On? Even to be Free enough to have respect for other teachers? I must be honest in honoring my true feelings. There is horror and betrayal even in seeing someone who has devoted their whole life and soul to the evil wickedness of this guru worship. I cannot bear being in proximity to one with these religious beliefs. I know my capacity, my feelings and their extension. I have to write this truth for there is so much hurt within it. Children turned against parents, friends turned against friends, siblings turned against siblings, all this, the guru's awful damage. A mother's last statement about her dearest son who was taken by this guru, "He is dead to me," certainly is the apex of this tragedy. The dreadful grief of it is a spiritual irritation that outweighs much of life's natural joy. I cannot bear to see anyone in those "clutches." Keep your perspective!

The poison of the guru, what arrogant assumptions and not accurate. I did not want to be like this guru as he accused me. Yes, I was a young poet who imitated a professor and a writer who strangely turned out to be... I heard American disciples talk of the disciples from one country as those "fools." Indians of course were thought to be the highest and best. Those from another country were seldom talked about perhaps because there were so few. This guru would not condescend to help. Even my letter was obvious to this guru, a comment on his anger. Yet Swami is genuine enough to write someone in pain. How silly was the mockery between disciples, X. for example, his name just now returned to my mind, especially reminds me of that very unspiritual mocking of others and speaking to me saying that the disciples never thought I would change. What they did not know is that what they thought was a change was... And change to what? A submissive clone imitator! Now, in that case it was quite all right with this guru.

And his fury at one man who considered his guru was the guru's guru, pressing his belief in a human teacher connection that could only be fulfilled through him! This guru's teachings became redundant and boring to me. I had reached a wall where they were of no more help. I could not admit to myself that that is just the simple truth and accept that reality. I had to believe there was something wrong with me because of the poisonous self image that this guru instilled, by my giving away to him the power to do so in this kind of relation and the trust in him to do the same. All, because I questioned. Blessed Divine Mother, grant me to finally think and feel on the Purity of my own Atma without the cursed shadow of this dark teacher in mind! Grant me this gift of all things!

You would think that if this were truly good, that as a teacher he would pray (sankalpa, making a powerful wish) for the well being of those who had gone off and release them of the obvious pain and sense of failure, but this could never be the case with this guru and his disciples, who could only think of those who have "turned away" as being polluted, cursed or fools. It is not their way to see the vaster expanse of compassion. I am sure that my insecure relation would add fear to this and never be able to admit to himself that his relation has actually come to abhor this guru and those who worship him and the demonic superstitions and fanaticism that he allows to surround him. My trust was turned into betrayal and then despair and finally scorn for this deception became the cure for this deception.

So I looked to trust someone new. I was blessed or lucky. I met Ramakrishna's Swamis who did not delude me! I learned then to Trust My own True Self.

318

Really, perhaps it is regional cultural attitude, but it seems more like a fugue of arrogance in these disciples and their guru. Could any of them see, at all, I did not want that fugue of solipsism! This guru would mock the Buddhist scrolls of one who was there calling it a squirrel. This kind of teacher always keeps you on the edge, as the other in stupidity, until you leave and become your own Teacher/Self!

I can go into the Infinite Love and feel it for Real. I never needed a guru to do that! The Spiritual as your Innateness is not that huge of a mystery. I am thinking of the Atma arrogance and really if you did not get it as he thought you should get it, then he was distinctly angry at you, displeased with you. In truth, should a teacher of the spiritual act that way? In reality, if I do not question these behaviors of teachers, who will? There should be a standard with teachers also as with students, a standard of kindness in their teaching. Yet what is more often learned? When someone I knew returned from their visit to India their arrogance had increased one hundred times or more. Is that spiritual?

Forgive me now Mother, I only must work my woeful anguish away. These notes reveal the Zhi Khro of my mind, the peace and wrath, the mind sentiments and the spiritual feelings, two sided as they look, still I work hard to find Truth. What does it mean? Doctrines of gods and demons in battle over their misinterpretations of Immortality? No, don't be absurd. Peace and Wrath are two forces in Non-Dual Dakini Dance that both reveal Reality as Pure Mind, since the apparent both-ness, issue out from and come from the same Pure Mind. I was stupid enough to devote myself to the arrogance of a guru, so what else could humiliate me more! My stupidity has helped my Humility and this feeling is Wise to itself.

Vedanta says a guru is a necessity. But is Vedanta right? For Buddhists say the Doctrine of Atma is demonic in that it keeps you from the Luminous Dharmakaya! And there are those who have well realized all and everything that Vedanta has to offer without a guru. Ramakrishna is one, "His own Pure Mind..." But then there are Vedantist who say Sakyamuni was "Gayasura," the demon of Gaya (Bodha Gaya), for he taught a

319

newer and more pure Vedanta, busting tradition apart and freeing it of Atma solipsists, which is what most gurus are! The most repellent thing of all, a disciple of the guru's guru felt that Truth is the innate birthright of one and all, but this guru had to reply saying that he did not think that he had gone that far (meaning it in the negative sense). Astounding, if the guru did not control you and be the sole dispenser of Truth then there was his displeasure, at least that is how it appeared to me. And to think that Truth is not True in everyone, unless a guru gives it to you is mind boggling. I do not deny that I had negative self feeling before I went to this teacher. Yet, as a spiritual teacher whose teachings should act as a healing from self illusion, I found just the opposite.

My relation used to refer to Tibetan stuff (religion and people) as being dirty. This is because of the neurotic prejudiced ideas instilled by this particular form of guruism. Swami Vivekananda wrote, "I hate only one thing in the world-- hypocrisy." And so when I wanted to send my story The Tibetan to this guru there was not a soul who would carry it to India because they didn't want to be associated with me by fear of their spiritual defilement, but more so it was because the guru would associate them with me, but finally there was one unique man who took it with him to India. He was just a kind person and always had been. But otherwise this was the result of this so called darshan of Atma which is the spiritual and divine Principle as the Real Self of all, but apparently it has nothing to do with how you treat others according to what goes on around this guru. There was always a way for the guru to insult you. I asked about putting the passion of fire into my spiritual life and he jumped down my throat about the choice of the word "fire." I could not even open my mouth to ask a question without him bitting my head off. What good is a spiritual teacher you cannot talk to, so I wrote poetry to try and capture what I thought was spiritual experience. One morning I asked him, "How are you?" He was so affronted by this simple and sincere inquiry that he scaldingly said to me that he was always the same. But it was not so, he could change his mood like anyone. But disciples are convinced by the guru to believe otherwise, that their emotions are for the disciple's benefit and not really what a guru is doing or feeling, and this is a deception and a denial of human reality. If you question it you are considered a heretical fool. Even when a guru claims they are only human, deep down you are not expected to really believe this. It goes on and on. In one of my early manuscripts I used the expression of a fish swimming in the Ocean to describe sahaja and as I would have known now, he had to insult and belittle that choice of words. Latter I found Ramakrishna using the same metaphor to describe his spiritual feelings. As a writer I felt suffocated in the company of this teacher. Writing and publishing my phenomenal thoughts and feelings was permitted, but anything of a spiritual nature, even poetry, was restricted. So I shaped my spiritual feelings in clouds of phenomenal thoughts so I would not have to endure those restrictions. Under that shadow my writing would have never come into its own light, which is to say I myself would have remained in darkness.

From what my subconscious speaks in my dreams and what my conscious mind says in all honesty, I see him as powerful but vain and now I know what Ramakrishna also thinks about the matter, My spiritual friend Ramakrishna puts it succinctly, "The vanities of all others may gradually die out, but the vanity of a saint regarding his sainthood is hard indeed to wear away." (Sayings of Ramakrishna : Sri Ramakrishna Math). Or the vanity of a sage regarding his sagehood in this case and it was no doubt this vanity which would become so mad and blaming of others. I cannot say that this was spiritual. I think that all that neurotic vanity and psychotic imitation is perhaps some of the reason why Swami Vivekananda wrote, "What I am most afraid of is the worship-room." That is that true and real spirituality would be reduced to the worship and adoration of a person and in such psychologically imbalanced ways that the person (guru) becomes more important than the Truth or Reality. To worship a guru is like worshiping the Sun (simply a star), it is still materialism. Where the Truth of Spiritual Reality is just that, Spiritual, not material, as a human being is a material being at least in the way of mind, body and behavior.

The denied fact is that one who plays the teacher role as a

tulku, a lama or a guru often hurts others by assuming this stance. But those who share knowledge from a position of human equality and spiritual friendship help others a great amount. There are examples of open and of restrictive teachers, but there are also those who will adhere to anything and call it good. It takes more courage to admit fear, doubt, ego, than to hide it and it is a better, purer, truer human teaching, by just being human. Love and Approval takes you much farther along the Way!

When one begins to reexamine this guru complex it almost appears as hilarious madness. But still sometimes things I have heard from gurus and teachers by the association of their ideas actually ruins the fresh spiritual opinions I might come across and prejudices my mind from seeing those sources in new and vigorous spiritual ways. But that is only the basic human psychology of deep rooted impressions. Joseph Campbell came across this problem of the guru dilemma and thought that following a guru was bad news when asked about the rise of religions and cults surrounding gurus, for he had observed the spiritually mind blown Americans that were just imitations of a guru and not their true selves. Mr. Campbell still felt that Tibetan Buddhism and Ramakrishna were paths that were good in the Asian spectrum and he was a life long friend of Nikhilananda helping also to translate The Gospel of Sri Ramakrishna. (See A Fire in the Mind and An Open Life)

It makes you wonder, Yogananda Paramahansa and Swami Rama in their combined surveys of spiritual teachers in India and Tibet, together met so many of the famous and not known teachers of those regions. But neither of these two spiritual people ever mention the guru's guru, if they met him at all. You would think they would have as both were with the spiritual instinct and intuition to find teachers. They both encountered a famous sage who was that guru's contemporary both living in the same region of India even. But even these two teachers never met one another as it is not the way of gurus to go and search out each other's company for generally the one who goes assumes the role of the one who is lesser, being that they are seeking out the other and gurus don't want to be lesser than the

322

other. Also do not forget that very rare are gurus who want to be friends with each other, friendship being agreement in its meaning and equality, and so one teaching would be as good as the other. Who wants that for people want to think their spirituality is the superior one. Yet, Tibetan lamas are often friends with each other and Ramakrishna is an exception to this for he went out looking for others such as Ganga Mata and Trailanga Swami, not for teaching but for company and spiritual companionship, connection.

You see this guru and his guru were both thought to be the highest kind of guru, the karana guru, the cause guru, who causes highest realization. Where karya (effect) gurus are thought only to show a path. But another Indian spiritual system states that the karana guru is your own True Self and the karya guru is the human being. Just the reverse. I suppose we decide which is which. But really I did not see anyone who was "caused" into the highest realization. Genuinely I could not see it as even this guru would say that Ramakrishna was not fully enlightened because of the nature of his death. But in Indian tradition Ramakrishna is most excellent so I feel this was just another way of disparaging all other spiritual systems other than one's own which is what gurus (and most religions) so often do to others.

I wish I could remember the name of the book I found so many years ago. A disciple of this guru came up behind me and looked over my shoulder and said that this was a forbidden book! Why? Because it spoke honestly from the little I read about guru's guru's house and spiritual community saying how narrow and fanatic his disciples appeared to be and really how puny their attitude was. This writer spoke about how they made such a big to do over that guru's little books. Another thing that is strange is that at least one if not two spiritual theories of this guru's guru were claimed or thought to be new and original but I have found these two theories in the spiritual ideas of the Tibetan Tilopa who lived centuries before. So it is clear now that those little books his guru wrote are not the be all and end all of spiritual truth.

All this makes me question reality, not denying what really exists around gurus. My friend Alfred Collins speaks the truth honestly and is much more real about what happens later, Jeffrey Masson also tells reality, of course Joseph Campbell. With these stories about this problem, how can they all be wrong, at least something is wrong. There is a reason for this because there are in fact problems with gurus otherwise why would people write of it when fear does not keep their stories hidden. Should I not write truthfully in the truth of my experience or should I cushion it out of fear? And as it goes I cannot go with X.'s solution. It was my solution, but it is not mine now. In his book I felt that he actually got it with his idea of loving and living love as what Love is, but he loses it I feel to avoid himself and lose himself in identity with a guru. The story also disparages his wife's spiritual search and stages of enlightenment in her spiritual path. It just comes down to Vedantic prejudice and superiority with its resultant arrogance. I still have to work hard not to be arrogant in thinking on the exclusive egotistical nature of this tradition's Vedantic presentation.

Self Trust is certainly paralyzed even by the so called best spiritual teachers if they for but one second assume the stance which is the mistake that is so succinctly described by Swami Vivekananda, "Great saints are the object-lessons of the Principle. But the disciples make the saint the Principle, and then they forget the Principle in the person." Indeed, it is so simple, the object (or personhood of a guru) lessens (as a distraction from the Real Spiritual Lesson) one's Experience. Are we unique in our wounds or does this kind of thing go on everywhere wherever the person emphasizes the person and not the Reality of the Immense All Pervasive Principle? For me this is the epitome of false reality! I went to see a dear and wonderful holy woman sage of great depth who loves Ramakrishna and Mother Kali. She meditated and said, "Its difficult to come back." I was moved by the truth of that. Yet, later she said in the sweetest voice, "Now bow to your guru." And of course everyone in the room bowed to her. It was sweet and almost cute, but I could not bow. If I bend forward, I deny Mother behind. If I search for Her above I miss Her below. So I sat with my head straight and did not bow.

When one goes to a guru one goes to find your Self, but the

strange thing is that you take with you the Self you hope to find! Then if the guru reflects to you a negative image or idea of Self then you might become fixed with that idea and that can be hell. Further, this can create the need for confirmation and affirmation from elsewhere which is contradictory to the original going to find the Self within. It is a strange and actually desperate process. So, being with a guru is not what it appears to be. It is not being with a body. You could be sitting next to an enlightened person on an airplane and never know it. It is not being with someone's mind. The obscuration of your own mind prevents that and worst yet the rigid opinions of the guru can even more so obscure you from your Own Peace. Being with the guru is really a figure of speech meaning that you are with the Self, your own Light, ever present within that removes the shadow of darkness for you. In stillness it is Peace. In movement it is Guidance.

Actually the entire journey of going to and being with can be and really must be taken within your own mind. One reason for this is that all externals are temporal locations. They are but ornaments as Dzogchen describes them. But your mind is always with you regardless of temporal locations. And more so your Pure Mind. Neurotic is needful. Psychotic is the replacement of you with something else. In this case the shadow form of a guru. So the needfulness is usually expressed as imitation of the idealized and idolized superiority of a guru. And the replacement of you is one of the strongest forms that can be demonstrated in the shape of dependency. Imitation and dependency are not the true Self. They are what Dzogchen calls slipping into mis-identities. And really, and honestly, so much of the behaviors of both gurus and their disciples are just that. They are substitutes for Reality and they are not Reality as the true Self. A great soul named Nityananda of Ganeshpuri expressed this annoying problem by saying that if disciples excrete in the palm of their own hand they have to come to him to ask what they should do with it. (See Nityananda: The Divine Presence) In truth one is looking to find and be with God, but you see, to project God unto the guru, which is what gurus tell you to do, can only end in disappointment. And this is how one feels betrayed. The needful displaced disciple will say that the more he (the guru) is the less I am and will relish this position. But one who has snapped to clarity about the untruth of this submissive state says the greater he is the less you are. You negate yourself and you negate God by the projection of a false reality, a God cult on the guru's personality. By this you negate the Equally Present Reality of Genuine God Consciousness, Existence and Love. As all these feelings here described in this chapter are the facts of my personal experience, it is still simply just my opinion.

When I first read about Swami X.'s (not a Ramakrishna swami) sexual embraces with young women I didn't believe it, but the second time I read a more detailed and respectable report I thought it must be true. But I felt less betrayal that he was sexually human, even closer to him, to his human nature, to know that he was human, than I felt from the betrayal of the guru I knew who was said to be able to reveal highest reality and but gave devaluation. A swami's vow is to give up home and hearth, marriage, money, fame and ego, for him to break his own vow affected me less. How can True Spirituality cause those injuries, the damaged feeling of betrayal, it cannot if it is true. Such guruism, gurudom, the guru chase, it is to leave the Elephant at Home and go looking for its footprints.

The agony that the dark teacher creates and that binds you to the worship of the shadow is a misery that must free itself from misery as the very suffering of it must find a solution in the Self. I give that Self to Mother! This misery is the devaluation a guru can cause you to feel. This can be reversed by seeing with a realistic sight, the entire tradition, from the Vedic horsemen's arrival in India thousands of years ago to the arrival of Indian religions to America within the last two hundred years. A guru might want to crumble you so you bend to his will, more than reveal the revelation of Truth itself. By de-idealizing and de-idolizing that which one thought was great back into just what it is, one can restore the true value of Self as your natural inheritance and not the guru's property or garbage that he made you feel you were to dispose of as he wishes. Please allow me to paraphrase an idea on one of the final genuine and truthfully revealing insights about the whole problem that Jeffrey Masson addresses in his brilliant book, My Father's Guru; A Journey through Spirituality and Disillusion. The guru insists on total submission. According to him there is no other way. You must magnify the guru's importance and completely diminish your own value, life and self, until you become one of the inner circle and you can start devaluing other people the way the guru devalued you.

These problems seem to be everywhere. I have experienced them also in Dzogchen. A lama empowered us to practice Trekchod and Thogal, but when asked about the nature of Thogal he was very mocking in his reply. Is this not a contradiction to the very essence of what was being taught. That is the way of some teachers and they claim this hypocrisy to be divinely inspired. But to be fair and true I also met a Dzogchen lama whose humility, truth, wisdom and genuine unpretentious nature touched me deeply.

A healing story is here. You see, in the Ashtavakra Samhita it is Ashtavakra who is the teacher of the King of Videha, Janaka. Yet, in the Tripura Rahasya, King Janaka is the teacher of Ashtavakra, the son of the sage of Kohoela. I asked this guru of this and in his anger I received yet another one of his blows. Most disciples thought these "blows" were of benefit, yet I thought and felt they were nothing but curses leaving deep wounds (crooks in the soul) and did not appear to be of benefit to others and I did not feel in myself these "blows" to be spiritually beneficial, in fact it was quite to the contrary, making one feel so spiritually worthless you hardly felt like continuing to live any longer. You see it almost appears that you just don't ask questions of a guru unless you know he knows the answer, for if it is not within a guru's arena of knowledge he will become quite pissed at you. Ashtavakra was the son/disciple of the sage of Kohoela and this sage, the father/guru once became enraged at his son/disciple and cursed him causing him to have eight crooked parts in his body. These crooks, wounds, injuries and damages that a guru's cursing and angry behaviors can do are so well pointed out in this story. Nevertheless you see, the sage of Kohoela was engaged in spiritual debate in the court of King

327

Janaka and he was defeated in the debate so he was sent to his death to be drowned in the sea. The old way of debate was that you either became the disciple of your conqueror or you had to kill yourself if you lost. It was very serious stuff. So, just in time, Ashtavakra comes and defeats the victor of his father/guru and so redeems his abusive teacher, which is a very interesting element to the story. In some way it seems an abused student must do this either through one's own honesty and truth or through an outright battle with oneself or debate with the soul. So continuing the story, Ashtavakra becomes somewhat puffed up in ego at the fact that he had saved the life of his father/guru. At this point there appears in the court of the King of Videha, a Bhairavi Woman, a Fierce Tantric Goddess Woman (or Dakini Lady) who proceeds to humble Ashtavakra and lead him on into a deeper and greater understanding of Truth! It is She who Teaches him! And then she tells him to learn the rest of the details from Janaka. And so here you have Ashtavakra in the stance of the student and Janaka in the role of the teacher. Janaka teaches him the rest and what he teaches is the Advaita of the Goddess describing Reality as She! Yes - the Goddess! This is the Tripura Rahasya story, in the Ashtavakra Samhita the roles are reversed. And so, roles can be reversed it seems. Pure Mind is the Only Constant! The student/teacher roles are relative to Pure Mind and in the sweetest simplicity what transcends the student/teacher roles is their spiritual friendship versatile enough to accept Pure Mind in either role, student or teacher, in each other! Ashtavakra, even though cursed, wounded by the guru's rage (his "eight crooks" is the meaning of his name), he still realizes Advaita by the Bhairavi Goddess' Grace and the healing spiritual friendship with Janaka. A final thought is that in Tantra it is said that in the Sahasrara (Pure Mind) there is no disciple and no guru, so from here you may also see how Janaka and Ashtavakra may have been both disciple and teacher to each other, for they were really identified in that level, the Pure Mind, and not merely as ego selves. By the way, those "intervals" claimed as unique insights, where between thoughts or feelings or in deep sleep as well as other conditions such as loving embrace, surprise, extreme fright or sorrow, where Pure Mind shines or illuminates, are described in great detail in the Tripura Rahasya!

Perhaps you will think I am only protecting my ego self with these ideas. I don't think so for these are realities that cannot be denied. Or you may think that I am just projecting my own inner sense of despair and tragedy upon the dark shadow symbol of a guru. If this were so then why would I have discovered what Ramakrishna has to say about the matter in the following chapter. And is not the weave of this all but a fabrication upon the Unfabricated Primordial? I seek the Spirituality which is not limited by anything, which is never marked by the teachers' marking nor mirrored in that reflection and not measured by an ideal. Unbound and unbinding, free, one may love the ideal, but Love carries you past the ideal, into Love alone, which stands free. This liberating Love is Mother Sakti Herself. If you think in your own measured and marked limitation that one must retain the reflecting mirrors of the past traditions as what is real in Spirituality, then let me remind you that before Hubble discovered that those tiny wisps of light were actually other galaxies, we foolishly thought that the Milky Way was the entire universe! How wrong that was, so how wrong might other so called realities be? And, is not this continuous Cutting Away of false realities what Trekchod is, so that one may Soar On in Thogal to better and truer Truth!

Ramakrishna's Solution to the Obscuration of the Guru

An obstruction is something that blocks or prevents, here, it is structures that obscure or obfuscate. An obscuration is something that darkens. An inherent or innate solution is one that you are born with, for you are always born with your own answer.

As to the guru exclusively being God, one person said, "You too are that same Rama." Ramakrishna replies in the voice of spiritual sanity, "For heaven's sake! Never say that." So it is with those who do not contradict True Spiritual Reality. It is so easy just to believe in what is put out there for you to believe rather than to Know your own Belief (Experience), for those who want Spirituality without the dark binding of the guru.

In the example of Ramakrishna's life the problems encountered in the teacher/deity dilemma did not arise in his Pure Relation of Pure Contact in the Pure Mind of the Divine Mother, the Goddess, Kali, Sakti. Never! For with and within the Humble Sage of Sakti to Her was Surrendered all Power of Spiritual Illumination! This Real Lama/Guru/Teacher is directly the Harmony Balance into the Absolute Ultimate which does not make any fabrication of any person or deity at all. (Refer to Kindly Bent To Ease Us for more on this idea.) Even the highest Teacher, the original teacher of Dzogchen, Samantha Bhadra in his primordial celestial abode who gave the Dzogchen to the subtle being Vajrasattva who in turn gave the Dzogchen to the human being Garab Dorje are all but a dream state compared to the Pure Mind.

Everyone projects the symbol of their highest importance on something or someone, a temple, an ashram, a place, a tree, a guru, a religion. This is the highest spiritual distraction, the cause of bewilderment. Then we fall down, down and down, into the mind spiraling further on, becoming lost then, since no projection can fulfill the need for Highest Importance (significance and meaning) and since you carry that Importance with you always in and as Life, but you will not see or further experience this Importance, as the Essence of Life (Love) until

330

projections drop out entirely. Nothing projected. Life is just Life, and I, in Humility and Surrender of I, accept what my life has been and best yet, what Life Is.

"He addressed Sri Ramakrishna as "Guruji" or teacher. The Master would sometimes resent this saying, "Who is a Guru and to whom? You are my Guru." But Shambhu would not give in and persisted in using the epithet till the end." (Life of Sri Ramakrishna) Besides Sakyamuni, Ramakrishna is one of the only ones who has gone beyond the contained and confined ideas about the what, who, why and the where for of a guru is. He transcends the boundaries. And he asks others to do so as well even though they persist in their stubbornness on the matter and contrary to his feelings of resenting the epithet. Amazing that such persons will not go beyond their limited ideas even though he asks them to do so. "Who" and "to whom," once we break beyond the constriction of this barrier we may perhaps see more as Ramakrishna sees. It is always in the "You" that one has the impulse to regard someone or something as guru. It is always in this dualism of a Me then a You. Once the dualism goes there is only Pure Mind and then Who is to teach Whom!

We will go beyond traditional injunctions to the Real Meaning. We will go beyond all that and understand it ourselves. Some subjects from The Gospel of Sri Ramakrishna will be given and the contradictions there in highlighted so that we may explore the clarity of what this is in the light of Sri Ramakrishna's eyes. God, Teacher, Guru, Dust, Disciple, Acharya, Inner Guide, Incarnation, Pure Mind, Pure Atman, Pure Buddhi, Pure Love, Pure Self, Refuge, Sakti, Sage, Divine Mother, Master, all these indeed, what do they really mean in Sri Ramakrishna's spiritual experiences.

A devotee has had a dream of a brahmin walking on water going to the City of the Divine Mother. Ramakrishna says to him in response, "Oh, my hair is standing on end! Please be initiated by a guru as soon as possible." What does it mean? Ramakrishna does not hold himself as a guru to initiate anyone. Yet he is obviously thrilled by the unfolding of Sakti within the content of the man's dream consciousness which was retold to him. But he does not say any particular guru, apparently any

331

will do in this case. Just get mantra initiation by this secondary formality where you can practice Mother Sakti's worship. The worship of Her in Pure Mind practice exalted by mantra repetition. Ramakrishna does not act as a guru, occupy his attention by thinking of himself as a guru, nor profess to be a guru. This is a highly important point to realize, a point made by one of the greatest beings ever to arise in the spiritual stratosphere.

"But you see, I do not care much for Gurus-personalities." (Swami Atulananda: Atman Alone Abides) He was one of the early swamis of the Ramakrishna Order. He was born in Holland. His mind is clear on this and he has grasped Ramakrishna's spiritual wisdom on the subject of the guru. Atulananda does not hold the guru at the height of spiritual concerns as so many have done to the loss of themselves. He actually states that he does not care for gurus. And he was not only initiated by Abhedananda but by the Holy Mother as well, and he also knew Swami Vivekananda. He knew all these great souls, but still he does not care for gurus!

"I fought with my Master for six long years with the result that I know every inch of the way." Swami Vivekananda. (The Master as I saw Him by Sister Nivedita) Why indeed a fight and what indeed is this fight. It is to see beyond the conception of a guru (or master) for the guru/master is a concept. Ramakrishna cries out for you to find this that is beyond the concept. Vivekananda had to fight for it. What does he come to know in the end? "Mother is the same as Brahman (the Absolute beyond all concepts) and has two natures: the conditioned and the unconditioned. As the former She is God, nature, and soul. As the latter She is unknown and unknowable... A bit of Mother, a drop, was Krishna; another was Buddha; another was Christ... Worship Her if you want love and wisdom." (Inspired Talks) Absolutely! The highest realization. Nothing but the Mother, the Divine Mother. Even these greatest of beings, avataras, enlightened ones, messiahs and not to forget gurus, are what? Drops, but bits of the Divine Mother! So it is natural to feel the fight within oneself with this conception of a guru, it pricked Ramakrishna's flesh. Why? Perhaps because of what

332

Vivekananda realized himself. "Great saints are the illustrations of the Principle. But the disciples make the saint the Principle and then they forget the Principle in the person." (Inspired Talks) How sad it is if in your spiritual life you do indeed forget Pure Mind and become lost in the illustration.

This Pure Mind is always within you, if you think, "O my mind is so impure," then you are simply identifying Pure Mind with an idea of impure mind and no idea, pure or impure, can change the Pure Mind within, which is the finest divine gift of the Blessed Mother whose Power encompasses every concept or idea infinite or finite. Ramakrisha was the most excellent example of the Pure Mind of Mother. The Divine Mother Kali's four arms or hands, as it were, are sometimes described as three of them being the cosmic process of creation, preservation and destruction or withdrawal of the universe back into Herself. And it is then Her fourth hand that is the saving grace of realization. In this I see Ramakrisha as that hand of Mother. What is he? An arm of Mother's finest Power in the Manifesting of Pure Mind.

Again the result is seen when coming out of the most excellent Ground of Reality as the best expression of Truth in Pure Mind. "There is no greater guru than you own mind." (Meditation and Spiritual Life) A statement of complete Truth made by Swami Brahmananda, one who knew Ramakrishna. Pure Mind is your one Eternal Companion and there is nothing greater than Pure Mind. "No guru is greater than your own mind." (The Eternal Companion) What more can be said really. Plenty and we will get to it.

The guru is supposed to be the one who removes the darkness, or the light (ru) that removes doubt (gu). But seldom is it said that in truth a guru can very well be the one who generates doubt, who creates bewilderment and who can obscure the Astonished Wonder in one's own Pure Mind, by the pull of conscious influence that cognises the delusion that a mere human being is a god or God. This creates fear no doubt, because you are then faced with accepting a fallible being as an infallible power. And this can never be reality because any being anywhere can fall, descend, lapse or make mistakes. Think about it. You see, fear is the great problem, essentially the great

333

fear and fright of death. Once this problem is solved in the Pure Certainty of Pure Mind we find the Self most pleasantly astonished within the Spiritual Amazement of Pure Wonder in Pure Mind. But you see when dealing with fear one must absolutely never forget that it is not the things, people or events that we resent in the experience of fear, but it is that we have fear at all that we resent fear. So deal with the answer to fear not all the complicated attachments that come along with the feeling. Once fear is gone, in those moments when the Astonishment of Beauty is discovered we find and live in Pure Mind more and more often.

Ramakrishna speaks on Pure Mind, Pure Buddhi and Pure Atma as All The Same! Buddhi! Bodha! Buddha! He says without any other indication that Sat Chid Ananda is the Only Teacher. If any addressed him as guru he would say, "Go away you fool! I have no disciples." As it was with Sakyamuni's saying, "Be a Light to Your Self. Rely on none for assistance. Worship none." As Vivekananda put it when he spoke of how often the Principle is forgotten in a person and then the person becomes emphasized over the Principle which is Truth. Pure Mind. But hardly anyone remembers this and no one does this and rarely do these people not worship Ramakrishna or Sakyamuni (or lesser examples), who were people like you and me.

"God (Or Kali) alone is the Master, and again, He (Or She) is the Servant." Most very profound when blessed Ramakrishna says it. Do you understand? There is no duality as both are God. But what is God? If you know that, then who is the Master? Could it be as simple as Love? Probably so. Bands of holy women and men are dancing at Her Feet, She who is Love. That is the thing. Are you one of them? For Ramakrishna, She was the "Ever Awake Teacher Within" his single mine of Power was Mother! If not this then where will your Experience of Self be? If it is not within your own Mine of Power! He/She who knows the Highest Advaitic Authority within his/her own experience, in accordance with Pure Reality no longer testifies to dragging the Pure Mind down into the form of a form, human or divine! Even the great Advaitic example, Gaudapada, admits this dragging

334

down is imagination. Something done out of human love and gratitude. "Salutation always implies duality and is possible only from the relative standpoint. The author, being full of human love and gratitude to the knowledge that enabled him to realize the Supreme Reality, drags it, as it were, to the relative plane by imagining it as a Person or Teacher and then adores it by saluting it, to set an example to the ignorant." (Nikhilananda's commentary to Gaudapada IV 100.) Non-dual salutation to your own Mine of Power is really where your respect should go and in Reality this is not an object outside of you but is your own Being. It is the Supreme Reality that enables you to Realize Reality, the adoration of This in the forms of person, teacher or deity is imagination as it is admitted here so sharply. Know this. Adore it, salute it outside of you if you are in need of the example for the ignorant!

At the Moment you realize it is You, Self, that all this is about, Joy sets in! It is as the old saying goes, follow the Voice of your own Soul, Self, Being, for that is where true Happiness dwells. In You. All the teachings are teaching just that. The difficulty in what Ramakrishna says is only on the surface of this obscuration, because on one side he says, "have faith in the guru" but on the other hand if any one calls him a guru he says, "Go away you fool!" The problem is perplexing but we will solve it. Truth can have no contradiction otherwise it is not complete Truth, so guru is not the Complete Truth (because of this contradiction). There are followers of pure Advaita who even "do not accept the Divine Incarnation" much less a reality (or illusion) of a guru. So the question is within the freedom of your mind, what do you accept?

You see, Ramakrishna is there and what it is that he wants you to accept is Pure True Reality, the glorious life giving Sun of your own Luminous Self, not him as a guru, or even him as an incarnation which was a title he was most reluctant to accept. Someone says to him, saying he is the incarnation, "You too are that same Rama." He replies, "For heaven's sake! Never say that." His heart was always on Truth, not on guruism, nor even the grandest possible distraction of being an incarnation.

The entire solution to this riddle can very well be realized by diving with full awareness into this exchange between Ramakrishna and M. So Ramakrishna is saying how he would roam the streets at night weeping for Mother, for the Goddess, to remove the limited sense of reasoning. You see, what is to be described here is so pure that the figuring and calculating mind can barely grasp the immediate beauty of its recognition. Ramakrishna goes on to say that everything can be gotten simply through Love. Yes. He speaks of the Veda and the Vedanta, the Tantra and the Purana and says, "One by one She has revealed all these to me." And then the astounding affirmation, "Yes, She has taught me everything." This is the epiphany of True Wisdom coming from the purest state of Pure Mind. She as the Reality of Ultimate Sat Chid Ananda reveals Reality directly to him.

It goes on with his seeing of himself alone amidst mountain high heaps of human skulls. It is the great fear, the great fright which is the death of all beings including himself that he must face, as it is, alone, and he goes through this to even deeper mysteries to be known. This was the acceptance that all ego must die and will die and what Mother, the Goddess will reveal is the truth beyond the boundary of death. We must Let Go of our distorted misunderstanding of the fear of death in order to Soar On!

The exchange continues. "Still another day She showed me an ocean. Taking the form of a salt doll, I was going to measure its depth. While doing this, through the grace of the guru I was turned to stone. Then I saw a ship and at once got into it. The helmsman was the guru. I hope you pray everyday to Satchidananda, who is the Guru. Do you?" M. responds most likely with awe and amazement, filled with respect, "Yes, sir." Ramakrishna goes on, "The guru was the helmsman in the boat. I saw that "I" and "you" were two different things. Again I jumped into the ocean, and was changed into a fish. I found myself swimming joyfully in the Ocean of Satchidananda. These are all deep mysteries. What can you understand through reasoning? You will realize everything when God Himself teaches you. Then you will not lack any knowledge." So there!

First of all it is the Goddess that shows him all this, the

ocean and the Ocean. One is the mind, the other is Pure Mind. The salt doll is the ego (mind) which when measuring the depth of the Ocean will disappear, that is melt into the Ocean. This was a favorite illustration of Ramakrisha's to explain nirvikalpa samadhi or that disappearance into Pure Mind. But you see he is turned to stone, metaphorically, the ego is kept in a firm state so that he can continue the experience before him and not go into the deepest state of Pure Mind where no ego exists, where it has melted in the Ocean, otherwise where and who would be the experiencer of the further coming experience. It is by the "grace of the guru" that Ramakrishna says this happened. It certainly does not seem that he is speaking to us of a human being. I sincerely believe that he is telling us of the inner grace of the inner guru, the "Inner Guide" that he would speak of elsewhere. And I see in perfect evidence and accordance that this experience is one that is just like the one of the Siva like sadhu (the figure of a young Sannyasin, which was his own Self, and that looked just like him exactly) that earlier emerged forth from his own Pure Mind to teach, reveal and uncover highest spiritual reality to him. Referring to this experience. It is said that his Pure Mind became his Guru. "The Brahmani, Tota Puri and the others came and taught me afterwards what I had already known." He says that these human teachers came later only to maintain traditions and injunctions it seems, to maintain them by his honoring of them. He did not need them at all but you see the simple minds of the world have a hard time believing in spontaneous spiritual experience coming out of Pure Mind and they need some traditional lineage history to verify the nature of spiritual experience. Ramakrishna says there could be no other reason for accepting the naked one, Tota Puri, and the other teachers. So we have now established that this helmsman guru is another shape of Pure Mind in emanation just like the figure of the young sannyasin.

Remember, and never forget that it is the Goddess of his own Pure Mind that is showing him all these things and the Shower of a thing is always More, Greater, than the thing that is shown. The ocean, the salt doll, the stone, the helmsman guru and the grace of that power are all things that She is showing him. This helmsman of the ship is the one who works the rudder, so one may say this is the inner steering power of his Pure Mind, turning and guiding the ship of mind through the ocean of mind. Wonderful.

Next he goes from stone to get in the ship. More of the mystery is here. One must be fluid in order to get into a ship, into the fluid ocean of mind. So the ego has gone from a firm state which did not enter nirvikalpa samadhi to enter the ship of the mind. Even here, the ship as mind is something larger than the helmsman guru. And the ocean is something larger and more grand than the ship or the helmsman. But astoundingly we come to the Essence. Ramakrishna does not hope for M. that he should pray to Ramakrishna. Ramakrishna hopes that M. prays to Satchidananda who is the Real Guru. Even here he is speaking of the Pure Mind that he hopes M. will pray to, think upon and be one with. Here he is not even talking of the smaller power principle of the guru helmsman, but of the Guru! Who is none but God! Or the Goddess, as these expressions are interchangeable with Ramakrishna.

He again states that the guru is the rudder man (helmsman) of this boat, that is the boat of his mind sailing through the ocean of mind, perhaps all minds together. But here he says the "I" and the "You" are two different things, that is, at the level of mind, but we shall see that once he jumps into the Ocean of Satchidananda (Pure Mind) that sense of two different things goes. He, as an ego mind is now transformed, changed into a fish. The salt doll is a life form of a person composed of salt, a mock up if you would of a real person prior to its melting into Pure Awareness or Pure Mind, for we all are but mock ups until then. The salt person is turned into stone, that is frozen by the intensity of Pure Awareness as ego would be stopped in its tracks so to speak, but now we have a new metaphor, of a fish, one who can move with great ease through the Ocean (not ocean) of Pure Mind. His self, as the "myself" is joyful in its swimming in Pure Mind, in the Ocean of Pure Mind! Also, it should be evident and most obvious that here takes place a most beautiful spiritual transition. The salt doll, the stone, the passenger in the ship are all dualistic phenomenal stage relations to the helmsman's energy. Yet now we see that he jumps off, abandons the ship of the helmsman guru or the guiding guru's energy through this ocean of apparition in mind. He is now in the Joy of swimming in his own Pure Mind. But even this expression in the limitations of words cannot express this pure just Pure Mind feeling, you see, for he still speaks with an idea of the myself-mind. But that should not deter you from making the jump, the transition, the beautiful deepest mystery of change, back into what you have been along, Pure Mind. It is simply going from the ship of the ordinary ocean of mind into the Wondrous Ocean of Pure Mind! Or one can say that he is swimming in the Ocean of the Goddess, for She is the One who is Showing him all this.

Ramakrishna has said that Pure Atman, Pure Buddhi and Pure Mind are all the Same. So we hear him say also, "Pure Atman is the Great Cause." This is to say that Pure Mind is the Great Cause. Here Pure Mind is the Maha (great) karana, the Great cause of spiritual experience, enlightenment, knowledge, Love. Remember it is Karana which is the causing principle or kick to enlightenment. Again, "Pure Atman is the Cause of the cause." That is Pure Mind is the Cause of the cause of Spiritual Awakenment and of everything else. Here, he means by cause, the Primordial Energy (Sakti), She who causes enlightenment and it is the Pure Mind which is the Cause of this, your own Sakti in your own Enlightenment. "This Pure Atman alone is our real nature." So Ramakrishna is saying Pure Mind is our real nature. Everything else is what: illusion, reality, energy? So you decide yourself with your own Pure Mind.

Ramakrishna continues telling us that these are deep mysteries, indeed, an understatement, for perhaps these are the deepest of mysteries! And, as to this, what can you understand of these mysteries with your figuring, calculating, cause needing, reasoning mind? You cannot, for these are not things in the ocean of mere mind as waking, dreaming or deep sleep, but are in the Ocean of the Pure Mind! So he finishes his beautiful most outstanding expressions with the Truth that you will only realize all these things, that is everything, when God Himself teaches you. When the Goddess Herself teaches you. She who has shown him all this. She who is Pure Mind and the Only Teacher there Is! Now and in the end of all phenomenal states of consideration, Who can be capable of giving and showing the state of Pure Mind where you will not have any lack of knowledge. Everything else is but an apparition in Pure Mind, for what Ramakrishna's Advaita is saying is that Pure Mind is your Real Nature, and so, your guiding power itself when apparitions appear, to guide you out of apparition, out of its occurring, back to Pure Mind itself.

For the sake of thoroughness in explaining this dilemma let us drop down from the Height just above and with Ramakrishna's help, try to clear away the darkness of this causal dynamic of spiritual trauma and abuse that occurs with gurus. Totapuri could be very angry and even cruel. The case example of such behaviors is when he became so angry with the outcast man who lit his smoke from Totapuri's fire. Ramakrishna laughed at him, his Vedantic Advaitic state, for such a little thing could shake him out of his Peace. The Brahmani was a problem in that in her jealous grasping pride she felt that Ramakrishna was her own and no others. The angry father. The jealous mother. Is there no sanctuary from this madness that is not only in the dimension of spiritual teachers but itself present in no shortage with most the parents of the world. I have seen gurus look with disdain in their angry burning eyes. I have known gurus who could be quiet upset if they could not possess you as their own with their jealous pride. This is hardly spiritual and I think there is no excuse for such behavior, even when gurus tell you they are doing it for your own good.

First, think well on this. "He who is spiritually higher than others does not consider himself a guru." The footnote explains the meaning to be that if a person thinks of themselves as a guru which means heaviness they go down like the heavier pan of a balance. They drag their own self down with this identity. And they drag you down even further into delusion and despair. One may add to this also that the truly spiritually high person does not think of their own self in this dark delusion, but they also do not think of another person this way! Indeed, what happens to those who consider such a one as guru or who consider

340

themselves as guru? Disaster! For in Ramakrishna's own words, "He who says he is a guru is a man of mean intelligence." Most profound. He is intelligent, maybe more than you, but also he is mean and that is dangerous. You could get wrapped up with an intelligent and mean person who is saying with Advaitic delusion that they are the messenger or mouthpiece of God or even worse yet, that they are God! This is clarified by Ramakrishna of how wrong the attitude is, "A man cannot be a guru." Spirituality, as everything does, happens by the Power of the Spiritual Splendor itself, not by the will or proclamation of a human being. All a man can do is speak many words, when that is done, everything rests with the Primal Power of Adya Sakti! Not with human beings! In spite of any thing else that will be said one cannot deny these profound statements.

Again, "Three words- 'master', 'teacher', and 'father'- prick me like thorns." And again the same idea but expressed perhaps with even more force and feeling about the weight of the matter, "Do you know my attitude? As for myself, I eat, drink, and live happily. The rest the Divine Mother knows. Indeed, there are three words that prick my flesh: 'guru', 'master', and 'father' ." You cannot negate the power of these statements, nor can you eliminate the truth of the comment to these thoughts of self consideration, "And, 'I am the doer', 'I am the guru', 'I am the father'- this is ignorance." It is nothing but ignorance to consider yourself as guru or to consider another as guru again is nothing but the dark shadow of ignorance. The solution will be given as we continue.

Even more so with the same conviction, "If someone addresses me as guru, I say to him: "Go away, you fool! How can I be a teacher? There is no teacher except Satchidananda. There is no refuge except Him. He alone is the Ferryman to take one across the ocean of the world." What more can be said, how much clearer can it get? "It is not good to be a guru by profession." And, "The profession of a teacher is like that of a prostitute." They will have their students build houses and gardens around them while people throw themselves at their feet and still they will deny that they are prostitutes of Truth by profession. O yes I see how a fool would buy it! Even more, that it too would prick my flesh like a thorn! What deception!

Ramakrishna continues to say that reverence to an acharya makes him proud as he sits there erect and preaching to others who hear him, "This is a very bad attitude. He gets a little prestige and it ends there." Does it end there, for what damage does that pride do to those who come and listen? An acharya is one who is a preceptor of Reality, but even such a one as that can be a victim of their own pride! For he says, "It is not easy to get rid of the idea, 'I am the master'." And, "'I am the master, father and teacher' - all these ideas are begotten of ignorance." But there are those who claim they have gone beyond this in their pride. With Ramakrishna even though those around him called him master, he himself refused the title for it would prick the flesh. A powerful statement. For his true feeling was that God, in Form, yet Formless as Sat, Existence/Being as Life, Chid as Consciousness/Light and Ananda as Bliss and Love, is the only Master and that he was the servant of the Divine Mother. It is said that God laughs on two occasions, when a doctor thinks he heals, and when someone thinks they own a piece of Mother Earth, to this another may be added, when a human being thinks they are the Master, the Teacher.

Based on such powerful statements I think it is important to distinguish when Ramakrishna is speaking in the form of the traditional classic guru arena and when he is speaking on a much higher level out there on his own. He gave us a way out of the problem while himself living amidst the problem. For those who are afraid to confront this reality out of their superstitious foolish fear Ramakrishna tells us of how Ramanuja disagreed with his guru who was a non-dualist and how that led to the Qualified Non-Dualism of Ramanuja. Whether you agree with Ramanuja or not is not the point here. The point is that disagreement with his teacher led him out to his own Spirituality!

Ramakrishna was not a possessor of disciples. In some of his most human and humble statements I am moved to tears, "As for me, I consider myself as a speck of the dust of the devotee's feet." And when he was asked who he was he answered "I am the servant of your servant, the dust of the dust of your feet." And, "I have no disciples. I am the servant of the servant of

342

Rama." What could be purer, if he has no disciple he is not acting as a guru! I remember that Swami Aseshananda when asked when he would go back to India he replied that he would not, "I am here to serve the Americans." For one half of a century he did just that until he left the body. Furthermore Ramakrishna's genuine humility is seen, "There is not a fellow under the sun who is my disciple. On the contrary, I am everybody's disciple." How many teachers, or just people, do you know who are so humble on the contrary to what is thought to be the way we should go that they would feel themselves to be the disciple of the whole world and everyone in this world? For most want to possess disciples not be disciples.

With such honest and realistic statements Ramakrishna removes the sting of superstitious guru fear like that which is induced by such verses that say if you reject the guru you will be doomed to be reborn in a hell of wandering in a waterless jungle. Is that to reject a human or does it mean to reject God, Reality, Truth? Such statements can only be intended for the manipulation of others through fear. I remember a painting I saw of a guru hanging upside down in hell. These threats can work both ways. Yet Ramakrishna takes all the fear away by telling us the truth on this level. "As long as you do not feel that God is the Master, you must come back to the world, you must be born again and again. There will be no rebirth when you can truly say, 'O God, Thou art the Master.'" It sounds like the simplest religious formula for salvation, redemption or paradise that is a world wise experience of many systems. But there is more here than meets the eye. For one thing you see, mind by its own power can rarely get out of the mind's loop, yet by placing that power on Something Higher, one has created a space where mind can rest and Truly Feel that it does not have to grasp at itself. This grasping mind is really the only cloud between the self sense and Luminous Reality. Also, what is it that you want? To realize Atman, to not be reborn? It would seem so. Do we fear being reborn perhaps even as much as we fear dying itself? Why would you want to come back? Unless you are a Bodhisattva or a Vivekananda who just loves the world so much that they will come back again and again until it is empty of all

343

those who have not remembered God. It is a relaxing thought to know that Ramakrishna said he would come back one more lifetime to help. It puts away the stress and fear about getting out right now. Is it perhaps that this world is itself a mix of heaven and hell? It does indeed seem to be so. But really, hell is but self grasping, self loathing, self unforgivingness. And heaven is to be Open. You have rolled over to let the Real Master take over, and this is not a mere human being, nor a superhuman being, it is God (Goddess) whom the scriptures say is the One Super Being. It is Here that one puts the power and so does not simply transfer mere mind power to the mind power of another human being who is caught in the same loop as you, be they guru or not. And if this world is heaven and hell in actuality, it would seem that when we leave our bodies that the self grasping mind might separate to create its own hell and that the open heart would make its own heaven. So you can see just how important this is. And this is why I love the Dzogchen motivation which is to empty the depths of hell.

Really, all this could be put more simply. If you are in this world and you are reading this it would be evident that you have a human mother. But Who is your Real Mother if not the Divine Mother. Or substitute father with the same thought. Our parents or if you are a parent, are the ones who bring us forth, to bring forth is what parent means and this is so similar to guru, even lama can translate as soul mother who helps bring you forth. This is not the problem, what is the problem is that gurus so often claim they got it, you don't and you must come to them to get it, but they don't seem to give it, at least not in full, for if you went there to get it you have to remain in the position of getting and not gotten.

Ramakrishna states, "Yes, many need a guru." This does not say that everyone needs a guru, but there are many who do. For how many of us spring forth fully grown into this world without a mother? But a guru can be many things, experiences we have, people perhaps, even the form of your own mind can be a form of the guru or like Dattatreya who had twenty four gurus, twenty two of which were natural phenomena as well as birds, animals and so forth. He also learned from observing a prostitute at her

344

labor and a maiden in the kitchen working on her wedding day. Nevertheless, the concept of what a guru is expands here for what one is searching to see in the guiding helmsman guru energy is God, Reality, the Goddess Herself. And it is not so easy just to say that in the end that is what the guru is or to think that is what you are seeing now.

To this question there is the negative side, there is a positive outlook and there is the final solution which is the only truth about it in the end. I will try to go through it slowly so that you may get to the line of insight, remove the obscuration and come to the final inherent solution. As is your own mind, the guru energy is both light and dark. The symbol of Tao really embodies the light and dark guru energy very nicely. Yet the symbol itself points to Something beyond the symbol, and that is the great and wonderful, incomprehensible Oneness of All. That is the final solution, not the symbolic circle of light and dark energy. Really Ramakrishna's message here is to let go of the circle and get to the core reality of it all, that is the Truth, the Reality, God, Pure Mind, Pure Love, the Divine Mother. That is where we are leading ourselves to be.

Ramakrishna exclaims, "The Divine Mother has revealed to me the essence of the Vedanta." Amazing, for many would say that it was Totapuri who did this, but here we hear Ramakrishna saying that it was the Divine Mother. We could interpret this in the primary and secondary sense, in the way of the first cause and in the path of many effects. The secondary sense being our lives and the people and places, so forth, we meet along the way. The primary cause being the Divine Mother Herself. This is simple and beautiful, but if we want Truth free of contradictions it is going to get confusing along the way.

If God is the Guru of the guru wouldn't you rather go to the one who taught the guru? In any case Patanjali says, "In Him becomes Infinite that All Knowingness which in others is only a germ." Why take the germ, the seed, when you can have the whole Tree, the Entire Forest for that matter! But we hear from Ramakrishna also the more positive side of the guru tradition in quiet a few statements that are contradictory to the previous ones that are quoted. Is it two types of gurus that he is speaking of or

345

is it a phenomenal composite which exists in one person. If gurus are anything like you or me I would say it is a composite as well as a possible type casting for there can be on the surface apparently good and evil gurus, and there can be good and evil in a single guru.

We go on with him telling us about success in spiritual life "by looking at the guru as God" which is highly traditional sounding. In truth shouldn't we look on God everywhere, not just in a guru. That is again just the "germ." For, "The Divine Mother revealed to me in the Kali temple that it was She who had become everything." This is everything not just a single human form, but all forms and everything even beyond the realm of forms and that is what Pure Mind is as without forms. As M. confirms, "It was the Divine Mother of the Universe who revealed the Truth to him."

We find other traditional ideas, "The guru is like a companion who leads you by the hand." This should be your own Pure Mind, the Inner Guide, for a human hand might just lead you into the ravine of ego. "after the realization of God, one loses the distinction between the guru and the disciple." Let us take it at a higher level. How wonderful when you as ego-disciple lose the distinction between that one and the One Pure Mind! Dropping down to a lesser level how can there be no distinction between two human beings. "For the distinction between teacher (Pure Mind the Real Teacher) and disciple (ego mind) ceases to exist after the disciple (ego mind) attains Brahman (Pure Mind). The relationship between them remains as long as the disciple (ego mind) does not see God (Pure Mind)." Or as long as you are caught in the worship of a human form, how can you see God (Pure Mind) when you are doing that?

So again, "If a man is initiated by a human guru, he will not achieve anything if he regards his guru as a mere man." This is the traditional attitude but how does it go with, "A man cannot be a guru. Everything happens by the will of God." Is he not just a "mere man" as Ramakrishna says, "What power is there in man?" For the Goddess works Her work and yet human minds say that it is theirs. How strange is that height of anti-humility!

346

It is two extreme views, man as he naturally is and then a deification. It goes like this, "The guru should be regarded as the direct manifestation of God." But he who says 'I am the guru' is in "ignorance" which is darkness. And shall we regard as God, a guru, the very word of which "pricks" Ramakrishna's flesh! How can this contradiction exist? It cannot. "One can get human gurus by the million." So, are there a million manifestations of God? How can it be? One out of a million may be sincere and honest and genuine, but if we regard so many as guru manifestations is not the chance of deception so great? Shall we immolate them and adore them as manifestations where we deceive ourselves under the premise that Ramakrishna says in the saying so potent, "Like guru, like disciple" which is really a great key to unlocking the latch on the guru dilemma.

"It is Satchidananda that comes to us in the form of the guru," he says. But does not Satchidananda come to us in the form of everything, hold us, exist within us and surround us and beyond all that appearance is just Non-Duality itself. Again, "The Mother reveals to me that She Herself has become everything." Here we see Reality clearly. It is Mother who is none but Satchidananda itself. But then two questions arise. "He who says he is a guru is a man of mean intelligence," So are we to regard a mere man of mean intellect as a manifestation of God, as a form of Satchidananda? Also, Vilwamangal realized God through his love for a prostitute, Ramakrishna recalls, "He said to the prostitute: 'You are my guru. You have taught me how one should yearn for God.'" So then a form/manifestation of Satchidananda can even be a prostitute, as guru, as teacher, as the one who reveals God? It raises questions as it shows us that the light/dark teacher energy can be discovered for oneself just about anywhere and probably everywhere as Mother has become everything.

Then he speaks of the eight fetters. Shame, hatred, fear, caste pride, lineage pride, pride of good conduct, grief and secretiveness and says, "And they cannot be unfastened without the help of a guru." Yet in reality I have seen gurus cause these eight fetters. Making disciples ashamed of themselves, causing them to hate those who do not think the way they do, to fear the guru, to have pride in being in the caste and lineage of the guru, to think their conduct is superior to others and to be completely secretive and even lie about having a guru. It is true and you cannot deny that this happens.

Then again trying to reconcile tradition, "A man should have faith in the words of his guru." Does he not have to look into his guru's character. "'Though my guru visits a grog-shop, still he is the Embodiment of Eternal Bliss.'" The old saying about the grog shop is a figure of speech for any kind of bad behavior, abusive, cruel, demeaning, debasing, humiliating. It is an extreme request for how many of us do not look into another's character even when we accept a friend. Are you suppose to accept the guru's dark behavior as an example of how to get to God? This is a very old attitude traditionally accepted and I feel that it is what Ramakrishna means when he speaks of the "endless suffering" that can exist with gurus and disciples in the unripe relation. How can this be? Are we to have faith in such a person, when Ramakrishna says, "He who is spiritually higher than others does not consider himself a guru." For this is the heavier side of the balance which drags us down. Are we to be dragged down by a guru in order to know God. And if the spiritually higher person is not a guru then what are we looking for. I would seek the spiritually higher person rather than a guru, and indeed who might that be.

So then, we hear, "The guru is like a companion who leads you by the hand." And, "The guru is the thread that leads to God." But if we were to address Ramakrishna as the guru/companion/thread would he not say to us, "Go away, you fool! How can I be a teacher? There is no teacher except Satchidananda. There is no refuge except Him. He alone is the Ferryman to take one across the ocean of the world." Where does that lead us as we would be considered a fool by Ramakrishna? Is it that we have not continued to see that Satchidananda, this Endless Undying Life as our own Existence and Being, the Light of our own Consciousness inside and within and Bliss as our own Love, the Pure Mind, the Pure Buddhi, the Pure Atman, the Divine Mother, Shakti, is the only Refuge, the only Inner Guide. And even by addressing Ramakrishna with that word "guru' would we not prick his flesh?

How will you understand the solution? Where is the spiritually higher person, the one who is One in Mother? We hear further, "It is Satchidananda that comes to us in the form of the guru." Are we to think that Reality comes to us in this dark/light duplicitous person? Are we all such persons? "The guru is none other than Satchidananda." But what is not Satchidananda, even the angel of the bright morning star (venus) was once an archangel made of the light of God's creation before he became a dark shadow of the dark/light paradox in the human mind. Even those who would consider this form to be none but Satchidananda would be thought to be still fools by Ramakrishna, as they worship those of "mean intelligence." As he does not say this mean intelligence is in a false guru, but just in a guru. There are these dark implications as "a man cannot be a guru" but Satchidananda is guru, who is a man of "mean intelligence" "considered" by "fools" and so it pricks the flesh of Ramakrishna like a thorn. I cannot prick his flesh so I cannot accept the dark implication of this guru form. This is "prostitution" and the "profession" of pride. So guru sounds like none else than the world bewitching maya, a pricking, mean, assuming his human-hood is God, utterly illusion. Getting out is knowing, "God Himself is the Guru."

There is more. We go deeper with Ramakrishna through something even greater and more powerful than gurus, and that is Incarnations and with Incarnations comes Ishtas. "The farther you advance, the more you will realize that God alone has become everything. He alone does everything. He alone is the Guru and He alone is the Ishta. He alone gives us knowledge and devotion." The key is farther and further advancement, you are getting past the mere guru to the Guru. Even past ishtas and incarnations to God which is none other than Satchidananda (Pure Mind, Pure Atman, Pure Buddhi, Pure Brahman, all the same). Here, as Ramakrishna says, "The disciple no longer sees the guru." Nor does the guru see the disciple, nor is anything seen, ishtas, incarnations, not any dualism, only Pure Mind.

So again Ramakrishna says that Krishna, Christ, Buddha, Chaitanya, Rama, all were Incarnations, which are each an

Avatara (incarnation) which is nothing but Tara, a name of the Divine Mother, who has descended (ava). This is one of Kali's names at Dakshineswar also, as Bhavatarini, the Mother Savior. Indeed, and as Ramakrishna says, "The Incarnation of God is a part of the lila of Shakti." Very good, most illuminating! Even with, "So the greatest manifestation of God is through His Incarnations," one will find that these are but a part of the play (lila) of Shakti. Wonderful! With that should not all attention of the mind be placed there? These Incarnations are most often the Ishtas, but also those Gods and Goddesses who never incarnate into the human realm are often Ishtas. These Ishtas are divine personal forms of Satchidananda. These incarnations are so powerful as manifestation/forms that, "Whoever salutes an Incarnation, even once, obtains liberation." Ramakrishna says that it is Shakti that becomes such beings as these. "It is Shakti (the Divine Mother) that is born as an Incarnation." Not only that, but it is She, the Divine Mother who is all these Ishtas, the Gods and Goddesses who ever remain never born, that is unborn in human terminology. And to add to this beautiful understanding, "This attitude of regarding God as Mother is the last word in sadhana... the last word in spirituality." As it is the end of the journey of spiritual practice (sadhana) that we have been treading through.

So, within the voyage of Indian spiritual practice one comes to an advanced stage where Ramakrishna tells us, "When he obtains the vision of his Chosen Ideal (Ishta), it is really the guru who appears to him and says, 'This is that, that is to say, he points out to the disciple his Ishta. Uttering these words, the guru disappears into the form of the Ishta. The disciple no longer sees the guru." So there is much here to be understood. This Ishta is something that is beyond, further, higher than the guru and this guru is not the Guru as Ramakrishna describes, "Satchidananda Himself is the Guru." That is the Reality of Pure Mind is the only Teacher there is. Again it is that guiding energy which appears and then disappears, even so, no longer to be seen, as in having anything to do with, once the Ishta is known and experienced. But you see, even that guiding helmsman energy as an Ishta is not yet There where the Truest Teacher may

350

be. "The Vaishnavas say that Krishna alone is the Helmsman to take one across the ocean of the world. The Saktas retort: 'Oh, yes! Our Divine Mother is the Empress of the Universe. Why should She bother about a ferry-boat? Therefore She has engaged that fellow Krishna for the purpose (All laugh)." It is important to see the beauty of humor in that all are laughing here. Even the ishtas, incarnations, gods and goddesses are nothing but ferry boats to the Divine Mother (Shakti)!

Again we hear the same depth of insight, not in the Voice of Shakti, but in the Voice of Vedanta, "'Alekh' means That which cannot be pointed out or perceived by the sense-organs. According to this sect, Radha and Krishna are only two bubbles of the Alekh." He says more, "According to the Vedanta, there is no Incarnation of God. The Vedantists say that Rama and Krishna are but two waves in the Ocean of Satchidananda. In reality there are not two. There is only One." You see, in the One Pure Mind there is nothing else, that is all that is, and this is what you have been all along, so even Ishtas and Incarnations do not exist there or they exist as they are, as the One Itself, also aware of Pure Mind. You see, the Ishta Devata is only the Luminous Bright (Deva) God (Ishvara) or Goddess (Ishvari) Being (Ta) Existence (Ta). Here there is no darkness (gu) like there is with the guru. If the guru was at anytime thought to be a companion/thread, here we have more of an immense supporter and a huge rope. The Brightness of Being is better now, more in Pure Mind, like it is, as reflected in Vajrasattva (Refer to Ramakrishna's Sadhu of his own Pure Mind) and even deeper and more expansive into the Vastness with Samantha Bhadri and Samantha Bhadra. One is ready now to really take flight as Garuda (Pure Mind)!

Ramakrishna says it with even more power in the Cutting Through and Soaring On, "Their aim is to attain Nirvana. They are followers of Vedanta. They constantly discriminate, saying, 'Brahman alone is real, and the world illusory.' But this is an extremely difficult path. If the world is illusory, then you too are illusory. The teacher who gives the instruction is equally illusory. His words, too, are as illusory as a dream." This Truth is expressed at perhaps the highest level if one can say such a thing. It tallies perfectly with Gaudapada who gives zero space, no room for the error of thinking within duality's framework. It is extremely difficult for the mind has the tendency to drop down from this Pure Unfabricated Primordial View, to something easier to grasp at than the Pure Mind! Yet, if you want Pure Truth it is to be known in Pure Mind where duality has no grasp. You do not exist, nor does a teacher exist, only Pure Mind exists, at this spiritual level. "If any imagines illusory ideas such as teacher, the taught, and the teaching, then they will disappear. These ideas are for the purpose of instruction. Duality ceases to exist when Reality is known." Gaudapada I 18. Not only do you have to Cut Through and Soar On past the idea of being an idea of one who is taught, but also the teacher (as well as you) must be able to Cut Through and Soar On past the idea that he/she is holding to an idea that they are giving a teaching. This is really the Joyful stage of Spiritual life, there is not even any teaching that is apparently given or apparently received. There is only Pure Mind that you have been all along.

And this Pure Mind is the only Teacher. Gaudapada makes the same point with different words, "Atman is imagined as prana and other numberless ideas." All these imagined numberless ideas include your idea that what you are is someone who is seeking and looking to a teaching, or that a teacher is somewhere other than the Atman (Pure Mind), it goes on to numberless or infinite ideas that can be imagined in Pure Mind. "All this is due to maya, belonging to the effulgent Atman, by which it appears, Itself, to be deluded." Gaudapada II 19. This maya or obscuration is imagined in you, Pure Mind, and leaves the same way by no more imagination. "The birthless, dreamless, and sleepless Reality reveals Itself by Itself; for this Dharma (Atman) by its very nature is Self Luminous." Gaudapada IV 81. Pure Mind Itself reveals Pure Mind Itself, there are no others in the mix and if there are others in the mix that is imagination.

The point is again made forcefully, "The disciple grasps only that idea which is presented to him by his teacher. Atman assumes the form of what is taught and thus protects the disciple. Absorbed in that idea, he realizes it as Atman." Gaudapada II

29. So much is said here, for one thing, what idea is a teacher presenting to you for Pure Mind will assume the form of that idea even as imagination and even so in the shape of some protection or guardedness from Pure Mind. The absorption in that idea will be obscured by human conveyance and you will imagine (realize) that as Pure Mind. For in Truth, "All such ideas are always imagined in Atman." II 28. For what is presented by a teaching will color you with the idea that that is Pure Mind when most likely so, it is still imagination! The idea about assuming the form of what has been taught will usually be taken as a positive import, but few will see the razor sharp insight into Pure Mind that Gaudapada is conveying.

"It is the Self Luminous Atman who, through the power of Its own maya, imagines in Itself by Itself all the objects that the subject experiences within and without. It alone is the cognizer of objects. This is the decision of Vedanta." II 12. If Pure Mind can imagine in Itself by Itself all that then why can't you (the subject) un-imagine all that? Beautiful! It is your own maya that ravels and unravels the imagination of obscuration. It is only imagination. Go through it for it is the only way out past the obscuration into the Solution! "The objects perceived by the dreamer, not usually seen in the waking state, owe their existence to the peculiar conditions under which the cognizer, that is, the mind, functions for the time being, as with those residing in heaven. The dreamer, associating himself, with the dream conditions, perceives those objects, even as a man, well instructed here, goes from one place to another and sees the peculiar objects belonging to those places." II 8. Gaudapada holds nothing back as we dive into the depth of what is not Pure Mind, and hold to peculiar conditions, indeed, that are imagination of what is not Pure Mind, even as those Ishtas and Incarnations cognised for a time being as residing in heaven. Pure Mind will not let us drop down to imagination, even to dreaming that one is a man going from one place to another! It is the instruction you have received and accepted that jolts and jars imagination to think that it is so, when what we are is not physical, subtle or spiritual, not celestial heavens nor flesh and blood, for we are Pure Mind.

So with clarity to removing our having gotten lost in this idea, Ramakrishna makes his final statements with Exalted Awareness! And thank the Goddess that he does so as it is so rare that anyone has done so. "He who is the Lord of the Universe will teach everyone. If they need teaching, then He will be the Teacher. He is our Inner Guide." "There is only one Guru and that is Satchidananda. He Alone is the Teacher." "Satchidananda Himself is the Guru." "Satchidananda alone is the Guru." "God Himself is the Guru." "Take refuge in Chitsakti, the Mahamaya." "This is called Mahamaya, the Great Illusion. Therefore one must take refuge in the Divine Mother, the Cosmic Power Itself." "How is it ever possible for one man to liberate another from the bondage of the world? God alone, the Creator of this world-bewitching maya, can save men from maya. There is no other refuge but that great Teacher, Satchidananda." "Everything is due to the Sakti of the Divine Mother." "Sakti, Sakti... I have taken refuge at Thy feet, O Divine Mother; not I, but Thou." "Yes, She has taught me everything." Speaking of there being no lack of knowledge, "Then the Divine Mother supplies it without fail." "Have faith in the Divine Mother and you will attain everything." And is not the Divine Mother the Pure Mind Itself. "Sometimes I say to myself in the Kali temple, 'O Mother, the mind is nothing but Yourself.' Therefore Pure Mind, Pure Buddhi, and Pure Atman are one and the same thing." "He is aware that the Divine Mother knows everything." Ramakrishna's attitude was that of a five year old child in the Lap of the Divine Mother. As the perfectly present mind is in Pure Mind! "Do you know my attitude? As for myself, I eat, I drink, I live happily. The rest the Divine Mother knows." Where anything below the Pure Mind in Mother's Pure Light is as being the pricking of deception.

As all this that is said, that this is the one, and alone it is so, or if there is need, and where refuge should be taken and who supplies and knows and does and is everything, is made clear, so all else would be contradiction in comparison, if any were to compare themselves to the Height of Pure Mind, and it would prick the flesh of Ramakrishna, as also that one who does this pricking is considered to a be a fool who should go away. But as mind conception wants to believe something easier, faster to grasp, and more seductive in its comfort we hear, "It is said that those who serve others for twelve years or so become slaves." Again so much is said, one can be a slave to conception and most of us are, or to a human being, a system, a belief, and even most deadly, to the ego identifying with the deception Free State of Pure Mind, a slave to one's own ego idea of the Pure Self. You see, you see, you see, it is as simple as non-conceptuality! No conceptuality (vikalpa), and then the Pure Mind in Mother Light just sets in, yet really there is no setting in and not even an uncovering, once the barrier is free of conception the Mother Light that has always been so is noticed in that Cutting Through of conception, that Letting Go of conception (vikalpa). You see what is thought to be the offspring mind is nothing but conception and so once that is released Pure Mind is just naturally there as it always has been. In that very no (nir) conception (vikalpa) you are beginning to Soar On. Hold to no barrier of conception, that you or someone other is a child or offspring of Mother Light, or a conception of yourself or another as student or teacher. One does not say anything to oneself even in the slightest subtlest way. You are in the Dzogchen Mind now.

Now one last problem, "How is it ever possible for men who have not realized God or received His command, and who are not strengthened with divine strength, to save others from the prison house of the world." So Ramakrishna presents the idea. First, are not such beings just wonderful examples in natural human heritage and is it not how they should be regarded? Again, who will say to you, or if you say to yourself that you have received the command of God to teach, then who will identify with that idea. For as it was said, "He who is spiritually higher than others does not consider himself a guru." So who will tell you to consider that you or another is a guru who can preach and teach? Who can do this? Is it not ego? Then if one truly has such divine strength and spiritual power, then that spiritually higher person does not say! Astounding is the awareness in Pure Mind where no display of false conceptuality arises.

With all this in mind we can now ask who and what was Ramakrishna? Was he a demonstration of what is possible for everyone? Was he the heart example of Pure Mind? Was he the servant of everyone? A teacher who does not teach as an example that leaves no traces? A living symbol of true Spiritual Potential? Pure person in sweetest human heritage? The real Kalyana Mitram (beautiful spiritual friend)? Even to those whose conception had to fall into the limited view (limited in that Pure Mind is more, larger and immense than one Incarnation) that he was an Incarnation he responded, "I feel as if they had been my friends in a former incarnation." Wonderful, he does not hold them to the limitation of being self objects to his own personhood, but they are friends. This indeed is the enlightened expression of the true spiritually higher person! "I had a vision of the Sun. As He arose, the darkness vanished, and all men took refuge at His feet." Then the song continues, "O Mother, Savior of the helpless..." You see truly where refuge is taken! Not to him, but to the Luminous Sun of Reality! Not I, Not I, it is all you Mother! Yet then M. will confuse us with conceptuality in his enlightened viewing as he describes an "amazing transformation. His face shines with a heavenly light. His two hands are raised in the posture of granting boons and giving assurance to the devotees; it is the posture one sees in the images of the Divine Mother. His body is motionless (for there is only motion when there is conceptuality); he has no consciousness of the outer world. He sits facing the north. Is the Divine Mother of the Universe manifesting Herself through his person (though he feels this within he does not consider himself as such)? Speechless with wonder, the devotees look intently at Sri Ramakrishna, who appears to them to be the embodiment (Mother cannot be limited to a body) of the Divine Mother Herself."

Even as this view is at the height of beauty it is still conception (vikalpa) for when there is no vikalpa then there is no apprehender, nor apprehension, nor apprehended in regard to oneself as looking at Mother, apprehending Her, or Her being as something outside oneself as an apprehension. No conceptuality! But as Incarnation, Ishta, Teacher, then what does it mean? In Pure Mind the disciple in discipline to the guru configuration ceases and from only there do you know what that was! It is past tense for it no longer exists as it never was in the Pure Mind. It is like death, you die through it to see the Pure Mind. It is the Garuda Mind, the Pure Mind, that Cuts Through and Leaps Through everything that is not the Pure Mind. In Pure Mind the Incarnation/Ishta idea and the devotee idea ceases and from there you know what that was. Reposing in this ever liberated Pure Mind, Janaka exclaims to Ashtavakra, "Where is the disciple, and where is the preceptor; where, indeed..." The Avadhuta (the one who has shaken off the dust of duality) Dattatreya too makes the shout of freedom in Pure Mind, "Here is the Self, which is without grief and grieflessness. Here is the Supreme, without happiness and sorrow. The Supreme Truth is devoid of teacher and disciple. Why dost thou, who art the identity in all, grieve in thy heart?" And Swami Vivekananda would sing to Sri Ramakrishna, the Eight Verses on Nirvana, "Death or fear I have none,... neither disciple nor guru: I am Pure Knowledge and Bliss." This being none but the Pure Mind. The Paramahansa Upanishad validates the view from this Unfabricated Height not bound by Conceptuality, "He prostrates himself before none." Not incarnation, not ishta, not teacher, Pure Mind alone! The Amrita Bindu (Immortal Nectar Bliss Drop (Thigle)Upanishad also proclaims without fear the highest Pure Mind, "Neither am I a seeker." I am not a disciple, I am Pure Mind. And the Paramahamsa Upanishad comes back to strengthen the highest point of Pure Mind, "He should not have a body of disciples." Only a fool would consider himself a guru, for one should not have disciples.

Any conceptuality as disciple or teacher is merely dualistic narcissism. It is below Pure Mind. There is cosmic, individual and spiritual/religious narcissism. To conceptualize that we are no longer mere flesh and blood, heart and mind and that the goddesses and gods are causing us to be what we think we are is spiritual/religious narcissism. It comes to the mind by mirroring the idea of self on the luminous Parama Ishta Devata (Supreme Ideal/Concept of God) conceptuality. In Vedanta you even hear of the attaining of reality as becoming the Ego of Atman instead of the mere ego. Is this not simply individual narcissism as dualistic reflection of what one thinks the parama atman to be? Parama is supreme, how can we think ourselves supreme and be humble without the blot of ego blinding the sight/experience of Pure Mind? Then one rises into more misconception with the idea of being parama brahman, the supreme cosmic infinite and this is narcissism at its highest. These too obscure the solution of Pure Mind. Are you using your ego, if you love God in the guru, master, father then you are a fool and you prick the flesh of Ramakrishna. Is he trying to say as he does, that we must come to Pure Love for Pure Love, for Pure God, for Pure Self, for Pure Mind. Sakti! Kali! Buddhi! No human conceptual proliferation into the mix! You are called to Regard all as This! Not outside you, external or above, nor inner nor within, but all Pure Mind.

Ramakrishna's response to this is absolute Wonderment. "I see that everything is Rama Himself. And sometimes I say to myself, 'Whom shall I teach?'" Beautiful! The Height is incomprehensible! "You will realize everything when God Himself teaches you." God, Pure Mind, Sakti, the Divine Mother Herself. Absolutely no guruhood, not in awareness, not in act, nor assumption of guru function, not ever considering such as a guru. No guru narcissism of one who imagines they teach. Nor disciple narcissism of one who imagines they learn. What do you as Pure Mind have to learn or to teach, both being nothing but conceptual narcissism in regard to this direct and profound engaging in Reality.

What is the test of truth as to what has been said here? It is if the spiritual effect is good as to the Cause to the Pure Mind! Ramakrishna would praise Vivekananda. "He is independent even of me." This is most good, there was depth of spiritual love, but not dependence, domination, possessiveness, submission nor slavery between them going in either direction. And where do these wholesome spiritual attitudes bring us, not only in regard to Vivekananda, but to even his feelings for Ramakrishna as it would seem, "How often," he said, "does a man ruin his disciples, by remaining always with them! When men are once trained, it is essential that their leader leave them,

358

for without his absence they cannot develop themselves!" It is certainly the truth what Swami says and cannot be denied. It too goes along with his depth of spiritual insight, on the "automatic working of the mind" as "mind becoming the Guru" so "saturated" with the "principles" that it requires "no guidance." Here, Pure Mind is Teacher, not teacher in the little sense, but Teacher in the Immense Level. This "same automatic mentality" as Swami puts it rises from the "subjective source." It is the quick recognition "within upon the mind itself" as it is "really dictated by the higher wisdom of super-consciousness." Even in people unaware of this in themselves he could see the guidance from the super consciousness as subjective source, "in such things he saw a higher impulsion." Even in regard to things that commonly might be held in the standard of mistakes, "Not all ignorance was in his eyes equally dark." For we learn from the Pure Mind this way and that way, as the Truth of this is innate within us.

To define this Pure Mind in even more clarity we find Swami states. "Self is the Savior of self -- none else." And is not the Self the Pure Mind as we have been saying! Further more, "No one is greater. Realize that you are Brahman. Nothing has power except what you give it." Understand that you are Pure Mind and no being is greater than this and that anyone or anything only has power if you give it power out of your own mind. And what is this subjective source, this super consciousness, this automatic working of the mind, this spontaneous guidance, what indeed if not Mother Herself? She alone is the one who nourishes us, nurtures us, guides us, is our refuge and the one who gives enlightenment. Vivekananda speaks here, "And Whatever you ask Her for, She will assuredly bestow." "She can show Herself to us in any form at any moment." No person has this power being limited by the form of a person and by the boundary of the moment. But with Mother Shakti there is no limitation or boundary! Furthermore Ramakrishna gives us the last word, "Sometimes I say to myself in the Kali temple, 'O Mother, the mind is nothing but Yourself.' Therefore Pure Mind, Pure Buddhi, and Pure Atman are one and the same thing." But what obscures this spontaneous automatic

359

direct awareness of Her as well as Her higher impulses of guidance, "But who are you? It is the Divine Mother who has become all this. It is only as long as you do not know Her that you say, 'I', 'I'." It is the ego 'I' that obscures, this conceptuality of self, when it is the Divine Mother who has become all this and all this includes you, everything, but mostly Her as your Pure Mind, none but your Atman, and your awakened Buddhi. That is real Buddha and that is why Swami Vivekananda would say of Sakyamuni, "the one absolutely sane man that the world has ever seen. How he had refused worship! The Buddha was not a person but a realization, and to that, anyone of them might attain. And with his last breath he forbade them to worship any." "Buddha-hood is an achievement, not a person!" With such important emphasis, he said again, that Sakyamuni was the "only man in the world who was ever quite sane, the only sane man ever born." Where does that leave Ramakrishna? "In Buddha, he saw Ramakrishna Paramahamsa: in Ramakrishna, he saw Buddha." Remarkable, what freedom of Pure Mind!

But back to the "source" of it all! "A bit of Mother, a drop, was Krishna; another was Buddha; another was Christ. Worship Her if you want love and wisdom." This leads back again to our knowledge that even so, all the ishtas and incarnations are but a few drops, bits of Mother. She alone is the complete Picture! Vivekananda reminds us again with slightly different words, so that we will not become lost in all this that obscures our sight! "Great saints are illustrations of the Principle. But the disciples make the saint the Principle and then they forget the Principle in the person." That such a "spiritual friend" of Ramakrishna could say this, of him, of his own self to others, of Buddha, Krishna or any greatness there might be, is indeed the sign of genuine spiritual well being.

If we are to further define this Principle we turn to Swami's thoughts. "He is the Teacher of even the ancient teachers, not limited by time. The word that manifests Him is Om." (Patanjali 1 26-27) Swami illuminates this, "Yet though there are men teachers, god teachers, and angel teachers, they are all limited. We are forced to admit, finally, One Teacher who is not limited by time; and that Teacher, of infinite knowledge and without beginning or end, is called God." Which is most beautifully stated, and also by Ramakrishna, "O Mother! O Embodiment of Om!" In many extraordinary ways we are given what it is to approach the Pure Mind. Here, the Essence of this Innermost Ancient Teacher is revealed as well as the fact that men (humans), gods (incarnations) and angels (ishtas) are all secondary to the Living Power of what is Embodied inside Om!

This effect of true spiritual well being comes through with another extraordinary "friend" of Ramakrishna. "Swami Brahmananda used to say, 'There is no greater guru than your own mind.'" This comes from Yatiswarananda's chapter, "The Pure Mind as Guru." He continues, "It was this inner guru that Buddha asked his disciples to follow after his passing away. 'Be a lamp unto yourself' (Atmadipo Bhava), he told them." "Remember Buddha's instruction,: 'Roam about free and alone like the rhinoceros.'" "The higher Self is the best integrating power known to man. There is no need to run after this man and that man for one's peaceful existence." And with astounding clarity on both ishta and guru he remarks amazingly, "The trouble with most spiritual seekers is that they identify themselves with their own body and personality, and become devoted to a male or female Deity, and remain stuck there. And if they have a spiritual teacher, they cling to the form and personality of the teacher also. This is nothing but materialism, though given a spiritual color... this spiritual materialism must be transcended; but how to do it is the question." And the answer is the Pure Mind given so many times here in so many ways described. To me this insight that all this we have been discussing is "nothing but materialism" is one of the most extraordinary and remarkably vigorous, sound and wholesome I have found. He really tears away the bark of all those fragile and failing, worn out and worn down beliefs that have come along, with two words, "spiritual materialism."

Where shall we find a startling example of this spiritual materialism with Ramakrishna? "Kedar believed in certain queer practices... He held the Master's big toe in his hand, believing that in this way the Master's spiritual power would be transmitted to him." Ramakrishna responded to this, "Mother, what can he do to me by holding my big toe? Mother take him away." At these words Kedar's throat dried up. In a frightened tone he said to Ram, "What is the Master saying?" Such spiritual materialism cannot but cause a frightened distorted state. Is it not indeed a queer or weird practice, this guru worship? There is nothing in the toe. If anything happens at anytime anywhere it is the power of your own Veneration, your own Pure Mind itself. Yatiswarananda gives insight into why such deluded guru worship happens and how it obscures the Pure Mind, "In many people there seems to be an inherent fear of remaining alone. They always need a company of some sort or other. People are eager to talk to others and make others talk to them. The main cause of this tendency is the clinging to one's own little self. The ego is a complex bundle of ideas, memories and impulses, and therefore needs some kind of support. Ordinarily, people try to hold together the ego with the support of others. But those who have succeeded in integrating their personality from within do not need such external supports. The center of gravity of the personality in their case lies wholly within." Perfect. Pure Mind is that center of gravity. And here "others" are so often the gurus that are held with worshiping dependence as "external supports" in order to keep the little bundle intact and not Cut Through and Soar On with sound, vigorous and wholesome spirituality.

A teacher may give words, mantras, instructions or even answers on the highest level, but it is no one else but God who gives Experience. No one!, and that God is found in Pure Mind. "You are the Question, guru is the Book, and God is the Answer." Haridhosgiri. When you are the Answer you no longer need the book and when you are that Answer (Pure Mind) you no longer are the question! Pure Mind is the Real Ishta, the Real Guru, the Real God, for it is out of Pure Mind which arise these three as a conceptual reality, even so the conceptuality of the three states (waking, dreaming, deep sleep) as well. Down from here everything is materialism, because your own Pure Mind is the one pure teacher and pure reality. None other, and this is the True Eternal Companion.

The Pure Point of all this is to go beyond the impeding perplexity of all dualistic conceptuality, especially in relationship. There are five basic forms of moods in these relations of dualistic conceptuality. Serenity with the chosen spiritual ideal, serving another, friendship, child to parent, and sweethearts. These are shanta/shanti, dasya/dasyi, sakha/sakhi, vatsalya/vatsalyi, and the precious madhura bhava. (Sometimes a sixth mood of relation is added which is to see God, Pure Mind, Sakti even in an enemy.) We include both feminine and masculine forms here. And even though all mood forms are obvious what we have dwelt upon is the dasya/dasyi, the conceptual mood relation between teacher and student, mentor and the guided, tutor and taught, guru and sishya, lama and chela, sensei and deshi, shaman and apprentice, master and disciple, sifu and toedai, on and on it goes no matter what cultural conceptual context one may be experiencing. Can one have direct experience in Pure Mind when any dualistic conceptuality is present, whether it be causal spirituality, subtle spirituality or physical spirituality? Pure Mind is present in spite of these dualities.

It takes courage to admit that one may be trapped in conceptuality. This exists in even very high relation forms. "God Himself is the Supreme Guru, the Guru of the Guru," Swami Virajananda would say, but here, even though in its height it speaks Truth, still it is expressed through conceptuality, the God concept. One may think of Buddha and Jesus as descended emanations of Pure Mind. The Truth expressed by both is that there is nothing higher than Love for others, but that too is conceptual context. Again, Rama stands for, to do what must be done and Krishna is the demonstration of the supreme Letting Go into the Universal Form. But doing and letting go are also conceptuality. Even the regard for the Divine Mother exists in conceptuality. The teacher, the mantra, the ishta, to Pure Mind at last. Mother is my conceptuality in Real Spirituality.

The point is to be Free, free of Everything. A good guide, or a true ishta will want to help you to that stageless stage with all of his/her might. They will not glorify themselves. They will glorify Reality, Pure Mind. You must get beyond the paradox.

It is not the beyond nor the here and now. It is Something indecipherable to yourself, yet ever being yourself. Ramakrishna tells us, "If you worship with love even a brick or stone as God, then through His grace you can see Him." The brick or stone may appear to you as the guiding energy, but it is your own power of veneration that is the ishta that leads you on to see God, the Goddess and Pure Mind. When I met Swami Bhashyananda he said, "Have no anxiety. You are in the presence of God and the teacher." He put Principle before the person. He spoke of the big focus as God and then Truth and as the little focus as the teacher. He spoke of "letting go" and I would say too, that this is also of the little focus, perhaps even the big focus, to lead further on to soaring through Reality. I said, "In the final analysis Satchidananda is the only Teacher." And to me he replied, "In the final analysis Satchidananda is all that is." The Pure Non-Dual God without God conceptuality.

Again Ramakrishna states, "There is still another class of devotees, the svapnasiddha, who have had the vision of God in a dream." Svapna is the dream state. Sva is Self, Pure Mind, and siddha means attainment. So, even such a subtle or deeply spiritual vision of God will be in conceptuality because the dreamer is present there. If Non-Dual Pure Mind arises during such a Pure Mind dream, there is no more dreamer of conceptuality. Pure Mind can show through the dream state. I am still fond of my dream of Swami Aseshananda who within my conceptuality said, "Yes, Richard, you read. I shall interpret quickly." Yet when I visited him in Portland two things return to saturate my mind. One, I asked him about becoming the Sugar and tasting the Sugar. Sugar as Sweetness is a metaphor of Reality. He answered, "Ask the Divine Mother, She will Guide you." He made it clear, all Power to Her not to him. And second, "Your own Atma is the Divine Mother." Beautiful! Is it not one's own Pure Mind, the Guide, the Atma, the Divine Mother!

Again, the example I have found of one who teaches without boundaries, Ramakrishna, I quote, "The pure mind and pure intellect are one and the same. God is known by the pure mind. Didn't the sages and seers of olden times see God? They realized the All-pervading Consciousness by means of their inner consciousness." What is it that sees what is called God but the Pure Mind and what sees This can only be This. Those sages and seer poets had vigorous and invigorating direct contact. There is no other agency or guiding energy mentioned here. The Helmsman of their own Pure Mind was all that was needed. These Enlightened Ones existed before the idea of even the incarnation came into being. Ramakrishna did this in the Kali temple before the Divine Mother. Sakyamuni did this sitting under the sacred Tree. You too can do this free of all boundaries dark or light.

"Experience is the Greatest Teacher." Swami Aseshananda quoting Swami Vivekananda. And our own Experience is what we so often forget and lose in what pricks the flesh. Why would one go from what is the Greatest, to what annoys like a thorn? Nitya! Suddha! Buddha! Mukta! Ever Eternal. Ever Pure. Ever Awakened. Ever Free. "As a rope lying in darkness, about whose nature one remains uncertain, is imagined to be a snake or a line of water, so Atman is imagined in various ways." Gaudapada II 17 Eternity (Pure Mind) is Ever Present in the present, holding past and future, left and right in Its arms, stretching out as space in every direction Infinite. There are no real boundaries. To this the final light is shown by Ramakrishna, "It is the mind that becomes at last the spiritual teacher and acts as such."

Groundwork for The Ancient Method

This is the fourth part of the text Inherent Solutions To Spiritual Obscurations, following The Wonder of the Dakini Mind, Letting Go and Soaring On, Resolution in Pure Mind and now The Ancient Method.

What was dealt with before, as with Gaudapada, for example, who was the profound Epiphany of Upanishadic development, when he laid down the pure groundwork for the Advaitic experience in the four parts of his Karika, is now being continued. We shall look into the past, far into the past of what came before the time of Gaudapada and hopefully it will shed fresh light on old ground.

Referencing those histories and myths, we shall attempt to see the real Ramakrishna, the real Janaka, and the pure spontaneous, vigorous voice of the Upanishads. I hope the reader will find it of interest, this unworthy study, that has been done here on the spiritual poet (the kavi), the seven rishis (seers), the ten avataras (incarnations) and such magnificent spiritual heroes like Prahlada, Sukadeva, Vamadeva, Trisanku, and Uddalaka.

We will compare the Rk Veda and true history while making sense of the mythical overlay. With the court of king Janaka as the central point in time and place, we shall look at Yajnavalkya and Ashtavakra and other amazing figures who are presented.

Two words that appear in the text need more than a simple glossary definition. Vasana and Samskara. Samskara is usually translated as mental impression, as it deals with the conscious and subconscious imprints. Vasana is usually translated as hidden potential or hidden desire, as it deals more in the unconscious. The truest hidden potential or vasana is Self Knowledge, Knowing the Atman, the Pure Mind. With samskara, the strongest mental impression is usually that one thinks one is the ego. In samskara, these conscious and subconscious impressions, imprints, tendencies and potentialities are usually obvious. They are said to be left by causes no longer operating, that is from a previous life, but it seems they also come from this life too as impressions left from conception through childhood and onward. These are decorations of the mind obscuring Pure Mind. They are a continuity of impressions which make up character and personality. There are three types of samskaras. Vega: simply, impulse, that is to feel compelled towards something. Sthita Sthapaka: translated as elasticity, but is more the Steady Standing Ideas of Self in which you are cooked, baked, broiled or roasted. Bhavana: is the reproducing imagination, the after effect of a creation in the mind, which decorates Pure Mind and is regarded as real though actually is not. Now, Vasana is much more interesting. These vasanas are unconscious psychic knots (or bundles) of hidden or latent (buried) and yet to be manifested desires, potentials, and even skills or abilities. Even from previous lives and they are not always so obvious. Ramakrishna gives a good example. A washer boy dies and is reincarnated as a prince. So now he gets his princely playmates to go at a game with him. He lays down on the ground and has them beat on his back. Strange at first, but then you realize how he is recalling, at least the feeling memory of washing clothes by pounding them on the stones next to a river. Of course, the True Vasana within everyone is the vasana of their Real Atman, and everyone, like Vamadeva, eventually bursts through these vasanas to remember their True Self. Vasana also means dress, garment or cloth, which here means the thoughts in which the mind which is really Pure Mind, is clothed, garmented, and dressed as that which surrounds the mind keeping the view of Pure Mind shrouded. Vasana also means the sojourn, the dwelling or residence of the mind in its excursion out of Pure Mind knowing. Vasana is also a deep rooted attachment to a doctrine, belief or idea.

As it was with the first three parts of Inherent Solutions to Spiritual Obscurations, this is a further diving on into the questions presented, the Self Path?, or the teacher path?. The full text is available as a virtual book at 1st Books Library at www.1stbooks.com or through Ingram's "Books in Print" catalog, acquirable through twenty five thousand bookstores around the world, including Barnes and Noble, Amazon.com and Borders.

Part Four
THE ANCIENT METHOD

Ramakrishna, Janaka and the Upanishads

Subjects

Vamadeva
The Hawk
Dirghatamas
Bitter Rage and God Consciousness
Taking Heads
Friends in Truth
In Spite of It, Good Ideas
Traditional Behaviorism
Pure Upanishad
Trisanku
Direct Method
Janaka and Suka
Janaka and the Siddhas
Janaka and Yajnavalkya
Janaka and Ashtavakra
Janaka and the Ten Sikhs
Mandukyo
- A -
- U -
- M -
Aum
Prana, Sakti, Mother
Prahlada
Kaushitaki
My Self
Direct Dream Sight
Experience
Pure Rk Vedic Experience
Soma
Vac

Kabandha
The Salt Doll
Incarnations of God Consciousness
in Natural Powers
Incarnations of God Consciousness
Within Human Beings
The Seven Sages and the One Poet
Experience
Yet Another Cursing Guru
Mythic Phenomena
Origins of Thought
Sunahsepa
Ramakrishna and Yajnavalkya
The Darkening of Woman
Uddalaka
Mood of Spirit

The Ancient Method

Ramakrishna, Janaka and the Upanishads

How shall I begin this weighty subject, for the more I write, the more I find, for it is indeed, Immense! So I shall call on Mother to Help, if She wishes to do so! The idea that the Gods can constrict one's spiritual progress is there. It will be dealt with in the case of the poet seer (kavi) Vamadeva. But what is the Ancient Method? It is Direct Experience in (your own) Pure Mind! Like those "seers of old" as Ramakrishna calls them, who would rouse their minds to fly beyond the barriers of contraries ideas and superstitions that keep one from the direct experience, even if those barriers be the gods themselves.

Vamadeva

This is so in the case of Vamadeva. Other seer poets may or may not have had the depth of his insight/experience. You see, this Vamadeva was an extraordinary example of those "seers of old." He was born in utter poverty so much so that he had to live on dog entrails at some time. But this hardship did not deter his Pure Mind, the enlightenment in the Ancient Method. He is an exception to the rishi poets and his importance is thereby demonstrated by being twice quoted in the Upanishads. The Aitareya and the Brihadaranyaka which are two of the oldest. He is quoted because of the power of his example. In the Rig Veda the poets praise a Deity, some of them become identified with the Deity, and yet some go further on to More than just identity. Vamadeva makes it clear in the fourth mandala of the Rig Veda to which he is ascribed almost its entire authorship. R.V. IV 26. v.2 "I guided forth the loudly roaring waters and the Gods moved according to my pleasure." Here the Gods become his pleasure, for he is so identified beyond them that he is no longer their pleasure or sacrifice.

You see, the Gods like to be worshiped, all the Vedic gods, the Trimurti or triple faced, Brahma, Vishnu and Shiva, even

371

Krishna perhaps, but Krishna may have transcended this problem. I quote Swami Nikhilananda, "The rishi Vamadeva, too, became omniscient through the Knowledge of Atman. Even the gods cannot injure the knower of Atman, because he becomes their Atman, or self, too. The ignorant man who worships the gods, regarding them as other than his Atman, becomes subservient to them. The gods obstruct his spiritual progress." This is so powerful, the key to Pure Spiritual Experience. It is further said, along with the gods, that this term of words includes the gods, seers, men, etc., even teachers as it will be seen in this essay. The point is that the outer arena of powers and people may indeed obstruct the sight experience of Pure Mind if one allows one's mind to be subservient to these. We want the Great Identity not these lesser identities!

The Great Forest Upanishad states then, "The self was indeed Brahman in the beginning. It knew itself only as 'I am Brahman.' Therefore it became all. And whoever among the gods had this enlightenment, also became That (Brahman). It is the same with the seers (rishis), the same with men. The seer Vamadeva, having realized this (self) as That, came to know: 'I was Manu and the Sun.' And to this day, whoever in like manner knows the self as 'I am Brahman', becomes all this (universe). Even the gods cannot prevent his becoming this, for he has become their Self. Now, if a man worships another deity, thinking: 'He is one and I am another,' he does not know. He is like an animal to the gods. As many animals serve a man, so does each man serve the gods. Even if one animal is taken away, it causes anguish (to the owner); how much more so when many (are taken away)! Therefore it is not pleasing to the gods that men should know this" Brihadaranyaka Upanishad I. iv. 10. This is so astounding, remember that gods, etc., includes, seers, teachers, men. I myself seek to bring anguish to the gods that many will no longer be animals. So I write. Vamadeva had this individual spontaneous bursting forth to True Self so why not you, and him and her and even so, me as well. We all want a spiritual place where we are no longer animals to the gods.

Deussen translates the Rig Veda of Vamadeva as this, "I was once Manu, I was once the Sun." While Griffith gives us all of the first verse. "I was aforetime Manu, I was Surya. I am the sage Kaksivan, the holy singer. Kutsa, the son of Arjuni I master. I am the sapient Usana behold me." This is so interesting into the level of Vamadeva's mind. The height of his identity in the Great Identity is expressed in terms of the vigor of his poetry. Manu was the first man created by Brahma as mythology tells us. Yet even in the real history of humankind Vamadeva is identified with the first human. He knows his True Self was there then as much here now. He goes even further in the being of identity knowing himself there as Surya, the Sun, perhaps even the early Sun before even the Earth was created. The Essence (Mystery) in Vamadeva the seer poet is the same as in the Sun as well as your own head. He says also that he was Kakshivan the holy singer. Now, this Kakshivan or Kakshivat was the son of the poet/sage Dirghatamas who birthed him on (like horses, sired on, a strange patriarchal expression) King Bali's Queen, which is in the time of the Vamana Avatara, so it was a long time ago. Again Dirghatamas is the father of one of the seven sages, Gautama (not the Buddha), and this Dirghatamas is the son of Brihaspati, who was the son of Angiras. So Vamadeva identifies himself with having been this Kakshivat.

It goes on with him saying that he is master of Kutsa who was also a Rig Veda poet. But I do not know if they were contemporary and yet when Vamadeva speaks as "I master" he may not be singing the poetry himself of himself as a person, but as the Great Identity Itself which in that sense masters us all! Kutsa was legendary for being the favorite of Indra which I like to think of as a deity metaphor of Pure Mind and it is here that Griffith says that Vamadeva is identified as Indra when he says "I master." Or it could be the Parama Atma (Supreme Self) that Vamadeva is identified with when he speaks such verse as he says. The point is that it is so beautiful that he could be identified at all in that way! So we come to his remarkable exclamation that he also was Usana. The Markendeya Purana says that Usana is none other than Sukra, the teacher of the demons or asuras. Sukra is also a great poet so much so that he is identified as just Kavi, the Poet. This is interesting as well because Krishna latter

373

says in the Bhagavad Gita X. 37 "... and of seers I am Usanas the seer." This is also expressed by Krishna in the Srimad Bhagavatam, "... and of the wise I am Sukra." So we are coming across some astounding levels of identity, not only in regard to what is thought of as positive and negative, the gods and the demons, but to Immense Identity of having been and of being not only being confined to the person of one's own identity but of being, or sharing, or participating in that life and self of others. This is the extraordinary realization which is called under different headings, one being Bhavamukha, which subject we will deal with a few pages on.

But for now let us continue with Vamadeva whose name means the Beautiful One, the Shining or Generous One and how true that is when he among so many generously shares the Beauty of Direct Experience. Upanishad means "to sit down near the end." Some interpret this as to sit near the teacher, but others have taken this deeper to mean that one is sitting near the Rahasya, the Mystery, which is one's own Inner Mystery, the Tattva Jnana, the Knowledge of the Ultimate Principle, the Mystery of one's own Self which is what the Upanishads are the study of, so here you are sitting down near the mystery of your own Self, where you loosen or destroy that sense of separation from the Self which then is no longer a mystery (rahasya).

The Hawk

Vamadeva's True Mind is like the Hawk, like the Falcon which in his poetry are symbols of Indra (the Deity of Pure Mind or Pure Buddhi as Intellect). I quote the Aitareya Upanishad which quotes Vamadeva's fourth mandala of the Rig Veda, 27 v. 1. "While yet tarrying in my mother's womb, I have learnt all the births of these gods; Had a hundred iron fortresses held me back, Yet like a Hawk of swift flight I had escaped away." (Deussen's version) Now Griffith gives us his rendering, "I, As I lay within the womb, considered all generations of these Gods in order. A hundred iron fortresses confined me but forth I flew with rapid speed a Falcon." Vamadeva continues speaking of this Bird, this Bold One, which is not so different from the

374

Garuda, as you will see.

Now in this same Upanishad, the Aitareya, is given in context of this quote what is called the doctrine of the Three Births which is attributed to Vamadeva. I have actually come across three interpretations of this doctrine. One is natural birth, spiritual education and then death as the third birth. Another version says it is to be born as an offspring which is the first birth. Then to give birth of oneself in the offspring of another is the second. And the the third birth is death. The last version which I think is what Vamadeva actually meant was that the first birth is conception (since that is what is described in the Upanishad). The second birth is actually coming out of the womb. And the third birth is death. It is important to consider this doctrine of the three births in order to grasp Vamadeva. Even while in the mother's womb he came to know the birth or source, the generation or creation of all the Gods. The mother's womb is the place of Inner Grace for him as the temple of Mother Kali was for Ramakrishna and is not the Mother's Womb the most natural of Her temples from which worlds come forth. He had gone through one of many of the third births (deaths) and is now in the first birth, that of some stage of conception before natural birth where he experiences what is quoted in the Aitareya. But it is also here that he realizes, "I was once Manu, I was once the Sun," Kakshivat, Usanas, Kutsa and so forth as already described. Those one hundred strongholds or iron fortresses which tried to confine him while there in the womb from which he burst forth like a Hawk, the Falcon Mind of Indra are considered perhaps as a poetic one hundred barriers which could be previous identities of many bodies before or the many gods which try to bind him with their identities or perhaps the feeling of being so confined by the womb itself. Or more likely, the vasanas and samskaras, two very interesting words. Vasanas are thoughts that surround or clothe the mind in hidden desire potentials. Samskaras are mental or psychic impressions that make up the character. See Groundwork for complete definitions. At any rate it is a conglomeration of numerous forces of identity that would make one feel like an animal to the gods. Here, though, he has the turnaround or revolution in Mind

375

which sees more in the Way of Indra (Pure Mind). And that is the extraordinary thing of it all! I quote Nikhilananda's rendering, "About this a rishi has said: 'While still lying in the womb, I came to know all the births of the gods. A hundred strongholds, as if made of iron, confined me, yet I burst through them all swiftly, like a hawk.' Vamadeva spoke, in this wise, even while lying in the womb." In the full Rig Veda version Vamadeva goes on to describe that, "Not at his own free pleasure did he bear me." That is the Bold Falcon of his own Mind as Indra. This is to say that this realization did not come easily as "free pleasure." But it came like a loud cry from heaven hasting like the wind, wildly raging in his mind. This all happened in the mother's womb. And what the wind is there and the wild raging of the mind is in the womb can only be the spiritual echoes of Vamadeva's Mind.

The verse before this section of the Aitareya will help us to understand. "Therefore He (the Supreme Self) is called Idandra. Idandra, indeed, is His name. Him who is Idandra they call indirectly Indra. For the gods appear to be fond of cryptic epithets; yea, the gods appear to be fond of cryptic epithets." I iii 14. Idandra is Indra who perceives Himself! Not the perception of the eyes nor the mind, but the Pure Mind itself. These cryptic epithets also give us an opening as to how the hundred strongholds can be interpreted and also the obstructions of the gods in the way of blocking final realization in that they would keep us in a cryptic interpretation of the Self rather than a direct experience of the Self, for then they, like human teachers as well, would lose their power to keep others in sacrifice to them. The authority of Vamadeva is recognized for he himself recognized the Pure Mind even in the womb. As Deussen writes, this came by virtue of sastra drishti, an inspired conception, which is the Way of the Poets.

It is indeed no less than what Prahlada realized when he spoke forth his True Self saying that all the gods sing his praise for he is (identified) himself Vishnu. It is the very thing that Death himself sings in the Katha Upanishad. "Who but myself can know that Luminous Atman...?" And, "It is attained by him alone whom It chooses!" I ii 21 & 23. With this, any thoughtful person may know that Vamadeva has just been through death, has been death before, that is prior to the womb birth and so he too may say, who but myself and alone whom It chooses! Yet is it not the experience of one and all, death, so who alone is there that it does not choose. The echo comes again on the hasting wind of the Chhandogya Upanishad, "The gods meditate on that Self. Therefore all worlds belong to them and all desires." VIII xii 6. So what indeed comes to the one who knows their very Self in the Reality of one's own!

Coming into all this, from the Rig Veda to the formation of the first Upanishad centered as a description of happenings in the court of King Janaka, we find a difficult mixture of legend and reality, of history and myth. And one finds different opinions about who is who, parentages and lineages, ages of times, exactly how many kings lived between the life of one sage and another, and so forth, and that within lineages people in different times bear the same family name. Yet, the Rig Veda is honest in its history of two great wars waged upon the Dasas, the indigenous people of Harrapa (Hariyupia) and Mohenjodaro. The Dasa chief was Shamvara and the Aryan chief was Divodasa. In the first war it is said Indra destroyed 99 out of 100 city forts of the Dasas and with this Vamadeva even identifies with the Indra who did this in his Rigvedic poem, V 26 v 3. This disturbs me. The second war was thought to be waged upon Mohenjodaro by the Aryan chief Sudasa against the Dravidian chief Bheda. In this seven city forts were demolished putting an end to these wars. It is estimated that it took five hundred to one thousand years for this to be accomplished by the five tribes of the Indo Aryans. (See Rig Veda Summary by Rajmohon Nath).

This scholar makes an interesting comment on Vamadeva. "Vamadeva, praying to Ashvins while yet in the mother's womb, became super intelligent. Vamadeva is the seer of the 4th book of the Rig Veda. He was delivered by caesarean operation. He was the propounder of a new cult of supramental theory. By psychic training a man could become as powerful as the creator himself. Divinity is manifested as a human being, and every human being can become a divinity." What is curious is that one would think of a new cult all those thousands of years ago. And

377

of Usana who we described a little while ago he says there were two. One who is Sukra and another who was Kavi. But he gives this, "Kavi literally means poet. It is really the one from the core (Ku) of whose heart emerges forth (I) the feelings like stream in rhythm and harmony." Which is very good.

Dirghatamas

Now lets return to Dirghatamas who Rajmohon Nath says is the son of Ucathya whose parent was Ucitya who was the son of Ushija. He agrees that Dirghatamas is the father of Kakshivan, but says Gotama is parented by Rahugana. You can see there are sages and sages going back through history, but parentages don't always agree. It may only matter to those who live by a sense of consistency. That Dirghatamas is the author of the famous Asya Vamasya Hymn in the Rig Veda I 164 which is said to contain Rig Vedic mysticism in a nutshell. One line stands out at present, "To what is One, sages give many a title." Also rendered as, "Truth is One, sages name it variously." Nevertheless, it is Vipra that is written in Sanskrit. The Vipra or Kavi are the seer/composers, the Poets, literally, so it is the Poets who name Truth, the One, variously, and here are various Deities listed. Kavi is the Poet Path of Inspired Intuition, which is then given expression in vigorous powerful words of praise and of high identity with the deities that have been praised. These are the vipras, the poet/sages. These Vipras and Kavis are the Heroic Poets. "Ekam sad vipra bahudha vadanty - What is One, poets speak of in many ways." But as we shall see, these blessed words of the poet Dirghatamas are contradicted by the behavior of many of these sages. They fight among themselves, so it comes as no wonder to me that Ramakrishna backed off from letting himself be to heavily identified with all this. I quote Swami Saradananda, "... the Master asked the Mother (the Divine Mother) every day to take back from him the position of the teacher, which he regarded as totally worthless, though others yearn for it, on account of the attendant honors."

An example of this behavior is given even here with Dirghatamas. It is a strange little story. Brihaspati sought to

378

have sexual relation with Mamata, Dirghatamas was already in her womb and and shut her cervix with his legs. So Brihaspati cursed him and he was born blind as his name means one who is shrouded in the deepest darkness forever. Can you not see the selfish lust of the great sage and that his anger and cursing hurt the poet Dirghatamas. His sight is restored later after he is thrown in the sea for ravishing another's wife and then is rescued by King Bali. And after this he becomes known as Gautama.

Bitter Rage and God Consciousness

Vasistha and Visvamitra are notorious for their fighting and quarrels, so much so that their battles with one another are metaphorically retold as two war birds rending each other to shreds. Truth is One, but the behavior of sages can be astoundingly shocking. The envy and rival between these two is on a high scale of jealousy over which was the higher type of sage, a royal, a great or a God, Brahma rishi. Vasistha and Visvamitra battled each other desperately over a sacred magic cow. A cow? But others have said this cow is a symbol of the heartland of North India (Madhyadesa) which seems reasonable but really shows the petty behavior of two sages who are not only author poets of large portions of the Rig Veda but also are thought to be among the Seven Sages, a very sacred tradition to them. These are the Mind Born sons of God (Brahma) and Gautama is thought to be one of them, but he is parented by Rahugana in one history and by Dirghatamas in another, not God. So, it is convenient for diverging interpretations.

Another strange tale of Vasistha is here. Janaka's father was Nimi and Nimi's father was Ikshavatu who was a son of Manu the first man. It is here most interesting to note that Ikshavatu may have been of Mongolian descent, or he may have come from the Sakas (Indo Scythians) or the Yavanas (Indo Greeks), no one is sure. The Rig Veda shows an extraordinary race awareness of other peoples and cultures Nevertheless, Nimi is desiring to hold a sacred sacrifice and he asked his family priest Vasistha to perform it but Vasistha can not do it for a long time and it must be done, according to religious ideas. So King Nimi

379

asks another of the sacred seven sages to help, Gautama, and he does so. Vasistha is so awfully enraged that he curses King Janaka's father Nimi to death and as Nimi is dying, he in turn curses Vasistha to death. They both drop dead. Truth is One, but the behavior! There are certainly the anger prone personalities of these sages whose traditional behavior influence has set a standard of behavior even in today's sages I have found and felt at the blunt end, though they claim to be above influence or anger. This is certainly not the Kindness of the Buddha nor the Loving Heart of Sri Ramakrishna who both set completely different examples of behavior. A behavioral example. Ramakrishna speaks of how paramahamas like the company of children because their sweet and spontaneous characteristics are assumed by them. A paramahamsa is one who has flown beyond all delusion, but you see even here, they are, like any of us, influenceable!

Again, with Vasistha and Visvamitra there was the fight between them over King Trisanku of the Taittiriya Upanishad. He went to Vasistha seeking to have the Great Transference of Bodily Ascension into a Heavenly Region as the legend goes. Not unlike the Pho Wa Transference of Tibet. Vasistha said this was impossible. But after seeking out Visvamitra, Trisanku attained this state as the legend is told. We will talk of Trisanku latter as some of his spontaneous exclamations of Enlightenment are some of the grandest recorded in the Upanishads. These two are regarded as two of the Seven Original Sages and unfortunately they are often times referred to as irascible because of their jealousy and anger in regard to one another. Yet, when Lord Rama is learning the Yoga Vasistha of Advaita Vedanta they were said to have made amends.

Taking Heads

Truth is One, but the behavior! In the case of Yajnavalkya we see that he even took heads in debate, literally. Defeating Sakalya, his head was cut off, all over a debate on the nature of spiritual reality. This happened in King Janaka's court. He also threatens Gargi, the naked Bhairavi woman who debated with him. Yajnavalkya is also called irascible for his behaviors and when Janaka asked him why he was there, whether it was to debate philosophy or win the prize of thousands of cows (Janaka's reward for the best debater) he replied to Janaka that he was there for both. There is a difference between Ramakrishna and Yajnavalkya. The sage Yajnavalkya had two wives and desired to win the prize of wealth from Janaka. Ramakrishna renounced lust and gold. There is a difference. Perhaps that was the old way for some. Yet the behavior of Yajnavalkya taking heads was set in the tradition and the influence even went down to Shankara (and so to modern times as well, not in the sense of killing those who disagree but of abuse) who as we shall see did the same all in the name of Spiritual Reality. It is reprehensible and irascible!

Vidyaranya in his Jivanmuktiviveka makes a clear mark on the difference between Janaka (after Enlightenment) and Yajnavalkya. "For, though, in the case of Janaka, there was no recurrence of impure vasanas (sub or unconscious potentials), Yajnavalkya, Bhagiratha and others had enough of such recurrence. In Yajnavalkya and his opponents, Usasta, Kahola and others, there was considerable arrogance of learning, for, they took part in disputation with the object of vanquishing their opponents."

Even though a brilliant Non-Dualist, Shankara too took the lives of Buddhists he defeated in argument. It is repulsive in fact that a spiritual person would call upon killing. It is murder in fact! Swami Vivekananda gives the astoundingly healthy surveillance of this, "So Shankara had no need whatsoever of displaying this curious bit of pedantry on this subject, contrary to the Vedas. And such was his heart that he burnt to death lots of Buddhist monks - by defeating them in argument! And the Buddhists, too, were foolish enough to burn themselves to death, simply because they were worsted in argument! What can you call such an action on Shankara's part except fanaticism? But look at Buddha's heart! Ever ready to give his own life to save the life of even a kid (young animal) - what to speak of 'For the welfare of the many, for the happiness of the many!' See, what a large heartedness - what compassion!" There was a guru that I once knew whose disciples said that he reminded them of Shankara. Indeed, even this that Swami Vivekananda describes as fanaticism I would say as to his abuse. It was thought that those who were killed by Rama or Krishna were instantly liberated. This too sounded to me like an excuse to abuse others and yet not liberate them but increase their pain.

Vivekananda tells the truth of it again, "Shankara's intellect was sharp like a razor. He was a good arguer and a scholar, no doubt of that, but he had no great liberality; his heart too seems to have been like that. Besides, he used to take great pride in his Brahminism - much like a southern Brahmin of the priest class, you may say." Thank you and bless you Swami, for how true it is! Not just Shankara but the lineage of behavior he has put in motion. That pride and arrogance.

I would never criticize Love, Truth, and Reality. But I am certainly free to criticize the manners in which the conveyance of Truth may be attempted. The fearless Swami Vivekananda was very bold in his own thoughts on these deep spiritual problems. He writes, "Rama, Krishna, Buddha, Chaitanya, Nanak, Kabir, and so on are the true Avataras, for they had their hearts broad as the sky - and above all, Ramakrishna. Ramanuja, Shankara etc., seem to have been mere Pundits with much narrowness of heart. Where is that love, that weeping heart at the sorrow of others? - Dry pedantry of the Pundit - and the feeling of only oneself getting to salvation hurry-scurry!"

I once asked a south Indian teacher if the reason why one should not go to different teachers was that different Truths were conveyed. His reply was that it was not the Truth that was different but the personality through which It is conveyed. It was such spiritual irony really because here he was speaking of other teacher's personalities as being less than fit for conveying Truth and his personality could become such an angry personality that I found the conveyance of Truth there less than enlightening, less enriching. He would tell those there that one who contemplates the Witness without the teacher will end up schizophrenic. This can only be wrong for schizophrenia is an organic ailment not one brought about by any amount of contemplation, meditation or thinking. Besides, according to that idea the whole world would be schizophrenic just by thinking about God in the position of the Witness and that is not so. Another strange irony is that it was said that it would be better to write something that reflects this teacher alone. I did that and it was mocked. Now I do so with a truer voice.

This traditional arrogance is the Strangest thing on the face of the Earth, to have Spiritual Knowledge and then to be Unkind and Cruel! Is it something, a hint at what Ramakrishna speaks of as a cautionary note, about those who say, "I am not the body nor the mind. I am Brahman," but who deceive and drag others and themselves down. "He cannot understand his own state of mind." For he says he is one thing (Brahman) when he is really another (as body and mind) like a solipsistic psychosis, failing to unify the body and mind experience with the Spiritual Experience.

One may find the following comments of Ramakrishna to be an interesting paradox of viewpoints, "Kabir was a worshiper of the Impersonal God. He did not believe in Siva, Kali or Krishna. He used to make fun of them and say that Kali lived on the offerings of rice and banana, and that Krishna danced like a monkey when the gopis clapped their hands. (All laugh.)" What is interesting is that Swami Vivekananda wrote that Kabir was an Incarnation, and so here we see one incarnation making fun of other incarnations. If this is so among the field of interpersonal relationships with incarnations then why can't ordinary people like me have a right to our own feelings in regard not only to these but to much lesser souls in consequence?

Vivekananda boldly comes to our defense with his open mindedness, "My motto is to learn whatever good things I may come across anywhere. This leads many friends to think that it will take away from my devotion to the Guru. These ideas I count as those of lunatics and bigots. For all Gurus are one and are fragments and radiations of God, the Universal Guru." Lunatics and bigots, indeed Swami! And superstition as Ranade points out, admitting, "This last chapter, as has been pointed out above, ends with certain superstitious Brahminical practices." (Brihadaranyaka Upanishad). And on the Kaushitaki he remarks, "It contains a description of a number of social customs

383

of the time which are superstitious and which may therefore be regarded as irreligious." If this is the case then what else may be there as "superstitious?" We will see!

Friends in Truth

Ramakrishna says with rarest clarity avoiding the deep spiritual trauma of guru abuse, "There is not a fellow under the sun who is my disciple. On the contrary, I am everybody's disciple." Thus, true and real awakened spirituality does indeed live as a Reality without guru disciple monotony, the problem itself. Simply, how can one be dependent on another for one's own realization? Truth is One. Love must be free of all universal influences. And this Love comes down to us even so without superstition, without arrogance, without pride. The Nitya and the Lila are Two Aspects of the Same Reality. To See this is Vijnana! My spiritual friend, Swami Bhaskarananda and I were talking together. "Isn't the Lila seen in the Nitya as the serpent is seen in the Rope?" I asked. "But the Seer and the Seen are in the Lila, they are not in the Nitya." Swami replied. Replying with humility his thought stirred in my mind. So simple and true, I mused to myself, "The Witness-Seer and the Cosmic-Seen are within the Relative Waking Dream. In Dreamless Formless Sleep no otherness is seen or felt. The Nitya is very near! So much More So, the Self!" Swami engaged me again, "Some believe it was Totapuri who showed this to Ramakrishna, otherwise he would have been like Ramanuja, seeing Indivisible Oneness within Differentiation. Yet, it was the Divine Mother who brought Totapuri to Dakshineswar. 'Who' sees the Nitya, 'Who' sees the Lila, the One Without a Second. Human beings are like myths, born mortal, they are not the Immortal Infinite (Nirguna Kali Brahman) without Qualities!"

On another occasion Swami shared his Inner Self. Here is the thought, "As I am Bliss what need have I for samadhi." It is the automatic grace, the divine, the spiritual conveyance of Kali that matters. One Sunday I was visiting with my very dear spiritual friend Swami Bhaskarananda. I asked, "What is the difference between Bliss and Happiness?" He responded with uncommon force, "Bliss Is What You Are! The Atman (Real 'I') is what you are. The Atman is Bliss." My thoughtful conceptions were shattered as Swami explained that Bliss is silence, stillness, the cessation of all dualities, while happiness pertains to attaining an object of desire, Bliss is untouched by this. In a simple spontaneous way another question cognised within my thought, "If no one can know Brahman since it is Nirguna (without quality) and there is no dualistic other there, no second thing, thought, ego, then Who experiences nirvikalpa?" Swami's innate spiritual strength showed forth, "Nirvikalpa shows you what you are!" He explained that it is the door of samadhi, you are not the door, the door is a state, it is Bliss that is what you are. It is in fact only a door to what 'I' am, the Real You, the Atman as Brahman Consciousness.

Then Swami began to describe Sri Ramakrishna's experience with the Goddess Kali in a way of which I had never heard him speak. He said that in Reality the Goddess Kali, the Blissful Mother is this Chaitanya, Consciousness itself. I had never heard him speak with so much enthusiasm, energy, focus, excitement, feeling and love. He said Ramakrishna would see the Goddess Kali even in a prostitute, even in a cat. That the Goddess Kali was his chosen divine ideal form, so he was most accustomed to Her appearance, not shocked by Her four arms and Her lolling tongue. But who may say how She really looked to him, this Blissful Chaitanya, neither dual nor non dual.

I asked Swami of Nirodha, the Cessation of Mind. His brilliant spiritual insight shone forth, "But who makes the effort to perform Nirodha?" "The ego mind." I answered and he nodded and smiled. Is it not the same as the case may be with Pho Wa, Dzogchen or Samadhi, who makes the effort to get these but the ego mind! One goes from Buddhi (Bright Intellect) to Bodha (Luminous Consciousness) to Buddha (Awakened Illumination) but who indeed makes the effort and that one who makes the effort is not the one who thus goes There! No ego effort contaminates the Experience which just Happens as it is the Basis of Experience Itself. Whether it is Advaita or Dzogchen as the Maha Sandhi, the Great Fulfillment, it is as a

385

Living Understanding, not simply just a state that one enters, leaves and returns to at some other time.

In Spite of It, Good Ideas

Shankara was brilliant, no doubt, even though Vivekananda makes a healthy criticism of him. In his Laghu Vakya Vritti he explains four important points. One is that the conviction that one is the Infinite (Brahman) expressed in the individual context of the Atman (Self) becomes as strong as the conviction of ordinary people that they are the body. Another point is when he describes the moment to moment changing of phenomena like a string of pearls as modifications or thoughts, feelings, events, and as, "though hidden by modifications of the Intellect, can be clearly perceived in between any two modifications." That is this Reality is experienced between the rising and setting of two thoughts or two feelings or two mental events, just naturally as It is and so without the effort of Nirodha, as we just mentioned. And what is most Astounding is that Shankara describes what is Experienced there in the between place, as She, that is Pure Consciousness as She. Her, the Divine Mother, the Goddess! So it leads one to believe that Shankara must have written this after his conversion or accepting of the Goddess and not before that, because in the Vivekachudamani he has written of his prejudiced belief that a male body is better suited for enlightenment than a woman's body and that is regretful that he set that ridiculous idea in motion. Mother, Sakti, please don't make me like that, a hypocrite. May all my energy serve the Goddess. Lastly and surprisingly, in his text Shankara describes what I will describe more and more of as the Ancient Method. That is a mutual sharing of Reality in a healthy spiritual way where we meditate, discuss, enlighten one another and cherish this Spiritual Reality together as the Supreme End! And that is beautiful!

Traditional Behaviorism

To hearken back to the Rig Veda, they called upon Indra who is a deity no less of your own spiritual genius or Pure

386

Intellect. Indeed, as an inner metaphor poetically speaking, of your own innate Pure Mind, as the Leader, the Guide, the Helper, the Power of Illumination. I would quote Asrani in his light and clear expression, on this path over the other. "In this relative and dynamically evolving world, nobody can be regarded as absolutely perfect. Hence the cult of Faith in the Guru, as a Perfect Being, so common to Indian Yogic circles, is in the opinion of the writer, misplaced. It leads to imitation, among disciples. Boasting charlatans get, in this cult, a wide berth to ply their trade. The personalities of sincere disciples, get suppressed; they cannot actualize their potentialities, and give free scope to their creative genius. A neurotic skepticism in everything, will of course not do; nor a changing of the Guru, every now and then. A sane amount of Faith is like that of a university student, in his professor, or that of a patient, in the doctor, to whom he decides, after due enquiry, to go; a realistic and discriminative Faith."

In the last verse of the Svetasvatara Upanishad it is stated that the guru should be worshiped as God. Ranade, Deussen, Chakravarti and Max Muller all agree that this verse was added later. I quote Chakravarti, "Lastly, it is not necessary to quarrel with any one who intends to derive comfort by finding in this Upanishad the germs of the Bhakti doctrine. Not only do I agree with Max Muller that the last verse of this Upanishad, where highest devotion for God as well as for one's Guru is enjoined, is an addition, but I go much further and hold the view that there is no room for devotion, when the doctrine of Atman has been fully grasped." Not only is this verse not of the original Ancient Method of the Upanishad, but Ranade goes as far to say that all but the first chapter is added, "while the last chapter is the only unsectarian portion of the Upanishad which gives us a purely theistic view of the Godhead, and introduces the idea of Bhakti to Guru as to God." This may have been where it began, not an evolution of Spirituality but a manipulation, as this idea was introduced! Also the word Vedanta itself appears to be brought out for the first time in the second to last verse before the one saying a guru is God! Perhaps it was well meaning but perhaps it was the plan of such teachers to control others for the tradition follows even to this day with teachers of Vedanta who will become enraged if they cannot control you! I feel that Ramakrishna Stands for the Truth of the Ancient Method before this influence came to be, as Really his Spirituality was between him and the Divine Mother in the Primary and Great Sense of It and not with gurus who think they should be treated as God!

An incredible and extraordinary insight is given in the Maitri Upanishad which completely reminds me of Swami Vivekananda's amazingly powerful admonishment. "Great saints are illustrations of the Principle. But the disciples make the saint the Principle and then they forget the Principle in the person." So in this Upanishad you see, the sadhu's ego image is described, and for that matter this could be the illustration of a guru teacher's as well. "... He (the ego/ahamkara) wears on his head the crown of infatuation (or bewilderment, self infatuation), wears the earrings of greed and of envy (or jealousy) in his ears, carries in his hand the staff of sleepiness (laziness), drunkenness and deceitfulness; he is the pastmaster of deceitfulness, then he takes up the bow, the bow string of which is called anger, the frame (danda) of which is called avarice and he is used to kill the fellow beings with the arrow of demanding desire..." Chapter VI verse 28.

It is not the sadhu/teacher's ego image that is the Reality or the Teacher, the Guide, the Power of Truth. It is Immensity Itself that is the True Teacher, Power, Guide and Reality. So powerful is the Insight of the teachings, do not be deceived. In the same Maitri Upanishad a teaching is given about this Immensity! Chap. VII verse 11, Brahman, the Infinite is described as having four parts. One fourth of this part of the Infinite appears as the total universal collective of waking, dreaming and deep sleep states. The other three parts are the Unmanifest Infinite. So much more than what is seen by us! "The Great Self underwent duality in order to experience truth and untruth." These have been Deussen's renderings! What is described here is also originally given by the Rig Veda poet, Narayana, who sings, "So mighty is his Greatness; yea, greater than this is Purusha. All creatures are one fourth of him, three fourths eternal life in heaven. With three fourths Purusha went

388

up; one fourth of him again was here. Thence he rode out to every side over what eats not and what eats." Rig Veda. Mandala X. Song 90. Verse 3 & 4.

One Swami friend told me to write for myself not others. And that is what I do. I carve the path for myself to the Self and so by writing of it produce those experiences in the texture of my consciousness by the Loving Blessed Kindness of the Divine Mother. The poet sage Tukaram of more recent times (1608 - 1649 C.E.) is often cited as to emphasize guru devotion or guru worship, but the truth is that he had no human guru. He was given mantras and teachings by discarnate siddhas in dreams, not so much unlike Janaka as we shall see. Tukaram worshiped Lord Krishna, as the Pure Ideal of God Infinite and Immense, who lived two or three thousand years before him, not a human guru, there was no human contact there. Still, as the wondrous and kind Ramakrishna says, "Nothing is impossible for God!"

Pure Upanishad

In the Isa Upanishad we are told that one who has this Knowledge does not hate anyone. Verse 6. Wonderful. But is it not then a contradiction to what is Reality and what is the behavior of the sages we have discussed and will discuss. This Upanishad speaks most excellently of Vijnana, the unique knowledge that comprehends the light and the dark. And it speaks of two darknesses in regard to those who worship only the Unmanifest Eternal or those who worship the Manifest Relative, the Hiranya Garbha, or universal dream condition, the personal form of deity. The two darknesses describe those who are one sided to either extreme. Ramakrishna remarked that he accepted both the Nitya and the Lila, the Unborn Unmanifest Eternal and the Relative Manifestation. With this Upanishad we have the Unique Knowledge given and it is most interesting as the speaker/author/proclaimer of the Upanishad talks there in the last verse of the genuine text to his mind, as the consciousness of body is burnt to ashes, saying, "O Mind, remember, remember all that I have done." It is believed by Chakravarti and others that the last verse where praise of old Rig Vedic deities is given,

389

is an addition, put there by those who wished to emphasize their particular mental persuasion. So, with the Upanishads one may come across what is certainly original text and what is added for the sake of some person's desire to justify their belief system and often it is either for a religious ideal or to bolster up the need in people for the teacher tradition rather than spontaneous identity through Upanishadic conveyance or one's own immediate experience. When in the Isa, the truth is, that at the beginning it is the Golden Orb of Luminosity that it saluted and shown respect as Illuminator and Guide. None other! And there should be no doubt that this Luminosity is your own Pure Mind! As Ramakrishna would say, "Sometimes I say to myself in the Kali temple, 'O Mother, the mind is nothing but Yourself.' Therefore Pure Mind, Pure Buddhi, and Pure Atman are one and the same thing."

Among other thinkers on the Rig Veda, Rajmohon Nath openly admits the hard evidence that prior to the arrival of the soma drinking Vedic poet horsemen, Mohenjo Daro and Harrapa (among other ancient cities, ninety-nine all together), that Goddess worship was an already established religious or spiritual practice of these people. But then they will turn around and say that worship of the Divine Mother began in the seed of Vac, a Vedic poetess who was the daughter of Ambrina, or that Tantra started with the pleasure talk between Agastya and Lopamudra of the Rig Veda. They say one thing is preexistent and then attribute it to some other existent. Nevertheless, the Divine Mother, the Goddess is in the Kena Upanishad. Here, in parts three and four it is She who teaches the Tattva Rahasya, the Principle Mysterious, the Principle Secret! It is the Divine Mother that teaches the god Indra who is but Mind itself, the sweet lesson of Genuine Humility!

Again, in the Kena, we hear this, "We do not know It; we do not understand how anyone can teach It." I. 3. Saying one does not know It is saying that It cannot be conceptualized. That is simple enough. But we do not understand how anyone can teach It, for It is Pure Exclamation of Pure Experience! But in the next part one sees a contradiction because the Upanishad has been tampered with, in part II verses 1 through 5, there are the original verses of Pure Exclamation which describe this Reality as being past knowing and not knowing, "It is not known by those who know It; It is known by those who do not know It." II. 3. Which is not confusing at all for the poet is spontaneously remarking that knowing or rather conceptualizing does not grasp the Reality as Pure Mind, so the poet reverts to describing this as not knowing or rather not conceptualizing the Natural Experience. And that is Beautiful. But we see here that these verses are spontaneous and then later, perhaps by Shankara, these eloquent natural exclamations were reduced to a dialogue of a disciple with a teacher.

Chakravarti speaks with amazing truth and clarity, "The trouble arises when we come to the second khanda or part. I seriously question the propriety of one verse being put into the mouth of a person, to be called 'Teacher,' and another in the mouth of a person, to be called 'Pupil.' The manner in which all the verses of the first two parts of this Upanishad are composed, does not at all justify such an arrangement, unless a commentator is inclined to pick out some verses to be ascribed to a teacher, and some to a pupil, with the object of giving preference to one class of ideas over another." By doing this the aptness of what is revealed in the Upanishad is lost by dragging the Exclamation into the conditioned context of a teacher and pupil. Ranade throws some light on it, "The verse part of the Upanishad gives us a psychological argument for the existence of Atman as the inspirer of various sense functions; it also breaks the idols, literally and metaphorically, in favor of the worship of Ultimate Reality conceived as Atman." Yes indeed, and are not such teachers and gods, one and all but idols exterior to Reality! Ranade continues speaking of the Divine Mother as the "Damsel" who is no less "the proof of the Immeasurable Power which lies at the back of the forces of Nature." Is it not She who is the Real Guiding Power that is addressed in the Kena Upanishad, not an idol and not a person! Ranade continues, "The Upanishad also advises us to find the same reality in objective as well as subjective existence, in the flash of the lightning as in the motion of the mind." That "same reality" is the Divine Mother!

In the Katha Upanishad we come across the most interesting and enlightening paradigm. Nachiketa (the son/disciple) is sacrificed to Death by his father/guru. This is not unlike Sunahsepa's dilemma where his father/guru Ajigarta donates him to a death sacrifice to fulfill the obligatory promise of king Harischandra. We will deal with this story in more detail. That the seeker or son should approach Pure Death as Teacher rather than the limited relation with a human being is the remarkable thing here. In the Katha, Death is Directly the Conveyer. It is said here in the last verse that the King of Death is the one who taught Nachiketa the Wisdom of the Infinite Self and, "Thus it will be also with any other who knows, in this manner, the Inmost Self." How is it done? Simply, "Atman cannot be attained by speech, by the mind, or by the eye. How can It be realized in any other way than by the affirmation of him who says: 'He Is?'" II. 3. 12. Again, the remarkable direct spontaneous method is expressed, "It is attained by him alone whom It chooses." This is perfect. It is like Vamadeva's experience! Exactly so! You see, It Just Happens, and that is Sakti, the Divine Mother! Only a conscious cognitive limitation in a belief that you need a guru, lama, teacher, or explainer limits you to think you need an explainer to explain the taste of Sugar (Self). It is the Self and It needs no explainer! Nor can it have an explainer! The poetry of Death itself speaks, "Who but myself can know that luminous Atman?" I. 2. 21. Meaning only that when all is cleared or even so, slain or killed, from the limited mind, is the Pure Mind known! All conceptuality is dropped. Again the poetry of Death on the Infinite, "Who, then, knows where He is - He to whom brahmins (gurus) and kshattriyas (warriors) are mere food, and death itself a condiment?" I. 2. 25. To me this is the most striking of all, where Death exclaims that death itself, is but a condiment, wiping away even the limited idea or conception of death, for how can the Immortal Eternal know what death is, that is, that death is relative to the Eternal! Again the ecstasy of Death speaks, "You are, indeed, a man of true resolve. May we always have an inquirer like you!" I. 2. 9. The Mirror of Death as the annihilation of all conceptuality rejoices that there are those who would seek out this Truth. And as the young seeker does this, Death replies, "The Abode of Brahman, I believe, is open for Nachiketa." Which is the Ultimate validation and affirmation!

It is in this text that the path is described as difficult as a razor's edge. For, "The Atman cannot be attained by the study of the Vedas, or by intelligence, or by much learning of sacred books (which are activities done with a teacher). It is attained by him alone whom It chooses. To such a one Atman reveals It own form." I. 2. 23. But what is this form that is shown by the Purest Illuminator who is Death, of whose self, itself, disappears as a mere condiment. It is the Self which pushes out (creates) all form and fills it with meaning yet by which no form describes! And, is not the Divine Mother, all this, as She is to Ramakrishna! The Pure Mind of the Isa, the Mother Damsel in the Kena and of course, as Kali, She is the Devourer, the Death of all illusion! Blessed is that!

In the Pure God direction of the Ancient Method one does not suffer from two problems. Cult fanaticism and guru dependence. It is so, that in the Mandukyo Upanishad, neither religious fanatical prejudice nor leaning toward the dependence on a teacher is expounded upon at all, in its twelve essential and direct verses. As my friend Swami Bhaskarananda says, "Who glorifies the teacher is only glorifying his ego." As that glorification is simply fanaticism and dependence.

The first sage on the face of Mother Earth had to go to God or the Goddess, for who was there before that! In the Kaushitaki Upanishad, Pratardana goes directly to the God Indra, who is the god of the Pure Mind metaphorically speaking in the Rig Vedic context. It is from his own Pure Mind that he receives instruction on the nature of Reality, or from a god reflection in the revelation process of his own Pure Mind. This is the Ancient Method!

Now, in the Kaivalya Upanishad, it is said that Ashvalayana approaches Paramesthi or Brahma, the Pure Creator God to be taught by Him. In the Aruneyi Upanishad it says that Aruna's son (who would be Aruni Uddalaka) went to the Sphere of Brahma, God, the Creator to be taught. This is the Ancient Method. Other Upanishads that describe inquiry of a teacher are

393

something different.   As the Chhandogya Upanishad says speaking of the oldest path, the Direct God Path, "Brahma told the Knowledge of Self to Prajapati (Kasyapa)."   VIII 15. 1. Kasyapa is one of the original seven sages, and Ancient Method was not just for him and his spiritual kin of those olden days alone. Truth is truth at any time of history. Again, the example I have. found of one who teaches without boundaries, Ramakrishna, I quote, "The pure mind and pure intellect are one and the same. God is known by the pure mind. Didn't the sages and seers of olden times see God?   They realized the All-pervading   Consciousness   by   means   of   their   inner consciousness." This Pure Mind, this Pure Intellect, ever present in the Eternal Reality, is as True now, as it was for Kasyapa!

In the Mundaka Upanishad the Ancient Method is again told, in the first verse, where Brahma, the Maker of the Universe and the first of the gods, tells Atharva about the Knowledge of Brahman, the Infinite. The next verses describe how it was then told by him to another and then to another and so forth, but the Original Method is that of direct God Experience, with no human teacher, mediator or transmitter of knowledge. It was just between Atharva and God, or Reality as the case of spiritual insight and experience may be.   This Atharva is identified as Dadhyach Atharva of the Brihadaranyaka Upanishad by Ranade. So historically, this is not a mythical person, nor is his experience.

It is astounding how easy it was for Ramakrishna to be Bold in God Consciousness! Not unlike Vamadeva or Kasyapa. M. makes the remark of observing this, "Getting back into consciousness he says, 'Thou hast come, hast thou? Well, I am here too!' Who will pretend to fathom this mystery? Is this the language of the gods?"   (The Condensed Gospel of Sri Ramakrishna)   So with blessed Ramakrishna one can see the direct path of the Ancient Method clearly demonstrated as M. wonders if this is "the language of the gods" that is being shown in modern times.

In the Srimad Bhagavatam, Devahuti is one of the daughters of Manu and Satarupa, the first man and first woman. She gives birth to Kapila who is the founder of the Samkhya Philosophy.

So, you see how old it is thought to be.   But no teacher is described here for Kapila, no guru. He finds enlightenment on his own! Again, the story of Rsabha (the one who excels all others) is told. He was the first Jain of ancient prehistoric times, and the one who started Jainism long before Mahavira! He was the first Jina (Spiritual Hero Conqueror) recorded in their history. He is said to be the father of Jadabharata, after which India was named. I asked Swami Bhaskarananda of this and he said, "There are so many Bharatas."   It is this way with many of these names. The point here is that neither Kapila nor Rsabha are described as having teachers. They had Spontaneous Identity with the True Self (who is none other than the Supreme Teacher). It should be no less for you! I feel it is Just Seeing that What You Are is Spontaneously Born as You in Reality (as Pure Mind) like Kapila or Rsabha, who are but examples of possibilities within every human being!

In the Brihadaranyaka Upanishad it is described how Gautama (the original of the seven sages or one of the family of Gautamas) went to King Pravahana, the son of Jivala, to learn the famous mystical doctrines of this Upanishad on sexuality, death and rebirth or the journey of the soul in relation to natural wonders. The Upanishad talks for itself. "The king said, 'Then, verily, O Gautama, you should ask it in the prescribed way.' Gautama replied, 'I approach you as a disciple.' The ancients used to approach a teacher through mere declaration." VI 2. 7. Nikhilananda writes, "That is to say, not actually rendering any menial service, such as touching the teacher's feet." Excellent, but so much more is here as the pure path of the ancients! There is no worship of the teacher, the guru, as God! None of it! Gautama goes for learning, not to worship another man as God, which was latter suggested as the path in the Svetasvatara Upanishad as we have already described. The Ancient Method is the Direct Respect for that Amazement of Spirituality. It is to be overwhelmed by that Amazement! Not to throw yourself at a human being! It is to throw your mind into the Amazement of Knowledge and Truth!   The study of these Upanishads is marvelous because it connects the awareness within your own mind with something Very Old, Original, the First Breath of the

Beginning within you, if you will.

Echoes of the Mundaka Upanishad speak clearly, "He who chooses Atman - by him alone is Atman attained. It is Atman that reveals to the seeker Its true nature." III 2. 3. You see, it is none other than this, Pure Mind, Pure Buddhi, Pure Atman! Nothing else is the path, the method, but this! Even while in the womb, Vamadeva speaks of the direct path to Reality, to the Self that chooses the Self in the Self! "While still in the womb, I came to know all the births of all the gods. A hundred strongholds, as if made of iron, confined me, yet I burst through them all swiftly, like a hawk!" The divine hawk of Pure Mind may arise at any time. Excellent!

As P. Sankaranarayan states in his book What is Advaita, on the remarks of Vamadeva's enlightenment, "The first three of the foregoing rks show that Vamadeva attained to an experience of identity with all selves by reason of his Atmajnana. The fourth relates to his awareness of being Brahman and to the fact of his knowing the origin of all the devas by virtue of his non-difference from Brahman. He also says in the last rk that before his Brahmajnana, he got into countless forms which chained him to the world, and that after the dawn of jnana, he was released from bondage." With this, the thought of Yogabhrashta comes, that is when yoga is broken off due to death, but then the soul circulates back into a well to do family of a pious and spiritual nature where yoga may be continued, as Krishna describes in the Gita. It is thought to happen when a yogi or yogini has reached perhaps the fourth or fifth plane of Consciousness and then they die. But following on they carry what was attained before and begin again. Vamadeva certainly demonstrates this. It is thought that such a one does not require a guru but gets all guidance from the Power of the True Self! All spiritual knowledge arrives spontaneously.

Swami Vivekananda of course, was thought to be Yogabhrashta. He had some things to go through until he remembered. Ramakrishna says that before their birth he remembers going up to the realm of the seven rishis and whispering into one of the rishi's ears that he should accompany him (Ramakrishna) to Earth. In truth, is it not this way for all of

396

us, all of us coming from Spiritual Light, forgetting our True Self in the one hundred strongholds of illusion and mis-identity or conscious shapes of being human, then as "Self Chooses Self" we all simply Remember our Source and Real Being, Self, the Spiritual Light! It may be that the metaphor of reality is that we all incarnate or descend as Wisdom incarnate only to remember. But it is easier to accept the idea that there are humans who attain or become Wisdom itself and there are those who are indeed Wisdom incarnate! Which is it?

Trisanku

Like Vamadeva, Trisanku feels the Primordial Feeling which is nothing less than the Epiphany of the Eternal. In the highest achievable awareness Trisanku exclaims in the way of the Ancient Method, "I am the Mover of the Tree of the Universe. My fame rises high, like a mountain peak. My Root is the Supremely Pure Brahman. I am the Unstained Essence of the Self, like the Nectar of Immortality that resides in the Sun. I am the Brightest Treasure. I am the Shining Wisdom. I am Immortal and Undecaying." Thus did Trisanku proclaim the Knowledge of the Self. Taittiriya Upanishad. I. 10. 1. The "Tree" in fact is the five koshas individually and probably here more in the collective universal awareness. These five koshas are the physical body or all bodies, then the vital emotional body or bodies, the mental, the intellectual and finally the body or bodies of bliss. But there is only One Bliss spiritually speaking, not many collectively, though there are many partakers of this Bliss. These are the classic five sheaths of the soul: the sheath of food, prana, mind, pure intellect and bliss that are given in this Upanishad. Also there is the beautiful description of the multiplications of bliss. The Ecstatic Calculus! Say for example, the happiness of a householder multiplied becomes the happiness of a gandharva, that multiplied becomes the happiness of a deity, then a god, then all the way up to the happiness or bliss of the Creator and so on to the Beyond. Think of this. These progressive generations of bliss. It is you who generate in your self these higher and higher, deeper and deeper levels or multiplications of Joy. This is the ancient way, the direct way, It is the path of Self Effort. Do you need a teacher to teach this? No!

Moving on. Trisanku is aware of himself in the true sense as the "brightest treasure" and so is this not the most healthy estimation of Self Value in regard to one's real dignity which is so often lost in the whirl of the world! Again it is described that this feeling of realization or epiphany in the Eternal Self makes you feel like a mountain peak. I picture this as the Sun shining on the shoulders of a mountain range as the feeling is so vast and extensive as to the awareness of the Self!

More is there. "I am prior or older than the gods themselves." Remember what was said by Vamadeva. It is to even burst forth out of the consciousness of the gods or powers over you. This most certainly includes the teachers, rishis, poets and sages as well as all those powers of the gods. What you are in Truth is older, prior to and a greater and brighter treasure than the gods themselves. And how can it not be so when all that you experience is only experienced by your Self and not another, not a deity, not a god, not another human being, not a teacher, not a seer, not a poet!

Ranade seems to associate the great mystic Trisanku with the further remarkable exclamations of true Self awareness that are given in this Upanishad but Chakravarti states that they are part of a conversation between the seeker/sage Bhrigu and the God Varuna, so it would be God's own words. Either way, attributed to Trisanku or to God it is spoken from the level of God Consciousness, when describing someone who has known the non-duality of Brahman all they can say or sing is "Ah! Ah! Ah!" Wherever the mind wanders or goes, whatever shows itself in the intellect or the mind their remark is a para-linguistic wonder or astounded-ness, "Ah! Ah! Ah!" It is exactly like when Sri Ramakrishna would often say, "Ah me! Ah me! What a vision!"

There is much more that is said from the Height of Awareness. "I am the First Born of the True, prior to the Gods, and the navel of Immortality. He who gives me away, he alone preserves me. He who eats food - I, as food, eat him." This well indeed could be Trisanku's words for he speaks in the high consciousness of being prior to the gods and Varuna is one of the gods. Beautiful. Also, he has this magnificent awareness of being the one who eats all those beings and creatures who eat. That is the Infinite who devours all, like Mother Kali, in fact! You see, this Primordial Epiphany of being the One who is in fact the eater of all others who eat food is that it gives You the feeling that You are what eats everything in the End. And it is true in that all is eaten or interpreted by Self alone! Again, from this verse, who gives Truth freely to others preserves Truth in others by openly sharing it! Truth is the real food we are hungry for. This certainly reminds one of the instruction from Death to Nachiketa in the Katha Upanishad. "And death is but the condiment!"

The Taittiriya finishes. "I overpower the whole world. I am radiant as the Sun. Whoever knows this attains liberation. Such, indeed, is the Upanishad." III 10. 6. It is from this Height of Feeling/Perception that one may have the spiritual sensation of overpowering world consciousness or in fact, the consciousness in one's mind that perceives the world. Very interesting. And it is this knowledge that is what the Upanishads are stating in their direct way or interpretation. It gives the awareness that this Consciousness is such, "This he who is in this man, and that he who is in the yonder sun, both are one." III 10. 4. This is a wonderful vigorous verse or rk! It describes deeply the mysticism of the rishis. It is to have that beautiful sense of Self that extends out as far as the Sun. Vamadeva experienced this as well when his awareness reached a consciousness when he knew what he was was indeed even before the existence of the Sun itself! Amazing! What is in me, what is in my head as the energy in my brain is the same energy or Prana that is moving at the core of the star as a nuclear furnace. So it is the same in the furnace of my mind!

This Trisanku would appear to be the same King Trisanku that Vasistha cursed in his jealous and angry rage which he was so often tending to do and whose awful behavior has set down a traditional behaviorism which has stretched forth to many gurus and teachers of today. The myth legend states that after Trisanku asked Vasistha to perform bodily ascension for him to heaven that Vasistha said it could not be done and so the king went to Visvamitra and he performed the ritual of bodily transference for king Trisanku. This of course enraged Vasistha for he was a jealous and petty minded guru. So he cursed the king and that is why he is called Trisanku or thrice transgressed or three times cursed. You see the beauty of this story is that in spite of being cursed by a guru sage he discovered and experienced the highest kind of enlightenment. Also, Deussen writes that all these things such as raising corpses by consciousness transference, bodily ascension and such things like resurrection are but superstitions in the Upanishads and related legends. They are myths to tell a story in the extreme example of the measure!

Direct Method

This Highest Awareness must be attended with Humility or it is just arrogance. What Pippalada describes in the Prasna Upanishad after giving out all he can give out he says, "Thus far is what I know." He claims it is the Supreme Knowledge that he knows but there is the pleasant tone of humility attending his awareness!

One more amazing example of True Exclaiming is given by an anonymous speaker at the end of the Chhandogya Upanishad. "From the dark I come to the variegated, from the variegated I come to the dark." This is consciousness moving in the poet, from the Non-Dual into the many and back again. Or as Ramakrishna would say from the Nitya to the Lila and from the Lila to the Nitya. "Shaking off evil as a horse shakes dust from its hair, freeing myself from the body as the Moon frees itself from the mouth of Rahu." So fine, one may just shake off the idea of being just a body, for you are more than that and it is this limitation which is classified as evil. Indeed, for it restricts or confines our awareness. Also, it is an old and beautiful metaphor of the Moon, as Consciousness, that is momentarily eclipsed by the shadow of the Earth and this is an ancient dragon thought of as Rahu by the old ones. What swallows consciousness of true Self like a shadow but for the ego mind!

400

Yes. But one comes out of it when the shadow passes. It is interesting that when Sakyamuni's (the Buddha's) son was born he said, "O no, he is Rahula." Meaning that he is like a shadow that will devour the Moon of his spiritual search if he does not proceed on his quest but remains bound to the responsibilities of a householder. This Upanishad continues finally, "I fulfill all ends and obtain the Uncreated World of Brahman." This Uncreated which is never created as a duality in world consciousness is the High Awareness of the Self that is never born as it remains ever Unborn to the dual complex of life created in the mirror of energy as the current of life. This is the "navel of Immortality" which Trisanku so easily identifies his true Self with as being Just That!

This is your Destiny of Rare Occasion. This is the dream of life fulfilled as you pull the Observer of the True Self out of the shadow of the dream itself! It may also be Trisanku's method that this process of deeper and deeper Self Awareness comes as it is described in the Taittiriya Upanishad. "That Sushumna is the path for the Realization of Indra." I. 6. 1. Here, Indra is the Pure Mind Awareness as God Consciousness Itself. The sushumna is the central core nerve that moves up "through a piece of flesh which hangs down like a nipple between the two palates and ends where the skull splits and the roots of the hair lie apart." This is the ancient method of direct consciousness transference into the plane or dimension of Indra as Pure Mind. It is a mystic yogic nerve and gland like the pineal that is described as a nipple that excretes what may be a somatic feeling or nectar of well being that bestows the sense of a spiritual feeling to life. This nerve goes right through this "nipple" to Indra!

When Ramakrishna would state, "I now see that I and my Divine Mother have become one once for all." Is it so different than when Trisanku states that he is now identified as the "Mover of the Tree?" Both have raised consciousness to an awareness of Spiritual Identity! For it is the Goddess, the Divine Mother, that is the Prime Mover of the Unmoved, the Unborn, the Uncreated! Identity with Her, in the Purest Energy of Love, is the Essential Thing! And when Ramakrishna would state,

"Here (that is, within himself) there are two Persons. One is the Divine Mother - One is the Divine Mother, the other person is Her devotee. It is the second person who has been now taken ill. Do you understand this?" Is it not that second person that is as we all are, swallowed in the shadow of Rahu? And yet the true Identity in the Divine Mother is exclaimed in the freedom as a horse shaking the dust from itself! Fulfilling all within the world and yet knowing the Uncreated World of Infinite Mother!

Janaka and Suka

If one looks only in the condensed versions of these stories one will not find all the facts. For example, Ramakrishna tells the humorous story of how Suka went to Janaka and Janaka said you must pay me the teacher's fee first because after I teach you, you will not see any difference between the teacher and the student, and so not feel the need for payment. In all the translations of the Laghu Yoga Vasistha that I have there is not one that tells this story. But it is said that the complete recounting is given in the Yoga Vasistha Maha Ramayana.

Janaka, the King of Videha, is of central importance historically, because it was in his court that the oldest Upanishad, the Brihadaranyaka, was written, experienced, recounted. He loved philosophy and spirituality and invited all the great yogis and yoginis, poets and poetesses to his court to discuss Truth. Janaka is the father of Sita, the divine wife of the divine lord Rama. It is said that he found her sprung up from the Earth as a gift during a plowing ritual that he was performing. As Swami Dayatmananda has said, "All these stories are allegorical." That seems true, for to retain a purity around Sita, she is given this myth of a virgin birth, where "plowing" is perhaps a metaphor, an allegory of sexuality. Nevertheless this gives us the time period of Janaka, the first Upanishad, the great spiritual gathering in his court as being contemporary to the Ramayana. And the poetic beauty is that this wonderful Janaka adopted Sita as a gift from the Mother Earth.

So too is wonderful, this Suka, remarkable. He was the son of Vyasa the great sage and author of Brahma Sutras, the

402

collector of all the Vedic poems and other great works. Vyasa is in fact considered to be a minor avatara. Parasara was his father and Parasara's father was Manu, the first man, or one of the first men, so you see, it is a squeeze on history really for in studying these traditions one comes up on a time collapse where so many great people and events all seem to happen in this pond of time in the way back. So sorting it out in real time becomes quite a difficult task.

Suka had in fact already realized Advaita. It was firm in him, but his mind was still troubled so he asked his father/teacher about it and Vyasa was helpless to give him Peace so he sent his son to Janaka. This must have been after Janaka's episodes with Yajnavalkya, Ashtavakra and the Siddhas, for he teaches Suka of what he learned most especially from the Siddhas which we will deal with next. The remarkable thing is that Suka needed Janaka to take him to the next level so to speak and that Vyasa's limitations as a teacher are clearly shown by this!

A story was told by Ramakrishna in the "The Great Master." Suka was walking by a river where women where bathing naked. They had no embarrassment. When Vyasa walked by they felt embarrassed and ran to put their clothes on. When asked why, they said Suka had no consciousness of sexual differentiation, but you still do, Vyasa! So this event must have happened after Suka talked with Janaka, because before that Suka's problem was differentiating external appearances as we shall soon see. Even though Vyasa taught his son Advaita and the Srimad Bhagavatam which he recounts to king Parikshit latter, Vyasa's spirituality was limited. This is why Suka went to Janaka to learn what Vyasa, his father/guru did not know.

It is said that Suka needed Janaka because he could not affirm to himself what he already knew, which was not the Reality of the Advaitic Atma, but that the imagination of differentiation must cease when it ceases, that is that the subtle tendencies of the mind must cease their reveries in dualistic imagination. If Suka could have done this he would not have needed Janaka's healthy advice. And though it is said that Suka went into Nirvikalpa Samadhi for ten thousand years (an allegory) on Mount Maha Meru after this encounter with Janaka, Ramakrishna says, "According to some people... the utmost that Sukadeva and holy sages like him could ever do was to see and to touch the water of this Immortal Sea, and just taste a bit!" And, "If we say they could eat up eight or ten particles of this sugar (as a metaphor of Infinite Brahman), we have said enough in their favor." So what is the case in regarding Suka? He was certainly considered one of the most highly enlightened beings of all time. So much so that M. in the company of Ramakrishna says, "M. wondered if It is Sukadeva before him that talks of the Lord?" But elsewhere Ramakrishna in his amazing humility says, when addressed as a holy man, "You may say that about sages like Narada, Prahlada, or Sukadeva. I am like your son." And again Ramakrishna states, "Janaka was a jnani. He attained Knowledge by means of his sadhana. But Sukadeva was Knowledge itself."

Thinking on Janaka and Suka is a powerful healing story. Different versions are given. In the Srimad Devi Bhagavatam it is described how Suka is horrified by the behavior of Vasistha, and Nimi, who is an ancestor or perhaps even the father of Janaka, as Manu fathers Ikshavatu who begets Nimi who begets Janaka, but there are many Nimis, Ikshavatus and Manus. That is the story of their murdering each other by mutual cursing because Vasistha is jealous of Nimi asking Gautama to complete his necessary ritual. The story was given earlier. Strangely though Janaka gives no reply to Suka on this for perhaps he too was horrified by the noxious behavior of Vasistha and his disciple Nimi.

What Ramakrishna tells of Janaka attaining Knowledge by his own sadhana, means, his own solitary spiritual practice which will be described in more detail in the next heading of Janaka and the Siddhas. In this light it is strange too because Janaka breaks with more present day traditions that have been influenced by the last implanted verse of the Svetasvatara Upanishad, by himself having quite a few teachers. Yajnavalkya, Ashtavakra, the Pure Forms of the Siddhas and much to our surprise he even addresses Suka as the son of his guru, but I have never found any recorded instruction from

Vyasa to Janaka. Another account tells that he was instructed by Vasistha as well, which would mean he received spiritual teaching from the murderer of his father which seems highly improbable.

The highly important wisdom that Janaka tells Suka is the ceasing of imagination in differentiation, especially in regard to mental diversification on who is a friend and who is an enemy. This very important point will be discussed in more depth while explaining AUM, but for now what Suka learned was to bring the Advaita of the Nitya down into the Maya of the Lila. To See the Reality in All. For in the Vast Greatness how can we distinguish friend from enemy. To love and to hate only pulls consciousness away from its divine sinking into the sweet sugar of the Ocean of Immortality. In a divine yet round about way Janaka must have conveyed to Suka to not even find faults with Vasistha and Nimi, which would engage the mind, that is, which simply engages the mind in sankalpa or mental deliberations on the trammels of bondage, the delusion of Maya, the constant spinning and yearning for things that pull us out of Self, Atman, Brahman, Pure Consciousness.

Accordingly, what Suka actually learned is in my feeling what the Holy Mother Sri Sarada Devi taught as her last message before death. "But I tell one thing - if you want peace of mind do not find fault with others. Rather see your own faults. Learn to make the whole world your own. No one is a stranger. The whole world is your own." To this magnificent awareness a comment is given in Sri Sarada Devi: The Great Wonder. "If everybody would see his own faults will there be any fault left to be seen? We acquire faults by seeing faults. (Such as friend and enemy dualism like in Suka's case) So to see faults in others is a subversive act against oneself. ... But how is it possible not to find fault with others? It is one of the severest austerities one could take upon oneself. At the outset it seems to be an absurd task even. But as one sticks to the aspiration with grit, ways open up. This can be attempted in two ways: by self-projection and Vichara (discrimination). In the ultimate analysis self-projection is of course a misnomer. Because the Self that pervades everything cannot conceivably be projected. Yet what

405

we mean by self-projection in a relative sense is the discovery of the perennial affinity and even identity. As one advances in this sadhana one discovers that the very conception of 'others' is another name for illusion. Once one can get grounded at least in the conceptual understanding of this truth, one gradually learns to see that ultimately, there is nothing as 'others.' When 'others' cease to exist their faults also go with them. What remains is a vast ocean of being, of Self, nomenclatured diversely - a pleasant fair of the duplication of self. When I have learned to own other's faults as mine, I cannot be at war with others. The secret of oceanic love, the mystics develop, is that they realize the self in all that exists. Therefore they are always a fountain source of abiding peace. It may be that from the Vyavaharika stand-point (actual becoming or manifestation), the individual and his faults exist for all practical purposes. But the realization of self-identity with the 'others' who have faults works out a real and vital transformation in the quality of the seeing of the seer. He learns to see the virtues and vices with equal eye, he becomes Samadarshin (one with equal vision). He does not even see any vital difference between a man and an animal." So perfectly said and it was just this that Suka learned.

But now thinking in historical sobriety we say, Suka was taught by Janaka. Janaka is Sita's father, the wife of Rama, in the Era of the Ramayana. So it is said that Suka was called out of the depth of Nirvikalpa Samadhi, by Narada who sang for him and so the hairs on his body stood on end and he regained normal consciousness so he could recite the Srimad Bhagavatam which is mostly stories of Sri Krishna, to the King Parikshit who was installed as king after the conclusion of the Mahabharata war which is the Era of Krishna. The most conservative estimate between Rama and Krishna is two hundred years. No human being has lived that long. Were there two Sukas then? Or is this mythical phenomena? Myth equates with dream. History equates with reality, which we take seriously!

In Janaka's mutual sharing of the Experience with Suka he clearly speaks of the two paths, "O Sage, you have known it by yourself and have heard it from your sire again." The Self Path of the Ancient Method is described as Suka's first and primary encounter with Reality, while hearing it from his sire is described as something that happened again, or secondary. This Self Path is described as dawning spontaneously in this life due to one's natural efforts or because of the collective effect of previous lives (again Yogabhrashta). Yet ultimately it is the cessation of imagination with the otherness of duality that finishes off Suka's spiritual experience whereby he goes into Samadhi for ten thousand metaphorical years which could more imply the depth of his samadhi rather than the length.

Janaka and the Siddhas

If one has annihilated imagination wherein duality appears, wherein 'others' appear, then one's mind is in the Non-Dual. This is the full ceasing or annihilation, even so, the quenching of the firebrand of the three states of consciousness which are the waking, dreaming and deep sleep states! For Janaka this would have to include even the quenching of imagining the self projection of the Siddhas as the imagining of 'others.'

After his encounter with the siddhas Janaka makes the astounding observation, "The mind is, as it were, the root of the tree of samsara. I believe it to be none other than imagination. By ceasing imagination, I am awakened! I am wide awake!" This is Vidyaranya's rendering. One will remember that these are the words of Sakyamuni too, who came later, after Janaka and said, "I am awake," when he was asked what is his spiritual condition. It is exactly the same feeling in Dzogchen when imagination ceases (Alatasanti) and one gets the feeling of being Awake! It is no different and the remarkable feeling is that imagination stops and being "Awake" encounters you!

Vidyaranya again makes a remarkable and very telling observation, "The best among the best yogins, such as Janaka and Prahlada, belong to the class of practitioners with extremely unlimited ardor (so much too like Ramakrishna), for, they can, at a moment's thought, work themselves up into the condition of confirmed ecstatic Concentration. Uddalaka and others, of the lowest among the low sort, belong to the class of mildly ardent practitioners, for, they can find the condition of Concentration

407

only after considerable effort put forth in that direction." Amazing!

If my mind as of yet has not completely gone and left me, I remember reading in the full version of the Yoga Vasistha Maha Ramayana, that when Janaka was in his pleasure garden he was not alone as it is said in the condensed (laghu) versions of the story, but that he was indeed in loving embrace with his wife, when the five or six disembodied Siddhas appeared to his mind's vision and sang the vigorous and extraordinary songs of the Advaita to him. This is one of the most extraordinary spiritual events, and I take this as of the same caliber, as that of when Ramakrishna's own Pure Mind appeared to him in the form of a Shiva-like sadhu, and as he proclaims taught him everything, Vedanta, Tantra and all the rest, for it was nothing less than the Divine Mother who in fact was in the concentrated form of the young sadhu who appeared looking just like Sri Ramakrishna. This is the Highest Plane of spiritual teaching.

Here the self-projection of "others" has melted into the form of one's own mind and as one's own mind teaches one what is Spiritual Reality. This I believe is what happened to Janaka in his pleasure garden, whether or not as the story is differently told, he was making love to his wife or not. But why should it be such a surprise if he was in fact in sexual embrace with his consort? The Brihadaranyaka Upanishad where Janaka appears as the central figure around which the formation of first Upanishadic literature emerges, gives in its final chapters some the the most erotic and extraordinary sexual teachings one may find anywhere. Completely mystical, describing death, the soul's journey and rebirth through the sexual process of procreation. So why should it not be so that Janaka could be in the embrace of love making with his own beloved when the extraordinary discarnate Siddhas came and sang to him the songs of Reality. In the divine dance of heightened awareness due to loving embrace his mind may have been so tuned to a higher perception that this astounding awareness could have dawned upon him. Timid versions of puritanical blends would not want to include this aspect of the story for obvious reasons. I have seven translations of the story which give this timid version.

408

Besides, why should it be surprising that one version may not tell the whole story, Ramakrishna speaks of how Janaka requested Suka to pay him the teacher's fee before he taught him because after instruction he would see no need to pay Janaka because he would see no difference between Janaka and himself. It is humorous. But all the versions I have neglect to add this part of the story of Suka, not feeling its importance, as Ramakrishna felt.

On the two paths thoughts are given. Vidyaranya writes, "In the case of Janaka, however, through maturity of previous merit, Knowledge dawned upon him suddenly, as a result of his having heard the Siddha Gita, even like the fall of a fruit from heaven." That is how it comes to you on the Self Path, like a gift falling from heaven! Vidyaranya goes on to say that after this experience the recurrence of imagination never came back to Janaka. There is more, "What can I accomplish with effort? What imaginings are possible for me who am the Consciousness, Self Sustained and Ever Pure? I desire not what I have not; I care not to part from what I have; I stand in the Eternal Self in me; let that be mine which has been mine." Janaka has really soared high here. In the last line he realizes that it has already always been "mine" and he knows that he does not have to part with nor change any part of himself or desire to go anywhere, meet anyone, learn anything and so forth. As he is knowing his True Self as the Eternal Self why should any of that be a trouble to his consciousness? "Janaka addressed himself without the least attachment to results (in regard to any happening, event, encounter or occurrence), to whatever came up in the course of life, even like the Sun running its diurnal course. He relates himself not with the future, nor with what has gone by, he lives the present out with a smiling heart." Vidyaranya. So this sounds so much like Dzogchen, in the Whatever Arises is Just Fine! Janaka's realization is Pure Mind as Self. He need not chase out, nor change, for he is What Is. I am wide Awake!

K. Narayanaswami Aiyer translates, "There are two kinds of paths leading to Moksha (liberation). (Of the two paths to Jnana, a person is guided by a guru on one, and on the other, he is guided by himself) If without fail, one were to follow the path laid down by a teacher, delusion would wear away from him little by little and emancipation will result, either in the very birth of his initiation by his guru, or in some succeeding birth. On the other path, the mind, being fortified with a stainless, spontaneous knowledge, ceaselessly meditates upon it; and then there arises true Jnana, like a fruit falling unexpectedly from above." This Primary Self Path was Janaka's course to Spirituality! Note that following a teacher is slower "little by little" in its results.

So it is no doubt true that Janaka is most extraordinary as a householder, a king, and a spiritual seeker. Please allow me to borrow as a brief quotation in this critical article from Swami Venkatesananda's The Concise Yoga Vasistha. "Janaka attained whatever he did by dint of his own inquiry. Similarly, one should pursue the inquiry into the nature of truth till one reaches the very limits of such inquiry. Self Knowledge or Knowledge of Truth is not had by resorting to a guru (preceptor) nor by the study of scripture, nor by good works: it is attained only by means of inquiry inspired by the company of the wise and holy men. One's inner light alone is the means, naught else." So very beautiful! Two points are made. Resorting to a teacher is not the way. But sacred company is a different matter all together. It is companionship in the Experience, not resorting to another human being for the Experience. And remember the path of following a preceptor is the slower method.

More is said. When Janaka was in the garden, "Other Siddhas chimed forth: 'To look for Reality without, while relinquishing Reality within, is like going in quest of conch shells after discarding the Kaustubha Gem in one's hand." The Kaustubha is the gem that shines on Vishnu's breast/heart. This is so similar to the Dzogchen saying that rings the same truth, that going in search of the teacher is like leaving your Elephant at home and then going into the forest to look for its footprints. Precisely!

It is said that while Janaka was perambulating the garden he heard the songs of the discarnate Siddhas whose minds were one with the One Consciousness. This is echoed by Ramakrishna. "It is this divine power (Sakti) which the scriptures speak of as

410

the spiritual teacher, and it is to this power that man is called upon to offer his heart's reverence and adoration with unflinching faith." Swami Saradananda. Again from the same. "The spiritual teacher is One and not many. Although the receptacle of this power or bodies through which it is manifested are different, your spiritual teacher and mine are not different but One only, that One being none other than that Power." As with Ramakrishna, so with Janaka, and so too those receptacles or bodies may indeed be as discarnate siddhas for Janaka, as they were the numerous and various forms of Mother Sakti, that they were for Ramakrishna, especially the young sadhu that appeared to him like himself!

So we come to the question of the mental projection of a teacher out from the true dimension or profound consciousness of the Pure Mind! For Janaka all imagination, even of mind forms or siddha projections, were once and for all time renounced or given up and away! One may say these siddha projections or mind forms, coming out of Janaka's own head are just so similar to the Ancient Method of contacting what is believed to be God forms, like Pratardana learning from Indra previously described. For Janaka, once this Final Self Teaching of the Siddha Gita arose in him all his dualistic imagination was Gone! It was truly the Quenching of the Firebrand of the three states of consciousness in Turiya as Gaudapada describes so perfectly!

But there are two problems. One is fear of the disembodied or consciousness engaging with ghosts or departed souls too heavily, which is not so good, for that fear of being constantly observed can become neurotic. Besides, most of that would be dream fabrication or mental projection. So it seems that Janaka learned from the power of his own Mind as imagination in regard to the siddha projections.

The other problem is that Vasistha contradicts himself in what is said about the Self Path or Ancient Method as I call it, when he states so many times in the Yoga Vasistha that without a guru you cannot get to Truth. Unless he means by guru, also the siddha projections, for example. Janaka had teachers, but his Final Self Fulfillment came from his Own Self!

411

Quoting Ramakrishna, "When the mind rises to the fifth plane the aspirant wants to hear only about God. This is the Visuddha center of Yoga. The sixth plane and the center known by the yogi as Ajna are one and the same. When the mind rises there, the aspirant sees God. But still there is a barrier between God and the devotee. It is like the barrier of glass in a lantern, which keeps one from touching the light. King Janaka used to give instruction about Brahmajnana from the fifth plane. Sometimes he dwelt on the fifth plane, and sometimes on the sixth." What is of interest is what Ramakrishna calls the mind that rises. Yes, the rising of the mind to deeper and higher dimensions. Also, the barrier of glass between what is mind and Pure Mind. You can see through glass and so too can you see through mind. We see only by mind really and we can see through mind. When Janaka saw through his mind, it was in his own mind that the Siddhas appeared to teach. This is so important!

Of course Ramakrishna goes on to tell us that after passing the sixth plane, "The individual soul and the Supreme Soul become one." In fact they were always One and only the imagination of the mind put up the barrier of glass where it appeared like a reflection in consciousness that there was an illusion or imaginative separation and duality! Ramakrishna would also say that Janaka could fence with two swords, one of the Mind yoga and the other of the action yoga. Perhaps that is what is meant when we say Janaka could rule as a king without leaving the consciousness of Brahman. For after the siddhas appeared, he forever renounced any imaginative difference in his mind. He realized that everything and everyone everywhere were just eventually dust or nothingness anyway and so he lost all interest in maintaining an imagination about it. Vidyaranya writes of Janaka's thoughts, "Millions of Creators have come and gone. Myriads of heavens have vanished one after another. Potentates have been turned to dust. What hold have I on this life? Persons, by the closing or opening of whose eyelids, worlds were created or destroyed, have passed out of memory. (This recalls the Ashtavakra Gita.) Why then should the existence of persons of my type be noticed at all?"

412

That last line is the most vigorous song of most excellent Humility wherein the chance for mind to become Pure Mind arises and emerges forth like the Hawk! There is the surface thought and the true depth thought on Renunciation which is for the Sake of the Atma once and for all, the True Reality. It does not return to the imagination of "what if?" It Knows, without the "dust!" It is for the sake of knowing the Infinite beyond which even heaven or paradise are renounced knowing their temporal nature! As Swami Aseshananda said, "It is Love, Pure and Total, free of worldliness." Worldliness being that there is any possible satisfaction with phenomena. Love is not disgust. Love is the Pull toward the Infinite, not disgust with the finite.

My favorite saying of Swami Brahmananda is, "No guru is greater than your own Mind." This is certainly the Experience of Janaka and it was most certainly the Experience of Ramakrishna, as he knew that the Divine Mother was his own pure mind. That it was She who had become his own Atma! So, like Ramakrishna and Janaka we should Develop This! My friend Swami Bhaskarananda said it so purely and simply, in regard to what Spirituality is, it is to, "Develop your Mind." When Brahmananda was asked if it were possible to realize God without a guru he responded, "It is, but it is not so easy without a guru." Yet Janaka proves the Self Path, though more difficult, is more rewarding, direct, spontaneous, fulfilling, as a fruit falling directly from heaven into one's own hand. And as you may study, this barrier of glass, one will wonder, that sometimes people would have dreams of Swami Brahmananda where he would give them a mantra. They had never met him nor saw him before and when they arrived he in fact would tell them what that mantra was that they received to their amazement. You must conclude that in both the dreamer and the swami that the Pure Mind was working in mind as such, with an astounding wonder. I bring this up because of Janaka and his siddha projections which are not unlike the dreamer.

413

Janaka and Yajnavalkya

As it has been already described by Vidyaranya, that he felt Janaka was in fact a more advanced or developed soul than Yajnavalkya, for he was easily roused to the consciousness of the Atman, and once so, did not return to the state of imagination. Nevertheless, with Yajnavalkya, we find that recurrence of ego imagination, "For, though, in the case of Janaka, there was no recurrence of impure vasanas (sub or unconscious potentials), Yajnavalkya, Bhagiratha and others had enough of such recurrence. In Yajnavalkya and his opponents, Usasta, Kahola and others, there was considerable arrogance of learning, for, they took part in disputation with the object of vanquishing their opponents." And Yajnavalkya took heads in debate. Sakala lost his head and that is appalling. Yajnavalkya also defeated the nude Bhairavi woman Gargi, he bested over Ashtavakra's father Kahola, he leveled Asvala, the pupil of Saunaka, he even smashed one of his own gurus, Aruni Uddalaka, in debate. Artabhaga, Bhujyu, and Vidaghdha were among others that he sank into the shame of defeat. And as a result of his victories he was the one to take the thousand cows with ten padas of gold tied to each of their horns. Whoever he was he was clever and a powerful arguer.

In fact, Yajnavalkya is such an interesting character in that lineages are given in great detail for all other sages, but with Yajnavalkya, his lineage and where he came from is very difficult to trace. Even Deussen makes the comment of Yajnavalkya, "Whoever he was." But we must know who he was for it is in his explanation of the Doctrine to Janaka that the very first formation of Vedantic teachings is created, at least in written historical context. The gist of it is that he tells our friend Janaka about the Waking State, the Dream State, the Deep Sleep State, the Infinite Brahman (and the Prana), about Death and Rebirth. This was long before these thoughts were more defined in the Mandukyo Upanishad. All this is what is in the Great Forest Upanishad, the Brihad Aranyaka.

He is one of the first recorded Upanishadic thinkers. From

414

"where" did the clarity of his Doctrine arise, even the Mandukyo is a latter synthesis as we have said. Who was this man who first formulized the Three States, Death and Rebirth doctrines which were important enough to be recorded in the Brihadaranyaka Upanishad? Some have speculated that Yajnavalkya was not an Indo Aryan at all, not of the five tribes of Vedic seer/poets spoken of in the Rk Veda (the Turvasas, Yadus, Druhyu, Anu, and Puru). These were the Nahusas or five "Neighbors" mentioned in Rk Veda VI 46. v.7 It is thought he may have been Indo Scythian, Indo Greek, or even Mongolian or that he may have been of indigenous pre-Vedic origin perhaps coming from Harrapa or Mohenjo Daro. From where this mysterious figure Yajnavalkya came may remain a mystery. But whatever his origin was he had a remarkable knowledge of the Doctrine. Some have stretched it to say Yajnavalkya was the name of an early philosophical school and not a real historical figure which if one were to believe as a fact would cause you to question if Janaka was real. Janaka was real and his existence is an historical fact because it was around him and his court that tremendous events took place as the confluence of historical beings who came together to discuss and even verbally battle each other as to the dominance of their doctrines.

It is said that one of these spiritual battles occurred as it is recorded in the Great Forest Upanishad, between one of Yajnavalkya's gurus, Aruni Uddalaka who did not know the doctrine of meta-psychosis. Yet Yajnavalkya knew it even though his guru did not and so one is led by this to ask where did Yajnavalkya learn it? From the Mongolians? Or the Siberians? Or the Indus Valley people of Mohenjo Daro which was just one of ninety nine pre Aryan invasion cities that were in this area of the world as it is recorded in the Rk Veda itself. Some other origin of his doctrine may be the case, for it is a well known story, of how Yajnavalkya expressed his anti-brahminical attitude when he mocked the brahmins in saying that all they care about was if people would give them cows and give them gold. Yajnavalkya did not stick much with the Brahmins and found them to be a source of absurdity.

So it may be that Yajnavalkya was not born of the family

415

lineages (gotras) of the seven sages at all. He is really a quite interesting person. Another one of his three known gurus was not of this lineage at all. This may be another thought on why he is considered to have contradicted the Vedic path. Vashkala or Bhashkala was his aboriginal guru, that is Vashkala was non-Aryan and so by the Aryans was considered a Daitya (a demon) or an Asura (not of the gods). A contradiction of the Vedas would be to have a demon teacher, though this exaggeration is merely that a person has a different ethnic background. Even so as some form of compensation (perhaps because of Yajnavalkya's importance in the Upanishads) Vashkala is given a recension in the Rk Veda it is said, though he was not a Indo Aryan. Strangely the motto of the Rk Veda is, "Truth is One, though sages/poets name It differently." But this mostly applies to only their own poets. This is the religious narrowness of many systems indeed. So all others, it is believed, are destined to take a tour of hell. A black and white simplistic viewing of the world. But this was not Ramakrishna's way of open heartedly accepting that there are many paths to the same Truth. In fact he was so open he even acknowledged paths that were not his own way. He speaks of being taken to a Tantric Circle where things are done that Ramakrishna would not do, but still he says, "It is very honorable for husband and wife to assume the roles of bhairava and bhairavi."

Part of Yajnavalkya's teachings are the Two Wheels or paths as it seems. One wheel is the Daiva (Deva) path which is a course of divine dependence, in that one leans on a trust in the gods and gurus, etc. The Other Wheel is the way of Purusha Kara (The Ancient Method) which is the way of Self Effort, Self Exertion and Free Will. In my opinion most wonderful and as a matter of speculation Yajnavalkya may have discovered this himself or it may have been suggested to him by Vashkala. Who knows? But it is said that this Purusha Kara path was a preparation of the Way for the Buddha Sakyamuni, by Yajnavalkya.

Now we come to Yajnavalkya's third guru, Vaisampayana, the story of which is truly a healing one and quite amazing. This Vaisampayana is said to have assisted the minor avatara Vyasa

416

in making the Vedas into their present organization and the Mahabharata, so he is a teacher who would be considered to have some weight. Again we find the touch of anti-brahminism in Yajnavalkya. You see, this Vaisampayana had accidentally kicked to death his own sister's child. How that could happen accidentally I do not know for it is probably a cover up of Vaisampayana's rage for some reason or another. So this sage was then going to make a ritual to free himself of the bad karma and guilt of killing a child. Yajnavalkya said to him that he was an inefficient and wretched brahmin as he thought a ritual could free him of such a terrible deed. So he quarreled with his guru about this and as is usual in the case of these gurus, this guru became utterly enraged. Vaisampayana demanded that Yajnavalkya return all the knowledge he had learned from him. So Yajnavalkya gladly obliged the teacher and vomited on the ground all the teachings he had received from this teacher as he sputtered up the wisdom in the shape of bloody vomit. Interesting. As the story is told Vaisampayana's disciples turned into partridges and ate up all the blood and vomit and after once doing this they regurgitated the blood into disgorged texts which came to be known as the Black Yajur Veda because the book is obscure, formless and ill digested.

There is much in the first half of this story, for one, vomiting up the teacher's arrogance to cleanse oneself or free oneself of such clutches or limitations. Another is that the disciples of the guru become partridges, behave like partridges. Why so? As humans are want to do, they project their awful qualities onto animals. Here the partridges behave like the mindless collective of disciples that is so often the case. They scavenge the vomit of Yajnavalkya who has freed himself of the teacher's arrogance trying to make it into something reasonable to them in the context of re-vomiting it back as the texts. Of course as is the behavior of these arrogant sages, Vaisampayana cursed Yajnavalkya.

But the story goes on. Yajnavalkya goes to the forest to be alone with his self. Here in the sacred sanctuary of the forest Vishnu appears to Yajnavalkya. This is God, direct and true appearing to him. Some say it was Surya, the Energy of the Sun

417

that appeared to him. But both versions of the story say that whether or not it was God or the Sun, the appearance was that of Hayagriva, the Divine Horse, who is also considered to be a minor avatara in Hindu story cycles. This Hayagriva revealed the true texts to him, as it is, he restored and retaught Yajnavalkya what has come to be known as the White Yajur Veda. Also called the Vajasaneyi Samhita. From this point forward Yajnavalkya was renamed Vajasaneyi which means the complete collection of all strengths. This strength came to him only after he left his guru, an important thought. Also, in the simplest interpretation the story clearly shows the guru verses God controversy. From the guru he got the Black Veda (Knowledge) and from God he gets the White Veda. Not that these colors are distinguishable as a good and evil duality, but to make the point that it is higher, purer, and better to go directly to God! Did this happen before or after Yajnavalkya showed up at Janaka's court assembly for dialogue? Hard to say. The Yajur Veda is talked about in the Brihadaranyaka, that is one key. But then why would Yajnavalkya be called by that name then instead of Vajasaneyi? Unless that was a personal secret name. Another point is that the event with Hayagriva may have happened before Yajnavalkya/Vajasaneyi arrived there to Janaka because how else would he have been so Self Certain in his own Realization. And if this is not the case then he gave teachings to Janaka before his own full realization.

I have not found that Ramakrishna mentions Yajnavalkya when he recalls so many of those seers of old, like Suka, Janaka and Prahlada among others. I do not know why for sure, but Yajnavalkya had two wives. Maitreyi and Katyayani. I think there are many people who justify bigamy, polygamy and other such unfaithful acts because of this fact about Yajnavalkya. So it may be the case that Ramakrishna did not want to encourage that behavior by praising Yajnavalkya, but I do not know.

Also of interest is that Hayagriva in this story is the name of God. But in an earlier older story pertaining to the manifestation of the Fish Incarnation (Matsya Avatara) that saves the world from drowning in the great flood, it is Hayagriva that is the opposing demon in this story cycle. As you will eventually read

418

it is not unlike Krishna saying he was both Sukra (the opposing demon guru) and Vamana also named Upendra as the Vamana Avatara. In that early story cycle it is the Fish who speaks to Manu who was Satyavrata (promised to Truth) and learned from this fish god while floating on the water, the Supreme Science of the Spirit as it is called the Vedas.

The instructions in Truth that are embedded in these stories are profound and amazing, but you have to dig them out. As Yajnavalkya got his Best Experience from Hayagriva, so too Janaka got his Best Spiritual Awareness directly from the Siddha Gita, the Songs of the Siddhas, who proclaimed in their verses the basic fundamental teachings of Advaita. You are the Reality and so forth and so don't give yourself away to worry and so on! This Siddha or Self Attained Gita, was the More and the Most for Janaka, and it would most definitely appear that this Self Final Fulfillment in Janaka came after his encounter with both Yajnavalkya and Ashtavakra. Then, the Siddha Gita revelation happened to him and sometime after that Suka showed up for his conversation with Janaka. What was conveyed about the three states, death and rebirth and final Brahman, by Yajnavalkya to Janaka was not enough for him. Even though, at that time, after Janaka's hearing of what is in the Brihadaranyaka Upanishad, he offered himself and his whole kingdom to Yajnavalkya. This is because he was overwhelmed with emotion upon hearing this New Knowledge. But for Janaka's final realization that was not enough. The Siddha songs were what was enough! Nor was any teaching he may or may not have received from Vyasa nor even Ashtavakra, as we shall follow along, deeper into that. Yet, this Yajnavalkya's realization of the truth of Purusha Kara, Self Effort as the Ancient Method, indeed accords with the Sakyamuni Buddha's spiritual advice when he says that, "Nothing is gained by seeing me. Self Realization is worked out by your own Self Effort." So it is this Idea of the Ancient Method that continued!

419

Janaka and Ashtavakra

Now to get a glimpse of the historical time and place. The cycle story of Janaka and Ashtavakra is important enough to be retold in the Mahabharata (era of Krishna) even though their meeting in Janaka's court at Mithila (or Videha as it was also called) is in the era of the Ramayana. It is actually interesting that Ashtavakra does not have his own Upanishad because his dialogue on Advaita is at a higher level than Yajnavalkya's dialogue with Janaka. The Ashtavakra Samhita (or Gita sometimes) is one of the highest plane Advaita texts. Ramakrishna would have Swami Vivekananda read this book aloud to him so that the Swami's mind would become accustomed to Advaitic thinking.

So we have Aruna of the Upanishads, who was the father of Aruni Uddalaka also of the Upanishads. Uddalaka was the father of Svetaketu and Svetaketu was also his student. Their famous conversation is in the Chhandogya Upanishad. Now Svetaketu was the maternal uncle of Ashtavakra. Ashtavakra's mother was Sujata which makes her the daughter of Uddalaka and the sister of Svetaketu. One of Uddalaka's students was Ashtavakra's father. He was the sage of Kohoela, also called Kahola, Kahor or Kagola depending upon which linguistic pool intones his name. Kahola's father was the sage of the Kaushitaki Upanishad. "Next, Kahola, the son of Kaushitka, questioned him." That is questioned Yajnavalkya. Ashtavakra's father was one of those who were bested over or defeated by Yajnavalkya. Brihadaranyaka Upanishad. III 5. 1. So you see there were so many close relations here between these ancient souls.

A curative story is here. You see, in the Ashtavakra Samhita it is Ashtavakra who is the teacher of the King of Videha (or Mithila), Janaka. Yet, in the Tripura Rahasya, King Janaka is the teacher of Ashtavakra, the son of the sage of Kohoela. Ashtavakra was the son/disciple of the sage of Kohoela and this sage, the father/guru once became enraged at his son/disciple and cursed him causing him to have eight crooked parts in his body. These crooks, wounds, injuries and damages that a guru's cursing and angry behaviors can do are so well pointed out in this story. Nevertheless you see, the sage of Kohoela was engaged in spiritual debate in the court of King Janaka and he was defeated in the debate so he was sent to his death to be drowned in the sea. The old way of debate was that you either became the disciple of your conqueror or you had to kill yourself if you lost. It was very serious stuff. So, just in time, Ashtavakra comes and defeats the victor of his father/guru and so redeems his abusive teacher, which is a very interesting element to the story. In some way it seems an abused student must do this either through one's own honesty and truth or through an outright battle with oneself or debate with the soul. So continuing the story, Ashtavakra becomes somewhat puffed up in ego at the fact that he had saved the life of his father/guru. At this point there appears in the court of the King of Videha, a Bhairavi Woman, a Fierce Tantric Goddess Woman (or Dakini Lady) who proceeds to humble Ashtavakra and lead him on into a deeper and greater understanding of Truth! It is She who Teaches him! And then she tells him to learn the rest of the details from Janaka. And so here you have Ashtavakra in the stance of the student and Janaka in the role of the teacher. Janaka teaches him the rest and what he teaches is the Advaita of the Goddess describing Reality as She! Yes - the Goddess! This is the Tripura Rahasya story, in the Ashtavakra Samhita the roles are reversed. And so, roles can be reversed it seems. Pure Mind is the Only Constant! The student/teacher roles are relative to Pure Mind and in the sweetest simplicity what transcends the student/teacher roles is their spiritual friendship versatile enough to accept Pure Mind in either role, student or teacher, in each other! Ashtavakra, even though cursed, wounded by the guru's rage (his "eight crooks" is the meaning of his name), he still realizes Advaita by the Bhairavi Goddess' Grace and the healing spiritual friendship with Janaka. A final thought is that in Tantra it is said that in the Sahasrara (Pure Mind) there is no disciple and no guru, so from here you may also see how Janaka and Ashtavakra may have been both disciple and teacher to each other, for they were really identified in that level, the Pure Mind, and not merely as ego selves. By the way, those "intervals"

421

claimed as unique insights, where between thoughts or feelings or in deep sleep as well as other conditions such as loving embrace, surprise, extreme fright or sorrow, where Pure Mind shines or illuminates, are described in great detail in the Tripura Rahasya!

All excellent and most interesting! In Janaka's court Kahola was defeated by Yajnavalkya but as it is said Kahola held his peace or remained silent after that. Even teachers of today enjoy silencing the students out. But with Vandi, Kahola's victor in this story, the consequence was greater for he had to go and drown himself in the sea, because Vandi's father was Varuna (an ocean god). Nevertheless, when Ashtavakra came and debated with Vandi, defeating Vandi, he redeemed his father somehow and the curse of eight crooks was lifted from him. He did not punish Vandi which shows he had a kind heart unlike so many of these easily enraged wise men. It is also interesting in fact to know that Ashtavakra was only twelve years old when this event took place. And Svetaketu just a few years older than he. So when the Ashtavakra Samhita is recorded it is extraordinary to know that it is a conversation between the mature king Janaka and a twelve year old boy.

Ashtavakra and Yajnavalkya were not Janaka's only teachers. And one would think that Ashtavakra and Yajnavalkya probably crossed paths in Janaka's court, but there is no record of any kind of rift between them, which is good, as it is the tendency usually between jealous sages. One would think that they met because these court assemblies of Janaka's sound like they happened around the same time with losers of debate losing their heads or being drowned. So in the Brihadaranyaka, Yajnavalkya asks Janaka who are his other teachers and what he learned. Janaka names them and tells what he learned. Jitvan Sailini, Udanka Saulbhayana, Varku Varshini, Gardabhi Vipita Bharadvaja, Satyakama Jabala, and Vidagha Sakalya. Their last names are given as they are the sons and descendants. Interestingly, Vidagha is the son of Sakalya (or Sakala) and just before this questioning, it was this Sakala who lost his head to Yajnavalkya who said, "You ghost, that you think that the heart should be elsewhere than in ourselves." I very much like that

422

statement but the fact that Sakala had to lose his head over it is tragic, even ridiculous. And he was the father of one of Janaka's teachers and was also present for the debates.

There is something that Ramakrishna said that verifies the Tripura Rahasya version of the story of Janaka and Ashtavakra. "Sages like Janaka entered the world after attaining Knowledge. But still the world is a place of terror. Even a detached householder has to be careful. Once Janaka bent down his head at the sight of a bhairavi. He shrank from seeing a woman. The bhairavi said to him, 'Janaka, I see you have not yet attained Knowledge. You still differentiate between man and woman.'" So a number of revelations are here. It confirms the Bhairavi that came and humbled Ashtavakra, teaching him to restrain his arrogance and pride of learning, and apparently Janaka too. It shows that the Tantra was already existing at the time of the first Upanishadic thinkers in assembly. Since Janaka still "differentiated" he had not yet experienced the Siddha Gita. It is most likely that this Bhairavi was the naked Gargi who had debated with Yajnavalkya who returned latter another day, as it is recorded, with a stronger conviction of what she must do and say. Also, that prior to the spread of more patriarchal ideas, women were held as equals and as teachers at this time. Perhaps Gargi was a Tantric Bhairavi from Mohenjo Daro? It is not impossible and all this occurred before the advent of the absurd restrictions that women should not study the Upanishads or the Vedas. Also, all this took place before Janaka encountered with Suka which was after the Siddha Gita Self Awakening Experience, for only after that did Janaka completely cease with the imagination of "differentiation."

Two things of interest. At one point it is said that Janaka recognized a sage that he once knew, Budila, as being reincarnated in the form of an elephant he was riding. Maybe the sage wanted to help or serve Janaka. And another very important recognition is the similarity of experience between Vamadeva and Ashtavakra. You would remember how Vamadeva had spiritual awareness while even within his mother's womb. And also, Ashtavakra was cursed by his father's rage to have eight crooks in his body, because he

423

corrected his father's recitations of the Vedas from his mother's womb. Both Vamadeva and Ashtavakra maintained high previous awareness of spiritual states even as they returned into their mother's wombs for rebirth. If you believe in such things or just take them as instructional allegories.

Janaka and the Ten Sikhs

So, we have been tracing Janaka's life to the time when the deepest realization came to him as Self Awakening and Continuing to stay Awake as expressed in the Siddha Gita episode. We have found more or less when it came and how he expressed himself thereafter, as with Suka, and before as with Yajnavalkya and Ashtavakra and so forth. Janaka was always a humble being and his kingdom of Mithila or Videha as it was also called was famous for peace, generosity and prosperity.

Now, something very fascinating. I quote Swami Saradananda from "Sri Ramakrishna: The Great Master." Ramakrishna states an amazing belief about the ten teachers of the Sikhs. "They are all incarnations of the Rishi Janaka. The royal Janaka, I have been told by the Sikhs, had a desire in his mind on the eve of his liberation to do good to the people. He, therefore was born ten times as a guru, from Nanak to Govind and, having established religion among the Sikhs, became eternally united with the Supreme Brahman. There is no reason why this saying of the Sikhs should not be true." Incredible!

The "eve of his liberation" could be before the Siddha Gita dawned for him or it could mean his death. As Janaka desired to do good to the people, that is help people in a truly real spiritual way, I would see his continuing effort through ten rebirths as trying to keep the Ancient Method alive, so it would not become sunk in the spiritual quick sand of guru worship.

I quote J. S. Grewal, Guru Nanak in History, found in "More About Ramakrishna." "Guru Nanak was against the idea of human incarnation of God. Said Nanak, 'Burnt be the tongue that sayeth "God falleth into the womb." Guru Govind said, "Those who call me Supreme Lord will go to hell!" But the followers gradually deified Nanak and other Gurus. Finally they

424

came to believe that 'the Gurus present resemblance with the Avataras, or the prophets of God, or even God Himself.' Also Bhai Gurdas quite frequently posed an equation between the guru and God. For Bhai Gurdas, Nanak the guru was beyond time (Akal rup); he was like God." This is such an extraordinary thing. Not only posing the equation that gurus equal God, but that people believe this! Therefore they block within themselves of ever putting to practice the most effective way of the Ancient Method, which is in all things or matters of the heart or spirituality or anything, deal directly with your own God Consciousness. For the other course is truly hell on Earth where the tongue is burnt.

And if we say Janaka is really Nanak and so forth, then how far did his effort to help others really go. For the most part it was turned around on its head. I am sorry for you Janaka, but perhaps a few people will get to their own Siddha Gita. Keeping this in mind remember the poetry of Walt Whitman, "Only what nobody denies is so." But then we come up against two totally and completely different and contradictory belief systems. We are familiar with the Hindu system of guru worship, but also the Tibetans tell us even in Dzogchen that one should worship their lama/guru as the Buddha Himself! First, this is actually a contradiction to what the Buddha taught, for example, "Depend on no external assistance." And reinforcing the way of the Ancient Method most succinctly, "Be a Lamp to your Self!" So I must confess my alliance with the thoughts of Janaka as the reincarnated Sikh teachers, that to worship these humans as God or Buddha or some other deification is no less the destiny of hell and you should indeed have your tongue burnt out of your feeble minded, spiritually retarded, moronic head.

That you can make your self Humble is the Benefit, not that you go about losing your soul in the worship of a human being! Janaka was Humble and his way was the method of the Self Path directly to God or the Reality forms manifesting as Siddhas. He did not even worship them, he merely listened and meditated on what they said to him. In essence, "Your True Self, Janaka, is the Reality. Do not lose the Divine Jewel of the Kaustubha going about looking for conch shells." It is interesting to think

425

of those possibilities charged with the Compassion to help people that may cause the reincarnating of religious or even spiritual ideas to become once again buried in obscuration and mental formations even as the "100 iron fortresses or bodies" that Vamadeva broke through like a Hawk, to remember the True Self, in the directly encountered contact of the Ancient Method!

Mandukyo

The Mandukyo Upanishad speaks of nothing but Truth, in it there are no gods, no teachers, no praising of seers. It is just Truth. The Brihadaranyaka Upanishad in its list of lineages at the very end of the text, mentions two persons, one is Mandukayani and the other is Manduki. It is probably Manduki who is the author of the twelve verses that compose the Mandukyo Upanishad. Of course, Gaudapada thought these twelve verses were important enough to write his Karika on. The Mandukyo comprises the heart and mind essence/wisdom of all that is in the Upanishads and it is said that the study of this one Upanishad will bring about the states of enlightenment and liberation. This is stated in the Mukti Upanishad and has also been restated in many places as with Lord Rama and so forth. The Mandukyo is all that is needed. It is the direct expression of enlightenment without any gods or teachers. It is simply the pure expression of awakened enlightenment without any interference. It is twelve verses that explain the four states of consciousness as they relate to the primordial mantra Aum, as the symbol or actual power expression of Reality.

- A -

"The first quarter (pada) is called Vaisvanara, whose sphere of activity is the waking state, who is conscious of external objects, who has seven limbs and nineteen mouths, and who is the experiencer of gross objects." V. 3

"Vaisvanara Atman, whose sphere of activity is the waking state, is A, the first letter of Aum, on account of his all -

pervasiveness or on account of his being the first. He who knows this obtains all desires and becomes first among the great." V. 9

I pray that as I submit some thoughts to you that they will be of some value. By the Divine Mother's Grace may it become true. It has for a long time been my desire to write a comment on the Mandukyo ever since a dream of Swami Bhashyananda where he said in the dream, "The Mandukyo Upanishad is the Principle Training." There are variants in translations that bring forth some very subtle illuminations as one compares these.

Vaisvanara is most often meaning "Common to all" as all beings experience the waking state. We find the factor of identity in all beings as just being the waking state. It is the waking state that experiences the waking state. You as Pure Consciousness are a few steps back from the common experience of all, for there is more to you than just a common waking experience. Visva as vaisva means "beings" and Nara is enjoyment. So this waking state is the state of all beings enjoyment. Individually, it is Vaisvanara, your own consciousness in the waking state of enjoyment and then Universally it is Virat, the Totality of all being's waking states. This is the cosmic or universal view. One can simply say that all these beings in common are Vaisvanara Atman. The Self of the Waking State.

They are all "bahir prajna" that is conscious of the outside. The beauty of this is that consciousness (prajna) or what is conscious is simply looking outward. Let us not even bother ourselves with the small individual concept when we define "seven limbs (saptanga) and nineteen mouths (ekonavimsati mukhah)" even though individually we experience these and collectively it is the great universe before all in common. The seven limbs are the head, the eyes, the mouth, the breath, the middle part of the body, the kidneys and the feet. These are the cosmic person or the world soul identified as expressing itself in the totality. The heavens, the sun, fire, air, akasa, water, and earth as elements and forms of external existence are identified respectively, as the head, the eyes, the mouth and so forth in that order.

427

The nineteen mouths are the five organs of perception (taste, touch, smell, seeing and hearing). These are the jnana indriyas (organs of knowledge). They are called mouths because that is how consciousness feeds on, or tastes external experience and gets knowledge of it. Then the five organs of action (hands, feet, anus, vagina/penis, and the mouth) are how we as egos identify with the complexities of outer experience. We become identified as actors in action (karma) and so these action organs are called karma indriyas. Then the five pranas or living and life giving energies are there. One moves upward (prana), one downward (apana), one centrally circulates (samana), one moves pervasively through the gross and subtle body (vyana) and the last lifts consciousness into the dream state and deep sleep and at the end of the lifetime helps this consciousness move out of the gross body in death (udana). Then is antar karana, the inner cause of the four functions of consciousness which as a cause, cause us to perceive all this objectively and subjectively. Whether or not this inner cause is present in an individual or not present, the Reality or Brahman still exists. So whether you are living or dead, Reality is Present! The cause of your inner view does not change anything. It does not create Reality.   It does not destroy Reality. It is just your momentary temporal view point.   And this view point consists of the four inner cause functions of mind, intellect, ego and memory (manas, buddhi, ahamkara and chitta). These are the nineteen mouths by which the cosmic totality of what is common to all beings, enjoys, tastes, feeds or eats the world, devouring the consciousness of which the universe is made. This view centers awareness where you are, as a conscious (prajna) being amidst the organs or mouths of mind, intellect, ego, and memory, the five pranas, and the ten organs of action and perception. It is within these that you are experiencing Self (Atman) as World (Virat)!

As we examine the Rk Vedic experience a little later on, we shall see more of the beauty of this natural cosmic wonder which is described in the experience we have through the seven limbs and the nineteen mouths, where the whole universe appears to be one Huge Sacrifice (of ego)! This cosmic way of viewing Self is nothing less than what Krishna showed Arjuna in the Gita and

428

Uddhava in the Bhagavatam, as the Visva Virat Swarupa, which translates as the Individual Universal Self Form of the Great Universe. Of course this was identified in the person or personality of Sri Krishna. Krishna then became for Arjuna the focus of this view of what is merely the seven limbs and the nineteen mouths and all the personalities and deities, humans and animals and so forth that are within this cosmic totality as Krishna identifies himself with various select and beautiful parts of it all. It is really just simply the cosmological view of Beauty and Immensity as what the Waking State is in Full!

In the Goddess' Bhagavatam you will find the Goddess Herself showing to all the Gods, Her Universal Visva Virat Swarupa. Vyasa tells a king about this and as he explains you see that it is the same as Krishna's Visva Virat, yet Her Personality is there instead of Krishna's. And She speaks of Hring, the ancient Tantric formula. H is the Waking State. R is the Dream State. I is the Deep Sleep State. And Ng is the Turiya! What is there is the same as in the Mandukyo. Which came first is a grand question, that is Hring or Aum!

Then we come to Ramakrishna's Bhavamukha. Mukha again is mouth or in this case, "face." It is the Mood or Bhava of Facing Immensity. Even as the Visva Virat Swarupa! It is empathic Seeing and Feeling from the Turiya Standpoint, of the Universal Collective of Waking, Dreaming and Deep Sleep. An extraordinary Condition of Spiritual Awareness.

So, this awareness is not so different from what Suka learned. That is to not differentiate the Self into the singular isolated condition of the ego. His judgment in that context dropped and then he found Peace. It is then seeing and feeling the Being of the Universal Form (Visvarupa) as the total, complete Vaisvanara Self, whose center of focus is the right eye as Gaudapada has written. This is also described in the Chhandogya Upanishad V. 13. 1 - 2. You find this condition of awareness also beautifully and most poetically described by the experiencer of the Svetasvatara Upanishad. "All faces are His faces; all heads, His heads; all necks, His necks." And, "They call It the First, the Great, the Full." This is the "A" of Aum in the awareness of Reality in the state (waking) represented by the

429

letter "A." "The Purusha with a thousand heads, a thousand eyes, a thousand feet, compasses the Earth on all sides and extends beyond it by ten fingers breadth." The poetry of the boundless beyond! It goes on, "His hands and feet are everywhere; His eyes, heads, and faces are everywhere; His ears are everywhere; He exists compassing all." "I know the Great Purusha, who is Luminous like the Sun." The same continues in this Astoundedness, "Thou art woman, Thou art man... Thou art the dark blue bee; Thou art the green parrot with red eyes; Thou art the thunder cloud... There is one Unborn (Prakriti) - red, white and black (the three gunas within this) which gives birth to many creatures like itself." You see it is the dynamic identity with all personalities, names and forms as being this One Vaisvanara Atman.

The Rk Veda gives its beautiful description of this experience of awareness. "A thousand heads had Purusha, a thousand eyes, a thousand feet... With three-fourths Purusha went up; one fourth of Him again was here... The moon was gendered from his mind, and from his eye the Sun had birth. Indra and Agni from his mouth were born, and Vayu from his breath. Forth from his navel came mid-air (atmosphere); the sky was fashioned from his head; Earth from his feet, and from his ears the regions (of space). Thus they formed the worlds." Rk Veda X. 90.

Ramakrishna tells of the entire experience of this Reality as described with utter directness and clarity. "Do you know what I see! I see Him as All. Man and other creatures, - they appear as veritable figures skin-bound, - with the Lord within, - shaking the head or moving the hands and feet!" That is the best and most direct of explanations as to the all pervasiveness of "A" which is Apti. With the awareness of the Infinite or God within this "A" as what it represents, the waking state, you yourself become the First, the Best among the Great, the All Pervasive, as you realize the Equalness of the Presence of the Infinite throughout the waking state. It is now you who are among the great, the foremost, the first. All that emanates as the waking state is Vaisvanara Atman and that is what you are!

Then there is, "ca bhavati adih," which I would put as Adi!.

with emphasis here as Adi is the Primordial, the First, the Original! Then "bhavati" is that you feel this Primordial as your Self in the Waking State! And as the entire waking state itself! This is so beautiful. Such an Awareness. Also as a result of this awareness the Upanishad says, "Apnoti ha vai sarvan kaman" which means all the desires of the world, the universe, are fulfilled or satisfied as the Visva enjoyer or experiencer of the waking state is now identified in the mood feeling of the Primordial and the All Pervasive. As you see your Self in all that is, how can you not experience all desires as satisfied? Who knows this, "yah evam veda" that is, who knows this Identity! As this identity, is that you know your Self, Infinite among this first-ness, this best-ness and Primordial!

When Ramakrishna would speak of seeing the Nitya in the Lila it was meaning that you should see the Eternal in the Relative. The same as we have been writing. Now, sometimes he would refer to the Lila as the twenty four cosmic principles that manifest from the Mother Prakriti. One version is this. These are the five physical elements. The five subtle elements. The ten organs of action and knowing. And the four functions of consciousness; all that was described above, yet Mahat (Cosmic or Universal Intelligence) is exchanged for chitta, the memory in the mind stuff. Comparing these seven limbs and nineteen mouths, another version gives us the twenty four principles as: The five great elements (prapanco bhutas) of earth, water, fire, air and ether in their subtle pre-physical conditions (tanmatras). The five (panca) sense objects or perceptions which correspond to each element: earth to smell, water to taste, fire to seeing, air to touch, and ether to sound. Then the ten indriyas of action and perception. And mind, intellect, ego and instead of chitta, memory, we have Avyakta, the Unmanifest Mother Prakriti, which is pure Deep Sleep where the three gunas (slowness, motion, and peace) are not stirring. Other systems add more to this Purusha Viewing and Prakriti "principles." Ignorance and the five bindings of time, space, desire, limited knowledge and power; to which the corresponding freedoms are: eternity where there was time, infinity where there was space, bliss where desire has dropped, and of course full knowledge and power. The next

431

principles rising up are knowledge, God Consciousness, Ubiquitous Awareness and Sakti and Shiva. There are many different views overlapping, increasing or expounding the same ideas more or less.

By realizing these all as "principles" you are immediately put into the "viewing" which Purusha has, who is looking at these "principles." The form of Aum as the designated letters and states of consciousness viewed in divisionistic seeing is the lower Lila (if one would even say lower, as that is divisionistic) and then the higher Nitya is the Eternal Great Oneness, where even the idea of self (individual) goes! It is the great vital Prana (Energy) that Connects!, these two, as we shall hear more of that!

- U -

"The second quarter (pada) is Taijasa, whose sphere of activity is the dream state, who is conscious (prajna) of internal objects, who is endowed with seven limbs and nineteen mouths, and who is the experiencer of subtle objects." V. 4

"Taijasa Atman, whose sphere of activity is the dream state, is U, the second letter of Aum, on account of his superiority or intermediateness. He who knows this attains a superior knowledge, receives equal treatment from all, and finds in his family no one ignorant of Brahman." V. 10

The second quarter is Taijasa sthana or abode or place of dream. As waking was its own, now there is dream. Dominic Goodall gives the translation of experiencing what is subtle as being "composed of light" (taijasa) which is a beautiful execution of the word.

It is Taijasa for the individual and Hiranya Garbha (Luminous Womb) or sometimes Sutra Atma (Self as Inner Controller or as the Thread throughout All) for the universal or total gathering of all dream states. Taijasa or Hiranya Garbha is "antah prajna" or inward conscious, as the consciousness is inward or subjective now, as it was objective in the waking state. As human beings we must go from the objective and then to rest in the subjective and then back to the objective. So curious isn't

432

it.

When it comes to the expression of the "seven limbs and the nineteen mouths" in regard to the dream state one may more so regard these as the vasanas (hidden desires) and samskaras (mind impressions, see Groundwork) of the waking state experience of the seven limbs and the ten organs of action and perception/knowledge. Of course, the five pranas and the four psychic functions are there too, but as no contact with the ten external organs, for they have gathered together inwardly, as pratyahara. As Swami Sharvananda gives in his translation of the Mandukyo saying for one that Taijasa is literally, "one of shining element," and the "enjoyer of mental impressions only or the enjoyer of loneliness" as the whole world and all that exists is only in one's own mind. For in the dream state certainly the five pranas are functioning within, but most certainly and without doubt, so are the four functions of consciousness: mind, intellect, ego and memory. They are generally stirring now in this mind world composed of light, or self reflection, in the mirror of consciousness, as Taijasa is like a fire perceived in a mirror. Some Upanishads give fourteen mouths as it were, dropping the five pranas. As waking was Emanation, this is the realm of Splendour. And Gaudapada states that this dream state is centered in the throat chakra, as it appears, perhaps because it is downward and inward from the consciousness in the head behind the right eye, the center focus for the waking state. Curious. One may say this is the realm of the god Indra as a Deity of the mind, intellect, ego and memory, because these are what rule the indriyas or ten organs of perception and movement. More purely speaking, this is Indra as Mind, over the organs (indriyas) in terms of Rk Vedic context. Also realize that if we are speaking of Krishna's or the Goddess' Swarupa Virat it is done in reference to the subtle dimension of dream in the universal Hiranya Garbha or Sutra Atma context. This again aligns perfectly with Ramakrishna's Bhavamukha Feeling of Immensity, as an Immensity within just the realm of thoughts or ideas, or feelings of empathy throughout all minds within the universal dream mind referred to already.

By realization of the Brahman, the Infinite within the Atma

433

of the dream state represented by the designation of the letter "U" some results are described or rather even promised to the realizer of this level of Consciousness within dream consciousness. We see the term "superior knowledge" for example. Which could in fact be described more accurately as exalted knowledge because dream is the realm of just ideas, where waking was in reference to physical objects and ideas (thoughts). Dream is exalted, Utkarsat, because it is an excellence of being naturally just ideas and so it is also "Ubhayatvat" or intermediate. As "A" is first and foremost, so "U" is exalted excellence being intermediate between the waking and the deep sleep state. The phrase from the Upanishad is such, "Utkarsati ha vai jnanasantatim" as one of the promised results. This could mean exalted in superior knowledge, but it also may mean the heightening or exaltation of the current of knowledge. Or even more so, the exalting (ukarsat) of jnana (spiritual knowledge or spiritual wisdom) santa (peace, tranquility, calmness). This really gives insight into one of these results being the heightening of the current of peace and wisdom within oneself, that is your own self, in the dream state. And this result does of course, come also into the waking state.

Now comes the statement that one is treated equally alike by all, equally as by friends, equally as by enemies. Sometimes this is translated as he or she becomes equal to Brahman. Or that one, oneself, treats all alike, or sees Oneness in all perceptions and mood feelings. The statement is "ca bhavati samanah" which means that one has the mood (bhava) of sameness, and with this, is not, or is no longer an object of envy to enemies nor to friends. It may be one's own attitude. Or it may mean that since everyone is but a being of dream, the mood of sameness, (sama rasa or sama bhava) in that regard is there in one's own self. This is really what Suka learned from Janaka. And it is certainly Sri Sarada's no fault finding in others as no one is a stranger and so there are no friend and enemy divisions in the mind or imagination. Ramakrishna makes the point perfectly clear, in reference to his other insight of God shaking in all heads and moving all hands and feet. "I had once a like perception: One Substance, I felt, had taken the form of the cosmos with all

434

living creatures: like a house of wax, with gardens, roads, men, cows and the rest, all made of wax and nothing but wax!"

This is certainly "bhava saman" the mood/feeling of Sameness whether it is in regard to the dream or waking state, the feeling carries through. Like Suka, who came to the place within his mind of no more imagination in differentiation over friend or enemy. No wonder Janaka said "Give me the teacher's fee first because after I teach you, you will see no difference between your own self and the teacher." That is, even so, the grand humor of Janaka's remark to Suka! I wrote in some previous essays such thoughts on this as, "Why does my friend, the Dreamer, think of Self as Luminous Consciousness? The Old One said, "He/She is treated Equally by all, no one is a friend, no one is an enemy. No one is born in my lineage who is not a Sage or Sagess, because in Dream Consciousness, all things are "Seen" as that Self Luminous Flame of Self! That is the Mystery explained." (Turiya Letters) Then, "Mandukyo states in this Upanishad (a most quick and simple expression of Reality) that the person who recognizes the identity of the letter "U" of Aum as being the same as the Taijasa State attains great things. Such things as superior knowledge, is treated equally by all alike and no one in his/her future families of generations is born without knowing the Nature of Reality. Superior Knowledge seems natural enough. A good thing to have. To be seen by all alike, to be treated by all alike is a curious comment, which might really mean that one who has experienced Taijasa and knows it well, actually sees everyone and everything as Dream Creations or Dream Images. So in that way the Taijasa person sees all alike and is seen by all alike. Beautiful! From the higher level, the Conscious Cosmic Dreamer is dreaming up everyone, everything, the Whole Universe. As to the comment on future generations, I do not have the wisdom to understand it. Perhaps a change in Dream Consciousness can actually effect genetic material of future generations. or in some way, the understanding of the Self Luminous Dream State can attract good and high souls to be reborn in one's own family. Who can say for sure, but something is meant there. To say it even more simply, Satchidananda is the Luminosity shining in the Three

435

States." (Dream Techniques) And, "In other words they are the elements of Dream Consciousness, "U." They are the stuff, the substance of the Dream State. The one who realizes the meaning of "U" in this context is said to have no enemy, all are friend, because the recognition has taken place in consciousness that all beings are waves of dream consciousness which emanate as ideations, images and cognitions in consciousness." (Emanation and Source) Then, "As it is, the Witness just watches the reflection of mind in the dream state, but watches more closely than a mirror watches the image in it. For the seeing or perception of the Witness is non-dual. The dream state is the activity of the subtle body when the waking or physical body is at rest. This subtle body is of course arrayed with the spectrum of sense perceptions, for that is why we see and hear and so forth in the dream state. But it may be more the thought or memory of these perceptions. The subtle body is nothing but mind, intellect, the ego connection and memory. The Witness witnesses these functions undisturbed by them. To know or keep aware of the Witness when the subtle body functions is a high understanding, a beautiful non-dual connection with the Pure Divine undisturbed. When one can do this the result is a knowledge that knows what is Real in everyone and everybody. The equality of each soul is understood by directly realizing the dream nature within each being. Their natural phenomenal cognitive dilemma. And so this person possessed of this understanding treats all beings equally and to that precious person all treatment towards that person is perceived equally for it is nothing but dream itself, the inner conscious movement in identity with one and all. So why should one react, this way or that way, since it is only the energy of the dream state which is equal to all beings. By this attitude, during dream, your consciousness retains the Witness Power and so does not become involved in egotistical corruptions, distortions, projections, or unaddressed questions that may arise as perplexing dualistic paradoxical symbols in dream consciousness." (from The Mirage and The Mirror)

Certainly, "ca bhavati samanah" explains how no one remains an enemy and all are friends, at this stage of Consciousness, in the conscious (prajna) being, who is pulled into the dream state. The verse, "None is born in his line who is not a knower of Brahman," is repeated also in the Mundaka Upanishad III. 3rd from last verse. It is stated, but not even Shankara explains what it means. So all the knots of the heart are untied, wrong view and grief are crossed over, one becomes Brahman the Immortal or rather one sees the True Reality of the Infinite and the Immortal (the Nitya). The verse is "Asya kule (in one's line or family, or lineage) yah evam veda (who knows this, "U" full of Pure Consciousness) na bhavati abrahmavit (none is born who is not a knower of Brahman)." This is certainly amazing and almost unimaginable, as it would say, the eventual and inevitable birth of nothing but enlightened beings takes place as time moves on, as mind itself changes matter itself at the quantum genetic level. Perhaps that is so! Who knows. Yet for now I give another thought for this "na bhavati abrahmavit." Bhava can mean becoming as in a mood or feeling or conceptional condition. And it can also mean actual birth in the sense of a physical, subtle or even causal existence or realm (such as a heaven region). That is not the point. I feel that it means, "No mood of not being Brahman." Or, "No feeling of not being in Brahman," more precisely. No feeling (na bhavati) that is not Brahman (abrahmavit). Nothing that comes in his or her wake is not Brahman. Nothing is not the Infinite. All events or all that is born in one's wake is the Infinite. This is spectacularly Beautiful! Nothing is born in your wake as family (as Saradadevi says that the Whole World is your family and none is a stranger) that is not the Infinite. So thereafter everything is seen in the Infinite and as the Infinite and so effects physical lineage and energy in its wave motions or wakes, equality in mind, and a higher current of knowing and feeling.

The Prasna Upanishad speaks of this dream state God-like Energy, the Taijasa Light, "There, in dreams, that god, the mind experiences glory." IV. 5. This "god of the mind" is, metaphorically, none but Indra, who is the Lightning and Thunder of Pure Mind. And this God Light is the Luminous Prana. You see, the bahir mukhas, the outward mouths of the ten indriyas are not functioning in the awareness of consciousness in the dream state. Only the antar mukhas or the inward mouths are

437

functioning as in devouring this luminous Prana which is manifesting in the four psychic functions; ego, intellect, mind and memory. The functions of these "mukhas" gives us a direct clue into the nature of "Bhavamukha!" But in Bhavamukha one is not in the individual function, you are experiencing through the universe in total with great and full empathic feeling for the Self as True in all! In the same verse, IV 5., it says, after describing the inner nature of the dream state, "He sees all, himself being all." This is because in dream your own consciousness is all that exists for you, even though, within that, you imagine the differentiation of other people or deities, or places and events.

Again one finds in the Brihadaranyaka Upanishad, "And when he dreams, he takes away a little of the the impressions of this all embracing world, the waking state, himself makes the body unconscious, and creates a dream body in its place, revealing his own brightness by his own light - and he dreams. In this state, the person becomes self illumined." IV. 3. 9. This is Taijasa, take note, "revealing his own brightness, by his own light... the person becomes self illumined." The Chhandogya extends this even into the dream of the after death state where it describes, "If he desires the world of the ancestors, by his mere thought the ancestors come to him. Having obtained the world of the ancestors he is happy." It goes on describing "if he desires," the world of the mothers, or brothers, or sisters, or friends, or perfumes and garlands, or food and drink, or song and music, or the world of women, or a country one longs for, then, "by the mere thought of it that appears in consciousness." VIII. 2. 1 - 10.

- M -

"That is the state of deep sleep wherein one asleep neither desires any object nor sees any dream. The third quarter is Prajna, whose sphere is deep sleep, in whom all experiences become unified, who is verily a mass of consciousness, who is full of bliss and experiences bliss, and who is the door leading to the knowledge of dreaming and waking." V. 5

"He is the Lord of all. He is the knower of all. He is the inner controller. He is the source of all; from him all beings originate and in him they finally disappear." V. 6

"Prajna Atman, whose sphere is deep sleep, is M, the third letter of Aum, because both are the measure and also because in them all become one. He who knows this is able to measure all and also comprehends all within himself." V. 11

In the Prajna there is only One Mouth (Mukha) and that is Consciousness. All the gods and so forth are gone! There are no more seven limbs, there are no more nineteen mouths. Even mind, intellect, ego and memory have slowed down into the "mass of consciousness" (prajnanaghanah). As the individual, this state is called Prajna Atman, the Atman in the deep sleep. As the universal this is called Isvara astoundingly enough which is God Consciousness as the Unmanifest before creation (Avyakta). The seat of this Wisdom (prajna) is the heart. Deep in the heart is the experience of deep sleep.

This one Principle as Consciousness in deep sleep is called Ceto Mukha, a beautiful word meaning the face, mouth or door of consciousness, that is a door into the oneness as a mass of consciousness or a mass of joy (anandabhuk) or a door or facing back into the waking and dreaming states. This "anandabhuk" is one who has become freed from the extreme of effort and so is naturally happy. This prajna of deep sleep is also "ekibhutah," (one element) undifferentiated, which is most important to know for it is our imagination in the waking and dreaming states that create in that imagination all the differentiation. But in deep sleep it goes, for this sthana or place/abode/sphere is undifferentiated. It is anandamaya also for it is full of joy. These are characteristics of deep sleep described by the poet of the Mandukyo Upanishad.

It is described that one in deep sleep does not desire any desire nor see any dream. Recall what the Chhandogya said that by the mere thought of the thing or desire for the thing the thing in case appears, but here there is no desire for any desire and so no dream objects appear. One is then oneself this ekibhutah, anandabhuk, prajnanaghanah, and anandamaya as you are then in cetomukha. Excellent. In its grandest depth this is equated with

439

Isvara (God Consciousness) Unmanifest.

We find also that this Prajna or Isvara is nothing but Pure Energy, that is Pure Prana! Gaudapada has stated this fact. And it is said, "When a person has entered into deep sleep, as it is called, then, my dear, he becomes united with Pure Being (Sat), he has gone to his own Self. That is why they say he is in deep sleep (Svapiti); it is because he has gone (Apiti) to his own Self (Svam). Just as a bird tied by a string to the hand of the bird catcher first flies in every direction, and then finding no rest anywhere, settles down at the place where it is bound, so also the mind, that is the individual soul reflected in the mind, my dear, after flying in every direction and finding no rest anywhere, settles down in the Prana (Pure Being), for the mind, the individual soul is fastened to the Prana as Pure Being." Chhandogya VI 8. 1 - 2.

This Prana as Pure Being is the Immense Divine Energy. Prana is Life itself, not just flesh, blood and bone, it is everything: the psyche, the feelings, the spiritual. How, who, can designate the Immense Expanse of Prajna Atman as the Prana, within the dream or waking mind conception? This is why it is called the Measure (Miti) of the Universe in full for one becomes in the Place where the Universe is absorbed, merged and united (Apiti). Very important you see. As it is said, "...ca Bhavati apitih" which is the feeling/mood of becoming the place where the entire universe is absorbed, merged, united. This is the Immense Prana. And this is Miti, the Measure of all things, for all things are reduced to Here! The poetry of the Upanishad is beautiful. It was stated that "Apti" is the All Pervasive as an awareness of the first and foremost primary Self, but now even that, as the waking expanse, is absorbed and merged into the bhava of Apiti, the place which is also "Esah Yoni" the Source of all, and "yoni" here is the womb of none but the Divine Mother.

Ramakrishna makes it clear. "The Mother showed me that there exists only One, and not two." This One is the Measure (Miti) of all that is and this One is the Place of merging, absorbing and uniting as "Va Apiti." This is none but "Esah Yoni" the Womb of the Mother. As the Brahma Sutra Bhasya

440

states, I 4. 27. "And because Brahman is declared to be the Source (Yoni)." That is the Mother's Yoni which makes everything. And so that is none other than Sakti as Her Divine Energy, as the Pure Prana, but as the "apiti bhava" in that mood/feeling, you know it as your own Self. That is the point you see, from this place (yoni), "Minoti ha vai idam sarvam" you are able to measure and to know and to comprehend the whole universe in your Self as this is the Oneness and the Peace of all in the place of comprehension. It is Isvara and it is the Self in Isvara!

This Bhava Apiti is to Become One in the Pure Prana, the Mother, the Sakti, the Yoni. This is described as "Esah Antaryami," the Inner Controller or Director of all beings for this is within all beings! This is the Source (yoni) of all (sarvasya). It is sarvesvarah, the Isvara of the whole world, and sarvajnah, the Omniscient Knower of all the world (sarva)! When Ramakrishna speaks of the Mother as the One, he is really speaking of the higher level of complete comprehension of Aum. But until we have clarified the Fourth (Turiya) for ourselves, this level of understanding is very good as it is usable and pragmatic.

The saying is that, enlightened persons behave as if in deep sleep, for they are unaware or non-knowing of dualities of any kind, well that is good, but with this thought of Pure Prana we can take this a little further by saying that this person behaves as if they are in Pure Prana. This gives the experience a Living Energy, as if one were behaving, as they are, One in Mother!

The deep sleep state is described again in the Prasna Upanishad, "When the jiva is overcome by light, he sees no dreams; at that time, in this body, arises happiness." IV 6. The light referred to is the Light of Brahman appearing in the undifferentiated mass of consciousness and joy, as pure being. Beautiful. "Whatever one is thinking at the time of death, with that one enters into Prana. Prana joined with fire, together with the soul, leads to whatever world has been fashioned by thought." III 10. Out of the Pure Prana all the worlds are fashioned by thought. From this Place of Pure Prana these all come forth and arise! This is the extraordinary measure of comprehension in the "place" as everything becomes One in the

Pure Prana and then arises or is fashioned out of this Pure Prana.

This is the origin and dissolution of all beings, where "they finally disappear." Dominic Goodall translates it as "both the origin and the end of contingent beings." Of course, this is Isvara! As to the originating, the Prasna says, "He (Purusha or Pure Soul) created Prana, from Prana faith, space, air, fire, water, earth, the organs, mind, food, from food virility, austerity, the Vedic verses, sacrifice, the worlds; and in the worlds He created names." VI 4. All that one may dream or fashion by thought! The Virat!, which is Apti (the All Pervasive) and which becomes One in the Apiti (The Place where it is all Merged or United)!

To behave in this Pure Prana of Deep Sleep, let all that has come before you die! This is the real meaning of the corpse pose (asana) or posturing in the Pure Prana, as it is the origin and the end of all that is between, then what in the world can affect you as you are in the Place of Peace in the Pure Prana!

Yajnavalkya states, "Vayu (or the Prana as Hiranya Garbha in the Immensity) O Gautama, is that Sutra (Thread). By Vayu, as by a thread, O Gautama, are this world, the other world (death) and all beings held together. Therefore, O Gautama, they say of a person who dies that his limbs have been loosened; for they are held together by Vayu (Prana as breath/air) as by a thread." What is fashioned in thoughts out of this Pure Prana, Yajnavalkya describes, "There are in this body nerves (nadis) called hita, which are as fine as a hair divided into a thousand parts and are filled with white, blue, brown, green, and red fluids. They are the seat of the subtle body, which is the storehouse of impressions. Now, when he feels as if he were being killed or overpowered, or being chased by an elephant, or falling into a pit, in short, when he fancies at that time, through ignorance, whatever frightful thing he has experienced in the waking state, that is the dream state. So also, when he thinks he is a god, as it were, or a king, as it were, or thinks, "This universe is myself and I am all," that is the highest state." IV 3. 20.

Yajnavalkya goes on to describe deep sleep where, "where the gods are no more the gods" or mothers, fathers, killers, beggars, monks and so forth are no longer! He continues saying in deep sleep that "seeing is no longer seeing but there is no cessation for the seer," likewise, as in seeing, in smelling, tasting, speaking, hearing, thinking, touching, knowing, anything of the doing of all waking and dreaming. Then he finishes telling king Janaka, "In deep sleep it becomes transparent like water, the Witness, One and Without a Second. This is the World of Brahman, Your Majesty. This is the supreme attainment, this is its supreme glory, this is the highest world, this is its supreme bliss. On a particle of this bliss other creatures live." IV 3. 32. That is to say on a particle of the Bliss of Pure Prana, all other creatures live! So, Esah Yoni is Sakti and from a particle of Her Pure Bliss or Prana Energy is created the entire Luminous Womb of Hiranya Garbha and out of the same Prana, the World, Virat!

- Aum -

"The Fourth (Turiya) is without parts and without relationship; It is the cessation of phenomena; It is all good and non-dual. This Aum is verily Atman. He who knows this merges his self in Atman - yea, he who knows this." V. 12

"Turiya is not that which is conscious (prajna) of the inner (subjective) world, nor that which is conscious (prajna) of the outer (objective) world, nor that which is conscious (prajna) of both, nor is it that which is a mass of consciousness. It is not simple consciousness nor is It unconsciousness. It is unperceived, unrelated, incomprehensible, uninferable, unthinkable, and indescribable. The essence of Consciousness manifesting as the self in the three states. It is the cessation of all phenomena. It is all peace, all bliss, and non-dual. This is what is known as the Fourth (Turiya). This is Atman and this has to be realized." V. 7.

"All this is, indeed, Brahman. This Atman is Brahman. This same Atman has four quarters." V.2.

"The same Atman explained before as being endowed with four quarters is now described from the standpoint of the syllable Aum. Aum, too, divided into parts, is viewed from the standpoint of the letters. The quarters of Atman are the same as

443

the letters of Aum and the letters are the same as the quarters. The letters are A, U, and M." V. 8.

"Harih AUM! AUM, the Word, is all this. A clear explanation of it is as follows. All that is past, present, and future is, indeed, Aum. And whatever else there is, beyond the threefold division of time - that also is truly Aum." V. 1.

This Turiya, the Fourth, is pure Satchidananda. This is Atman in context of the individual. This is Brahman, the Infinite, in context of the Universe. This is the Nitya in Ramakrishna's wording. All that came before is the Lila, that is the waking, dreaming and deep sleep conditions. Here, all the three letters become unified in the experience of what is represented by the Higher OM! The Eternal! The Nitya, for now the Lila is seen in its clarified state, Clearly, as it is raised to the consciousness of the Eternal!, leaving behind its relative (Lila) condition. This is Pure Self Feeling, Being Great Bliss!

In the Gita, Krishna says, "Of words, I am the monosyllable "OM." X 25. This is the Supreme Identity. In the Srimad Devi Bhagavatam, Hring, is the Fulfillment and completion of the monosyllable, in the Goddess, the Divine Mother. Ramakrishna says to Mother Kali, "The mind is nothing but Yourself." He also says to Her, "You are the Embodiment of OM." So does it mean that the "mind" itself is nothing but the embodiment of OM! Elsewhere you will find him saying that OM is a step down from the Reality he is experiencing! And of the Mother he will say that the "Vedas and the Vedanta are so far below Thee." Mother is the Essence of Consciousness manifesting in the Three States and it is to this that attention, feeling and thought are focused and with that the experience arises! The Emphasis is on this Essence of Consciousness!

Turiya is described as the "cessation of all phenomena," but this cessation is not the nirodha cessation of the mind alone. It is more than that. This, in which all phenomena ceases is "prapancopa saman," which is really the awareness or the reaching of the state of consciousness in which the world of the five elements (prapanco) is made or seen or becomes "Saman" or Sameness! This is Astounding, the Universe becomes or is seen to be and to have always been this Sameness. That is Samarasa,

444

the flavor, mood, or taste of Sameness! All this is resolved into This, which is Pure Existence, Pure Consciousness, Pure Bliss (Sat Chid Ananda)!

The center of location for this experience is said to be in the head or just above it in the poetry of "ten fingers breadth above," but no less we experience this in the heart, the throat, and the eyes! As feeling, as vigorous poetic declaration and as what is seen as the world. In the head it is the high Awareness of Atman and Brahman as the Immensity!

As we continue we go further on with Vamadeva, while in the womb, with no help from anyone, on his own, he burst through the net of ideas like a free flying hawk and to this Swami Gambhirananda's translation adds to this amazing state, "What a Wonder!" not unlike Ramakrishna all alone in the Kali temple with no help from another. From the womb to the dissolution of the body, we go through and we get deeper and deeper states of Self Depth like Vamadeva, like Ramakrishna! Going through every imaginable stage, state, deity conceptions and life all surrounding, one comes to know, "All these have Consciousness as the giver of their reality; all these are impelled by Consciousness; the universe has Consciousness as its eye, and Consciousness is its end. Consciousness is Brahman. He (Vamadeva or anyone like him) having realized Oneness with Pure Consciousness soared on from this world (the three states), and having obtained all desires in yonder heavenly world, became Immortal, yea, became Immortal." Aitareya Upanishad III. 1. 3 - 4. The Wonder and the Capacity to do this is in your own Energy (Prana)!

Really, not even Turiya describes the Reality! Is there Something Greater than Atman? The Katha Upanishad challenges this simple knowing, "Beyond the senses are the objects; beyond the objects is the mind; beyond the mind, the intellect; beyond the intellect; the Great Atman; beyond the Great Atman, the Unmanifest, beyond the Unmanifest, the Purusha. Beyond the Purusha there is nothing; this is the end, the Supreme Goal," I 3. 10 -11. This Unmanifest (Avyakta) is the Unborn spoken of in the Rk Veda. Is this the Shunyata? Perhaps and perhaps not. What is Greater than the Great Atman?

445

Even though the translation notes say this term indicates Hiranya Garbha (or Sutra Atma), one is still lead to wonder! The Unborn (Ajati) Non-Dual (Advaita) Brahman is Greater than the individual Atman, and so we remain Humble!

Then where is the Experience? "The sages realize that Indescribable Supreme Joy as 'This is That.' How can I realize It? Is It Self Luminous? Does It shine brightly or not?" Katha II 2. 14. It is luminous, it is the brightness of one's own mind in fact, expressing itself there and then, as now it is! But since it is the Purest of the Pure in Consciousness it may be somewhat difficult to define with simple consciousness (ordinary cognition). That is why it is ungraspable and unthinkable (agrahyam and acintyam). One translator says, it is beyond all empirical dealings, another says it has no relation to anything, and another says it has no commerce with the world (avyavaharyam). It cannot be related to anything, being the Supreme behind everything! It is not cognitive nor is it non-cognitive (na prajnam naprajnam), not outer waking, inner dreaming nor a mass of deep sleep. It has no distinctions, it is incapable of being spoken about in words because there are no distinctive marks, for it is the Ever Pure (Pure Mind)!

It is important not to become too technical for this is not an intellectual experience and such only keeps the mind in figuring. That is why it is acintyam (unthinkable), so be as Vamadeva soaring past the thinkable into what has never been born to thought or thinking. That is why it is called the Essence of Consciousness throughout the three states, yet, not of the three states!

The results that are given such as becoming the first and foremost among the great, being all pervasive, exalting the current of knowledge, being treated equally by friend and enemy, having no one (nor any feeling or thing) born in your wake that is not aware of, nor felt to be Brahman, being one with the Measure and Source of all, these are just secondary results given by way of praising the Primary and True Reality! It is the adoration of what is truly Adorable, the Reality! The Prasna Upanishad gives further praising of results on recognition of the spiritual content and meaning of A, U, and M. "If he meditates

446

on one letter (A), then, being enlightened by that alone, he quickly comes back to the earth after death." "If, again, he meditates on the second letter (U), he attains the mind, and is led up to the Intermediate Space, to the Plane of the Moon (which is the symbol for the Region of the Mind)." "Again, he who meditates on the highest Person (M) through this syllable Aum consisting of three letters, becomes united with the Effulgent Sun." Shaking off all limitations like Vamadeva, he becomes the Supreme Purusha, Higher than the High, pervading everywhere! "The three letters of Aum, if employed separately, are mortal (leading back into death); but when joined together in meditation on the Total Reality and used properly on the activities of the external, internal, and intermediate states (waking, deep sleep and dream as intermediate), the knower trembles not!" "The wise person, meditating on Aum, attains this world (of the Infinite)... through the syllable Aum he realizes that which is tranquil, free from decay, death, and fear, and which is the Highest." Prasna V 2 - 7.

Prana, Sakti, Mother

As you are, in your True Self, Already the Reality, it is just getting your Prana into the straight and narrow with the Divine Mother. Or I should say with Her, into the curved and the wide as the Most Encompassing. Prana is your own Living Energy. One cannot know this enough and though Brahman is spoken of as the support of the Prana, Ramakrishna would say that what you call Brahman he calls Kali, Sakti, the Divine Mother. So there is no duality!

It is Prana, not person! Deep Sleep is the Prajna of Isvara! And this is Pure Prana! All that is waking and dreaming and deep sleep is nothing but Prana. The eyes, speech, mind and energy all directly question the Creator or Creatrix! This is your own, not another person between. Nothing between you and Mother, not even a between imagination. No mediator here. Direct Experience. No mediatory principle, idea, god, goddess, sound, teacher, seer, etc. It is the state of the Seer! The Rk Poet! "I was Manu. I was the Sun." And even More. I was the

447

Infinite! I am the Infinite! This is Love at its Best! The Foremost! Pure Energy! Pure Sakti! Pure Kali! Pure Prana!

This Pranava which is the name of Aum, is your own mind, energy, feeling and life! The Energy of Aum as Mind takes you directly into the Supreme. Have no doubt. This is without formations in Consciousness, like gods, ideas, etc. The Chhandogya addresses this Reality, "The Prana, indeed, is the Oldest, the Greatest." V 1. 1. This is before all persons, deities, anything! This Living Energy, Sakti, is what makes everything or anyone Dear to one's self! "The prana moves by prana. The prana gives the prana to the prana." For She is solely independent in Her Energy! "Prana is father, mother, brother, sister, teacher and brahmin." "If anyone says something unbecoming to a father, mother, brother, sister, teacher or brahmin, then people say: "Shame on you! Verily you are a slayer of your father, mother, brother, sister, a slayer of your teacher, a slayer of a brahmin." "But if, when the Prana has departed from them, one shoves them together with a poker and burns every bit of them, no one would say: "You are a slayer of your father, mother, brother, sister, teacher or brahmin." VII 15. 1 - 3.

It means above all these Prana is what is important and what gives meaning and feeling to anything at all. The expressions of Living Energy.

"Take the Upanishad as the Bow, the great weapon, and place upon it the arrow sharpened by meditation. Then, having drawn it back with a mind directed to the thought of Brahman, strike that mark, O my Good Friend, that which is the Imperishable! Aum is the Bow; the Atman is the Arrow; Brahman is said to be the Mark. It is to be struck by an undistracted mind. Then the Atman becomes One with Brahman, as the Arrow with the Target!" Mundaka II 2. 3 -4. That is it!

Prahlada

Prahlada resolved and pledged himself to worship Vishnu Narasimha as himself. Perhaps only an asura, a daitya, a demon can do this. The story of Prahlada is my favorite, perhaps because honestly as an ego I too see myself in that ego as being asuric. It is an aspect within all of us and the story of Prahlada addresses this with honesty and liberates us from it. Prahlada appears to be a eudemonist, a good hearted demon who is a genius, always seeking to do good for the sake of the happiness of others and of self (which is within others). It is such a story so old that in its wisdom it teaches grand truths. Ramakrishna would say to those who addressed him as a holy man from whom they should take the dust of his feet, "You may speak that way about sages like Dhruva, Prahlada, Narada, or Kapila, but who am I?" What astounding Humility, so rare in the history of humanity! Again, "Prahlada realized, 'I am It (God the Absolute). He also realized, 'I am Thy servant, Thou art my Lord.' This Love solves the problem of life." O how true that is, how true. Again speaking of those like Prahlada, "Apart from the Divine Mother they are as good as non-entities." This is very important to keep in mind as we dive into the wonder of Prahlada.

Krishna in the Gita states, "Of the Daityas I am Prahlada," which commands the height of identity and the importance of Prahlada's example. You see, Daitya or Asura is loosely translated as demon. Yet in the meshes of history and myth one finds that the Gods (Devas or Suras) are those who are Inwardly Tranquil and the Demons are those immersed in their own self reflection. Two aspects of human nature, one, inner peace, the other, ego attraction or narcissism.

The essence of the story is this. To protect Prahlada from his father king and his two inimical gurus, Narasimha Vishnu (God in the form of the Man Lion) appears or emerges out of the stone pillar to kill them all with His vajra like claws and teeth. Then Prahlada in the Pure Practice of the Ancient Method, forgets himself as being a Daitya demon, and becomes One in his identity with the All Self of Vishnu! We will describe what that is as we go on.

Narasimha appears for Prahlada's Sake, in reference to you this means, Pure Mind appears for your Sake, out of the Pillar of Reality to kill the ego (demon) that obscures your own Reality.

449

One may ask the healthy questions, "Was it an actual event or is it a myth? Or was this like Ramakrishna's Shiva like sadhu that appeared out of the consciousness of his own mind to teach him Advaita, Tantra and all that he latter was told again by the teachers that came to him?" I see a deep similarity.

There are two Narasimha Upanishads that describe the ritual diagrammatic visualization of cognitive power forms of Narasimha. The second or higher Upanishad describes Aum as being the Embodiment of Narasimha. (like Aum is the Embodiment of Mother or the Embodiment of Krishna.) The first Upanishad describes Aum-Narasimha in the condition of qualities within time past, present and future (saguna) and the second leads one, at the conclusion, to the nirguna or transcendent of the time state in Oneness, in the formless, or what is beyond time, is also Aum in the nirguna (free of qualities relating to time). All this is Aum! Yet, you see, that in this Practice, you yourself and none other, are Prahlada. That is how the cognition is generated!

Remember Vidyaranya's insight, "The best among the best Yogins, such as Janaka and Prahlada, belong to a class of practitioners with extremely unlimited ardor, for, they can, at a moment's thought, work themselves up into the condition of confirmed ecstatic Concentration." We see this in Prahlada in spite of an inimical father king and malignant gurus. For we hear from the story, that Prahlada was so sensitive to a moment's thought, that if he simply heard the syllable "Ka" or saw it written, that he would go into the ecstasy of Krishna. No, Krishna had not been actually born until long long later in time, perhaps the letter reminded Prahlada of a Krishna to come. Sometimes these stories are not time bound to the reality of time in which we apparently live and they indicate a higher awareness of "realities" that may be termed a matter of faith rather than historical fact. But this should not diminish us, but enhance us. In history, we see Ramakrishna being so sensitive to words, the name of Mother, could throw him into ecstasy, and his unlimited ardor for Her, could certainly, at a moment's thought bring his mind into the confirmed Consciousness of Bliss!

Now, as it is with Kasyapa, being the father of so many

gods, and demons, and human beings and so forth, he is raised mythically almost to the level of God the Creator, here we find that with Diti he sired the two brothers Hiranyaksha and Hiranyakasipu. The first brother (a demon who controlled the world for a time) was killed by the Boar incarnation óf Vishnu. It was Hiranyakasipu who was Prahlada's father/king. Prahlada's two gurus were Sanda and Amarka. The king told the gurus never to let Prahlada call directly upon Vishnu. But they could not stop him and so the king would become enraged, for he felt his life might be threatened by Vishnu too (since he, like his brother before him, was a demon, you see). Nevertheless, Prahlada disobeys or turns away from the gurus and worships God directly! This is a great, and a tremendous and invaluable lesson!

Even as a demon it is said that Prahlada came to be born on the Earth with a tenderness like a flower dropping upon grass. Nothing could hurt him (not father/kings nor gurus) as Vishnu was always in his heart. Now you come to this idea of the Daityas or Asuras as human beings, or the Dasas which were one of the names given in the Rk Veda for the people of Mohenjo Daro and Harrapa and the other ninety seven cities that were there in this part of the world. So we might just have a simple demonization of other people, you see, as alienation and xenophobia, which was not uncommon in the Rk Veda. So, Prahlada and the others in the story were not demons at all, they were just an "other people," and so demonized to that extent in the view of opposing religious beliefs in some way. So contradictory to what Ramakrishna felt, in that, all paths lead to Truth (eventually)!

So the king (and the gurus) in their common fury devised ways in which to kill Prahlada (drowning, trampling, thrown from a height and so forth) but every way they tried to killed Prahlada he felt the presence of Vishnu there and was protected. I quote the Srimad Bhagavatam translated by Swami Prabhavananda. "As Prahlada stood there he forgot he was a Daitya and had a mortal body; he felt that he was the universe and that all the powers of the universe emanated from him; he, himself, was the ruler of nature. Time passed thus, in one

451

unbroken ecstasy of bliss, until gradually Prahlada began to remember that he had a body and that he was Prahlada. As soon as he became once more conscious of the body, he saw that God was within and without, and everything appeared to him as Vishnu." Perfect!

The king rallied the two gurus again, to try and stop Prahlada from his worship and ecstasy in God Consciousness. It did not work and Prahlada would say God is everywhere. The king said if this is so then make God appear out of this stone pillar. Narasimha emerged and toothed and clawed the king and the gurus to death and anyone else in his untamable rage that dared to harm Prahlada. The anger of Narasimha was only cooled when Prahlada got in His lap and embraced Him and kissed him as the Man Lion returned these affections. Then He promised Prahlada that after the dissolution or dropping of his body that he would attain the Pure State of Vishnu. Until that time he was installed as king in the throne of the Daityas. Is it not a metaphor of God Consciousness being over ego consciousness?

Hiranyakasipu hated Vishnu because in the form of the Boar he had killed his younger brother Hiranyaksha. So the king did so much yoga that the God Brahma had to come to him and grant him a favor. This was not to die by any imaginable means. Narasimha was unimaginable, half man, half lion, coming out of a pillar.   There is always a way to get around these commitments of deities, for humans generally cannot outwit the Gods! Except for those like Vamadeva who just blast them out of consciousness. The king wanted his flesh to live forever, that is generally the mistake of the narcissistic mind, you see, and why extreme preservation of the flesh is considered to be a dark pursuit.

There is another aspect of the story. It is said that Narada, the sage of Love, came and would sing to Prahlada's mother while Prahlada was still in the womb. He sang to him songs of spiritual teaching.   This reminds one of Vamadeva's and Ashtavakra's knowledge while still in the womb. Perhaps it is metaphorical and instructional for all of us, every being, because if one is in the womb, one has come from somewhere, the Great Light experienced in the previous death cycle, or somewhere and as such is experiencing vasanas in the dream state condition of being in the womb and yet has not completely burst forth as an independent waking state being! The potential experienced by those such as Prahlada, or Vamadeva is within each of us, to experience at any time, not just within the womb. Another question is raised. Narada is taught by Sanatkumara in the Chhandogya Upanishad. This episode is circa the era of Rama and maybe even Krishna. There is debate about that. But Prahlada and Narasimha were long, long before that era. So one must wonder if this was added later or if again we are experiencing the time slip found in so many of these stories.

Swami Ramakrishnananda writes of Prahlada, "Although a Daitya by birth, he was really a God by nature and so long as he reigned, there was no quarrel between them. Everyone was impartial under his rulership." The story of Prahlada is told in the Laghu Yoga Vasistha and starts after Narasimha emerged from the pillar and killed all the delusion assaulting Prahlada. It is here that Prahlada begins even a deeper meditation, that is perhaps deeper than the one prior to the emerging or coming forth of Narasimha from the stone pillar. That one was profound but this one seems to have more depth. Nevertheless it takes place after the death of Hiranyakasipu who is thought by some to have been a Shiva worshiper, for at Mohenjo Daro they had the concept of Shiva and the Goddess long before the Aryan arrivals. In reaction to this the Shiva devotees have the myth that Shiva came as Sarabha, part man, beast and bird who punished Narasimha for killing Hiranyakasipu. Will this quarreling never end? Hiranyakasipu means golden (luminous) robed, his younger brother Hiranyaksha means golden (luminous) eyed, or golden yaksha (a king of demons). All names given by the Indo Aryans to those who were strange to them. It is said that the famous Kasyapa, one of the strongest of the seven sacred rishis, with Diti, was the father of Hiranyaksha and Hiranyakasipu. But we think they were Dasas from Harrapa or Mohenjo Daro, so this story of their parents may have possibly been a taking or absorbing of one culture into another, by way of making the story more their own, for Kasyapa and Diti are Indo Aryan!

The extreme importance of Prahlada is that he brings forth

453

God on his own. God appears in the form of Narasimha, the lion man which is nothing but the courage and truth of one's own Pure Mind in the Ancient Method. So now Prahlada dives into the Depth. He will worship Vishnu as his own Self. This idea he created in his mind. Prahlada's mind swung between the beauty of the senses, as demons will do, and the full complete Reality. So he doubled his worship of the Primordial Cause. He arrived at the Final Inquiry of Atman and asked the questions, "Who am I? What was I before I was born? What is the nature of the "I" that engages its Identity with the world, the body, the mind and so then stays and runs, cries and laughs, exults and is afflicted?" (Note that this is the method that has been suggested by such souls as Brahmajna Ma and Ramana Maharshi. Now you know where this Ancient Method originated!) Prahlada arrived at the thought, "I cognize my Reality. Ha, Ha, Ha, now I have known my True Self. All souls from Brahma to a blade of grass end as the Universe ends in the great dissolution, so how can ideas such as "I" or "You" which pertain to the mind exist at all. All jivas are but "I" and the "Pratyagatman" (One's Inward and Inmost Self, one's own Soul) their Inner Controller has no other to lean on, so I offer salutation to them all as my own Self! I am the Kutastha (the Witness). I am the Brahman (Infinite). I shine devoid of difference. I am Thou and Thou art I! Prostration to My Self who have attained Reality without obscuration! I, who can cognize all! Conceptions of duality and non-duality have fallen from my Incomparable State of Kevala (Independence), the ego has flown away, Thou art I and I am Thou, the Final Seat of Understanding. The cause of Creation! The causeless Cause! The Imperishable Cause!"

And so it said in the Laghu Yoga Vasistha, Prahlada remained in Nirvikalpa Samadhi for five thousand years, of course this is symbolic because of historical reality. But what is so interesting is that it is said Patala became like Satyaloka itself which is that because of Prahlada's understanding of Reality, Hell itself became Heaven! The Universe had turned around. If hell is quiescent then a decline begins. The gods and demons both feared that they would have to give up their forms and enter the undifferentiated state of Pure Reality and because of that the

Universe would stop. Such was the power of Prahlada's Realization by the Ancient Method.

So Vishnu Narasimha appears once again and tells Prahlada he must come down from his tremendous Samadhi and start to rule again as king of the demons. It is beautifully described that he slowly started to recover from the Depth of this Samadhi, the Sakti of Consciousness descended back into the Brahmarandhra, the aperture of God at the top of the skull and this divine Sakti Energy pervaded through his nadis (spiritual nerves) and started to perceive and experience perception through the nine apertures, (seven in the head, two eyes, ears, nostrils and mouth, and then the two openings at the base of the spine, between the hips). Like a reflection upon glass his Mind became active and the Prana and Apana began to percolate through his nerves and organs, generating complete perception of the world again. He glowed with Life.

Vishnu Narasimha appeared again and said to Prahlada that he should rule his kingdom (Is it hell or the Dasa kingdom?) and when his body died and dissolved that he would return to the deep state of this Identity. Until then he should live as one with half closed eyes, liberated while yet living, behaving as one whose vasanas (See Groundwork) have disappeared in deep sleep, for in deep sleep one does not entertain thoughts nor dreams. Which is to say, as one whose impressions and deep psychic knots of differentiation have gone!

It is such a profound story. Prahlada was a brilliant diamond among the best jewels of gods or demons. He turned the world around where the gods delighted in the faces of demonesses and the demons delighted in the faces of goddesses. He worshiped Vishnu as Vishnu, God as God, and knew, "I am Vishnu." He who is known as Prahlada, whose name means pleasurable excitement, the feeling of Joy, gladdening, delighting, and cheerful, is none other than Vishnu for there is no separative idea of duality. "And those gods are really singing my own praise, as I am Vishnu. He am I and I salute Him." All he wanted was to be able to consider the Limitless and the Infinite! He engaged himself then and there in that direct inquiry of the Ancient Method! And there he realized, there is no conceptualization of

455

the Omnipresent Self! "I salute this Self which is its own Light, in the Limitless Space of Consciousness!" What gives rise to the delusion that expresses itself in such ideas of "you" or "I", what even is life or death, with body or without body! "I salute the Self! Salutations to My Self! Om is the One Non-Dual Consciousness!" Prahlada understood the secret, "Whatever comes, let it come; whatever goes, let it go." In Vishnu and in my own excellent Self Effort I have Realized Reality. "O Self! I salute You! I embrace You: Who but you is my friend and relative in the three worlds?" He had forgotten his True Nature thinking he was a demon, and now he has forgotten he was a demon, and remembered his True Nature! O Self, You are the Supreme Point in which the Whole Universe Exists!

He inquired in the Ancient Method, "Who am I? How could all this happen? And yet be free from all that? O Self, you apparently have fallen asleep and you are apparently awakened by your own energy! For the purpose of becoming aware of the experiences being undergone!" He went through to the Real explaining to himself the use of such words as "I", "When you yourself adore yourself or describe yourself for your own delight!"

Prahlada knew that pleasure and pain perceived through Equanimity was a different consciousness than when perceived through ignorance and that it is impossible to describe! A thousand years went by in the Depth of Samadhi. The demons thought Prahlada to be dead for in Nirvikalpa Samadhi outwardly there are no signs of life. The gods in heaven had nothing to fear and with nothing to fear (the demons), there was no hate and so the universe would come to a standstill in the Transcendent Condition. So Vishnu comes and arouses Prahlada's consciousness, so that the Prana (life force) began to vibrate in the crown of Prahlada's head. As he awakened back into the world mind he realized that those who think themselves stupid, weak or miserable are fit to die. Yet, for those whose mind has reached the cessation of mind phenomena state, for them alone, life is appropriate in the state of Great Joy, not death! Prahlada knew he was bodiless, not a demon, not a god, not a man! From hence forth he lived as an enlightened person

456

in the state of deep sleep, with eyes half closed, perceiving no distinctions. "I was in the state of Consciousness which Spontaneously Arose in Me. The entire universe is My Self so nothing is to be acquired and nothing is to be abandoned."

Harmony between the gods and demons was regained, and friendship between the goddesses and demonesses returned. The world was at Peace for a time. It is said that Prahlada attained Vishnu as Self and Self as Vishnu through the method of Self Effort, the Foremost Means! For, "If it is true that gurus can spiritually uplift the world without Self Effort, then why do not gurus uplift camels and bulls?"

Have you seen the picture of Ramakrishna with half closed eyes, the one where he is sitting? That is what is meant. I picture Prahlada there in the Deepest Depth of Self, like the picture of Ramakrishna standing there in Great Joy, being physically supported by Hriday. The first telling of this story is from K. Narayanaswami Aiyer's rendering. The second telling of this story is briefly quoted by me, telling of it, from Swami Venkatesananda's version.

Kaushitaki

Not a single leaf falls except by the Will of what is Absolute! Whatever happens with gods or gurus, friends or enemies, husbands and wives, life or death, anything, Know This! "Atman does not become higher or greater through good, nor does Atman become lower or less through evil deeds, but it is Atman who makes him, whom he wishes to take higher up from this world, to do good deeds and it is Atman who makes him, whom he wants to lead downwards, to do evil deeds." Kaushitaki Upanishad III verse 8. My rendered variation of Deussen's translation.

Atman is not increased by good, nor diminished by the small. Deussen uses "he" to say Atman. This is valid. The Self encompasses good and evil as gods and demons both are seen in Krishna's Universal Form. From Atman is the cause of good, from Atman the cause of evil. "he does not distress himself with the thought: Why did I not do what is good? Why did I do what

457

is evil? Whoever knows this regards both of these (i.e. good and evil) as Atman (and thus strengthens It); indeed he cherishes both these as Atman." Taittiriya. III 9. 1. This is the Self! This one should Know! "The Great Unborn Self.... It does not become greater through good deeds or smaller through evil deeds." Brihadaranyaka. IV 4. 22.

My Self

If one word I could speak to the question of what is my religion, as I was dying, the answer to that would be, "Love." What I have seen?, is not so extraordinary! It is just to know what one is seeing, as all seeing, is in Consciousness, feeling in Love, being in Mystery! In that regard, in that veneration.

If I really believe in Ramakrishna I will go by his example and experience! Yes! The answers have always been with me. I have been, to my Joy, this whole life trying to express this! Knowing this gives me Peace. Perhaps all I have experienced is only a reminder to continue what I was doing from previous lives, triggered in my mind by such questions asked of me like, "What culture were you born in?"

What I seek? It is She who gives the Sweetest Tear of Oneness, Beauty and Love! Whether it be the Atman as Self Sense or the Unending Openness of the Vast Expanse! Fullness! and Void! My Purpose is to Serve the Goddess with all forms of my Energy!

Everything predicts, prophesies, reveals, reflects and empowers the Fulfillment of You! Conviction is in the Bones! Confidence is in the Mind! Certainty is in the Soul! Courage is in the Spirit!

I am Humbled by my own Ignorance!, so what need have I of instructions, deities or teachers!

Direct Dream Sight

Taijasa is the one of shining element in the aloneness of your own Mind as the experience of Reality in itself as your own mind is experienced. A Goddess approached me in the dream.

She said, "Teach me Tantra." So I showed Her many old texts that were brown with age. She said again, "Teach me the Tantra!" So I said to Her that Aseshananda says, "The Divine Mother is the Ever Presence of Beauty, Strength and Spirituality! The Holy Mother is a person." At that the dream Goddess was Satisfied! This is the Answer I have sought always as to what is the path to Truth in this Ancient Method I am so ineffectually attempting to describe, to practice and To Be!

Experience

Instead of turning to seek out conch shells, make the Decision to Turn to Your Own Jewel (Pure Mind). Then Soar On with this Jewel as "That Mind Pure Mind" Humble and Surrendered! "You will go beyond all this and will be able to understand everything yourself. It is the mind that becomes at last the spiritual teacher and acts as such." "The power of the spiritual teacher is the Power of the Universal Mother and that power is either lying dormant or is awake in all men." You will go past, "the hidden complex truths of spirituality." "Your spiritual teacher and mine are not different but One only, that One being none other than that Power. It is this Divine Power (Sakti) which the scriptures speak of as the spiritual teacher, and it is to this Power that man is called upon to offer his heart's reverence and adoration with unflinching faith." Ramakrishna. Quoting Swami Saradananda.

Pure Rk Vedic Experience

All this, from the gods, all into the Unborn. Though Agni, Indra and Soma are deities, they represent deeper elements. Agni is as the Luminosity of Being and Fire itself. Indra is now Pure Thought as Pure Intellect, the mere Witness Observer without mental action and the Thunder and Lightning of Pure Mind. Soma is the bliss of Bliss. Prithivi (Mother Earth), Varuna (the Oceans), Surya (the Sun), Vayu (the Air/Atmosphere), the Ashvins (Day and Night) and the Diks (the Directions), and Mitra (Prana as the Living Day), Ushas (Dawn),

Ratri (Night), Savitri (Sun Goddess). Aditi (Boundless Free Mother Sun) and the twelve Adityas; Vishnu (Preserver), Indra (Intellect), Visvavat (World Tree), Mitra (Living Day), Varuna (Ocean), Pusan (Nourisher), Tvastar (Architect), Bhaga (Cherished Share of Tribe), Aryaman (Solar Prana in the Eyes), Dhatar (Arranger), Savitri (Sun), and Amsa (Distributor). Rahus (the Artists), Tvastar (the Cosmic Architect), Maruts, (Thunder, Lightning, and Tempest), Prithivi (Mother Earth), Chandra (Moon) and Dyaus (Sky) all (there are more deity concepts, so many, everything), all the forms of God Consciousness in Direct Experience. Of great interest is that it is the poet seer Kasyapa, who by embracing Aditi, caused Her to give birth to the Adityas. Imagine; Indra, Vishnu, Varuna and the others, born of the poet sage and the Sun!

The Height of experience in the ecstasy of death is explained in two courses. The path of the Sun and that of the Moon. This Solar Northern course leads to the realm of Brahma where one may retain a subtle or causal form for a while and yet then eventually merge and unite with the Formless Reality after a time. The Lunar Southern course is one where the soul is in the realm of the gods and or ancestors for a time and yet then as it is believed, through light, the soul goes into rain and then food, which is eaten and then reborn through the parents. These are cosmic pathways described in the Gita by Krishna and in the Upanishads. Yajnavalkya gives an elaborate and beautiful description of this process more in reference to the three states of consciousness, in his dying and rebirth doctrine.

I wrote in Dragon Sight: A Cremation Poem, "the Jewel, the Essence Giver, you did not follow the Northern Solar Course, through pingala, the Path of Prana, Pure Energy, into the Realms of Brahma, nor did you follow the Southern Lunar Course through ida, Rayi, the Path of Energy Returning, to the forms of substance. Mother Divine you returned to Yourself... Undying." The Prana Course pulls one's consciousness toward heaven, the gods, and eventual liberation into the formless. The path of Rayi or returning energy as consciousness is described with a sweet poetic beauty in the Upanishads, which may be actual, but as Ranade and Chakravarti comment might just be superstitious.

460

Nevertheless, the soul leaves the body, the body is cremated, the soul enjoys for a time in the Lunar course, the enjoyment of the gods, goddesses and or ancestors, if you like, then through the returning descent by the course of the Moon around the Earth, the soul falls back as rain, the rain goes into the ground, out of which food is produced. The food is eaten by a woman and a man, this food becomes ovum and sperm, it is given into the woman and then birth comes forth. "Woman, O Gautama, is the fire, her sexual organ is the fuel, what invites is the smoke, the vulva is the flame, what is done inside is the embers, the pleasures are the sparks." Chhandogya V 8. 1. And so life or consciousness comes back, returns.

Sexuality, birth, death and rebirth or the intense possibility of liberation are described so well in this and the Brihadaranyaka Upanishad. The path that bypasses both the Northern or Southern courses is the path of Om, the unified consciousness moving upward through the sushumna, through the crown aperture of the skull spreading out into the Infinite. Aum or Om is the Power in how this is done. Krishna describes the process of its application in the Gita. It is leaving the body behind, through the yogi's Eye, the Sun of true Seeing in Luminosity or if you prefer as I do, the Yogini's Divine Spiritual Eye, which does not follow the courses of the solar nerve (pingala) or the lunar nerve (ida), but follows the udana straight up the sushumna, as you see, into Infinite Dispersion! The Katha Upanishad tells of the Sushumna coming out of the one hundred spokes (of the nerve complex in the body) as the only course to liberation, for the other nerves, as consciousness travels these, only lead back to death, or life again as duality, in following these pathways of death. The Maitri describes seven sounds that are heard when this happens in yoga: a river, a bell, a brazen vessel, a wheel, the croaking of frogs, the pattering of rain, and a voice that comes from a place of seclusion. (Ranade's rendering) That would be your Inmost Self teaching you, in that voice!

As it was described in the Prasna Upanishad, the awareness of Consciousness in "A" leads back to human rebirth. That same awareness of Consciousness in "U" leads to the lunar course, the symbolic Moon region of ancestors circulating in that dream like world around the Earth. And the awareness of Consciousness within "M" leads to the realm of the Gods as the solar luminosity of Brahma's heaven. But the unified awareness of Consciousness within Aum as the Fourth, the Turiya of Pure Consciousness, the Atman in Brahman, through the divine eye of yoga, leads to freedom as spiritual liberation in the awareness of Self, Truth, Infinity! Of which there is no ending! Other developments and associations give "A" as Fire. "U" as the Moon. And "M" as the Sun. This triad of lights merge into the One Light of Truth! The Real Light!

Some certainly believe they can control the process through yogic concentration like Tibetan lamas who consciously come back through the after death bardo into the sidpa bardo into human life or redirect their consciousness into the Nirvana of no rebirth or at least a higher deity region. Yet in reality, it is only the Divine Mother who knows the course of the soul. And yet through the natural powers of the Gods, She may perhaps in the case that the Gods remain in your experience, Guide Us. So you see I had this dream of a Tibetan yogi and we were talking and I could not tell if I were teaching him or he me. We simultaneously shared our talk on the "Two Currents" as the Prana and Rayi courses, the Prana and Apana and were saying mutually that, "when these two currents come to a standstill, that is Death or Samadhi." This dream felt good, affirming, and validating. I awoke in a pleasant mood.

For it is indeed the Experience of the Infinite in the Immanent, which is Nature and the Cosmos. Ramakrishna simplifies for us the whole difficulty of grasping the problem of death. As he said to Sarada his wife, "I have only gone from one room to the next." And whether these rooms be these immense spiritual regions or these grand cosmic pathways, or something much simpler than that, our state is still Guided by the Divine Mother. It is She who reveals Pure Consciousness that follows neither a Northern or Southern course, but goes right up into the Unborn Purest State of Love, Real Being, and Spiritual Light. So have no fear or worry.

It is all God. It is all Mother. Whatever you prefer. It is all Consciousness Absolute and Unborn! Seeing this in the "seven

462

limbs" is part of the Rk Vedic experience. Heaven is his head. The Sun is his eye. Space is his body. Air is his breath. Fire is his speech. Water is his lower region. Earth is his feet. A little different from the description in the section - A -, yet the point is well taken. All that is around us and surrounds us is God or the Gods as you may prefer and to whatever is your level. And not only in the surrounding universe experience of seven limbs seen as manifest God, but more even into the internal experience of one's own limbs or mouths, as we see. He has "seven limbs" and "nineteen mouths," and to this the Vedantasara of Sadananda gives us a beautiful illumination making everything Deity!

In verse 115 it is described how Sound and Hearing are actually the manifestation of the Directions or Quarters, the Diks. Everything is a god. Everything is raised to a Consciousness of Deity. Touch and Sensitivity is nothing but the Deity of Vayu, the Air. Color or Sight is the Deity Surya, the Sun. Taste and the Tongue is Varuna, the Ocean Deity. Everything is connected and interconnected in us. Smell and the Nose are the Ashvins which circulate as Day and Night like our breath circulates in and out through the two nostrils. So, the five senses and the objects of perception as well as the vasanic impression of these has been raised to Deity consciousness. These are the jnana indriyas or knowledge organs (mouths).

Next comes the organs of action, the karma indriyas. Speaking is nothing but Agni, the Sacred Fire. The hands themselves and acceptance with the hands are nothing but Indra. The feet and walking are Vishnu. Then excretion and the anus are Yama, the deity of death. The sex organs and enjoyment are the god Prajapati, another name for the Creator. So far, the karma and jnana indriyas make ten mouths deified in us as created beings.

The next four mouths making fourteen mouths which a few Upanishads identify as the mouths or experiencers of the waking and dreaming states, having left out the five pranas which in the beauty of pranic thought are not five divergences but One Energy (which is felt in deep sleep). Now, of the four psychic functions, the Mind is nothing but the deity of the Moon, Chandra. Intellect is the god Brahma, the Creator. Egoism is

Shiva himself. And the Memory is Vishnu and nothing but, for our memories indeed support us, as Vishnu supports the universe. I suppose egoism is what is destroyed in Shiva, leaving only Consciousness. Intellect is obvious as it creates our world or rather the perception of how and what we see or notice at any given time. And Moon as Mind is certainly symbolic as the mind is reflecting the light of Consciousness. (Of course, the Trimurti conception of the three gods, Brahma, Vishnu and Shiva as triple function is a later sequence of development in Upanishadic writing and not so purely present in Rk Vedic originality. The triple idea was there but not so pronounced.)

The five pranas completing the nineteen mouths. Prana, apana, samana, vyana and udana. Upward, downward, centrally circulating, pervading all the system and what lifts consciousness into dream away from the ten outer mouths or helps to carry the soul (atma) up at death, respectively. Ten mouths of karma and jnana indriyas. Five mouths of energy. And four functions of consciousness make up the "nineteen mouths." But really Prana is One Energy felt in its fullness in the state of deep sleep. Universally this is called Isvara, God Consciousness, out of which the potential of recreation of the waking and dreaming states individually and collectively, are reborn, remade, remanifest! And this is where they dissolve and return. So in this view Isvara is a higher function than Brahma, Vishnu and Shiva, containing these three within its higher condition.

So, really, when we dream we are dreaming of what was perceived by these deities as impressions or vasanas in the one of shining element as one's own mind alone. This is a clue to how all the universe is within your own consciousness. So as Vedantasara gives it, all these fourteen or nineteen mouths and all surroundings are the Gods. All these gods merge in the Prana which equates with and in the Deep Sleep State is called Prajna, whose secret name meaning is true Wisdom. This state is potential in remanifesting the waking and dreaming states which are composed of nothing but the Gods, and so that is why the Brahma Sutras and the the Mandukyo call this "Yoni" which is the Womb of all!

You see it is Consciousness that is the real taster (mouth), hearing and hearer, the seer of seeing and so forth. The eyes, the ears and so forth are not existing in deep sleep or they have been reduced to their true essence as just Consciousness or they have become One in this Consciousness in the state of deep sleep. Out of this (Yoni) whatever is imagined appears, like it was described in the Chhandogya, where whatever is thought appears in thought, in the after death state or the dream mind state, or the waking, dream and sleep state. This advice or description of enlightened awareness is to behave as if one were in deep sleep with half closed eyes, is indeed the behavior of Isvara as the Eye of God, who sees only what is God in all that is nothing but God!

In the old Rk Vedic view Indra is really the Chief of all the Gods. And Indra is just the Mind deified as the Discerner, and the Organizer of all the gods in function. Remember, "that god, the mind, dreams" then in the dream state. It is the impression of the "seven limbs and nineteen mouths" left in Indra which is the dream state. Do you see the connection Indra is Chief of the Indriyas, the nineteen mouths as organs of functioning life processes? It is so simple!

The old Rk Vedic Poet Path saw everything coming out of this Indra as Mind, Agni as Fire or Luminosity aroused, Soma as Creative Joy and all the rest. God would burst forth for them, the poets. Their thoughts would soar in the divine spiritual freedom of bold vigorous poetic expressions of their identity, awareness and feeling with the Gods and Goddesses or the Great Unborn, and so like Vamadeva, they were no longer animals to the Gods, but became the Gods and even More in the Unborn!

Soma

I will say in truth that what the Soma is in its natural fact, is one's Own Joyful Creative Motion of continuing constant Insight into the Divine which is the source of Soma as that Creative Joy. It is in the relationship of Brahma (Creator), and Prana (Pure Energy), to Soma expressing the wonderment of insight in Indra as the luminosity of Experience, then as Agni and so forth through all the Gods! It is the Creative Joy of God Consciousness always ever moving around the Center of Pure

465

Consciousness and so the Joy that comes forth from Pure Consciousness and its manifest creative energy and delight is this Soma, a great deity held in esteem by the Rk Vedic poets.

But the Soma was also the red bull with white spots, a plant, that was pressed with stones and drained through a cloth and was drank at ceremonial sacred circles. It was most likely the amanita muscaria. The Rig Veda Summary describes two opinions. That of the sage poets who mocked those who needed to drink the Soma and those who drank the Soma. So, when the Buddha came, he was addressing a long time preexisting problem. Buddha destroyed the excessive use of Soma drinking. But there was a drink that brought forth a deep feeling of physical well being, even a sense of immortality in one's consciousness and a dreamlike inebriation.

The real Soma is Spiritual Joy! Soma made the poets feel One with the Gods, or even more, the Unborn Pure Reality, and so they would see all Creation, Heaven and Earth as if coming out from them(Selves), as the Poets, of course! It was the creation of early Religion and yet Religion is within the oldest beings on the Face of Mother Earth who forever and ever, have been looking and searching to Relink (religion's meaning) with their Source! It would seem that, in that poetic vision of divine insight, that it was only the fright and ignorance of other people who could not see the Divine World that you were seeing, at that moment, was indeed, the only barrier. So as Soma there was a drink. As Soma Pavamana it was the Luminosity (Pavamana or Brightness) of Creative Joy.

The poet Lava, realizes his identity with Indra, the Pure Mind and with the One Unborn! He drinks the Soma and he experiences the Creative Joy in the Motion of Mind to Pure Mind and as Pure Mind knowing himself exalted as Indra, for he now speaks as Indra. Rk Veda X 119. "The Heavens and Earth themselves have not grown equal to one half of me! Have I not drunk of Soma juice? I in my Grandeur have surpassed the Heavens and all the spacious Earth! Have I not drunk of Soma juice? Aha! This spacious Earth I will deposit either here or there! Have I not drunk of Soma juice? In one short moment I will destroy the Earth in fury here or there! Have I not drunk of

466

Soma juice? One of my flanks is in the Sky, I let the other trail below! Have I not drunk of Some juice?" So you can clearly see from this example the Height of Feeling that is described by the poet in the Moment of Divine Insight as Indra, and the kind of godly feeling produced with this awareness in consciousness!

Many spiritual ideas can be understood from the Height of this kind of Consciousness. For example, how one of the seven sages, Kasyapa, could be identified as being the One who birthed the Kurma Avatara, the Incarnation of God as the Turtle who kept the world from drowning in the flood. A human being giving birth to such a symbolic creature! Even more so one might comprehend in a glimpse of Insight the True Teaching Power of the Immense Spirit as Ramakrishna saw This in his state of Bhavamukha! Or the Immense Creative Power of the Brahman, the Infinite, where Vamadeva while knowing that, "I was Manu. I was the Sun," felt he was Kutsa's master, the poet Usana and Kakshivat too.

Vak

Not only Vamadeva, but Vak, the daughter of Ambrina, gives the vigor of Light in Rk Vedic verse. She raises herself in Identity to the Goddess of Atma Jnana (Self Knowledge) in song and speaks not as a woman sagess and poetess but as the Goddess of Speech Herself (Vak) which is coincidentally her name as well. In Rk Veda X 71., She tells to us in the Voice of the Pure Mind, "One man has never seen Vak and yet he sees! One man has hearing but he has never heard Her! But to another She has shown Her Beauty as a fond well dressed woman to her husband." In different ways Pure Mind is known by some and not by others, but when it is known it comes like a woman to her husband, completely natural in its arrival. "No part in Vak has he who has abandoned his own dear friend who knows the truth of Friendship." Like, Prahlada one knows the Self in Pure Mind is the best of Dear Friends. Now the mutual sharing of the Ancient Method and two kinds of knowers are described. "When friendly Brahmins sacrifice together with mental impulse which the heart has fashioned, They leave one (you or others) far

467

behind in their attainments and some who count as Brahmins wander elsewhere." Perhaps these second types are not knowers at all but only wanderers!

Again in Rk Veda X 125. Vak gives her vigorous poetry not as the woman that she is but as the Goddess Herself. "I am the Queen, the Gatherer up of Treasures, most thoughtful (or the Most Conscious and Aware), the First of those who merit worship (Primary among the Gods). Thus the Gods have established Me in many Places (as She is Everywhere) with many homes to enter and abide in (as every potential place for enlightenment and its preservation). Through Me alone all eat the food that feeds them (Is it not so, Mother!) each man who sees, breathes, hears the Word Outspoken. They know it not but they dwell beside Me (aware or unaware She is Here). Hear one and all, the Truth as I declare It! I, in truth, Myself announce and utter the Word (Aum) that Gods and Men alike shall welcome! I make the man I love exceedingly mighty (any human or god, woman or man), make him (or her) a sage, a rishi (seer poet) and a Brahman (one who knows the Infinite). I have penetrated Earth and Heaven (Mother is within both and All). On the world's Summit I bring forth the Father (that is at the Beginning, in the Height, She creates God), My home is in the waters, in the Ocean (as everywhere and as where life starts). Thence I extend over all existing creatures, and touch even yonder Heaven with my forehead (again the All pervasive First Most "A") I breathe a strong breath like the wind and tempest (Prana as all life giving Energy), the while I hold together all Existence! Beyond this wide Earth and beyond the Heavens I have become so Mighty in My Grandeur!" The Awareness of Vak the Poetess is raised to that State where she speaks as She, the Goddess!

Kabandha

Uddalaka, Yajnavalkya's teacher, is talking and tells of this. "In the country of Madra, in the house of Patanchala, of the line of Kapi we lived... His wife was possessed by a gandharva. We asked him, the gandharva: "Who are you?" He said: I am

468

Kabandha, the son of Atharvan." Brihadaranyaka III 7. 1. Well, they continue to talk with the gandharva (a male love spirit), an apsarasa is a female love spirit, they both enjoy sexuality, music and so forth, some munis (sages) are said to tread the path of the apsarasas and gandharvas. So, the questioner (in the first telling it is the daughter who has a gandharva and Bhujyu questions the gandharva named Sudhavan of the Angiras family, asking of the limit of the world and where are Parikshit's family) at this time is rather debunked by the gandharva (or the woman) in his knowledge about the Sutra Atman (the Thread of Self) or the Self as the Inner Director and Controller of all creation, life, the entire universe. So, some very interesting ideas are here. Let us be free of all superstition first! Is this really a disembodied gandharva love spirit who is a spiritual teacher or one who can give teachings to Uddalaka or Bhujyu? Or is this a disguise for the the woman's Spiritual Power? She tests and debunks Uddalaka making it clear to him that there is a Power greater than he! Is this a phenomena of Spontaneous Self Awareness and Teaching couched in myth and superstition so as not to make it that a woman here is more spiritually alert and awakened than a man? I am thinking that is what it is, for I do not believe in possession.

The Salt Doll

Yajnavalkya speaks to his beloved wife Maitreyi in the Brihadaranyaka. II 4. 12. "As a lump of salt dropped into the water becomes dissolved in water and cannot be taken out again, but wherever we taste the water it tastes salt, even so my dear, this Great, Endless, Infinite Reality is Pure Intellect alone! This self comes out as a separate entity from these elements and with their destruction this separate existence also is destroyed. After attaining Oneness it has no more consciousness. That is what I say my Dear." This was a favorite illustration of Ramakrishna's as to the salt doll that went to measure the Deep of the Ocean and could not come back to explain how deep it is, the Infinite, because the salt doll has dissolved.

Now if that gandharva, Kabandha had really understood the

Infinite Inner Controller would not his consciousness too have dissolved in that Inner Controller and so no longer would have been holding to the subtle form of a gandharva, unless the craving for enjoyments is so high that such a subtle existence is generated! The thought is an interesting one! We are all just lumps of salt compared to the Shores of the Infinite!

Ramakrishna is said to have spent six months in this Nirvikalpa Samadhi where the "salt doll" has dissolved, yet I found it of great interest to see in the Yoga Vasistha that Uddalaka was one other too who spent six months in Nirvikalpa Samadhi. This is when the Mahad Yasah (Great Glory) Shines even free of the highest and pure stage of Pure Intellect. "He has no master in the world." Svetasvatara VI 9. "No one can grasp Him above, across, or in the middle. There is no likeness of Him. His name is Great Glory (Mahad Yasah). His form is not an object of vision; no one beholds Him with the eyes. They who, through Pure Intellect and Knowledge of Unity based upon reflection, realize Him as abiding in the heart become Immortal." IV 19 - 20. This One, though addressed as God, is Reality, and the Author of all that is in time and so there cannot be found any likeness of this Pure Reality within Time, no gods, no teachers, no poets, no nothing! Not even the purest of the Purest Intellect!

The Chhandogya says This is the "Tajjalan." From "Tad" (Brahman) the universe arises "ja" and disappears "li' and so the universe is Brahman create, living, breathing "an" and moving as past, present and future never distinct from Brahman.

Incarnations of God Consciousness in Natural Powers

Have modern beings forgotten the Voice of God Consciousness that is ever speaking within Immanent Nature? Do we no longer hear and listen, see and feel in our bones the Voice, Directly and Purely? The Fish, Tortoise and Boar Avataras represent the emergence of early life from the Ocean, the development of the amphibian and then the full air breathing land animal. It is evolution as myth. Again the half man, half lion is the stage of animal and human emergence. (Narasimha story told under subtitle Prahlada.) The Dwarf represents the

470

young or early human. Parasurama is human and yet savage. Rama and Krishna together are the representation of the development of warrior and lover, of prince and king, of dignity and cosmic awareness! Buddha is the perfectly Peaceful human being. And Kalki is perhaps an expectation of further development toward complete resolution of all Consciousness as a Krishna and Kali mix! Was this Ramakrishna?

In these Avataras one finds interesting stages where Veda (or just Knowledge) is lost, found, regained, protected, demonstrated, revived, emerges and so forth. I think the line of Avataras reflect what are stages of spiritual development couched in myth, uncovered by our development, regained and so forth, in like as Knowledge.

The Fish, Matsya, is Consciousness submerged, and so this Consciousness is raised by God (or Consciousness) itself. This fact stands out even though there was a time when the world or some of it was flooded from glaciers melting.

The Tortoise, Kurma, is really God or Consciousness supporting the subconscious from sinking. The gods and demons use the serpent Vasuki to churn the Ocean on the back of the turtle, who is supporting a bit of land. The gods and demons bring forth the Nectar (Amrita) of Immortality from the Ocean of the unconscious. More than nectar is brought up: the cup of the gods, the fortune and wealth of the Goddess, the moon on Shiva's forehead, the most attractive apsarasa Rambha, the sacred white horse, the Kaustubha jewel, the wish fulfilling tree, the cow of plenty (kamadhenu: granting all desires), the white elephant, the conch shell, the bow, all these rise forth from the churning of the unconscious. As we all must do in fact, as to clarify our own consciousness.

The Boar, Varaha, is a step further on. It is the divine stubbornness of Consciousness ever rising upward. Nothing can keep it down. It is the vigor of Consciousness that destroys delusion or containment of the spirit, as all the avataras function in this way. We find that Kasyapa and Diti together birthed Hiranyaksha and Hiranyakasipu who are brothers. As it is being gradually mentioned here and there, Kasyapa and Diti are the parents of so many, even the Kurma, Tortoise avatara is parented

471

by Kasyapa. Hiranyakasipu's brother, Hiranyaksha had conquered the world, as demons want and are so attracted to the world, they usually want to conquer it. And so he does and of course the gods become threatened by this. So Vishnu comes in the form of a boar and impales him with his golden tusks. You see, Hiranyaksha had received a boon from doing his austerities and this was of course invulnerability and immortality as demons are so inclined to try very hard to preserve their mortal frames. But in the conditions of this boon he forgot to mention that one thing, a boar, and so Vishnu appeared in that form. Are demons forgetful or is it that we cannot outwit the Spiritual? As his brother also, Hiranyakasipu, in the story of Prahlada and Narasimha, listed every possibility that could destroy him, but he never thought of a half man, half lion! The lesson is, we are clever, but never as clever as What Humbles us all!

I feel that the myths relating to these two brothers are actually dealing with how difficult it was for the Indo Aryans to conquer and uproot Mohenjo Daro and the other cities, for it took some five hundred to one thousand years to do this, and mythologically, we find these tales of invulnerability and immortality.

You see, Kasyapa and Diti birthed the brothers Hiranyaksha, and Hiranyakasipu, who was Prahlada's father. Prahlada gives birth to Vairochana who fathers Bali. Bali is the significant character in the Dwarf incarnation. But first, it seems that the Man Lion, or the Narasimha incarnation is one of bringing forth Individual Consciousness Awareness, as was seen in the detailed story of Prahlada, a very important one. One interesting note of thought is that the Mandukyo and the Mundaka Upanishads state of a knower of Brahman, "No one ignorant of Brahman is ever born in his family." Prahlada was certainly a knower of the best stage, yet the Chhandogya describes Vairochana, his son, as not being enlightened at all, but very comfortable with the idea that the body is reality. But the Yoga Vasistha describes Vairochana as being somewhat enlightened. So this is a contradiction of example.

The Dwarf, Vamana or Upendra is the Emergence of Self out of a complex myth illustration. It embodies the three steps of

472

God, which are the three states of consciousness. And it is a story teaching Humility! Now it is evident that Bali is a Dasa, one from Mohenjo Daro and he is said to be an Asura, a demon, as all others not Aryan were identified. So once again the Dasa asuras have conquered what was known as the world. Indra becomes very threatened (a Vedic anxiety) by Bali's power. Bali is a very generous demon. He is a very good hearted demon, like his grandfather Prahlada. Kasyapa and Diti give birth to the dwarf boy Upendra (the Younger of Indra) or Vamana (Beautiful One). Vamana goes to Bali and asks for a favor, three steps of land. Bali, of course, being so generous, says yes. In two steps he covers heaven and earth with his miraculous stride. Bali in his grand humility offers his own head to honor the promise of three steps and so the dwarf boy takes that third step and covers Bali and all the kingdom of demons described as Patala. But Upendra later gives back this area of the universe to Bali. Malabar people still celebrate Bali as their king every year.

This story shows God or Consciousness conquering with Kind and Gentle Intelligence. There are some very interesting points also. Sukra is Bali's guru and he tries and tries to warn Bali and turn him away from honoring or making his generous promise to God. Here the guru is a dark distraction. In the Yoga Vasishtha it s described how Sukra learned the art of bodily resurrection. It is the demon science of the demon guru for they are so concerned with preserving the flesh since the body is the ideal of reality. Well, even so, Sukra is later given the planet Venus as planetary reminder of his life. Even of more interest is Krishna saying in the Gita and the Bhagavatam, "of the Wise, I am Sukra." Sukra is also Kavi, the Poet and even thought to be one of the mind born sons of Brahma (God). But here too, Krishna is Vamana, the Avatara of Vishnu, so in Spiritual Essence they are the same being, as demonstration of the Continuity of Consciousness in preserving the idea of Reality of Earth. So Krishna is identified as both the antagonistic guru Sukra who tries to turn Bali away from the direct God encounter, and Krishna is also the Kind Insight of Upendra, so being both, he closes up of the gap of duality!

473

Unbelievable procreative powers are projected on Kasyapa. He is said to be a Mind Born Son of Brahma, yet other accounts say his human father is Marici who is one of the seven sages from the previous cycle (manvantara). It is confusing. Kasyapa married Aditi, a Vedic Goddess, and birthed other Gods: Vishnu, Indra, Visvavat, Mitra, Varuna, Pusan, Tvastar, Bhaga, Aryaman, Dhatr, Savitri, and Amsa. With other wives he gives birth to the gandharvas and apsarasas, demons, ghosts, numerous celestial and terrestrial animals, snakes, birds, buffaloes, cattle, hawks, vultures, even vegetables and trees. It is truly astounding and even more, it is said that Kasyapa and Diti reincarnate to become the parents of Rama (Dasaratha and Kausalya) and then reincarnate again to become the parents of Krishna (Vasudeva and Devaki). Kasyapa is even said to be the father of Narada. Some accounts say he is the father of one of the Manus (Vaivasvata) or the father of the father of the human race. The last verse of the Chhandogya says Kasyapa was taught directly by God (Brahma) and that Kasyapa taught the first man, Manu. So he indicates the Ancient Method in a deep way. The seer Ambhini learns of Reality from the Sun, again the Ancient Method. (Brihadaranyaka VI 5. 3.) The lineages of teachers gets quite confusing, so perhaps that is why the enlightened scholar Ranade doest not give much credence to those lineages. Other Kasyapas are also described as the families (gotras) often used the same name again and again.

The Yoga Vasistha tells us of Bali's awakening in meeting Upendra as God. The negative distraction of the guru did not interfere. He learned Humility to the Deep of God without which all efforts are but pouring offerings into piles of ashes. He realized the grand fun and joy of life and that no one has bound him, in any manner whatsoever and that he does not even need to long for liberation since it is ever present. Even though he met with God, he gives up any dependence on God, and prefers the Ancient Method of self exertion and grinding one's own teeth to attain Reality. Nevertheless he continued to rule in his arena and as it is said, fondly sported with women.

Incarnations of God Consciousness Within Human Beings

474

Parasu Rama comes next, demonstrating the Continuity of Consciousness as he has Meeting with Lord Rama. There is no break in God Consciousness. The axe (parasu) problem is here as demonstrating how difficult it is to get over the most challenging samskaras (psychic impressions).

Parasurama is the son of Jamadagni and Renuka. Bhrgu birthed Aurva who birthed Rcika who birthed Jamadagni. Visvamitra also is born from this branch. Two of the seven sages come from the older cycle of seven sages. Jamadagni is one of these. It will make more sense latter.

One day Renuka was at a river and she looked upon the king of the Gandharvas, Chitraratha. Lord Krishna has said, "Of the Gandharvas, I am Chitraratha." Of note, is, there is human joy, the joy of the manes (ancestors), above that the joy of the apsarasas and gandharvas, then the joy of gods attained by humans through ritual, the natural born gods, the Joy of Pure Prana and Brahman the Infinite. The manes are ancestor souls once human now somewhat deity-like. The Vedic deity Aryaman, the solar energy in our eyes, is the chief of the manes. Nevertheless, getting back to the story. Jamadagni gets so enraged and furious at Renuka that he tells his sons to kill her, no one will, but Parasurama takes up the axe and slays his own mother. The curse of this most serious samskara will not leave his hand. The axe is stuck there.

Now there is such strange contradiction. Visvamitra is married to Dhrti, one day he sees the Apsarasa Menaka and enjoys her giving birth to Sakuntala who was immortalized by the poet Kalidasa. Sakuntala latter married a human king and gave birth to one of the Bharatas who founded the first empire in North India. The contradiction is that Renuka is murdered by the sage's fury and Visvamitra is praised for helping to birth a king. Renuka only looked upon the gandharva who was actually one of Krishna's many swarupas (Self Forms).

You will find in the Upanishads verses that say the knowledge of Brahman will kill your enemies. Of course, this is metaphorical of delusion. Still, Ramakrishna worshiped the Divine Mother, in Maya itself and She revealed Reality to him without these feelings of antagonism. Other famous rishis killed women by turning them to stone. Such wicked acts are justified by saying these sages are maintaining dharma, but I do not see that killing like that is dharmic! Marici cursed Dharmavrata to stone, when she stopped rubbing his feet to greet the Creator Brahma. A guru, jealous of her Direct Encounter with God! Indra in a lustful mood seduced Ahalya, so Gautama cursed her to turn to stone which is to die. And Visvamitra cursed the apsarasa Rambha turning her to stone when Indra sent her to distract him. Gautama became so excited at the sight of the apsarasa Urvasi his seed fell on the ground and Krpa and Krpi were born. On another occasion Visvamitra became enchanted with the apsarasa Ghrtaci and made love to her for ten years. So with all this Jamadagni's action of killing by command is quite hypocritical!

The story goes on, king Kartaviraya comes and steals Jamadagni's wish granting cow (Kamadhenu?) and so the sage sends his son to kill the king. Parasurama returns and the sage says I will grant you a wish. Restore my Mother. Renuka is brought back to life. Kartaviraya's son out of his rage comes and kills Jamadagni. Parasurama becomes enraged and kills every living kshattriya he can find. After this he gives the land to Kasyapa, the sage. Sometime after this the axe falls from his hand. He meets Lord Rama (as Vishnu incarnate and reincarnate we have a double avatara), but he is jealous of Rama for breaking the bow of Shiva in Janaka's court to win Sita. These two avataras fight each other and Lord Rama knocks him senseless. He retires to the forest for twelve years. He teaches Arjuna war arts. He fights Bhisma in the Mahabharata. Mythologically and in consistent history you see a time problem of course. This avatara is living through his own, Rama's era (which is consistent) and then Krishna's era. Certainly, Parasurama is still a manifestation of some lesson in God Consciousness through the stage of savage horror. I feel sorry for him.

The Incarnations of Rama, Krishna and Buddha are so well known I do not find it of need to go into great detail. Some lists give Balarama instead of Buddha. He was the elder brother of

Lord Krishna, which gives you a double incarnation, God in two places. Other minor avataras include Dhanvantari appearing from the ocean, Hayagriva told in the story of Yajnavalkya, Kapila, the Samkhya philosopher, Mohini, an enchantress who duped the demons to give back the nectar of the gods, Nara - Narayana, the two brothers who are the Man Lion split and reborn. Nara from the human half and Narayana from the lion half. Vyasa, the Vedic scholar, Jagannatha, world lord, Panduranga Vitthala or Vithoba, like a little Krishna, Ranganatha, Varadaraja, Venkatesa, Visvaksena and a few others.

Rama is symbolic of God not Knowing he is God. So much like us all. He is the dignity of the warrior. He needed teaching from Vasistha and he cooled the rage between Vasistha and Visvamitra. It is of deep interest to me to note that his arch rival Ravana is actually a son of Pulastya, a rishi of the sacred seven from a previous cycle, mothered by Puspotkata, showing an interesting relation between the antagonist and the savior descending both from the sages. Also Hanuman, may have been a Dravidian or even perhaps a Cro Magnon.

In Krishna one finds the development of Consciousness as the Lover and as Cosmic Consciousness. Krishna as Krishna really needed no teachers. They were as in the case of Ramakrishna, only a formality. Two accounts are given with Krishna. The Chhandogya describes a Krishna, son of Devaki, who is taught by Angiras? Probably not our Krishna. Then the Bhagavatam describes Krishna studying the Vedas with Sandipani, but as with Ramakrishna, the disciple is of more value to the guru than the guru is to the disciple, for the legend tells that Krishna raised the dead son of Sandipani back to life. Ramakrishna did not raise the dead, but he taught his gurus more than they taught him. It is of deep spiritual interest that Ramakrishna said, "He who was Rama and he who was Krishna is now Ramakrishna, but not in your Vedantic sense." He told this to Vivekananda on his death. Can one know one's prior spiritual origin? Is it a Continuity of a conscious personality? Is it an intentional soul returning? Certainly it is a Continuity of Consciousness!

In the Buddha Sakyamuni you find Perfect Awareness, Peace, Love and Compassion manifest. Vivekananda said he was the "most Sane man" the world has known. He rejected all teachers (Arada and Rudraka) other than the Self! The current of No Harm to others was put into motion. But for many reasons, the Hindu belief system could not abide the Buddha. Ideas arose that the Gods felt humans had become too clever and questioned the Vedas and since the Gods (or maybe the gurus) worried humans would stop worshiping them they sent the Buddha to confuse human beings with the doctrine of the Void. Other absurd and ridiculous things have been said. That he was a devious advocate of human beings and wished to destroy the worship of the gods and so taught that pleasure is heaven, bodily suffering is hell, and death is but peaceful rest, which is not the doctrine of Buddha at all! Added to this is that the Goddess Lakshimi appeared with him on Earth as most beautiful women who came to make men lose themselves in sex lust. This is all deceptive and untrue statements about the Buddha.

Kalki is the Incarnation to come as it is thought. I think in truth it is that we should come to the Consciousness of Fulfillment in the Now of Kali destroying all that is not Absolute Truth! But the common syndrome is that Kalki is Vishnu (Krishna) returning to Earth on a white flying horse swinging a sword to destroy all who have turned against dharma. To me it seems like a cross pollination of the Christian ideal in the Book of Revelations. I think it is toxically apocalyptic and fearful. The description is the end of an age with enough to describe the world as it is now to generate some fear. Truth and Love disappear. All becomes but outward empty show and pretense. Meanness and killing become very prevalent by the example of kings (politicians). Marriage becomes sex based and not for the reason of love. Materialism rises. Religion and Sacred ritual practices decline. And to our relief which we have not yet seen, people are reduced to a primitive state, wearing bark for clothes and eating only roots and fruits. And neither women nor men then live past the age of twenty three years. This is suppose to be the Kali yuga, where all has become dark. It sounds of an atomic apocalypse. But it may have already passed, in reality, as calculation based on the Sun's twenty four thousand year orbit around another nearby Star. According to this Christ appeared right smack dead in the middle of the Kali yuga. And that time has passed. So don't freak out and panic in the sweat of millennial fever.

The Seven Sages and the One Poet

For years I have thought about what Ramakrishna has said about before his birth, going to the region of the seven sages, whispering into one of their ears to come with him, and that is how Vivekananda was born. Remember, Vivekananda has said that he would not rest until everyone has realized God, such was his Love for humanity and his fearlessness of being reborn!

These seven sages are the legendary Mind Born sons of God, the Creator Brahma, but strangely enough all of them have previous human fathers as we shall see. So you can be at rest that no one has yet sprung out of God like a flower from the ground, unless you consider millions of years and more as that process. All this is metaphorical, so the Mind Born sages are born out of the Pure Mind within one and all, as a Spontaneous demonstration of the Ancient Method of Direct Awareness.

The Brihadaranyaka II 2. 4. describes the mystery of the human head as a bowl containing spiritual secrets. The seven sages dwell here. The right ear is Gautama, the left Bharadvaja. The right eye is Visvamitra, the left is Jamadagni. The right nostril is Vasistha, the left is Kasyapa. And the tongue or mouth is Atri. Who would you say was Vivekananda based on this symbolically sage empowered head? I think of it more as character based. Kasyapa was it seems the most powerful of all and any of the seven sages. He gave Birth to Gods like Indra and Vishnu by joining with the Sun (Aditi) and his character is good. He did not go into rage like Vasistha and Visvamitra. He did not curse like Gautama, nor kill like Jamadagni. Bharadvaja perhaps? Or Atri, who with Anasuya gave birth to Dattatreya, who was an Incarnation of Brahma, Vishnu and Shiva together?

I was thinking it could be the sage of the right eye because as Gaudapada says this is the seat of waking state experiences and that is where we are unknowing of our God Reality within because we are distracted out. But here are questionable things about Visvamitra and there was never anything questionable about Swami Vivekananda! So perhaps he was Kasyapa because of his power or Atri! I thought too for a long time that Swami may have been one of the First Born of God, as the legend says of them who sprang forth from Hiranya (Luminous) Garbha (Womb) of the Pure Prana which is the First Manifestation of the Infinite Brahman, uninterested in the world! So latter the seven sages were Mind Born with more instinct for the world as that is evident. The four first born are: Sanaka, Sanandana, Sanatana and Sanatkumara (who is Narada's legendary teacher). They are four eternally youthful beings who just meditate all the time enjoying Bliss. The seven sages and the four Manus (first men) were created latter and they helped give birth to creation as they were bestowed with the power to create gods, other humans, animals, planets, vegetable, herbs, fruits and so forth. (See Nikhilananda's Bhagavad Gita page 238.)

All right then. The Real Rishi is the Eka Rishi, the One, The Poet, the Prana. Rk Veda X 82. 2. "Their offerings Joy in rich juice where they value One, only One, beyond the Seven Rishis." This is extremely good as the poet Visvakarman who is named in the deity Visvakarman (World Maker) describes the importance and final Value of the One! The Prasna Upanishad also describes, II. 11. "Thou art vratya, O Prana and the Eka Rishi Fire that devours butter." Butter is life and nourishment. Here too "vratya" is one who receives no worship, for Prana was before any created being was made and so who was there to give worship. This is the One, or the Energy Power of the One. This is the Power of Aum! Aum is Pranava!

Today the seven rishis are said to have their abodes on, or as, the seven stars of Ursa Major. Their wives on the Pleiades. Connecting this to the rishis being the seven portals of the head you find the attempt to portray to the mind a vast extent of connection and interconnection which fulfills itself in awakening to the sweet and immense Power of All Pervasive Prana! It is a cosmic poetic picture of inter-connection.

If we look back into the more recent past of three previous

cycles (manvantaras) we find there are thirteen sacred sages, that appear alternately in group combinations of seven. The Puranas give fourteen manvantaras or cycles of the seven sages going back in time. Some names are recycled over and over and there are so many other names as well. These sage cycles exist within yugas (other cycles) and these exist within Kalpas that are the days and nights of God that extend to the life span of the Universe as the Life Span of a Creator.

The most recent list is this, with their wives. Visvamitra and Dhrti. Jamadagni and Renuka. Bharadvaja and Vira. Gautama and Ahalya. Atri and Anasuya. Vasistha and Arundhati. Kasyapa and Diti (a human), Aditi (the Sun). The majority have more than one wife. To this primary list are added in alternate variations going back to the second and third cycle and even further with the same names and additions like Medhatithi, Vyasa, Dattoli, Abhimanyu, Kaushitka, Rsyasrnga, and so forth. But these are very old ones. To stay with the recent second and third, to the list we add Agastya and Lopamudra (both poets of the Rk Veda famous for the seductive sex verses), Marici and Sambhuti (with a different woman he fathered Kasyapa), Pulastya and Priti, Kratu and Sannati (who birthed the Valakhilyas of the Rk Veda), Pulaha and Ksama, Angiras and Smtri (Dirghatamas, Gautama and Bharadvaja are born in this line) and Bhrgu and Khyati (Jamadagni and Visvamitra are born in this line). Other lineage trees say Visvamitra was born of the sage Kaushitka who has an Upanishad named after him.

So you see it is quiet complex as a lineage. Bhrgu is said to have learned how to make fire from the dwellers at Mohenjo Daro. Atharvan too. That knowledge goes back thirty five, forty, maybe forty five thousand years. So these lineages are really old. And maybe not so well kept, but pretty good considering their age.

To make the deeper meaning and purpose of the Rishis more clear, please permit me to quote from John E. Mitchiner's spectacular text, Traditions of the Seven Rsis. "... their self-transformation and reabsorption into Brahman brings with it a realization that the very nature of Brahman is dynamic, creative, and ever impelling to motion and change. Brahman is not a static concept or entity, but - like Prana itself - a dynamically creative force." And, "The Rsis' attainment of the center of the turning wheel brings with it the acknowledgement that this center is itself not the negation but the affirmation of motion; indeed, the center is motion, and it is this very motion of the center which provides the impetus for and is itself embodied in the turning wheel." And lastly, "This, then, becomes the goal of the ascetic and mystic within the Rsis traditions: to merge with Brahman or the Absolute, and thence to become identified with the creative self expansion of Brahman within creation." I quote these because they are so helpful in understanding what Ramakrishna meant by the Eternal in the Relative and the Relative in the Eternal. The Nitya and the Lila!

Experience

It is to know past and beyond the evidence of death, the Truth of Love, the absolute most Absolute, as Oneness and Togetherness with the Beloved. No less than, Such Faith in what Ramakrishna has demonstrated and what the Divine Mother Is, that surpasses death in this Togetherness! Even that I should Know Her past the death of my beloved girl woman, for Death comes inevitably to one and all, to accept this as Her Teaching! There is More Power Felt in Trusting My Own Pure Mind Contact as one person who has Come Here! That you think and feel you are missing something is chasing for conch shells and that takes you out from the Goddess Experience, the Kaustubha Jewel, You Are Having Right Now! As Ramakrishna speaks the Truth of Truth, "Whatever appears in the Pure Mind is the voice of God. That which is Pure Mind is also Pure Buddhi; that, again, is Pure Atman, because there is nothing pure but God. But in order to realize God one must go beyond dharma and adharma." Or "go beyond" your measuring of what you think is good or evil, the right or wrong path, the god and guru direction or not, for what do we know of anyone's real condition anyway. And only God (Atman, Buddhi, Pure Mind) is "pure," nothing else!

Yet Another Cursing Guru

Narada sang to Suka and pulled him out of his Samadhi so he could recite the Bhagavatam to King Parikshit at the conclusion of the Mahabharata War. One story was of King Ambarisa. He performed a sacrifice as kings would do. He was supposed to wait for the sage Durvasa before he drank water to break the fast. The king waited and waited. The sage was late, so the king took a little water and terminated the sacrifice and fast. Of course, the sage cursed him in the heat of violent anger, as these sages so often do. The curse took the form of a demon coming to devour Ambarisa, but the king remained clam trusting in God (Krishna) so the demon turned around and went at Durvasa. You would think these sages would learn that cursing people will always come back at them. Durvasa had an unusual enlightenment realizing it was wrong to curse his devotee which is rare for so many of these gurus. He also feared the demon and so begged Ambarisa's forgiveness and of course the kind king did so and the demon (created by the sage's rage) disappeared.

The fright of yet another spiritual personality who might be kind and yet might be abusive. No more gambling with spiritual feeling. I am my own Spiritual Empowerment, vigorous poet easily aroused to the Vast Expanse and Who but the Divine Mother shall say I am permitted to Transfer Consciousness and Know the States of Death already described in my poetry!

I live in my own Siddha Gita within my own Kaustubha Jewel and so deciding not to go to the woman guru or the reincarnated lama. Still hoping and searching for a perfect teacher makes for disappointment. Conserve my Energy here! As psychic powers were said to be in this lama I took Ramakrishna's advice. He watched with a special eye for new mental powers being manifested and "he forbade them to follow those practices for some time, lest egoism should arise in their minds and make them lose sight of the aim of God Realization."

Spiritually, nothing new or unique would be received. Though I miss the Dzogchen sisters and brothers, it is more the

483

company of those in the sacred task. I cannot deal with yet another spiritual personality. Whether I see a lama or guru or not!, it does not change the Unfabricated Primordial! Luminous Spiritual Energy or Pure Void Vast! Is This Solid or Void? Only Sakti will Answer!

Go beyond traditions, Upanishads or otherwise! "Sri Ramakrishna used to say in corroboration of this point: "The state of this place (meaning his own experiences) has gone much beyond what is written in the Vedas and Vedanta." It is, "at Her feet," we come forth, "out of pure Love for Her," as and in, "a sport of Self with the Self," to live in "a mood beyond all moods and ideas."

Mythic Phenomena

It is said that the wonderful poet Tukarama at the time of his realization had the experience of remembering himself in the Bodiless form of Pure Consciousness as being there a witness to Suka's complete Realization on the mountain. This is like Vamadeva and Trisanku and Vac's high states of Consciousness. Beautiful.

Accounts give that Tukarama turned his human body into a Body of Light, so much so just like the Tibetan Jaluspa. But another account says Tukarama drowned in a river when his time came and his body was lost. Faith in myth or reality? It is the same with Suka who is said to have dissolved his body into the Eternal Infinite, just as in the Great Pho Wa transfer of Tibetan yoga. Is it faith in myth or reality? Whatever elevates you!, phenomena or reality. Perhaps rainbow body death is like this, mythic to keep faith alive. Faith should depend on Faith not powers.

The reincarnated lama as claimed, wearing his sunglasses is said to have left his hand print in a rock and drove a wooden staff into solid rock like Excalibur. I saw a photograph of Yeshe Tsogyal's footprint left in solid rock, but to me it looked chiseled and ill formed, funky, not human. Still people want to believe so bad. I was told a long while back of a yogi who was said to be three hundred years old. He would smoke five or six cigarettes held together at one time and drink scalding hot coffee. Like that I don't believe he was three hundred years old. It was a delusion to keep faith alive, like another yogi who was said to be only two hundred and fifty years old. Has that ever been so? "These are physical things and have nothing to do with God." Ramakrishna.

Please do not be contradictory or anxious with that decision, in the non action of engaging those who claim such claims. And please do not be disappointed or wondering if anywhere there would be hope fulfilled genuinely in these concerns. As the Poetess Vac said of this wondering, "And some wander elsewhere." A curiosity with miracles? Or just to be Happy in the Decision of Self, your own Siddha Gita, for the Goddess works Her Miracle of Creation and we notice this not, as we become fascinated with hand prints and old age (true or not), distracting ourselves from Her Wonder Divine and Everywhere!

Origins of Thought

I am still pleasantly amazed that in this part of the world so much fine thought came forth. Original yoga may have come from Mohenjo Daro culture as the very old stone seal of the yogi is from there. And as Mohenjo Daro was the seat of the worship of the Seven Mothers, the Sapta Matrkas, it is most likely the birth zone of Tantra too, as these people worshiped the Divine Mother in the Goddess. There were also Buddhas before Sakyamuni who were said to have practiced Dzogchen. Dipankara being one of those, meditating on the Dzogchen of fire and silence. And the Jain heroes (Viras) also came forth from here with a long pre-Vedic history. From both the Buddhas and the Viras came the Doctrine of Love and Compassion for others in the practice of No Harm (A-himsa)!

Samkhya sprung forth from here through Kapila and yet as Purusha is included in the Upanishads, the doctrine of Kapila is not Vedic.

The Veda arrived in India. And like a dear friend who would like to think they know everything about everything, the Veda would like to claim to be the origin of all good and high

485

thoughts that ever came from this area of the world. But it is probably not so. The creation of a tradition of seven sages may in fact be the design to incorporate the reflection, into male formed Vedic tradition, of a quality of the Seven Mothers of Mohenjo Daro. But who knows since it was all so long ago.

There are thirteen original Upanishads. The Brihadaranyaka, the Chhandogya, the Isa, Kena, Katha, the Aitareya, the Taittiriya, the Prasna, Mundaka and Mandukyo, the Maitri, Kaushitaki and the Svetasvatara. These, except for the tamperings that have been explained are to be trusted as authentic. There are one hundred and eight, to some lists even giving two hundred in total of the number of Upanishads. There is even an Allah Upanishad from the sixteenth century. In fact, some Upanishads were lost in their original Sanskrit and were regained by translating them back from Arabic. What does it tell you? There are now as later developments: Vedanta, Yoga, Sanyasa, Vishnu and Shiva Upanishads. Some have even claimed authorship of an Upanishad in this century. There is even a sweet little book called the Ramakrishna Upanishad which tells of his life and teachings.

Chakravarti writes, "It is unfortunate that the commentators, Sankara and Ramanuja, with their theological bias, should have twisted the Great Doctrine, and kept the world long deprived of the benefit of its inspiration and guidance." I find this true as well in what the Upanishads are saying! It is a message that comes from back and back and back in time from a place where the human mind comprehends the Spiritual Reality in the Self. It is Ati, the Highest. It is Advaita, the Non-Dual. It is as old as the name for Dzogchen, Maha Sampatra, the Entire and Great Receptacle of (your own) Pure Mind. It is Maha Sandhi, the Great Gain, the Great Fulfillment!

Chakravarti continues, "While Sankara was deluded and proclaimed his theory of Maya and destroyed the world. Ramanuja lacked in courage and imagination, and tried to perpetuate the individual. Between the two time honored commentators, the Atman philosophy, containing the highest truths for all time, regarding God, the world and the soul, stood completely mangled." Remarkable, for even as Yajnavalkya

486

defeated his own teacher Uddalaka in philosophical battle, we may see a defeat here, taking place even now, of doctrine twisting which keeps people from the profound message of the Upanishads.

He continues, speaking of Ramanuja who could not deny the reality of the world, like Sankara could, destroying it at the mental level, "... he had a difficult task to perform - to maintain, on the one hand, the integrity of the Atman philosophy, and, on the other, to keep in tact the current trend of thoughts by which he was surrounded, amongst which the maintenance of a deity for human worship, was not the least. The Upanishads boldly preached that there were no gods, no deity to be worshiped. The gods who had been so long thriving on human ignorance, had been dashed to the ground." He writes of rising past the old views, "The initiative always comes from the advance few, who undauntingly travel out of the ordinary rut, and the need for it is felt more than ever in the present times." For the truth is, "But since the philosophers of the Upanishads were able to get at these truths with the help of concentration, they frankly stated that these truths could be perceived by deep concentration by everyone."

Sunahsepa

The story of Sunahsepa is so invaluable it is told again and again. The Rk Veda of course is where the songs of Sunahsepa are found. The Srimad Devi Bhagavatam, the Markendeya Purana and the Aitareya Brahmana all give the story. I would have never understood the story if it were not for the brilliant genius of Dr. Alfred Collins who interprets it with spiritual truth and psychological clarity in From Brahma To A Blade of Grass.

There are different interpreters of the story, some are of questionable account. Yet the story is this. Harischandra wants a son. He begs the god Varuna for a child. The god say yes, but when the son reaches a certain age he must be sacrificed to Varuna. The time comes. Hariscandhra does not want to do this and his son Rohitas runs away to the forest. So he asks Ajigarta, the poor and hungry brahmin guru and father of Sunahsepa for

487

help. Ajigarta says that the king can sacrifice his son Sunahsepa for one hundred cows. Okay, but when it comes to killing Sunahsepa, the king cannot do this because of his tender heart. So Ajigarta says for one hundred more cows he will do it. He approaches for the kill. Sunahsepa sings songs to Varuna. His three bindings tying him to the sacrificial post fall off (some interpreters say these three bindings are symbols for the three knots that obstruct spiritual passage through the sushumna and the chakras as knots of the three states of waking, dreaming and deep sleep). Sunahsepa runs over and jumps in Visvamitra's lap for refuge. This could be seeking refuge in another more kind teacher, but it could be a symbol for seeking God directly, as the songs of Varuna are what break the three bindings. Visvamitra adopts Sunahsepa as his own, but fifty out of his one hundred sons don't accept this adoption. So Visvamitra curses them, as these sages are so want to do.

The invaluable message of this story told over and over again is to never allow yourself to be the sacrificial object of the guru/father. It is to not be the guru's object or self-object of servant sacrifice. As Ramakrishna put it, to be in the "clutches" of such a guru. It is interesting, this story is so old, that the Srimad Devi Bhagavatam says that Vamadeva himself was there and that Vamadeva thought it was appropriate that Sunahsepa be adopted by Visvamitra. The same text gives a variation in the story saying that Harischandra needed to do this sacrifice for the sake of getting rid of a disease, rather than fulfilling his agreement with Varuna. But the first version is older and probably more accurate.

The story certainly gives warning of how evil and deadly it can be to find oneself in the "clutches" of such gurus who are given to spiritual rage and would think of you as dog genitals which is what Sunahsepa means. This is something I cannot abide in my understanding; how such rage can coexist with enlightenment. I am left with the thought that maybe it is not enlightenment, no matter how clever, intelligent or ingenious it may sound.

Ramakrishna and Yajnavalkya

Yajnavalkya says, "Atman alone is real and all else is "artam" a tinsel show." (Ranade's rendering) Brihadaranyaka III 4. 2. And now Ramakrishna says that the Mother showed him, "Brahman alone is real and all else is illusory." Is the Divine Mother illusory? No. She is the Brahman! Yajnavalkya described to Janaka that when the lights of the sun, the moon, fire and sound have gone out then the Light of the Self is what guides a person. This too is Mother. Yajnavalkya describes the Inner Thread Puller, the Atman, moving without moving, thinking without thinking, dreaming and yet unaffected by dream, and waking, yet unaffected by waking, is what is making all of us jump about, our hands and feet going this way or that! This is Mother, She is Brahman, all else, whether it be gods, gurus, or the whole universe, is just a tinsel show, real in itself but a show! Is this yet still, but a solipsistic soliloquy, in Consciousness here, as the world here created is made for the Sake of (Mystical) Experience! Or what Ramakrishna says, "Whatever appears in Pure Mind is the voice of God."

It is the Mother Who is Brahman the Infinite, The Absolute Most Absolute. She is the Arche, the leading, the foremost, the beginning, the oldest, as the first mold of Consciousness and That which is so ancient She has never been molded. Her Knowledge just comes! "Being Brahman, he merges in Brahman." For It is what you Are! "The subtle, Ancient Path, stretching far away has been touched (reached) by me; nay, I have realized it myself." The Janaka within you has always attained it. Having "entered this perilous and perplexing place (the body)... we have somehow realized Brahman." And such a person, "no longer wishes to hide himself from It... the Ancient, the Primordial Brahman! ... through the Mind alone is Brahman realized... diversity leads from death to death." Brihadaranyaka IV 4. 8 - 19.

The Darkening of Woman

The Chhandogya shows contempt for woman as a birth giver in its conclusion, "May I never go to the red and toothless, all devouring, slippery place, yea, may I never go to it." With Ramakrishna, words like "yoni" of which the above verse is describing, would throw him into a state of ecstasy, as even these words, would spark and ignite his mind to the Divine Mother. It is so different in comparison, one is exalted, the other is disgusted. Disgust brings you down, contempt is not liberation of the mind. Only an arrogant ego would think it not so!

Ramakrishna could not stand to see women suffer in any way whatsoever. So when the sexual rituals described in both the Brihadaranyaka (especially) and the Chhandogya recommend hitting the spouse with the hand and if she does not give in for the ritual even then, a stick is advised to beat her into submission. This kind of abuse was completely appalling and revolting to Ramakrishna, as it should be to you. The Yajnavalkya Upanishad (a most questionable latter development) says to Janaka, "Women, pleasing and cruel, are the fuel for hell fire... Silly women are the nets spread by the hunter... Women are the bait stuck in the fish hook... What possibly is charming in a woman who is a doll made of flesh, a cage of limbs which is moved by machinery..." There is more, but enough is said.

Can this be the voice of Yajnavalkya who speaks so tenderly and lovingly to his wife Maitreyi, in the Brihadaranyaka? I do not think so. It must be a corrupt and revolting addition, as many thoughts have been added to the original Upanishads. Is this the voice of the one who says to Maitreyi that it is for the Sake of the Atman, that all these are "dear" and are loved; wife, gods, teachers, pleasures and wealth? Ramakrishna describes the clarity of knowing the Pure Feeling, "Whether you love me or not, I love you. This is Love for Love's Sake!"

What is it that gives love the force of Love? It is none the less than what is at the High Peak! "Then the Atman becomes disembodied and immortal the Spirit, the Supreme Atman, the Prana, Brahman the Light!" Brihadaranyaka IV 4. 7. This is the Energy, the Power and the Reality of Love! There is no contempt, disgust or hatred in this! The mysterious Yajnavalkya states that it is for the Sake of This that all is dear and loved! It is what Walt Whitman said expanding himself as Love for all in his poem "Song of Myself." Ranade explains it as, "In every act of mental affection, the Atman is calling unto the Atman." Or Pure Mind calling unto Pure Mind! As the end of all endeavor is to realize this Love that is so obvious!

For when you read in the Narasimha Purva Tapaniya Upanishad that a teacher who teaches Upanishad (the secret) to a woman or one of lowest cast, will go to hell after death! Can you believe that and if you do you are a fool! It is nothing but rambling stupidity!

Even so there is contradiction even in this contempt, of course! Vasistha tells in the Yoga Vasistha that he has been born thirty one times before as Vasistha and now he is for a thirty second time, Vasistha again. Contempt for the red slippery place! When a sage like Vasistha is reborn just by Mitra and Varuna's seed falling on the ground! Other rishis too, are mythically born spontaneously from seed just falling into a pot, when a rishi gets excited seeing an apsarasa!

Even though Vasistha is Enlightened he still reincarnates. This is really the Buddhist Ideal of Returning Compassion and what Vivekananda said, that he would not rest but come again and again until everyone knows what God is! It makes it easier for us who will naturally reincarnate. One Indian friend of mine, her mother, through some superstitious signs felt that for absolute certainty she would not ever again reincarnate! Perhaps it is so! Who knows the potential of Cognitive Belief and its Power! Another friend, once a monk, was certain he would reincarnate again. Both are directions of Consciousness as Power!

Uddalaka

A teacher may be of help at some time, but Truth is up to You. And the teacher is still in the duality of the mind. Besides that Swami Vivekananda says that you can get it all just from your Self! Is not the Self there in every one of us, purely at One, in Bliss, within the Prana Pure as Deep Sleep? The Ribhu Gita of the Rk Vedic poet sage completely destroys the idea/illusion of the guru. So does the Avadhuta Gita of Dattatreya, the son of the Rk Vedic sages Atri and Anasuya, and though he learns from

491

twenty four teachers, all within Nature, from three humans he learns, by watching: a child, a prostitute and a maiden, and though he learns spiritual truths by observing, they are unaware that he is learning from them. Is not this the best way? And of course, the Pure Advaita of the Ashtavakra Gita, the conversation of exclamation between Janaka and Ashtavakra, destroys the guru idea. How rare, how great, how splendid are those who renounce any kind of guru messiahship. Ramakrishna rejected it! Swami Saradananda writes, "The Master asked the Mother every day to take back from him the position of the teacher, which he regarded as totally worthless, though others yearn for it, on account of the attendant honors."

As Vidyaranya observes, Uddalaka was slower in catching on than Janaka or Prahlada. Here is his story. Though the Brihadaranyaka says that Uddalaka learned from Aruna, in the last section, we find the Laghu Yoga Vasistha saying that he got Supreme Experience through his own effort! He went to a mountain, he dived into his own question, "When will I come to This?" following the Ancient Method! It came to him through the Extraordinary Power of Aum, proving the Truth of the Mandukyo Upanishad, as that carried him through amazing levels of experience and awareness, ultimately up to two stages. Cit Samanya, the Infinite Universal Consciousness and Sat Samanya, the Infinite Universal Being. Remember, this Uddalaka was Yajnavalkya's teacher, who Yajnavalkya defeated in the court of Janaka, so this story must have happened after that, as it will be obvious.

He is described in the story as sitting there in the forest like the Buddha. This must be a latter addition because it is said that Yajnavalkya's doctrine of Purusha Kara, the the Act, Agent, or Effort of one's own Soul, was a way of preparing for the Buddha who would demonstrate this in great ways. Uddalaka observed everything like Dattatreya did. He then practiced the Ancient Method of inner questioning, "Am I all this?" or is there no "I?" Both leading to the examining of the Self! Who am I, what am I made from, what is myself and who made it? The ego is sorrow. I know I am not the body, it is obvious, because a corpse does not function. In all time, everything happens everywhere, in

492

every imaginable way.

And so with half closed eyes he sounded the Aum. The Prana filled him to the crown opening of his head. His body felt like it was roaming, floating through space. The second sound of Aum made him feel as if his body, its very bones, were but pure ashes burnt by Prana, feeling the Oneness of all perceptions in equal treatment. The third sound of Aum brought the nectar of Prana like a cool breeze from the region of the moon, like rain upon the ashes that were left of his body! From these ashes he rose forth in the divine dignity of identifying with Vishnu, feeling as if he had four arms like that God. He realized that all previous ideas were but the mental fabric of past experience. His mind stayed in his heart, not going out, it felt like deepest sleep, but brilliant light shone forth from there and he then experienced the Totality of the Universe existing as nothing but Universal Consciousness. Like a wave merging in the Ocean! With this Uddalaka became enlightened, losing ego, beyond description like the salt doll melted in the sea.

He beheld within the Universal Consciousness, all the many gods and sages, the Creator, the Preserver,and the Destroyer. He paid no attention and went beyond even that state. One taste of This and the delight of heaven compared is sour. Uddalaka remained for six months in this state. He declined again the invitation to heaven. He remained with Equal Vision. This is similar to Ramakrishna's six months in Nirvikalpa Samadhi!

Uddalaka came down to consciousness and thought that he would now drop the body, give it up! In a mountain cave he closed the nine apertures of the body so the Prana could not escape to outward consciousness and remained completely merged in Nirvikalpa Samadhi again, for six months, as Universal Being! This is probably more like Ramakrishna's six months in Nirvikalpa Samadhi. Still, even the greatest joys of heaven were worthless in comparison for him. Uddalaka then died away from the body. This might have happened to Ramakrishna, but a knowing yogi came and would force feed him to keep consciousness in the body and so he came back down. The story goes to say the Goddess came and took the corpse of Uddalaka and placed it on Her Crown! The story concludes saying that study and teachers are good, but that with a clear intellect ("Pure Buddhi, Pure Mind, Pure Atman, all the Same!"), sharp and keen, you will attain everything without any other aid. It is the same in Janaka's story of the Siddhas. "Truth is not had by going to a guru. One's own Inner Luminosity is the means, nothing else!" Uddalaka's journey sounds much like Totapuri's. It took Tota forty years to get Nirvikalpa. Where Ramakrishna got That in one day, for the Goddess had already taught him That when She appeared as the young sadhu who looked just like Ramakrishna and taught him. This was his own Pure Mind coming forth as Her, and indeed this is a modern example of the Ancient. Method. So it seems that Vidyaranya would have certainly included Ramakrishna in the class of Prahlada and Janaka who were so easily roused to Consciousness!

Mood of Spirit

In the Srimad Devi Bhagavatam one finds that Narada is taught directly by the Goddess, but the Chhandogya has Narada learning from one of the first born divine beings, Sanatkumara. When a human speaks with another human it is the path of ordinary learning. When a human speaks to a God or Goddess it is the Path of Self Reflection as the projection of Consciousness in the Reflection of the Goddess! As to the meaning of the word Buddha, Budh or Awake and Ta, to Notice or to Understand. So this is to simply Notice What is Really Awake!

Even the Gods and Demons both as described in the Chhandogya go directly themselves to What Is Awake, here, the Creator, Brahma. Indra and Vairochana both go to Brahma to learn, though each to a different Depth. Vairochana was happy with the waking state, while Indra went through the dream and deep sleep state to know the Atman in Turiya.

Find your own Spiritual Mood, the Bhava of your own Ancient Method, even as the Source of Kali if you wish! You are Free! Let It Be and Be Happy, Be in the Joy that you Are! When I was young, Ramakrishna found me, meeting Ranganathananda. I lost Ramakrishna for years. Yet

494

Ramakrishna found me again when I met Atmavratananda and then to Bhashyananda. Nothing happens without the Will of God or the Goddess! Not even a single leaf may fall! Om Hring Rtam! The Power of Aum and Hring which are the Same Moves Everything That Happens (Rta)!

Adiswarananda said that he told me in forty minutes what it took him forty years to distill and understand. How generous! I wrote of that in "The Deathless Self and the Dramatics of the Psyche." He said that who his guru was, was not important! And he told me to never give up writing even if it is only a hobby. Swahananda told me to defend my position which is intellectual! Aseshananda said, "Your own Atma is the Divine Mother," making me realize that Mother (Ma) moves (at) in me as the Atma! And Chetanananda shared his insight into Bhavamukha. Aparananda taught me Joy! Bhaskarananda has shown me the good reality of the spiritual friend! While Swami Gahanananda answered the question of an American experiencing Kali, simply with, "Why not!" And Bhashyananda said, "Have no fear or anxiety. You are in the Presence of God," to me and my beloved.

Swami Abhedananda said the same thing to others. Have no fear or anxiety! And, "In that Brahman, there is neither the patient nor the physician nor medicine. In the realm of maya, these, the patient, the physician and the medicine, all will remain distinct. Even to the End of the Non-Dual Idea it is "Anal Hawk!" "Not am I, but Thou!" "The divine lover is such a man that he considers him (his body, the temple of God, the Sahaja) as great, and so he does not care even for the state of Indra, the Ruler of the Gods. He is a divine lover, who lives all the time with a smiling face, and thinks this world as an ocean of Love. The divine lover does not care for any caste, nor any praising nor good name, and if any blame is given to him, he lives with his heart full of divine sentiment, without being affected by anything, shortcoming or defect; and the key or source of joy and happiness remains in his own hand, that is, in his control, without depending on others." Aum! The End!

495

Glossary

Advaita   Non-Duality.   An example.   If you are in a lighted room you see many objects.   Turn the light off and you see only darkness which naturally occurs in the nirodha of deep sleep. Advaita is one step more.   You are the Light, the very Seer Self perceiving the the dark and the many.   And Gaudapada's third section to his Karika commentary.

Agama Prakarana   First section of Gaudapada explaining Aum.

Ajata/Ajati   the masculine and feminine meaning the unborn, never born to dualism

Alatasanti   Quenching the Firebrand, Gaudapada's fourth section

Alaya-vijnana   the store house consciousness, like the unconscious, but more extensive, storing in the house of the mind the entire expanse of creation.

Amanibhava   the mood free of the mind

Antara Bhava   the inner mood in the after death state

Arada   Sakyamuni's savikalpa samadhi teacher

Ashtavakra   a great Advaitic thinker, friend of Janaka

Asparsa   No contact, no grasping at duality

Ati Yoga   highest yoga, same as Dzogchen

Atma or Atman   the true Self, the genuine Self

Avasthatraya   the three states: waking, dreaming and deep sleep

Avatara   an incarnation

Bardo the between state between any two conditions

Bhagavati Tanu   the pure Spiritual Body of the Divine Mother

Bhava   mood, feeling, attitude

Bhavagra   the Summit of Mood, Feeling, or Attitude, the Summit of Becoming

Bhavamukha   the Supreme Mood of Facing the Infinite

Bija   seed of a mantra, or of creation itself or anything in between

Bindu   point or drop or essence

Bodha   Consciousness

Bodhichitta   Compassionate Consciousness

Bodhisattva a compassionate person

Brahma the Creator aspect of God Consciousness

Brahmacharya vow of celibacy

Brahman Infinite Reality

Brahmani Bhairavi Ramakrishna's Tantra teacher

Bu the offspring mind

Buddha Awakened

Buddhi intellect

Chikhai Clear Light of Death

Chodpa a sacrifice of cutting away obscurations

Chonyid what appears in the after death state after the Clear Mother Light

Dakini the Tibetan Goddess (Divine Mother)

Dattatreya a very ancient Advaitic soul, an incarnation, a contemporary of Janaka

Dharma has many meanings: right action in life, right course of life, the path, the teachings, the soul (jiva) in the confluence of the karmic "I" compound and at last Reality itself.

Dharma Dhatu Reality Indestructible, Foundational Supreme Essence

Dharmakaya Reality Actuality Dimension

Dharmata when whatever appears in the here or the here after is seen only in the Light of the Mother Reality

Garab Dorje the great Dzogchen thinker

Garuda the spiritual divine bird which represents the flight of one's own mind

Gaudapada the great Advaitic thinker

Heruka a wrathful psychic spiritual image, a wrathful yidam

Indra the intellect as a divine deity

Ishta a chosen Spiritual Ideal

Isvara the Godhead over creation

Janaka the king, the Advaitic thinker, the father of Sita who was Rama's wife and the friend of Ashtavakra

Jigme Lingpa the great Dzogchen thinker and composer of the Longchen Nyingthig

Jiva the individual soul bound by karmic confluences

Jnana Pure Knowledge, Pure Wisdom

Kali the Divine Mother

497

Kama the desire for pleasure

Karma cause and effect

Karmic "I" the jiva/dharma confluence of identity based on the temporal conjunctions of cause and effect

Karunam Pure Compassion

Khadroma the Dakini as one who goes or dances in the sky of Pure Mind

Kung Zhi same as Alaya-vijnana, the base out of which manifests the Zhi Khro

Kuntu Zang Mo/Po pure spiritual Dharmakaya Divine Mother and Father

Kutastha the Witness Consciousness dynamically engaged with the appearance and disappearance of the three states of waking, dreaming and deep sleep

Lila the Relative, the Play of the Divine Mother

Longchen Nyingthig the Dzogchen teachings of the Heart Essence of the Vast Expanse

Longchenpa the great Dzogchen thinker and writer

Longchen Rabjampa same as Longchenpa

Ma the Divine Mother, the Natural Light of Pure Mind

Madhura Bhava the Mood of Lovers

Maha Mudra the Great Gesture

Maha Sukha Kaya Great Bliss Actuality Dimension

Maha Vidya Goddesses there are ten Great Wisdom Goddesses: Kali, Tara, Tripura Sundari, Bhuvaneswari, Tripura Bhairavi, Chinnamasta, Dhumavati, Bagla Mukhi, Matangi, and Kamala. They are all manifestations of the Radiant Excellent Wisdom of the Divine Mother

Manjushri the Gentle Lord of the Dharmakaya

Mantra Diksha initiation into a mantra

Mara Buddhist term for illusion or death's illusion

Ma-rigpa ignorance (avidya)

Maya cosmic illusion where in Real identity gets lost

Nadi spiritual nerve canals, channels, systems

Nirmanakaya Emanation Actuality Dimension

Nirodha cessation of relative phenomenal mind

Nirvana without waves, peace

Nirvikalpa without conceptuality

498

Nitya the Eternal Innate Reality

Padma leks grub (1608 - ?) the excellent Dzogchen thinker and writer, author of the extraordinary manuscript, The Sun's Life Giving Force or The Explanation of The Intrinsic Meaning of The Indestructible Light That Is The Sublime And Most Mysterious And Unsurpassable Message Of All Spiritual Pursuits For the translation see Herbert Guenther's amazing book, Meditation Differently.

Pho Wa Chenpo the Great Transference of Consciousness at Death

Prana the Vital Life Energy

Prajna or prajna Supreme Wisdom and deep sleep

Prajna Paramita the doctrine and the Goddess of Supreme Wisdom

Prajnata a seed of Consciousness

Prakriti the Energy Behind Mother Nature and all that manifests as Nature, physical, subtle, cosmic

Pratyeka a solitary practitioner

Ramakrishna 1836 - 1886, the mystic of Dakshineswar who devoted his whole life to the Divine Mother

Rigpa the clear light of wisdom (vidya)

Rudraka Sakyamuni's nirvikalpa teacher

Sadhaka one who does spiritual practice to ground oneself in Reality

Sada Shiva the always and ever present Consciousness as Shiva

Sahajakaya the Natural Innate Self Reality Actuality Dimension

Sakshi The Witness Consciousness which is not engaged with the coming and going of the three states of consciousness, waking, dreaming and deep sleep

Sakti the Primordial Mother Reality and Her Power

Sakyamuni name of the human being who became the awakened Buddha, meaning the sage of the Sakya clan

Samantha Bhadri/Bhadra the Divine Mother and Father as the Primordial Ground Luminosity

Sambhogakaya Resplendent Actuality Dimension

Samsara the circle/cycle wheel of birth and death and birth throughout any of the potential worlds

Samskara See Groundwork for The Ancient Method

Sat Chid Ananda Existence Life, Consciousness Knowledge and Love Joy Bliss, the Reality

Savikalpa with conceptuality

Shankara the Advaitic philosopher and writer

Shiva God Consciousness in the Destroyer aspect

Sidpa any region or stage of beginning to reincarnate

Six Traditions of the Hindus: Veda, Vedanta, Yoga, Samkhya, Logic, and Atomics.

Shunyata the Luminous Void

Sri Vidya the Supreme Wisdom of the Divine Mother

Sugata Suchness, Reality Just As It Is

Sva Bhava Mood of the True Self

Svabhavakaya Mood of the True Self Actuality Dimension

Taijasa the dream state as the luminous fire of consciousness

Tantra the doctrines of the Divine Mother

Tara the Goddess who descends (ava) out of Compassion to reveal Reality and end suffering

Tatha Gata Garbha the Womb (Garbha) of Reality (Tatha) thus Gone to the Other Shore (Gata)

Tayi All Light, Gaudapada's final conclusion

Thigle an essence, point or drop of conceptuality

Thogal Soaring On

Tilopa the great Tibetan mystic

Totapuri Ramakrishna's nirvikalpa mentor

Trekchod Letting Go

Trikaya the three Actuality Dimensions of Nirmana, Sambhoga and Dharmakaya recognized in the Suchness of Inseparability

Trung Pe Resurrection, resuscitation, translation and Cutting or Leaping, Leaping or Soaring

Turiya the Fourth State, Pure Consciousness, the True Self as Sat Chid Ananda

Twelve Causings please see page 75-76

Twenty Four Cosmic Principles from Kapila's Samkhya system. Five Elements: Earth, Water, Fire, Air and Ether. Five Subtle Elements or Sense Perceptions, like Quantum counterparts to the above list. Five Action Organs: Hands, Feet, Sex, Anus, and Mouth. Five Sense Organs: Eyes, Ears, Skin,

Tongue and Nose and their Perceptual Fields. And then the Inner Organ: Mind, Intellect, Ego Identity and Memory. Sometimes, Mahat (cosmic intelligence) or Avyakta (the Great Unmanifest) are exchanged for the principle of memory (chitta)

Unmani to become suddenly without relative phenomenal mind

Vaitathya Prakarana Gaudapada's second subject heading, On Illusion

Vajrakaya Indestructible Reality Actuality Dimension

Vajrasattva a subtle plane Sambhogakaya deity reflection of what is one's own Pure Mind

Vajrayogini the Great Dakini of the Dharmakaya of Pure Mind

Vasana See Groundwork for The Ancient Method

Vijnana the special or unique wisdom that sees both the Eternal and the Relative within the Divine Mother

Viraja Homa the spiritual cremation of all ties and connections before one renounces the world

Vishnu the Preserver aspect of God Consciousness

Visva the waking state as the outward natural and cosmic universe surrounding

Yamantaka one who is victorious over death (yama)

Yeshes the Pure Wisdom of the Divine Mother

Yidam a psychological/psychic image which may be either peaceful or wrathful

Zhi Reality as the Base or Foundation of all, the Ground Luminosity

Zhi Khro the cognitive manifestations of the peaceful and wrathful deitesses and deities arising from the Base of the Ground Luminosity itself.

References as Sources
of Inspiration, for Facts and Ideas
and in Quotations
for The Wonder of The Dakini Mind,
Letting Go and Soaring On,
and Resolution in Pure Mind

Swami Ashokananda. Avadhuta Gita. Sri Ramakrishna Math. 1981. Quoted.

Swami Atulananda. Atman Alone Abides. Sri Ramakrishna Math. 1978. "I do not care for gurus..." Quoted.

Aurobindo. On Yoga II Tome One. Sri Aurobindo International University Centre. 1958. Quoted in text.

Arthur and Ellen Avalon. Hymns to the Goddess. Ganesh and Co. 1913. The expression Kama-Kala in the Turiya state comes from this text. The names Author and Ellen Avalon were aliases for Mr. and Mrs. John G. Woodroffe.

Mayah Balse. Mystics and Men of Miracles in India. HaPi Press. 1976. Quoted in text.

Richard Maurice Bucke, M.D. Cosmic Consciousness Causeway Books. 1900. Ideas about Walt Whitman found in this interesting text.

Joseph Campbell. An Open Life. Perennial Library. 1989. Ideas on what can happen with teachers comes from this text of this very good, honest and genuine man.

Paul Carus, Editor. Buddha: His Life and Teachings. Crescent Books. 1959. A good source of ideas and facts about the Buddha's life.

C. M. Chen. The Meditation of the Tara. Mrs. Pauline M. Janes. Mr. Stanley Moskowitz. Mr. Edger Freeman. 1956. All but one or two things about Tara come from this book which holds no copyright claim for it is a gift to everyone.

Alfred Collins. From Brahma to a Blade of Grass: Towards an Indian Self Psychology. Journal of Indian Philosophy. 1991. Quoted in text. Extremely inspirational idea source.

Alfred Collins. Fatherson: A Self Psychology of the Archetypal Masculine. Chiron Publications. 1994. Most inspirational. Ideas about the rage of a spiritual teacher.

W.Y. Evans-Wentz. The Tibetan Book of the Dead. Oxford University Press. 1927. (The Bardo Thodol: The Hearing About Liberation While in the After Death Plane) "Walk with your head erect. Know thyself in the bardo." Quoted. Also an endless source of inspiration, ideas and facts for this text.

W.Y. Evans - Wentz. The Tibetan Book of the Great Liberation. Oxford University Press. 1954. (Naked Awareness or Seeing Mind in its Nakedness) Stories and examples of Padmasambhava come from this remarkable book.

W.Y. Evans-Wentz. Tibetan Yoga and Secret Doctrines. Oxford University Press. 1935. Sarah, Milarepa, and Tilopa are quoted. Also inspirational and an idea source.

A. Foucher. The Life of the Buddha. Wesleyan University Press. 1963. "I, who am here, at this moment, I know what is." quoted. Very inspirational source of ideas.

Swami Gabhirananda. The Mandukya Karika. Sri Ramakrishna Math. 1987. Quotations of Swami Aseshananda on Gaudapada come from this excellent text.

Swami Gambhirananda. Brahma Sutra Bhasya. Advaita Ashrama. 1965. Ideas of Audulomi, and others are quoted.

Swami Gambhirananda. Eight Upanisads. Advaita Ashrama. 1996. An endless and continuous source of light which is massively quoted from Gaudapada's Karika

Herbert V. Guenther. Kindly Bent To Ease Us. Dharma Publishing. 1976. A massive source of inspiration and ideas.

Herbert V. Guenther. The Life and Teaching of Naropa. Shambhala Publications. 1963. Most excellent. Most powerful source of inspiration for the Dakini and Tilopa.

Herbert Guenther. Meditation Differently: Phenomenological - Psychological Aspects of Tibetan Buddhist (Mahamudra and sNying-thig) Practices from Original Tibetan Sources. Motilal Banarsidass Publishers. 1992. I cannot begin to even tell you how much a source of inspiration, ideas and facts this wondrous text has been. It is a continuous and endless source of spiritual light. Dr. Guenther's translation of Padma's The Sun's Life Giving Force... is the second main source of inspiration and guidance for this manuscript. The expressions of the "Barrier Free Approach" for Trekchod and the "Final Leap Approach" for Thogal come from this text. Also the idea that the Nirmanakaya is a "guiding image" comes from this book as well as many of the expressions as to what the "Lamps" are such as "Self Kindled Wisdom Lamp," the "Openness and Singularity," "Ecstatic Intensity," "Acumen and Appreciation," "Peak Towering Over All" ideas and what the thigle are, much of my information in Spontaneous Arrivals comes from here as the Four Thogals through Body, Speech and Mind. Also the expression of "whatever comes to presence," is from this text. I am deeply indebted to Dr. Guenther. May he live in perfect health and peace for nine centuries so that he may continue writing!

Herbert V. Guenther. Wholeness Lost and Wholeness Regained: Forgotten Tales of Individuation from Ancient Tibet. State University of New York Press. 1994. Inspiration as a source of natural wisdom.

Janet Gyatso. Apparitions of the Self: The Secret Autobiographies of a Tibetan Visionary. A Translation and Study of Jigme Lingpa's Dancing Moon in the Water and Dakki's Grand Secret - Talk. Princeton University Press. 1998. I cannot begin to tell you how wonderfully excellent this book is for me. Extreme Inspiration. Profound Ideas from here are expressed, for example, the ideas about the "apparitions" of other beings and even one's own self, the expression of "spacing out" in Dzogchen and the comment of Jigme Lingpa that "whatever happens is just fine," come from this remarkable manuscript.

Geshe Kelsang Gyatso, Guide to Dakini Land. Tharpa Publications. 1991. An extraordinary fascinating source of inspiration.

Captain M. U. Hatengdi and Swami Chetanananda. Nityananda: The Divine Presence. Rudra Press. 1984. An idea is expressed from this book.

Linda Johnsen. Daughters of the Goddess. Yes International Publishers. 1994. Brahmajna Ma's idea about the guru process.

Anne Carolyn Klein. Meeting the Great Bliss Queen.

Buddhists, Feminists, And The Art Of Self. Beacon Press. 1995. This wonderful book is most inspiring filled with eloquent ideas.

Stephen and Robin Larsen. A Fire in the Mind. Doubleday. 1991. Some ideas about Joseph Campbell's thought on the affect of spiritual teachers.

M. The Condensed Gospel of Sri Ramakrishna. Sri Ramakrishna Math. 1911. (1897.) The remarkable definition of the Dakini comes from this text.

M. and Translated by Swami Nikhilananda. The Gospel of Sri Ramakrishna. Ramakrishna - Vivekananda Center. New York. 1942. The main source of inspiration, ideas and massively quoted numerous times. I cannot tell you my gratitude for this amazing extraordinary text filled to the brim with continuous spiritual light!

Swami Madhavananda. Minor Upanishads. Advaita Ashrama. 1968. Quoted.

Jeffrey Moussaieff Masson. My Father's Guru: A Journey through Spirituality and Disillusion. Addison - Wesley Publishing Company. 1993. Very inspirational. A source of healing. Ideas come from this bold and honest book that are in the text.

Lopon Tenzin Namdak. Heart Drops of Dharmakaya. Snow Lion Publications. 1993. A most excellent source of inspiration.

Swami Nikhilananda. Life of Sri Ramakrishna. Advaita Ashrama. 1924. This text is an endless source of inspiration and ideas. A superior spiritual light which is quoted in this manuscript.

Swami Nikhilananda. The Mandukyopanisad with Gaudapada's Karika. Sri Ramakrishna Math. 1936. An endless continuous source of spiritual light which is heavily quoted.

Translated by Swami Nikhilananda. The Upanishads. Bonanza Books. 1952. Most excellent source of ideas and information, especially on Gaudapada.

Swami Nityaswarupananda. Astavakra Samhita. Advaita Ashrama. 1969. This high Advaitic text is quoted.

Sister Nivedita. The Master As I Saw Him. Udbodhan Office. 1910. Quotations of Swami Vivekananda come from this wondrous text.

Namkhai Norbu and Kennard Lipman. Primordial Experience. Shambhala Publications. 1983. A very powerful inspiration.

E, Mansell Pattison, M.D. Clinical Psychiatry and Religion. Little, Brown and Company. 1969. The nine characteristics of religious/mystical experience are found in this text.

Swami Prabhavananda. The Eternal Companion Spiritual Teachings of Swami Brahmananda. Sri Ramakrishna Math. 1931. Quotation about the pure mind as guru.

Swami Prajnanananda. Christ the Saviour and Christ Myth. Ramakrishna Vedanta Math. 1961. Ideas about what may have happened after the crucifixion come from this source.

Richard Chambers Prescott. The Skills of Kalee. Grascott. 1995. Disturbing Delights: Waves of the Great Goddess. Volume Five. Grascott. 1993. Dragon Sight: A Cremation Poem. Grascott. 1992. Quoted.

Dr. Kenneth Ring. Heading Toward Omega: In Search of the Meaning of the Near Death Experience. Quill. 1984. The expression "Omega Prototype" comes from this fascinating work.

Swami Rudrananda. (Albert Rudolph) Spiritual Cannibalism. The Overlook Press. 1978. Two ideas of Rudi's are expressed in the text.

Swami Saradananda. Sri Ramakrishna: The Great Master. Sri Ramakrishna Math. 1952. An invaluable source of spiritual light which is also quoted in this manuscript.

Swami Ramanananda Saraswati. Tripura Rahasya: The Mystery Beyond the Trinity. T. N. Venkataraman. 1971. Stories of Janaka and Ashtavakra are retold. Ideas about the Goddess.

Sayings of Sri Ramakrishna. Sri Ramakrishna Math. 1965. The quote about the vanity of a saint.

Swami Sarvananda. Mandukyopanisad: With a Summary of Gaudapada's Karika) Sri Ramakrishna Math. 1976. A profound source of ideas on Gaudapada's consideration of Sakyamuni.

Robert E. Spiller. The Cycle of American Literature.

Mentor. 1955. The ideas about Walt Whitman's four stages of spiritual development come from this text.

Swami Tapasyananda. Sankara Dig Vijaya. Sri Ramakrishna Math. 1980. Stories of Shankara come from here.

Tulku Thondup. Longchen Nyingthig Ngondro. Library of Tibetan Works and Archives. 1982. A massive source of inspiration, facts and ideas on Dzogchen.

Tulku Thondup. The Practice of Dzogchen. Snow Lion Publications. 1989. Extremely inspirational.

Rai Bahadur Srisa Chandra Vasu. The Siva Samhita. Munshiram Manoharlal Publishers. 1914. Ideas about the comparrison of Maha Shunyata and Turiya.

Swami Vivekananda. The Complete Works of Swami Vivekananda. Advaita Ashrama. 1907. A massive source of spiritual light which is quoted many times from Inspired Talks and Raja Yoga and a letter or two from Swami.

Swami Virajananda. Towards the Goal Supreme. Vedanta Press. 1950. "God alone is the Supreme Guru..." Quoted.

Tenzin Wangyal. Wonders of the Natural Mind. Station Hill. 1993. A powerful source of inspiration and ideas.

Walt Whitman. Complete Poetry and Selected Prose. Leaves of Grass. Edited by James E. Miller Jr. Houghton Mifflin Company. 1959. So many times quoted. Continuous as an inspiration of spiritual light and source of ideas.

Sir John. George Woodroffe. The Serpent Power. Ganesh and Co. 1918. Inspiration. Facts and Ideas are expressed from this text. Also, from his commentary on The Tibetan Book of the Dead, the interpretation of Antara Bhava.

Swami Yatiswarananda. Meditation and Spiritual Life. Sri Ramakrishna Ashrama. 1979. Many ideas and quotations come from this excellent sober text.

Paramahansa Yogananda. Autobiography of a Yogi. Self - Realization Fellowship. 1946. Inspirational. Ideas. And stories of Sri Yukteswar are recounted.

Swami Yogeshananda. The Lotus and The Flame: Monastic Teachings of Swami Aseshananda. The Eternal Quest, Inc. 1996. Some quotes from Swami Aseshananda.

References for
The Ancient Method

K. Narayanaswami Aiyer. Laghu Yoga Vasistha. Adyar Library. 1896.

P. Sheshadari Aiyer. Spiritual Teachings of Swami Abhedananda. Ramakrishna Vedanta Math. 1962.

Swami Aparananda. Laghu Vakya Vritti. Sri Ramakrishna Kutir. Almora, Himalayas. 1953.

U. A. Asrani. Yoga Unveiled. Motilal Banarsidass. 1977.

Sures Chandra Chakravarti. M.A. B. L. The Philosophy of the Upanishads. University of Calcutta. 1935.

Dr. Alfred Collins. From Brahma to a Blade of Grass. Journal of Indian Philosophy. 1991.

Paul Deussen. The Philosophy of the Upanishads. Dover. 1906. Sixty Upanisads of the Veda. Motilal Banarsidass. 1897.

Swami Gabhirananda. The Mandukya Karika. Sri Ramakrishna Math. 1987.

Swami Gambhirananda. Brahma Sutra Bhasya. Advaita Ashrama. 1965. Eight Upanishads. Advaita Ashrama. 1966.

Dominic Goddall. Hindu Scriptures. University of California Press. 1996.

Theodore Goldstucker. Sanskrit and Culture. Susil Gupta LTD. 1955.

Ralph T. H. Griffith. Hymns of the Rgveda. Chowkhamba Sanskrit Series. 1896.

Swami Harshananda. Hindu Gods and Goddesses. Sri Ramakrishna Math. 1987.

M. The Condensed Gospel of Sri Ramakrishna. Sri Ramakrishna Math. 1911.

M. and Translated by Swami Nikhilananda. The Gospel of Sri Ramakrishna. Ramakrishna - Vivekananda Center. New York. 1942.

Swami Madhavananda. Minor Upanishads. Advaita Ashrama. 1968.

John E. Mitchiner. Tradition of The Seven Rsis. Motilal Banarsidass. 1982.

Rajmohon Nath. Rig Veda Summary. Anjan Kumar Nath. 1966.

Swami Nikhilananda. Vedantasara of Sadananda. Advaita Ashrama. 1949.

Swami Nikhilananda. The Bhagavad Gita. Ramakrishna Vivekananda Center. 1952.

Swami Nikhilananda. The Mandukyopanisad with Gaudapada's Karika. Sri Ramakrishna Ashrama. 1936.

Swami Nikhilananda. The Upanishads. Abridged Edition. Harper Torchbooks. 1963.

Swami Nityaswarupananda. Astavakra Samhita. Advaita Ashrama. 1969.

F. Eden Pargiter. The Markendeya Purana. Indological Book House. 1981.

Swami Prabhananda. More About Ramakrishna. Advaita Ashrama. 1993

Swami Prabhavananda. Srimad Bhagavatam. Sri Ramakrishna Math Madras. 1986.

Swami Prajnanananda. Thoughts on Yoga, Upanishad and Gita. The Class Lectures of Swami Abhedananda. Ramakrishna Vedanta Math. 1970.

Richard Chambers Prescott. The Mirage and the Mirror. 1998. Disturbing Delights: Waves of the Great Goddess. Vol. 6. Turiya Letters. Vol. 7. Dream Techniques. Vol. 19. Emanation and Source. 1993 & 1994 Dragon Sight: A Cremation Poem. 1992 Grascott Publishing.

Dr. C. Kunhan Raja. Asya Vamasya Hymn; The Riddle of the Universe: Rgveda I 164. Ganesh and Company. 1956.

C. Rajagopalachari. Mahabharata. Bharatiya Vidya Bhavan. 1950. Ramayana. 1951.

Swami Ramakrishnananda. God and Divine Incarnations. Sri Ramakrishna Math. 1947.

Prof. A. A. Ramanathan. The Samnyasa Upanisads. Adyar Library. 1978.

R. D. Ranade A Constructive Survey of Upanishadic Philosophy. Bharatiya Vidya Bhavan. 1926.

P. Sankaranarayanan. What is Advaita? Bharatiya Vidya Bhavan. 1971.

Sri Sarada Devi: The Great Wonder. By Apostles, Monks, Savants, Scholars, Devotees. Ramakrishna Mission New Delhi. 1984.

Swami Saradananda. Sri Ramakrishna: The Great Master. Sri Ramakrishna Math. 1952.

Swami Sarvananda. Mandukyopanisad. Sri Ramakrishna Math. 1976.

Pandit S. Subrahmanya Sastri and T. R. Srinivasa Ayyangar. Jiva Mukti Viveka of Vidyaranya. Adyar Library. 1978.

Swami Sharvananda. Mundaka and Mandukya Upanishads. Sri Ramakrishna Math 1920.

Margaret and James Stutley. Dictionary of Hinduism. Harper and Row. 1977.

Swami Venkatesananda. The Concise Yoga Vasistha. State University of New York Press. 1984.

Swami Vijnanananda. The Srimad Devi Bhagawatam. Munshiram Monaharal. 1986.

Swami Vivekananda. The Complete Works of Swami Vivekananda. Advaita Ashrama. 1907.

Benjamin Walker. Hindu World: An Encyclopedic Survey of Hinduism. George Allen and Unwin Ltd. 1968.

About the Author

Richard Chambers Prescott is a writer and publisher of twenty books of poetry. He has had five plays published by Aran Press in Kentucky and over seventy essays and articles published from the U. S. A. to India. His essay, The Lamp of the Turiya, has been translated into Dutch and published in the Amsterdam journal, Vedanta. Over the last several years, some articles and essays have been printed in Prabuddha Bharata and The New Times. The intent of his writing is to join the spiritual and psychological aspects of human nature. He has donated to the publication of a text on the woman saint, Gauri Ma. Grascott Publishing has published two books of humor by Swami Bhaskarananda, The Danger of Walking on Water and One Eyed Vision. Some of his collected essays have been published in the texts, such as, Because of Atma: Essays on Self and Empathy and the work entitled Measuring Sky Without Ground: On the Goddess Kali, Sri Ramakrishna and Human Potential. His manuscript, The Goddess and The God Man: An Explorative Study of the Intimate Relationship of the Goddess Kali with Sri Ramakrishna of Dakshineswar came later and is perhaps the crown of those creations. Then, The Mirage and the Mirror was born out of continuous pondering on the Goddess. His most recent text is Inherent Solutions to Spiritual Obscurations, which is a comparison of Tibetan Dzogchen and Indian Advaita in four parts, The Wonder of the Dakini Mind, Letting Go and Soaring On, Resolution in Pure Mind and the Ancient Method.

His early seven books of poetry, The Sage, Moonstar, Neuf Songes, The Carouse of Soma, Lions and Kings, Allah Wake Up, and Night Reaper, are on the passionate emergence, the coming forth of spiritual desire, Neuf Songes (Nine Dreams), being the crest wave of that time. Kings and Sages is a poetic sojourn through discoveries in East Indian doctrines. Three Waves is a poetic text on the transformation of tragedy into the love of life, that then becomes spirituality. The Imperishable is a collection of Tantric and Vedantic essays. The Dark Deitess is a sensitive text on the enigmatic stages of Goddess worship.

Years of Wonder is a recounting of time spent in searching for the spiritual. Dream Appearances is a one-fourth of a century study and examination of the spiritual connection within the dream state. Remembrance Recognition and Return is a record of personal spiritual return to the Goddess. The seven Dragon books: Tales, Dreams, Prayers, Songs, Maker, Thoughts, and Dragon Sight: A Cremation Poem are an evolution of the creative mind culminating with the poetic affection for non-dualism and the composition of his own cremation poem. Kalee Bhava :The Goddess and Her Moods, The Skills of Kalee, Kalee: The Allayer of Sorrows and Living Sakti: Attempting Quick Knowing in Perpetual Perception and Continuous Becoming are purely expressions for the Goddess, conveying states, emotions, methods, techniques, direct insights, fresh discoveries, and a few personal spiritual ideas. Disturbing Delights: Waves of the Great Goddess are twenty-one journal volumes which are written, illustrated, and published by Mr. Prescott. Tales of Recognition is seven stories of spiritual journeys through the past and the future, death consciousness and return. Spare Advice is a short novel on the tragic comedy of two souls searching for truth. Racopa and the Rooms of Light is a play taking place in the after death condition. Hanging Baskets is a comedy about psychiatry. Writer's Block and Other Gray Matters, written with his marriage companion, S. Elisabeth Grace, is a collection of comedy drama one acts. The Resurrection of Quantum Joe is a comedy on physics. The Horse and The Carriage is a comedy on disparagement. Mr. Prescott has been published side by side with other journalists, some professors, and renunciate women and men in the text Eternal Platform by the Ramakrishna Mission Ashrama in Ramharipur, India. He has also been published in the journal text Matriarch's Way and Vitals Signs: The International Association for Near Death Studies. He has just recently had an essay entitled Sri Ramakrishna As Personal Companion published in Global Vedanta. His works are in some libraries, universities and spiritual sanctuaries in the U.S.A., Europe, Russia, South America, and India. Writing has been his spiritual practice for thirty years. Including all volumes, he has over eighty published manuscripts, most of which are privately distributed. His works, of over twenty years, are now mentioned in the International Poet's Encyclopaedia, Cambridge, England. As of 1999, he is forty-seven years old and has been married for eighteen years.

I must thank a few friends for their kind letters, which have daily encouraged me to continue and complete this text:

Barbara G. Walker Author of The Women's Encyclopedia of Myths and Secrets: "Naturally, I am pleased by any profession of reverence for the Goddess."

Rufus C. Camphausen Author of The Divine Library: "You have so specialized a knowledge that I wonder what country (I mean culture) you've been born and raised in."

Swami Chetanananda: "Never give up writing --it is a good habit that clears understanding and keeps the mind in a higher plane, and it may also help others."

Swami Tyagananda: "We appreciate your efforts in trying to express different aspects of Vedanta philosophy."

Tenzin Wangyal Rinpoche, Author of Wonders of the Natural Mind and The Tibetan Yogas of Dream and Sleep: "And thank you for your books for our Ligmincha library. They will greatly benefit other people."

Dr. Raymond Moody Author of Life After Life: "I truly appreciate your thoughtfulness."

William Bond Author of Gospel of the Goddess: "Looking through your poems in Dragon Thoughts they seem to me to feel the same as the Tao Te Ching which has been a "Bible" for me over the years." "Thank you for Measuring Sky Without Ground. Looking through your book I do agree with most of what you say. Although I do have a different idea about getting rid of the ego. I feel man needs to develop his ego to learn how to love himself and how to become an individual. Until he reaches a state where he is so secure in his love of himself, that he no longer needs to search for "ego gratification." In this secure state he is able to now be humble and surrender to the Great Mother knowing he will not be swallowed up by Her and start to learn how to love others." And, "Thank you for your two books, it does amaze me how many books you are able to write on Kali."

Dr. Alfred Collins Author of Fatherson and From Brahma to a Blade of Grass:"I see again that you are a talented writer; some of the poems are very expressive and moving. I suppose your style is something like Walt Whitman's, among American writers." "Thanks for Measuring Sky... very interesting, very sincere."

Swami Bhashyananda: "I have gone through the manuscripts with great interest. You have genuine writing ability and the talent for using your imagination to express some of your spiritual intuitions. I was impressed to read what you have written. The thoughts are very valuable and elevating."

Swami Chidbhasananda on, The Lamp of the Turiya, from Because of Atma. "It is really a masterpiece coming from the bottom of your experience, and there is no artificial make-up in your composition. Our additional thanks and gratitude to your Kindself."

Amy Richards, assistant to Gloria Steneim: "So thank you for writing and also for sharing your humanity."

Anonymous by request of Author: "You are so kind, so wildly generous. We send our blessings on your work and writing hand."

Helen Fedro - Publisher: "The pieces I examined were very intriguing."

Swami Swahananda, Vedanta Society of Southern California, on The Lamp of the Turiya, from Because of Atma : "A very scholarly presentation."

Jo Kyle - Publisher: "We found your work most interesting and inspiring."

Artemis - Publisher: "I think you are trying to compete with Tolstoy or producing the equivalent of the Holy Koran. The pieces are superb."

Swami Atmavratananda: "I love your various books."

Sushri Braja Parikari Didiji: "I read your article, it was really very good."

Swami Vamanananda, Ramakrishna Mission Ashrama, West Bengal: "We would appeal to your goodself to contribute an article from your powerful pen and certainly it will add worth and prestige to our volume."

Swami Varadananda: "I wanted to thank you for the article on "The Indian Idea of Death," which you sent me. You are doing good work in spreading Sri Ramakrishna's message. As people become exposed to the teachings of Vedanta from various sources, it will gradually make an impression. By publishing your article in a non - Vedanta magazine, you have reached a whole new audience, which had perhaps never heard about these ideas."

Jerry Zientara - Librarian: "I shall also gladly point the books out to students and researchers interested in Tantra, Goddess Worship, and Spirituality outside the Western traditions."

Carola F. Sautter - Publisher: "This project seems to us to be an important one."

Arthur P. Young, Director, Northern Illinois University Libraries: "I am very pleased to acknowledge your recent contribution of materials. These are most welcome since they assist us in instructional and research programs of the university. It was good of you to remember us."

Swami Tathagatananda, Vedanta Society of New York: "I sincerely congratulate you for writing about Ramakrishna. Although we are working here for one hundred years, still, I am sorry to mention, very few intellectual Americans are showing their genuine interest in making a successful attempt to project the universal idealism of Ramakrishna. In the twenty-first century, we are reaching the Global Village which requires our cosmopolitan outlook to be fit for this Global Village. But the old ideas, thoughts and prejudices are still very prominently molding our lifestyle. This is quite natural. But still, you are doing your best through your creative writing to make people more liberal and universal. May God bless you with enthusiasm and right perspective."

Barry Scott, Ohio University Libraries: "Your contribution will enrich the Libraries' collections and help us to better serve the Ohio University Community. We appreciate your interest and hope you will continue your support of the Ohio University Libraries."

Swami Manishananda: "I am enjoying your book Measuring

Sky Without Ground immensely. Your phrases are excellent. I especially like imagery such as "our souls kidnapped by crusty old belief systems."

Dr. Stanley Krippner, Saybrook Institute, Graduate School and Research Center: "We all appreciate your generosity. Thanks for the unique books. I am sure our students will find the books interesting, as is usual with your publications."

Swami Yatatmananda, Sri Ramakrishna Math, Mylapore, India: "We greatly appreciate your kind gesture. The books are an invaluable addition to our Library. The books have an attractive get up and bold prints which make reading them a pleasure. The topics chosen are also of immense interest and we are sure that a lot of our members will benefit from the addition of these books. Thanking you."

Dr. Miriam Robbins Dexter, author of Whence The Goddess and editor of Varia on the Indo-European Past and The Kurgan Culture and The Indo-Europeanization of Europe by Marija Gimbutas: "Thanks very much for the copies of your book. I will be giving a workshop in Greece in two days and I shall bring copies of your books with me to give to colleagues. My best." "Kalee... if you send a signal my circuit is open." In Kalee Bhava and The Skills of Kalee, both inspired books of meditations, Richard Prescott speaks with directness and deep feeling to the immanent Goddess Kali." "Your Tales of Recognition were charming. I particularly enjoyed Racopa the Tibetan and The Spiritual Wars of the Planet Earth. I appreciate the positive hopeful quality of your work. Your meditations give a beautifully personal and spiritual picture of you - that you rejoice in being a poet, and a writer of prose. I particularly enjoy the fact that the Goddess calls you Her "honey boy" - recalling Inanna calling Dumuzi Her "honey man."

Swami Prapannananda, Vedanta Society of Sacramento: "I appreciate your kind thoughts. The books will be kept in the reading room. I wish you continued success in your writing and publishing work. With our greetings and best wishes."

Northwestern University Library, Illinois: "Thank you very much."

Elizabeth Usha Harding, Kali Mandir, author of Kali: The

Black Goddess of Dakshineswar: "Just wanted to thank you very much for the gift of the books. We really appreciate it and they will be in the library. Jai Ma."

Swami Shivarupananda, The Ramakrishna Vedanta Centre, England: "Thank you for the books which we received this morning. They will be a welcome addition to our library."

Dr. Allen R. Freedman, Vedanta Society of Western Washington: "On behalf of the Vedanta Society I would like to thank you very much for your kind and generous donation of your latest book Living Sakti to our society. Please accept my best wishes. Yours in Thakur, Ma and Swamiji."

Carolyn H. Aamot, University of Washington: Your generosity is very much appreciated. Thank you again."

Lakshmi Narayan, Krotona Library, "We appreciate your kind donation to Krotona Library. Thanking you again."

Ramakrishna Ashrama, Argentina: "Very interesting. Thank you very much."

Mangala Takacs, Vedanta Society of Southern California, San Diego: "Swami Atmarupananda asked me to write to you to thank you for copies of Because of Atma and Living Sakti that you sent for our Library. I find your statement of purpose quite interesting - the world needs more original manuscripts! Best wishes in your publishing work. Yours in Peace."

Swami Dayatmananda of the Ramakrishna Vedanta Centre in the U.K.: "Mother is working through you no doubt."

Ramakrishna Ashrama, Argentina: "Appreciating your analysis and thoughts on some interesting topics we placed your books in our public and personal libraries here."

Dr. Bruce Greyson, M.D. University of Connecticut: "Thank you for letting me see the enclosed selections of articles on existence, consciousness, and the mysteries of life and death. I enjoyed reading them, and as a clinical psychiatrist, I was particularly impressed by the wisdom and compassion in your article, Depression: A Spiritual Dilemma."

Haragano, author and teacher: "Dearest Ricky, poet visionary, and dear companion to a wonderful lady, thank you for sharing your poetry and dreams with me and others of our kind."

Such dear inspirations as theirs have helped me to put my thoughts into the illustration of words that form this text.

Swami Chetanananda, The Vedanta Society of St. Louis: "Thank you for sending us copies of your book The Goddess and the God Man. I shall keep one copy for myself, and place the others in our library and book store. I wish you good luck in spreading the message of Vedanta through your Grascott Publishing Company."

The Bear Tribe: "Thank you for your gift. We will be glad to enjoy them and have them in our library."

Swami Yogeshananda: "I do look forward to absorbing the fascinating comments in Dragon Sight and also finishing Measuring Sky Without Ground which I have begun."

Aoumiel: "Thank you very much for the new volumes for my library! As always, I enjoy reading your perspective on the balance of light and dark in the Divine. Bright Blessings to you and your work. I hope your heartfelt writings get a wide distribution."

Swami Atmaramananda, Prabuddha Bharata, India: "We are glad to receive your gift of Measuring Sky Without Ground for our library and bookstore. The packet arrived last week."

The Ramakrishna Vedanta Centre, England: "Swami Dayatmananda would like to thank you for your kindness in sending to us your recent books which we received this morning. Very much appreciated!"

Effie Brown, Shenoa Retreat, California: "I am sure we will enjoy these unique and interesting books. It was very kind of you to remember us in this way."

Diane Kent, Salt Spring Centre, BC, Canada: "Thank you very much for your book donation. I dipped into the covered for a few moments and saw the work of a true Kali devotee. It will be a pleasure to read and I'm sure that many of our guests will enjoying reading them."

Swami Prabuddhananda, Vedanta Society of Northern California: "I was glad to receive your packet of books - The Goddess and the God Man and Disturbing Delights. Thank you for sending me these books."

Susana Andrews, Tantra Magazine: "I am delighted. Thank

you for your generous gift of publications and also for your gift of service to the Goddess."

Swami Atmavratananda, Vivekananda Vihar, New York: "So fulfilled to see you are so filled with our Maha Kali. Yours in Love and Peace."

Swami Chidbhasananda, Vedanta Centrum R.V.V.N., The Netherlands: "We acknowledge with grateful thanks the receipt of The Goddess and the God Man and Disturbing Delights. Again, with our hearty thanks. May Sri Ramakrishna, Holy Mother and Swamiji shower their choicest Blessings on you and your family, is our earnest prayer at Their Feet!"

Cassia Berman, author of, Divine Mother Within Me: "everything I read, Ma authentically shines and plays through. I rejoice to find a kindred spirit and it means so much to me that you have been enjoying my work too. Those books are like a silver treasure chest, in every drawer of which Ma is sparkling. Thank you."

Lakshmi Narayan, Head Librarian, Krotona Library: "We acknowledge with deep gratitude your donation to the Krotona Library."

St. John, Secretary, The Lama Foundation: "Thank you so much for the books. People have already carted them off to read! Please keep us in your thoughts and prayers."

Karin J. Miles, Director, Cloud Mountain Retreat Center: "We do appreciate your recognition of our Dharma library, and your generous gift. It is certain that the books will be reviewed and read by at least some of the practitioners who pass through this Center. Thank you for your kindness."

Self Realization Fellowship, The Mother Center: "Our Encinitas Ashram Center informed us of your generous donation of a number of books for our library. It was kind of you to think of us. Please accept our gratitude for your thoughtfulness. May God bless you always. In divine friendship."

Swami Adiswarananda, The Ramakrishna Vivekananda Center, New York: "Please accept our thanks to you for your gift of Measuring Sky Without Ground. We appreciate your kind thoughts. I wish you continued success in your writing and publishing work. With our greetings and all best wishes."

Indralaya Library,Orcas Island: "Thank you for your donation... they are very much appropriate and appreciated. Always a treat to have new ideas offered."

Carolyn H. Aamot, University of Washington Libraries: "On behalf of the University of Washington Libraries, it is my privilege to express our gratitude. We welcome your interest in the University Libraries and value your support. Contributions of materials help enrich our collection for the many students, faculty and others who daily rely on its resources for study and research. Please be assured that your publications will be carefully reviewed for addition to our holdings."

Joni Cooke, Shoden, Mount Baldy Zen Center: "Thank you very much for this lovely silver book. We are not encouraged to read here at the monastery however, I just took a brief look through your collected titles and my sense is that it is wonderful that you are out there publishing exactly what pleases and interests you. I hope things go well in your publishing business, and I will put "The Mirage and the Mirror" in our library."

Self Realization Fellowship, Mother Center: "Thank you for your thoughtfulness and generosity. Our ashram in Encinitas received your donation also and asked us to convey their gratitude for your kindness. May the love of God be with you always, guiding you in all your worthwhile endeavors. In divine friendship."

Swami Murugananda, Satchidananda Ashram - Yogaville: "Thank you for your donation of spiritual books to our library. They are now all classified and cataloged and on our shelves for use by our community."

Ramakrishna Ashrama, Argentina: "Swami Pareshanandaji and all of us here are very thankful for sending copies of your latest creation, "The Mirage and the Mirror." We wish you a new year of more and more deep and bright thoughts. With all affection."

The Ramakrishna Mission Institute of Culture, Gol Park, Calcutta: We acknowledge with thanks the receipt of the books noted below which you have sent for use is our library. We are sure our readers will find the books useful."

Swami Shivarupananda, Vedanta Centre, England: Thank

you once again for the copies of "The Mirage and the Mirror", received with gratitude and appreciation. Yours in the Eternal."

Subhabrata, Mothers Trust/Mothers Place: "The Mirage and the Mirror will be a very valuable addition to our library. We are grateful for your continuing contributions to the ashram. We send our blessings and best wishes to you and hope to hear from you soon. Yours in service of Mother."

Dr. Kenneth Ring, Author of Life After Death and Heading Toward Omega : "I very much respect the learning you so easily express concerning the nature of death and the state of consciousness it engenders. And I am glad you are continuing to be one of those authors of the modern book of the dead and thereby helping to bring the ancient wisdom to a new generation of beings." "I am happy to know that you continue to be a prolific writer and weaver of story-magic."

Linda Johnsen, author of Daughters of the Goddess: The Women Saints of India: "Reading over the expressions of your soul, I also felt an intense poignancy. In this culture who is there to be inspired by words such as yours, by visions such as Hers? We live in such a wasteland, Richard. And at the same time this spiritual desert is a heaven world Mother has created for us so that we can do sadhana (spiritual practice) well fed in heated homes. I accept Her blessing of contemporary American life with gratitude and despair. The Divine One will never let us go. May we never let go of Her! Bowing to the Goddess in you." & "I certainly wish I was as continuously inspired as you and could keep producing books at such a prodigious rate! And all for the glory of Mother." "Thanks so much for Measuring Sky Without Ground. What a wonderful title! I especially appreciated your point that, "Mother is not a lesser form that needs destroying." When Ramakrishna attacked the form of Kali with the sword of discrimination, it was Kali's own sword he was using, jnana sakti."

Penny Slinger, artist and author of numerous books, The Path of the Mystic Lover being but one of her titles: "No one can write as you do without it being forged in the bliss of Her divine fire, no one comes to Her knowledge without being prepared to offer themselves in the flames... only they know the passion of this surrender! Beautiful poet, I salute you, for you are doing the work, the great work of preparing the vessel so She may flow through.. oh how I too ardently long for there to be nothing left of me but the Goddess! I honor you for honoring Her." & "I appreciated Dragon Sight deeply... I have absorbed it and pay homage to you for not only attempting but actually executing such a work. Thank goodness, thank Goddess, for beings like you."

Swami Dayatmananda of the Ramakrishna Vedanta Centre in the U.K.: "Mother is working through you no doubt." & "Advaita is one philosophy which is the goal and the path. I think it harmonizes all other religious paths in love and understanding. You have caught the spirit of this marvelous philosophy aright. May the Lord now graciously grant you its right realization is my fervent prayer."

Swami Bhaskarananda, author of The Essentials of Hinduism, on Measuring Sky Without Ground: "People are victims of their conditioning. That is the reason why people of the East and people of the West sometimes think differently. Richard Chambers Prescott has grown up in the West. He has had Western conditioning. Yet his inquiring mind has taken him to the shores of Eastern knowledge - particularly the knowledge of Hindu philosophy and religion. He is one of the few Western friends I know who have tried to explore the wealth of Hindu wisdom with the mind of an ardent and admiring student, and not that of a chance traveler or a supercilious surface-taster. The articles contained in this book clearly reflect his open-mindedness, impartial self-examination, and mental enrichment attained through the exploration of both Eastern and Western wisdom. Rudyard Kipling once said, "Oh, East is East, and West is West, and ne're the twain shall meet." Mr. Prescott has proved him wrong. In him the wisdom of the East and the wisdom of the West seem to have blended together in perfect harmony." And, "Your writings are very precise and clear, and therefore, they will help readers to understand some of the Vedantic ideas more easily. Please keep up the good work!"

Swami Muktirupananda, Advaita Ashrama, the Himalayas: Editor for Prabuddha Bharata: "I have gone through all of your review articles, they are very good and reveal the depth of the writer. Please try to share your mature thoughts with the reader of this spiritual journal." "So many books have been coming out from your facile pen and rich brain. I will keep the copies of your books in our Advaita Library. You have rightly pointed out that Turiya is the state of pure beingness. It is eternal existence without any name and form. It is the ego with the sense of 'I am this' and 'I am that', that thinks it undergoes changes. This information we have gathered in our heads about ourselves gives us the idea that we are limited, powerless. But, these definitions that one is American, or Christian, or husband, or wife, rich or poor, are added to one's pure beingness. These are external descriptions gathered in the course of time. We believe we are these definitions and suffer. Behind all these external decorations there is One who existed prior to all these. To see thoughts appearing in the mind, there must be somebody to see. So he must be in existence before there was any thought. 'You' as pure being exist prior to all thoughts. This pure being cannot be defined, because of it, everything else arises. It is prior to all. Spiritual practice is to throw out all we have accumulated from the external world. When all that rubbish stuff is thrown out, when the mind is cleaned what remains is Reality, beyond all words."

Swami Smarananananda, General Secretary, Belur Math: "Glad to receive your letter dated nil together with three copies of books. Thank you. The books have been kept in our Math Library and Probationers' Training Centre Library. With best wishes and greetings."

See other works of Richard Chambers Prescott at 1st Books Library http://www.1stbooks.com Or as a perfect bound book through Ingram's Books in Print Catalog at most major bookstores.

Printed in the United States
1213200002B/76